Lecture Notes in Computer Science 10805

Advanced Research in Computing and Software Science

Subline of Lecture Notes in Computer Science

Dirk Beyer · Marieke Huisman (Eds.)

Tools and Algorithms for the Construction and Analysis of Systems

24th International Conference, TACAS 2018 Held as Part of the European Joint Conferences on Theory and Practice of Software, ETAPS 2018 Thessaloniki, Greece, April 14–20, 2018 Proceedings, Part I

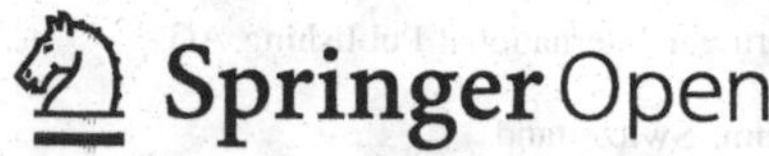

Editors
Dirk Beyer
Ludwig-Maximilians-Universität München
Munich
Germany

Marieke Huisman
University of Twente
Enschede
The Netherlands

ISSN 0302-9743 ISSN 1611-3349 (electronic)
Lecture Notes in Computer Science
ISBN 978-3-319-89959-6 ISBN 978-3-319-89960-2 (eBook)
https://doi.org/10.1007/978-3-319-89960-2

Library of Congress Control Number: 2018940138

LNCS Sublibrary: SL1 – Theoretical Computer Science and General Issues

Printed on acid-free paper

This Springer imprint is published by the registered company Springer International Publishing AG part of Springer Nature
The registered company address is: Gewerbestrasse 11, 6330 Cham, Switzerland

ETAPS Foreword

Welcome to the proceedings of ETAPS 2018! After a somewhat coldish ETAPS 2017 in Uppsala in the north, ETAPS this year took place in Thessaloniki, Greece. I am happy to announce that this is the first ETAPS with gold open access proceedings. This means that all papers are accessible by anyone for free.

ETAPS 2018 was the 21st instance of the European Joint Conferences on Theory and Practice of Software. ETAPS is an annual federated conference established in 1998, and consists of five conferences: ESOP, FASE, FoSSaCS, TACAS, and POST. Each conference has its own Program Committee (PC) and its own Steering Committee. The conferences cover various aspects of software systems, ranging from theoretical computer science to foundations to programming language developments, analysis tools, formal approaches to software engineering, and security. Organizing these conferences in a coherent, highly synchronized conference program facilitates participation in an exciting event, offering attendees the possibility to meet many researchers working in different directions in the field, and to easily attend talks of different conferences. Before and after the main conference, numerous satellite workshops take place and attract many researchers from all over the globe.

ETAPS 2018 received 479 submissions in total, 144 of which were accepted, yielding an overall acceptance rate of 30%. I thank all the authors for their interest in ETAPS, all the reviewers for their peer reviewing efforts, the PC members for their contributions, and in particular the PC (co-)chairs for their hard work in running this entire intensive process. Last but not least, my congratulations to all authors of the accepted papers!

ETAPS 2018 was enriched by the unifying invited speaker Martin Abadi (Google Brain, USA) and the conference-specific invited speakers (FASE) Pamela Zave (AT & T Labs, USA), (POST) Benjamin C. Pierce (University of Pennsylvania, USA), and (ESOP) Derek Dreyer (Max Planck Institute for Software Systems, Germany). Invited tutorials were provided by Armin Biere (Johannes Kepler University, Linz, Austria) on modern SAT solving and Fabio Somenzi (University of Colorado, Boulder, USA) on hardware verification. My sincere thanks to all these speakers for their inspiring and interesting talks!

ETAPS 2018 took place in Thessaloniki, Greece, and was organised by the Department of Informatics of the Aristotle University of Thessaloniki. The university was founded in 1925 and currently has around 75000 students; it is the largest university in Greece. ETAPS 2018 was further supported by the following associations and societies: ETAPS e.V., EATCS (European Association for Theoretical Computer Science), EAPLS (European Association for Programming Languages and Systems), and EASST (European Association of Software Science and Technology). The local organization team consisted of Panagiotis Katsaros (general chair), Ioannis Stamelos,

Lefteris Angelis, George Rahonis, Nick Bassiliades, Alexander Chatzigeorgiou, Ezio Bartocci, Simon Bliudze, Emmanouela Stachtiari, Kyriakos Georgiadis, and Petros Stratis (EasyConferences).

The overall planning for ETAPS is the main responsibility of the Steering Committee, and in particular of its Executive Board. The ETAPS Steering Committee consists of an Executive Board and representatives of the individual ETAPS conferences, as well as representatives of EATCS, EAPLS, and EASST. The Executive Board consists of Gilles Barthe (Madrid), Holger Hermanns (Saarbrücken), Joost-Pieter Katoen (chair, Aachen and Twente), Gerald Lüttgen (Bamberg), Vladimiro Sassone (Southampton), Tarmo Uustalu (Tallinn), and Lenore Zuck (Chicago). Other members of the Steering Committee are: Wil van der Aalst (Aachen), Parosh Abdulla (Uppsala), Amal Ahmed (Boston), Christel Baier (Dresden), Lujo Bauer (Pittsburgh), Dirk Beyer (Munich), Mikolaj Bojanczyk (Warsaw), Luis Caires (Lisbon), Jurriaan Hage (Utrecht), Rainer Hähnle (Darmstadt), Reiko Heckel (Leicester), Marieke Huisman (Twente), Panagiotis Katsaros (Thessaloniki), Ralf Küsters (Stuttgart), Ugo Dal Lago (Bologna), Kim G. Larsen (Aalborg), Matteo Maffei (Vienna), Tiziana Margaria (Limerick), Flemming Nielson (Copenhagen), Catuscia Palamidessi (Palaiseau), Andrew M. Pitts (Cambridge), Alessandra Russo (London), Dave Sands (Göteborg), Don Sannella (Edinburgh), Andy Schürr (Darmstadt), Alex Simpson (Ljubljana), Gabriele Taentzer (Marburg), Peter Thiemann (Freiburg), Jan Vitek (Prague), Tomas Vojnar (Brno), and Lijun Zhang (Beijing).

I would like to take this opportunity to thank all speakers, attendees, organizers of the satellite workshops, and Springer for their support. I hope you all enjoy the proceedings of ETAPS 2018. Finally, a big thanks to Panagiotis and his local organization team for all their enormous efforts that led to a fantastic ETAPS in Thessaloniki!

February 2018 Joost-Pieter Katoen

Preface

TACAS 2018 is the 24th edition of the International Conference on Tools and Algorithms for the Construction and Analysis of Systems conference series. TACAS 2018 is part of the 21st European Joint Conferences on Theory and Practice of Software (ETAPS 2018). The conference is held in the hotel Makedonia Palace in Thessaloniki, Greece, during April 16–19, 2018.

Conference Description. TACAS is a forum for researchers, developers, and users interested in rigorously based tools and algorithms for the construction and analysis of systems. The conference aims to bridge the gaps between different communities with this common interest and to support them in their quest to improve the utility, reliability, flexibility, and efficiency of tools and algorithms for building systems. TACAS solicits five types of submissions:

- Research papers, identifying and justifying a principled advance to the theoretical foundations for the construction and analysis of systems, where applicable supported by experimental validation
- Case-study papers, reporting on case studies and providing information about the system being studied, the goals of the study, the challenges the system poses to automated analysis, research methodologies and approaches used, the degree to which goals were attained, and how the results can be generalized to other problems and domains
- Regular tool papers, presenting a new tool, a new tool component, or novel extensions to an existing tool, with an emphasis on design and implementation concerns, including software architecture and core data structures, practical applicability, and experimental evaluations
- Tool-demonstration papers (6 pages), focusing on the usage aspects of tools
- Competition-contribution papers (4 pages), focusing on describing software-verification systems that participated at the International Competition on Software Verification (SV-COMP), which has been affiliated with our conference since TACAS 2012

New Items in the Call for Papers. There were three new items in the call for papers, which we briefly discuss.

- *Focus on Replicability of Research Results.* We consider that reproducibility of results is of the utmost importance for the TACAS community. Therefore, we encouraged all authors of submitted papers to include support for replicating the results of their papers.
- *Limit of 3 Submissions.* A change of the TACAS bylaws requires that each individual author is limited to a maximum of three submissions as an author or co-author. Authors of co-authored submissions are jointly responsible for respecting this policy. In case of violations, all submissions of this (co-)author would be desk-rejected.

– *Artifact Evaluation.* For the first time, TACAS 2018 included an optional artifact evaluation (AE) process for accepted papers. An artifact is any additional material (software, data sets, machine-checkable proofs, etc.) that substantiates the claims made in a paper and ideally makes them fully replicable. The evaluation and archival of artifacts improves replicability and traceability for the benefit of future research and the broader TACAS community.

Paper Selection. This year, 154 papers were submitted to TACAS, among which 115 were research papers, 6 case-study papers, 26 regular tool papers, and 7 were tool-demonstration papers. After a rigorous review process, with each paper reviewed by at least 3 program committee (PC) members, followed by an online discussion, the PC accepted 35 research papers, 2 case-study papers, 6 regular tool papers, and 2 tool-demonstration papers (45 papers in total).

Competition on Software Verification (SV-COMP). TACAS 2018 also hosted the 7th International Competition on Software Verification (SV-COMP), chaired and organized by Tomas Vojnar. The competition again had a high participation: 21 verification systems with developers from 11 countries were submitted for the systematic comparative evaluation, including two submissions from industry. This volume includes short papers describing 9 of the participating verification systems. These papers were reviewed by a separate program committee (PC); each of the papers was assessed by four reviewers. One session in the TACAS program was reserved for the presentation of the results: the summary by the SV-COMP chair and the participating tools by the developer teams.

Artifact-Evaluation Process. The authors of each of the 45 accepted papers were invited to submit an artifact immediately after the acceptance notification. An artifact evaluation committee (AEC), chaired by Arnd Hartmanns and Philipp Wendler, reviewed these artifacts, with 2 reviewers assigned to each artifact. The AEC received 33 artifact submissions, of which 24 were successfully evaluated (73% acceptance rate) and have been awarded the TACAS AEC badge, which is added to the title page of the respective paper. The AEC used a two-phase reviewing process: Reviewers first performed an initial check of whether the artifact was technically usable and whether the accompanying instructions were consistent, followed by a full evaluation of the artifact. In addition to the textual reviews, reviews also provided scores for consistency, completeness, and documentation. The main criterion for artifact acceptance was consistency with the paper, with completeness and documentation being handled in a more lenient manner as long as the artifact was useful overall. Finally, TACAS provided authors of all submitted artifacts the possibility to publish and permanently archive a "camera-ready" version of their artifact on https://springernature.figshare.com/tacas, with the only requirement being an open license assigned to the artifact. This possibility was used for 20 artifacts, while 2 more artifacts were archived independently by the authors.

Acknowledgments. We would like to thank all the people who helped to make TACAS 2018 successful. First, the chairs would like to thank the authors for submitting their papers to TACAS 2018. The reviewers did a great job in reviewing papers: They contributed informed and detailed reports and took part in the discussions during the virtual PC meeting. We also thank the steering committee for their advice.

Special thanks go to the general chair, Panagiotis Katsaros, and his overall organization team, to the chair of the ETAPS 2018 executive board, Joost-Pieter Katoen, who took care of the overall organization of ETAPS, to the EasyConference team for the local organization, and to the publication team at Springer for solving all the extra problems that our introduction of the new artifact-evaluation process caused.

March 2018

Dirk Beyer
Marieke Huisman
(PC Chairs)
Goran Frehse
(Tools Chair)
Tomas Vojnar
(SV-COMP Chair)
Arnd Hartmanns
Philipp Wendler
(AEC Chairs)

Organization

Program Committee

Wolfgang Ahrendt	Chalmers University of Technology, Sweden
Dirk Beyer (Chair)	Ludwig-Maximilians-Universität München, Germany
Armin Biere	Johannes Kepler University Linz, Austria
Lubos Brim	Masaryk University, Czech Republic
Franck Cassez	Macquarie University, Australia
Alessandro Cimatti	FBK-irst, Italy
Rance Cleaveland	University of Maryland, USA
Goran Frehse	University of Grenoble Alpes – Verimag, France
Jan Friso Groote	Eindhoven University of Technology, The Netherlands
Gudmund Grov	Norwegian Defence Research Establishment (FFI), Norway
Orna Grumberg	Technion — Israel Institute of Technology, Israel
Arie Gurfinkel	University of Waterloo, Canada
Klaus Havelund	Jet Propulsion Laboratory, USA
Matthias Heizmann	University of Freiburg, Germany
Holger Hermanns	Saarland University, Germany
Falk Howar	TU Clausthal/IPSSE, Germany
Marieke Huisman (Chair)	University of Twente, The Netherlands
Laura Kovacs	Vienna University of Technology, Austria
Jan Kretinsky	Technical University of Munich, Germany
Salvatore La Torre	Università degli studi di Salerno, Italy
Kim Larsen	Aalborg University, Denmark
Axel Legay	IRISA/Inria, Rennes, France
Yang Liu	Nanyang Technological University, Singapore
Rupak Majumdar	MPI-SWS, Germany
Tiziana Margaria	Lero, Ireland
Rosemary Monahan	National University of Ireland Maynooth, Ireland
David Parker	University of Birmingham, UK
Corina Pasareanu	CMU/NASA Ames Research Center, USA
Alexander K. Petrenko	ISP RAS, Russia
Zvonimir Rakamaric	University of Utah, USA
Kristin Yvonne Rozier	Iowa State University, USA
Natasha Sharygina	USI Lugano, Switzerland
Stephen F. Siegel	University of Delaware, USA
Bernhard Steffen	University of Dortmund, Germany
Stavros Tripakis	University of California, Berkeley, USA
Frits Vaandrager	Radboud University, The Netherlands
Tomas Vojnar	Brno University of Technology, Czech Republic

Heike Wehrheim	University of Paderborn, Germany
Thomas Wies	New York University, USA
Damien Zufferey	MPI-SWS, Germany

Program Committee and Jury — SV-COMP

Tomáš Vojnar (Chair)
Peter Schrammel (representing 2LS)
Jera Hensel (representing AProVE)
Michael Tautschnig (representing CBMC)
Vadim Mutilin (representing CPA-BAM-BnB)
Mikhail Mandrykin (representing CPA-BAM-Slicing)
Thomas Lemberger (representing CPA-Seq)
Hussama Ismail (representing DepthK)
Felipe Monteiro (representing ESBMC-incr)
Mikhail R. Gadelha (representing ESBMC-kind)
Martin Hruska (representing Forester)
Zhao Duan (representing InterpChecker)
Herbert Oliveira Rocha (representing Map2Check)
Veronika Šoková (representing PredatorHP)
Franck Cassez (representing Skink)
Marek Chalupa (representing Symbiotic)
Matthias Heizmann (representing UAutomizer)
Alexander Nutz (representing UKojak)
Daniel Dietsch (representing UTaipan)
Priyanka Darke (representing VeriAbs)
Pritom Rajkhowa (representing VIAP)
Liangze Yin (representing Yogar-CBMC)

Artifact Evaluation Committee (AEC)

Arnd Hartmanns (Chair)
Philipp Wendler (Chair)
Pranav Ashok
Maryam Dabaghchian
Daniel Dietsch
Rohit Dureja
Felix Freiberger
Karlheinz Friedberger
Frederik Gossen
Samuel Huang
Antonio Iannopollo
Omar Inverso
Nils Jansen
Sebastiaan Joosten

Eunsuk Kang
Sean Kauffman
Ondrej Lengal
Tobias Meggendorfer
Malte Mues
Chris Novakovic
David Sanan

Additional Reviewers

Aarssen, Rodin
Alzuhaibi, Omar
Andrianov, Pavel
Asadi, Sepideh
Ashok, Pranav
Bacci, Giovanni
Bainczyk, Alexaner
Baranowski, Marek
Barringer, Howard
Ben Said, Najah
Benerecetti, Massimo
Benes, Nikola
Bensalem, Saddek
Berzish, Murphy
Biewer, Sebastian
Biondi, Fabrizio
Blahoudek, František
Blicha, Martin
Bosselmann, Steve
Bruttomesso, Roberto
Butkova, Yuliya
Casagrande, Alberto
Caulfield, Benjamin
Ceska, Milan
Chen, Wei
Chimento, Jesus Mauricio
Cleophas, Loek
Cordeiro, Lucas
Dabaghchian, Maryam
Darulova, Eva
de Vink, Erik
Delzanno, Giorgio
Dietsch, Daniel
Du, Xiaoning
Dureja, Rohit
Dvir, Nurit
Ehlers, Rüdiger
Elrakaiby, Yehia
Enea, Constantin
Faella, Marco
Falcone, Ylies
Fedotov, Alexander
Fedyukovich, Grigory
Fox, Gereon
Freiberger, Felix
Frenkel, Hadar
Frohme, Markus
Genaim, Samir
Getman, Alexander
Given-Wilson, Thomas
Gleiss, Bernhard
Golden, Bat-Chen
González De Aledo, Pablo
Goodloe, Alwyn
Gopinath, Divya
Gossen, Frederik
Graf-Brill, Alexander
Greitschus, Marius
Griggio, Alberto
Guthmann, Ofer
Habermehl, Peter
Han, Tingting
Hao, Jianye
Hark, Marcel
Hartmanns, Arnd
Hashemi, Vahid
He, Shaobo
Heule, Marijn
Hoenicke, Jochen
Holik, Lukas
Horne, Ross
Hou, Zhe Hou
Hyvärinen, Antti
Inverso, Omar
Irfan, Ahmed
Jabbour, Fadi
Jacobs, Swen
Jansen, Nils
Jensen, Peter Gjøl
Joshi, Rajeev
Jovanović, Dejan
Kan, Shuanglong
Kang, Eunsuk
Kauffman, Sean
Klauck, Michaela
Kopetzki, Dawid
Kotelnikov, Evgenii
Krishna, Siddharth
Krämer, Julia
Kumar, Rahul
König, Jürgen
Lahav, Ori
Le Coent, Adrien
Lengal, Ondrej
Leofante, Francesco
Li, Jianwen
Lime, Didier
Lin, Yuhui
Lorber, Florian
Maarek, Manuel
Mandrykin, Mikhail
Marescotti, Matteo

Markey, Nicolas
Meggendorfer, Tobias
Meyer, Philipp
Meyer, Roland
Micheli, Andrea
Mjeda, Anila
Moerman, Joshua
Mogavero, Fabio
Monniaux, David
Mordan, Vitaly
Murtovi, Alnis
Mutilin, Vadim
Myreen, Magnus O.
Navas, Jorge A.
Neele, Thomas
Nickovic, Dejan
Nies, Gilles
Nikolov, Nikola S.
Norman, Gethin
Nyman, Ulrik
Oortwijn, Wytse
Pastva, Samuel
Pauck, Felix
Pavlinovic, Zvonimir
Pearce, David
Peled, Doron
Poulsen, Danny Bøgsted
Power, James
Putot, Sylvie
Quilbeuf, Jean
Rasin, Dan
Reger, Giles
Reynolds, Andrew
Ritirc, Daniela
Robillard, Simon
Rogalewicz, Adam
Roveri, Marco
Ročkai, Petr
Rüthing, Oliver
Šafránek, David
Salamon, Andras Z.
Sayed-Ahmed, Amr
Schieweck, Alexander
Schilling, Christian
Schmaltz, Julien
Seidl, Martina
Sessa, Mirko
Shafiei, Nastaran
Sharma, Arnab
Sickert, Salomon
Simon, Axel
Sloth, Christoffer
Spoto, Fausto
Sproston, Jeremy
Stan, Daniel
Taankvist, Jakob Haahr
Tacchella, Armando
Tetali, Sai Deep
Toews, Manuel
Tonetta, Stefano
Traonouez, Louis-Marie
Travkin, Oleg
Trostanetski, Anna
van den Bos, Petra
van Dijk, Tom
van Harmelen, Arnaud
Vasilev, Anton
Vasilyev, Anton
Veanes, Margus
Vizel, Yakir
Widder, Josef
Wijs, Anton
Willemse, Tim
Wirkner, Dominik
Yang, Fei
Zakharov, Ilja
Zantema, Hans

Contents – Part I

Theorem Proving

SAT and SMT I

Deductive Verification

Software Verification and Optimisation

Model Checking

Machine Learning

Contents – Part II

Concurrent and Distributed Systems

SAT and SMT II

Security and Reactive Systems

Temporal Logic and Mu-calculus

7th Competition on Software Verification (SV-COMP)

Theorem Proving

Unification with Abstraction and Theory Instantiation in Saturation-Based Reasoning

Giles Reger[1(✉)], Martin Suda[2], and Andrei Voronkov[1,2,3]

[1] University of Manchester, Manchester, UK
giles.reger@manchester.ac.uk
[2] TU Wien, Vienna, Austria
[3] EasyChair, Manchester, UK

Abstract. We make a new contribution to the field by providing a new method of using SMT solvers in saturation-based reasoning. We do this by introducing two new inference rules for reasoning with non-ground clauses. The first rule utilises theory constraint solving (an SMT solver) to perform reasoning within a clause to find an instance where we can remove one or more theory literals. This utilises the power of SMT solvers for theory reasoning with non-ground clauses, reasoning which is currently achieved by the addition of often prolific theory axioms. The second rule is *unification with abstraction* where the notion of unification is extended to introduce constraints where theory terms may not otherwise unify. This abstraction is performed lazily, as needed, to allow the superposition theorem prover to make as much progress as possible without the search space growing too quickly. Additionally, the first rule can be used to discharge the constraints introduced by the second. These rules were implemented within the Vampire theorem prover and experimental results show that they are useful for solving a considerable number of previously unsolved problems. The current implementation focuses on complete theories, in particular various versions of arithmetic.

1 Introduction

Reasoning in quantifier-free first-order logic with theories, such as arithmetic, is hard. Reasoning with quantifiers and first-order theories is very hard. It is undecidable in general and Π_1^1-complete for many simple combinations, for example linear (real or integer) arithmetic and uninterpreted functions [16]. At the same

This work was supported by EPSRC Grants EP/K032674/1 and EP/P03408X/1. Martin Suda and Andrei Voronkov were partially supported by ERC Starting Grant 2014 SYMCAR 639270. Martin Suda was also partially supported by the Austrian research projects FWF S11403-N23 and S11409-N23. Andrei Voronkov was also partially supported by the Wallenberg Academy Fellowship 2014 – TheProSE. Part of this work was done when Andrei Voronkov was part-time employed by Chalmers University of Technology.

D. Beyer and M. Huisman (Eds.): TACAS 2018, LNCS 10805, pp. 3–22, 2018.
https://doi.org/10.1007/978-3-319-89960-2_1

time such reasoning is essential to the future success of certain application areas, such as program analysis and software verification, that rely on quantifiers to, for example, express properties of objects, inductively defined data structures, the heap and dynamic memory allocation. This paper presents a new approach to theory reasoning with quantifiers that (1) uses an SMT solver to do *local* theory reasoning within a clause, and (2) extends unification to avoid the need to explicitly separate theory and non-theory parts of clauses.

There are two directions of research in the area of reasoning with problems containing quantifiers and theories. The first is the extension of SMT solvers with *instantiation* heuristics such as E-matching [9,12]. The second is the extension of first-order reasoning approaches with support for theory reasoning (note that the instantiation heuristics from SMT solvers are not appropriate in this context, as discussed in [26]). There have been a number of varied attempts in this second direction with some approaches extending various calculi [2,3,7,8,13,16,28] or using an SMT solver to deal with the ground part of the problem [20]. This second approach includes our previous work developing AVATAR modulo theories [21], which complements the approach presented in this paper as explained later. A surprisingly effective approach to theory reasoning with first-order theorem provers is to add *theory axioms* (i.e. axioms from the theory of interest). Whilst this has no hope of being complete, it can be used to prove a large number of problems of interest. However, theory axioms can be highly prolific in saturation-based proof search and often swamp the search space with irrelevant consequences of the theory [22]. This combinatorial explosion prevents theory axioms from being useful in cases where *deep* theory reasoning is required. This paper provides a solution that allows for a combination of these approaches i.e. the integration with an SMT solver, the use of theory axioms, and the heuristic extension of the underlying calculi.

Our paper contains two main ideas and we start with examples (which we revisit later) to motivate and explain these ideas. The first idea is motivated by the observation that the theory part of a first-order clause might already be restricting the interesting instances of a clause, sometimes uniquely, and we can use this to produce simpler instances that are useful for proof search. For example, the first-order clause

$$14x \not\simeq x^2 + 49 \vee p(x)$$

has a single solution for x which makes the first literal false with respect to the underlying theory of arithmetic, namely $x = 7$. Therefore, every instance of this clause is a logical consequence of its single instance

$$p(7)$$

in the underlying theory. If we apply standard superposition rules to the original clause and a sufficiently rich axiomatisation of arithmetic, we will most likely end up with a very large number of logical consequences and never generate $p(7)$, or run out of space before generating it. For many clauses the solution will not be unique but can still provide useful instances, for example by taking the clause

$$7 \leq x \vee p(x)$$

and using its instance

$$7 \leq 0 \vee p(0)$$

we can derive the clause

$$p(0).$$

This clause does not represent all solutions for $7 \leq x$, but it results in a clause with fewer literals. Moreover, this clause is ground and can be passed to an SMT solver (this is where this approach complements the work of AVATAR modulo theories).

Finally, there are very simple cases where this kind of approach can immediately find inconsistencies. For example, the clause

$$x \leq 0 \vee x \leq y$$

has instances making it false, for example via the substitution $\{x \mapsto 1, y \mapsto 0\}$.

As explained in Sect. 3, these observations lead to an instantiation rule that considers clauses to be in the form $T \rightarrow C$, where T is the theory part, and uses an SMT solver to find a substitution θ under which T is valid in the given theory, thus producing the instance $C\theta$. Which, in the case where $C = \bot$, can find general inconsistencies.

The second rule is related to the use of *abstraction*. By an *abstraction* we mean (variants of) the rule obtaining from a clase $C[t]$, where t is a non-variable term, a clause $x \not\simeq t \vee C[x]$, where x is a new variable. Abstraction is implemented in several theorem provers, including the previous version of our theorem prover VAMPIRE [18] used for experiments described in this paper.

Take, for example, the formula

$$(\forall x : int.\ p(2x)) \rightarrow p(10)$$

which is `ARI189=1` from the TPTP library [33]. When negated and clausified, this formula gives two unit clauses

$$p(2x) \quad \text{and} \quad \neg p(10),$$

from which we can derive nothing without abstracting at least one of the clauses.

If we abstract $p(10)$ into $p(y) \vee y \not\simeq 10$ then a resolution step would give us $2x \not\simeq 10$ and simple evaluation would provide $x \not\simeq 5$, which is refutable by equality resolution. However, the abstraction step is necessary. Some approaches rely on *full abstraction* where theory and non-theory symbols are fully separated. This is unattractive for a number of reasons which we enumerate here:

1. A fully abstracted clause tends to be much longer, especially if the original clause contains deeply nested theory and non-theory symbols. Getting rid of long clauses was one of the motivations of our previous AVATAR work on *clause splitting* [34] (see this work for why long clauses are problematic for resolution-based approaches). However, the long clauses produced by abstraction will share variables, reducing the impact of AVATAR.

2. The AVATAR modulo theories approach [21] ensures that the first-order solver is only exploring part of the search space that is theory-consistent in its ground part (using a SMT solver to achieve this). This is effective but relies on ground literals remaining ground, even those that mix theory and non-theory symbols. Full abstraction destroys such ground literals.
3. As mentioned previously, the addition of theory axioms can be effective for problems requiring shallow theory reasoning. Working with fully abstracted clauses forces us to make first-order reasoning to treat the theory part of a clause differently. This makes it difficult to take full advantage of theory axiom reasoning.

The final reason we chose not to fully abstract clauses in our work is that the main advantage of full abstraction for us would be that it deals with the above problem, but we have a solution which we believe solves this issue in a more satisfactory way, as confirmed by our experiments described in Sect. 5.

The second idea is to perform this abstraction *lazily*, i.e., only where it is required to perform inference steps. As described in Sect. 4, this involves extending unifications to produce theory constraints under which two terms will unify. As we will see, these theory constraints are exactly the kind of terms that can be handled easily by the instantiation technique introduced in our first idea.

As explained above, the contributions of this paper are

1. a new instantiation rule that uses an SMT solver to provide instances consistent with the underlying theory (Sect. 3),
2. an extension of unification that provides a mechanism to perform *lazy* abstraction, i.e., only abstracting as much as is needed, which results in clauses with theory constraints that can be discharged by the previous instantiation technique (Sect. 4),
3. an implementation of these techniques in the Vampire theorem prover (described in Sects. 3 and 4),
4. an experimental evaluation that demonstrate the effectiveness of these techniques both individually and in combination with the rest of the powerful techniques implemented within Vampire (Sect. 5).

An extended version of this paper [32] contains further examples and discussion. We start our presentation by introducing the necessary background material.

2 Preliminaries and Related Work

First-Order Logic and Theories. We consider a many-sorted first-order logic with equality. A *signature* is a pair $\Sigma = (\Xi, \Omega)$ where Ξ is a set of *sorts* and Ω a set of *predicate* and *function* symbols with associated argument and return sorts from Ξ. *Terms* are of the form c, x, or $f(t_1, \ldots, t_n)$ where f is a *function symbol* of arity $n \geq 1$, $t_1, \ldots, t_n$ are terms, c is a zero arity function symbol (i.e. a constant) and x is a variable. We assume that all terms are well-sorted. Atoms are of the form $p(t_1, \ldots, t_n), q$ or $t_1 \simeq_s t_2$ where p is a predicate symbol of arity n, $t_1, \ldots, t_n$ are terms, q is a zero arity predicate symbol and for each sort $s \in \Xi$, $\simeq_s$ is the *equality symbol for the sort s*. We write simply $\simeq$ when s is known from the context or irrelevant. A *literal* is either an atom A, in which case we call it *positive*, or a negation of an atom $\neg A$, in which case we call it *negative*. When L is a negative literal $\neg A$ and we write $\neg L$, we mean the positive literal A. We write negated equalities as $t_1 \not\simeq t_2$. We write $t[s]_p$ and $L[s]_p$ to denote that a term s occurs in a term t (in a literal L) at a position p.

A *clause* is a disjunction of literals $L_1 \vee \ldots \vee L_n$ for $n \geq 0$. We disregard the order of literals and treat a clause as a multiset. When $n = 0$ we speak of the *empty clause*, which is always false. When $n = 1$ a clause is called a *unit clause*. Variables in clauses are considered to be universally quantified. Standard methods exist to transform an arbitrary first-order formula into clausal form (e.g. [19] and our recent work in [25]).

A *substitution* is any expression θ of the form $\{x_1 \mapsto t_1, \ldots, x_n \mapsto t_n\}$, where $n \geq 0$. $E\theta$ is the expression obtained from E by the simultaneous replacement of each x_i by t_i. By an expression we mean a term, an atom, a literal, or a clause. An expression is *ground* if it contains no variables. An *instance of E* is any expression $E\theta$ and a *ground instance* of E is any instance of E that is ground. A *unifier* of two terms, atoms or literals E_1 and E_2 is a substitution θ such that $E_1\theta = E_2\theta$. It is known that if two expressions have a unifier, then they have a so-called most general unifier.

We assume a standard notion of a (first-order, many-sorted) *interpretation* $\mathcal{I}$, which assigns a non-empty domain $\mathcal{I}_s$ to every sort $s \in \Xi$, and maps every function symbol f to a function $\mathcal{I}_f$ and every predicate symbol p to a relation $\mathcal{I}_p$ on these domains so that the mapping respects sorts. We call $\mathcal{I}_f$ the *interpretation of f in $\mathcal{I}$*, and similarly for $\mathcal{I}_p$ and $\mathcal{I}_s$. Interpretations are also sometimes called *first-order structures*. A *sentence* is a closed formula, i.e., with no free variables. We use the standard notions of validity and satisfiability of sentences in such interpretations. An interpretation is a *model* for a set of clauses if (the universal closure of) each of these clauses is true in the interpretation.

A *theory* $\mathcal{T}$ is identified by a class of interpretations. A sentence is *satisfiable* in $\mathcal{T}$ if it is true in at least one of these interpretations and *valid* if it is true in all of them. A function (or predicate) symbol f is called *uninterpreted* in $\mathcal{T}$, if for every interpretation $\mathcal{I}$ of $\mathcal{T}$ and every interpretation $\mathcal{I}'$ which agrees with $\mathcal{I}$ on all symbols apart from f, $\mathcal{I}'$ is also an interpretation of $\mathcal{T}$. A theory is called *complete* if, for every sentence F of this theory, either F or $\neg F$ is valid in this theory. Evidently, every theory of a single interpretation is complete. We can define satisfiability and validity of arbitrary formulas in an interpretation in a standard way by treating free variables as new uninterpreted constants.

For example, the theory of integer arithmetic fixes the interpretation of a distinguished sort $s_{int} \in \Xi_{IA}$ to the set of mathematical integers $\mathbb{Z}$ and analogously assigns the usual meanings to $\{+, -, <, >, *\} \in \Omega_{IA}$. We will mostly deal with theories in which their restriction to interpreted symbols is a complete theory, for example, integer or real linear arithmetic. In the sequel we assume that $\mathcal{T}$ is an arbitrary but fixed theory and give definitions relative to this theory.

Abstracted Clauses. Here we discuss how a clause can be separated into a theory and non-theory part. To this end we need to divide symbols into theory and non-theory symbols. When we deal with a combination of theories we consider as *theory symbols* those symbols interpreted in at least one of the theories and all other symbols as *non-theory symbols.* That is, non-theory symbols are uninterpreted in all theories.

A non-equality literal is a *theory literal* if its predicate symbol is a theory symbol. An equality literal $t_1 \simeq_s t_2$ is a theory literal, if the sort s is a theory sort. A *non-theory literal* is any literal that is not a theory literal. A literal is *pure* if it contains only theory symbols or only non-theory symbols. A clause is *fully abstracted*, or simply *abstracted*, if it only contains pure literals. A clause is *partially abstracted* if non-theory symbols do not appear in theory literals. Note that in partially abstracted clauses theory symbols are allowed to appear in non-theory literals.

A non-variable term t is called a *theory term* (respectively *non-theory term*) if its top function symbol is a theory (respectively non-theory) symbol. When we say that a term is a theory or a non-theory term, we assume that this term is not a variable.

Given a non-abstracted clause $L[t] \vee C$ where L is a theory literal and t a non-theory term (or the other way around), we can construct the equivalent clause $L[x] \vee C \vee x \not\simeq t$ for a fresh variable x. Repeated application of this process will lead to an abstracted clause, and doing this only for theory literals will result in a partially abstracted clause. In both cases, the results are unique (up to variable renaming).

The above abstraction process will take $a + a \simeq 1$, where a is a non-theory symbol, and produce $x+y \simeq 1 \vee x \not\simeq a \vee y \not\simeq a$. There is a simpler equivalent fully abstracted clause $x + x \simeq 1 \vee x \not\simeq a$, and we would like to avoid unnecessarily long clauses. For this reason, we will assume that abstraction will abstract syntactically equal subterms using the same fresh variable, as in the above example. If we abstract larger terms first, the result of abstractions will be unique up to variable renaming.

Superposition Calculus. Later we will show how our underlying calculus, the superposition and resolution calculus, can be updated to use an updated notion of unification. For space reasons we do not replicate this calculus here (but it is given in our previous work [15]). We do, however, draw attention to the following *Equality Resolution* rule

$$\frac{s \not\simeq t \vee C}{C\theta} \quad \theta \text{ is a most general unifier of } s \text{ and } t$$

as, without modification, this rule will directly undo any abstractions. This rule will be used in Sect. 3 to justify ignoring certain literals when performing instantiation.

Saturation-Based Proof Search (and Theory Reasoning). We introduce our new approach within the context of saturation-based proof search. The general idea in saturation is to maintain two sets of *Active* and *Passive* clauses. A saturation-loop then selects a clause C from *Passive*, places C in *Active*, applies *generating inferences* between C and clauses in *Active*, and finally places newly derived clauses in *Passive* after applying some retention tests. The retention tests involve checking whether the new clause is itself redundant (i.e. a tautology) or redundant with respect to existing clauses.

To perform theory reasoning within this context it is common to do two things. Firstly, to *evaluate* new clauses to put them in a common form (e.g. rewrite all inequalities in terms of $<$) and evaluate ground theory terms and literals (e.g. $1+2$ becomes 3 and $1<2$ becomes *false*). Secondly, as previously mentioned, relevant theory axioms can be added to the initial search space. For example, if the input clauses use the $+$ symbol one can add the axioms $x+y \simeq y+x$ and $x+0 \simeq x$, among others.

3 Generating Simpler Instances

In the introduction, we showed how useful instances can be generated by finding substitutions that make theory literals false. We provide further motivation for the need for instances and then describe a new inference rule capturing this approach.

There are some very simple problems that are difficult to solve by the addition of theory axioms. Consider, for example, the following conjecture valid in the theory of integer arithmetic:

$$(\exists x)(x+x \simeq 2),$$

which yields the following unit clause after being negated for refutation

$$x+x \not\simeq 2.$$

It takes Vampire almost 15 s to refute this clause using theory axioms (and non-trivial search parameters) and involves the derivation of intermediate theory consequences such as $x+1 \simeq y+1 \vee y+1 \leq x \vee x+1 \leq y$. In contrast, applying the substitution $\{x \mapsto 1\}$ immediately leads to a refutation via evaluation.

The generation of instances in this way is not only useful where theory axiom reasoning explodes, it can also significantly shorten proofs where theory axiom reasoning succeeds. For example, there is a proof of the problem DAT101=1 from the TPTP library using theory axioms that involves generating just over 230 thousand clauses. In contrast, instantiating an intermediate clause

$$\mathsf{inRange}(x, \mathsf{cons}(1, \mathsf{cons}(5, \mathsf{cons}(2, \mathsf{nil})))) \vee x < 4 \qquad (1)$$

with $\{x \mapsto 4\}$ solves the problem after generating just 171 clauses.

Theory Instantiation. From the above discussion it is clear that generating instances of theory literals may drastically improve performance of saturation-based theorem provers. The problem is that the set of all such instances can be infinite, so we should try to generate only those instances that are likely not to degrade the performance.

There is a special case of instantiation that allows us to derive from a clause C a clause with fewer literals than C. We can capture this in the following *theory instantiation* inference rule where the notion of *trivial literal* has not yet been defined.

$$\frac{P \vee D}{D\theta}\ (\mathit{TheoryInst})$$

such that

1. P contains only pure theory literals;
2. $\neg P\theta$ is valid in $\mathcal{T}$ (equivalently, $P\theta$ is unsatisfiable in $\mathcal{T}$).
3. P contains no literals trivial in $P \vee D$;

The second condition ensures that $P\theta$ can be safely removed. This also avoids making a theory literal valid in the theory (a theory tautology) after instantiation. For example, if we had instantiated clause (1) with $\{x \mapsto 3\}$ then the clause would have been evaluated to *true* (because of $3 < 4$) and thrown away as a theory tautology.

The third condition avoids the potential problem of simply undoing abstraction. For example, consider the unit clause $p(1, 5)$ which will be abstracted as

$$x \not\simeq 1 \vee y \not\simeq 5 \vee p(x, y). \qquad (2)$$

The substitution $\theta = \{x \mapsto 1, y \mapsto 5\}$ makes the formula $x \simeq 1 \wedge y \simeq 5$ valid. Its application, followed by evaluation produces $p(x, y)\theta = p(1, 5)$, i.e. the original clause.

More generally, a clause does not need to be abstracted to contain such literals. For example, the clause

$$x \not\simeq 1 + y \vee p(x, y)$$

might produce, after applying *TheoryInst* (without the third condition) and evaluation, the instance $p(1, 0)$, but it can also be used to produce the more general clause $p(y + 1, y)$ using equality resolution.

Based on the above discussion we define literals that we do not want to use for applying *TheoryInst* since we can use a sequence of equality resolution steps to solve them. Let C be a clause. The set of *trivial literals in* C is defined recursively as follows. A literal L is trivial in C if

1. L is of the form $x \not\simeq t$ such that x does not occur in t;
2. L is a pure theory literal;
3. every occurrence of x in C apart from its occurrence in $x \not\simeq t$ is either in a literal that is not a pure theory literal, or in a literal trivial in C.

We call such literals trivial as they can be removed by a sequence of equality resolution steps. For example, in clause (2) both $x \not\simeq 1$ and $y \not\simeq 5$ are trivial. Consider another example: the clause

$$x \not\simeq y + 1 \vee y \not\simeq z \cdot z \vee p(x, y, z).$$

The literal $x \not\simeq y + 1$ is trivial, because, apart from this literal, x occurs only in the non-theory literal $p(x, y, z)$. The literal $y \not\simeq z \cdot z$ is also trivial, because y occurs only in non-theory literal $p(x, y, z)$ and in a trivial literal $x \not\simeq y + 1$.

It is easy to argue that all pure theory literals introduced by abstraction are trivial.

Implementation. To use *TheoryInst*, we apply the following steps to each given clause C:

1. abstract relevant literals;
2. collect (all) non-trivial pure theory literals $L_1, \ldots, L_n$;
3. run an SMT solver on $T = \neg L_1 \wedge \ldots \wedge \neg L_n$;
4. if the SMT solver returns
   - a model, we turn it into a substitution θ such that $T\theta$ is valid in $\mathcal{T}$;
   - *unsatisfiable*, then C is a theory tautology and can be removed.

Note that the abstraction step is not necessary for using *TheoryInst*, since it will only introduce trivial literals. However, for each introduced theory literal $x \not\simeq t$ the variable x occurs in a non-theory literal and inferences applied to this non-theory literal may instantiate x to a term s such that $s \not\simeq t$ is non-trivial. Let us now discuss the implementation of each step in further detail.

Selecting Pure Theory Literals. In the definition of *TheoryInst* we did not specify that P contains *all* pure theory literals in the premise. The reason is that some pure theory literals may be unhelpful. For example, consider

$$x \simeq 0 \vee p(x).$$

Here the SMT solver could select any value for x, apart from 0. In general, positive equalities are less helpful than negative equalities or interpreted predicates as they restrict the instances less. We introduce three options to control this selection:

- `strong`: Only select *strong* literals where a literal is strong if it is a negative equality or an interpreted literal.
- `overlap`: Select all strong literals and additionally those theory literals whose variables overlap with a strong literal.
- `all`: Select all non-trivial pure theory literals.

At this point there may not be any pure theory literals to select, in which case the inference will not be applied.

Interacting with the SMT solver. In this step, we replace variables in selected pure theory literals by new constants and negate the literals. Once this has been done, the translation of literals to the format understood by the SMT solver is straightforward (and outlined in [21]). We use Z3 [11] in this work.

Additional care needs to be taken when translating partial functions, such as division. In SMT solving, they are treated as total underspecified functions. For example, when $\mathcal{T}$ is integer arithmetic with division, interpretations for $\mathcal{T}$ are defined in such a way that for all integers a, b and interpretation $\mathcal{I}$, the theory also has the interpretation defined exactly as $\mathcal{I}$ apart from having $a/0 = b$. In a way, division by 0 behaves as an uninterpreted function.

Due to this convention, Z3 may generate an arbitrary value for the result in order to satisfy a given query. As a result, Z3 can produce a model that is output as an ordinary solution except for the assumptions about division by 0. For example solving $2/x = 1$ can return $x = 0$. If we accept that $x \simeq 0$ is a solution, the theorem prover may become unsound. As an example, consider a problem consisting of the following two clauses

$$1/x \not\simeq 0 \vee p(x) \qquad 1/x \simeq 0 \vee \neg p(x).$$

The example is satisfiable as witnessed by an interpretation that assigns false to $p(z)$ for every real number z and interprets $1/0$ as a non-zero real, e.g. 1. However, the *TheoryInst* rule could produce conflicting instances $p(0)$ and $\neg p(0)$ of the two clauses, internally assuming $1/0 = 0$ for the first instances and $1/0 \neq 0$ for the second.

To deal with this issue, we assert that $s \not\simeq 0$ whenever we translate a term of the form t/s. This implies that we do not pass to the SMT solver terms of the form $t/0$.

Instance Generation. The next step is to understand when and how we can turn the model returned by the SMT solver into a substitution making T valid. Recall that T can contain

1. interpreted symbols that have a fixed interpretation in $\mathcal{T}$, such as 0 or +;
2. other interpreted symbols, such as division;
3. variables of T.

In general, there are no standards on how SMT solvers return models or solutions. We assume that the model returned by the underlying SMT solver can be turned into a conjunction S of literals such that

1. S is satisfiable in $\mathcal{T}$;
2. $S \rightarrow T$ is valid in $\mathcal{T}$.

Note that checking that T is satisfiable and returning T as a model satisfies both conditions, but does not give a substitution that can be used to apply the *TheoryInst* rule.

To apply this rule, we need models of a special form defined below. A conjunction S of literals is said to be in *triangle form* if S has the form

$$x_1 \simeq t_1 \wedge \ldots \wedge x_n \simeq t_n \tag{3}$$

such that for all $i = 1, \ldots, n$ the variable x_i does not occur in $t_i, \ldots, t_n$. Any model S in a triangle form can be converted into a substitution θ such that $x_i\theta = t_i\theta$ for all $i = 1, \ldots, n$. Note that $S\theta$ is then valid, hence (by validity of $S \rightarrow T$), $T\theta$ is valid too, so we can use θ to apply *TheoryInst*.

Practically, we must evaluate the introduced constants (i.e. those introduced for each of the variables in the above step) in the given model. In some cases, this evaluation fails to give a numeric value. For example, if the result falls out of the range of values internally representable by VAMPIRE or when the value is a proper algebraic number, which currently also cannot be represented internally by our prover. In this case, we cannot produce a substitution and the inference fails.

Theory Tautology Deletion. As we pointed out above, if the SMT solver returns *unsatisfiable* then C is a theory tautology and can be removed. We only do it when we do not pass to the solver additional assumptions related to division by 0.

4 Abstraction Through Unification

As shown earlier, there are cases where we cannot perform a necessary inference step, because we are using a *syntactic* notion of equality rather than a *semantic* one. We have introduced an inference rule (*TheoryInst*) able to derive $p(7)$ from the clause

$$14x \not\simeq x^2 + 49 \vee p(x),$$

but unable to deal with a pair of clauses such as

$$r(14y) \qquad \neg r(x^2 + 49) \vee p(x),$$

as it only performs theory reasoning *inside* a clause whereas this requires us to reason *between* clauses. Semantically, the terms $14y$ and $x^2 + 49$ can be made equal when $y = x = 7$ so we would like to get the result $p(7)$ here also.

Notice that if the clauses had been abstracted as follows:

$$r(u) \vee u \not\simeq 14y \qquad \neg r(v) \vee v \not\simeq x^2 + 49 \vee p(x),$$

then the resolution step would have been successful, producing

$$u \not\simeq 14y \vee u \not\simeq x^2 + 49 \vee p(x)$$

which could be given to *TheoryInst* to produce $p(7)$. One solution would be to store clauses in abstracted form, but we argued earlier why this is not suitable and later confirm this experimentally. Instead of abstracting fully we incorporate the abstraction process into unification so that only abstractions necessary for a particular inference are performed. This is a *lazy* approach, i.e., we delay abstraction until it is needed.

Algorithm 1. Unification algorithm with constraints

function $\mathsf{mgu_{Abs}}(l, r)$
  let $\mathcal{E}$ be a set of equations; $\mathcal{E} := \{l = r\}$
  let $\mathcal{D}$ be a set of disequalities; $\mathcal{D} := \emptyset$
  let θ be a substitution; $\theta := \{\}$
  loop
    if $\mathcal{E}$ is empty **then return** (θ, D), where D is the disjunction of literals in $\mathcal{D}$
    Select an equation $s = t$ in $\mathcal{E}$ and remove it from $\mathcal{E}$
    if s coincides with t **then** do nothing
    else if s is a variable and s does not occur in t **then**
      $\theta := \theta \circ \{s \mapsto t\}$; $\mathcal{E} := \mathcal{E}\{s \mapsto t\}$
    else if s is a variable and s occurs in t **then** fail
    else if t is a variable **then** $\mathcal{E} := \mathcal{E} \cup \{t = s\}$
    else if s and t have different top-level symbols **then**
      if `canAbstract`(s, t) **then** $\mathcal{D} := \mathcal{D} \cup \{s \not\simeq t\}$
      else fail
    else if $s = f(s_1, \ldots, s_n)$ and $t = f(t_1, \ldots, t_n)$ for some f **then**
      $\mathcal{E} := \mathcal{E} \cup \{s_1 = t_1, \ldots, s_n = t_n\}$

Unification with Abstraction. Here we define a partial function $\mathsf{mgu_{Abs}}$ on pairs of terms and pairs of atoms such that $\mathsf{mgu_{Abs}}(t, s)$ is either undefined, in which case we say that it *fails* on (s, t), or $\mathsf{mgu_{Abs}}(t, s) = (\theta, D)$ such that

1. θ is a substitution and D is a (possibly empty) disjunction of disequalities;
2. $(D \vee t \simeq s)\theta$ is valid in the underlying theory (and even valid in predicate logic).

Algorithm 1 gives a unification algorithm extended so that it implements $\mathsf{mgu_{Abs}}$. The algorithm is parameterised by a `canAbstract` predicate. The idea here is that some abstractions are not useful. For example, consider the two clauses

$$p(1) \qquad \neg p(2).$$

Allowing 1 and 2 to unify and produce $1 \not\simeq 2$ is not useful in any context. Therefore, `canAbstract` will always be false if the two terms are always non-equal in the underlying theory, e.g. if they are distinct numbers in the theory of arithmetic. Beyond this obvious requirement we also want to control how prolific such unifications can be. Therefore, we include the following options here:

- `interpreted_only`: only produce a constraint if the top-level symbol of both terms is a theory symbol,
- `one_side_interpreted`: only produce a constraint if the top-level symbol of at least one term is a theory symbol,
- `one_side_constant`: only produce a constraint if the top-level symbol of at least one term is a theory symbol and the other is an uninterpreted constant,
- `all`: allow all terms of theory sort to unify and produce constraints.

Updated Calculus. So far we have only considered resolution as a rule that could use this new form of unification, but in principle it can be used wherever we use unification. In the extended version of this paper [32] we describe how to update the full superposition and resolution calculus to make use of unification with abstraction. Here we give the rules for resolution and factoring:

$$\frac{\underline{A} \vee C_1 \quad \underline{\neg A'} \vee C_2}{(D \vee C_1 \vee C_2)\theta} \ \textbf{Resolution-wA} \qquad \frac{\underline{A \vee A'} \vee C}{(D \vee A \vee C)\theta} \ \textbf{Factoring-wA}$$

where, for both inferences, $(\theta, D) = \mathsf{mgu}_{\mathsf{Abs}}(A, A')$ and A is not an equality literal.

Now given the problem from the introduction involving $p(2x)$ and $\neg p(10)$ we can apply Resolution-wA to produce $2x \not\simeq 10$ which can be resolved using evaluation and equality resolution as before. We note at this point that a further advantage of this updated calculus is that it directly resolves the issue of losing proofs via eager evaluation, e.g. where $p(1+3)$ is evaluated to $p(4)$, missing the chance to resolve with $\neg p(x+3)$.

Implementation. In VAMPIRE, as in most modern theorem provers, inferences involving unification are implemented via *term indexing* [30]. Therefore, to update how unification is applied we need to update our implementation of term indexing. As the field of term indexing is highly complex we only give a sketch of the update here.

Term indices provide the ability to use a *query term t* to extract terms that unify (or match, or generalise) with t along with the relevant substitutions. Like many theorem provers, VAMPIRE uses substitution trees [14] to index terms. The idea behind substitution trees is to abstract a term into a series of substitutions required to generate that term and store these substitutions in the nodes of the tree. To search for unifying terms we perform a backtracking search over the tree, composing substitutions from the nodes when descending down edges and checking at each node whether the query term is consistent with the current substitution. This involves unifying subterms of the query term against terms at nodes and a backtrackable result substitution must be maintained to store the results of these unifications. The result substitution must be backtracked as appropriate i.e. when backtracking past the point of unification.

To update this process we do two things. Firstly, wherever previously a unification failed we will produce a set of constraints using Algorithm 1. Secondly, alongside the backtrackable result substitution we maintain a backtrackable stack of constraints so that whenever we backtrack past a point where we made a unification that produced some constraints we remove those constraints from the stack.

5 Experimental Results

We present experimental results evaluating the effectiveness of the new techniques. Our experiments were carried out on a cluster on which each node is equipped with two quad core Intel processors running at 2.4 GHz and 24 GiB of memory.

Table 1. Evaluation of the 24 meaningful combination of the three tested options

fta	uwa	thi	solutions	fta	uwa	thi	solutions
on	off	all	252	off	one_side_interpreted	strong	387
on	off	overlap	265	off	off	all	392
on	off	strong	266	off	one_side_constant	strong	397
on	off	off	276	off	one_side_constant	overlap	401
off	all	all	333	off	interpreted_only	overlap	407
off	all	overlap	351	off	one_side_interpreted	off	407
off	all	strong	354	off	interpreted_only	strong	409
off	one_side_interpreted	all	364	off	one_side_constant	off	417
off	all	off	364	off	off	overlap	428
off	one_side_constant	all	374	off	interpreted_only	off	430
off	interpreted_only	all	379	off	off	strong	431
off	one_side_interpreted	overlap	385	off	off	off	450

Comparing New Options. We were interested in comparing how various proof option values affect the performance of a theorem prover. We consider the two new options referred to here by their short names: uwa (unification with abstraction) and thi (theory instantiation). In addition, we consider the boolean option fta (full theory abstraction), applying full abstract to input clauses as implemented in previous versions of VAMPIRE.

Making such a comparison is hard, since there is no obvious methodology for doing so, especially considering that VAMPIRE has over 60 options commonly used in experiments (see [24]). The majority of these options are Boolean, some are finitely-valued, some integer-valued and some range over other infinite domains. The method we used here was based on the following ideas, already described in [17].

1. We use a subset of problems with quantifiers and theories from the SMTLIB library [5] (version 2016-05-23) that (i) do not contain bit vectors, (ii) are not trivially solvable, and (iii) are solvable by some approach.
2. We repeatedly select a random problem P in this set, a random strategy S and run P on variants of S obtained by choosing possible values for the three options using the same time limit.

We consider combinations of option values satisfying the following natural conditions: either fta or uwa must be off, since it does not make sense to use unification with abstraction when full abstraction is performed. This resulted in 24 possible combinations of values. We ran approximately 100 000 tests with the time limit of 30 s, which is about 4000 tests per a combination of options. The results are shown in Table 1.

It may seem surprising that the overall best strategy has all the three options turned off. This is due to what we have observed previously: many SMTLIB problems with quantifiers and theories require very little theory reasoning. Indeed, VAMPIRE solves a large number of problems (including problems unsolvable by

Table 2. Results from finding solutions to previously unsolved problems.

SMT-LIB

Logic	New solutions	Uniquely solved
ALIA	1	0
LIA	14	0
LRA	4	0
UFDTLIA	5	0
UFLIA	28	14
UFNIA	13	4

TPTP

Category	New solutions	Uniquely solved
ARI	13	0
NUM	1	1
SWW	3	1

existing SMT solvers) just by adding theory axioms and then running superposition with no theory-related rules. Such problems do not gain from the new options, because new inference rules result only in more generated clauses. Due to the portfolio approach of modern theorem provers, our focus is on cases where new options are *complementary* to existing ones.

Let us summarise the behaviour of three options, obtained by a more detailed analysis of our experimental results.

Full Theory Abstraction. Probably the most interesting observation from these results is that the use of full abstraction (fta) results in an observable degradation of performance. This confirms our intuition that unification with abstraction is a good replacement for abstraction. As a result, we will remove the fta option from VAMPIRE.

Unification with Abstraction. This option turned out to be very useful. Many problems had immediate solutions with uwa turned on and no solutions when it was turned off. Further, the value all resulted in 12 unique solutions. We have decided to keep the values all, interpreted_only and off.

Theory Instantiation. This option turned out to be very useful too. Many problems had immediate solutions with thi turned on and no solutions when it was turned off. We have decided to keep the values all, strong and off.

Contribution of New Options to Strategy Building. Since modern provers normally run a portfolio of strategies to solve a problem (strategy scheduling), there are two ways new strategies can be useful in such a portfolio:

1. by reducing the overall schedule time when problems are solved faster or when a single strategy replaces one or more old strategies;
2. by solving previously unsolved problems.

While for decidable classes, such as propositional logic, the first way can be more important, in first-order logic it is usually the second way that matters. The reason is that, if a problem is solvable by a prover, it is usually solvable with a short running time.

We ran VAMPIRE trying to solve, using the new options, problems previously unsolved by VAMPIRE. We took all such problems from the TPTP library [33] and SMT-LIB [5] and Table 2 shows the results. In the table, new solutions are meant with respect to what VAMPIRE could previously solve and uniquely solved stands for the number of new problems with respect to what can be solved by other entrants into SMT-COMP[1] and CASC[2] where the main competitors are SMT solvers such as Z3 [11] and CVC4 [4] and ATPs such as Beagle [6] and Princess [28,29].

With the help of the new options VAMPIRE solved 20 problems previously unsolved by any other theorem prover or SMT solver.

6 Related Work

We review relevant related work. A more thorough review can be found in [32].

SMT Solving. SMT solvers such as Z3 [11] and CVC4 [4] implement E-matching [9,12], model based quantifier instantiation [9,12] and conflict instantiation [27] to handle quantifiers. Although complete on some fragments, these instantiation techniques are generally heuristic and cannot be directly applied in our setting (see [26]).

In $DPLL(\Gamma)$ [10] a superposition prover is combined with an SMT solver such that ground literals implied by the SMT solver are used as hypotheses to first-order clauses.

AVATAR Modulo Theories. Our previous work on AVATAR Modulo Theories [21] uses the AVATAR architecture [23,34] for clause splitting to integrate an SMT solver with a superposition prover. The general idea is to abstract the clause search space as a SMT problem and use a SMT solver to decide on at least one literal per clause to have in the current search space of the superposition prover. To abstract the clause search space, non-ground components (sub-clauses sharing variables) are abstracted as propositional symbols whilst ground literals are translated directly. The result is that the superposition prover only deals with a set of clauses that is theory-consistent in its ground part.

Theory Resolution. Stickel's Theory Resolution [31] is a generalisation of the resolution inference rule whose aim is to exclude the often prolific theory axioms from the explicit participation on reasoning about the uninterpreted part of a given problem. In [32] we show that the theory resolution rule is a re-definition of $\mathcal{T}$-sound inferences. Given this, it is too abstract per se to bear practical relevance to our approach.

[1] http://smtcomp.sourceforge.net/.
[2] http://www.cs.miami.edu/~tptp/CASC/.

Hierarchic Superposition. Hierarchic Superposition (HS) [3] is a generalisation of the superposition calculus for black-box style theory reasoning. The approach uses full abstraction to separate theory and non-theory parts of the problem and introduces a conceptual hierarchy between uninterpreted reasoning (with the calculus) and theory reasoning (delegated to a theory solver) by making pure theory terms smaller than everything else. HS guarantees refutational completeness under certain conditions that can be rather restrictive, e.g., the clauses $p(x)$ and $\neg p(f(c))$ cannot be resolved if the return sort of function f is a theory sort. The strategy of *weak abstractions* introduced by Baumgartner and Waldmann [7] partially addresses the downsides of the original approach. However, their approach requires some decisions to be made, for which there currently does not seem to be a practical solution. See [32] for more details.

Other Theory Instantiation. SPASS+T [20] implements a theory instantiation rule that is analogous to E-matching in the sense that it uses ground theory terms from the search space to perform instantiations as a last resort. This is not related to our approach.

Unification Modulo Theories. There is a large amount of work on unification modulo various theories, such as AC. This work is not related since we are not looking for the set of all or most general solutions to unification. Instead, we postpone finding such solutions by creating constraints, which can then be processed by the SMT solver.

7 Conclusion

We have introduced two new techniques for reasoning with problems containing theories and quantifiers. The first technique allows us to utilise the power of SMT solving to find useful instances of non-ground clauses. The second technique presents a solution to the issue of full abstraction by lazily abstracting clauses to allow them to unify under theory constraints. Our experimental results show that these approaches can solve problems previously unsolvable by VAMPIRE and other solvers.

There are two directions for future research that we believe will further increase the power of this technique. Firstly, to explore the relationship between this approach and the AVATAR modulo theories work and, secondly, to relax the restriction of theory instantiation to single concrete models.

References

1. Akbarpour, B., Paulson, L.C.: Extending a resolution prover for inequalities on elementary functions. In: Dershowitz, N., Voronkov, A. (eds.) LPAR 2007. LNCS (LNAI), vol. 4790, pp. 47–61. Springer, Heidelberg (2007). https://doi.org/10.1007/978-3-540-75560-9_6
2. Althaus, E., Kruglov, E., Weidenbach, C.: Superposition modulo linear arithmetic SUP(LA). In: Ghilardi, S., Sebastiani, R. (eds.) FroCoS 2009. LNCS (LNAI), vol. 5749, pp. 84–99. Springer, Heidelberg (2009). https://doi.org/10.1007/978-3-642-04222-5_5
3. Bachmair, L., Ganzinger, H., Waldmann, U.: Refutational theorem proving for hierarchic first-order theories. Appl. Algebra Eng. Commun. Comput. **5**, 193–212 (1994)
4. Barrett, C., Conway, C.L., Deters, M., Hadarean, L., Jovanović, D., King, T., Reynolds, A., Tinelli, C.: CVC4. In: Gopalakrishnan, G., Qadeer, S. (eds.) CAV 2011. LNCS, vol. 6806, pp. 171–177. Springer, Heidelberg (2011). https://doi.org/10.1007/978-3-642-22110-1_14
5. Barrett, C., Stump, A., Tinelli, C.: The Satisfiability Modulo Theories Library (SMT-LIB) (2010). www.SMT-LIB.org
6. Baumgartner, P., Bax, J., Waldmann, U.: Beagle – a hierarchic superposition theorem prover. In: Felty, A.P., Middeldorp, A. (eds.) CADE 2015. LNCS (LNAI), vol. 9195, pp. 367–377. Springer, Cham (2015). https://doi.org/10.1007/978-3-319-21401-6_25
7. Baumgartner, P., Waldmann, U.: Hierarchic Superposition with weak abstraction. In: Bonacina, M.P. (ed.) CADE 2013. LNCS (LNAI), vol. 7898, pp. 39–57. Springer, Heidelberg (2013). https://doi.org/10.1007/978-3-642-38574-2_3
8. Bonacina, M.P., Lynch, C., de Moura, L.M.: On deciding satisfiability by theorem proving with speculative inferences. J. Autom. Reasoning **47**(2), 161–189 (2011)
9. de Moura, L., Bjørner, N.: Efficient E-matching for SMT solvers. In: Pfenning, F. (ed.) CADE 2007. LNCS (LNAI), vol. 4603, pp. 183–198. Springer, Heidelberg (2007). https://doi.org/10.1007/978-3-540-73595-3_13
10. de Moura, L., Bjørner, N.: Engineering DPLL(T) + Saturation. In: Armando, A., Baumgartner, P., Dowek, G. (eds.) IJCAR 2008. LNCS (LNAI), vol. 5195, pp. 475–490. Springer, Heidelberg (2008). https://doi.org/10.1007/978-3-540-71070-7_40
11. de Moura, L., Bjørner, N.: Z3: an efficient SMT solver. In: Ramakrishnan, C.R., Rehof, J. (eds.) TACAS 2008. LNCS, vol. 4963, pp. 337–340. Springer, Heidelberg (2008). https://doi.org/10.1007/978-3-540-78800-3_24
12. Detlefs, D., Nelson, G., Saxe, J.B.: Simplify: a theorem prover for program checking. J. ACM **52**(3), 365–473 (2005)
13. Ganzinger, H., Korovin, K.: Theory instantiation. In: Hermann, M., Voronkov, A. (eds.) LPAR 2006. LNCS (LNAI), vol. 4246, pp. 497–511. Springer, Heidelberg (2006). https://doi.org/10.1007/11916277_34
14. Graf, P.: Substitution tree indexing. In: Hsiang, J. (ed.) RTA 1995. LNCS, vol. 914, pp. 117–131. Springer, Heidelberg (1995). https://doi.org/10.1007/3-540-59200-8_52
15. Hoder, K., Reger, G., Suda, M., Voronkov, A.: Selecting the selection. In: Olivetti, N., Tiwari, A. (eds.) IJCAR 2016. LNCS (LNAI), vol. 9706, pp. 313–329. Springer, Cham (2016). https://doi.org/10.1007/978-3-319-40229-1_22

16. Korovin, K., Voronkov, A.: Integrating linear arithmetic into superposition calculus. In: Duparc, J., Henzinger, T.A. (eds.) CSL 2007. LNCS, vol. 4646, pp. 223–237. Springer, Heidelberg (2007). https://doi.org/10.1007/978-3-540-74915-8_19
17. Kovács, L., Robillard, S., Voronkov, A.: Coming to terms with quantified reasoning. In: Proceedings of the 44th ACM SIGPLAN Symposium on Principles of Programming Languages, POPL 2017, Paris, France, 18–20 January 2017, pp. 260–270. ACM (2017)
18. Kovács, L., Voronkov, A.: First-order theorem proving and VAMPIRE. In: Sharygina, N., Veith, H. (eds.) CAV 2013. LNCS, vol. 8044, pp. 1–35. Springer, Heidelberg (2013). https://doi.org/10.1007/978-3-642-39799-8_1
19. Nonnengart, A., Weidenbach, C.: Computing small clause normal forms. In: Robinson, A., Voronkov, A. (eds.) Handbook of Automated Reasoning (in 2 volumes), pp. 335–367. Elsevier and MIT Press, Cambridge (2001)
20. Prevosto, V., Waldmann, U.: SPASS+T. In: Proceedings of the FLoC 2006 Workshop on Empirically Successful Computerized Reasoning, 3rd International Joint Conference on Automated Reasoning, vol. 192, CEUR Workshop Proceedings, pp. 19–33 (2006)
21. Reger, G., Bjørner, N., Suda, M., Voronkov, A.: AVATAR modulo theories. In: 2nd Global Conference on Artificial Intelligence, GCAI 2016, EPiC Series in Computing, vol. 41, pp. 39–52. EasyChair (2016)
22. Reger, G., Suda, M.: Set of support for theory reasoning. In: IWIL Workshop and LPAR Short Presentations, Kalpa Publications in Computing, vol. 1, pp. 124–134. EasyChair (2017)
23. Reger, G., Suda, M., Voronkov, A.: Playing with AVATAR. In: Felty, A.P., Middeldorp, A. (eds.) CADE 2015. LNCS (LNAI), vol. 9195, pp. 399–415. Springer, Cham (2015). https://doi.org/10.1007/978-3-319-21401-6_28
24. Reger, G., Suda, M., Voronkov, A.: The challenges of evaluating a new feature in vampire. In: Proceedings of the 1st and 2nd Vampire Workshops, EPiC Series in Computing, vol. 38, pp. 70–74. EasyChair (2016)
25. Reger, G., Suda, M., Voronkov, A.: New techniques in clausal form generation. In: 2nd Global Conference on Artificial Intelligence, GCAI 2016, EPiC Series in Computing, vol. 41, pp. 11–23. EasyChair (2016)
26. Reger, G., Suda, M., Voronkov, A.: Instantiation and pretending to be an SMT solver with Vampire. In: Proceedings of the 15th International Workshop on Satisfiability Modulo Theories, CEUR Workshop Proceedings, vol. 1889, pp. 63–75 (2017)
27. Reynolds, A., Tinelli, C., de Moura, L.M.: Finding conflicting instances of quantified formulas in SMT. In: Formal Methods in Computer-Aided Design, FMCAD 2014, Lausanne, Switzerland, 21–24 October 2014, pp. 195–202 (2014)
28. Rümmer, P.: A constraint sequent calculus for first-order logic with linear integer arithmetic. In: Cervesato, I., Veith, H., Voronkov, A. (eds.) LPAR 2008. LNCS (LNAI), vol. 5330, pp. 274–289. Springer, Heidelberg (2008). https://doi.org/10.1007/978-3-540-89439-1_20
29. Rümmer, P.: E-matching with free variables. In: Bjørner, N., Voronkov, A. (eds.) LPAR 2012. LNCS, vol. 7180, pp. 359–374. Springer, Heidelberg (2012). https://doi.org/10.1007/978-3-642-28717-6_28
30. Sekar, R., Ramakrishnan, I., Voronkov, A.: Term indexing. In: Robinson, A., Voronkov, A. (eds.) Handbook of Automated Reasoning, vol. II, pp. 1853–1964. Elsevier Science, Amsterdam (2001). Chap. 26
31. Stickel, M.E.: Automated deduction by theory resolution. J. Autom. Reasoning **1**(4), 333–355 (1985)

32. Suda, M., Reger, G., Voronkov, A.: Unification with abstraction and theory instantiation in saturation-based reasoning. EasyChair Preprint no. 1. EasyChair (2017). https://easychair.org/publications/preprint/1
33. Sutcliffe, G.: The TPTP problem library and associated infrastructure. J. Autom. Reasoning **43**(4), 337–362 (2009)
34. Voronkov, A.: AVATAR: the architecture for first-order theorem provers. In: Biere, A., Bloem, R. (eds.) CAV 2014. LNCS, vol. 8559, pp. 696–710. Springer, Cham (2014). https://doi.org/10.1007/978-3-319-08867-9_46

Efficient Verification of Imperative Programs Using Auto2

Bohua Zhan(✉)
Technical University of Munich,
Munich, Germany
zhan@in.tum.de

Abstract. Auto2 is a recently introduced prover for the proof assistant Isabelle. It is designed to be both highly customizable from within Isabelle, and also have a powerful proof search mechanism. In this paper, we apply auto2 to the verification of imperative programs. We describe the setup of auto2 for both stages of the proof process: verification of a functional version of the program, and refining to the imperative version using separation logic. As examples, we verify several data structures, including red-black trees, interval trees, priority queues, and union-find. We also verify several algorithms making use of these data structures. These examples show that our framework is able to verify complex algorithms efficiently and in a modular manner.

1 Introduction

Verification of imperative programs has been a well-studied area. While work on separation logic addressed the main theoretical issues, verification in practice is still a tedious process. Even if we limit to the case of sequential programs with relatively simple memory-allocation patterns, verification is still difficult when a lot of mathematical reasoning is required to justify the underlying algorithm. Such reasoning can quickly go beyond the ability of automatic theorem provers. Proof assistants such as Isabelle and Coq provide an environment in which human users can guide the computer through the proof. However, such a process today often requires a lot of low-level reasoning with lists, sets, etc, as well as dealing with details of separation logic. We believe much work can still be done to provide more automation in this area, reducing the amount of time and expertise needed to perform verifications, with the goal of eventually making verification of complex algorithms a routine process.

The auto2 prover in Isabelle is introduced by the author in [28]. Its approach to automation in proof assistants is significantly different from the two main existing approaches: tactics and the use of external automatic theorem provers (as represented by Sledgehammer in Isabelle). Compared to Sledgehammer, auto2 is highly customizable: users can set up new reasoning rules and procedures at any point in the development of a theory (for example, our entire setup for separation logic is built outside the main auto2 program). It also works

D. Beyer and M. Huisman (Eds.): TACAS 2018, LNCS 10805, pp. 23–40, 2018.
https://doi.org/10.1007/978-3-319-89960-2_2

directly with higher-order logic and types available in Isabelle. Compared to tactics, auto2 uses a saturation-based search mechanism, that is closer to the kind of search performed in automatic theorem provers, and from experience has been more powerful and stable than the backtracking approach usual in the tactics framework.

In this paper, we apply auto2 to the verification of imperative programs. We limit ourselves to sequential programs with relatively simple memory-allocation patterns. The algorithms underlying the programs, however, require substantial reasoning to justify. The verification process can be roughly divided into two stages: verifying a functional version of the program, and refining it to an imperative version using separation logic.

The main contributions of this paper are as follows.[1]

- We discuss the setup of auto2 to provide automation for both stages of this process. For the verification of functional programs, this means automatically proving simple lemmas involving lists, sets, etc. For refining to the imperative program, this means handling reasoning with separation logic.
- Using our setup, we verify several data structures including red-black trees, interval trees, priority queues, and union-find. We also verify algorithms including Dijkstra's algorithm for shortest paths and a line-sweeping algorithm for detecting rectangle intersection. These examples demonstrate that using our approach, complex algorithms can be verified in a highly efficient and modular manner.

We now give an outline for the rest of the paper. In Sect. 2, we give an overview of the auto2 prover. In Sect. 3, we discuss our setup of auto2 for verification of functional programs. In Sect. 4, we review the Imperative HOL framework in Isabelle and its separation logic, which we use to describe and verify the imperative programs. In Sect. 5, we discuss our setup of auto2 for reasoning with separation logic. In Sect. 6, we briefly describe each of the case studies, showing some statistics and comparison with existing verifications. Finally, we review related work in Sect. 7, and conclude in Sect. 8.

2 Overview of the auto2 Prover

The auto2 prover is introduced in [28]. In [29], several additional features are described, in an extended application to formalization of mathematics. In this section, we summarize the important points relevant to this paper.

Auto2 uses a saturation-based proof search mechanism. At any point during the search, the prover maintains a list of *items*, which may be derived facts, terms that appeared in the proof, or some other information. At the beginning, the statement to be proved is converted into contradiction form, and its assumptions form the initial state. The search ends successfully when a contradiction is derived. In addition to the list of items, the prover also maintains several additional tables, three of which will be described below.

[1] Code available at https://github.com/bzhan/auto2.

2.1 Proof Steps

Proof steps are functions that produce new items from existing ones. During the development of an Isabelle theory, proof steps can be added or removed at any time. At each iteration of the proof search, auto2 applies the current list of proof steps to generate new items. Each new item is given a *score* and inserted into a priority queue. They are then added to the main list of items at future iterations in increasing order of score. The score is by default computed from the size of the proposition (smaller means higher priority), which can be overriden for individual proof steps.

Adding new proof steps is the main way to set up new functionality for auto2. Proof steps range from simple ones that apply a single theorem, to complex functions that implement some proof procedure. Several proof steps can also work together to implement some proof strategy, communicating through their input and output items. We will see examples of all these in Sects. 3 and 5.

2.2 Rewrite Table

Among the tables maintained by auto2, the most important is the *rewrite table*. The rewrite table keeps track of the list of currently known (ground) equalities. It offers two main operations: deciding whether two terms are equivalent, and matching up to known equalities (E-matching). The latter is the basic matching function used in auto2: whenever we mention matching in the rest of the paper, it is assumed to mean E-matching using the rewrite table.

We emphasize that when a new ground equality is derived, auto2 does *not* use it to rewrite terms in the proof state. Instead, the equality is inserted into the rewrite table, and *incremental* matching is performed on relevant items to discover new matches.

2.3 Property and Well-Formedness Tables

We now discuss two other important tables maintained by auto2: the property table and the well-formedness table.

Any predicate (constant of type `'a ⇒ bool`) can be registered as a *property* during the development of a theory. During the proof, the *property table* maintains the list of properties satisfied by each term appearing in the proof. Common examples of predicates that we register as properties include sortedness on lists and invariants satisfied by binary search trees.

For any function, we may register certain conditions on its arguments as *well-formedness conditions* of that function. Common examples include the condition `a ≥ b` for the term `(a - b)::nat`, and `i < length xs` for the term `xs ! i` (`i`'th element of the list `xs`). We emphasize that registering well-formedness conditions is for the automation only, and does not imply any modification to the logic. During the proof, the *well-formedness table* maintains the list of well-formedness conditions that are known for each term appearing in the proof.

The property and well-formedness tables allow proof steps to quickly lookup certain assumptions of a theorem. We call assumptions that can be looked-up in this way *side conditions*. We will see examples of these in Sect. 3.1, and another important application of the well-formedness table in Sect. 3.2.

2.4 Case Analysis

The need for case analysis introduces further complexities. New case analysis is produced by proof steps, usually triggered by the appearance of certain facts or terms in the proof. We follow a saturation-based approach to case analysis: the list of cases (called *boxes*) is maintained as a part of the proof state, and derivation in all boxes are performed in parallel. More precisely, every item (and entry in the tables) is assigned to some box, according to the set of additional assumptions needed to derive that item. When a contradiction is derived in a box with additional assumption P, the fact $\neg P$ is added to its parent box. The proof finishes only if a contradiction is derived in the initial box (with no additional assumptions).

2.5 Proof Scripts

Auto2 defines its own language of proof scripts, which is similar to, but independent from the Isar proof language in Isabelle. The main differences between auto2 and Isar are that auto2 scripts do not contain names of tactics (all subgoals are proved using auto2), labels for intermediate goals, or names of previous theorems.

Examples of auto2 scripts are given in Sect. 3.4. We explain the basic commands here (all commands in auto2 scripts begin with an `@` sign, to distinguish them from similar Isar commands).

- `@have P`: prove the intermediate goal P. Afterwards, make P available in the remainder of the proof block.
- `@case P`: prove the current goal with additional assumption P. Afterwards, make $\neg P$ available in the remainder of the proof block.
- `@obtain x where P(x)`: here `x` must be a fresh variable. Prove the intermediate goal $\exists x.\ P(x)$. Afterwards, create variable x and make fact $P(x)$ available in the remainder of the proof block.
- `@with ... @end`: create a new proof block. That is, instead of proving the subgoal in the previous command directly using auto2, prove it using the commands between `@with` and `@end`.
- `@induct`, `@prop_induct`, etc: commands for several types of induction. Each type of induction has its own syntax, specifying which variable or proposition to apply induction on. We omit the details here.

3 Verification of Functional Programs

Proofs of correctness of functional programs involve reasoning in many different domains, such as arithmetic, lists, sets, maps, etc. The proof of a single lemma may require results from more than one of these domains. The design of auto2 allows automation for each of these domains to be specified separately, as a collection of proof steps. During the proof, they work together by communicating through the common list of items and other tables maintained by the prover.

In this section, we discuss our setup of auto2 for verification of functional programs. It is impossible to describe the entire setup in detail. Instead, we will give some examples, showing the range of functionality that can be supported in auto2. At the end of the section, we give an example showing the strength of the resulting automation.

We emphasize that the aim here is not to implement complete proof procedures, or to compete with highly-optimized theory solvers for efficiency. Instead, we simply aim for the prover to consistently solve tasks that humans consider to be routine. Since we are in an interactive setting, we can always ask the user to provide intermediate goals for more difficult proof tasks.

3.1 Simple Proof Steps

Most of the proof steps added to auto2 apply a single theorem. Such proof steps can be added easily to auto2 (for example, a forward reasoning rule can be added by setting the `forward` attribute to a theorem). We describe some basic examples in this section.

Forward and Backward Reasoning. The most basic kind of proof steps apply a theorem in the forward or backward direction. For example, the theorem

$$\texttt{sorted (x \# xs)} \Longrightarrow \texttt{y} \in \texttt{set xs} \Longrightarrow \texttt{x} \leq \texttt{y}$$

is added as a *forward* proof step. This proof step looks for pairs of facts in the form `sorted (x # xs)` and $\texttt{y} \in \texttt{set xs}$ (using E-matching, same below). For every match, it outputs the fact $\texttt{x} \leq \texttt{y}$ as a new item (to be added to the main list of items at a future iteration).

In contrast, the theorem

$$\texttt{sorted xs} \Longrightarrow \texttt{j < length xs} \Longrightarrow \texttt{i} \leq \texttt{j} \Longrightarrow \texttt{xs ! i} \leq \texttt{xs ! j}.$$

should be added as a *backward* proof step. This proof step looks for facts of the form $\neg(\texttt{xs ! i} \leq \texttt{xs ! j})$ (equivalently, goal to prove $\texttt{xs ! i} \leq \texttt{xs ! j}$). For every match, it looks for the assumption `sorted xs` in the property table, and `j < length xs` in the well-formedness table (it is the well-formedness condition of the subterm `xs ! j`). If both side conditions are found, the proof step outputs fact $\neg(\texttt{i} \leq \texttt{j})$ (equivalently, goal to prove $\texttt{i} \leq \texttt{j}$).

Another type of proof step adds a new fact for any term matching a certain pattern. For example, for the theorem

$$\texttt{n < length xs} \Longrightarrow \texttt{xs ! n} \in \texttt{set xs},$$

the corresponding proof step looks for terms of the form `xs ! n`. For every match, it looks for the assumption `n < length xs` in the well-formedness table, and output `xs ! n ∈ set xs` if the assumption is found. This particular setup is chosen because assumptions of the form `y ∈ set xs` appears frequently in practice.

Rewrite Rules. Rewrite rules form another major class of proof steps. They add new equalities to the rewrite table, usually after matching the left side of the equality. As an example, consider the theorem for evaluation of list update:

```
i < length xs ⟹ xs[i := x] ! j = (if i = j then x else xs ! j).
```

The corresponding proof step looks for terms of the form `xs[i := x] ! j`. For every match, it looks for the assumption `i < length xs` in the well-formedness table (this is the well-formedness condition of `xs[i := x]`). If the assumption is found, the proof step outputs the equality. When the equality is pulled from the priority queue at a later iteration, it is added to the rewrite table.

For the theorem evaluating the length of list update:

```
length (xs[i := x]) = length xs
```

we add a slightly different proof step: it produces the equality whenever it finds the term `xs[i := x]`, without waiting for `length (xs[i := x])` to appear. This can be justified by observing that it is useful to know the length of any list appearing in the proof, as it is mentioned in the assumptions of many theorems.

Generating Case Analysis. Another class of proof steps generate case analysis on seeing certain terms or facts in the proof state. For example, there is a proof step that looks for terms of the form `if P then b else c`, and creates case analysis on `P` for every match.

Case analysis may also be created to check well-formedness conditions. Usually, when we register a well-formedness condition, auto2 will look for the condition in the list of items during the proof. However, sometimes it is better to be more proactive, and try to prove the condition whenever a term of the given form appears. This is achieved by creating a case analysis with the condition as the goal (or equivalently, with the negation of the condition as the assumption).

3.2 Normalization of Natural Number Expressions

In this section, we give an example of a more complex proof step. It compares expressions on natural numbers by normalizing both sides with respect to addition and subtraction.

Mathematically, the expression $a-b$ on natural numbers is undefined if $a < b$. In Isabelle (and many other proof assistants), it is simply defined to be zero. This means many equalities involving subtraction on natural numbers that look obvious are in fact invalid. Examples include $a - b + b = a$, which in Isabelle is false if $a < b$.

This substantially complicates normalization of expressions on natural numbers involving subtraction. In general, normalization of such an expression agrees with intuition as long as the expression is well-formed, in the sense of Sect. 2.3. Following the terminology in [29, Sect. 3.3], we say a *well-formed term* is a term together with a list of theorems justifying its well-formedness conditions, and a *well-formed conversion* is a function that, given a well-formed term, returns an equality rewriting that term, together with theorems justifying well-formedness conditions on the right side of the equality. Well-formed conversions can be composed in the same way as regular conversions (rewriting procedures). In particular, we can implement normalization for expressions on natural numbers with respect to addition and subtraction as a well-formed conversion.

This is in turn used to implement the following proof step. Given any two terms s, t of type `nat` involving addition and subtraction, look for their well-formedness conditions in the well-formedness table. If all well-formedness conditions for subtraction are present, normalize s and t using the well-formed conversion. If their normalizations are the same, output the equality $s = t$. Such proof steps, when combined with proof scripts, allow the user to rapidly perform arithmetic manipulations.

3.3 Difference Logic on Natural Numbers

Difference logic is concerned with propositions of the form $a \leq b + n$, where n is a constant. A collection of such inequalities can be represented as a directed graph, where nodes are terms and weighted edges represent inequalities between them. A collection of inequalities is contradictory if and only if the corresponding graph contains a negative cycle, which can be determined using the Bellman-Ford algorithm.

In auto2, we implement difference logic for natural numbers using special items and proof steps. While less efficient than a graph-based implementation, it is sufficient for our purposes, and also interacts better with other proof steps. Each inequality on natural numbers is represented by an item of type `NAT_ORDER`, which contains a triple `<a,b,n>` recording the terms on the two sides and the difference. The transitivity proof step looks for pairs of items of the form `<a,b,m>` and `<b,c,n>`, and produces the item `<a,c,m+n>` for each match. The resolve proof step looks for items of the form `<a,a,n>`, where `n` is less than zero, and derives a contradiction for each match.

3.4 Example

As an example, we show a snippet from the functional part of the verification of the union-find data structure. Union-find is implemented on an array `l`, with `l ! i` equal to `i` if `i` is the root of its component, and the parent of `i` if otherwise. `rep_of i` denotes the root of the component containing `i`. The compress operation is defined as:

```
ufa_compress l x = l[x := rep_of l x]
```

The main properties of *ufa_compress* are stated and proved using auto2 as follows:

```
lemma ufa_compress_invar:
  "ufa_invar l ⟹ x < length l ⟹ l' = ufa_compress l x ⟹ ufa_invar
l'" @proof
  @have "∀i<length l'. rep_of_dom (l', i) ∧ l' ! i < length l'" @with
    @prop_induct "ufa_invar l ∧ i < length l"
  @end
@qed

lemma ufa_compress_aux:
  "ufa_invar l ⟹ x < length l ⟹ l' = ufa_compress l x ⟹
   i < length l' ⟹ rep_of l' i = rep_of l i"
@proof @prop_induct "ufa_invar l ∧ i < length l" @qed

lemma ufa_compress_correct:
  "ufa_invar l ⟹ x < length l ⟹ ufa_α (ufa_compress l x) = ufa_α l"
  by auto2
```

The only hints that needs to be provided by the human to prove these lemmas are how to apply the induction (specified using the *@prop_induct* command). By comparison, in the AFP library [14], the corresponding proofs require 20 tactic invocations in 42 lines of Isar text.

4 Imperative HOL and Its Separation Logic

In this section, we review some basic concepts from the Imperative HOL framework in Isabelle and its separation logic. See [3,13,14] for details.

4.1 Heaps and Programs

In Imperative HOL, procedures are represented as Haskell-style monads. They operate on a heap (type *heap*) consisting of a finite mapping from addresses (natural numbers) to natural numbers, and a finite mapping from addresses to lists of natural numbers (in order to support arrays). Values of any type *'a* can be stored in the heap as long as one can specify an injection from *'a* to the natural numbers. This means records with multiple fields, such as nodes of a search tree, can be stored at a single address. Along with native support for arrays, this eliminates any need for pointer arithmetic.

The type of a procedure returning a value of type *'a* is given by

```
datatype 'a Heap = Heap "heap ⇒ ('a × heap) option"
```

The procedure takes as input a heap h, and outputs either *None* for failure, or *Some* (r, h'), where r is the return value and h' is the new heap. The *bind* function for sequencing two procedures has type

```
'a Heap ⇒ ('a ⇒ 'b Heap) ⇒ 'b Heap.
```

Imperative HOL does not have native support for while loops. Instead, basic applications use recursion throughout, with properties of recursive procedures proved by induction. We will follow this approach in our examples.

4.2 Assertions and Hoare Triples

The type *partial heap* is defined by `pheap = heap` $\times$ `nat set`. The partial heap (h, as) represents the part of the heap h given by the set of addresses as.

An assertion (type `assn`) is a mapping from `pheap` to `bool`, that does not depend on values of the heap outside the address set. The notation $(h, as) \models P$ means "the assertion P holds on the partial heap (h, as)".

Some basic examples of assertions are:

- `true`: holds for all valid partial heaps.
- `emp`: the partial heap is empty.
- $\uparrow(b)$: the partial heap is empty and b (a boolean value) holds.
- $p \mapsto_r a$: the partial heap contains a single address pointing to value a.
- $p \mapsto_a xs$: the partial heap contains a single address pointing to list xs.

The *separating conjunction* on two assertions is defined as follows:

$$P * Q = \lambda(h, as).\, \exists u\, v.\, u \cup v = as \wedge u \cap v = \emptyset \wedge (h, u) \models P \wedge (h, v) \models Q.$$

This operation is associative and commutative, with unit `emp`. Existential quantification on assertions is defined as:

$$\exists_A x.\, P(x) = \lambda(h, as).\, \exists x.\, (h, as) \models P(x).$$

Assertions of the form $\uparrow(b)$ are called *pure* assertions. In [14], conjunction, disjunction, and the magic wand operator on assertions are also defined, but we will not use them here.

A Hoare triple is a predicate of type

$$\texttt{assn} \Rightarrow \texttt{'a Heap} \Rightarrow (\texttt{'a} \Rightarrow \texttt{assn}) \Rightarrow \texttt{bool},$$

defined as follows: <P> c <Q> holds if for any partial heap (h, as) satisfying P, the execution of c on (h, as) is successful with new heap h' and return value r, and the new partial heap (h', as') satisfies $Q(r)$, where as' is as together with the newly allocated addresses.

From these definitions we can prove the Hoare triples for the basic commands, as well as the *frame rule*

$$\text{<}P\text{>}\ c\ \text{<}Q\text{>} \Longrightarrow \text{<}P * R\text{>}\ c\ \text{<}\lambda x.\, Q(x) * R\text{>}.$$

In [14], there is further setup of a tactic `sep_auto` implementing some level of automation in separation logic. We do not make use of this tactic in our work.

5 Automation for Separation Logic

In this section, we discuss our setup of auto2 for separation logic. The setup consists of a collection of proof steps working with Hoare triples and entailments, implemented in around 2,000 lines of ML code (including specialized matching for assertions). While knowledge of auto2 is necessary to implement the setup, we aim to provide an easy-to-understand interface, so that no knowledge of the internals of auto2, or of details of separation logic, is needed to use it for concrete applications.

5.1 Basic Approach

Our basic approach is to analyze an imperative program in the forward direction: starting at the first command and finishing at the last, using existing Hoare triples to analyze each line of the procedure. To simplify the discussion, suppose the procedure to be verified consists of a sequence of commands $c_1; \ldots; c_n$. Let P_0 be the (spatial) precondition of the Hoare triple to be proved.

To reason about the procedure, we use existing Hoare triples for $c_1, \ldots, c_n$ (these may include the induction hypothesis, if some of c_i are recursive calls). We write each Hoare triple in the following standard form:

$$<p_1 \ * \cdots \ * \ p_m \ * \uparrow (a_1) \ * \cdots \ * \uparrow (a_k)>$$
$$c$$
$$<\lambda r.\ \exists_A \boldsymbol{x}.\ q_1 \ * \cdots \ * \ q_n \ * \uparrow (b_1) \ * \cdots \ * \uparrow (b_l)>$$

Here $p_1 \ * \cdots \ * \ p_m$ is the *spatial* part of the precondition, specifying the shape of the heap before the command, and $\uparrow (a_1) \ * \cdots \ * \uparrow (a_k)$ is the *pure* part of the precondition, specifying additional constraints on the abstract values (we assume that all variables appearing in a_i also appear in p_i or c). The assertions $q_1 \ * \cdots \ * \ q_n$ and $\uparrow (b_1) \ * \cdots \ * \uparrow (b_l)$ (depending on the return value r and possibly new data-variables $\boldsymbol{x}$) are the spatial and pure parts of the postcondition. They provide information about the shape of the heap after the command, and constraints on abstract values on that heap.

Applying the Hoare triple for c_1 involves the following steps:

1. Match the pattern c with the command c_1, instantiating some of the arbitrary variables in the Hoare triple.
2. Match the spatial part of the precondition with P_0. This is the *frame-inference* step: the matching is up to the associative-commutative property of separating conjunction, and only a subset of factors in P_0 need to be matched. Each match should instantiate all remaining arbitrary variables in the Hoare triple.
3. Generate case analysis (discussed at the end of Sect. 3.1) to try to prove each of the pure conditions a_i.
4. After all pure conditions are proved, apply the Hoare triple. This creates new variables for the return value r and possible data variables $\boldsymbol{x}$. The procedure is replaced by $c_2; \ldots; c_n$ and the precondition is replaced by $q_1 \ * \cdots \ * \ q_n$. The pure assertions $b_1, \ldots, b_l$ in the postcondition are outputed as facts.

On reaching the end of the imperative program, the goal reduces to an entailment, which is solved using similar matching schemes as above.

5.2 Inductively-Defined Assertions

Certain assertions, such as those for linked lists and binary trees, are defined inductively. For example, the assertion for binary trees (with a key-value pair at each node) is defined as follows:

```
btree Tip p = ↑(p = None)
btree (tree.Node lt k v rt) (Some p) =
      (∃A lp rp. p ↦r Node lp k v rp * btree lt lp * btree rt rp)
btree (tree.Node lt k v rt) None = false
```

Here `btree` t p is an assertion stating that the memory location p contains a functional data structure t. The term `tree.Node lt k v rt` represents a functional binary tree, where `lt` and `rt` are subtrees, while the term `Node lp k v rp` represents a record on the heap, where `lp` and `rp` are pointers. When working with inductively-defined assertions like this, the heap can be divided into spatial components in several ways. For example, a heap satisfying the assertion

$$p \mapsto_r \texttt{Node lp k v rp * btree lt lp * btree rt rp} \tag{1}$$

also satisfies the assertion

$$\texttt{btree (tree.Node lt k v rt) p.} \tag{2}$$

The former considers the heap as three components, while the latter considers it as one component.

We follow the policy of always using assertions in the more expanded form (that is, (1) instead of (2)). This means matching of assertions must also take into account inductive definitions of assertions, so that the assertion (1) will match the pattern `btree ?t p * ?P` as well as (for example) the pattern `btree ?t lp * ?P`. This is realized by maintaining a list of inductive definitions of assertions in the theory, and have the special matching function for assertions refer to this list during matching.

5.3 Modularity

For any data structure, there are usually two levels at which we can define assertions: the concrete level with definition by induction or in terms of simpler data structures, and the abstract level describing what data the structure is supposed to represent.

For example, in the case of binary trees, the concrete assertion `btree` is defined in the previous section. At the abstract level, a binary tree represents a mapping. The corresponding assertion `btree_map` is defined by:

```
btree_map M p = (∃At. btree t p * ↑(tree_sorted t) * ↑(M = tree_map t)),
```

where `tree_map` t is the mapping corresponding to the binary tree t with key-value pairs at each node. For each operation on binary trees, we first prove a Hoare triple on the concrete assertion `btree`, then use it to derive a second Hoare triple on the abstract assertion `btree_map`. For example, for the insertion operation, we first show:

```
<btree t b> btree_insert k v b <btree (tree_insert k v t)>
```

where *tree_insert* is the functional version of insertion on binary trees. Using this Hoare triple, and the fact that *tree_insert* preserves sortedness and behaves correctly with respect to *tree_map*, we prove

```
<btree_map M b> btree_insert k v b <btree_map (M {k → v})>
```

Similarly, for tree search, the Hoare triple on the concrete assertion is:

```
<btree t b * ↑(tree_sorted t)>
btree_search x b
<λr. btree t b * ↑(r = tree_search t x)>
```

This Hoare triple, along with properties of *tree_search*, is used to prove the Hoare triple on the abstract assertion:

```
<btree_map M b> btree_search x b <λr. btree_map M b * ↑(r = M⟨x⟩)>"
```

After the Hoare triples for *btree_map* are proved, the definition of *btree_map*, as well as the Hoare triples for *btree*, can be hidden from auto2 by removing the corresponding proof steps. This enforces modularity of proofs: auto2 will only use Hoare triples for *btree_map* from now on, without looking into the internal implementation of the binary tree.

5.4 Example

With the above setup for separation logic, auto2 is able to prove the correctness of the imperative version of compression in union-find after specifying how to apply induction (using the *@prop_induct* command):

```
uf_compress i ci p = (
  if i = ci then return ()
  else do {
    ni ← Array.nth p i;
    uf_compress ni ci p;
    Array.upd i ci p;
    return ()
  })

lemma uf_compress_rule:
  "ufa_invar l ⟹ i < length l ⟹ ci = rep_of l i ⟹
   <p ↦a l>
   uf_compress i ci p
   <λ_. ∃A l'. p ↦a l' * ↑(ufa_invar l' ∧ length l' = length l ∧
            (∀i<length l. rep_of l' i = rep_of l i))>"
@proof @prop_induct "ufa_invar l ∧ i < length l" @qed
```

Note that the imperative procedure performs full compression along a path, rather than a single compression for the functional version in Sect. 3.4. By comparison, the corresponding proof in the AFP requires 13 tactic invocations (including 4 invocations of *sep_auto*) in 34 lines of Isar text.

6 Case Studies

In this section, we describe the main case studies performed to validate our framework. For each case study, we describe the data structure or algorithm that is being verified, its main difficulties, and then give comparisons to existing work. Statistics for the case studies are summarized in the following table. On a laptop with two 2.0 GHz cores and 16 GB of RAM, it takes auto2 approximately 14 min to process all of the examples.

	#Imp	#Def	#Thm	#Step	Ratio	#LOC
Union-find	49	7	26	42	0.86	244
Red-black tree	270	27	83	173	0.64	998
Interval tree	84	17	50	83	0.99	520
Rectangle intersection	33	18	31	111	3.36	417
Indexed priority queue	83	10	53	84	1.01	477
Dijkstra's algorithm	44	19	62	150	3.41	549

The meaning of the fields are as follows:

- #Imp is the number of lines of imperative code to be verified.
- #Def is the number of definitions made during the verification (not counting definitions of imperative procedures).
- #Thm is the number of lemmas and theorems proved during the verification.
- #Step is the number of "steps" in the proof. Each definition, lemma, and intermediate goal in the proof script counts as one step (so for example, a lemma proved with one intermediate goal counts as two steps). We only count steps where auto2 does some work, omitting for example variable definitions.
- Ratio: ratio between #Step and #Imp, serving as a measure of the overhead of verification.
- #LOC: total number of lines of code in the theories (verification of functional and imperative program). This can be used to make approximate comparisons with other work.

6.1 Union-Find

Our verification follows closely that in the AFP [14]. As in the example in the AFP, we do not verify that the array containing the size of components has reasonable values (important only for performance analysis). Two snippets of auto2 proofs are shown in previous sections. Overall, we reduced the number of lines in the theory by roughly a half. In a further example, we applied union-find to verify an algorithm for determining connectivity on undirected graphs (not counted in the statistics).

6.2 Red-Black Tree

We verified the functional red-black tree given by Okasaki ([21], for insertion) and Kahrs ([18], for deletion). Both functional correctness and maintenance of invariants are proved. We then verified an imperative version of the same algorithm (imperative in the sense that no more memory is allocated than necessary). This offers a stringent test for matching involving inductively defined assertions (discussed in Sect. 5.2). For the functional part of the proof, we used the technique introduced by Nipkow [19] for proving sortedness and proper behavior on the associated maps using the inorder traversal as an intermediary.

Functional red-black tree has been verified several times in proof assistants [2,19]. The imperative version is a common test-case for verification using automatic theorem provers [17,22–24]. It is also verified "auto-actively" in the SPARK system [9], but apparently not in proof assistants such as Coq and Isabelle.

6.3 Interval Tree and Rectangle Intersection

Interval tree is an augmented data structure, with some version of binary search tree serving as the base. It represents a set of intervals S, and offers the operation of determining whether a given interval i intersects any of the intervals in S. See [8, Sect. 14.3] for details. For simplicity, we verified interval tree based on an ordinary binary search tree.

As an application of interval trees, we verify an algorithm for detecting rectangle intersection (see [8, Exercise 14.3-7]). Given a collection S of rectangles aligned to the x and y axes, one can determine whether there exists two rectangles in S that intersect each other using a line-sweeping algorithm as follows. For each rectangle $[a, b] \times [c, d]$, we create two operations: adding the interval $[a, b]$ at time c, and removing it at time d. The operations for all rectangles are sorted by time (breaking ties by putting insertion before deletion) and applied to an initially empty interval tree. There is an intersection if and only if at some point, we try to insert an interval which intersects an existing interval in the tree. Formal verification of interval trees and the line-sweeping algorithm for rectangle intersection appear to be new.

6.4 Indexed Priority Queue and Dijkstra's Algorithm

The usual priority queue is implemented on one array. It supports insertion and deleting the minimum. In order to support decreasing the value of a key (necessary for Dijkstra's algorithm), we need one more "index" array recording locations of keys. Having two arrays produce additional difficulty in having to verify that they stay in sync in all operations.

The indexed priority queue is applied to verify a basic version of Dijkstra's algorithm. We make several simplifying assumptions: the vertices of the graph are natural numbers from 0 to $n - 1$, and there is exactly one directed edge between each ordered pair of vertices, so that the weights of the graph can be represented as a matrix. Since the matrix is unchanged during the proof, we also do not put it on the heap. Nevertheless, the verification, starting from the definition of graphs and paths, contains all the essential ideas of Dijkstra's algorithm.

The indexed priority queue and Dijkstra's algorithm are previously verified using the refinement framework in [12,20]. It is difficult to make precise comparisons, since the approach used in the refinement framework is quite different, and Dijkstra's algorithm is verified there without the above simplifying assumptions. By a pure line count, our formalization is about 2-3 times shorter.

7 Related Work

This paper is a continuation of the work in [28,29]. There is already some verification of imperative programs in [28]. However, they do not make use of separation logic, and the examples are quite basic. In this paper, we make full use of separation logic and present more advanced examples.

The refinement framework, introduced by Lammich in [13], can also be used to verify programs in Imperative-HOL. It applies refinement and data abstraction formally, verifying algorithms by step-wise refinement from specifications to concrete implementations. It has been used to verify several advanced graph algorithms [11,15,16]. Our work is independent from the refinement framework. In particular, we use refinement and data abstraction only in an ad-hoc manner.

Outside Imperative-HOL, there are many other frameworks based on tactics for automating separation logic in proof assistants. Examples include [1,4–7,14, 27]. As discussed in the introduction, our framework is implemented on top of the auto2 prover, which follows a quite different approach to automation compared to tactics.

Finally, there are many systems for program verification using automatic theorem provers. The main examples include [10,25,26]. The basic approach is to generate verification conditions from user-supplied annotations, and solve them using SMT-based provers. Compared to such systems, we enjoy the usual advantages of working in an interactive theorem prover, including a small trusted kernel, better interaction when proving more difficult theorems, and having available a large library of mathematical results.

8 Conclusion

In this paper, we described the setup of the auto2 prover to provide automation for verification of imperative programs. This include both the verification of a functional version of the program, and refining it to the imperative version using separation logic. Using our framework, we verified several data structures and algorithms, culminating in Dijkstra's shortest paths algorithm and the line-sweeping algorithm for detecting rectangle intersection. The case studies demonstrate that auto2 is able to provide a great deal of automation in both stages of the verification process, significantly reducing the length and complexity of the proof scripts required.

Acknowledgements. The author would like to thank Adam Chlipala, Peter Lammich, and Tobias Nipkow for discussions and feedback during this project, and to the referees for their helpful comments. For the first half of this project, the author was at MIT and was supported by NSF Award No. 1400713. During the second half, the author is at TU Munich, and is supported by DFG Koselleck grant NI 491/16-1.

References

1. Appel, A.: Tactics for separation logic, January 2006. http://www.cs.princeton.edu/~appel/papers/septacs.pdf
2. Appel, A.: Efficient verified red-black trees (2011). http://www.cs.princeton.edu/~appel/papers/redblack.pdf
3. Bulwahn, L., Krauss, A., Haftmann, F., Erkök, L., Matthews, J.: Imperative functional programming with Isabelle/HOL. In: Mohamed, O.A., Muñoz, C., Tahar, S. (eds.) TPHOLs 2008. LNCS, vol. 5170, pp. 134–149. Springer, Heidelberg (2008). https://doi.org/10.1007/978-3-540-71067-7_14
4. Cao, J., Fu, M., Feng, X.: Practical tactics for verifying C programs in Coq. In: Leroy, X., Tiu, A. (eds.) CPP 2015, pp. 97–108 (2015)
5. Charguéraud, A.: Characteristic formulae for the verification of imperative programs. In: ICFP, pp. 418–430. ACM (2011)
6. Chlipala, A.: Mostly-automated verification of low-level programs in computational separation logic. In: PLDI 2011, pp. 234–245 (2011)
7. Chlipala, A., Malecha, G., Morrisett, G., Shinnar, A., Wisnesky, R.: Effective interactive proofs for higher-order imperative programs. In: Proceedings of the 14th ACM SIGPLAN International Conference on Functional Programming (ICFP 2009), pp. 79–90, August 2009
8. Cormer, T.H., Leiserson, C.E., Rivest, R., Stein, C.: Introduction to Algorithms, 3rd edn. MIT Press, Cambridge (1989)
9. Dross, C., Moy, Y.: Auto-active proof of red-black trees in SPARK. In: Barrett, C., Davies, M., Kahsai, T. (eds.) NFM 2017. LNCS, vol. 10227, pp. 68–83. Springer, Cham (2017). https://doi.org/10.1007/978-3-319-57288-8_5
10. Filliâtre, J.-C., Paskevich, A.: Why3 — Where programs meet provers. In: Felleisen, M., Gardner, P. (eds.) ESOP 2013. LNCS, vol. 7792, pp. 125–128. Springer, Heidelberg (2013). https://doi.org/10.1007/978-3-642-37036-6_8
11. Lammich, P.: Verified efficient implementation of Gabow's strongly connected component algorithm. In: Klein, G., Gamboa, R. (eds.) ITP 2014. LNCS, vol. 8558, pp. 325–340. Springer, Cham (2014). https://doi.org/10.1007/978-3-319-08970-6_21
12. Lammich, P.: Refinement based verification of imperative data structures. In: Avigad, J., Chlipala, A. (eds.) CPP 2016, pp. 27–36 (2016)
13. Lammich, P.: Refinement to imperative/HOL. In: Urban, C., Zhang, X. (eds.) ITP 2015. LNCS, vol. 9236, pp. 253–269. Springer, Cham (2015). https://doi.org/10.1007/978-3-319-22102-1_17
14. Lammich, P., Meis, R.: A separation logic framework for imperative HOL. In: Archive of Formal Proofs, November 2012. http://afp.sf.net/entries/Separation_Logic_Imperative_HOL.shtml. Formal proof development
15. Lammich, P., Sefidgar, S.R.: Formalizing the Edmonds-Karp algorithm. In: Blanchette, J.C., Merz, S. (eds.) ITP 2016. LNCS, vol. 9807, pp. 219–234. Springer, Cham (2016). https://doi.org/10.1007/978-3-319-43144-4_14

16. Lammich, P., Tuerk, T.: Applying data refinement for monadic programs to Hopcroft's algorithm. In: Beringer, L., Felty, A. (eds.) ITP 2012. LNCS, vol. 7406, pp. 166–182. Springer, Heidelberg (2012). https://doi.org/10.1007/978-3-642-32347-8_12
17. Le, Q.L., Sun, J., Chin, W.-N.: Satisfiability modulo heap-based programs. In: Chaudhuri, S., Farzan, A. (eds.) CAV 2016, Part I. LNCS, vol. 9779, pp. 382–404. Springer, Cham (2016). https://doi.org/10.1007/978-3-319-41528-4_21
18. Kahrs, S.: Red-black trees with types. J. Funct. Program. **11**(4), 425–432 (2001)
19. Nipkow, T.: Automatic functional correctness proofs for functional search trees. In: Blanchette, J.C., Merz, S. (eds.) ITP 2016. LNCS, vol. 9807, pp. 307–322. Springer, Cham (2016). https://doi.org/10.1007/978-3-319-43144-4_19
20. Nordhoff, B., Lammich, P.: Formalization of Dijkstra's algorithm. Archive of Formal Proofs, January 2012. https://www.isa-afp.org/entries/Dijkstra_Shortest_Path.html
21. Okasaki, C.: Red-black trees in a functional setting. J. Funct. Program. **9**(4), 471–477 (1999)
22. Pek, E., Qiu, X., Madhusudan, P.: Natural proofs for data structure manipulation in C using separation logic. In: PLDI 2014, pp. 440–451 (2014)
23. Piskac, R., Wies, T., Zufferey, D.: Automating separation logic with trees and data. In: Biere, A., Bloem, R. (eds.) CAV 2014. LNCS, vol. 8559, pp. 711–728. Springer, Cham (2014). https://doi.org/10.1007/978-3-319-08867-9_47
24. Qiu, X., Garg, P., Ştefănescu, A., Madhusudan, P.: Natural proofs for structure, data, and separation. In: PLDI 2013, pp. 231–242 (2013)
25. Leino, K.R.M.: Dafny: an automatic program verifier for functional correctness. In: Clarke, E.M., Voronkov, A. (eds.) LPAR 2010. LNCS (LNAI), vol. 6355, pp. 348–370. Springer, Heidelberg (2010). https://doi.org/10.1007/978-3-642-17511-4_20
26. Jacobs, B., Piessens, F.: The VeriFast program verifier. Technical report CW-520, Department of Computer Science, Katholieke Universiteit Leuven, Belgium, August 2008
27. Tuerk, T.: A separation logic framework for HOL. Technical report UCAM-CL-TR-799, University of Cambridge, Computer Laboratory, June 2011
28. Zhan, B.: AUTO2, a saturation-based heuristic prover for higher-order logic. In: Blanchette, J.C., Merz, S. (eds.) ITP 2016. LNCS, vol. 9807, pp. 441–456. Springer, Cham (2016). https://doi.org/10.1007/978-3-319-43144-4_27
29. Zhan, B.: Formalization of the fundamental group in untyped set theory using auto2. In: Ayala-Rincón, M., Muñoz, C.A. (eds.) ITP 2017. LNCS, vol. 10499, pp. 514–530. Springer, Cham (2017). https://doi.org/10.1007/978-3-319-66107-0_32

Frame Inference for Inductive Entailment Proofs in Separation Logic

Quang Loc Le[1(✉)], Jun Sun[2], and Shengchao Qin[1]

[1] Teesside University, Middlesbrough, UK
{Q.Le,S.Qin}@tees.ac.uk
[2] Singapore University of Technology and Design, Singapore, Singapore
sunjun@sutd.edu.sg

Abstract. Given separation logic formulae A and C, frame inference is the problem of checking whether A entails C and simultaneously inferring residual heaps. Existing approaches on frame inference do not support inductive proofs with general inductive predicates. In this work, we present an automatic frame inference approach for an expressive fragment of separation logic. We further show how to strengthen the inferred frame through predicate normalization and arithmetic inference. We have integrated our approach into an existing verification system. The experimental results show that our approach helps to establish a number of non-trivial inductive proofs which are beyond the capability of all existing tools.

1 Introduction

Separation logic (SL) [20,37] has been well established for reasoning about heap-manipulating programs (like linked-lists and trees). Often, SL is used in combination with inductive predicates to precisely specify data structures manipulated by a program. In the last decade, a large number of SL-based verification systems have been developed [1,3,6,8,13,18,19,24,29,33,36]. In these systems, SL is typically used to express assertions about program states. The problem of validating these assertions can be reduced to the *entailment* problem in SL, i.e., given two SL formulas Δ_a and Δ_c, to check whether $\Delta_a \models \Delta_c$ holds. Moreover, SL provides the frame rule [20], one prominent feature to enable compositional (a.k.a. modular) reasoning in the presence of the heap:

$$\text{FRAME RULE}\ \frac{\{P\}c\{Q\}}{\{P{*}F\}c\{Q{*}F\}}$$

where c is a program, P, Q and F are SL formulas, and $*$ is the separating conjunction in SL. Intuitively, $P{*}F$ states that P and F hold in disjoint heaps. This conjunction allows the frame rule to guarantee that F is unchanged under the action of c. This feature of SL is essential for scalability [6,21,44] as it allows the proof of a program to be decomposed (and reused) into smaller ones, e.g., proofs of procedures. To automate the application of the frame rule, SL-based

D. Beyer and M. Huisman (Eds.): TACAS 2018, LNCS 10805, pp. 41–60, 2018.
https://doi.org/10.1007/978-3-319-89960-2_3

proof systems rely on a generalized form of the entailment, which is referred to as frame inference [1,8,12,33,39]. That is, given Δ_a and Δ_c, to check whether Δ_a entails Δ_c and simultaneously generate the residual heap, which is a satisfiable frame Δ_f capturing properties of the memory in Δ_a that is not covered by Δ_c. This problem, especially if Δ_a and Δ_c are constituted by general inductive predicates, is highly non-trivial as it may require inductive reasoning. Existing approaches [1,33] are limited to specific predicates e.g., linked lists and trees. The systems reported in [8,12,39] do not adequately support the frame inference problem for inductive entailments in separation logic with predicate definitions and arithmetic.

In this work, we propose a sound approach for frame inference which aims to enhance modular verification in an expressive SL fragment with general inductive predicates and Presburger arithmetic. Intuitively, given an entailment $\Delta_a \models \Delta_c$, our goal is to infer a satisfiable frame axiom Δ_f such that $\Delta_a \models \Delta_c * \Delta_f$ holds. Our approach works as follows. We first augment the entailment checking with an *unknown* second-order variable $\mathtt{U_f}(\bar{t})$ as a place-holder of the frame, where $\bar{t}$ is a set of pointer-typed variables common in Δ_a and Δ_c. That is, the entailment checking becomes $\Delta_a \models \Delta_c * \mathtt{U_f}(\bar{t})$. Afterwards, the following two steps are conducted. Firstly, we invoke a novel proof system to derive a *cyclic* proof for $\Delta_a \models \Delta_c * \mathtt{U_f}(\bar{t})$ whilst inferring a predicate which $\mathtt{U_f}$ must satisfy so that the entailment is valid. We show that the cyclic proof is valid if this predicate is satisfiable. Secondly, we strengthen the inferred frame with shape normalization and arithmetic inference.

For the first step, we design a new cyclic proof system (e.g., based on [2,3]) with an automated *cut rule* so as to effectively infer the predicate on $\mathtt{U_f}$. A cyclic proof is a derivation tree whose root is the given entailment checking and whose edges are constructed by applying SL proof rules. A derivation tree of a cyclic proof may contain virtual *back-links*, each of which links a (leaf) node back to an ancestor. Intuitively, a back-link from a node l to an internal node i means that the proof obligation at l is induced by that at i. Furthermore, to avoid potentially unsound cycles (i.e., self-cycles), a global soundness condition must be imposed upon these derivations to qualify them as genuine proofs. In this work, we develop a sequent-based cyclic proof system with a *cyclic cut* rule so as to form back-links effectively and check the soundness condition eagerly. Furthermore, we show how to extract lemmas from the proven cyclic proofs and reuse them through lemma application for an efficient proof system. These synthesized lemmas work as *dynamic cuts* in the proposed proof system.

For the second step, we strengthen the inferred predicate on the frame $\mathtt{U_f}(\bar{t})$ so that it becomes more powerful in establishing correctness of certain programs. In particular, the inferred frame is strengthened with predicate normalization and arithmetic inference. The normalization includes predicate split (i.e., to expose the spatial separation of the inferred frame) and predicate equivalence (i.e., to relate the inferred frame with user-supplied predicates). The arithmetic inference discovers predicates on pure properties (size, sum, height, content and bag) to support programs which require induction reasoning on both shape and data properties.

Lastly, we have implemented the proposal and integrated it into a modular verification engine. Our experiments show that our approach infers strong frames which enhances the verification of heap-manipulating programs.

2 Preliminaries

In this section, we present the fragment of SL which is used as the assertion language in this work. This fragment, described in Fig. 1, is expressive enough for specifying and verifying properties of a variety of data structures [24–26, 35, 41]. We use $\bar{t}$ to denote a sequence of terms and occasionally use a sequence (i.e., $\bar{t}$) to denote a set when there is no ambiguity. A formula Φ in our language is a disjunction of multiple clauses Δ, each of which is a conjunction of a spatial predicate κ and a pure (non-heap) constraint π. The spatial predicate κ captures properties of the heap whereas π captures properties of the data. κ can be an empty heap `emp`, or a points-to predicate $r{\mapsto}c(\bar{v})$ where c is a data structure, or a user-defined predicate $\mathtt{P}(\bar{t})$ or a spatial conjunction $\kappa_1{*}\kappa_2$. `null` is a special heap location. A pure constraint π is in the form of (dis)equality α (on pointers) and Presburger arithmetic ϕ. We write $v_1 \neq v_2$ and $v \neq \mathtt{null}$ for $\neg(v_1 = v_2)$ and $\neg(v = \mathtt{null})$, respectively. We often omit the pure part of a formula Φ when it is `true`. For standardizing the notations, we use uppercase letters for unknown (to-be-inferred) predicates, (e.g., $\mathtt{P}(\bar{t})$) and lowercase letters (e.g., $p(\bar{t})$) for known predicates.

Formula	$\Phi ::= \Delta \mid \Phi_1 \vee \Phi_2 \qquad\qquad \Delta ::= \exists\bar{v}\cdot(\kappa\wedge\pi)$
Spatial	$\kappa ::= \mathtt{emp} \mid x{\mapsto}c(\bar{v}) \mid \mathtt{P}(\bar{t}) \mid \kappa_1{*}\kappa_2$
Pure	$\pi ::= \mathtt{true} \mid \mathtt{false} \mid \alpha \mid \phi \mid p(\bar{t}) \mid \exists v\cdot\pi \mid \forall v\cdot\pi \mid \neg\pi \mid \pi_1{\wedge}\pi_2 \mid \pi_1{\vee}\pi_2$
Equality	$\alpha ::= v_1{=}v_2 \mid v{=}\mathtt{null}$
Pres. arith.	$\phi ::= a \mid \phi_1{=}\phi_2 \mid \phi_1{\leq}\phi_2$
	$a ::= k^{\mathtt{int}} \mid v \mid k^{\mathtt{int}}{\times}a \mid a_1{+}a_2 \mid -a \mid max(a_1,a_2) \mid \min(a_1,a_2)$
Lemma	$\iota ::= P(\bar{v}){\wedge}\pi \bowtie \exists\bar{w}{\cdot}\kappa{\wedge}\pi \qquad \bowtie ::= \rightarrow \mid \leftarrow \mid \leftrightarrow$

Fig. 1. Syntax

A user-defined (inductive) predicate $\mathtt{P}(\bar{v})$ with parameters $\bar{v}$ is defined in the form of a disjunction, i.e., $\mathtt{pred}\ \mathtt{P}(\bar{v}) \equiv \Phi$, where each disjunct in Φ is referred to as a branch. In each branch, variables that are not in $\bar{v}$ are implicitly existentially-quantified. We use function $\mathtt{unfold}(\mathtt{P}(\bar{t}))$ to replace an occurrence of inductive predicates by the disjuncts in the definition of `P` with actual/formal parameters renaming. For example, the following predicates `lseg` and `lsegn` are defined to express list segments where every node contains the same value 1, given data structure `node{int val; node next; }`.

```
pred lseg(root,l)≡emp∧root=l ∨ ∃ q·root↦node(1,q)*lseg(q,l);
pred lsegn(root,l,n)≡emp∧root=l∧n=0 ∨ ∃ q· root↦node(1,q)*lsegn(q,l,n−1);
```

where `root` is the head, l the end of the segment and n the length of the segment.

In our framework, we may have lemmas to assist program verification. A lemma ι of the form $\Delta_l \rightarrow \Delta_r$, which means that the entailment $\Delta_l \models \Delta_r$ holds. We write $A \leftrightarrow B$, a short form of $A \rightarrow B$ and $B \rightarrow A$, to denote a two-way lemma. If $A \leftrightarrow B$, A is semantically equivalent to B. We use E and F to denote an entailment problem.

In the following, we discuss semantics of the SL fragment. Concrete heap models assume a fixed finite collection *Node*, a fixed finite collection *Fields*, a disjoint set *Loc* of locations (i.e., heap addresses), a set of non-address values *Val* such that `null` $\in$ *Val* and $Val \cap Loc = \emptyset$. The semantics is given by a satisfaction relation: $s,h \models \Phi$ that forces the stack s and heap h to satisfy the constraint Φ where $h \in Heaps$, $s \in Stacks$, and Φ is a formula. *Heaps* and *Stacks* are defined as follows.

$$Heaps \stackrel{\text{def}}{=} Loc \rightharpoonup_{fin} (Node \times Fields \rightarrow Val \cup Loc)$$
$$Stacks \stackrel{\text{def}}{=} Var \rightarrow Val \cup Loc$$

The details of semantics of this SL fragment follow the one in [25].

```
1 node append(node x, node y)
2   requires lln(x,i)*lln(y,j)∧i>0
3   ensures lln(res,i+j);
4 {//lln(x,i)*lln(y,j)∧i>0
5   node t=last(x);
  //ll_last(x,t,i)*lln(y,j)∧i>0
6   t->next=y;
  //α:lsegn(x,t,i−1)*t↦node(y)*lln(y,j)∧i>0
7   return x; }

8 node last(node x)
9    requires lln(x,n)∧n>0
10   ensures ll_last(x,res,n);
11 { if(!x->next) return x;
12   else return last(x->next); }
```

Fig. 2. Code of `append`.

3 Illustrative Example

In the following, we first discuss the limitation of the existing entailment procedures [1,8] to the frame inference problem. Given an entailment, these procedures deduce it until the following subgoal is obtained: $\Delta_a \vdash$`emp` $\wedge$ `true`. Then, they conclude that Δ_a is the residual frame. However, these approaches provide limited support for proofs of induction. While [1] provides inference rules as a sequence of inductive reasoning for hardwired lists and trees, our previous work [8] supports inductive proofs via user-supplied lemmas [30]. Hence, it is very hard for these procedures to automatically infer the frame for the entailments which require proofs of induction.

We illustrate our approach via the verification of the `append` method shown in Fig. 2, which appends a singly-linked list referred to by `y` to the end of the singly-linked list referred to by `x`. It uses the auxiliary procedure `last` (lines 8–12) to obtain the pointer referring to the last node in the list. Each node object x has a data value `x->data` and a next pointer `x->next`. For simplicity, we assume that every node in the x list and the y list has data value 1. The correctness of append and last is specified using our fragment of SL with a pre-condition (requires) and a post-condition (ensures). The auxiliary variable res denotes the return value of the procedure. Note that these specifications refer to the user-provided predicates lln and ll_last, which are defined as follows.

$$\texttt{pred lln(root,}n\texttt{)} \equiv \texttt{emp}\wedge\texttt{root=null}\wedge n{=}0 \vee \exists\, q{\cdot}\texttt{root}{\mapsto}\texttt{node}(1,q){*}\texttt{lln}(q,n{-}1);$$
$$\texttt{pred ll\_last(root,}l,n\texttt{)} \equiv \texttt{l}{\mapsto}\texttt{node}(1,\texttt{null})\wedge\texttt{root}{=}l\wedge n{=}1$$
$$\vee\ \exists q{\cdot}\ \texttt{root}{\mapsto}\texttt{node}(1,q){*}\texttt{ll\_last}(q,l,n{-}1);$$

Intuitively, the predicate lln(root,n) is satisfied if root points to a singly-linked list with n nodes. The predicate ll_last(t,p,n) is satisfied if t points to a list segment with last element p and length n. In our framework, we provide a library of commonly used inductive predicates (and the corresponding lemmas), including for example the definitions for list segments lseg and lsegn introduced earlier. Given these specifications, we automatically deduce predicates on the intermediate program states (using existing approaches [8]), shown as comments in Fig. 2, as well as the following three entailment checks that must be established in order to verify the absence of memory errors and the correctness of the method append.

$$\texttt{E}_1{:}\texttt{lln}(x,i){*}\texttt{lln}(y,j)\wedge i{>}0 \vdash \exists\, n_1{\cdot}\texttt{lln}(x,n_1)\wedge n_1{>}0$$
$$\texttt{E}_2{:}\texttt{ll\_last}(x,t,i){*}\texttt{lln}(y,j)\wedge i{>}0\ \vdash\ \exists\, q,v{\cdot}t{\mapsto}\texttt{node}(v,q)$$
$$\texttt{E}_3{:}\texttt{lsegn}(\texttt{res},t,i{-}1){*}t{\mapsto}\texttt{node}(1,y){*}\texttt{lln}(y,j)\wedge i{>}0\ \vdash\ \texttt{lln}(\texttt{res},i{+}j)$$

$\texttt{E}_1$ aims to establish a local specification at line 5 which we generate automatically. $\texttt{E}_2$ must be satisfied so that no null-dereference error would occur for the assignment to t->next at line 6. $\texttt{E}_3$ aims to establish that the postcondition is met. Frame inference is necessary in order to verify the program. In particular, frame inference for $\texttt{E}_2$ is crucial to construct a precise heap state after line 6, i.e., the state α in the figure, which is necessary to establish $\texttt{E}_3$. Furthermore, the frame of $\texttt{E}_3$ (which is inferred as emp) helps to show that this program does not leak memory. As the entailment checks $\texttt{E}_2$ and $\texttt{E}_3$ require both induction reasoning and frame inference, they are challenging for existing SL proof systems [3,8,9,12,15,31,36,40]. In what follows, we illustrate how our system establishes a cyclic proof with frame inference for $\texttt{E}_2$.

Frame Inference. Our frame inference starts with introducing an unknown predicate (a second-order variable) $\texttt{U}_1(x,t,q,v,y)$[1] as the initial frame, which is a placeholder for a heap predicate on variables x, t, q and y (i.e., variables referred to in $\texttt{E}_2$). That is, $\texttt{E}_2$ is transformed to the following entailment checking problem:

$$\texttt{F}_2{:}\ \texttt{ll\_last}(x,t,i){*}\texttt{lln}(y,j)\wedge i{>}0 \vdash_{L_0} \exists q,v{\cdot}t{\mapsto}\texttt{node}(v,q){*}\texttt{U}_1(x,t,q,v,y)$$

where L_0 is a set of induction hypotheses and sound lemmas. This set is accumulated automatically during the proof search and used for constructing cyclic

[1] In implementation, we add # annotation into instantiated variables and non-heap variables to guide proof search which are not shown here.

proofs and lemma application. If a hypothesis is proven, it becomes a lemma and may be applied latter during the proof search. in this example, initially $L_0 = \emptyset$. The proposed proof system derives a cyclic proof for the entailment problem and, at the same time, infers a set of constraints $\mathcal{R}$ for $\mathtt{U}_1(x,t,q,v,y)$ such that the proof is valid if the system $\mathcal{R}$ is satisfiable. Each constraint in $\mathcal{R}$ has the form of logical implication i.e., $\Delta_b \Rightarrow \mathtt{U}(\bar{v})$ where Δ_b is the body and $\mathtt{U}(\bar{v})$ is the head (a second-order variable). For $\mathtt{F}_2$, the following two constraints are inferred, denoted by σ_1 and σ_2.

$$\sigma_1\text{: } \mathtt{lln}(y,j) \wedge t{=}x \wedge q{=}\mathtt{null} \wedge v{=}1 \ \Rightarrow \mathtt{U}_1(x,t,q,v,y)$$
$$\sigma_2\text{: } x_2 {\mapsto} \mathtt{node}(1,x) {*} \mathtt{U}_1(x,t,q,v,y) \Rightarrow \mathtt{U}_1(x_2,t,q,v,y)$$

We then use a decision procedure (e.g., $\mathbf{S2SAT_{SL}}$ [25,26] or [4]) to check the satisfiability of $\sigma_1 \wedge \sigma_2$. Note that we write a satisfiable definition of $(\Delta_1 {\Rightarrow} \mathtt{U}(\bar{v})) \wedge (\Delta_2 {\Rightarrow} \mathtt{U}(\bar{v}))$ in the equivalent form of $\mathtt{U}(\bar{v}) \equiv \Delta_1 \vee \Delta_2$. For instance, the above constraints are written as:

$$\mathtt{U}_1(\mathtt{root},t,q,v,y) \equiv \mathtt{lln}(y,j) \wedge \mathtt{root}{=}t \wedge q{=}\mathtt{null} \wedge v{=}1$$
$$\vee\ \exists q_1 \cdot \mathtt{root} {\mapsto} \mathtt{node}(1,q_1) {*} \mathtt{U}_1(q_1,t,q,v,y);$$

Note that, in the above definition of $\mathtt{U}_1$, the separation of those heap-lets referred to by $\mathtt{root}$, y and q is not explicitly captured. Additionally, relations over the sizes are also missing. Such information is necessary in order to establish the left-hand side of $\mathtt{E}_3$. The successful verification of $\mathtt{E}_3$ in turn establishes the post-condition of method **append**. In the following we show how to strengthen the inferred frame.

Frame Strengthening. We strengthen $\mathtt{U}_1$ with spatial separation constraints on the pointer variables *root*, y and q. To explicate the *spatial* separation among these pointers, our system generates the following equivalent lemma and splits $\mathtt{U}_1$ into two disjoint heap regions (with $*$ conjunction):

$$\mathtt{U}_1(\mathtt{root},t,q,v,y) \equiv \mathtt{U}_2(\mathtt{root},t) {*} \mathtt{lln}(y,j) \wedge q{=}\mathtt{null} \wedge v{=}1$$

where $\mathtt{U}_2$ is a new auxiliary predicate with an inferred definition:

$$\mathtt{U}_2(\mathtt{root},t) \equiv \mathtt{emp} \wedge \mathtt{root}{=}t \vee \exists\, q_1 \cdot\ \mathtt{root} {\mapsto} \mathtt{node}(1,q_1) {*} \mathtt{U}_2(q_1,t)$$

Next, our system detects that $\mathtt{U}_2$ is equivalent to the user-defined predicate $\mathtt{lseg}$, and generates the lemma: $\mathtt{U}_2(\mathtt{root},t) {\leftrightarrow} \mathtt{lseg}(\mathtt{root},t)$. Relating $\mathtt{U}_2$ to $\mathtt{lseg}$ enhances the understanding of the inferred predicates. Furthermore, as shown in [9], this relation helps to reduce the requirements of induction reasoning among equivalent inductive predicates with different names. Substituting $\mathtt{U}_2$ with the equivalent $\mathtt{lseg}$, $\mathtt{U}_1$ becomes:

$$\mathtt{U}_1(\mathtt{root},t,q,v,y) \equiv \mathtt{lseg}(\mathtt{root},t) {*} \mathtt{lln}(y,j) \wedge q{=}\mathtt{null} \wedge v{=}1$$

This definition states that frame $\mathtt{U}_1$ holds in two disjoint heaps: one list segment pointed to by $\mathtt{root}$ and a list pointed to by y. After substitution the entailment $\mathtt{F}_2$ becomes

$$\mathtt{ll\_last}(x,t,i) {*} \mathtt{lln}(y,j) \wedge i{>}0 \vdash_{L_0} \mathtt{t} {\mapsto} \mathtt{node}(1,\mathtt{null}) {*} \mathtt{lseg}(x,t) {*} \mathtt{lln}(y,j)$$

Next, we further strengthen the frame with pure properties, which is necessary to successfully establish the left hand side of E_3. In particular, we generate constraints to capture that the numbers of allocated heaps in the left hand side and the right hand side of F_2 are identical. Our system obtains these constraints through two phases. First, it automatically augments an argument for each inductive predicate in F_2 to capture its size property. Concretely, it detects that while predicates `ll_last` and `lln` have such size argument already, the shape-based frame `lseg` has not. As so, it extends `lseg(root,`t`)` to obtain the predicate `lsegn(root,`t,m`)` where the size property is captured by parameter m. Now, we substitute the `lsegn` into F_2 to obtain:

$$\texttt{ll\_last}(x,t,i)*\texttt{lln}(y,j)\wedge i{>}0 \vdash_{L_0} \exists k{\cdot} t{\mapsto}\texttt{node}(1,\texttt{null})*\texttt{lsegn}(x,t,k)*\texttt{lln}(y,j)$$

After that, we apply the same three steps of frame inference to generate the size constraint: constructing unknown predicates, proving entailment and inferring a set of constraints and checking satisfiability. For the first step, the above entailment is enriched with one unknown (pure) predicate: $\texttt{P}_1(i,j,k)$ which is the place-holder for arithmetical constraints among size variables i, j and k. The augmented entailment checking is:

$$\begin{array}{l}\texttt{ll\_last}(x,t,i)*\texttt{lln}(y,j)\wedge i{>}0\\ \quad\vdash_{L_0} \exists k{\cdot}\texttt{lsegn}(x,t,k)*t{\mapsto}\texttt{node}(1,\texttt{null})*\texttt{lln}(y,j)\wedge\texttt{P}_1(i,j,k)\end{array}$$

Secondly, our system successfully derives a proof for the above entailment under condition that the following disjunctive set of two constraints is satisfiable.

$$\begin{array}{l}\sigma_3\text{: } i{=}1\wedge k{=}0 \Rightarrow \texttt{P}_1(i,j,k)\\ \sigma_4\text{: } i_1{=}i{-}1\wedge k_1{=}k{-}1\wedge i{>}0\wedge\texttt{P}_1(i_1,j,k_1) \Rightarrow \texttt{P}_1(i,j,k)\end{array}$$

$$\textsf{EMP}\ \frac{\pi_a \Longrightarrow \pi_c}{\textbf{emp}\wedge\pi_a \vdash_L \textbf{emp}\wedge\pi_c \rightsquigarrow \textbf{true}} \qquad \textsf{CCUT}\ \frac{\Delta_l{\to}\Delta_r{\in}L \quad \Delta_{a_1}\rho \vdash_L \Delta_l \rightsquigarrow \mathcal{R}_1 \quad \Delta_r\rho{*}\Delta_{a_2} \vdash_L \Delta_c \rightsquigarrow \mathcal{R}_2}{\Delta_{a_1}{*}\Delta_{a_2} \vdash_L \Delta_c \rightsquigarrow \mathcal{R}_1\wedge\mathcal{R}_2}\ \text{gsc}$$

$$\textsf{PRED-M}\ \frac{\Delta_a \vdash_L \Delta_c\wedge\textbf{freeEQ}([\bar{v}/\bar{w}]) \rightsquigarrow \mathcal{R}}{\texttt{P}(r,\bar{v}){*}\Delta_a \vdash_L \texttt{P}(r,\bar{w}){*}\Delta_c \rightsquigarrow \mathcal{R}} \qquad \textsf{M}\ \frac{\Delta_a \vdash_L \Delta_c\wedge\textbf{freeEQ}([\bar{v}/\bar{w}]) \rightsquigarrow \mathcal{R}}{x{\mapsto}c(\bar{v}){*}\Delta_a \vdash_L x{\mapsto}c(\bar{w}){*}\Delta_c \rightsquigarrow \mathcal{R}}$$

$$\textsf{RU}\ \frac{\begin{array}{c}(x{\mapsto}c(\bar{w}) \text{ or } x{=}\textbf{null} \text{ or } x{=}q) \in \Delta_a\\ \texttt{unfold}(\texttt{P}(x,\bar{v})) = \{\Delta_1,..,\Delta_n\} \quad \exists i{\in}\{1...n\}\cdot\Delta_a \vdash_L \Delta_i{*}\Delta_c \rightsquigarrow \mathcal{R}_i\end{array}}{\Delta_a \vdash_L \texttt{P}(x,\bar{v}){*}\Delta_c \rightsquigarrow \mathcal{R}_i}$$

$$\textsf{LU}\ \frac{\begin{array}{c}(x{\mapsto}c(\bar{w}) \text{ or } x{=}\textbf{null} \text{ or } x{=}q){\in}\Delta_c \quad \texttt{unfold}(\texttt{P}(x,\bar{v})){=}\{\Delta_1,..,\Delta_n\}\\ L'_i{=}L\cup\{(\texttt{P}(x,\bar{v}){*}\Delta_a \to \Delta_c)\} \quad \forall i{\in}\{1...n\}\cdot\Delta_i{*}\Delta_a \vdash_{L'_i} \Delta_c \rightsquigarrow \mathcal{R}_i\end{array}}{\texttt{P}(x,\bar{v}){*}\Delta_a \vdash_L \Delta_c \rightsquigarrow \bigwedge\mathcal{R}_i}$$

Fig. 3. Basic inference rules for entailment procedure (where gsc is global soundness condition)

Lastly, to check whether the $\sigma_3 \wedge \sigma_4$ is satisfiable, we automatically compute the closure form for $\sigma_3 \wedge \sigma_4$ as: $\mathtt{P}_1(i,j,k) \equiv k{=}i{-}1 \wedge i{>}0$. This formula is satisfiable and substituted into the frame as: $\mathtt{lsegn}(x,t,k) * \mathtt{lln}(y,j) \wedge q{=}\mathtt{null} \wedge v{=}1 \wedge k{=}i{-}1 \wedge i{>}0$.

4 Frame Inference

In this section, we present our approach for frame inference in detail. Given an entailment $\Delta_a \vdash \Delta_c$, where Δ_a is the antecedent (LHS) and Δ_c is the consequence (RHS), our system attempts to infer a frame Δ_f such that when a frame is successfully inferred, the validity of the entailment $\Delta_a \vdash \Delta_c * \Delta_f$ is established at the same time.

Our approach has three main steps. Firstly, we enrich RHS with an unknown predicate in the form of $\mathtt{U}(\bar{v})$ to form the entailment $\Delta_a \vdash_L \Delta_c * \mathtt{U}(\bar{v})$ where $\bar{v}$ includes all free pointer-typed variables of Δ_a and Δ_c and L is the union of a set of user-supplied lemmas and a set of induction hypotheses (initially $\emptyset$). Among these, the parameters are annotated with $\#$ following the principle that instantiation (and subtraction) must be done before inference. The detail is as follows: (i) all common variables of Δ_a and Δ_c are $\#$-annotated; (ii) points-to pointers of Δ_c are $\#$-annotated; (iii) the remaining pointers are not $\#$-annotated. In the implementation, inference of frame predicates is performed incrementally such that shape predicates are inferred prior to pure ones. Secondly, we construct a proof of the entailment and infer a set of constraints $\mathcal{R}$ for $\mathtt{U}(\bar{v})$. Thirdly, we check the satisfiability of $\mathcal{R}$ using the decision procedure in [25, 26].

In the following, we present our entailment checking procedure with a set of proof rules shown in Figs. 3 and 4. For each rule, the obligation is at the bottom and its reduced form is on the top. In particular, the rules in Fig. 3 are used for entailment proving (i.e., to establish a cyclic proof) and the rules in Fig. 4 are used for predicate inference.

$$\textbf{AF}\ \frac{\begin{array}{c}\sigma \equiv \mathtt{R}(r,\bar{t}) * \mathtt{U_i}(r_i,\bar{t}_i\#) * \mathtt{U_f}(\bar{w},\bar{t'},\bar{z}\#,r\#) \wedge \nabla(\bar{w} \cup \{r,r_i\},\pi_1) \Rightarrow \mathtt{U}(r,\bar{w},\bar{z}\#)\\ r_i \in \bar{t} \quad \bar{t'}{=}\bar{t} \backslash (\bar{w} \cup \bar{z} \cup \{r\}) \quad \kappa_1 \wedge \pi_1 \vdash_L \mathtt{U_f}(\bar{w},\bar{t'},\bar{z}\#,r\#) * \kappa_2 \wedge \pi_2 \leadsto \mathcal{R}\end{array}}{\mathtt{R}(r,\bar{t}) * \mathtt{U_i}(r_i,\bar{t}_i\#) * \kappa_1 \wedge \pi_1 \vdash_L \mathtt{U}(r,\bar{w},\bar{z}\#) * \kappa_2 \wedge \pi_2 \leadsto \sigma \wedge \mathcal{R}}$$

$$\textbf{AF-F}\ \frac{\begin{array}{c}\sigma \equiv \mathtt{U}(r,\bar{w},\bar{z}\#) \Rightarrow \mathtt{R}(r,\bar{t}) * \mathtt{U_i}(r_i,\bar{t}_i\#) * \mathtt{U_f}(\bar{w},\bar{t'},\bar{z}\#,r\#) \wedge \nabla(\bar{w} \cup \{r,r_i\},\pi_1)\\ r_i \in \bar{t} \quad \bar{t'}{=}\bar{t} \backslash (\bar{w} \cup \bar{z} \cup \{r\}) \quad \mathtt{U_f}(\bar{w},\bar{t'},\bar{z}\#,r\#) * \kappa_1 \wedge \pi_1 \vdash_L \kappa_2 \wedge \pi_2 \leadsto \mathcal{R}\end{array}}{\mathtt{U}(r,\bar{w},\bar{z}\#) * \kappa_1 \wedge \pi_1 \vdash_L \mathtt{R}(r,\bar{t}) * \mathtt{U_i}(r_i,\bar{t}_i\#) * \kappa_2 \wedge \pi_2 \leadsto \sigma \wedge \mathcal{R}}$$

Fig. 4. Inference rules with predicate synthesis.

Given an entailment check in the form of $\Delta_a \vdash_L \Delta_c$, the rules shown in Fig. 3 are designed to subtract the heap (via the rules [M] and [PRED−M]) on both sides until their heaps are empty. After that, it checks the validity for the implication of two pure formulas by using an SMT solver, like Z3 [27], as shown in rule [EMP]. Algorithmically, this entailment checking is performed as follows.

- **Matching.** The rules [M] and [PRED−M] are used to match up identified heap chains. Starting from identified root pointers, the procedure keeps matching all their reachable heaps. It unifies corresponding fields of matched roots by using the following auxiliary function freeEQ(ρ): freeEQ($[u_i/v_i]_{i=1}^n$) = $\bigwedge_{i=1}^n \{u_i = v_i\}$.
- **Unfolding.** The rules [LU] and [RU] are used to derive alternative heap chains. While rule [LU] presents the unfolding in the antecedent, [RU] in the consequent.
- **Applying Lemma.** Rule [CCUT] derives yet other alternative heap chains. For LHS which has at least one UD predicate, we attempt to apply a lemma as an alternative search using [CCUT] rule. We notice that as we assume that a lemma which is supplied by the user is valid, applying this lemma does not requires the global condition.

Cyclic Proof. The proof rules in Fig. 3 are designed to establish cyclic proofs. In the following, we briefly describe a cyclic proof technique enhancing the proposal in [2].

Definition 1 (Pre-proof). *A* pre-proof *of entailment E is a pair ($\mathcal{T}_i$, $\mathcal{L}$) where $\mathcal{T}_i$ is a derivation tree and $\mathcal{L}$ is a back-link function such that: the root of $\mathcal{T}_i$ is E; for every edge from E_i to E_j in $\mathcal{T}_i$, E_i is a conclusion of an inference rule with a premise E_j. There is a back-link between E_c and E_l if there exists $\mathcal{L}(E_l)$ $= E_c$ (i.e., $E_c = E_l\,\theta$ with some substitution θ) ; and for every leaf E_l, E_l is an axiom rule (without conclusion).*

If $\mathcal{L}(E_l) = E_c$, E_l (resp. E_c) is referred as a bud (resp. companion).

Definition 2 (Trace). *Let ($\mathcal{T}_i$, $\mathcal{L}$) be a pre-proof of $\Delta_a \vdash_L \Delta_c$; $(\Delta_{a_i} \vdash_{L_i} \Delta_{c_i})_{i\geq 0}$ be a path of $\mathcal{T}_i$. A trace following $(\Delta_{a_i} \vdash_{L_i} \Delta_{c_i})_{i\geq 0}$ is a sequence $(\alpha_i)_{i\geq 0}$ such that each α_i (for all $i \geq 0$) is an instance of the predicate $\mathtt{P}(\bar{t})$ in the formula Δ_{a_i}, and either:*

- *α_{i+1} is the subformula containing an instance of $\mathtt{P}(\bar{t})$ in $\Delta_{a_{i+1}}$;*
- *or $\Delta_{a_i} \vdash_{L_i} \Delta_{c_i}$ is the conclusion of an unfolding rule, α_i is an instance predicate $\mathtt{P}(\bar{t})$ in Δ_{a_i} and α_{i+1} is a subformula $\Delta[\bar{t}/\bar{v}]$ which is a definition rule of the inductive predicate $\mathtt{P}(\bar{v})$. i is a progressing point of the trace.*

To ensure that a pre-proof is sound, a global *soundness condition* must be imposed to guarantee well-foundedness.

Definition 3 (Cyclic proof). *A pre-proof ($\mathcal{T}_i$, $\mathcal{L}$) of $\Delta_a \vdash_L \Delta_c$ is a cyclic proof if, for every infinite path $(\Delta_{a_i} \vdash_{L_i} \Delta_{c_i})_{i\geq 0}$ of $\mathcal{T}_i$, there is a tail of the path p=$(\Delta_{a_i} \vdash_{L_i} \Delta_{c_i})_{i\geq n}$ such that there is a trace following p which has infinitely progressing points.*

Brotherston *et al.* proved [2] that $\Delta_a \vdash \Delta_c$ holds if there is a cyclic proof of $\Delta_a \vdash_\emptyset \Delta_c$ where Δ_a and Δ_c do not contain any unknown predicate.

In the following, we explain how cyclic proofs are constructed using the proof rules shown in Fig. 3. [LU] and [CCUT] are the most important rules for forming back-links and then pre-proof construction. While rule [LU] accumulates possible companions and stores them in historical sequents L, [CCUT] links a bud with a companion using some substitutions as well as checks the global soundness condition eagerly. Different to the original cyclic system [3], our linking back function only considers companions selected in the set of historical sequents L. Particularly, $\Delta_l \rightarrow \Delta_r \in L$ is used as an intelligent cut as follows. During proof search, a subgoal (i.e., $\Delta_{a_1} * \Delta_{a_2} \vdash_L \Delta_c$) may be matched with the above historical sequent to form a cycle and close the proof branch using the following principle. First, $\Delta_l \vdash \Delta_r$ is used as an induction hypothesis. As so, we have $\Delta_l \rho * \Delta_{a_2} \models \Delta_r \rho * \Delta_{a_2}$ where ρ are substitutions including those for avoiding clashing of variables between Δ_r and Δ_{a_2}. If both $\Delta_{a_1} * \Delta_{a_2} \vdash_L \Delta_l \rho * \Delta_{a_2}$ and $\Delta_r \rho * \Delta_{a_2} \vdash_L \Delta_c$ are proven, then we have:

$$\Delta_{a_1} * \Delta_{a_2} \Longrightarrow \Delta_l \rho * \Delta_{a_2} \Longrightarrow \Delta_r \rho * \Delta_{a_2} \Longrightarrow \Delta_c .$$

Thus, the subgoal $\Delta_{a_1} * \Delta_{a_2} \vdash_L \Delta_c$ holds. We remark that if a hypothesis is proven, it can be applied as a valid lemma subsequently.

In our system, often a lemma includes universally quantified variables. We thus show a new mechanism to instantiate those lemmas that include universally quantified variables. We denote constraints with universal variables as universal guards $\forall G$. A universal guard $\forall G$ is equivalent to an *infinite* conjunction $\bigwedge_\rho G[\rho]$. Linking a leaf with universal guards is not straightforward. For illustration, let us consider the following bud $\mathtt{B_0}$ and the universally quantified companion/lemma $\mathtt{C_0} \in L$.

$\mathtt{B_0}$:$\mathtt{lsegn}(\mathtt{root},\mathtt{null}, n) \wedge n{=}10 \vdash_L \exists r {\cdot} \mathtt{lsegn}(\mathtt{root}, r, 3) * \mathtt{lsegn}(r, \mathtt{null}, 7)$
$\mathtt{C_0}$:$\forall a, b {\cdot} \mathtt{lsegn}(\mathtt{root},\mathtt{null}, n) \wedge n{=}a{+}b \wedge a{\geq}0 \wedge b{\geq}0$
$\quad \rightarrow \exists r {\cdot} \mathtt{lsegn}(\mathtt{root}, r, a) * \mathtt{lsegn}(r, \mathtt{null}, b)$

As shown in rule [CCUT], to link $\mathtt{B_0}$ back to $\mathtt{C_0}$, the LHS of these two entailments must be implied through some substitution. To obtain that, we propose *lemma instantiation*, a sound solution for universal lemma application. Based on the constraints in the LHS of the bud, our technique instantiates a universally quantified guard (of the selected companion/lemma) before linking it back. Concretely, we replace the universal guard by a *finite* set of its instances; an instantiation of a formula $\forall \bar{v} G(\bar{t})$ is $G(\bar{t})[\bar{w}/\bar{v}]$ for some vector of terms $\bar{w}$. These instances are introduced based on the instantiations in both LHS and RHS of the corresponding bud e.g., $n = 10 \wedge a = 3 \wedge b = 7$ in $\mathtt{B_0}$.

Frame Inference. The two inference rules shown in Fig. 4 are designed specifically to infer constraints for frame. In these rules, $\bigtriangledown(\bar{w}, \pi)$ is an auxiliary function that existentially quantifies free variables in π that are not in the set $\bar{w}$. This function extracts relevant arithmetic constraints to define data contents of the unknown predicates. $\mathtt{R}(r,\bar{t})$ is either $r {\mapsto} c(\bar{t})$ or a known (defined) predicate $\mathtt{P}(r,\bar{t})$, or an unknown predicate $\mathtt{U}'(r,\bar{t},\bar{w}_\#)$. The # in the unknown predicates is used to guide inference and proof search. We only infer on pointers without #-annotation. $\mathtt{U_f}(\bar{w}, \bar{t'})$ is another unknown predicate which is generated to infer the shape of pointers $\bar{w}$. Inferred pointers are annotated with $\#$ to avoid double inference. A new unknown predicate $\mathtt{U_f}$ is generated only if there exists at least one parameter not to be annotated with $\#$ (i.e., $\bar{w}\cup\bar{t}'\neq\emptyset$). To avoid conflict between the inference rules and the other rules (e.g., unfolding and matching), root pointers of a heap formula must be annotated with $\#$ in unknown predicates. For example, in our system while $x{\mapsto}\mathtt{c_1}(y){*}\mathtt{U_1}(x\#,y)$ is legal, $x{\mapsto}\mathtt{c_1}(y){*}\mathtt{U_1}(x,y)$ is illegal. Our system applies subtraction on the heap pointed to by x rather than inference for the following check: $x{\mapsto}\mathtt{c_1}(\mathtt{null}){\vdash_L}x{\mapsto}\mathtt{c_1}(y){*}\mathtt{U_1}(x\#,y)$.

Soundness. The soundness of the inference rules in Fig. 3 has been shown in unfold-and-match systems for general inductive predicates [3,8]. In the following, we present the soundness of the inference rules in Fig. 4. We introduce the notation $\mathcal{R}(\Gamma)$ to denote a set of predicate definitions $\Gamma=\{\mathtt{U_1}(\bar{v}_1)\equiv\Phi_1,..\mathtt{U}_n(\bar{v}_n)\equiv\Phi_n\}$ satisfying the set of constraints $\mathcal{R}$. That is, for all constraints $\Delta_l \Rightarrow \Delta_r \in \mathcal{R}$, (i) Γ contains states $(s_i,\ h_i)$, a predicate definition for each unknown predicate appearing in Δ_l and Δ_r; (ii) by interpreting all unknown predicates according to Γ, then it is provable that Δ_l implies Δ_r (i.e., there exists $s_i \subseteq s,\ h_i \subseteq h$ for $i \in \{1..n\}$, and $s,h \models \Delta_l$ implies $s,h \models \Delta_r$), written as $\Gamma : \Delta_l \vdash \Delta_r$.

Lemma 1. *Given the entailment judgement $\Delta_a \vdash_{\{\}} \Delta_c \rightsquigarrow \mathcal{R}$, if there is Γ such that $\mathcal{R}(\Gamma)$, the entailment $\Gamma{:}\Delta_a{\vdash}\Delta_c$ holds.*

The soundness of the predicate synthesis requires that if definitions generated for unknown predicates are satisfiable, then the entailment is valid.

Theorem 1. *Given the entailment judgement $\Delta_a \vdash_\emptyset \Delta_c \rightsquigarrow \mathcal{R}$ $\Delta_a(\Gamma) \vdash \Delta_c(\Gamma)$ holds if there exists a solution Γ of $\mathcal{R}$.*

Theorem 1 follows from the soundness of the rules in Fig. 3 and Lemma 1.

5 Extensions

In this section, we present two ways to strengthen the inferred frame, by inferring pure properties and by normalizing inductive predicates.

Pure Constraint Inference. The inferred frame is strengthened with pure constraints following two phases. We first enrich the shape-base frame with pure properties such as size, height, sum, set of addresses/values, and their combinations. After that, we apply the same three steps in Sect. 4 to infer relational assumptions on the new pure properties. Lastly, we check satisfiability of these assumptions using FixCalc [34].

In the following, we describe how to infer size properties given a set of dependent predicates. We can similarly infer properties on height, set of addresses and values properties. We first extend an inductive predicate with a size function to capture size properties. That is, given an inductive predicate $\mathtt{P}(\bar{v}) \equiv \bigvee \Delta_i$, we generate a new predicate $\mathtt{Pn}$ with a new size parameter n as: $\mathtt{Pn}(\bar{v},n) \equiv \bigvee(\Delta_i{\wedge}n{=}\mathit{sizeF}(\Delta_i))$ where function sizeF is inductively defined as follows.

$$sizeF(r{\mapsto}c(\bar{t}))=1 \quad sizeF(\exists\bar{v}\cdot\ \kappa\wedge\pi)=sizeF(\kappa)$$
$$sizeF(\texttt{emp})=0 \quad sizeF(\kappa_1{*}\kappa_2)=sizeF(\kappa_1)+sizeF(\kappa_2)$$
$$sizeF(\texttt{P}(\bar{t}))=t_s \text{ where } t_s\in\bar{t} \text{ and } t_s \text{ is a size parameter}$$

To support pure properties, we extend the proposed cyclic proof system with bi-abduction for pure constraints which was presented in [43]. In particular, we adopt the abduction rules to generate relational assumptions over the pure properties in LHS and RHS. These rules are applied exhaustively until no more unknown predicates occur.

Normalization. We aim to relate the inferred frame to existing user-provided predicates if possible as well as to explicate the heap separation (a.k.a. pointer non-aliasing) which may be implicitly constrained through predicates. Particularly, we present a lemma synthesis mechanism to explore relations between inductive predicates. Our system processes each inductive predicate in four steps. First, it generates *heap-only* conjectures (with quantifiers). Secondly, it enriches these conjectures with unknown predicates. Thirdly, it invokes the proposed entailment procedure to prove these conjectures, infer definitions for the unknown predicates and synthesize the lemmas. Last, it strengthens the inferred lemma with pure inference.

In the following, we present two types of normalization. This first type is to generate equivalence lemmas. This normalization equivalently matches a new generated predicate to an existing predicate in a given predicate library. Under the assumption that a library of predicates is provided together with advanced knowledge (i.e., lemmas in [1]) to enhance completeness. This normalization helps to reuse this knowledge for the new synthesized predicates, and potentially enhance the completeness of the proof system. Intuitively, given a set S of inductive predicates and another inductive predicate P (which is not in S), we identify all predicates in S which are equivalent to P. Heap-only conjecture is generated to explore the equivalent relation between two predicates, e.g., in the case of $\texttt{P}(x,\bar{v})$ and $\texttt{Q}(x,\bar{w})$: $\forall\bar{v}{\cdot}\texttt{P}(\texttt{root},\bar{v}){\rightarrow}\exists\bar{w}{\cdot}\texttt{Q}(\texttt{root},\bar{w})$. The shared root parameter x has been identified by examining all permutations of root parameters of the two predicates. Moreover, our system synthesizes lemmas incrementally for the combined domains of shape and pure properties. For example, with **lln** and **lsegn**, our system generates the following lemma afterwards: $\texttt{lsegn}(\texttt{root},\texttt{null},n){\leftrightarrow}\texttt{lln}(\texttt{root},n)$.

The other type of normalization is to generate separating lemmas. This normalization aims to expose hidden separation of heaps in inductive definitions. This paragraph explores parallel or consequence separate relations over inductive predicates parameters. Two parameters of a predicate are *parallel* separating if they are both root parameters e.g., r_1 and r_2 of the predicate zip2 as follows.

$$\begin{aligned}\texttt{zip2}(r_1,r_2,n) \equiv\ & \texttt{emp}\wedge r_1{=}\texttt{null}\wedge r_2{=}\texttt{null}\wedge n{=}0\\ \vee\ & r_1{\mapsto}c_1(q_1){*}r_2{\mapsto}c_1(q_2){*}\texttt{zip2}(q_1,q_2,n{-}2);\end{aligned}$$

Two arguments of a predicate are *consequence* separating if one is a root parameter and another is reachable from the root in all base formulas derived by unfolding the predicate (e.g., those of the predicate `ll_last`). We generate these separating lemmas to explicate separation globally. As a result, the separation of actual parameters is externally visible to analyses. This visible separation enables strong updates in a modular heap analysis or frame inference in modular verification. Suppose r_1, r_2 are consequence or parallel parameters in $\mathtt{Q}(r_1, r_2, \bar{w})$, heap conjecture is generated as:

$$\mathtt{Q}(r_1, r_2, \bar{w}) \rightarrow \mathtt{Q_1}(r_1)*\mathtt{Q_2}(r_2)*\mathtt{Q_3}(\bar{w})$$

This technique could be applied to synthesize spit/join lemmas to transform predicates into the fragment of linearly compositional predicates [14, 15]. For example, our system splits the predicate `zip2` into two separating singly-lined lists through the following equivalent lemma: $\mathtt{zip2}(\mathtt{root},r_2,n) \leftrightarrow \mathtt{lln}(\mathtt{root},n)*\mathtt{lln}(r_2,n)$.

6 Implementation and Experiments

We have implemented the proposed ideas into a procedure called **S2ENT** for entailment checking and frame inference, based on the **SLEEK** [8]. **S2ENT** relies on the SMT solver Z3 [27] to check satisfiability of arithmetical formulas. We have also integrated **S2ENT** into the verifier **S2** [24]. We have conducted two sets of experiments to evaluate the effectiveness and efficiency of **S2ENT**. The first set of experiments are conducted on a set of inductive entailment checking problems gathered from previous publications [1,5,9]. We compare **S2ENT** with the state-of-the-art tools to see how many of these problems can be solved. In the second set of experiments, we apply **S2ENT** to conduct modular verification of a set of non-trivial programs. The experiments are conducted on a machine with the Intel i3-M370 (2.4 GHz) processor and 3 GB of RAM.

Entailment Proving. In Table 1, we evaluate **S2ENT** on a set of 36 *valid* entailment problems that require induction reasoning techniques. In particular, Ent 1–5 were taken from Smallfoot [1], Ent 6–19 from $\mathtt{Cyclic}_{SL}$ [3,5], Ent 20–28 from [9], and Ent 29–36 were generated by us. We evaluate **S2ENT** against the existing proof systems presented for user-defined predicates. While the tools reported in [8,12,36] could handle a subset of these benchmarks if users provide auxiliary lemmas/axioms, [15] was designed neither for those inductive predicates in Ent 6–28 nor frame problems in Ent 29–36. The only two tools which we can compare **S2ENT** with are $\mathtt{Cyclic}_{SL}$ [3] and **songbird** [40].

The experimental results are presented in Table 1. The second column shows the entailment problems. Column *bl* captures the number of back-links in cyclic proofs generated by **S2ENT**. We observe that most of problems require only one back-link in the cyclic proofs, except that Ent 4 requires two back-links and Ent 13–15 of mutual inductive odd-even singly linked lists require three back-links. The last three columns show the results of $\mathtt{Cyclic}_{SL}$, **songbird** and **S2ENT** respectively. Each cell shown in these columns is either CPU times (in seconds) if the tool proves successfully, or TO if the tool runs longer than 30 s, or X if the

Table 1. Inductive entailment checks

Ent	Proven	bl	[3]	[40]	Ours
1	$\texttt{lseg}(x,t)*\texttt{lseg}(t,\texttt{null}) \vdash \texttt{lseg}(x,\texttt{null})$	1	0.03	0.04	0.06
2	$\texttt{lseg}(x,t)*\texttt{t}\mapsto c_1(y)*\texttt{lseg}(y,\texttt{null}) \vdash \texttt{lseg}(x,\texttt{null})$	1	0.03	0.04	0.08
3	$\texttt{lseg}(x,t)*\texttt{lseg}(t,y)*\texttt{y}\mapsto c_1(\texttt{null}) \vdash \texttt{lseg}(x,\texttt{null})$	1	0.03	1.36	0.11
4	$\texttt{lseg}(x,t)*\texttt{lseg}(t,y)*\texttt{bt}(y)\wedge y{\neq}\texttt{null} \vdash \texttt{lseg}(x,y)*\texttt{bt}(y)$	2	TO	0.12	0.21
5	$\texttt{lseg}(x,t)*\texttt{lseg}(t,y)*\texttt{lseg}(y,z)\wedge y{\neq}z \vdash \texttt{lseg}(x,y)*\texttt{lseg}(y,z)$	1	3.00	0.48	0.57
6	$\texttt{x}\mapsto c_1(y)*\texttt{rlseg}(y,z) \vdash \texttt{rlseg}(x,z)$	1	0.02	0.04	0.10
7	$\texttt{nlseg}(x,z)*\texttt{z}\mapsto c_1(y) \vdash \texttt{nlseg}(x,y)$	1	0.02	0.04	0.04
8	$\texttt{nlseg}(x,z)*\texttt{nlseg}(z,y) \vdash \texttt{nlseg}(x,y)$	1	0.03	0.04	0.06
9	$\texttt{glseg}(x,z)*\texttt{z}\mapsto c_1(y) \vdash \texttt{glseg}(x,y)$	1	0.02	0.04	0.04
10	$\texttt{glseg}(x,z)*\texttt{glseg}(z,y) \vdash \texttt{glseg}(x,y)$	1	0.02	0.04	0.04
11	$\texttt{dlseg}(u,v,x,y) \vdash \texttt{glseg}_2(u,v)$	1	0.07	0.04	0.04
12	$\texttt{dlseg}(w,v,x,z)*\texttt{dlseg}(u,w,z,y) \vdash \texttt{dlseg}(u,v,x,y)$	1	0.04	0.03	0.11
13	$\texttt{listo}(x,z)*\texttt{listo}(z,\texttt{null}) \vdash \texttt{liste}(x,\texttt{null})$	3	0.06	0.04	0.06
14	$\texttt{liste}(x,z)*\texttt{liste}(z,\texttt{null}) \vdash \texttt{liste}(x,\texttt{null})$	3	0.18	0.04	0.12
15	$\texttt{listo}(x,z)*\texttt{liste}(z,y) \vdash \texttt{listo}(x,y)$	3	4.33	0.03	0.88
16	$\texttt{binPath}(x,z)*\texttt{binPath}(z,y) \vdash \texttt{binPath}(x,y)$	1	0.03	0.05	0.06
17	$\texttt{binPath}(x,y) \vdash \texttt{binTreeSeg}(x,y)$	1	0.12	X	0.08
18	$\texttt{binTreeSeg}(x,z)*\texttt{binTreeSeg}(z,y) \vdash \texttt{binTreeSeg}(x,y)$	1	0.20	0.07	0.66
19	$\texttt{binTreeSeg}(x,y)*\texttt{binTree}(y) \vdash \texttt{binTree}(x)$	1	0.06	0.05	0.03
20	$\texttt{tmp}(x,size) \vdash \exists y \cdot \texttt{ls}(x,y,size)$	1	NA	0.73	0.39
21	$\texttt{sortll}(x,min) \vdash \texttt{ll}(x)$	1	NA	0.1	0.05
22	$\texttt{sortlln}(x,min,size) \vdash \texttt{lln}(x,size)$	1	NA	0.55	0.12
23	$\texttt{sortlln}(x,min,size) \vdash \texttt{sortll}(x,min)$	1	NA	TO	0.08
24	$\texttt{lsegn}(x,y,sz_1)*\texttt{lsegn}(y,z,sz_2) \vdash \texttt{lsegn}(x,z,sz_1+sz_2)$	1	NA	10.49	0.12
25	$\texttt{lsegn}(x,y,size_1)*\texttt{lsn}(y,size_2) \vdash \texttt{lsn}(x,size_1+size_2)$	1	NA	10.59	0.10
26	$\texttt{lsegn}(x,tl,n_1)*\texttt{tl}\mapsto c_1(y)*\texttt{lseg1}(y,ty,n_2) \vdash \texttt{lseg1}(x,ty,n_1+n_2+1)$	1	NA	16.76	0.10
27	$\texttt{avl}(x,size,height,bal) \vdash \texttt{btn}(x,size)$	1	NA	X	0.08
28	$\texttt{tll}(x,ll,lr,size) \vdash \texttt{btn}(x,size)$	1	NA	0.13	0.07
29	$\texttt{ll\_last}(x,y) \vdash y\mapsto c_1(\texttt{null})$	1	NA	NA	0.18
30	$\texttt{ll\_last\_size}(x,y,size) \vdash y\mapsto c_1(\texttt{null})$	1	NA	NA	0.23
31	$\texttt{zip2}(x,y) \vdash \texttt{ll}(x)$	1	NA	NA	0.23
32	$\texttt{zip2n}(x,y,size) \vdash \texttt{lln}(x,size)$	1	NA	NA	0.46
33	$\texttt{zip3}(x,y) \vdash \texttt{ll}(y)$	1	NA	NA	0.39
34	$\texttt{sortll}(x,min)*\texttt{sortll}(y,min_1) \vdash \texttt{ll}(x)$	1	NA	NA	0.13
35	$\texttt{sortlln}(x,min1,size1)*\ \texttt{slln}(y,min2,size2) \vdash \texttt{sll}(x,min1)$	1	NA	NA	0.27
36	$\texttt{tll}(x,ll,lr,size)*\texttt{ll}(y) \vdash \texttt{btn}(x,size)$	1	NA	NA	0.56

tool returns a false positive, or NA if the entailment is beyond the capability of the tool. *In summary, out of the 36 problems,* $\texttt{Cyclic}_{SL}$ *solves 18 (with one TO - Ent 4);* `songbird` *solves 25 (with two false positive - Ent 17 and 27 and one TO - Ent 23); and* `S2ENT` *solves all 36 problems.*

In Table 1, each entailment check in Ent 1–19 has `emp` as frame axioms (their LHS and RHS have the same heaps). Hence, they may be handled by existing inductive proof systems like [3,9,15,40]. In particular, Ent 1–19 include shape-only predicates. The results show that $\texttt{Cyclic}_{SL}$ and `songbird` ran a bit faster than `S2ENT` in most of the their successful cases. It is expected as `S2ENT` requires additional steps for frame inference. Each entailment check in Ent 20–28 includes inductive predicates with pure properties (e.g., size and sortedness). While $\texttt{Cyclic}_{SL}$ can provide inductive reasoning for arithmetic and heap domains separately [5], there is no system proposed for cyclic proofs in the combined domain. Hence, these problems are beyond the capability of $\texttt{Cyclic}_{SL}$. Ent 20 which requires mutual induction reasoning is the motivating example of `songbird` (agumented with size property) [40]. In particular, `sortll` represents a sorted list with smallest value `min`, and tll is a binary tree whose nodes point to their parents and leaves are linked by a linked list [19,24]. S2ENT solves each entailment incrementally: shape-based frame and then pure properties. The results show that S2ENT was more effective and efficient than songbird.

Each entailment check in Ent 29–36 requires both inductive reasoning and frame inference. These checks are beyond the capability of all existing entailment procedures for SL. S2ENT generates frame axioms for inductive reasoning. The experiments show that the proposed proof system can support efficient and effective reasoning on both shape and numeric domains as well as inductive proofs and frame inference.

Modular Verification for Memory Safety. We enhance the existing program verifier S2 [24] with S2ENT to automatically verify a range of heap-manipulating programs. We evaluate the enhanced S2 on the C library Glib open source [16] which includes non-GUI code from the GTK+ toolkit and the GNOME desktop environment. We conduct experiments on heap-manipulating files, i.e., singly-linked lists (gslist.c), doubly-linked lists (glist.c), balanced binary trees (gtree.c) and N-ary trees (gnode.c). These files contain fairly complex algorithms (e.g., sortedness) and the data structures used in gtree.c and gnode.c are very complex. Some procedures of gslist.c and glist.c were evaluated by tools presented in [9, 31, 36] where the user had to manually provide a large number of lemmas to support the tool. Furthermore, the verification in [9] is semi-automatic, i.e., verification conditions were manually generated. Besides the tool in [9], tools in [31,36] were no longer available for comparison.

Table 2. Experiments on Glib library

	LOC	#Pr	wo.		w.		
			#√	Sec.	#syn	#√	Sec.
gslist.c	698	52	41	8.93	126	47	12.47
glist.c	784	51	39	19.41	132	46	30.01
gtree.c	1204	40	36	57.31	96	36	60.88
gnode.c	1128	65	52	37.78	174	53	53.40

In Table 2 we show, for each file the number of lines of code (excluding comments) LOC and the number of procedures #Pr. We remark that these procedures include tail-recursive procedures which are translated from loops. The columns (#√) (and sec.) show the number of procedures (and time in seconds) for which S2 can verify memory safety without (wo.) and with (w.) S2ENT. Column #syn shows the number of synthesized lemmas that used the technique in Sect. 5. With the lemma synthesis, the number of procedures that can be successfully verified increases from 168 (81%) to 182 (88%) with a time overhead of 28% (157 s/123 s).

A closer look shows that with S2ENT we are able to verify a number of challenging methods in gslist.c and glist.c. By generating separating lemmas, S2ENT successfully infers shape specifications of methods manipulating the last element of lists (i.e., g_slist_concat in gslist.c and g_list_append in glist.c). By generating equivalence lemmas, matching a newly-inferred inductive predicate with predefined predicates in S2 is now extended beyond the shape-only domain. Moreover, the experimental results also show that the enhanced S2 were able to verify 41/52 procedures in gslist.c and 39/51 procedures in glist.c. In comparison, while the tool in [9] could semi-automatically verify 11 procedures in gslist.c and 6 procedures in glist.c, with user-supplied lemmas the tool in [31] could verify 22 procedures in gslist.c and 10 procedures in glist.c.

7 Related Work and Conclusion

This work is related to three groups of work. The first group are those on entailment procedures in SL. Initial proof systems in SL mainly focus on a decidable fragment combining linked lists (and trees) [1,7,11,13,14,17,22,29,32,33]. Recently, Iosif *et al.* extend the decidable fragment to restricted inductive predicates [19]. Timos et al. [42] present a comprehensive summary on computational complexity for entailments in SL with inductive predicates. Smallfoot [1] and GRASShopper [33] provide systematic approaches for frame inference but with limited support for (general) inductive predicates. Extending these approaches to support general inductive predicates is non-trivial. GRASShopper is limited to a GRASS-reducible class of inductive predicates. While Smallfoot system has been designed to allow the use of general inductive predicates, the inference rules in Smallfoot are hardwired for list predicates only and a set of new rules must be developed for a proof system targeting general inductive predicates. SLEEK [8] and jStar [12] support frame inference with a soundness guarantee for general inductive predicates. However, they provide limited support for induction using user-supplied lemmas [12,30]. Our work, like [8,36], targets an undecidable SL fragment including (arbitrary) inductive predicates and numerical constraints; we trade completeness for expressiveness. In addition to what are supported in [8,36], we support frame inference with inductive reasoning in SL by providing a system of cyclic proofs.

The second group is work on inductive reasoning. Lemmas are used to enhance the inductive reasoning of heap-based programs [5,12,30]. They are used as alternative unfoldings beyond predicates' definitions [5,30], external inference rules [12], or intelligent generalization to support inductive reasoning [3]. Unfortunately, the mechanisms in these systems require users to supply those additional lemmas that might be needed during a proof. SPEN [15] synthesizes lemmas to enhance inductive reasoning for some inductive predicates with bags of values. However, it is designed to support some specific classes of inductive predicates and it is difficult to extend it to cater for general inductive predicates. For a solution to inductive reasoning in SL, Smallfoot [1,3,5] presents subtraction rules that are consequent from a set of lemmas of lists and trees. Brotherston *et al.* propose cyclic proof system for the entailment problem [2,3]. Similarly, the circularity rule has been introduced in matching logic [38], Constraint Logic Programming [9] and separation logic combined with predicate definitions and arithmetic [40]. Furthermore, work in [39] supports frame inference based on an ad-hoc mechanism, using a simple unfolding and matching. Like [3,9,40], our system also uses historical sequents at case split steps as induction hypotheses. Beyond these systems [3,9,15,40], `S2ENT` infers frames for inductive proofs systematically; and thus it gives a better support for modular verification of heap-manipulating programs. Moreover, we show how we can incrementally support inductive reasoning for the combination of heap and pure domains. In contrast, there are no formalized discussions in [5,9,40] about inductive reasoning for the combined domains; while [5] supports these domains separately, [9,40] only demonstrates their support through experimental results.

The third group is on lemma synthesis. In inductive reasoning, auxiliary lemmas are generated to discover theorems (e.g. [10,23,28]). The key elements of these techniques are heuristics used to generate equivalent lemmas for sets of given functions, constants and datatypes. In our work, we introduce lemma synthesis to strengthen the inductive constraints. To support theorem discovery, we synthesize equivalent and separating lemmas. This mechanism can be extended to other heuristics to enhance the completeness of modular verification.

Conclusion. We have presented a novel approach to frame inference for inductive entailments in SL with inductive predicates and arithmetic. The core of our proposal is the system of lemma synthesis through cyclic proofs in which back-links are formed using the cut rule. Moreover, we have presented two extensions to strengthen the inferred frames. Our evaluation indicates that our system is able to infer frame axioms for inductive entailment checking that are beyond the capability of the existing systems.

Acknowledgements. This research is partially supported by project T2MOE1704 from Ministry of Education, Singapore.

References

1. Berdine, J., Calcagno, C., O'Hearn, P.W.: Symbolic execution with separation logic. In: Yi, K. (ed.) APLAS 2005. LNCS, vol. 3780, pp. 52–68. Springer, Heidelberg (2005). https://doi.org/10.1007/11575467_5
2. Brotherston, J.: Cyclic proofs for first-order logic with inductive definitions. In: Beckert, B. (ed.) TABLEAUX 2005. LNCS (LNAI), vol. 3702, pp. 78–92. Springer, Heidelberg (2005). https://doi.org/10.1007/11554554_8
3. Brotherston, J., Distefano, D., Petersen, R.L.: Automated cyclic entailment proofs in separation logic. In: Bjørner, N., Sofronie-Stokkermans, V. (eds.) CADE 2011. LNCS (LNAI), vol. 6803, pp. 131–146. Springer, Heidelberg (2011). https://doi.org/10.1007/978-3-642-22438-6_12
4. Brotherston, J., Fuhs, C., Gorogiannis, N., Pérez, J.N.: A decision procedure for satisfiability in separation logic with inductive predicates. In: Proceedings of CSL-LICS (2014)
5. Brotherston, J., Gorogiannis, N., Petersen, R.L.: A generic cyclic theorem prover. In: Jhala, R., Igarashi, A. (eds.) APLAS 2012. LNCS, vol. 7705, pp. 350–367. Springer, Heidelberg (2012). https://doi.org/10.1007/978-3-642-35182-2_25
6. Calcagno, C., Distefano, D., O'Hearn, P.W., Yang, H.: Compositional shape analysis by means of bi-abduction. In: Proceedings of the 36th Annual ACM SIGPLAN-SIGACT Symposium on Principles of Programming Languages, pp. 289–300. ACM (2009)

7. Chen, T., Song, F., Wu, Z.: Tractability of separation logic with inductive definitions: beyond lists. In: Meyer, R., Nestmann, U. (eds.) 28th International Conference on Concurrency Theory (CONCUR 2017), vol. 85, pp. 37:1–37:17 (2017)
8. Chin, W.N., David, C., Nguyen, H.H., Qin, S.: Automated verification of shape, size and bag properties via user-defined predicates in separation logic. SCP **77**(9), 1006–1036 (2012)
9. Chu, D.-H., Jaffar, J., Trinh, M.-T.: Automatic induction proofs of data-structures in imperative programs. In: PLDI 2015 (2015)
10. Claessen, K., Johansson, M., Rosén, D., Smallbone, N.: Automating inductive proofs using theory exploration. In: Bonacina, M.P. (ed.) CADE 2013. LNCS (LNAI), vol. 7898, pp. 392–406. Springer, Heidelberg (2013). https://doi.org/10.1007/978-3-642-38574-2_27
11. Cook, B., Haase, C., Ouaknine, J., Parkinson, M., Worrell, J.: Tractable reasoning in a fragment of separation logic. In: Katoen, J.-P., König, B. (eds.) CONCUR 2011. LNCS, vol. 6901, pp. 235–249. Springer, Heidelberg (2011). https://doi.org/10.1007/978-3-642-23217-6_16
12. Distefano, D., Parkinson, M.: jStar: towards practical verification for java. In: OOPSLA 2008, pp. 213–226. ACM, New York (2008)
13. Enea, C., Lengál, O., Sighireanu, M., Vojnar, T.: Compositional entailment checking for a fragment of separation logic. In: Garrigue, J. (ed.) APLAS 2014. LNCS, vol. 8858, pp. 314–333. Springer, Cham (2014). https://doi.org/10.1007/978-3-319-12736-1_17
14. Enea, C., Lengál, O., Sighireanu, M., Vojnar, T.: Compositional entailment checking for a fragment of separation logic. Formal Meth. Syst. Des. **51**(3), 575–607 (2017)
15. Enea, C., Sighireanu, M., Wu, Z.: On automated lemma generation for separation logic with inductive definitions. In: Finkbeiner, B., Pu, G., Zhang, L. (eds.) ATVA 2015. LNCS, vol. 9364, pp. 80–96. Springer, Cham (2015). https://doi.org/10.1007/978-3-319-24953-7_7
16. Glib. version 2.38.2 (2013). https://developer.gnome.org/glib/. Accessed 13 Oct 2017
17. Gu, X., Chen, T., Wu, Z.: A complete decision procedure for linearly compositional separation logic with data constraints. In: Olivetti, N., Tiwari, A. (eds.) IJCAR 2016. LNCS (LNAI), vol. 9706, pp. 532–549. Springer, Cham (2016). https://doi.org/10.1007/978-3-319-40229-1_36
18. Holik, L., Lengál, O., Rogalewicz, A., Šimáček, J., Vojnar, T.: Fully automated shape analysis based on forest automata. In: Sharygina, N., Veith, H. (eds.) CAV 2013. LNCS, vol. 8044, pp. 740–755. Springer, Heidelberg (2013). https://doi.org/10.1007/978-3-642-39799-8_52
19. Iosif, R., Rogalewicz, A., Simacek, J.: The tree width of separation logic with recursive definitions. In: Bonacina, M.P. (ed.) CADE 2013. LNCS (LNAI), vol. 7898, pp. 21–38. Springer, Heidelberg (2013). https://doi.org/10.1007/978-3-642-38574-2_2
20. Ishtiaq, S., O'Hearn, P.W.: BI as an assertion language for mutable data structures. In: ACM POPL, London, pp. 14–26, January 2001
21. Jacobs, B., Smans, J., Philippaerts, P., Vogels, F., Penninckx, W., Piessens, F.: VeriFast: a powerful, sound, predictable, fast verifier for C and Java. In: Bobaru, M., Havelund, K., Holzmann, G.J., Joshi, R. (eds.) NFM 2011. LNCS, vol. 6617, pp. 41–55. Springer, Heidelberg (2011). https://doi.org/10.1007/978-3-642-20398-5_4

22. Jansen, C., Katelaan, J., Matheja, C., Noll, T., Zuleger, F.: Unified reasoning about robustness properties of symbolic-heap separation logic. In: Yang, H. (ed.) ESOP 2017. LNCS, vol. 10201, pp. 611–638. Springer, Heidelberg (2017). https://doi.org/10.1007/978-3-662-54434-1_23
23. Johansson, M., Dixon, L., Bundy, A.: Conjecture synthesis for inductive theories. J. Autom. Reason. **47**(3), 251–289 (2011)
24. Le, Q.L., Gherghina, C., Qin, S., Chin, W.-N.: Shape analysis via second-order bi-abduction. In: Biere, A., Bloem, R. (eds.) CAV 2014. LNCS, vol. 8559, pp. 52–68. Springer, Cham (2014). https://doi.org/10.1007/978-3-319-08867-9_4
25. Le, Q.L., Sun, J., Chin, W.-N.: Satisfiability modulo heap-based programs. In: Chaudhuri, S., Farzan, A. (eds.) CAV 2016. LNCS, vol. 9779, pp. 382–404. Springer, Cham (2016). https://doi.org/10.1007/978-3-319-41528-4_21
26. Le, Q.L., Tatsuta, M., Sun, J., Chin, W.-N.: A decidable fragment in separation logic with inductive predicates and arithmetic. In: Majumdar, R., Kunčak, V. (eds.) CAV 2017. LNCS, vol. 10427, pp. 495–517. Springer, Cham (2017). https://doi.org/10.1007/978-3-319-63390-9_26
27. de Moura, L., Bjørner, N.: Z3: an efficient SMT solver. In: Ramakrishnan, C.R., Rehof, J. (eds.) TACAS 2008. LNCS, vol. 4963, pp. 337–340. Springer, Heidelberg (2008). https://doi.org/10.1007/978-3-540-78800-3_24
28. McCasland, R., Bundy, A., Serge, A.: Automated discovery of inductive theorems. Stud. Logic Grammar Rhetor. **10**(23), 135–149 (2007)
29. Navarro Pérez, J.A., Rybalchenko, A.: Separation logic modulo theories. In: Shan, C. (ed.) APLAS 2013. LNCS, vol. 8301, pp. 90–106. Springer, Cham (2013). https://doi.org/10.1007/978-3-319-03542-0_7
30. Nguyen, H.H., Chin, W.-N.: Enhancing program verification with lemmas. In: Gupta, A., Malik, S. (eds.) CAV 2008. LNCS, vol. 5123, pp. 355–369. Springer, Heidelberg (2008). https://doi.org/10.1007/978-3-540-70545-1_34
31. Pek, E., Qiu, X., Madhusudan, P.: Natural proofs for data structure manipulation in C using separation logic. In: Proceedings of the 35th ACM SIGPLAN Conference on Programming Language Design and Implementation, pp. 440–451. ACM, New York (2014)
32. Pérez, J.A.N., Rybalchenko, A.: Separation logic + superposition calculus = heap theorem prover. In: PLDI, pp. 556–566 (2011)
33. Piskac, R., Wies, T., Zufferey, D.: Automating separation logic using SMT. In: Sharygina, N., Veith, H. (eds.) CAV 2013. LNCS, vol. 8044, pp. 773–789. Springer, Heidelberg (2013). https://doi.org/10.1007/978-3-642-39799-8_54
34. Popeea, C., Chin, W.-N.: Inferring disjunctive postconditions. In: Okada, M., Satoh, I. (eds.) ASIAN 2006. LNCS, vol. 4435, pp. 331–345. Springer, Heidelberg (2007). https://doi.org/10.1007/978-3-540-77505-8_26
35. Qin, S., He, G., Chin, W.-N., Craciun, F., He, M., Ming, Z.: Automated specification inference in a combined domain via user-defined predicates. Sci. Comput. Program. **148**(C), 189–212 (2017)
36. Qiu, X., Garg, P., Ştefănescu, A., Madhusudan, P.: Natural proofs for structure, data, and separation. In: PLDI, pp. 231–242. ACM, New York (2013)
37. Reynolds, J.C.: Separation logic: a logic for shared mutable data structures. In: Proceedings of the 17th Annual IEEE Symposium on Logic in Computer Science, LICS 2002, pp. 55–74. IEEE Computer Society, Washington, DC (2002)
38. Rosu, G., Stefanescu, A.: Checking reachability using matching logic. In: OOPSLA 2012, pp. 555–574. ACM, New York (2012)
39. Rowe, R.N.S., Brotherston, J.: Automatic cyclic termination proofs for recursive procedures in separation logic. In: CPP (2017)

40. Ta, Q.-T., Le, T.C., Khoo, S.-C., Chin, W.-N.: Automated mutual explicit induction proof in separation logic. In: Fitzgerald, J., Heitmeyer, C., Gnesi, S., Philippou, A. (eds.) FM 2016. LNCS, vol. 9995, pp. 659–676. Springer, Cham (2016). https://doi.org/10.1007/978-3-319-48989-6_40
41. Tatsuta, M., Le, Q.L., Chin, W.-N.: Decision procedure for separation logic with inductive definitions and Presburger arithmetic. In: Igarashi, A. (ed.) APLAS 2016. LNCS, vol. 10017, pp. 423–443. Springer, Cham (2016). https://doi.org/10.1007/978-3-319-47958-3_22
42. Antonopoulos, T., Gorogiannis, N., Haase, C., Kanovich, M., Ouaknine, J.: Foundations for decision problems in separation logic with general inductive predicates. In: Muscholl, A. (ed.) FoSSaCS 2014. LNCS, vol. 8412, pp. 411–425. Springer, Heidelberg (2014). https://doi.org/10.1007/978-3-642-54830-7_27
43. Trinh, M.-T., Le, Q.L., David, C., Chin, W.-N.: Bi-abduction with pure properties for specification inference. In: Shan, C. (ed.) APLAS 2013. LNCS, vol. 8301, pp. 107–123. Springer, Cham (2013). https://doi.org/10.1007/978-3-319-03542-0_8
44. Yang, H., Lee, O., Berdine, J., Calcagno, C., Cook, B., Distefano, D., O'Hearn, P.: Scalable shape analysis for systems code. In: Gupta, A., Malik, S. (eds.) CAV 2008. LNCS, vol. 5123, pp. 385–398. Springer, Heidelberg (2008). https://doi.org/10.1007/978-3-540-70545-1_36

Verified Model Checking of Timed Automata

Simon Wimmer(✉) and Peter Lammich(✉)

Fakultät für Informatik,
Technische Universität München,
Munich, Germany
{wimmers,lammich}@in.tum.de

Abstract. We have constructed a mechanically verified prototype implementation of a model checker for timed automata, a popular formalism for modeling real-time systems. Our goal is two-fold: first, we want to provide a reference implementation that is fast enough to check other model checkers against it on reasonably sized benchmarks; second, we strive for maximal feature compatibility with the state-of-the-art tool UPPAAL. The starting point of our work is an existing highly abstract formalization of reachability checking of timed automata. We reduce checking of UPPAAL-style models to the problem of model checking a single automaton in this abstract formalization, while retaining the ability to perform on the fly model-checking. Using the Isabelle Refinement Framework, the abstract specification of the model checker is refined, via multiple intermediate steps, to an actual imperative implementation in Standard ML. The resulting tool is evaluated on a set of standard benchmarks to demonstrate its practical usability.

1 Introduction

Timed automata [1] are a widely used formalism for modeling real-time systems, which is employed in a class of successful model checkers such as UPPAAL [2]. These tools can be understood as trust-multipliers: we trust their correctness to deduce trust in the safety of systems checked by these tools. However, mistakes have previously been made. This particularly concerns an approximation operation that is used by model-checking algorithms to obtain a finite search space. The use of this operation induced a soundness problem in the tools employing it [3], which was only discovered years after the first model checkers were devised.

Our ongoing work[1] addresses this issue by constructing a fully verified model checker for timed automata, using Isabelle/HOL [4]. Our tool is not intended to replace existing model checkers, but to serve as a reference implementation against which other implementations can be validated. Thus, it must provide sufficient performance to check real world examples. To this end, we use the

[1] https://github.com/wimmers/munta.

D. Beyer and M. Huisman (Eds.): TACAS 2018, LNCS 10805, pp. 61–78, 2018.
https://doi.org/10.1007/978-3-319-89960-2_4

Isabelle Refinement Framework (IRF) [5,6] to obtain efficient imperative implementations of the algorithms required for model checking.

Our work starts from an existing abstract formalization of *reachability* checking of timed automata [7]. To close the gap to a practical model checker, we need to address two types of issues: efficient implementation of abstract model checking algorithms, and expressiveness of the offered modeling formalism. Two kinds of algorithms deserve special attention here. The first are operations to manipulate Difference Bound Matrices (DBMs) [2], which represent abstract states. With the help of the IRF, we obtain efficient implementations of DBMs represented as arrays. The second are search algorithms that govern the search for reachable states. These algorithms are interesting in their own right, since they make use of *subsumption*: during the search process an abstract state can be ignored if a larger abstract state was already explored. We provide a generalized framework for different variants of search algorithms, including a version which resembles UPPAAL's unified passed and waiting list [2].

We aim to offer a modeling formalism that is comparable in its expressiveness to the one of UPPAAL. To accomplish this goal while keeping the formalization effort manageable, we opt to accept UPPAAL *bytecode* as input. At the current state of the project we have formalized the semantics of a subset of the bytecode produced by UPPAAL. We support the essential modeling features: networks of automata with synchronization, and bounded integer state variables. We apply a product construction to reduce models of this formalism to a single timed automaton. As in real model checkers, the whole construction is computed *on the fly*. However, not every bytecode input designates a valid automaton. To this end, we employ a simple *program analysis* to accept a sufficiently large subset of the valid inputs.

We conducted experiments on a small number of established benchmark models. The throughput of our model checker — the number of explored states per time unit — is within an order of magnitude of a version of UPPAAL running a comparable algorithm.

1.1 Isabelle/HOL

Isabelle/HOL [4] is an interactive theorem prover based on Higher-Order Logic (HOL). You can think of HOL as a combination of a functional programming language with logic. Although Isabelle/HOL largely follows ordinary mathematical notation, there are some operators and conventions that should be explained. Like in functional programming, functions are mostly curried, i.e. of type $\tau_1 \Rightarrow \tau_2 \Rightarrow \tau$ instead of $\tau_1 \times \tau_2 \Rightarrow \tau$. This means that function application is usually written $f\ a\ b$ instead of $f(a, b)$. Lambda terms are written in the standard syntax $\lambda x.\ t$ (the function that maps x to t) but can also have multiple arguments $\lambda x\ y.\ t$, paired arguments $\lambda(x, y).\ t$, or dummy arguments $\lambda\_.\ t$. Type variables are written $'a$, $'b$, etc. Compound types are written in postfix syntax: τ *set* is the type of sets of elements of type τ. In some places in the paper we have simplified formulas or code marginally to avoid distraction by syntactic or technical details, but in general we have stayed faithful to the sources.

1.2 Related Work

The basis of the work presented in this paper is our existing formalization of timed automata [7]. We are aware of one previous proof-assistant formalization of timed automata using PVS [8,9]. This work has the basic decidability result using regions and claims to make some attempt to extend the formalization towards DBMs. Another line of work [10,11] aims at modeling the class of p-automata [12] in Coq and proving properties of concrete p-automata within Coq. A similar approach was pursued with the help of Isabelle/HOL in the CClair project [13]. In contrast, our formalization [7] focuses on the foundations of timed automata model checking. In particular, it encompasses a formalization of the relevant DBM algorithms and the rather intricate developments towards the correctness proof for the approximation operation.

We are not aware of any previous formalizations or verified implementations of timed automata model checking. The first verification of a model checker we are aware of is by Sprenger for the modal μ-calculus in Coq [14]. Our important forerunner, however, is the CAVA project [15–17] by Esparza et al. It sets out for similar goals as we do but for *finite state LTL* model checking. A significant part of the refinement technology that we make use of was developed for this project, and it was the first project to demonstrate that verification of model checking can yield practical implementations. Compared to CAVA, our work offers several novelties: we target model checking of timed automata, which have an infinite state space; we use imperative data structures, which is crucial for efficient DBMs; finally, we implemented complex search algorithms with subsumption. Additionally, we operate on automata annotated with UPPAAL bytecode, which has interesting ramifications: for the product construction, and because we need to ensure that the input actually defines a timed automaton.

2 Timed Automata and Model Checking

2.1 Transition Systems

We take a very simple view of transition systems: they are simply a relation $\rightarrow$ of type $'a \Rightarrow 'a \Rightarrow \mathit{bool}$. We model *(finite) runs* as *inductive* lists, and *infinite runs* as *coinductive* streams. We write $a \rightarrow xs \rightarrow b$ to denote the $\rightarrow$-run from a to b using the intermediate states in the list xs, and $a \rightarrow^{ys}$ to denote the infinite $\rightarrow$-run starting in a and then continuing with states from the stream ys. Additionally, we define:

$$a \rightarrow^{+} b = (\exists xs.\ a \rightarrow xs \rightarrow b) \text{ and } a \rightarrow^{*} b = (a \rightarrow^{+} b \vee a = b).$$

We define the five *CTL* properties that are supported by UPPAAL, $\mathbf{A}\Diamond$, $\mathbf{A}\Box$, $\mathbf{E}\Diamond$, $\mathbf{E}\Box$, and $\dashrightarrow$, as properties of infinite runs[2] starting from a state. For instance,

$$\mathbf{A}\Diamond\ \phi\ x = (\forall xs.\ x \rightarrow^{xs} \Longrightarrow ev\ (holds\ \phi)\ (x \cdot xs)),$$

and

$$\phi \dashrightarrow \psi = \mathbf{A}\Box\ (\lambda x.\ \phi\ x \Longrightarrow \mathbf{A}\Diamond\ \psi\ x),$$

where *ev* specifies that a property on a stream eventually holds, and *holds* constrains *ev* to the current state instead of the remainder stream. It then is trivial to prove identities such as $\mathbf{E}\Box\ \phi\ x = (\neg\, \mathbf{A}\Diamond\ (Not \circ \phi)\ x)$.

2.2 Timed Automata

Compared to standard finite automata, timed automata introduce a notion of clocks. Figure 1 depicts an example of a timed automaton. We will assume that clocks are of type *nat*. A *clock valuation* u is a function of type $nat \Rightarrow real$.

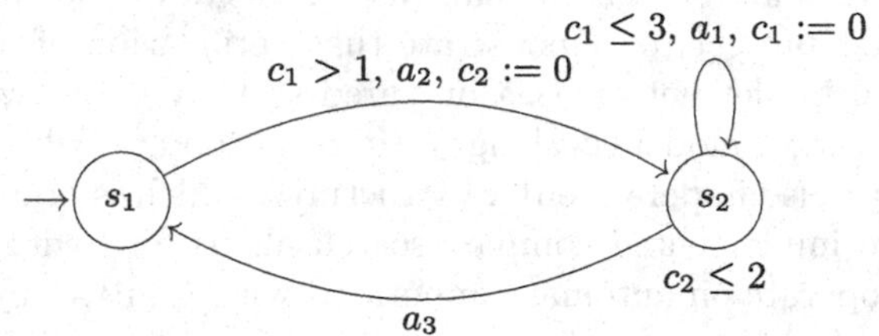

Fig. 1. Example of a timed automaton with two clocks.

Locations and transitions are guarded by *clock constraints*, which have to be fulfilled to stay in a location or to take a transition. Clock constraints are conjunctions of constraints of the form $c \sim d$ for a clock c, an integer d, and $\sim \in \{<, \le, =, \ge, >\}$. We write $u \vdash cc$ if the clock constraint cc holds for the clock valuation u. We define a timed automaton A as a pair $(\mathcal{T}, \mathcal{I})$ where $\mathcal{I}$ is an assignment of clock constraints to locations (also named invariants); and $\mathcal{T}$ is a set of transitions written as $A \vdash l \longrightarrow^{g,a,r} l'$ where l and l' are start and successor location, g is the guard of the transition, a is an action label, and r is a list of clocks that will be reset to zero when the transition is taken. States of timed automata are pairs of a location and a clock valuation. The operational semantics define two kinds of steps:

- Delay: $(l, u) \rightarrow^{d} (l, u \oplus d)$ if $d \ge 0$ and $u \oplus d \vdash \mathcal{I}\ l$;
- Action: $(l, u) \rightarrow_{a} (l', [r \rightarrow 0]u)$
  if $A \vdash l \longrightarrow^{g,a,r} l'$, $u \vdash g$, and $[r \rightarrow 0]u \vdash \mathcal{I}\ l'$;

[2] This is fairly standard in the literature [2,3,12,18] but differs slightly from the implementation in UPPAAL.

where $u \oplus d = (\lambda c.\ u\ c + d)$ and $[r \to 0]u = (\lambda c.\ \mathsf{if}\ c \in r\ \mathsf{then}\ 0\ \mathsf{else}\ u\ c)$. For any (timed) automaton A, we consider the transition system

$$(l, u) \to_A (l', u') = (\exists d \geq 0.\ \exists a\ u''.\ (l, u) \to^d (l, u'') \wedge (l, u'') \to_a (l', u')).$$

That is, each transition consists of a delay step that advances all clocks by some amount of time, followed by an action step that takes a transition and resets the clocks annotated to the transition. We write $A, s_0 \models \phi$ if ϕ holds in state s_0 w.r.t. $\to_A$. Note that it is crucial to combine the two types of steps in order to reason about liveness. Consider the automaton from Fig. 1 and assume the two kinds of steps could be taken independently. Then the automaton has a run on which some predicate P holds everywhere if and only if $P\ s_1$ holds.

2.3 Model Checking

Due to the use of clock valuations, the state space of timed automata is inherently infinite. Thus, model checking algorithms for timed automata are based on the idea of abstracting from concrete valuations to *sets* of clock valuations of type $(\mathit{nat} \Rightarrow \mathit{real})\ \mathit{set}$, often called *zones*. The initial decidability result [1] partitioned the state space into a quotient of zones, the so-called regions, and showed that these yield a sound and complete abstraction[3]. However, practical model checking algorithms rather explore the state space in an *on-the-fly* manner, computing successors directly on zones, which are typically represented symbolically as Difference Bound Matrices (DBMs). DBMs are simply a matrix-form representation of clock constraints, which contain exactly one conjunct for each pair of clocks. To represent constraints on single clocks, an artificial **0**-clock is added, which is assumed to be assigned 0 in any valuation.

The delicate part of this method is that the number of reachable zones could still be infinite. Therefore, an over-approximation is applied to zones to obtain a finite search space. We call the transition system of zones the *zone graph*, and the version where over-approximations are applied the *abstract zone graph* [18]. The soundness argument for this method (due to over-approximation completeness is trivial), starts from the region construction and then introduces the notion of the *closure* of a zone, which is defined to be the union of all regions intersecting with a zone. It can be shown from the correctness of the region construction that closures yield a sound over-approximation of zones. Finally, one shows that the result of applying the over-approximation operator to zones is always contained in the closure, thus inheriting soundness from the soundness of closures. We have formalized this argument and all of the material summarized in this section in previous work [7]. It only covers the case of reachability, but we will demonstrate how to extend the soundness argument to liveness below.

[3] We use the same notions as in [7]. Soundness: for every abstract run, there is a concrete instantiation. Completeness: every concrete run can be abstracted.

3 A First Glance at the Model Checker

This section provides a first overview of our model checker, its construction, and the correctness theorem we proved. The input to our checker consists of a model, i.e. a network of Timed Automata, and a formula to be checked against the model. To achieve high compatibility with UPPAAL, guards and updates can be formulated in UPPAAL bytecode[4]. This intermediate representation is computed by UPPAAL from the original C-style input before the actual model checking process is started. Given such an input, our tool will first determine whether the input is valid and lies in the supported fragment. This is achieved by a simple program analysis. As input formulae, our model checker accepts the same (T)CTL fragment that is supported by UPPAAL, but restricts formulae to not contain clocks. While this is not a principal limitation of our work, it reduced the complexity of our first prototype. If the input is invalid, our tool answers with "invalid input", else it determines whether

$$\mathit{conv}\ N, (\mathit{init}, s_0, u_0) \vDash_{\mathit{max\_steps}} \phi$$

holds for the all-zero valuation u_0 under the assumption that the automaton is deadlock-free[5], and answers with true/false. Here, N is the input automaton, *conv* converts all integer constants to reals (as the semantics are specified on reals), and ϕ is the input formula. The relation $\vDash_{\mathit{max\_steps}}$ is a variant of $\vDash$ lifted to networks of timed automata with shared state and UPPAAL bytecode annotations. It is indexed with the maximum number of steps that any execution of a piece of UPPAAL bytecode can use (i.e. *max_steps* is the *fuel* available to executions). The vector of start locations *init*, and the shared state s_0 (part of the input) describe the initial configuration.

The actual model checking proceeds in two steps. First, a product construction converts the network to a *single* timed automaton, expressed by HOL functions for the transition relation and the invariant assignment. Second, according to the formula, a model checking algorithm is run on the single automaton. We need three algorithms: a reachability checker for $\mathbf{E}\Diamond$ and $\mathbf{A}\Box$, a loop detection algorithm for $\mathbf{E}\Box$ and $\mathbf{A}\Diamond$, and a combination of both to check $\dashrightarrow$-properties. Note that the aforementioned HOL functions are simply *functional programs* that construct the product automaton's state and invariant assignments *on-the-fly*. The final correctness theorem we proved can be stated as follows:

$$\begin{array}{l}\{\mathit{emp}\}\\ \quad \mathit{precond\_mc}\ p\ m\ k\ \mathit{max\_steps}\ I\ T\ \mathit{prog}\ \mathit{formula}\ \mathit{bounds}\ P\ s_0\\ \{\lambda \mathit{Some}\ r \Rightarrow \mathit{valid\_input}\ p\ m\ \mathit{max\_steps}\ I\ T\ \mathit{prog}\ \mathit{bounds}\ P\ s_0\ \mathit{na}\ k\ \wedge\\ \quad\quad (\neg\ \mathit{deadlock}\ (\mathit{conv}\ N)\ (\mathit{init}, s_0, u_0) \Longrightarrow\\ \quad\quad\quad r = \mathit{conv}\ N, (\mathit{init}, s_0, u_0) \vDash_{\mathit{max\_steps}} \mathit{formula})\\ \quad \mid \mathit{None} \Rightarrow \neg\ \mathit{valid\_input}\ p\ m\ \mathit{max\_steps}\ I\ T\ \mathit{prog}\ \mathit{bounds}\ P\ s_0\ \mathit{na}\ k\}\end{array}$$

[4] For the time being, the bytecode needs to be pre-processed slightly, mainly to rename textual identifiers to integers.

[5] Adding a check for deadlocked states to our algorithms would be conceptually simple but is left for future work.

This Hoare triple states that the model checker terminates and produces the result *None* if the input is invalid. If the input is valid and deadlock free, it produces the result *Some* r, where r is the answer to the model checking problem.

4 Single Automaton Model Checking

In this section, we describe the route from the abstract semantics of timed automata to the implementation of an actual model checker. The next section will describe the construction of a single timed automaton from the UPPAAL-model.

4.1 Implementation Semantics

Although we have established that the DBM-based semantics from Sect. 2 can only explore finitely many zones, it is still "too infinite": the automaton and DBMs are described by real constants, and operations on DBMs are performed on infinitely many dimensions (i.e. clocks). Thus, we introduce an *implementation semantics*, in which automata are given by integer constants, and where the number of clocks is fixed. We prove equivalence of the semantics in two steps: first, we show that DBM operations need only be performed on the clocks that actually occur in the automaton; second, we show that all computations can be performed on integers, provided the initial state only contains integers.

For the former step, we simplify the operations under the assumptions that they maintain *canonicity* of DBMs. A DBM is canonical if it stores the tightest derivable constraint for each pair of clocks, i.e.

$$\mathit{canonical}\ M\ n = (\forall i\ j\ k.\ i \le n \land j \le n \land k \le n \longrightarrow M\ i\ k \le M\ i\ j + M\ j\ k).$$

During model checking, the Floyd-Warshall algorithm is used to turn a DBM into its canonical counterpart.

For the latter step, we use Isabelle's integrated parametricity prover [19] to semi-automatically transfer the operations from reals to integers.

As an example, Fig. 2 displays the refinement steps of the *up* operation, which computes the time successor of a zone Z, i.e. the set $\{u \oplus d \mid u \in Z \land d \ge 0\}$.

$$\begin{array}{l} \mathit{up}\ M = (\lambda i\ j. \\ \quad \textsf{if}\ i > 0\ \textsf{then if}\ j = 0\ \textsf{then}\ \infty \\ \quad \textsf{else}\ \min(M\ i\ 0 + M\ 0\ j)(M\ i\ j) \\ \quad \textsf{else}\ M\ i\ j) \end{array}$$

(a)

$$\begin{array}{l} \mathit{up}_1\ M = (\lambda i\ j. \\ \quad \textsf{if}\ i > 0 \land j = 0 \\ \quad \textsf{then}\ \infty \\ \quad \textsf{else}\ M\ i\ j) \end{array}$$

(b)

$$\begin{array}{l} \mathit{up}_2\ M\ n = \mathit{fold} \\ \quad (\lambda i\ M.\ M((i,0) := \infty)) \\ \quad [1..{<}n+1]\ M \end{array}$$

(c)

$$\begin{array}{l} \mathit{up}_3\ M\ n = \mathit{imp\_for'}\ 1\ (n+1) \\ \quad (\lambda i\ M.\ \mathit{mtx\_set}\ (n+1)\ M\ (i,0)\ \infty) \\ \quad M \end{array}$$

(d)

Fig. 2. Refinement stages of the *up* operation for computing time successors.

In the step from *up* to up_1, the assumption that the input DBM is canonical is introduced. In up_2, which is the version used in the implementation semantics, the operation is constrained to clocks 1 to n. Finally, in up_3, the matrices are implemented as arrays and the fold is implemented as a foreach loop.

At this point, a naive exploration of the transitive closure of the implementation semantics would already yield a simple but inefficient model checker. The rest of this section outlines the derivation of a more elaborate implementation that is close to what can be found in UPPAAL.

4.2 Semantic Refinement of Successor Computation

We further refine the implementation semantics to add two optimizations to the computation of successor DBMs: to canonicalize DBMs it is sometimes sufficient to only "repair" single rows or columns instead of running the full Floyd-Warshall algorithm; moreover, we can terminate the computation early whenever we discover a DBM that represents an empty zone (as it will remain empty). Both arguments are again carried out on the semantic level.

4.3 Abstraction of Transition Systems with Closures

Recall that the correctness of the reachability analysis on the abstract zone graph in Sect. 2 was obtained arguing that the region closure of zones forms a sound over-approximation of zones, which in turn is larger than the abstract zone graph. We want to reuse the same kind of argument to also argue that there exists a cycle in the abstract zone graph if and only if there is a cycle in the automaton's transition system. This proof is carried out in a general abstract framework for transition systems and their abstractions.

We consider a concrete step relation $\rightarrow_C$ over type *'a* and what is supposed to be its simulation, a step relation $\rightarrow_{A_1}$ over type *'a set*. We say that $\rightarrow_{A_1}$ is *post-stable* [20] if $S \rightarrow_{A_1} T$ implies

$$\forall s' \in T.\ \exists s \in S.\ s \rightarrow_C s',$$

and that $\rightarrow_{A_1}$ is *pre-stable* [20] if $S \rightarrow_{A_1} T$ implies

$$\forall s \in S.\ \exists s' \in T.\ s \rightarrow_C s'.$$

In the timed automata setting, for instance, the simulation graph is post-stable and the region graph is pre-stable.

Lemma 1. *If* $\rightarrow_{A_1}$ *is post-stable and we have* $a \rightarrow_{A_1} as \rightarrow_{A_1} a$ *with* a *finite and non-empty, then there exist* xs *and* $x \in a$ *such that* $x \rightarrow_C xs \rightarrow_C x$.

Proof. Let $x \to y = (\exists xs.\ x \to_C xs \to_C y)$. As $\to_{A_1}$ is post-stable, every a has an ingoing $\to$-edge. Because a is finite we can thus find an $\to$-cycle in a, and obtain the claim.

Lemma 2. *If $\to_{A_1}$ is pre-stable and we have $a \to_{A_1} as \to_{A_1} a$ and $x \in a$, then there exist xs such that $x \to_C^{xs}$ and xs passes through a infinitely often.*

Proof. By coinduction. From pre-stability we can find $x_1 \in a$ such that $x \to_C^+ x_1$, from x_1 we find $x_2 \in a$ such that $x_1 \to_C^+ x_2$, and so forth.

We can now consider doubly-layered abstractions as in the case for regions and zones. That is, we add a second simulation $\to_{A_2}$ and two predicates P_1 and P_2 that designate valid states of the first and second simulation layer, respectively. Then we define the *closure* $\mathcal{C}$ of a state of the second layer as

$$\mathcal{C}\ a = \{x \mid P_1\ x \wedge a \cap x \neq \emptyset\} \text{ and } a \to_{\mathcal{C}} b = (\exists x\ y.\ a = \mathcal{C}\ x \wedge b = \mathcal{C}\ y \wedge x \to_{A_2} y).$$

We assume that $\to_{A_1}$ is pre-stable w.r.t. $\to_{\mathcal{C}}$ and that $\to_{\mathcal{C}}$ is post-stable w.r.t. $\to_{A_1}$. Along with some side conditions on P_1 and P_2[6] we can prove:

Theorem 1. *If $a_0 \to_{A_2} as \to_{A_2} a \to_{A_2} bs \to_{A_2} a$ and $P_2\ a$, then there exist $x \in \bigcup(\mathcal{C}\ a_0)$ and xs such that $x \to_C^{xs}$ and xs passes through $\bigcup(\mathcal{C}\ a)$ infinitely often.*

Proof. We first apply $\mathcal{C}$ to the second layer states and get a path of the form: $\mathcal{C}\ a_0 \to_{\mathcal{C}} as' \to_{\mathcal{C}} \mathcal{C}\ a \to_{\mathcal{C}} bs' \to_{\mathcal{C}} \mathcal{C}\ a$ for some as' and bs'. From Lemma 1 and post-stability, we obtain a path of the form $a_{0_1} \to_{A_1} as_1 \to_{A_1} a_1 \to_{A_1} bs_1 \to_{A_1} a_1$ with $a_{0_1} \in \mathcal{C}\ a_0$ and $a_1 \in \mathcal{C}\ a$. By applying Lemma 2 and pre-stability, we obtain the desired result.

This is the main theorem that allows us to run cycle detection on the abstract zone graph during model checking: the other direction is trivial, and the theorem can be directly instantiated for regions and (abstracted) zones. There is a slight subtlety here since we only guarantee $x \in \bigcup(\mathcal{C}\ a_0)$. However we typically have $\mathcal{C}\ a_0 = a_0$, as all clocks are initially set to zero.

4.4 Implementation of Search Algorithms

We first implement the three main model checking algorithms abstractly in the nondeterminism monad provided by the IRF. On this abstraction level, we can use such abstract notions as sets and specify the algorithm for an arbitrary (finite) transition system $\to$. We only showcase the implementation of our cyclicity checker (used for $\mathbf{A}\Diamond$ and $\mathbf{E}\Box$). The techniques used for the other algorithms are similar. The code for our cyclicity checker is displayed in Listing 1.1.

[6] P_1 states are distinct and there are only finitely many of them. For every P_2 state, there is an overlapping P_1 state.

```
dfs P = do {
  (P, ST, r) ← rec_T (λdfs (P, ST, v).
    do {
      if ∃v' ∈ set ST. v' ≼ v then return (P, ST, True)
      else do {
        if ∃v' ∈ P. v ≼ v' then return (P, ST, False)
        else do {
          let ST = v · ST;
          (P, ST', r) ←
            foreach {v' | v → v'} (λ(_, _, b). ¬b)
              (λv' (P, ST, _). dfs (P, ST, v'))
              (P, ST, False);
          assert (ST' = ST);
          return (insert v P, tl ST', r)
        }
      }
    })(P, [], a₀);
  return (r, P)}
```

Listing 1.1. Cyclicity Checker

We claim that this closely resembles the pseudo-code found, e.g., in [21]. The algorithm takes a passed set, and produces a new passed set in addition to the answer. This can be used in the algorithm for checking $\dashrightarrow$-properties. The crux of the algorithm is the use of the subsumption operator $\preceq$, to check whether smaller states are already subsumed by larger states that we may have discovered earlier (for timed automata, this would correspond to set inclusion on zones). We assume that $\preceq$ is a pre-order and monotone w.r.t. $\rightarrow$. Then, using the IRF's verification condition generator, we prove:

$$\begin{gathered}dfs\ P \leq \mathsf{SPEC}\ (\lambda(r, P').\ (r \Longrightarrow (\exists x.\ a_0 \rightarrow^* x \wedge x \rightarrow^+ x)) \\ \wedge(\neg\, r \Longrightarrow \neg\,(\exists x.\ a_0 \rightarrow^* x \wedge x \rightarrow^+ x) \wedge liveness\_compatible\ P')) \\ \text{if } liveness\_compatible\ P.\end{gathered}$$

The invariant we maintain for the passed set P is encoded in the predicate *liveness_compatible* P. We say that a state x is covered by P if there exists $x' \in P$ such that $x \preceq x'$. Then, informally, *liveness_compatible* P states that the successors of every node that is covered by P are also covered, and that there is no cycle through nodes that are covered by P. After specifying the correct loop invariant (using *liveness_compatible* as the main insight) and the termination relation, together with some key lemmas about the invariant, the verification conditions can be discharged nearly automatically.

In subsequent steps, we gradually refine this implementation to use more efficient data structures. The final version uses a function to compute a list of successors, and is able to *index* the passed set and the stack according to a key function on states (this corresponds to the location part of states in the abstract zone graph). The refinement theorem can be stated as:

$$dfs\_map\ P \leq\ \Downarrow (Id \times_r map\_set\_rel)\ (dfs\ P')\ \text{if}\ (P, P') \in map\_set\_rel.$$

That is, *dfs_map* is a refinement of *dfs*, where the passed set is data-refined w.r.t. the relation *map_set_rel*. This relation describes the implementation of passed sets indexed by keys.

These refinement steps are conducted inside the nondeterminism monad of the IRF. The final step leads into the heap-monad of Imperative HOL [22], which supports imperative data structures. Here, the *Sepref* tool [6] replaces functional by imperative data structures and generates a refinement theorem automatically.

Maps are implemented via hash tables, which poses a challenge for the implementation as the maps contain objects stored on the heap. This was not supported by the existing implementation in the Imperative Collections Framework, due to sharing issues: when retrieving a value from the map, we cannot obtain ownership of the value while the map also retains ownership. This is even true if the value is read-only. One way to solve this problem would be to extend the separation logic that underlies the IRF to fractional permissions or read-only permissions. Our solution, however, is more ad-hoc: we simply restrict the operations that we perform on the hash map to insertions and an *extract* operation, which deletes a key-value pair from the map and returns the value (i.e. it combines lookup and delete). To define the map implementation, we use a trick similar to Chargueraud's ideas from [23]: we use a *heap assertion* that first connects an abstract map m with an intermediate map m_h of pointers to the elements, and then implements the map of pointers by a regular hash map m_i. Formally, the assertion is defined as:

$$hms\_assn\ A\ m\ m_i = (\exists_A m_h.\ is\_map\ m_h\ m_i * map\_assn\ A\ m\ m_h).$$

Here *is_map* is the assertion for an existing map implementation from the Imperative Collections Framework (which cannot store heap objects, but supports pointers), and $map\_assn\ A\ m\ m_h$ connects a map of abstract values with a map of pointers, where the relation between abstract values and pointed-to objects is defined by A.

Then, the final implementation is produced by proving that all map-related operations in *dfs_map* can be replaced by insert and extract operations, and letting Sepref synthesize the imperative variant, making use of our new hash map implementation. The key theorem on the final implementation is the following Hoare triple:

$$\begin{array}{l}\{emp\}\\ \quad dfs\_map\_impl'\ succsi\ a_0 i\ Lei\ keyi\ copyi\\ \{\lambda r.\ r = (\exists x.\ a_0 \rightarrow^* x \wedge x \rightarrow^+ x)\}\end{array}$$

It is expressed in a locale (Isabelle's module system) that assumes that $a_0 i$, *succsi*, etc., are the correct imperative implementations of a_0, the successor function, and so forth. Versions of the search algorithm for concrete transition systems are obtained by simply instantiating the locale with the operations of the transition system and their implementations.

4.5 Imperative Implementations of Model Checking Operations

Recall the refinement of the *up* operation (Fig. 2). It is crucial that up_2 is expressed as a fold-operation with explicit updates, as only then the IRF can extract an efficient imperative version with destructive updates and a foreach loop. The imperative implementation up_3 is, again, synthesized by the Sepref tool. As can be witnessed for up_3, the pattern $\mathit{fold}\ f\ [1\,..{<}\,n+1]$ is turned into a foreach loop. Technically, this is achieved by a set of rewrite rules that are applied automatically by the Sepref tool at the end of the synthesis process. The only hurdle for this kind of synthesis is that the dimension of DBMs needs to become a parameter of the refinement relations. For n clocks, we define

$$\mathit{mtx\_assn} = \mathit{asmtx\_assn}\ (n+1)\ \mathit{id\_assn}.$$

This specifies that our DBMs are implemented by square-arrays of dimension $n+1$, and their elements are refined by the identity relation.

The refinement theorem for up_3 is proved automatically by the Sepref tool:

$$(up_3, up_2) \in [\lambda(\_, i).\ i \leq n]\ \mathit{mtx\_assn}^d * \mathit{nat\_assn}^k \rightarrow \mathit{mtx\_assn}.$$

This theorem states that, if the specified dimension is in bounds, up_3 refines up_2. The $\cdot^d$ annotation indicates that the operation is allowed to overwrite (destroy) the input matrix on the heap. Symmetrically, the $\cdot^k$ annotation means that the second parameter is not overwritten (kept).

4.6 Code Extraction

Finally, Isabelle/HOL's code generator [24] is used to extract imperative Standard ML code from the Isabelle specifications generated by Sepref. Code generation involves some optimizations and rewritings that are carried out as refinement steps and proved correct, followed by pretty printing from the functional fragment of HOL and the heap monad to Standard ML.

5 From UPPAAL-Style Semantics to a Single Automaton

5.1 UPPAAL-Style Semantics

Due to the lack of documentation on the UPPAAL intermediate format, we define an approximation of this assembler-like language by reverse engineering. This is sufficient to check typical benchmarks, and gives a clearly defined semantics to the fragment that we cover. The language is defined as a simple data type *instr*. A *step* function of type *instr* $\Rightarrow$ *state* $\Rightarrow$ *state option* computes the successor state after executing an instruction, or fails. A state consists of an instruction pointer, the stack, the state of the shared integer variables, the state of the comparison flag, and a list of clocks that have been marked for reset. Using a fuel parameter, we execute programs by repeatedly applying the *step* function until we either reach a halt instruction, fail, or run out of fuel, which we also regard as a failed execution.

A special instruction *CEXP* is used to check whether an atomic clock constraint holds for a given valuation u. However, this instruction cannot simply be executed during model checking as it would need to work on zones instead of valuations. Unconstrained use of the *CEXP* instruction would allow for disjunctions of clock constraints on edges, which is not part of the standard timed automata formalism. Thus, in the same way as UPPAAL, we restrict the valid input programs to those that only yield conjunctions of clock constraints on edges. We then replace every *CEXP* instruction by a special meta instruction that sets the comparison flag to true. This amounts to enforcing a program execution where the clock constraint, which is expressed by a piece of bytecode, holds for a valuation. Edges are annotated with the conjunction of the atomic clock constraints encountered during execution. In the current version of our tool, we separate concerns for locations by using a state predicate, which is not allowed to use *CEXP* instructions, and a separate clock constraint. The two could be merged by using the same approach as for edges.

5.2 Program Analysis

As stated in the last section, we need to ensure that successful program executions can only induce conjunctive clock constraints. That is, we need to ensure that program executions can only be successful when all *CEXP* instructions that are encountered during execution evaluate to true. To this end, we use a naive analysis, which recognizes a subclass of these programs that is sufficiently large to cover common timed automata benchmarks. This analysis tries to identify what we call *conjunction blocks.* A conjunction block reaching from addresses pc_s to pc_t ends with a *halt* instruction at pc_t, starts with a *CEXP* instruction at pc_s and then is extended to pc_t by repeatedly using one of the following two patterns:

- a *copy* instruction to push the flag on the stack, followed by *CEXP* and an *and* instruction;
- a *copy* instruction, followed by a *jump-on-zero* instruction with pc_t as the destination, followed by *CEXP* and an *and* instruction.

We simultaneously show the two key properties of conjunction blocks via induction: if there is a conjunction block from pc_s to pc_t, then any successful execution starting from pc_s ends in pc_t, and every *CEXP* instruction that is encountered has to evaluate to true. Given a start address pc_s, the whole analysis works by computing an approximation of the set of possible addresses that can be reached from pc_s, say S, and then checking whether

$$\mathit{Min}\ \{pc \mid pc \in S \wedge (\exists ac.\ P_{pc} = \mathit{CEXP}\ ac)\}\ \text{to}\ \mathit{Max}\ S$$

is a conjunction block, where P_{pc} is the program instruction at address pc. A major limitation of this analysis is that it cannot approximate the reachable

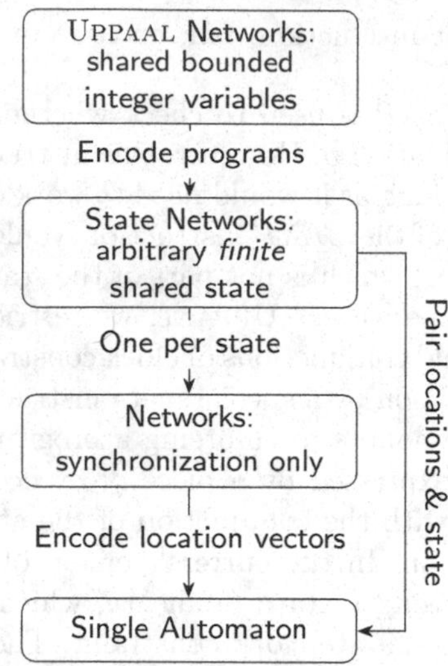

Fig. 3. Outline of the product construction.

set for *call* and *return* instructions, so we are not able to handle inputs that are compiled from UPPAAL programs with sub-routines. However, as the main objective of our work is not program analysis, we consider the current naive analysis sufficient to demonstrate the general viability of our approach.

5.3 Product Construction

The general shape of our product construction is outlined in Fig. 3. The first stage of the construction encodes the bytecode annotations as guards and updates on the shared state. The subsequent stage constructs a network of automata for *each shared state* by essentially filtering the transitions that are valid for a given state. For a simple network, the product can be constructed in the obvious way. However, this is only used in the correctness proof of the final step, which directly constructs a single automaton by pairing the location vector and the state.

The result of this construction is a highly contrived description of the single automaton. To obtain an efficiently executable version of this description, we specify an alternative functional implementation and prove the equivalence of the two.

6 Experimental Evaluation

We conducted experiments on some standard benchmark models for timed automata: a variant of Fischer's mutual-exclusion protocol, the FDDI token ring protocol, and the CSMA/CD protocol used in Ethernet networks. We tested one reachability and one liveness property for each model: $\mathbf{E}\Diamond(c > 1)$ and $P_1.b \dashrightarrow$

$P_1.c$ for Fischer's protocol; $\mathbf{E}\Diamond(\neg P_1.idle \wedge \neg P_2.idle)$ and $true \dashrightarrow z\_async_1$ for FDDI; and $\mathbf{E}\Diamond(P_1.abort \wedge P_2.send)$, and $collision \dashrightarrow active$ for CSMA/CD. We compare (c.f. Table 1) our tool against UPPAAL configured with two different approximation operators: difference (UPPAAL$_1$) and location-based (UPPAAL$_2$) extrapolation. We give the computation time in seconds and the number of explored states, as reported by our tool and UPPAAL[7]. Since the number of explored states differs significantly, we also calculated *throughput*, i.e. the number of explored states per second. The ratio of UPPAAL's throughput and our tool's throughput is given in the column *TR*. We specify the problem size as the number of automata in the network.

Table 1. Experimental results on a set of standard benchmarks.

Model	Prop	SAT	Size	Our tool		UPPAAL$_1$			UPPAAL$_2$		
				Time	#States	Time	#States	TR	Time	#States	TR
Fischer	R	N	5	6,61	38578	0,31	12363	6,83	0,04	3739	16,02
	L	Y	5	7,52	42439	0,31	20340	11,8	0,04	8149	40,1
		Y	6	485,9	697612	42,85	249295	4,1	1,53	67325	30,7
FDDI	R	N	8	16,04	6720	0,34	5416	37,6	0,31	5416	42,0
		N	10	142,8	29759	6,63	24210	17,5	6,44	24120	18,0
	L	Y	6	2,58	2083	0,05	2439	61,7	0,04	2439	68,7
		Y	7	6,50	3737	0,15	4944	57,0	0,14	4944	62,3
CSMA/CD	R	N	5	4,48	9959	0,03	2704	45,3	0,03	2769	40,6
		N	6	71,70	81463	1,70	17613	9,2	1,79	17939	8,8
	L	Y	5	4,93	11526	0,04	3802	42,4	0,04	3867	42,4
		Y	6	76,83	96207	1,78	23128	10,4	1,86	12603	10,1

The results indicate that our tool's throughput is around one order of magnitude lower than UPPAAL's. Encouragingly, the gap seems to decrease for larger models. However, for larger problem sizes of some models, we also start to run out of memory because our tool is not tuned towards space consumption. We do not have a convincing explanation for the difference in states explored by our tool and UPPAAL — particularly, because our tool already implements location-based extrapolation. Nevertheless, we conclude that the performance offered by our tool is reasonable for a reference implementation against which other tools can be validated: we can check medium sized instances of common benchmark models, which should be sufficient to scrutinize the functionality of a model checker.

[7] UPPAAL comes with a note suggesting that these numbers might be wrong for liveness properties.

7 Conclusion

We have derived an efficiently executable and formally verified model checker for timed automata. Starting from an abstract formalization of timed automata, we first reduced the problem to model checking of a single automaton, and then used stepwise refinement techniques to gradually replace abstract mathematical notions by efficient algorithms and data structures. Some of the verified algorithms and data structures, e.g. search with subsumption and Difference Bound Matrices, are interesting in their own right. Our experiments demonstrate that our tool's performance is suitable for validating other model checkers against it on medium sized instances of classic benchmark models. Using a simple program analysis, we can cover a subset of the UPPAAL bytecode that is sufficient to accept common models as an input.

Following the construction we expounded above, our checker can be improved on two different axes: advanced modeling feature such as broadcast channels or committed locations can be enabled by elaborating the product construction; using the refinement techniques that we demonstrated above, further improvements of the model checking algorithms can achieve better performance.

An alternative approach to tackle performance problems is to resort to certification of model checking results. For the simple CTL properties that are supported by our tool and UPPAAL, passed sets could be used as the certificates and the model checking algorithms could be reused for certificate checking. As the model checking algorithms for timed automata make use of subsumption, passed sets can contain significantly less states than the total number of states explored during model checking. We plan on exploring this avenue in the future.

Data Availability Statement. The datasets generated during and analyzed during the current study are available in the figshare repository [25]: https://doi.org/10.6084/m9.figshare.5917363.v1.

References

1. Alur, R., Dill, D.L.: A theory of timed automata. Theoret. Comput. Sci. **126**(2), 183–235 (1994)
2. Bengtsson, J., Yi, W.: Timed automata: semantics, algorithms and tools. In: Desel, J., Reisig, W., Rozenberg, G. (eds.) ACPN 2003. LNCS, vol. 3098, pp. 87–124. Springer, Heidelberg (2004). https://doi.org/10.1007/978-3-540-27755-2_3
3. Bouyer, P.: Untameable timed automata! In: Alt, H., Habib, M. (eds.) STACS 2003. LNCS, vol. 2607, pp. 620–631. Springer, Heidelberg (2003). https://doi.org/10.1007/3-540-36494-3_54
4. Nipkow, T., Wenzel, M., Paulson, L.C. (eds.): Isabelle/HOL. LNCS, vol. 2283. Springer, Heidelberg (2002). https://doi.org/10.1007/3-540-45949-9
5. Lammich, P., Tuerk, T.: Applying data refinement for monadic programs to Hopcroft's algorithm. In: Beringer, L., Felty, A. (eds.) ITP 2012. LNCS, vol. 7406, pp. 166–182. Springer, Heidelberg (2012). https://doi.org/10.1007/978-3-642-32347-8_12

6. Lammich, P.: Refinement to Imperative/HOL. In: Urban, C., Zhang, X. (eds.) ITP 2015. LNCS, vol. 9236, pp. 253–269. Springer, Cham (2015). https://doi.org/10.1007/978-3-319-22102-1_17
7. Wimmer, S.: Formalized timed automata. In: Blanchette, J.C., Merz, S. (eds.) ITP 2016. LNCS, vol. 9807, pp. 425–440. Springer, Cham (2016). https://doi.org/10.1007/978-3-319-43144-4_26
8. Xu, Q., Miao, H.: Formal verification framework for safety of real-time system based on timed automata model in PVS. In: Proceedings of the IASTED International Conference on Software Engineering, pp. 107–112 (2006)
9. Xu, Q., Miao, H.: Manipulating clocks in timed automata using PVS. In: Proceedings of SNPD 2009, pp. 555–560 (2009)
10. Paulin-Mohring, C.: Modelisation of timed automata in Coq. In: Kobayashi, N., Pierce, B.C. (eds.) TACS 2001. LNCS, vol. 2215, pp. 298–315. Springer, Heidelberg (2001). https://doi.org/10.1007/3-540-45500-0_15
11. Garnacho, M., Bodeveix, J.-P., Filali-Amine, M.: A mechanized semantic framework for real-time systems. In: Braberman, V., Fribourg, L. (eds.) FORMATS 2013. LNCS, vol. 8053, pp. 106–120. Springer, Heidelberg (2013). https://doi.org/10.1007/978-3-642-40229-6_8
12. Alur, R., Henzinger, T.A., Vardi, M.Y.: Parametric real-time reasoning. In: Proceedings of the Twenty-Fifth Annual ACM Symposium on Theory of Computing, pp. 592–601 (1993)
13. Castéran, P., Rouillard, D.: Towards a generic tool for reasoning about labeled transition systems. In: TPHOLs 2001: Supplemental Proceedings (2001). http://www.informatics.ed.ac.uk/publications/report/0046.html
14. Sprenger, C.: A verified model checker for the modal μ-calculus in Coq. In: Steffen, B. (ed.) TACAS 1998. LNCS, vol. 1384, pp. 167–183. Springer, Heidelberg (1998). https://doi.org/10.1007/BFb0054171
15. Esparza, J., Lammich, P., Neumann, R., Nipkow, T., Schimpf, A., Smaus, J.-G.: A fully verified executable LTL model checker. In: Sharygina, N., Veith, H. (eds.) CAV 2013. LNCS, vol. 8044, pp. 463–478. Springer, Heidelberg (2013). https://doi.org/10.1007/978-3-642-39799-8_31
16. Neumann, R.: Using promela in a fully verified executable LTL model checker. In: Giannakopoulou, D., Kroening, D. (eds.) VSTTE 2014. LNCS, vol. 8471, pp. 105–114. Springer, Cham (2014). https://doi.org/10.1007/978-3-319-12154-3_7
17. Brunner, J., Lammich, P.: Formal verification of an executable LTL model checker with partial order reduction. J. Autom. Reasoning **60**(1), 3–21 (2018)
18. Herbreteau, F., Srivathsan, B., Tran, T.T., Walukiewicz, I.: Why liveness for timed automata is hard, and what we can do about it. In: Lal, A., Akshay, S., Saurabh, S., Sen, S. (eds.) FSTTCS 2016, vol. 65. LIPIcs. Schloss Dagstuhl - Leibniz-Zentrum für Informatik, pp. 48:1–48:14 (2016)
19. Huffman, B., Kunčar, O.: Lifting and transfer: a modular design for quotients in Isabelle/HOL. In: Gonthier, G., Norrish, M. (eds.) CPP 2013. LNCS, vol. 8307, pp. 131–146. Springer, Cham (2013). https://doi.org/10.1007/978-3-319-03545-1_9
20. Bouajjani, A., Tripakis, S., Yovine, S.: On-the-fly symbolic model checking for real-time systems. In: Proceedings of the 18th IEEE Real-Time Systems Symposium (RTSS 1997), 3–5 December 1997, San Francisco, CA, USA, pp. 25–34 (1997)
21. Behrmann, G., Larsen, K.G., Rasmussen, J.I.: Beyond liveness: efficient parameter synthesis for time bounded liveness. In: Pettersson, P., Yi, W. (eds.) FORMATS 2005. LNCS, vol. 3829, pp. 81–94. Springer, Heidelberg (2005). https://doi.org/10.1007/11603009_7

22. Bulwahn, L., Krauss, A., Haftmann, F., Erkök, L., Matthews, J.: Imperative functional programming with Isabelle/HOL. In: Mohamed, O.A., Muñoz, C., Tahar, S. (eds.) TPHOLs 2008. LNCS, vol. 5170, pp. 134–149. Springer, Heidelberg (2008). https://doi.org/10.1007/978-3-540-71067-7_14
23. Charguéraud, A.: Higher-order representation predicates in separation logic. In: Proceedings of the 5th ACM SIGPLAN Conference on Certified Programs and Proofs, CPP 2016, St. Petersburg, FL, USA, pp. 2–14. ACM, New York (2016). https://doi.org/10.1145/2854065.2854068
24. Haftmann, F., Nipkow, T.: Code generation via higher-order rewrite systems. In: Blume, M., Kobayashi, N., Vidal, G. (eds.) FLOPS 2010. LNCS, vol. 6009, pp. 103–117. Springer, Heidelberg (2010). https://doi.org/10.1007/978-3-642-12251-4_9
25. Wimmer, S., Lammich, P.: Verified model checking of timed automata - artifact (2018)

SAT and SMT I

Chain Reduction for Binary and Zero-Suppressed Decision Diagrams

Randal E. Bryant(✉)

Computer Science Department, Carnegie Mellon University,
Pittsburgh, PA 15213, USA
Randy.Bryant@cs.cmu.edu

Abstract. Chain reduction enables reduced ordered binary decision diagrams (BDDs) and zero-suppressed binary decision diagrams (ZDDs) to each take advantage of the others' ability to symbolically represent Boolean functions in compact form. For any Boolean function, its chain-reduced ZDD (CZDD) representation will be no larger than its ZDD representation, and at most twice the size of its BDD representation. The chain-reduced BDD (CBDD) of a function will be no larger than its BDD representation, and at most three times the size of its CZDD representation. Extensions to the standard algorithms for operating on BDDs and ZDDs enable them to operate on the chain-reduced versions. Experimental evaluations on representative benchmarks for encoding word lists, solving combinatorial problems, and operating on digital circuits indicate that chain reduction can provide significant benefits in terms of both memory and execution time.

1 Introduction

Decision diagrams (DDs) encode sets of values in compact forms, such that operations on the sets can be performed on the encoded representation, without expanding the sets into their individual elements. In this paper, we consider two classes of decision diagrams: reduced ordered binary decision diagrams (BDDs) [4] and zero-suppressed binary decision diagrams (ZDDs) [11,12]. These two representations are closely related to each other, with each achieving more compact representations for different classes of applications. We present extensions to both representations, such that BDDs can take advantage of the source of compaction provided by ZDDs, and vice-versa.

Both BDDs and ZDDs encode sets of binary sequences of some fixed length n, defining a Boolean function over n variables. We can bound their relative sizes as follows. Suppose for some function, we encode it according to the different DD types. For function f, let $T(f)$ indicate the number of nodes (including leaf nodes) in the representation of type T. Let $R_f(T_1, T_2)$ denote the relative sizes when representing f using types T_1 and T_2:

$$R_f(T_1, T_2) = \frac{T_1(f)}{T_2(f)}$$

D. Beyer and M. Huisman (Eds.): TACAS 2018, LNCS 10805, pp. 81–98, 2018.
https://doi.org/10.1007/978-3-319-89960-2_5

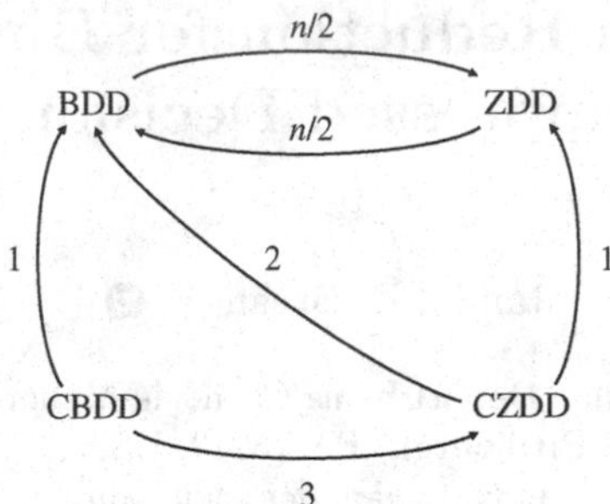

Fig. 1. Size bound relations between different representations

Comparing BDDs and ZDDs, Knuth [9] has shown that for any function f:

$$R_f(\mathrm{BDD}, \mathrm{ZDD}) \leq n/2 + o(n) \tag{1}$$

$$R_f(\mathrm{ZDD}, \mathrm{BDD}) \leq n/2 + o(n) \tag{2}$$

As these bounds show, ZDDs may be significantly (a factor of $n/2$) more compact than BDDs, or vice-versa. In practice, the comparative advantage of one representation over the other can be very significant, given that the size of the data structure is often the limiting factor in the use of DDs.

In this paper, we introduce two new representations: *chain-reduced ordered binary decision diagrams* (CBDDs), and *chain-reduced zero-suppressed binary decision diagrams* (CZDDs). The key idea is to associate two levels with each node and to use such nodes to encode particular classes of linear chains found in BDDs and ZDDs. Chain reduction can be defined in terms of a set of reduction rules applied to BDDs and ZDDs, giving bounds for any function f

$$R_f(\mathrm{CBDD}, \mathrm{BDD}) \leq 1 \tag{3}$$

$$R_f(\mathrm{CZDD}, \mathrm{ZDD}) \leq 1 \tag{4}$$

We show bounds on the relative sizes of the representations as:

$$R_f(\mathrm{CBDD}, \mathrm{CZDD}) \leq 3 \tag{5}$$

$$R_f(\mathrm{CZDD}, \mathrm{BDD}) \leq 2 \tag{6}$$

These relations are summarized in the diagram of Fig. 1. In this figure, each arc from type T_1 to type T_2 labeled by an expression E indicates that $R_f(T_1, T_2) \leq E + o(E)$. We also show these bounds are tight, by demonstrating parameterized families of functions that achieve the bounding factors of (5) and (6).

These results indicate that the two compressed representations will always be within a small constant factor (2 for CZDDs and 3 for CBDDs) of either a BDD or a ZDD representation. While one representation may be more slightly compact than the other, the relative advantage is bounded by a constant factor, and hence choosing between them is less critical.

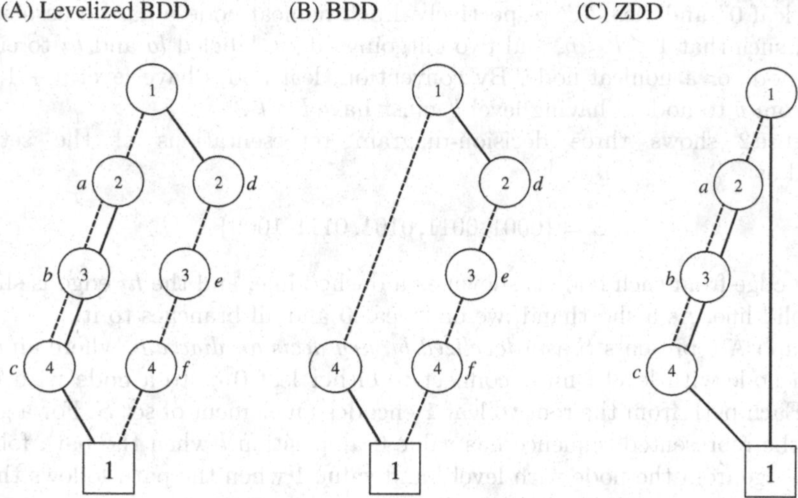

Fig. 2. Reductions in BDDs and ZDDs. Each reduces the representation size with edges between nonconsecutive levels.

This paper defines the two compressed representations, derives the bounds indicated in (5) and (6) and presents extensions of the core BDD and ZDD algorithms to their chained versions. It describes an implementation based on modifications of the CUDD BDD package [14]. It presents some experimental results and concludes with a discussion of the merits of chaining and possible extensions.

2 Related Work

In independent work, van Dijk and his colleages devised a hybrid of BDDs and ZDDs they call *tagged BDDs* [6]. Their representation augments BDDs by associating a variable with each edge, in addition to the variable associated with each node, enabling them to represent both BDD and ZDD reductions along each edge. For any function, a tagged BDD is guaranteed to have no more nodes than either its BDD or its ZDD representation. They avoid the constant factor in node growth that CBDDs or CZDDs may require, at the cost of requiring storage for three variables per node (one for the node, and one for each of the outgoing edges) versus two. Choosing between their representation or ours depends on a number of implementation factors. Both achieve the larger goal of exploiting the reductions enabled by both BDDs and ZDDs.

3 BDDs and ZDDs

Both BDDs and ZDDs encode sets of binary sequences of length n as directed acyclic graphs with two leaf nodes, labeled with values **0** and **1**, which we refer to as "leaf **0**" and "leaf **1**," respectively. Each nonleaf node v has an associated level l, such that $1 \leq l \leq n$, and two outgoing edges, labeled *lo* and *hi* to either a leaf node or a nonleaf node. By convention, leaf nodes have level $n + 1$. An edge from v to node u having level l' must have $l < l'$.

Figure 2 shows three decision-diagram representations of the set S, defined as:

$$S = \{0001, 0011, 0101, 0111, 1000\} \tag{7}$$

The *lo* edge from each node is shown as a dashed line, and the *hi* edge is shown as a solid line. As a shorthand, we omit leaf **0** and all branches to it.

Graph A represents S as a *levelized binary decision diagram*, where an edge from a node with level l must connect to either leaf **0** or to a node with level $l+1$. Each path from the root to leaf **1** encodes an element of set S. For a given path, the represented sequence has value 0 at position l when the path follows the *lo* edge from the node with level l and value 1 when the path follows the *hi* edge.

Graph A has nodes forming two linear chains: a DON'T-CARE *chain*, consisting of nodes a and b, and an OR *chain*, consisting of nodes d, e, and f. A DON'T-CARE chain is a series of DON'T-CARE nodes, each having its two outgoing edges directed to the same next node. In terms of the set of represented binary sequences, a DON'T-CARE node with level l allows both values 0 and 1 at sequence position l. An OR chain consists of a sequence where the outgoing *hi* edges for the nodes all go the same node—in this case, leaf **0**. An OR chain where all *hi* edges lead to leaf **0** has only a single path, assigning value 0 to the corresponding positions in the represented sequence. We will refer to this special class of OR chain as a ZERO *chain*.

BDDs and ZDDs differ from each other in the interpretations they assign to a *level-skipping edge*, when a node with level l has an edge to a node with level l' such that $l + 1 < l'$. For BDDs, such an edge is considered to encode a DON'T-CARE chain. Thus, graph B in Fig. 2 shows an BDD encoding set S. The edge on the left from level 1 to level 4 is equivalent to the DON'T-CARE chain formed by nodes a and b of graph A. For ZDDs, a level skipping edge encodes a ZERO chain. Thus, graph C shows a ZDD encoding set S. The edge on the right from level 1 to the leaf encodes the ZERO chain formed by nodes d, e, and f of graph A. Whether the set is encoded as a BDD or a ZDD, one type of linear chains remains. Introducing chain reduction enables BDDs and ZDDs to exploit both DON'T-CARE and OR (and therefore ZERO) chains to compress their representations.

4 Chain Patterns and Reductions

Figure 3 shows the general form of OR and DON'T-CARE chains, as were illustrated in the examples of Fig. 2. These chains have levels ranging from t to b, such that $1 \leq t < b \leq n$. Each form consists of a linear chain of nodes followed by two nodes f and g with levels greater than b. Nodes f and g are drawn as triangles to indicate that they are the roots of two subgraphs in the representation. In an OR chain, the *lo* edge from each node is directed to the next node in the chain, and the *hi* edge is directed to node g. The chains eliminated by ZDDs are a special case where $g = \mathbf{0}$. In a DON'T-CARE chain, both the *lo* and the *hi* edges are directed toward the next node in the chain.

As was illustrated in Fig. 2, having edges that skip levels allows BDDs to compactly represent DON'T-CARE chains and ZDDs to eliminate OR chains when $g = \mathbf{0}$. The goal of chain reduction is to allow both forms to compactly represent both types of chains. They do so by associating two levels with each node, as indicated in Fig. 3(C). That is, every nonleaf node has an associated pair of levels $t:b$, such that $1 \leq t \leq b \leq n$. In a *chain-reduced ordered binary decision diagram* (CBDD), such a node encodes the OR chain pattern shown in Fig. 3(A), while in a *chain-reduced zero-suppressed binary decision diagram* (CZDD), such a node encodes the DON'T-CARE chain pattern shown in Fig. 3(B). A node with levels t and b such that $t = b$ encodes a standard node with respect to the indicated variable.

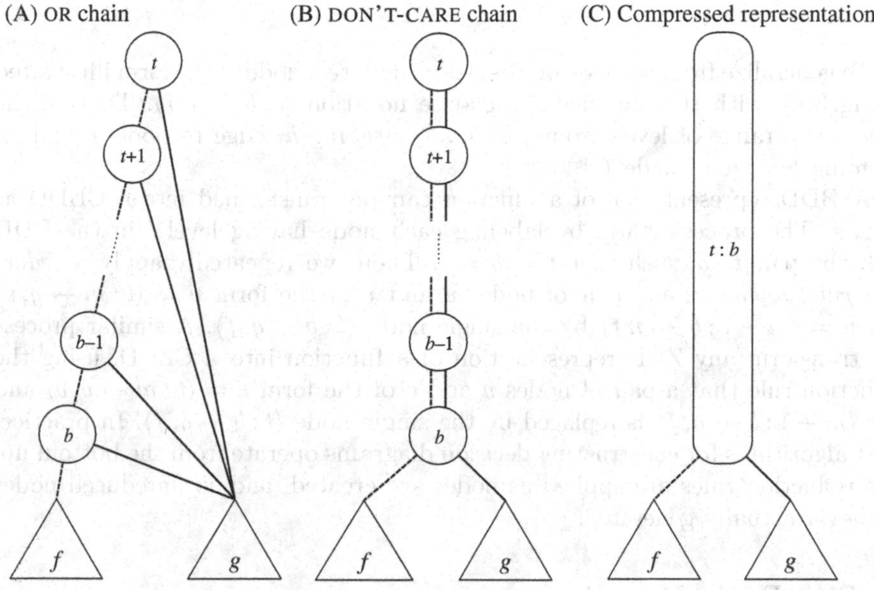

Fig. 3. Chain patterns. These patterns remain after BDD reduction (A), and ZDD reduction (B), but can be represented in compressed form (C).

Figure 4 shows the effect of chain reduction, starting with the levelized graph A. In the CBDD (B), a single node f' replaces the OR chain consisting of nodes d, e, and f. In the CZDD (C), the DON'T-CARE chain consisting of nodes a and b is incorporated into node c to form node c'. These new nodes are drawn in elongated form to emphasize that they span a range of levels, but it should be emphasized that *all* nodes in a chained representation have an associated pair of levels.

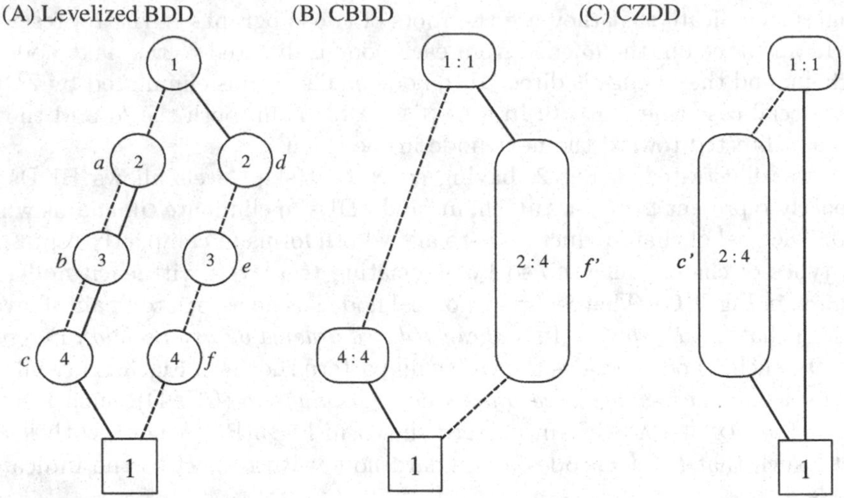

Fig. 4. Chain Reduction Examples. Each now reduces both chain types.

To generalize from these examples, let us denote a node of the form illustrated in Fig. 3(C) with the modified if-then-else notation $\langle t : b \rightarrow g, f \rangle$. That is, the node has a range of levels from t to b, an outgoing *hi* edge to node g, and an outgoing *lo* edge to node f.

A BDD representation of a function can be transformed into a CBDD as follows. The process starts by labeling each node having level l in the BDD with the pair $t : b$, such that $t = b = l$. Then, we repeatedly apply a *reduction rule*, replacing any pair of nodes u and v of the form $u = \langle t : m \rightarrow g, v \rangle$ and $v = \langle m+1 : b \rightarrow g, f \rangle$ by the single node $\langle t : b \rightarrow g, f \rangle$. A similar process can transform any ZDD representation of a function into a CZDD, using the reduction rule that a pair of nodes u and v of the form $u = \langle t : m \rightarrow v, v \rangle$ and $v = \langle m+1 : b \rightarrow g, f \rangle$ is replaced by the single node $\langle t : b \rightarrow g, f \rangle$. In practice, most algorithms for constructing decision diagrams operate from the bottom up. The reduction rules are applied as nodes are created, and so unreduced nodes are never actually generated.

5 Size Ratio Bounds

These reduction rules allows us to bound the relative sizes of the different representations, as given by (5) and (6).

First, let us consider (5), bounding the relative sizes of the CBDD and CZDD representations of a function. Consider a graph G representing function f as a CZDD. We can generate a CBDD representation G' as follows. G' contains a node v' for each node v in G. However, if v has levels $t : b$, then v' has levels $b : b$, because any DON'T-CARE chain encoded explicitly in the CZDD is encoded implicitly in a CBDD.

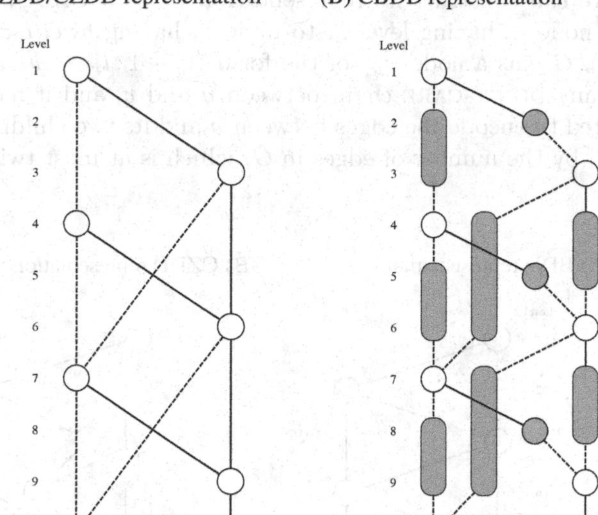

Fig. 5. Worst case example for effectiveness of CBDD compression. The implicit ZERO chains in the ZDD (A) must be explicitly encoded in the CBDD (B), increasing its size by a factor of 3.

Consider an edge from node u to node v in G, where the nodes have levels $t_u : b_u$ and $t_v : b_v$, respectively. If $t_v = b_u + 1$, then there can be an edge directly from u' to v'. If $t_v < b_u + 1$, then we introduce a new node to encode the implicit zero chain in G from u to v. This node has the form $\langle b_u + 1 : t_v - 1 \rightarrow \mathbf{0}, v' \rangle$ and has an edge from u' to it.

The size of G' is bounded by the number of nodes plus the number of edges in G. Since each node in G has at most two outgoing edges, we can see that G' has at most three times the number of nodes as G. Graph G' may not be reduced, but it provides an upper bound on the size of a CBDD relative to that of a CZDD.

This bound is tight—Fig. 5 illustrates the reduced representations for a family of functions, parameterized by a value k ($k = 3$ in the example), such that the function is defined over $3k + 2$ variables. The ZDD and CZDD representations are identical (A), having $2k + 3$ nodes (including both leaf nodes.) The CBDD representation has $6k + 2$ nodes (B). We can see in this example that the CBDD requires nodes (shown in gray) to encode the ZERO chains that are implicit in the ZDD.

Second, let us consider (6), bounding the relative sizes of the CZDD and BDD representations of a function. Consider a graph G representing function f

as a BDD. We can construct its representation G' as a CZDD. Consider each edge G from node u, having level l_u to node v, having level l_v. Let $r = lo(v)$ and $s = hi(v)$. G' has a node w_{uv} of the form $\langle l_u + 1 : l_v \rightarrow w_{vs}, w_{vr} \rangle$. That is, w_{uv} encodes any DON'T-CARE chain between u and v, and it has edges to the nodes generated to encode the edges between v and its two children. The size of G' is bounded by the number of edges in G, which is at most twice the number of nodes.

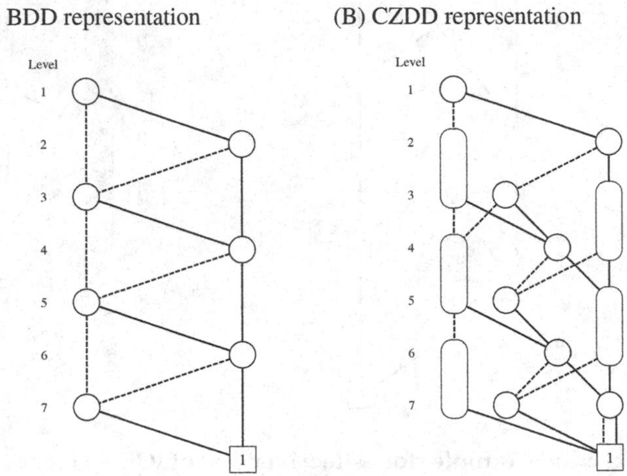

Fig. 6. Worst case example for effectiveness of CZDD compression. The nodes in the BDD (A) must be duplicated to encode the incoming DON'T-CARE chains (B), increasing the size by a factor of 2.

This bound is also tight—Fig. 6 illustrates the reduced representations for a family of functions, parameterized by a value k ($k = 3$ in the example), such that the function is defined over $2k + 1$ variables. The BDD representations (A) has $2k + 3$ nodes (including both leaf nodes). The CZDD representation has $4k + 3$ nodes (B). We can see that most of the nodes in the BDD must be duplicated: once with no incoming DON'T-CARE chain, and once with a chain of length one.

As can be seen in Fig. 1, these bounds contain an asymmetry between BDDs and ZDDs and their compressed forms. The bound of 3 holds between CBDDs and CZDDs, and hence by transitivity between CBDDs and ZDDs, while the bound of 2 holds only between CZDDs and BDDs. The general form of the OR chain (Fig. 3(A)), where g is something other than $\mathbf{0}$, cannot be directly encoded with CZDD nodes.

6 Operating on CBDDs and CZDDs

The APPLY algorithms for decision diagrams operate by recursively expanding a set of argument decision diagrams according to a Shannon expansion of the represented functions [4,5]. These algorithms allow functions to be combined according to standard binary Boolean operations, as well as by the if-then-else operation ITE.

As notation, consider a step that expands k argument nodes $\{v_i | 1 \leq i \leq k\}$ where $v_i = \langle t_i : b_i \rightarrow g_i, f_i \rangle$. For example, operations AND, OR, and XOR use the APPLY algorithm with $k = 2$, while ternary operations, such as ITE use $k = 3$. A step can be summarized as follows:

1. If one of the terminal cases apply, then return the result.
2. If the computed cache contains an entry for this combination of operation and arguments, then return the previously computed result.
3. Recursively compute the result:
   (a) Choose splitting level(s) based on the levels of the arguments.
   (b) Generate *hi* and *lo* cofactors for each argument.
   (c) Recursively compute the *hi* and *lo* values of the result using the APPLY algorithm with the *hi* cofactors and the *lo* cofactors, respectively.
   (d) Determine the result node parameters based on the computed *hi* and *lo* cofactors, the splitting level(s), and the reduction rules.
   (e) Either reuse an existing node or create a new one with the desired level(s) and *hi* and *lo* children.
4. Store an entry in the computed cache.
5. Return the computed value.

In generalizing from conventional BDDs and ZDDs to their chained versions, we need only modify 3(a) (splitting), 3(b) (cofactoring), and 3(d) (combining) in this sequence. In the following presentation, we first give formal definitions and then provide brief explanations.

For CBDDs, we define the splitting levels t and b as:

$$t = \min_{1 \leq i \leq k} t_i \tag{8}$$

$$b = \min_{1 \leq i \leq k} \begin{cases} b_i, & t_i = t \\ t_i, & t_i = n+1 \\ t_i - 1, & \text{else} \end{cases}$$

We then define the two cofactors for each argument node v_i, denoted $lo(v_i, t:b)$ and $hi(v_i, t:b)$, according to the following table:

Case	Condition	$lo(v_i, t:b)$	$hi(v_i, t:b)$
1	$b < t_i$	v_i	v_i
2	$b = b_i$	f_i	g_i
3	$t_i \leq b < b_i$	$\langle b+1 : b_i \rightarrow g_i, f_i \rangle$	g_i

These three cases can be explained as follows:

Case 1: Splitting spans levels less than the top level of v_i. Since level-skipping edges encode DON'T-CARE chains, both cofactors equal the original node.

Case 2: Splitting spans the same levels as node v_i. The cofactors are therefore the nodes given by the outgoing edges.

Case 3: Splitting spans a subset of the levels covered by node v_i. We construct a new node spanning the remaining part of the encoded OR chain for the *lo* cofactor and have g_i as the *hi* cofactor.

Recursive application of the APPLY operation on the cofactors generates a pair of nodes u_0 and u_1. Using the variable levels t and b defined in (8), these are combined to form a result node u, defined as follows:

$$u = \begin{cases} u_0, & u_0 = u_1 & \text{Case 1} \\ \langle t : b' \rightarrow u_1, w_0 \rangle\,, & u_0 = \langle b+1, b' \!: \rightarrow u_1, w_0 \rangle & \text{Case 2} \\ \langle t : b \rightarrow u_1, u_0 \rangle\,, & \text{else} & \text{Case 3} \end{cases} \tag{9}$$

These three cases can be explained as follows:

Case 1: The *hi* and *lo* cofactors are identical, and so the don't-care reduction rule can be applied.

Case 2: Chain compression can be applied to create a node that absorbs the *lo* cofactor.

Case 3: No special rules apply.

Similar rules hold for applying operations to CZDDs, although there are important differences, due to the different interpretations of level-skipping edges.

We define the splitting levels t and b as:

$$t = \min_{1 \leq i \leq k} t_i \tag{10}$$

$$b = \min_{1 \leq i \leq k} \begin{cases} b_i, & t_i = t \\ n+1, & v_i = \mathbf{0} \\ t, & \text{else} \end{cases}$$

The cofactors for argument node v_i are defined according to the following table:

Case	Condition	$lo(v_i, t : b)$	$hi(v_i, t : b)$
1	$b < t_i$	v_i	$\mathbf{0}$
2	$b = b_i$	f_i	g_i
3	$t_i \leq b < b_i$	$\langle b+1 : b_i \rightarrow g_i, f_i \rangle$	$\langle b+1 : b_i \rightarrow g_i, f_i \rangle$

These three cases can be explained as follows:

Case 1: The splitting spans levels less than the top level of v_i. Since level-skipping edges encode ZERO chains, the *lo* cofactor equals the original node and the *hi* cofactor equals leaf **0**.

Case 2: The splitting spans the same levels as node v_i. The cofactors are therefore the nodes given by the outgoing edges.

Case 3: The splitting spans a subset of the levels covered by node v_i. We construct a new node spanning the remaining part of the encoded DON'T-CARE chain for both cofactors.

Recursive application of the APPLY operation on the cofactors generates a pair of nodes u_0 and u_1. Using the variable ranges t and b defined in (10), these are combined to form a result node u, defined as follows:

$$u = \begin{cases} u_0, & u_1 = \mathbf{0} \text{ and } t = b & \text{Case 1} \\ \langle t : b-1 \rightarrow u_0, u_0 \rangle, & u_1 = \mathbf{0} \text{ and } t < b & \text{Case 2} \\ \langle t : b' \rightarrow w_1, w_0 \rangle, & u_0 = u_1 = \langle b+1, b' : \rightarrow w_1, w_0 \rangle & \text{Case 3} \\ \langle t : b \rightarrow u_1, u_0 \rangle, & \text{else} & \text{Case 4} \end{cases} \tag{11}$$

These four cases can be explained as follows:

Case 1: The zero-suppression rule can be applied to return a direct pointer to u_0

Case 2: The zero-suppression rule can be applied, but we must construct a node encoding the DON'T-CARE chain between levels t and $b-1$.

Case 3: Chain compression can be applied to create a node that absorbs the *lo* cofactor.

Case 4: No special rule applies.

7 Experimental Results

We implemented both CBDDs and CZDDs by modifying version 3.0.0 of the CUDD BDD package [14]. When compiled for 64-bit execution, CUDD stores a 32-bit field `index` in each node, where this index is translated into a level according to the variable ordering. For our implementation, we split this field into two 16-bit fields `index` and `bindex` to (indirectly) encode the top and bottom levels of the node. Thus, there was no storage penalty for the generalization to a chained form.

CUDD uses complement edges when representing BDDs [2,13]. Complement edges can potentially reduce the size of a BDD by a factor of two, invalidating the size ratio bounds derived in (5) and (6). For our experimental results, we therefore use a representation based on CUDD's support for *Algebraic Decision Diagrams* (ADDs) [1]. ADDs generalize BDDs by allowing arbitrary leaf values. Restricting the leaf values to 0 and 1 yields conventional BDDs without complement edges.

To evaluate the effectiveness of chain reduction, we chose three different categories of benchmarks to compare the performance of BDDs, ZDDs, and their chained versions. One set of benchmarks evaluated the ability of DDs to represent information in compact form, a second to evaluate their ability to solve combinatorial problems, and a third to represent typical digital logic functions. All experiments were performed on a 4.2 GHz Intel Core i7 processor with 32 GB of memory running the OS X operating system.

7.1 Encoding a Dictionary

As has been observed [9], a list of words can be encoded as a function mapping strings in some alphabet to either 1 (included in list) or 0 (not included in list). Strings can further be encoded as binary sequences by encoding each symbol as a sequence of bits, allowing the list to be represented as a Boolean function. We consider two possible encodings of the symbols, defining the *radix* r to be the number of possible symbols. A *one-hot* encoding (also referred to as a "1-of-N" encoding) requires r bits per symbol. Each symbol is assigned a unique position, and the symbol is represented with a one in this position and zeros in the rest. A *binary* encoding requires $\lceil \log_2 r \rceil$ bits per symbol. Each symbol is assigned a unique binary pattern, and the symbol is represented by this pattern. Lists consisting of words with multiple lengths can be encoded by introducing a special "null" symbol to terminate each word.

Eight benchmarks were derived from two word lists to allow comparisons of different encoding techniques and representations. The first list is a set of English words in the file `/usr/share/dict/words` found on Macintosh systems. It contains 235,886 words with lengths ranging from one to 24 symbols, and where the symbols consist of lower- and upper-case letters plus hyphen. We consider two resulting symbol sets: a *compact* form, consisting of just the symbols found in the words plus a null symbol (54 total), and an *ASCII* form, consisting of all 128 ASCII characters plus a null symbol. The second word list is from an online list of words employed by password crackers. It consists of 979,247 words ranging in length from one to 32 symbols, and where the symbols include 79 possible characters. Again, we consider both a compact form and an ASCII form. The choice of one-hot vs. binary encoding has a major effect on the number of Boolean variables required to encode the words. With a one-hot encoding, the number of variables ranges between 1,296 and 4,128, while it ranges between 144 and 256 with a binary representation. To generate DD encodings of a word list, we first constructed a trie representation the words and then generated Boolean formulas via a depth-first traversal of the trie.

Figure 7 shows the number of nodes required to represent word lists as Boolean functions, according to the different lists, encodings, and DD types. The entry labeled "(C)ZDD" gives the node counts for both ZDDs and CZDDs. These are identical, because there were no DON'T-CARE chains for these functions. The two columns on the right show the ratios between the different DD types. Concentrating first on one-hot encodings, we see that the chain compression of CBDDs reduces the size compared to BDDs by large factors (15.50–34.03).

One-hot	Node counts			Ratios	
	BDD	CBDD	(C)ZDD	BDD:CBDD	CBDD:CZDD
Compact word list	9,701,439	626,070	297,681	15.50	2.10
ASCII word list	23,161,501	626,071	297,681	37.00	2.10
Compact password list	49,231,085	2,321,572	1,130,729	21.21	2.05
ASCII password list	79,014,931	2,321,792	1,130,729	34.03	2.05

Binary	Node counts			Ratios	
	BDD	CBDD	(C)ZDD	BDD:CBDD	CBDD:CZDD
Compact word list	1,117,454	1,007,868	723,542	1.11	1.39
ASCII word list	1,464,773	1,277,640	851,580	1.15	1.50
Compact password list	4,422,292	3,597,474	2,506,088	1.23	1.44
ASCII password list	4,943,940	4,307,614	2,875,612	1.15	1.50

Fig. 7. Node counts and ratios of node counts for dictionary benchmarks

Compared to ZDDs, representing the lists by CBDDs incurs some penalty (2.05–2.10), but less than the worst-case penalty of 3. Increasing the radix from a compact form to the full ASCII character set causes a significant increase in BDD size, but this effect is eliminated by using the zero suppression capabilities of CBDDs, ZDDs, and CZDDs.

Using a binary encoding of the symbols reduces the variances between the different encodings and DD types. CBDDs provide only a small benefit (1.11–1.23) over BDDs, and CBDDs are within a factor of 1.50 of ZDDs. Again, chaining of ZDDs provides no benefit. Observe that for both lists, the most efficient representation is to use either ZDDs or CZDDs with a one-hot encoding. The next best is to use CBDDs with a one-hot encoding, and all three of these are insensitive to changes in radix. These cases demonstrate the ability of ZDDs (and CZDDs) to use very large, sparse encodings of values. By using chaining, CBDDs can also take advantage of this property.

Although the final node counts for the benchmarks indicate no advantage of chaining for ZDDs, statistics characterizing the effort required to derive the functions show a significant benefit. Figure 8 indicates the total number of operations and the total time required for generating ZDD and CZDD representations of the benchmarks. The operations are computed as the number of times the program checks for an entry in the operation cache (step 2 in the description of the APPLY algorithm). There are many operational factors that can affect the number of operations, including the program's policies for operation caching and garbage collection. Nevertheless, it is some indication of the amount of activity required to generate the DDs. We can see that chaining reduces the number of operations by factors of 8.87–13.30. The time required depends on many attributes of the DD package and the system hardware and software. Here we see that chaining improves the execution time by factors of 1.35–15.26.

With unchained ZDDs, many of the intermediate functions have large DON'T-CARE chains. For example, the ZDD representation of the function x, for variable x, requires $n+2$ nodes—one for the variable, $n-1$ for the DON'T-CARE chains

One-hot	Operations			Time (secs.)		
	ZDD	CZDD	Ratio	ZDD	CZDD	Ratio
Compact word list	142,227,877	12,097,435	11.76	48.78	15.04	3.24
ASCII word list	375,195,184	28,574,814	13.13	173.56	21.84	7.95
Compact password list	806,017,001	62,785,274	12.84	713.15	46.73	15.26
ASCII password list	1,383,534,557	104,059,626	13.30	658.21	57.81	11.39

Binary	Operations			Time (secs.)		
	ZDD	CZDD	Ratio	ZDD	CZDD	Ratio
Compact word list	15,701,738	1,826,171	8.60	13.11	9.70	1.35
ASCII word list	20,921,746	2,139,574	9.78	14.40	10.20	1.41
Compact password list	66,489,058	7,499,615	8.87	52.52	30.62	1.72
ASCII password list	75,556,080	7,936,321	9.52	50.77	30.33	1.67

Fig. 8. Impact of chaining on effort required to generate DD representations of word lists.

before and after the variable, and two leaf nodes. With chaining, this function reduces to just four nodes: the upper DON'T-CARE chain is incorporated into the node for the variable, and a second node encodes the lower chain. Our dictionary benchmarks have over 4,000 variables, and so some of the intermediate DDs can be more than 1,000 times more compact due to chaining.

7.2 The 15-Queens Problem

A second set of benchmarks involved representing all possible solutions to the n-queens problem [12] as a Boolean function. This problem attempts to place n queens on a $n \times n$ chessboard in such a way that no two queens can attack each other. For our benchmark we chose $n = 15$ to stay within the memory limit of the processor being used.

Once again, there are two choices for encoding the positions of queens on the board. A *one-hot* encoding uses a Boolean variable for each square. A *binary* encoding uses $\lceil \log_2 n \rceil = 4$ variables for each row, encoding the position of the queen within the row.

Our most successful approach for encoding the constraints with Boolean operations worked from the bottom row to the top. At each level, it generated formulas for each column and diagonal expressing whether it was occupied in the rows at or below this one, based on the formulas for the level below and the variables for the present row.

We considered two ways of ordering the variables for the different rows. The *top-down* ordering listed the variables according to the row numbers 1 through 15. The *center-first* ordering listed variables according to the following row number sequence:

$$8, 9, 7, 10, 6, 11, 5, 12, 4, 13, 3, 14, 2, 15, 1.$$

Our hope was that ordering the center rows first would reduce the DD representation size. This proved not to be the case, but the resulting node counts are instructive.

One-hot		Node counts			Ratios	
Ordering	Graph(s)	BDD	CBDD	CZDD	BDD:CBDD	CBDD:CZDD
Top-down	Final	51,889,029	10,529,738	4,796,504	4.93	2.20
Top-down	Peak	165,977,497	39,591,936	18,625,659	4.19	2.13
Center-first	Final	65,104,658	12,628,086	5,749,613	5.16	2.20
Center-first	Peak	175,907,712	42,045,602	19,434,105	4.18	2.16

Binary		Node counts			Ratios	
Ordering	Graph(s)	BDD	CBDD	CZDD	BDD:CBDD	CBDD:CZDD
Top-down	Final	13,683,076	11,431,403	7,383,739	1.20	1.55
Top-down	Peak	43,954,472	38,898,146	26,682,980	1.13	1.46
Center-first	Final	17,121,947	14,185,276	9,054,115	1.21	1.57
Center-first	Peak	46,618,943	41,362,659	28,195,596	1.13	1.47

Fig. 9. Node counts and ratios of node counts for 15-queens benchmarks

Figure 9 shows the node counts for the different benchmarks. It shows both the size of the final function representing all solutions to the 15-queens problem, as well as the peak size, computed as the maximum across all rows of the combined size of the functions that are maintained to express the constraints imposed by the row and those below it. For both the top-down and the center-first benchmarks, this maximum was reached after completing row 3. Typically the peak size was around three times larger than the final size.

For a one-hot encoding, we can see that CBDDs achieve factors of 4.18–5.16 compaction over BDDs, and they come within a factor of 2.20 of CZDDs. For a binary encoding, the levels of compaction are much less compelling (1.13–1.20), as is the advantage of CZDDs over BDDs. It is worth noting that the combination of a one-hot encoding and chaining gives lower peak and final sizes than BDDs with a binary encoding.

One-hot		Node counts		Ratios
Ordering	Graph(s)	ZDD	CZDD	ZDD:CZDD
Top-down	Final	4,796,504	4,796,504	1.00
Top-down	Peak	18,632,019	18,625,659	1.00
Center-first	Final	5,749,613	5,749,613	1.00
Center-first	Peak	73,975,637	19,434,105	3.81

Binary		Node counts		Ratios
Ordering	Graph(s)	ZDD	CZDD	ZDD:CZDD
Top-down	Final	7,383,739	7,383,739	1.00
Top-down	Peak	26,684,315	26,682,980	1.00
Center-first	Final	9,054,115	9,054,115	1.00
Center-first	Peak	33,739,362	28,195,596	1.20

Fig. 10. Effect of chaining for ZDD representations of 15-queens benchmarks

	Node counts			Ratios	
Circuit	BDD	ZDD	CZDD	ZDD:BDD	CZDD:BDD
c432	31,321	48,224	41,637	1.54	1.33
c499	49,061	49,983	48,878	1.02	1.00
c880	23,221	52,436	32,075	2.26	1.38
c1908	17,391	18,292	17,017	1.05	0.98
c2670	67,832	261,736	85,900	3.86	1.27
c3540	3,345,341	4,181,847	3,538,982	1.25	1.06
c5315	636,305	898,912	681,440	1.41	1.07
c6288	48,181,908	48,331,495	48,329,117	1.00	1.00
c7552	4,537	37,689	4,774	8.31	1.05

Fig. 11. Node counts and ratios of node counts for digital circuit benchmarks

Figure 10 compares the sizes of the ZDD and CZDD representations of the 15-queens functions. We can see that the final sizes are identical—there are no DON'T-CARE chains in the functions encoding problem solutions. For the top-down ordering, CZDDs also offer only a small advantage for the peak requirement. For the center-first ordering, especially with a one-hot encoding, however, we can see that CZDDs are significantly (3.81×) more compact. As the construction for row 3 completes, the variables that will encode the constraints for rows 2 and 5 remain unconstrained, yielding many DON'T-CARE chains. Once again, this phenomenon is much smaller with a binary encoding.

7.3 Digital Circuits

BDDs are commonly used in digital circuit design automation, for such tasks as verification, test generation, and circuit synthesis. We selected the circuits in the ISCAS '85 benchmark suite [3]. These were originally developed as benchmarks for test generation, but they have also been widely used as benchmarks for BDDs [7,10]. We generated variable orderings for all but last two benchmarks by traversing the circuit graphs, using the fanin heuristic of [10]. Circuit c6288 implements a 16 × 16 multiplier. For this circuit, the ordering of inputs listed in the file provided a feasible variable ordering, while the one generated by traversing the circuit exceeded the memory limits of our machine. For c7552, neither the ordering in the file, nor that provided by traversing the graph, generated a feasible order. Instead, we manually generated an ordering based on our analysis of a reverse-engineered version of the circuit described in [8]

Figure 11 presents data on the sizes of the DDs to represent all of the circuit outputs. We do not present any data for CBDDs, since these were all close in size to BDDs. We can see that the ZDD representations for these circuits are always larger than the BDD representations, by factors ranging up to 8.31. Using CZDDs mitigates that effect, yielding a maximum size ratio of 1.38.

8 Observations

Our experiments, while not comprehensive, demonstrate that chaining can allow BDDs to make use of large, sparse encodings, one of the main strengths of ZDDs. They also indicate that CZDDs may be the best choice overall. CZDDs have all of the advantages of ZDDs, while avoiding the risk of intermediate functions growing excessively large due to DON'T-CARE chains. They are guaranteed to stay within a factor of 2× of BDDs. Even for digital circuit functions, we found this bound to be conservative—all of the benchmarks stayed within a factor of 1.4×.

Acknowledgements. This work was supported, in part, by NSF STARSS grant 1525527.

References

1. Bahar, R.I., Frohm, E.A., Gaona, C.M., Hachtel, G.D., Macii, E., Pardo, A., Somenzi, F.: Algebraic decision diagrams and their applications. In: Proceedings of the International Conference on Computer-Aided Design, pp. 188–191, November 1993
2. Brace, K.S., Rudell, R.L., Bryant, R.E.: Efficient implementation of a BDD package. In: Proceedings of the 27th ACM/IEEE Design Automation Conference, pp. 40–45, June 1990
3. Brglez, F., Fujiwara, H.: A neutral netlist of 10 combinational benchmark circuits and a target translator in Fortran. In: 1985 International Symposium on Circuits And Systems (1985)
4. Bryant, R.E.: Graph-based algorithms for Boolean function manipulation. IEEE Trans. Comput. **C-35**(8), 677–691 (1986)
5. Bryant, R.E.: Binary decision diagrams. In: Clarke, E.M., Henzinger, T.A., Veith, H., Bloem, R. (eds.) Handbook of Model Checking. Springer, Heidelberg (2017). https://doi.org/10.1007/978-3-319-10575-8
6. van Dijk, T., Wille, R., Meolic, R.: Tagged BDDs: combining reduction rules from different decision diagram types. In: Formal Methods in Computer-Aided Design, pp. 108–115 (2017)
7. Fujita, M., Fujisawa, H., Kawato, N.: Evaluation and improvements of Boolean comparison method based on binary decision diagrams. In: Proceedings of the International Conference on Computer-Aided Design, pp. 2–5, November 1988
8. Hansen, M., Yalcin, H., Hayes, J.P.: Unveiling the ISCAS-85 benchmarks: a case study in reverse engineering. IEEE Des. Test **16**(3), 72–80 (1999)
9. Knuth, D.E.: The Art of Computer Programming: Combinatorial Algorithms, Part I, vol. 4A. Addison Wesley, Reading (2011)
10. Malik, S., Wang, A., Brayton, R.K., Sangiovanni-Vincentelli, A.L.: Logic verification using binary decision diagrams in a logic synthesis environment. In: Proceedings of the International Conference on Computer-Aided Design, pp. 6–9, November 1988
11. Minato, S.: Zero-suppressed BDDs for set manipulation in combinatorial problems. In: Proceedings of the 30th ACM/IEEE Design Automation Conference, pp. 272–277, June 1993

12. Minato, S.: Binary Decision Diagrams and Applications for VLSI CAD. Kluwer Academic Publishers, Norwell (1995)
13. Minato, S., Ishiura, N., Yajima, S.: Shared binary decision diagrams with attributed edges for efficient Boolean function manipulation. In: Proceedings of the 27th ACM/IEEE Design Automation Conference, pp. 52–57, June 1990
14. Somenzi, F.: Efficient manipulation of decision diagrams. Int. J. Softw. Tools Technol. Transf. **3**(2), 171–181 (2001)

CDCLSym: Introducing Effective Symmetry Breaking in SAT Solving

Hakan Metin[1(✉)], Souheib Baarir[1,2,3], Maximilien Colange[3], and Fabrice Kordon[1]

[1] Sorbonne Université, CNRS UMR 7606 LIP6, 75005 Paris, France
hakan.metin@lip6.fr
[2] Université Paris Nanterre, Nanterre, France
[3] LRDE, EPITA, Le Kremlin-Bicêtre, France

Abstract. SAT solvers are now widely used to solve a large variety of problems, including formal verification of systems. SAT problems derived from such applications often exhibit symmetry properties that could be exploited to speed up their solving. *Static symmetry breaking* is so far the most popular approach to take advantage of symmetries. It relies on a symmetry preprocessor which augments the initial problem with constraints that force the solver to consider only a few configurations among the many symmetric ones.

This paper presents a new way to handle symmetries, that avoid the main problem of the current static approaches: the prohibitive cost of the preprocessing phase. Our proposal has been implemented in `MiniSym`. Extensive experiments on the benchmarks of last six SAT competitions show that our approach is competitive with the best state-of-the-art static symmetry breaking solutions.

Keywords: Boolean satisfiability · Static symmetry breaking Dynamic symmetry breaking · Symmetry based reduction

1 Introduction

Nowadays, Boolean satisfiability (SAT) is an active research area finding its applications in many contexts such as planning decision [14], hardware and software verification [3], cryptology [19], computational biology [17], etc. Hence, the development of approaches that could treat increasingly challenging SAT problems has become a focus.

State-of-the-art complete solvers of SAT problems are based on the well-known *Conflict Driven Clauses Learning (CDCL)* algorithm [18], itself inspired from the Davis–Putnam–Logemann–Loveland algorithm [6]. These are complete backtracking based search algorithms that welcome any heuristic/optimisation

The datasets generated during and/or analysed during the current study are available in the figshare repository: https://doi.org/10.6084/m9.figshare.5901025.v1.

D. Beyer and M. Huisman (Eds.): TACAS 2018, LNCS 10805, pp. 99–114, 2018.
https://doi.org/10.1007/978-3-319-89960-2_6

pruning of parts of the explored search tree. In this paper, we are interested in exploiting the symmetry properties of SAT problems to perform such a pruning.

Symmetries in SAT Solving. SAT problems often exhibit symmetries[1], and not taking them into account forces solvers to needlessly explore isomorphic parts of the search space.

For example, the "pigeonhole problem" (where n pigeons are put into $n - 1$ holes, with the constraint that each pigeon must be in a different hole) is a highly symmetric problem. Indeed, all the pigeons (resp. holes) are swappable without changing the initial problem. Trying to solve it with a standard SAT solver, like MiniSAT [10], turns out to be very time consuming (and even impossible, in reasonable time, for high values of n). Here, such a standard solver ignores the symmetry property of the problem, and then potentially tries all variables combinations; this eventually leads to a combinatorial explosion.

Symmetries of a SAT problem are classically obtained through a reduction to an equivalent graph automorphism problem. Technically, the SAT problem is converted to a colored graph, then it is passed to a tool, like `saucy3` [13] or `bliss` [12], to compute its automorphism group.

A common approach to exploit such symmetries is to pre-compute and enrich the original SAT problem with *symmetry breaking predicates (sbp)*. These added predicates will prevent the solver from visiting equivalent (isomorphic) parts that eventually yield the same results [1,5]. This technique, called *static symmetry breaking*, has been implemented first in the state-of-the-art tool `SHATTER` [2] and then improved in `BREAKID` [8]. However, while giving excellent results on numerous symmetric problems, these approaches still fail to solve some classes of symmetric problems.

Another class of approaches exists, known as *dynamic symmetry breaking* techniques. They intervene directly during the search exploration. It concerns, to mention but a few, the injection of symmetric versions of *learned clauses* [7,21], particular classes of symmetries [20], or speeding up the search by inferring symmetric facts [9]. These approaches succeeded in treating particular and hand crafted problems but, to the best of our knowledge, none of them is competitive face to the *static symmetry breaking* methods.

Drawbacks of the Static-Based Approaches. In the general case, the size of the *sbp* can be exponential in the number of variables of the problem so that they cannot be totally computed. Even in more favorable situations, the size of the generated *sbp* is often too large to be effectively handled by a SAT solver [15]. On the other hand, if only a subset of the symmetries is considered then the resulting search pruning will not be that interesting and its effectiveness depends heavily on the heuristically chosen symmetries [4]. Besides, these approaches are preprocessors, so their combination with other techniques, such as *symmetry*

[1] Roughly speaking, a SAT problem exhibits symmetries when it is possible to swap some variables while keeping the original problem unchanged.

propagation [9], can be very hard. Also, tuning their parameters during the solving turns out to be very difficult. For all these reasons, some classes of SAT problems cannot be solved yet despite exhibiting symmetries.

Proposed Solution. To handle these issues, we propose a new approach that reuses the principles of the static approaches, but operates dynamically: the symmetries are broken during the search process without any pre-generation of the *sbp*. To do so, we elaborate the notions of *symmetry status tracking* and *effective symmetric breaking predicates* (*esbp*).

The approach is implemented using a couple of components: (1) a *Conflict Driven Clauses Learning (CDCL) search engine*; (2) *a symmetry controller*. Roughly speaking, the first component performs the classical search activity on the SAT problem, while the second observes the engine and maintains the status of the symmetries. When the controller detects a situation where the engine is starting to explore a redundant part[2], it orders the engine to operate a backjump. The detection is performed thanks to *symmetry status tracking* and the backjump order is given by a simple injection of an *esbp* computed on the fly.

The main advantage of such an approach is to cope with the heavy (and potentially blocking) pre-generation phase of the static-based approaches, but also offers opportunities to combine with other dynamic-based approaches, like the *symmetry propagation* technique [9]. It also gives more flexibility for adjusting some parameters on the fly. Moreover, the overhead for non symmetric formulas is reduced to the computation time of the graph automorphism.

The extensive evaluation of our approach on the symmetric formulas of the last six SAT contests shows that it outperforms the state-of-the-art techniques, in particular on unsatisfiable instances, which are the hardest class of the problem.

Content of the Paper. The remainder of the paper is organized as follows. Section 2 is dedicated to preliminaries and definitions. Section 3 discusses the details of our CDCLSym algorithm. Section 4 highlights our tooling support and evaluations. Section 5 concludes this work and gives directions for future work.

2 Preliminaries and Definitions

This section introduces some definitions. First, we define the problem of Boolean satisfiability. Then, we introduce the notions of ordering and monotonicity that provide a lexicographical order to assignments. These are central concepts to the definition of a representative assignment.

Finally, we introduce two core notions that are required to define our new algorithm: (i) *Reducer, inactive and active permutation*, and (ii) the *effective symmetry breaking predicates* (*esbp*).

[2] Isomorphic to a part that has been/will be explored.

2.1 Basics on Boolean Satisfiability

A *Boolean variable*, or *propositional variable*, is a variable that has two possible values: true or false (noted $\top$ or $\bot$, respectively). A *literal* l is a propositional variable or its negation. For a given variable x, the positive literal is represented by x and the negative one by $\neg x$. A *clause* ω is a finite disjunction of literals represented equivalently by $\omega = \bigvee_{i=1}^{k} l_i$ or the set of its literals $\omega = \{l_i\}_{i \in [\![1,k]\!]}$. A clause with a single literal is called *unit clause*. A *conjunctive normal form (CNF) formula* φ is a finite conjunction of clauses. A CNF can be either noted $\varphi = \bigwedge_{i=1}^{k} \omega_i$ or $\varphi = \{\omega_i\}_{i \in [\![1,k]\!]}$. We denote $\mathcal{V}_\varphi$ ($\mathcal{L}_\varphi$) the set of variables (literals) used in φ (the index in $\mathcal{V}_\varphi$ and $\mathcal{L}_\varphi$ is usually omitted when clear from context).

For a given formula φ, an *assignment* of the variables of φ is a function $\alpha : \mathcal{V} \mapsto \{\top, \bot\}$. As usual, α is *total*, or *complete*, when all elements of $\mathcal{V}$ have an image by α, otherwise it is *partial*. By abuse of notation, an assignment is often represented by the set of its true literals. The set of all (possibly partial) assignments of $\mathcal{V}$ is noted $Ass(\mathcal{V})$.

The assignment α *satisfies* the clause ω, denoted $\alpha \models \omega$, if $\alpha \cap \omega \neq \emptyset$. Similarly, the assignment α satisfies the propositional formula φ, denoted $\alpha \models \varphi$, if α satisfies all the clauses of φ. Note that a formula may be satisfied by a partial assignment. A formula is said to be *satisfiable* (SAT) if there is at least one assignment that satisfies it; otherwise the formula is *unsatisfiable* (UNSAT).

Example. Let $\varphi = \{\{x_1, x_2, x_3\}, \{x_1, \neg x_2\}, \{\neg x_1, \neg x_2\}\}$ be a formula. φ is satisfied under the assignment $\alpha = \{x_1, \neg x_2\}$ (meaning $\alpha(x_1) = \top$ and $\alpha(x_2) = \bot$) and is reported to be SAT. Note that the assignment α, making φ SAT, does not need to be complete because x_3 is a *don't care variable* with respect to α.

2.2 Ordering and Monotonicity

In order to exploit the symmetry properties of a SAT problem, we need to introduce an ordering relation between the assignments.

Definition 1 (Assignments ordering). *We assume a total order, $\prec$, on $\mathcal{V}$. Given two assignments $(\alpha, \beta) \in Ass(\mathcal{V})^2$, we say that α is strictly smaller than β, noted $\alpha < \beta$, if there exists a variable $v \in \mathcal{V}$ such that:*

- *for all $v' \prec v$, either $v' \in \alpha \cap \beta$ or $\neg v' \in \alpha \cap \beta$.*
- *$\neg v \in \alpha$ and $v \in \beta$.*[3]

Note that $<$ coincides with the lexicographical order on *complete* assignments. Furthermore, the $<$ relation is monotonic as expressed in the following proposition.

Proposition 1 (Monotonicity of assignments ordering). *Let $(\alpha, \alpha', \beta, \beta') \in Ass(\mathcal{V})^4$ be four assignments.*

$$If\ \alpha \subseteq \alpha'\ and\ \beta \subseteq \beta',\ then\ \alpha < \beta \implies \alpha' < \beta'$$

[3] We could have chosen as well $v \in \alpha$ and $\neg v \in \beta$ without loss of generality.

Proof. The proposition follows on directly from Definition 1.

It is worth noting that this last proposition is the key property for the efficient implementation of our algorithm.

2.3 Symmetry Group of a Formula

The group of permutations of $\mathcal{V}$ (i.e. bijections from $\mathcal{V}$ to $\mathcal{V}$) is noted $\mathfrak{S}(\mathcal{V})$. The group $\mathfrak{S}(\mathcal{V})$ naturally acts on the set of literals: for $g \in \mathfrak{S}(\mathcal{V})$ and a literal $\ell \in \mathcal{L}$, $g.\ell = g(\ell)$ if ℓ is a positive literal, $g.\ell = \neg g(\neg \ell)$ if ℓ is a negative literal. The group $\mathfrak{S}(\mathcal{V})$ also acts on (partial) assignments of $\mathcal{V}$ as follows: for $g \in \mathfrak{S}(\mathcal{V})$, $\alpha \in Ass(\mathcal{V})$, $g.\alpha = \{g.\ell \mid \ell \in \alpha\}$. Let φ be a formula, and $g \in \mathfrak{S}(\mathcal{V})$. We say that $g \in \mathfrak{S}(\mathcal{V})$ is a symmetry of φ if for every *complete* assignment α, $\alpha \models \varphi$ if and only if $g.\alpha \models \varphi$. The set of symmetries of φ is noted $S(\varphi) \subseteq \mathfrak{S}(\mathcal{V})$.

Let G be a subgroup of $\mathfrak{S}(\mathcal{V})$. The *orbit of α under* G (or simply the *orbit of* α when G is clear from the context) is the set $[\alpha]_G = \{g.\alpha \mid g \in G\}$. The lexicographic leader (*lex-leader* for short) of an orbit $[\alpha]_G$ is defined by $min_<([\alpha]_G)$. This *lex-leader* is unique because the lexicographic order is a total order.

The optimal approach to solve a symmetric SAT problem would be to explore only one assignment per orbit (for instance each *lex-leader*). However, finding the *lex-leader* of an orbit is computationally hard [16].

What we propose here is a best effort approach that tries to eliminate, *dynamically*, the *non lex-leading* assignments with a minimal computation effort. To do so, we first introduce the notions of *reducer*, *inactive* and *active* permutation with respect to an assignment α.

Definition 2 (Reducer, inactive and active permutation). *A permutation g is a* reducer *of an assignment α if $g.\alpha < \alpha$ (hence α cannot be the lex-leader of its orbit. g reduces it and all its extensions). g is* inactive *on α when $\alpha < g.\alpha$ (so, g cannot reduce α and all the extensions). A symmetry is said to be* active *with respect to α when it is neither inactive nor a reducer of α.*

Proposition 2 restates this definition in terms of variables and is the basis of an efficient algorithm to keep track of the status of a permutation during the solving. Let us, first, recall that the *support*, $\mathcal{V}_g$, of a permutation g is the set $\{v \in \mathcal{V} \mid g(v) \neq v\}$.

Proposition 2. *Let $\alpha \in Ass(\mathcal{V})$ be an assignment, $g \in \mathfrak{S}(\mathcal{V})$ a permutation and $\mathcal{V}_g \subseteq \mathcal{V}$ the support of g. We say that g is:*

1. a reducer *of α if there exists a variable $v \in \mathcal{V}_g$ such that:*
   - *$\forall\, v' \in \mathcal{V}_g$, s. t. $v' \prec v$, either $\{v', g^{-1}(v')\} \subseteq \alpha$ or $\{\neg v', \neg g^{-1}(v')\} \subseteq \alpha$,*
   - *$\{v, \neg g^{-1}(v)\} \subseteq \alpha$;*
2. inactive *on α if there exists a variable $v \in \mathcal{V}_g$ such that:*
   - *$\forall\, v' \in \mathcal{V}_g$, s. t. $v' \prec v$, either $\{v', g^{-1}(v')\} \subseteq \alpha$ or $\{\neg v', \neg g^{-1}(v')\} \subseteq \alpha$,*
   - *$\{\neg v, g^{-1}(v)\} \subseteq \alpha$;*
3. active *on α, otherwise.*

When g is a *reducer* of α we can define a predicate that contradicts α yet preserves the satisfiability of the formula. Such a predicate will be used to discard α, and all its extensions, from a further visit and hence pruning the search tree.

Definition 3 (Effective Symmetry Breaking Predicate). *Let $\alpha \in Ass(\mathcal{V})$, and $g \in \mathfrak{S}(\mathcal{V})$. We say that the formula ψ is an effective symmetry breaking predicate (esbp for short) for α under g if:*

$$\alpha \not\models \psi \text{ and for all } \beta \in Ass(\mathcal{V}), \beta \not\models \psi \Rightarrow g.\beta < \beta$$

The next definition gives a way to obtain such an effective symmetry-breaking predicate from an assignment and a reducer.

Definition 4 (A construction of an *esbp*). *Let φ be a formula. Let g be a symmetry of φ that reduces an assignment α. Let v be the variable whose existence is given by item 1. in Proposition 2. Let $U = \{v', \neg v' \mid v' \in \mathcal{V}_g \text{ and } v' \preceq v\}$. We define $\eta(\alpha, g)$ as $(U \cup g^{-1}.U) \setminus \alpha$.*

Example. Let us consider $\mathcal{V} = \{x_1, x_2, x_3, x_4, x_5\}$, $g = (x_1\, x_3)(x_2\, x_4)$, and a partial assignment $\alpha = \{x_1, x_2, x_3, \neg x_4\}$. Then, $g.\alpha = \{x_1, \neg x_2, x_3, x_4\}$ and $v = x_2$. So, $U = \{x_1, \neg x_1, x_2, \neg x_2\}$ and $g^{-1}.U = \{x_3, \neg x_3, x_4, \neg x_4\}$ and we can deduce than $\eta(\alpha, g) = (U \cup g^{-1}.U) \setminus \alpha = \{\neg x_1, \neg x_2, \neg x_3, x_4\}$.

Proposition 3. *$\eta(\alpha, g)$ is an effective symmetry-breaking predicate.*

Proof. It is immediate that $\alpha \not\models \eta(\alpha, g)$.

Let $\beta \in Ass(\mathcal{V})$ such that $\beta \wedge \eta(\alpha, g)$ is UNSAT. We denote a α' and β' as the restrictions of α and β to the variables in $\{v' \in \mathcal{V}_g \mid v' \preceq v\}$. Since $\beta \wedge \eta(\alpha, g)$ is UNSAT, $\alpha' = \beta'$. But $g.\alpha' < \alpha'$, and $g.\beta' < \beta'$. By monotonicity of $<$, we thus also have $g.\beta < \beta$.

It is important to observe that the notion of *ebsp* is a refinement of the classical concept of *sbp* defined in [2]. In particular, like *sbp*, *esbp* preserve satisfiability.

Theorem 1 (Satisfiability preservation). *Let φ be a formula and ψ an ebsp for some assignment α under $g \in S(\varphi)$. Then,*

$$\varphi \text{ and } \varphi \wedge \psi \text{ are equi-satisfiable.}$$

Proof. If $\varphi \wedge \psi$ is SAT then φ is trivially SAT. If φ is SAT, then there is some assignment β that satisfies φ. Without loss of generality, β can be chosen to be the lex-leader of its orbit under $S(\varphi)$. Thus, g does not reduce β, which implies that $\beta \models \psi$.

3 CDCLSym Algorithm

This section describes how to augment the state-of-the-art CDCL algorithm with the aforementioned concepts to develop an efficient symmetry-guided SAT solving algorithm. We first recall how the CDCL algorithm works. We then explain how to extend it with a *symmetry controller* component which guides the behavior of CDCL algorithm depending on the status of symmetries.

3.1 Classical CDCL

A Conflict-Driven Clause Learning (CDCL) algorithm is depicted in Algorithm 1. The parts in red (grey in B&W printings) should be ignored for the moment.

The algorithm walks a binary search tree. It first applies unit propagation to the formula φ for the current assignment α (line 4). A conflict at level 0 indicates that the formula is not satisfiable, and the algorithm reports it (lines 8–9). If a conflict is detected, it is analyzed, which provides a *conflict clause* explaining the reason for the conflict (line 11). This clause is learnt (line 14), as it does not change the satisfiability of φ, and avoids encountering a conflict with the same causes in the future. The analysis is completed by the computation of a backjump point to which the algorithm backtracks (line 15). Finally, if no conflict appears, the algorithm chooses a new decision literal (line 18–19). The above steps are repeated until the satisfiability status of the formula is determined.

It is out of the scope of this paper to detail the existing variations for the conflict analysis and for the decision heuristic.

```
1  function CDCLSym(φ: CNF formula, SymController: symmetry controller)
     returns ⊤ if φ is SAT and ⊥ otherwise
2    dl ← 0 ;                                          // Current decision level
3    while not all variables are assigned do
4        isConflict ← unitPropagation();
5        SymController.updateAssign(currentAssignment());
6        isReduced ← SymController.isNotLexLeader(currentAssignment());
7        if isConflict || isReduced then
8            if dl == 0 then
9                return ⊥;                             // φ is UNSAT
10           if isConflict then
11               ω ← analyzeConflict();
12           else
13               ω ← SymController.generateEsbp(currentAssignment());
14           addLearntClause(ω);
15           dl ← backjumpAndRestartPolicies();
16           SymController.updateCancel(currentAssignment());
17       else
18           assignDecisionLiteral();
19           dl ← dl + 1;
20   return ⊤;                                         // φ is SAT
```

Algorithm 1. The CDCLSym SAT Solving Algorithm.

3.2 Symmetry-Guided Search

As explained earlier, the main problem of the static approaches is that they generate many *sbp* that are not effective in the solving (size of the generated formulas, overburden of the unit propagation procedure, etc.).

The idea we bring is to break symmetries *on the fly*: when the current partial assignment can not be a prefix of a *lex-leader* (of an orbit), an *esbp* (see Definition 3) that prunes this forbidden assignment and all its extensions is generated.

We implement this approach using two components that communicate with each other: the SAT-solving engine itself, and a *symmetry controller*. The symmetry controller is initially given a set of symmetries G[4]. It observes the behavior of the SAT engine and updates its internal data according to the current assignment, to keep track of the status of the symmetries. This observation is *incremental*: whenever a literal is assigned or cancelled, the symmetry controller updates the status of all the symmetries. This corresponds to lines 5 and 16 of Algorithm 1. When the controller detects that the current assignment can not be a *lex-leader* (line 6), it generates the corresponding *esbp* (line 13).

In the remainder of this section, we detail the functions composing the symmetry controller.

Symmetries Status Tracking. The `updateAssign`, `updateCancel` and `isNotLexLeader` functions (see Algorithm 2) track the status of symmetries based on Proposition 2; there, resides the core of our algorithm.

All these functions rely on the *pt* structure: a map of variables indexed by permutations. Initially, $pt[g] = \min(\mathcal{V}_g)$ for all $g \in G$ and all permutations are marked *active*.

For each permutation, g, the symmetry controller keeps track of the smallest variable $pt[g]$ in the support of g such that $pt[g]$ and $g^{-1}(pt[g])$ do not have the same value in the current assignment. If one of the two variables is not assigned, they are considered not to have the same value.

When new literals are assigned, only active symmetries need to have their $pt[g]$ updated (line 2). This update is done thanks to a while loop (lines 4–5).

When literals are cancelled, we need to update the status of symmetries for which some variable v before $pt[g]$, or $g^{-1}(v)$, becomes unassigned (lines 9–10). Symmetries that were inactive may be reactivated (line 11).

The current assignment is not a *lex-leader* if some symmetry g is a reducer. This is detected by comparing the value of $pt[g]$ with the value of $g^{-1}(pt[g])$ (line 16). The function `isNotLexLeader` also marks symmetries as *inactive* when appropriate (lines 18–19).

Generation of the *esbp*. When the current assignment cannot be a *lex-leader*, some symmetry g is a reducer. The function `generateEsbp` computes the

[4] The generators of the group of symmetries.

```
function updateAssign(α: assignment)
    foreach active g ∈ G do
        v ← pt[g];
        while {v, g⁻¹(v)} ⊆ α or {¬v, ¬g⁻¹(v)} ⊆ α do
            v ← next variable in V_g;
        pt[g] ← v

function updateCancel(α: assignment)
    foreach g ∈ G do
        u ← min{v ∈ V_g | {v, ¬v} ∩ α = ∅ or {g⁻¹(v), ¬g⁻¹(v)} ∩ α = ∅};
        if u ⪯ pt[g] then
            mark g as active;
            pt[g] ← u;

function isNotLexLeader(α: assignment)
    foreach active g ∈ G do
        v ← pt[g];
        if {v, ¬g⁻¹(v)} ⊆ α then
            return ⊤;                          // g is a reducer
        if {¬v, g⁻¹(v)} ⊆ α then
            mark g as inactive ;   // g can't reduce α or its extentions
    return ⊥

function generateEsbp(α: assignment) returns ω: generated esbp
    ω ← {};
    g ← the reducer of α detected in isNotLexLeader;
    v ← min(V_g);
    u ← pt[g];
    while u ≠ v do
        if v ∈ α then ω ← ω ∪ {¬v} else ω ← ω ∪ {v};
        if g⁻¹(v) ∈ α then ω ← ω ∪ {¬g⁻¹(v)} else ω ← ω ∪ {g⁻¹(v)};
        v ← next variable in V_g
    ω ← ω ∪ {¬v, g⁻¹(v)};
    return ω
```

Algorithm 2. The functions keeping track of the status of the symmetries and generating the *esbp*.

$\eta(\alpha, g)$ defined in Definition 4, which is an effective symmetry-breaking predicate by Proposition 3. This will prevent the SAT engine to explore further the current partial assignment.

3.3 *Lex-leader* Forcing

Our algorithm prevents as much as possible the solver from visiting *non lex-leaders* assignments. To do so, we propose an additional heuristic that delays the visit of *non lex-leaders* partial assignments.

Let us consider a permutation g and an assignment α. Assume there exists a variable $v \in \mathcal{V}_g$, with, for all $v' \in \mathcal{V}_g$, such that $v' \prec v$, either $\{v', g^{-1}(v')\} \subseteq \alpha$ or $\{\neg v', \neg g^{-1}(v')\} \subseteq \alpha$ and $v \in \alpha$. Let $\alpha' = \alpha \cup \{\neg g^{-1}(v)\}$. Then g is a reducer of α', which would generate $\eta(\alpha', g)$ (Proposition 2 and Definition 4).

A way to prevent α from becoming a *non lex-leader* is to force the literal $g^{-1}(v)$ into α. This can be easily done by learning $\eta(\alpha', g)$ when the current assignment is α. The same reasoning holds when $\neg g^{-1}(v) \in \alpha$ and $v \notin \alpha$.

3.4 Illustrative Example

Let us illustrate the previous concepts and algorithms on a simple example. Let $\mathcal{V} = \{v_1 \prec v_2 \prec v_3 \prec v_4 \prec v_5 \prec v_6\}$, and a set of symmetries $G = \{g_1 = (v_1 v_5 v_3)(v_2 v_4),\ g_2 = (v_1 v_6)(v_4 v_5)\}$ (written in cycle notation). Their respective supports are, $\mathcal{V}_{g_1} = \{v_1, v_2, v_3, v_4, v_5\}$ and $\mathcal{V}_{g_2} = \{v_1, v_4, v_5, v_6\}$.

On the assignment $\alpha = \emptyset$, both permutations are active and $pt[g_1] = pt[g_2] = v_1$. When the solver updates the assignment to $\alpha = \{v_6\}$, both permutations remain active and $pt[g_1] = pt[g_2] = v_1$. On the assignment $\alpha = \{v_6, v_1\}$, the symmetry controller updates $pt[g_2]$ to v_5, while $pt[g_1]$ remains unchanged. On the assignment $\alpha = \{v_6, v_1, \neg v_3\}$, $g_1.\alpha = \{v_6, v_5, \neg v_1\}$, which is smaller than α (because $v_1 \in \alpha$ and $\neg v_1 \in g.\alpha$): g_1 is a reducer of α. The symmetry controller then generates the corresponding *esbp* $\omega = \{\neg v_1, v_3\}$. Alternatively, when *lex-leader* forcing is active, from the assignment $\alpha = \{v_6, v_1\}$, the symmetry controller could force the value of the variable v_3, by learning the same *esbp* $\omega = \{\neg v_1, v_3\}$.

4 Implementation and Evaluation

In this section, we first highlight some details on our implementation of the symmetry controller. Then, we experimentally assess the performance of our algorithm against three other state-of-the-art tools.

4.1 cosy: An Efficient Implementation of the Symmetry Controller

We have implemented our method in a C++ library called cosy (1630 LoC). It implements a symmetry controller as described in the previous section, and can be interfaced with virtually any CDCL SAT solver. cosy is released under GPL v3 licence and is available at https://github.com/lip6/cosy.

Heuristics and Options. Let us recall that finding the optimal ordering of variables (with respect to the exploitation of symmetries) is NP-hard [15], so the choice for this ordering is heuristic. cosy offers several possibilities to define this ordering:

- a naive ordering, where variables are ordered by the lexicographic order of their names;

- an ordering based on occurrences, where variables are sorted according to the number of times they occur in the input formula. The lexicographic order of variables names is used for those having the same number of occurrences;
- an ordering based on symmetries, where variables belonging to the same orbit (under the given set of symmetries) are grouped together. Orbit are ordered by their numbers of occurrences.

The ordering of assignments we use in this paper orders negative literals before positive ones (thus, $\{\neg v\} < \{v\}$), but using the converse ordering does not change the overall method. However, it can impact the performance of the solver on some instances, so that it is an option of the library.

All the symmetries we used for the presentation of our approach are permutations of variables. Our method straightforwardly extends to permutations of literals, also known as *value permutations* [4]. Another option allows to activate the *lex-leader* forcing described in Sect. 3.3.

Integration in `MiniSAT`. We show how to integrate `cosy` to an existing solver, through example of `MiniSAT` [10].

First, we need an adapter that allows the communication between the solver and `cosy` (30 LoC). Then, we adapt Algorithm 1 to the different methods and functions of `MiniSAT`. In particular, the function `updateAssign` is moved into the `uncheckEnqueue` function of `MiniSAT` (2 LoC). The `updateCancel` function is moved to the `cancelUntil` function of `MiniSAT` that performs the backjumps (2 LoC). The `isNotLexLeader` and `generateEsbp` functions are integrated in the `propagate` function of `MiniSAT` (30 LoC). This is to keep track of the assignments as soon as they occur, then the *esbp* is produced as soon as an assignment is identified as not being *lex-leader*. Initialization issues are located in the main function of `MiniSAT` (15 LoC).

The integration of `cosy` increases `MiniSAT` code by 3%.

4.2 Evaluation

This section presents the evaluation of our approach. All experiments have been performed with our modified `MiniSAT` called `MiniSym`. The symmetries of the SAT problem instances have been computed by two different state-of-the-art tools `saucy3` [13] and `bliss` [12]. For a given group of symmetries, the first tool generates less permutations to represent the group than the second one, but it is slower than the other one.

We selected from the last six editions of the SAT contests [11], the CNF instances for which `bliss` finds at least 2% of the variables are involved in some symmetries that could be computed in at most 1000 s of CPU time. We obtained a total of 1350 symmetric instances (discarding repetitions) out of 3700 instances in total.

All experiments have been conducted using the following conditions: each solver has been run once on each instance, with a time-out of 5000 s (including the execution time of the symmetries generation except for `MiniSAT`) and limited to 8 GB of memory. Experiments were executed on a computer with an Intel Xeon X7460 2.66 GHz featuring 24 cores and 128 GB of memory, running a Linux 4.4.13, along with g++ compiler version 6.3.

We compare `MiniSym` using the occurrence order, value symmetries, and without *lex-leader* forcing, against:

- `MiniSAT`, as the reference solver without symmetry handling [10];
- `Shatter`, a symmetry breaking preprocessor described in [2], coupled with the `MiniSAT` SAT engine;
- `breakID`, another symmetry breaking preprocessor, described in [8], also coupled with the `MiniSAT` SAT engine.

Each SAT solution was successfully checked against the initial CNF. For UNSAT situations, there is no way to provide an UNSAT certificate in presence of symmetries. Nevertheless, we checked our results were also computed by the other measured tools. Unfortunately, out of the 1350 benchmarked formulas, we have no proof or evidence for the 15 UNSAT formulas computed by `MiniSym` only.

Results are presented in Tables 1, 2, and 3. We report the number of instances solved within the time and memory limits for each solver and category. We separate the UNSAT instances (Table 1) from the SAT ones (Table 2). Besides the reference with no symmetry (column `MiniSAT`), we have compared the performance of the three tools when using symmetries computed by `saucy3` (see Tables 1a and 2b), and `bliss` (see Tables 1a and 2b). Rows correspond to groups of instances: from each edition of the SAT contest, and when possible, we separated applicative instances (app$\langle x \rangle$ where $\langle x \rangle$ indicates the year) from hard combinatorial ones (hard$\langle x \rangle$). This separation was not possible for the editions 2015 and 2017 (all2015 and all2017). The total number of instances for each bench is indicated between parentheses. For each row, the cells corresponding to the tools solving the most instances (within time and memory limits) are typeset in bold and greyed out. Table 3 shows the cumulative and average PAR-2 times of the evaluated tools.

Table 1. Comparison of different approaches on the UNSAT instances of the benchmarks of the six last editions of the SAT competition.

Benchmark	MiniSAT	Shatter	BreakID	MiniSym
app2016 (134)	18	19	**20**	17
app2014 (161)	23	23	22	**24**
app2013 (145)	6	8	8	**10**
app2012 (367)	115	115	**120**	**120**
hard2016 (128)	8	17	**50**	42
hard2014 (107)	9	24	**30**	29
hard2013 (121)	12	24	**48**	29
hard2012 (289)	86	84	88	**93**
all2017 (124)	8	14	**15**	14
all2015 (65)	9	8	8	**10**
TOTAL (no dup)	261	302	**371**	345

(a) With `saucy3`

Benchmark	MiniSAT	Shatter	BreakID	MiniSym
app2016 (134)	18	**21**	18	19
app2014 (161)	23	21	20	**24**
app2013 (145)	6	7	10	**11**
app2012 (367)	115	106	114	**123**
hard2016 (128)	8	11	**79**	77
hard2014 (107)	9	45	40	**53**
hard2013 (121)	12	51	**56**	54
hard2012 (289)	86	69	90	**93**
all2017 (124)	8	14	**15**	**15**
all2015 (65)	**9**	7	8	8
TOTAL (no dup)	261	324	415	**439**

(b) With `bliss`

Table 2. Comparison of different approaches on the SAT instances of the benchmarks of the six last editions of the SAT competition.

Benchmark	MiniSAT	Shatter	BreakID	MiniSym
app2016 (134)	20	**22**	21	20
app2014 (161)	**24**	**24**	**24**	22
app2013 (145)	34	35	35	**43**
app2012 (367)	121	112	119	**126**
hard2016 (128)	**0**	**0**	**0**	**0**
hard2014 (107)	14	**17**	**17**	14
hard2013 (121)	23	23	**24**	22
hard2012 (289)	135	141	**143**	138
all2017 (124)	23	20	26	**27**
all2015 (65)	**7**	5	**7**	6
TOTAL (no dup)	325	323	**337**	335

(a) With saucy3

Benchmark	MiniSAT	Shatter	BreakID	MiniSym
app2016 (134)	20	20	**22**	20
app2014 (161)	**24**	**24**	23	22
app2013 (145)	**34**	32	30	33
app2012 (367)	**121**	112	120	118
hard2016 (128)	**0**	**0**	**0**	**0**
hard2014 (107)	14	14	17	**18**
hard2013 (121)	23	24	**26**	25
hard2012 (289)	135	134	141	**142**
all2017 (124)	23	25	26	**29**
all2015 (65)	**7**	5	6	6
TOTAL (no dup)	325	316	334	**336**

(b) With bliss

Table 3. Comparison of PAR-2 times (in seconds) of the benchmarks on the six last editions of the SAT competition.

Solver	PAR-2 sum	PAR-2 avg
MiniSAT	8 074 348	5 981
Shatter	7 770 434	5 756
BreakID	6 909 999	5 119
MiniSym	7 229 700	5 355

(a) With saucy3

Solver	PAR-2 sum	PAR-2 avg
MiniSAT	8 074 348	5 981
Shatter	7 517 556	5 569
BreakID	6 444 954	4 774
MiniSym	6 245 448	4 626

(b) With bliss

We observe that MiniSym with saucy3 solves the most instances in only half of the UNSAT categories. However, with bliss, MiniSym solves the most instances in all but four of the UNSAT categories; it then also solves the highest number of instances among its competitors. This shows the interest of our approach for UNSAT instances. Since symmetries are used to reduce the search space, we were expecting that it will bring the most performance gain for UNSAT instances.

The situation for SAT instances is more mitigated (Table 2), especially when using saucy3. Again, this is not very surprising: our method may cut the exploration of a satisfying assignment because it is not a *lex-leader*. This delays the discovery of a satisfying assignment. The other tools suffer less from such a delay, because they rely on symmetry breaking predicates generated in a pre-processing step. Also, when seeing the global results of MiniSAT, we can globally state that the use of symmetries in the case of satisfiable instances only offers a marginal improvement.

We observe that performances our tool are better with bliss than with saucy3 (see Fig. 1). We explain it as follows: saucy3 is known to compute fewer generators for the group of symmetries than bliss. Since, the larger the symmetries set is, the earlier the detection of an *evidence* that an assignment is not a *lex-leader* will be, we generate less symmetry-breaking predicates (only the effective ones). This is shown in Table 4; MiniSym generates an order of magnitude fewer predicates than breakID.

We also conducted experiments on highly symmetrical instances (all variables are involved in symmetries), whose results are presented in Table 5.

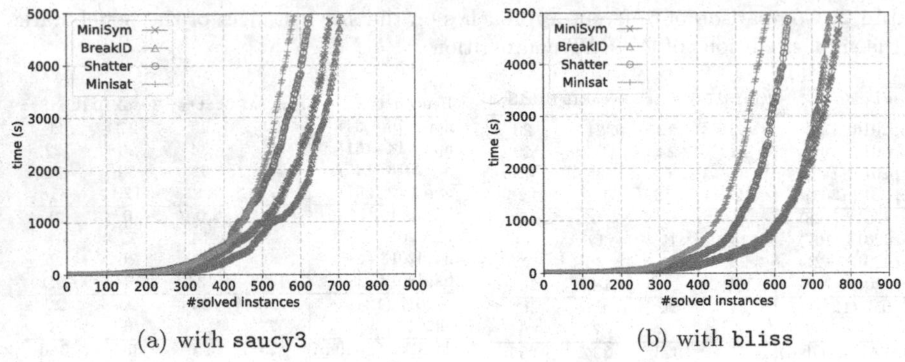

(a) with saucy3

(b) with bliss

Fig. 1. Cactus plot total number of instances

Table 4. Comparison of the number of generated SBPs each time breakID and MiniSym both compute a verdict (number of verdicts between parentheses).

Number of SBPs	BreakID	MiniSym
UNSAT (316)	12 088 433	1 579 623
SAT (312)	13 839 689	359 352

(a) With saucy3

Number of SBPs	BreakID	MiniSym
UNSAT (399)	2 576 349	913 339
SAT (320)	12 179 513	457 452

(b) With bliss

Table 5. Comparison of the tools on 99 highly symmetric UNSAT problems.

Benchmark	MiniSAT	Shatter	breakID	MiniSym
battleship(6)	**5**	**5**	**5**	**5**
chnl(6)	4	**6**	**6**	**6**
clqcolor(10)	3	4	5	**6**
fpga(10)	6	**10**	**10**	**10**
hole(24)	10	12	**23**	11
hole shuffle(12)	1	2	**12**	3
urq(6)	1	2	**6**	2
xorchain(2)	1	1	**2**	**2**
TOTAL	31	42	**69**	45

(a) With saucy3

Benchmark	MiniSAT	Shatter	breakID	MiniSym
battleship(6)	5	5	5	**6**
chnl(6)	4	**6**	**6**	**6**
clqcolor(10)	3	5	8	**10**
fpga(10)	6	**10**	**10**	**10**
hole(24)	10	**24**	**24**	23
hole shuffle(12)	1	3	**7**	4
urq(6)	1	2	**6**	5
xorchain(2)	1	1	**2**	**2**
TOTAL	31	56	**68**	66

(b) With bliss

The performance of breakID on this benchmark is explained by a specific optimization for the *total symmetry groups* that are found in these examples, that is neither implemented in Shatter nor in MiniSym. However, the difference between breakID and MiniSym is rather thin when using bliss. Our tool still outperforms Shatter on this benchmark.

5 Conclusion

This paper presented an approach dealing with the symmetries when they appear in SAT problems. It borrows from the state-of-the-art static-based approaches their basic principle, i.e., the adding of *symmetry breaking predicates* to the original problem, but performed in an incremental and dynamic way. This is possible thanks to the *dynamic tracking of symmetries status* and *on-the-fly generation of effective symmetry breaking predicates*.

Our approach outperforms other state-of-the-art static methods, as shown by an extensive evaluation on the symmetric problems gathered from the last six SAT competitions.

This approach is implemented in the C++ library called cosy. It is an off-the-shelf component that can be interfaced with virtually any CDCL SAT solver. cosy is released under GPL licence and is available at https://github.com/lip6/cosy.

We now plan to focus on combining our approach with *symmetry propagation* [9]. It seems that such a combination could be implemented thanks to minor changes on our algorithm. This would allow to integrate the acceleration mechanisms provided by the *symmetry propagation*, therefore obtaining a better pruning of the search three.

Another track for future work, is to evaluate the possibility of changing the order of variables dynamically: for example, following the order used by the solver when it chooses its decision variables.

References

1. Aloul, F., Ramani, A., Markov, I., Sakallah, K.: Solving difficult instances of Boolean satisfiability in the presence of symmetry. IEEE Trans. CAD Integr. Circuits Syst. **22**(9), 1117–1137 (2003)
2. Aloul, F., Sakallah, K., Markov, I.: Efficient symmetry breaking for Boolean satisfiability. IEEE Trans. Comput. **55**(5), 549–558 (2006)
3. Biere, A., Cimatti, A., Clarke, E., Zhu, Y.: Symbolic model checking without BDDs. In: Cleaveland, W.R. (ed.) TACAS 1999. LNCS, vol. 1579, pp. 193–207. Springer, Heidelberg (1999). https://doi.org/10.1007/3-540-49059-0_14
4. Biere, A., Heule, M., van Maaren, H.: Handbook of Satisfiability, vol. 185. IOS Press, Amsterdam (2009)
5. Crawford, J., Ginsberg, M., Luks, E., Roy, A.: Symmetry-Breaking Predicates for Search Problems, pp. 148–159. Morgan Kaufmann, San Francisco (1996)
6. Davis, M., Logemann, G., Loveland, D.: A machine program for theorem-proving. Commun. ACM **5**(7), 394–397 (1962)
7. Devriendt, J., Bogaerts, B., Bruynooghe, M.: Symmetric explanation learning: effective dynamic symmetry handling for SAT. In: Gaspers, S., Walsh, T. (eds.) SAT 2017. LNCS, vol. 10491, pp. 83–100. Springer, Cham (2017). https://doi.org/10.1007/978-3-319-66263-3_6
8. Devriendt, J., Bogaerts, B., Bruynooghe, M., Denecker, M.: Improved static symmetry breaking for SAT. In: Creignou, N., Le Berre, D. (eds.) SAT 2016. LNCS, vol. 9710, pp. 104–122. Springer, Cham (2016). https://doi.org/10.1007/978-3-319-40970-2_8
9. Devriendt, J., Bogaerts, B., de Cat, B., Denecker, M., Mears, C.: Symmetry propagation: improved dynamic symmetry breaking in SAT. In: IEEE 24th International Conference on Tools with Artificial Intelligence, ICTAI 2012, Athens, Greece, 7–9 November 2012, pp. 49–56 (2012)

10. Eén, N., Sörensson, N.: An extensible SAT-solver. In: Giunchiglia, E., Tacchella, A. (eds.) SAT 2003. LNCS, vol. 2919, pp. 502–518. Springer, Heidelberg (2004). https://doi.org/10.1007/978-3-540-24605-3_37
11. Järvisalo, M., Le Berre, D., Roussel, O., Simon, L.: The international SAT solver competitions. AI Mag. **33**(1), 89–92 (2012)
12. Junttila, T., Kaski, P.: Engineering an efficient canonical labeling tool for large and sparse graphs. In: Applegate, D., Brodal, G.S., Panario, D., Sedgewick, R. (eds.) Proceedings of the Ninth Workshop on Algorithm Engineering and Experiments and the Fourth Workshop on Analytic Algorithms and Combinatorics, pp. 135–149. SIAM (2007)
13. Katebi, H., Sakallah, K.A., Markov, I.L.: Symmetry and satisfiability: an update. In: Strichman, O., Szeider, S. (eds.) SAT 2010. LNCS, vol. 6175, pp. 113–127. Springer, Heidelberg (2010). https://doi.org/10.1007/978-3-642-14186-7_11
14. Kautz, H.A., Selman, B., et al.: Planning as satisfiability. In: ECAI, vol. 92, pp. 359–363 (1992)
15. Luks, E., Roy, A.: The complexity of symmetry-breaking formulas. Ann. Math. Artif. Intell. **41**(1), 19–45 (2004)
16. Luks, E.M., Roy, A.: The complexity of symmetry-breaking formulas. Ann. Math. Artif. Intell. **41**(1), 19–45 (2004). https://doi.org/10.1023/B:AMAI.0000018578.92398.10
17. Lynce, I., Marques-Silva, J.: SAT in bioinformatics: making the case with haplotype inference. In: Biere, A., Gomes, C.P. (eds.) SAT 2006. LNCS, vol. 4121, pp. 136–141. Springer, Heidelberg (2006). https://doi.org/10.1007/11814948_16
18. Marques-Silva, J.P., Sakallah, K., et al.: GRASP: a search algorithm for propositional satisfiability. IEEE Trans. Comput. **48**(5), 506–521 (1999)
19. Massacci, F., Marraro, L.: Logical cryptanalysis as a SAT problem. J. Autom. Reason. **24**(1), 165–203 (2000)
20. Sabharwal, A.: SymChaff: exploiting symmetry in a structure-aware satisfiability solver. Constraints **14**(4), 478–505 (2009)
21. Schaafsma, B., Heule, M.J.H., van Maaren, H.: Dynamic symmetry breaking by simulating Zykov contraction. In: Kullmann, O. (ed.) SAT 2009. LNCS, vol. 5584, pp. 223–236. Springer, Heidelberg (2009). https://doi.org/10.1007/978-3-642-02777-2_22

Automatic Generation of Precise and Useful Commutativity Conditions

Kshitij Bansal[1(✉)], Eric Koskinen[2], and Omer Tripp[1]

[1] Google, Inc., New York, USA
kbk@google.com, trippo@google.com
[2] Stevens Institute of Technology, Hoboken, USA
eric.koskinen@stevens.edu

Abstract. Reasoning about commutativity between data-structure operations is an important problem with applications including parallelizing compilers, optimistic parallelization and, more recently, Ethereum smart contracts. There have been research results on automatic generation of commutativity conditions, yet we are unaware of any fully automated technique to generate conditions that are both sound and effective.

We have designed such a technique, driven by an algorithm that iteratively refines a conservative approximation of the commutativity (and non-commutativity) condition for a pair of methods into an increasingly precise version. The algorithm terminates if/when the entire state space has been considered, and can be aborted at any time to obtain a partial yet sound commutativity condition. We have generalized our work to left-/right-movers [27] and proved relative completeness. We describe aspects of our technique that lead to *useful* commutativity conditions, including how predicates are selected during refinement and heuristics that impact the output shape of the condition.

We have implemented our technique in a prototype open-source tool Servois. Our algorithm produces quantifier-free queries that are dispatched to a back-end SMT solver. We evaluate Servois through two case studies: (i) We synthesize commutativity conditions for a range of data structures including Set, HashTable, Accumulator, Counter, and Stack. (ii) We consider an Ethereum smart contract called BlockKing, and show that Servois can detect serious concurrency-related vulnerabilities and guide developers to construct robust and efficient implementations.

1 Introduction

Reasoning about the conditions under which data-structure operations commute is an important problem. The ability to derive sound yet effective commutativity

K. Bansal—This work was partially supported by NSF award #1228768. Author was at New York University when part of the work was completed.

E. Koskinen—Support in part by NSF CCF Award #1421126, and CCF Award #1618542. Some of the research was done while author was at IBM Research.

O. Tripp—Some of the research was done while author was at IBM Research.

D. Beyer and M. Huisman (Eds.): TACAS 2018, LNCS 10805, pp. 115–132, 2018.
https://doi.org/10.1007/978-3-319-89960-2_7

conditions unlocks the potential of multicore architectures, including parallelizing compilers [30,34], speculative execution (*e.g.* transactional memory [19]), peephole partial-order reduction [37], futures, etc. Another important application domain that has emerged recently is Ethereum [1] smart contracts: efficient execution of such contracts hinges on exploiting their commutativity [14] and block-wise concurrency can lead to vulnerabilities [31]. Intuitively, commutativity is an important property because linearizable data-structure operations that commute can be executed concurrently: their effects do not interfere with each other in an observable way. When using a linearizable HashTable, for example, knowledge that `put(x,'a')` commutes with `get(y)` provided that $\mathtt{x} \neq \mathtt{y}$ enables significant parallelization opportunities. Indeed, it's important for the commutativity condition to be sufficiently granular so that parallelism can be exploited effectively [12]. At the same time, to make safe use of a commutativity condition, it must be sound [23,24]. Achieving both of these goals using manual reasoning is burdensome and error prone.

In light of that, researchers have investigated ways of verifying user-provided commutativity conditions [22] as well as synthesizing such conditions automatically, *e.g.* based on random interpretation [6], profiling [33] or sampling [18]. None of these approaches, however, meet the goal of computing a commutativity condition that is both *sound* and *granular* in a *fully automated* manner.

In this paper, we present a refinement-based technique for synthesizing commutativity conditions. Our technique builds on well-known descriptions and representations of abstract data types (ADTs) in terms of logical $(Pre_m, Post_m)$ specifications [10,16,17,20,26,28] for each method m. Our algorithm iteratively relaxes under-approximations of the commutativity *and* non-commutativity conditions of methods m and n, starting from false, into increasingly precise versions. At each step, we conjunctively subdivide the symbolic state space into regions, searching for areas where m and n commute and where they don't. Counterexamples to both the positive side and the negative side are used in the next symbolic subdivision. Throughout this recursive process, we accumulate the commutativity condition as a growing disjunction of these regions. The output of our procedure is a logical formula φ_m^n which specifies when method m commutes with method n. We have proven that the algorithm is sound, and can also be aborted at any time to obtain a partial, yet useful [19,33], commutativity condition. We show that, under certain conditions, termination is guaranteed (relative completeness).

We address several challenges that arise in using an iterative refinement approach to generating precise and useful commutativity conditions. First, we show how to pose the commutativity question in a way that does not introduce additional quantifiers. We also show how to generate the predicate vocabulary for expressing the condition φ_m^n, as well as how to choose the predicates throughout the refinement loop. A further question that we address is how predicate selection impacts the conciseness and readability of the generated commutativity conditions. Finally, we have generalized our algorithm to left-/right-movers [27], a more precise version of commutativity.

We have implemented our approach as the SERVOIS tool, whose code and documentation are available online [2]. SERVOIS is built on top of the CVC4 SMT solver [11]. We evaluate SERVOIS through two case studies. First, we generate commutativity conditions for a collection of popular data structures, including Set, HashTable, Accumulator, Counter, and Stack. The conditions typically combine multiple theories, such as sets, integers, arrays, etc. We show the conditions to be comparable in granularity to manually specified conditions [22]. Second, we consider BlockKing [31], an Ethereum smart contract, with its known vulnerability. We demonstrate how a developer can be guided by SERVOIS to create a more robust implementation.

Contributions. In summary, this paper makes the following contributions:

- The first sound and precise technique to automatically generate commutativity conditions (Sect. 5).
- Proof of soundness and relative completeness (Sect. 5).
- An implementation that takes an abstract code specification and automatically generates commutativity conditions using an SMT solver (Sect. 6).
- A novel technique for selecting refinement predicates that improves scalability and the simplicity of the generated formulae (Sect. 6).
- Demonstrated efficacy for several key data structures as well as the BlockKing Ethereum smart contract [31] (Sect. 7).

An extended version of this paper can be found in [8].

Related Work. The closest to our contribution in this paper is a technique by Gehr *et al.* [18] for learning, or inference, of commutativity conditions based on black-box sampling. They draw concrete arguments, extract relevant predicates from the sampled set of examples, and then search for a formula over the predicates. There are no soundness or completeness guarantees.

Both Aleen and Clark [6] and Tripp *et al.* [33] identify sequences of actions that commute (via random interpretation and dynamic analysis, respectively). However, neither technique yields an explicit commutativity condition. Kulkarni et al. [25] point out that varying degrees of commutativity specification precision are useful. Kim and Rinard [22] use Jahob to verify manually specified commutativity conditions of several different linked data structures. Commutativity specifications are also found in dynamic analysis techniques [15]. More distantly related is work on synthesis of programs [32] and of synchronization [35,36].

2 Example

Specifying commutativity conditions is generally nontrivial and it is easy to miss subtle corner cases. Additionally, it has to be done pairwise for all methods. For ease of illustration, we will focus on the relatively simple Set ADT, whose state consists of a single set S that stores an unordered collection of unique elements. Let us consider one pair of operations: (i) `contains`(x)`/bool`, a side-effect-free check whether the element x is in S; and (ii) `add`(y)`/bool` adds y to S if it is not already there and returns true, or otherwise returns false. `add` and `contains` clearly commute if they refer to different elements in the set. There is another case that is less obvious: `add` and `contains` commute if they refer to the same element e, as long as in the pre-state $e \in S$. In this case, under both orders of execution, `add` and `contains` leave the set unmodified and return false and true, respectively. The algorithm we describe in this paper completes within a few seconds, producing a precise logical formula φ that captures this commutativity condition, *i.e.* the disjunction of the two cases above: $\varphi \equiv x \neq y \vee (x = y \wedge x \in S)$. The algorithm also generates the conditions under which the methods *do not* commute: $\tilde{\varphi} \equiv x = y \wedge x \notin S$. These are precise, since φ is the negation of $\tilde{\varphi}$.

A more complicated commutativity condition is generated by our tool Servois for Ethereum smart contract BlockKing. Method $\mathsf{enter}(\mathsf{val}_1, \mathsf{sendr}_1, \mathsf{bk}_1 ...)$ (Fig. 3, Sect. 7) does not commute with itself $\mathsf{enter}(\mathsf{val}_2, \mathsf{sendr}_2, \mathsf{bk}_2 ...)$ *iff*:

$$\bigvee \begin{cases} \mathsf{val}_1 \geq 50 \wedge \mathsf{val}_2 \geq 50 \wedge \mathsf{sendr}_1 \neq \mathsf{sendr}_2 \\ \mathsf{val}_1 \geq 50 \wedge \mathsf{val}_2 \geq 50 \wedge \mathsf{sendr}_1 = \mathsf{sendr}_2 \wedge \mathsf{val}_1 \neq \mathsf{val}_2 \\ \mathsf{val}_1 \geq 50 \wedge \mathsf{val}_2 \geq 50 \wedge \mathsf{sendr}_1 = \mathsf{sendr}_2 \wedge \mathsf{val}_1 = \mathsf{val}_2 \wedge \mathsf{bk}_1 \neq \mathsf{bk}_2 \end{cases}$$

This disjunction enumerates the non-commutativity cases and, as discussed in Sect. 7, directly identifies a vulnerability.

Capturing precise conditions such as these by hand, and doing so for many pairs of operations, is tedious and error prone. This paper instead presents a way to automate this. Our algorithm recursively subdivides the state space via predicates until, at the base case, regions are found that are either entirely commutative or else entirely non-commutative. Returning to our Set example, the conditions we incrementally generate are denoted φ and $\tilde{\varphi}$, respectively. The following diagram illustrates how our algorithm proceeds to generate the commutativity conditions for `add` and `contains` (abbreviated as m and n).

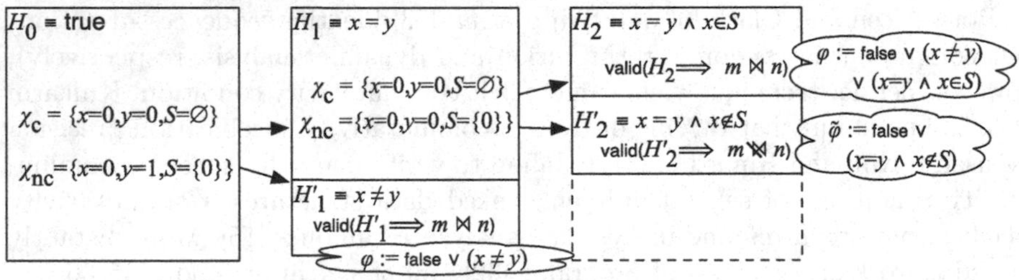

In this diagram, each subsequent panel depicts a partitioning of the state space into regions of commutativity (φ) or non-commutativity ($\tilde{\varphi}$). The counterexamples χ_c, χ_{nc} give values for the arguments x, y and the current state S.

We denote by H the logical formula that describes the current state space at a given recursive call. We begin with H_0 = true, φ = false, and $\tilde{\varphi}$ = false. There are three cases for a given H: (*i*) H describes a precondition for m and n in which they *always* commute; (*ii*) H describes a precondition for m and n in which they *never* commute; or (*iii*) neither of the above. The latter case drives the algorithm to subdivide the region by choosing a new predicate.

We now detail the run of this refinement loop on our earlier Set example. We elaborate on the other challenges that arise in later sections. At each step of the algorithm, we determine which case we are in via carefully designed validity queries to an SMT solver (Sect. 4). For H_0, it returns the commutativity counterexample: $\chi_c = \{x = 0, y = 0, S = \emptyset\}$ as well as the non-commutativity counterexample $\chi_{nc} = \{x = 0, y = 1, S = \{0\}\}$. Since, therefore, $H_0 = \mathsf{true}$ is neither a commutativity nor a non-commutativity condition, we must refine H_0 into regions (or stronger conditions). In particular, we would like to perform a *useful* subdivision: Divide H_0 into an H_1 that allows χ_c but disallows χ_{nc}, and an H'_1 that allows χ_{nc} but not χ_c. So we must choose a predicate p (from a suitable set of predicates $\mathcal{P}$, discussed later), such that $H_0 \wedge p \Rightarrow \chi_c$ while $H_0 \wedge \neg p \Rightarrow \chi_{nc}$ (or vice versa). The predicate $x = y$ satisfies this property. The algorithm then makes the next two recursive calls, adding p as a conjunct to H, as shown in the second column of the diagram above: one with $H_1 \equiv \mathsf{true} \wedge x = y$ and one with $H'_1 \equiv \mathsf{true} \wedge x \neq y$. Taking the H'_1 case, our algorithm makes another SMT query and finds that $x \neq y$ implies that `add` always commutes with `contains`. At this point, it can update the commutativity condition φ, letting $\varphi := \varphi \vee H'_1$, adding this H'_1 region to the growing disjunction. On the other hand, H_1 is neither a sufficient commutativity nor a sufficient non-commutativity condition, and so our algorithm, again, produces the respective counterexamples: $\chi_c = \{x = 0, y = 0, S = \emptyset\}$ and $\chi_{nc} = \{x = 0, y = 0, S = \{0\}\}$. In this case, our algorithm selects the predicate $x \in S$, and makes two further recursive calls: one with $H_2 \equiv x = y \wedge x \in S$ and another with $H'_2 \equiv x = y \wedge x \notin S$. In this case, it finds that H_2 is a sufficiently strong precondition for commutativity, while H'_2 is a strong enough precondition for non-commutativity. Consequently, H_2 is added as a new conjunct to φ, yielding $\varphi \equiv x \neq y \vee (x = y \wedge x \in S)$. Similarly, $\tilde{\varphi}$ is updated to be: $\tilde{\varphi} \equiv (x = y \wedge x \notin S)$. No further recursive calls are made so the algorithm terminates and we have obtained a precise (complete) commutativity/non-commutativity specification: $\varphi \vee \tilde{\varphi}$ is valid (Lemma 2).

Challenges and Outline. While the algorithm outlined so far is a relatively standard refinement, the above generated conditions were not immediate. We now discuss challenges involved in generating sound *and* useful conditions.

(Section 4) A first question is how to pose the underlying commutativity queries for each subsequent H in a way that avoids the introduction of additional quantifiers, so that we can remain in fragments for which the solver has complete decision procedures. Thus, if the data structure can be encoded using theories that are decidable, then the queries we pose to the SMT solver are guaranteed to be decidable as well. $Pre_m/Post_m$ specifications that are partial would introduce quantifier alternation, but we show how this can be avoided by, instead, transforming them into total specifications.

(Section 5) We have proved that our algorithm is sound even if aborted or if the ADT description involves undecidable theories. We further show that termination implies completeness, and specify broad conditions that imply termination.

(Section 6) Another challenge is to prioritize predicates during the refinement loop. This choice impacts not only the algorithm's performance, but also the quality/conciseness of the resulting conditions. Our choice of next predicate p is governed by two requirements. First, for progress, $p/\neg p$ must eliminate the counterexamples to commutativity/non-commutativity due to the last iteration. This may still leave multiple choices, and we propose two heuristics – called *simple* and *poke*—with different trade-offs to break ties.

(Section 7) We conclude with an evaluation on a range of popular data structures and a case study on boosting the security of an Ethereum smart contract.

3 Preliminaries

States, Actions, Methods. We will work with a state space Σ, with decidable equality and a set of *actions* A. For each $\alpha \in A$, we have a transition function $(\!|\alpha|\!) : \Sigma \rightharpoonup \Sigma$. We denote a single transition as $\sigma \xrightarrow{\alpha} \sigma'$. We assume that each such action arc completes in finite time. Let $\mathfrak{T} \equiv (\Sigma, A, (\!| \bullet |\!))$. We say that two *actions* α_1 and α_2 *commute* [15], denoted $\alpha_1 \bowtie \alpha_2$, provided that $(\!|\alpha_1|\!) \circ (\!|\alpha_2|\!) = (\!|\alpha_2|\!) \circ (\!|\alpha_1|\!)$. Note that $\bowtie$ is with respect to $\mathfrak{T} = (\Sigma, A, (\!| \bullet |\!))$. Our formalism, implementation, and evaluation all extend to a more fine-grained notion of commutativity: an asymmetric version called left-movers and right-movers [27], where a method commutes in one direction and not the other. Details can be found in [8]. Also, in our evaluation (Sect. 7) we show left-/right-mover conditions that were generated by our implementation.

An action $\alpha \in A$ is of the form $m(\bar{x})/\bar{r}$, where m, $\bar{x}$ and $\bar{r}$ are called a *method*, *arguments* and *return values* respectively. As a convention, for actions corresponding to a method n, we use $\bar{y}$ for arguments and $\bar{s}$ for return values. The set of methods will be finite, inducing a finite partitioning of A. We refer to an action, say $m(\bar{a})/\bar{v}$, as *corresponding* to method m (where $\bar{a}$ and $\bar{v}$ are vectors of values). The set of actions corresponding to a method m, denoted A_m, might be infinite as arguments and return values may be from an infinite domain.

Definition 1. *Methods m and n* commute, *denoted $m \bowtie n$ provided that $\forall \bar{x}\ \bar{y}\ \bar{r}\ \bar{s}.\ m(\bar{x})/\bar{r} \bowtie n(\bar{y})/\bar{s}$.*

The quantification $\forall \bar{x}\bar{r}$ above means $\forall m(\bar{x})/\bar{r} \in A_m$, i.e., all vectors of arguments and return values that constitute an action in A_m.

Abstract Specifications. We symbolically describe the actions of a method m as pre-condition Pre_m and post-condition $Post_m$. Pre-conditions are logical formulae over method arguments and the initial state: $[\![Pre_m]\!] : \bar{x} \to \Sigma \to \mathbb{B}$. Post-conditions are over method arguments, and return values, initial state and final state: $[\![Post_m]\!] : \bar{x} \to \bar{r} \to \Sigma \to \Sigma \to \mathbb{B}$. Given $(Pre_m, Post_m)$ for every method m, we define a transition system $\mathfrak{T} = (\Sigma, A, (\!| \bullet |\!))$ such that $\sigma \xrightarrow{m(\bar{a})/\bar{v}} \sigma'$ *iff* $[\![Pre_m]\!]\ \bar{a}\ \sigma$ and $[\![Post_m]\!]\ \bar{a}\ \bar{v}\ \sigma\ \sigma'$.

Since our approach works on deterministic transition systems, we have implemented an SMT-based check (Sect. 7) that ensures the input transition system is deterministic. Deterministic specifications were sufficient in our examples. This is unsurprising given the inherent difficulty of creating efficient concurrent implementations of nondeterministic operations, whose effects are hard to characterize. Reducing nondeterministic data-structure methods to deterministic ones through symbolic partial determinization [5,13] is left as future work.

Logical Commutativity Formulae. We will generate a commutativity condition for methods m and n as logical formulae over initial states and the arguments/return values of the methods. We denote a logical commutativity formula as φ and assume a decidable interpretation of formulae: $[\![\varphi]\!] : (\sigma, \bar{x}, \bar{y}, \bar{r}, \bar{s}) \to \mathbb{B}$. (We tuple the arguments for brevity.) The first argument is the initial state. Commutativity *post*- and *mid*-conditions can also be written [22] but here, for simplicity, we focus on commutativity *pre*-conditions. We may write $[\![\varphi]\!]$ as φ when it is clear from context that φ is meant to be interpreted.

We say that φ_m^n is a *sound commutativity condition*, and $\hat{\varphi}_m^n$ a sound *non*-commutativity condition resp., for m and n provided that

$$\forall \sigma \bar{x}\bar{y}\bar{r}\bar{s}.\ [\![\varphi_m^n]\!]\ \sigma\ \bar{x}\ \bar{y}\ \bar{r}\ \bar{s} \Rightarrow m(\bar{x})/\bar{r}\ \bowtie\ n(\bar{y})/\bar{s}, \text{ and}$$
$$\forall \sigma \bar{x}\bar{y}\bar{r}\bar{s}.\ [\![\hat{\varphi}_m^n]\!]\ \sigma\ \bar{x}\ \bar{y}\ \bar{r}\ \bar{s} \Rightarrow \neg(m(\bar{x})/\bar{r}\ \bowtie\ n(\bar{y})/\bar{s}), \text{ resp.}$$

4 Commutativity Without Quantifier Alternation

Definition 1 requires showing equivalence between different compositions of potentially partial functions. That is, $(\!|\alpha_1|\!) \circ (\!|\alpha_2|\!) = (\!|\alpha_2|\!) \circ (\!|\alpha_1|\!)$ if and only if:

$$\forall \sigma_0\ \sigma_1\ \sigma_{12}.\ (\!|\alpha_1|\!)\sigma_0 = \sigma_1 \wedge (\!|\alpha_2|\!)\sigma_1 = \sigma_{12} \ \Rightarrow\ \exists \sigma_3.\ (\!|\alpha_2|\!)\sigma_0 = \sigma_3 \wedge (\!|\alpha_1|\!)\sigma_3 = \sigma_{12}$$
$$\textit{(and a symmetric case for the other direction)}$$

Even when the transition relation can be expressed in a decidable theory, because of $\forall\exists$ quantifier alternation in the above encoding (which is undecidable in general), any procedure requiring such a check would be incomplete. SMT solvers are particularly poor at handling such constraints.

We observe that when the transition system is specified as Pre_m and $Post_m$ conditions, and the $Post_m$ condition is *consistent* with Pre_m, then it is possible to avoid quantifier alternation. By consistent we mean that whenever Pre_m holds, there is always some state and return value for which $Post_m$ holds (*i.e.* for which the procedure does not abort).

$$\forall \bar{a}\ \sigma.\quad Pre_m(\bar{a}, \sigma) = \mathsf{true} \ \Rightarrow\ \exists \sigma'\ \bar{r}.\ Post_m(\bar{a}, \bar{r}, \sigma, \sigma').$$

That is, the procedure terminates for every Pre_m, which holds in particular for all of the specifications in the examples we considered (see Sect. 7). This allows us to perform a simple transformation on transition systems to a lifted domain, and enforce a definition of commutativity in the lifted domain $m\ \hat{\bowtie}\ n$ that is equivalent to Definition 1. This new definition requires only *universal* quantification, and as such, is better suited to SMT-backed algorithms (Sect. 5).

Definition 2 (Lifted transition function). *For $\mathfrak{T} = (\Sigma, A, (\!|\bullet|\!))$, we lift $\mathfrak{T}$ to $\hat{\mathfrak{T}} = (\hat{\Sigma}, A, (\!|\!|\bullet|\!|\!))$ where $\hat{\Sigma} = \Sigma \cup \{err\}$, $err \notin \Sigma$, and $(\!|\!|\alpha|\!|\!) : \hat{\Sigma} \to \hat{\Sigma}$, as:*

$$(\!|\!|\alpha|\!|\!)\hat{\sigma} \equiv \begin{cases} err & if\ \hat{\sigma} = err \\ (\!|\alpha|\!)\hat{\sigma} & if\ \hat{\sigma} \in \mathbf{dom}((\!|\alpha|\!)) \\ err & otherwise \end{cases}$$

Intuitively, $(\!|\!|\alpha|\!|\!)$ wraps $(\!|\alpha|\!)$ so that err loops back to err, and the (potentially partial) $(\!|\alpha|\!)$ is made to be total by mapping elements to err when they are undefined in $(\!|\alpha|\!)$. It is not necessary to lift the actions (or, indeed, the methods), but only the states and transition function. Once lifted, for a given state $\hat{\sigma}_0$, the question of *some* successor state becomes equivalent to *all* successor states because there is exactly one successor state.

Abstraction. Pre-/post-conditions ($Pre_m, Post_m$) are suitable for specifications of potentially partial transition systems. One can translate these into a new pair ($\widehat{Pre_m}, \widehat{Post_m}$) that induces a corresponding lifted transition system that is total and remains deterministic. These lifted specifications have types over lifted state spaces: $[\![\widehat{Pre_m}]\!] : \bar{x} \to \hat{\Sigma} \to \mathbb{B}$ and $[\![\widehat{Post_m}]\!] : \bar{x} \to \bar{r} \to \hat{\Sigma} \to \hat{\Sigma} \to \mathbb{B}$. Our implementation performs this lifting via a translation denoted LIFT from ($Pre_m, Post_m$) to:

$$\widehat{Pre_m}(\bar{x}, \hat{\sigma}) \equiv \text{true}$$

$$\widehat{Post_m}(\bar{x}, \bar{r}, \hat{\sigma}, \hat{\sigma}') \equiv \bigvee \begin{cases} \hat{\sigma} = \text{err} \wedge \hat{\sigma}' = \text{err} \\ \hat{\sigma} \neq \text{err} \wedge Pre_m(\bar{x}, \hat{\sigma}) \wedge \hat{\sigma}' \neq \text{err} \wedge Post_m(\bar{x}, \bar{r}, \hat{\sigma}, \hat{\sigma}') \\ \hat{\sigma} \neq \text{err} \wedge \neg Pre_m(\bar{x}, \hat{\sigma}) \wedge \hat{\sigma}' = \text{err} \end{cases}$$

(We abuse notation, giving $\hat{\sigma}$ as an argument to Pre_m, etc.) It is easy to see that the lifted transition system induced by this translation $(\hat{\Sigma}, (\!|\!|\bullet|\!|\!))$ is of the form given in Definition 2. In [8], we show how our tool transforms a counter specification into an equivalent lifted version that is total.

We use the notation $\hat{\bowtie}$ to mean $\bowtie$ but over lifted transition system $\hat{\mathfrak{T}}$. Since $\hat{\bowtie}$ is over total, determinsitic transition functions, $\alpha_1 \mathrel{\hat{\bowtie}} \alpha_2$ is equivalent to:

$$\forall \hat{\sigma}_0.\ \hat{\sigma}_0 \neq \text{err} \Rightarrow (\!|\!|\alpha_2|\!|\!)\ (\!|\!|\alpha_1|\!|\!)\ \hat{\sigma}_0 = (\!|\!|\alpha_1|\!|\!)\ (\!|\!|\alpha_2|\!|\!)\ \hat{\sigma}_0 \tag{1}$$

The equivalence above is in terms of state equality. Importantly, this is a universally quantified formula that translates to a ground satisfiability check in an SMT solver (modulo the theories used to model the data structure). In our refinement algorithm (Sect. 5), we will use this format to check whether candidate logical formulae describe commutative subregions.

Lemma 1. *$m \bowtie n$ if and only if $m \mathrel{\hat{\bowtie}} n$.* (All proofs in [8].)

5 Iterative Refinement

We now present an iterative refinement strategy that, when given a lifted abstract transition system, generates the commutativity and the non-commutativity conditions. We then discuss soundness and relative completeness and, in Sects. 6 and 7, challenges in generating precise *and* useful commutativity conditions.

The refinement algorithm symbolically searches the state space for regions where the operations commute (or do not commute) in a conjunctive manner, adding on one predicate at a time. We add each subregion H (described conjunctively) in which commutativity always holds to a growing disjunctive description of the commutativity condition φ, and each subregion H in which commutativity never holds to a growing disjunctive description of the non-commutativity condition $\tilde{\varphi}$.

The algorithm in Fig. 1 begins by setting $\varphi = \mathsf{false}$ and $\tilde{\varphi} = \mathsf{false}$. Refine begins a symbolic binary search through the state space H, starting from the entire state: $H = \mathsf{true}$. It also may use a collection of predicates $\mathcal{P}$ (discussed later). At each iteration, Refine checks whether the current H represents a region of space for which m and n always commute: $H \Rightarrow m \mathrel{\hat{\bowtie}} n$ (described below). If so, H can be disjunctively added to φ. It may, instead be the case that H represents a region of space for which m and n never commute: $H \Rightarrow m \mathrel{\hat{\not\bowtie}} n$. If so, H can be disjunctively added to $\tilde{\varphi}$. If neither of these cases hold, we have two counterexamples. χ_c is the counterexample to commutativity, returned if the validity check on Line 2 fails. χ_{nc} is the counterexample to *non*-commutativity, returned if the validity check on Line 4 fails.

```
1  REFINE^m_n(H, P) {
2      if valid(H ⇒ m ⋈̂ n) then
3          φ := φ ∨ H;
4      else if valid(H ⇒ m ⋈̸̂ n) then
5          φ̃ := φ̃ ∨ H;
6      else
7          let (χc, χnc) = counterexs. to ⋈̂ and ⋈̸̂
8          let p = CHOOSE(H, P, χc, χnc) in
9              REFINE^m_n(H ∧ p, P \ {p});
10             REFINE^m_n(H ∧ ¬p, P \ {p});
11 }
12 main { φ := false;  φ̃ := false;
13         try { REFINE^m_n(true, P); }
14         catch (InterruptedExn e) { skip; }
15         return(φ, φ̃); }
```

Fig. 1. Algorithm for generating commutativity φ and non-commutativity $\tilde{\varphi}$.

We now need to subdivide H into two regions. This is accomplished by selecting a new predicate p via the Choose method. For now, let the method Choose and the choice of predicate vocabulary $\mathcal{P}$ be parametric. Refine is sound regardless of the behavior of Choose. Below we give the conditions on Choose that ensure relative completeness, and in Sect. 7 we discuss our particular strategy. Regardless of what p is returned by Choose, two recursive calls are made to Refine, one with argument $H \wedge p$, and the other with argument $H \wedge \neg p$. The algorithm is exponential in the number of predicates. In Sect. 6 we discuss prioritizing predicates.

The refinement algorithm generates commutativity conditions in disjunctive normal form. Hence, any finite logical formula can be represented. This logical language is more expressive than previous commutativity logics that, because they were designed for run-time purposes, were restricted to conjunctions of inequalities [25] and boolean combinations of predicates over finite domains [15].

Checking a Candidate H_m^n. Our algorithm involves checking whether ($H_m^n \Rightarrow m \hat{\bowtie} n$) or ($H_m^n \Rightarrow m \hat{\not\bowtie} n$). As shown in Sect. 4, we can check whether H_m^n specifies conditions under which $m \bowtie n$ via an SMT query that does not introduce quantifier alternation. For brevity, we define:

$$\mathsf{valid}(H_m^n \Rightarrow m \hat{\bowtie} n) \equiv \mathsf{valid}\begin{pmatrix} \forall \hat{\sigma}_0\ \bar{x}\ \bar{y}\ \bar{r}\ \bar{s}.\ H_m^n(\hat{\sigma}_0, \bar{x}, \bar{y}, \bar{r}, \bar{s}) \Rightarrow \\ m(\bar{x})/\bar{r}\ n(\bar{y})/\bar{s}\ \hat{\sigma}_0 = n(\bar{y})/\bar{s}\ m(\bar{x})/\bar{r}\ \hat{\sigma}_0 \end{pmatrix}$$

Above we assume as a black box an SMT solver providing valid. Here we have lifted the universal quantification within $\hat{\bowtie}$ outside the implication.

We can similarly check whether H_m^n is a condition under which m and n *do not* commute. First, we define negative analogs of commutativity:

$$\begin{aligned} \alpha_1 \hat{\not\bowtie} \alpha_2 &\equiv \forall \hat{\sigma}_0.\ \hat{\sigma}_0 \neq \mathsf{err} \Rightarrow (\!|\alpha_2|\!)\ (\!|\alpha_1|\!)\ \hat{\sigma}_0 \neq (\!|\alpha_1|\!)\ (\!|\alpha_2|\!)\ \hat{\sigma}_0 \\ m \hat{\not\bowtie} n &\equiv \forall \bar{x}\ \bar{y}\ \bar{r}\ \bar{s}.\ m(\bar{x})/\bar{r} \hat{\not\bowtie} n(\bar{y})/\bar{s} \end{aligned}$$

We thus define a check for when φ_m^n is a *non*-commutativity condition with:

$$\mathsf{valid}(H_m^n \Rightarrow m \hat{\not\bowtie} n) \equiv \mathsf{valid}\begin{pmatrix} \forall \hat{\sigma}_0\ \bar{x}\ \bar{y}\ \bar{r}\ \bar{s}.\ H_m^n(\hat{\sigma}_0, \bar{x}, \bar{y}, \bar{r}, \bar{s}) \Rightarrow \hat{\sigma}_0 \neq \mathsf{err} \Rightarrow \\ m(\bar{x})/\bar{r}\ n(\bar{y})/\bar{s}\ \hat{\sigma}_0 \neq n(\bar{y})/\bar{s}\ m(\bar{x})/\bar{r}\ \hat{\sigma}_0 \end{pmatrix}$$

Theorem 1 (Soundness). *For each* REFINE_n^m *iteration:* $\varphi \Rightarrow m \hat{\bowtie} n$, *and* $\tilde{\varphi} \Rightarrow m \hat{\not\bowtie} n$.

All proofs available in [8]. Soundness holds regardless of what CHOOSE returns and even when the theories used to model the underlying data-structure are incomplete. Next we show termination implies completeness:

Lemma 2. *If* REFINE_n^m *terminates, then* $\varphi \vee \tilde{\varphi}$.

Theorem 2 (Conditions for Termination). REFINE_n^m *terminates if 1.* **(expressiveness)** *the state space Σ is partitionable into a finite set of regions* $\Sigma_1, ..., \Sigma_N$, *each described by a finite conjunction of predicates* ψ_i, *such that either* $\psi_i \Rightarrow m \hat{\bowtie} n$ *or* $\psi_i \Rightarrow m \hat{\not\bowtie} n$; *and 2.* **(fairness)** *for every* $p \in \mathcal{P}$, CHOOSE *eventually picks p (note that this does not imply that $\mathcal{P}$ is finite).*

Note that while these conditions ensure termination, the bound on the number of iterations depends on the predicate language and behavior of CHOOSE.

6 The SERVOIS Tool and Practical Considerations

Input. We use an input specification language building on YAML (which has parser and printer support for all common programming languages) with SMTLIB as the logical language. This can be automatically generated relatively easily, thus enabling the integration with other tools [10,16,17,20,26,28]. In [8], we show the Counter ADT specification, which was derived from the *Pre* and *Post* conditions used in earlier work [22]. The states of a transition system describing an ADT are encoded as list of variables (each as a name/type pair), and each method specification requires a list of argument types, return type, and *Pre* / *Post* conditions. Again, the Counter example can be seen in [8].

Implementation. We have developed the open-source SERVOIS tool [3], which implements REFINE, LIFT, predicate generation, and a method for selecting predicates (CHOOSE) discussed below. SERVOIS uses CVC4 [11] as a backend SMT solver. SERVOIS begins by performing some pre-processing on the input transition system. It checks that the transition system is deterministic. Next, in case the transition system is partial, SERVOIS performs the LIFT transformation (Sect. 4). An example of LIFT applied to Counter is in [8].

Next, SERVOIS automatically generates the predicate language (PGEN) in addition to user-provided hints. If the predicate vocabulary is not sufficiently expressive, then the algorithm would not be able to converge on precise commutativity and non-commutativity conditions (Sect. 5). We generate predicates by using terms and operators that appear in the specification, and generating well-typed atoms not trivially true or false. As we demonstrate in Sect. 7, this strategy works well in practice. Intuitively, *Pre* and *Post* formulas suffice to express the footprint of an operation. So, the atoms comprising them are an effective vocabulary to express when operations do or do not interfere.

Predicate Selection (CHOOSE)**.** Even though the number of computed predicates is relatively small, since our algorithm is exponential in number of predicates it is essential to be able to identify *relevant* predicates for the algorithm. To this end, in addition to filtering trivial predicates, we prioritize predicates based on the *two* counterexamples generated by the validity checks in REFINE. Predicates that distinguish between the given counter examples are tried first (call these *distinguishing* predicates). CHOOSE must return a predicate such that $\chi_c \not\Rightarrow H \wedge p$ and $\chi_{nc} \not\Rightarrow H \wedge \neg p$. This guarantees progress on both recursive calls. When combined with a heuristic to favor less complex atoms, this ensured timely termination on our examples. We refer to this as the *simple* heuristic.

Though this produced precise conditions, they were not always very concise, which is desirable for human understanding, and inspection purposes. We thus introduced a new heuristic which significantly improves the *qualitative* aspect of our algorithm. We found that doing a lookahead (recurse on each predicate one level deep, or *poke*) and computing the number of distinguishing predicates for the two branches as a good indicator of importance of the predicate. More precisely, we pick the predicate with lowest sum of remaining number of distinguishing predicates by the two calls. As an aside, those familiar with decision tree learning, might see a connection with the notion of entropy gain. This requires more calls to the SMT solver at each call, but it cuts down the total number of branches to be explored. Also, all individual queries were relatively simple for CVC4. The heuristic converges much faster to the relevant predicates, and produces smaller, concise conditions.

7 Case Studies

Common Data-Structures. We applied SERVOIS to Set, HashTable, Accumulator, Counter, and Stack. The generated commutativity conditions for these data structures typically combine multiple theories, such as sets, integers and arrays. We used the quantifier-free integer theory in SMTLIB to encode the abstract state and contracts for the Counter and Accumulator ADTs. For Set, the theory of finite sets [9] for tracking elements along with integers to track size; for HashTable, finite sets to track keys, and arrays for the HashMap itself. For Stack, we observed that for the purpose of pairwise commutativity it is sufficient to track the behavior of boundedly many top elements. Since two operations can *at most* either pop the top two elements or push two elements, tracking four elements is sufficient. All evaluation data is available on our website [2].

Depending on the pair of methods, the number of predicates generated by PGEN were (count after filtering in parentheses): Counter: 25–25 (12–12), Accumulator: 1–20 (0–20), Set: 17–55 (17–34), HashTable: 18–36 (6–36), Stack: 41–61 (41–42). We did not provide any hints to the algorithm for this case study. On all our examples, the *simple* heuristic terminated with precise commutativity conditions. In Fig. 2, we give the number of solver queries and total time (in paren.) consumed by this heuristic. The experiments were run on a 2.53 GHz Intel Core 2 Duo machine with 8 GB RAM. The conditions in Fig. 2 are those generated by the *poke* heuristic, and interested reader may compare them with the simple heuristic in [7]. On the theoretical side, our CHOOSE implementation is fair (satisfies condition 2 of Theorem 2, as Lines 9–10 of the algorithm remove from $\mathcal{P}$ the predicate being tried). From our experiments we conclude that our choice of predicates satisfies condition 1 of Theorem 2.

Although our algorithm is sound, we manually validated the implementation of SERVOIS by examining its output and comparing the generated commutativity conditions with those reported by prior studies. In the case of Accumulator and Counter, our commutativity conditions were identical to those given in [22]. For the Set data structure, the work of [22] used a less precise Set abstraction, so we instead validated against the conditions of [25]. As for HashTable, we validated that our conditions match those by Dimitrov *et al.* [15].

The BlockKing Ethereum Smart Contract. We further validated our approach by examining a real-world situation in which non-commutativity opens the door for attacks that exploit interleavings. We examined "smart contracts", which are programs written in the Solidity programming language [4] and executed on the Ethereum blockchain [1]. Eliding many details, smart contracts are like objects, and blockchain participants can invoke methods on these objects. Although the initial intuition is that smart contracts are executed sequentially, practitioners and academics [31] are increasingly realizing that the blockchain is a concurrent environment due to the fact the execution of one actor's smart contract can be split across multiple blocks, with other actors' smart contracts interleaved. Therefore, the execution model of the blockchain has been compared

	$m(\bar{x})$		$n(\bar{y})$	Simple	Poke	φ_n^m (Using Poke)
				Qs (time)	Qs (time)	
Counter	decrement	⋈	decrement	3 (0.1)	3 (0.1)	true
	increment	▷	decrement	10 (0.3)	34 (0.9)	$\neg(0 = c)$
	decrement	▷	increment	3 (0.1)	3 (0.1)	true
	decrement	⋈	reset	2 (0.1)	2 (0.1)	false
	decrement	⋈	zero	6 (0.1)	26 (0.6)	$\neg(1 = c)$
	increment	⋈	increment	3 (0.1)	3 (0.1)	true
	increment	⋈	reset	2 (0.0)	2 (0.1)	false
	increment	⋈	zero	10 (0.3)	34 (0.8)	$\neg(0 = c)$
	reset	⋈	reset	3 (0.1)	3 (0.1)	true
	reset	⋈	zero	9 (0.2)	30 (0.6)	$0 = c$
	zero	⋈	zero	3 (0.1)	3 (0.1)	true
Acum.	increase	⋈	increase	3 (0.1)	3 (0.1)	true
	increase	⋈	read	13 (0.3)	28 (0.6)	$c + x_1 = c$
	read	⋈	read	3 (0.0)	3 (0.0)	true
Set	add	⋈	add	10 (0.4)	140 (4.4)	$(y_1 = x_1 \wedge y_1 \in S) \vee \neg(y_1 = x_1)$
	add	⋈	contains	10 (0.4)	122 (3.6)	$x_1 \in S \vee (\neg(x_1 \in S) \wedge \neg(y_1 = x_1))$
	add	⋈	getsize	6 (0.2)	31 (0.9)	$x_1 \in S$
	add	⋈	remove	6 (0.2)	66 (2.2)	$\neg(y_1 = x_1)$
	contains	⋈	contains	3 (0.1)	3 (0.1)	true
	contains	⋈	getsize	3 (0.1)	3 (0.1)	true
	contains	⋈	remove	17 (0.5)	160 (4.8)	$S \setminus \{x_1\} = \{y_1\} \vee (... \wedge y_1 \in \{x_1\}) \vee ...$
	getsize	⋈	getsize	3 (0.1)	3 (0.1)	true
	getsize	⋈	remove	13 (0.3)	37 (1.0)	$\neg(y_1 \in S)$
	remove	⋈	remove	21 (0.7)	192 (6.4)	$S \setminus \{y_1\} = \{x_1\} \vee (... \wedge y_1 \in \{x_1\}) \vee ...$
HashTable	get	⋈	get	3 (0.1)	3 (0.1)	true
	get	⋈	haskey	3 (0.1)	3 (0.1)	true
	put	▷	get	13 (0.4)	74 (2.3)	$(H[x_1 \leftarrow x_2] = H \wedge y_1 \in keys)$ $\vee(\neg(H[x_1 \leftarrow x_2] = H) \wedge \neg(y_1 = x_1))$
	get	▷	put	10 (0.3)	48 (1.5)	$[H[y_1] = y_2] \vee [\neg(H[y_1] = y_2) \wedge \neg(y_1 = x_1)]$
	remove	▷	get	3 (0.1)	3 (0.1)	true
	get	▷	remove	13 (0.4)	40 (1.2)	$\neg(y_1 = x_1)$
	get	⋈	size	3 (0.1)	3 (0.1)	true
	haskey	⋈	haskey	3 (0.1)	3 (0.1)	true
	haskey	⋈	put	10 (0.3)	52 (1.6)	$[y_1 \in keys] \vee [\neg(y_1 \in keys) \wedge \neg(y_1 = x_1)]$
	haskey	⋈	remove	17 (0.5)	44 (1.3)	$[x_1 \in keys \wedge \neg(y_1 = x_1)] \vee [\neg(x_1 \in keys)]$
	haskey	⋈	size	3 (0.1)	3 (0.1)	true
	put	⋈	put	24 (0.9)	357 (13.5)	$... \vee (\neg(H[y_1] = y_2) \wedge \neg(y_1 = x_1))$
	put	⋈	remove	6 (0.3)	33 (1.2)	$\neg(y_1 = x_1)$
	put	⋈	size	6 (0.2)	23 (0.8)	$x_1 \in keys$
	remove	⋈	remove	21 (0.8)	192 (6.9)	$[keys \setminus \{x_1\} = \{y_1\}] \vee [...]$
	remove	⋈	size	13 (0.4)	37 (1.1)	$\neg(x_1 \in keys)$
	size	⋈	size	3 (0.1)	3 (0.1)	true
Stack	clear	⋈	clear	3 (0.1)	3 (0.1)	true
	clear	⋈	pop	2 (0.1)	2 (0.1)	false
	clear	⋈	push	2 (0.1)	2 (0.1)	false
	pop	⋈	pop	6 (0.2)	20 (0.6)	$nextToTop = top$
	push	▷	pop	72 (2.1)	115 (3.5)	$\neg(0 = size) \wedge top = x_1$
	pop	▷	push	34 (0.9)	76 (2.2)	$y_1 = top$
	push	⋈	push	13 (0.5)	20 (0.7)	$y_1 = x_1$

Fig. 2. Automatically generated commutativity conditions (φ_n^m). Right-moverness (▷) conditions identical for a pair of methods denoted by ⋈. **Qs** denotes number of SMT queries. Running time in seconds. Longer conditions have been truncated, see [7].

```
1  int warrior, warriorGold, warriorBlock, callback_result, king, kingBlock;
2  void enter(int val, int sendr, int bk, int rnd) {
3    if (val < 50) { send(sendr,val); return; }
4    warrior = sendr; warriorGold = val; warriorBlock = bk // write global variables
5    rpc_call("random number generator",__callback,res);
6    // Another call to enter() can execute while waiting for RPC
7    function __callback(int res_RN) {
8      // Most recent writer to warrior now reaps benefit of every callback
9      if (modFun(warriorBlock) == res_RN) {
10       king = warrior; kingBlock = warriorBlock; // winner } } }
```

Fig. 3. Simplified code for BlockKing in a C-like language.

to that of concurrent objects [31]. Unfortunately, many smart contracts are not written with this in mind, and attackers can exploit interleavings to their benefit.

As an example, we study the BlockKing smart contract. Figure 3 provides a simplification of its description, as discussed in [31]. This is a simple game in which the players—each identified by an address sendr—participate by making calls to BlockKing.enter(), sending money val to the contract. (The grey variables are external input that we have lifted to be parameters. bk reflects the caller's current block number and rnd is the outcome of a random number generation, described shortly.) The variables on Line 1 are globals, writable in any call to enter. On Line 3 there is a trivial case when the caller hasn't put enough value into the game, and the money is simply returned. Otherwise, the caller stores their address and value into the shared state. A random number is then generated and, since this requires complex algorithms, it is done via a remote procedure call to a third-party on Line 5, with a callback method provided on Line 7. If the randomly generated number is equal to a modulus of the current block number, then the caller is the winner, and warrior's (caller's) details are stored to king and kingBlock on Line 10.

Since random number generation is done via an RPC, players' invocations of enter can be interleaved. Moreover, these calls all write sendr and val to shared variables, so the RPC callback will always roll the dice for whomever most recently wrote to warriorBlock. An attacker can use this to leverage other players' investments to increase his/her own chance to win.

We now explore how Servois can aid a programmer in developing a more secure implementation. We observe that, as in traditional parallel programming contexts, if smart contracts are commutative then these interleavings are not problematic. Otherwise, there is cause for concern. To this end, we translated the BlockKing game into Servois format (see [8]). Servois took 1.4 s (on machine with 2.4 GHz Intel Core i5 processor and 8 GB RAM) and yielded the following *non-commutativity* condition for two calls to `enter`:

$$\texttt{enter}(\mathsf{val}_1, \mathsf{sendr}_1, \mathsf{bk}_1, \mathsf{rnd}_1) \not\bowtie \texttt{enter}(\mathsf{val}_2, \mathsf{sendr}_2, \mathsf{bk}_2, \mathsf{rnd}_2) \Leftrightarrow$$
$$\bigvee \begin{cases} \mathsf{val}_1 \geq 50 \wedge \mathsf{val}_2 \geq 50 \wedge \mathsf{sendr}_1 \neq \mathsf{sendr}_2 \\ \mathsf{val}_1 \geq 50 \wedge \mathsf{val}_2 \geq 50 \wedge \mathsf{sendr}_1 = \mathsf{sendr}_2 \wedge \mathsf{val}_1 \neq \mathsf{val}_2 \\ \mathsf{val}_1 \geq 50 \wedge \mathsf{val}_2 \geq 50 \wedge \mathsf{sendr}_1 = \mathsf{sendr}_2 \wedge \mathsf{val}_1 = \mathsf{val}_2 \wedge \mathsf{bk}_1 \neq \mathsf{bk}_2 \end{cases}$$

This disjunction effectively enumerates cases under which they contract calls *do not* commute. Of particular note is the first disjunct. From this first disjunct, whenever $\mathsf{sendr}_1 \neq \mathsf{sendr}_2$, the calls will not commute. Since in practice sendr_1 will always be different from sendr_2 (two different callers) and $\mathsf{val}_1 \geq 50 \wedge \mathsf{val}_2 \geq 50$ is the non-trivial case, the operations will almost never commute. This should be immediate cause for concern to the developer.

A commutative version of BlockKing would mean that there are no interleavings to be concerned about. Indeed, a simple way to improve commutativity is for each player to write their respective sendr and val to distinct shared state, perhaps via a hashtable keyed on sendr. To this end, we created a new version `enter_fixed` (see [8]). SERVOIS generated the following *non*-commutativity condition after 3.5 s.

$$\texttt{enter\_fixed}(\mathsf{val}_1, \mathsf{sendr}_1, \mathsf{bk}_1, \mathsf{rnd}_1) \not\bowtie \texttt{enter\_fixed}(\mathsf{val}_2, \mathsf{sendr}_2, \mathsf{bk}_2, \mathsf{rnd}_2) \quad \textit{iff}$$
$$\bigvee \begin{cases} \mathsf{val}_1 \geq 50 \wedge \mathsf{val}_2 \geq 50 \wedge \mathsf{val}_1 = \mathsf{val}_2 \wedge \mathsf{bk}_1 \neq \mathsf{bk}_2 \wedge \mathsf{sendr}_1 = \mathsf{sendr}_2 \\ \mathsf{val}_1 \geq 50 \wedge \mathsf{val}_2 \geq 50 \wedge \mathsf{val}_1 \neq \mathsf{val}_2 \wedge \mathsf{sendr}_1 = \mathsf{sendr}_2 \\ \mathsf{val}_1 \geq 50 \wedge \mathsf{val}_2 \geq 50 \wedge \mathsf{md}(\mathsf{bk}_2) = \mathsf{rnd}_2 \wedge \mathsf{md}(\mathsf{bk}_1) = \mathsf{rnd}_1 \wedge \mathsf{sendr}_1 \neq \mathsf{sendr}_2 \end{cases}$$

In the above non-commutativity condition, md is shorthand for modFun. In the first two disjuncts above, $\mathsf{sendr}_1 = \mathsf{sendr}_2$ which is, again, a case that will not occur in practice. All that remains is the third disjunct where $\mathsf{md}(\mathsf{bk}_2) = \mathsf{rnd}_2$ and $\mathsf{md}(\mathsf{bk}_1) = \mathsf{rnd}_1$. This corresponds to the case where *both* players have won. In this case, it is acceptable for the operations to not commute, because whomever won more recently will store their address/block to the shared king/kingBlock.

In summary, if we assume that $\mathsf{sendr}_1 \neq \mathsf{sendr}_2$, the non-commutativity of the original version is $\mathsf{val}_1 \geq 50 \vee \mathsf{val}_2 \geq 50$ (very strong). By contrast, the non-commutativity of the fixed version is $\mathsf{val}_1 \geq 50 \wedge \mathsf{val}_2 \geq 50 \wedge \mathsf{md}(\mathsf{bk}_2) = \mathsf{rnd}_2 \wedge \mathsf{md}(\mathsf{bk}_1) = \mathsf{rnd}_1$. We have thus demonstrated that the commutativity (and non-commutativity) conditions generated by SERVOIS can help developers understand the model of interference between two concurrent calls.

8 Conclusions and Future Work

This paper demonstrates that it is possible to automatically generate sound and effective commutativity conditions, a task that has so far been done manually or without soundness. Our commutativity conditions are applicable in a variety of contexts including transactional boosting [19], open nested transactions [29], and other non-transactional concurrency paradigms such as race detection [15], parallelizing compilers [30,34], and, as we show, robustness of Ethereum smart contracts [31]. It has been shown that understanding the commutativity of data-structure operations provides a key avenue to improved performance [12] or ease of verification [23,24].

This work opens several avenues of future research. For instance, leveraging the internal state of the SMT solver (beyond counterexamples) in order to generate new predicates [21]; automatically building abstract representation or making inferences such as one we made for the stack example; and exploring strategies to compute commutativity conditions directly from the program's code, without the need for an intermediate abstract representation [34].

References

1. Ethereum. https://ethereum.org/
2. Servois homepage. http://cs.nyu.edu/~kshitij/projects/servois
3. Servois source code. https://github.com/kbansal/servois
4. Solidity programming language. https://solidity.readthedocs.io/en/develop/
5. Abadi, M., Lamport, L.: The existence of refinement mappings. Theor. Comput. Sci. **82**, 253–284 (1991)
6. Aleen, F., Clark, N.: Commutativity analysis for software parallelization: letting program transformations see the big picture. In: Proceedings of the 14th International Conference on Architectural Support for Programming Languages and Operating Systems (ASPLOS-XII), pp. 241–252. ACM (2009)
7. Bansal, K.: Decision procedures for finite sets with cardinality and local theory extensions. Ph.D. thesis, New York University, January 2016
8. Bansal, K., Koskinen, E., Tripp, O.: Automatic generation of precise and useful commutativity conditions (extended version). CoRR, abs/1802.08748 (2018). https://arxiv.org/abs/1802.08748
9. Bansal, K., Reynolds, A., Barrett, C., Tinelli, C.: A new decision procedure for finite sets and cardinality constraints in SMT. In: Olivetti, N., Tiwari, A. (eds.) IJCAR 2016. LNCS (LNAI), vol. 9706, pp. 82–98. Springer, Cham (2016). https://doi.org/10.1007/978-3-319-40229-1_7
10. Barnett, M., Leino, K.R.M., Schulte, W.: The Spec# programming system: an overview. In: Barthe, G., Burdy, L., Huisman, M., Lanet, J.-L., Muntean, T. (eds.) CASSIS 2004. LNCS, vol. 3362, pp. 49–69. Springer, Heidelberg (2005). https://doi.org/10.1007/978-3-540-30569-9_3
11. Barrett, C., Conway, C.L., Deters, M., Hadarean, L., Jovanović, D., King, T., Reynolds, A., Tinelli, C.: CVC4. In: Gopalakrishnan, G., Qadeer, S. (eds.) CAV 2011. LNCS, vol. 6806, pp. 171–177. Springer, Heidelberg (2011). https://doi.org/10.1007/978-3-642-22110-1_14
12. Clements, A.T., Kaashoek, M.F., Zeldovich, N., Morris, R.T., Kohler, E.: The scalable commutativity rule: designing scalable software for multicore processors. ACM Trans. Comput. Syst. **32**(4), 10 (2015)
13. Cook, B., Koskinen, E.: Making prophecies with decision predicates. In: Proceedings of the 38th ACM SIGPLAN-SIGACT Symposium on Principles of Programming Languages, POPL 2011, Austin, TX, USA, 26–28 January 2011, pp. 399–410 (2011)
14. Dickerson, T., Gazzillo, P., Herlihy, M., Koskinen, E.: Adding concurrency to smart contracts. In: Proceedings of the ACM Symposium on Principles of Distributed Computing, PODC 2017, pp. 303–312. ACM, New York (2017)
15. Dimitrov, D., Raychev, V., Vechev, M.T., Koskinen, E.: Commutativity race detection. In: O'Boyle, M.F.P., Pingali, K. (eds.) ACM SIGPLAN Conference on Programming Language Design and Implementation, PLDI 2014, Edinburgh, United Kingdom, 09–11 June 2014, p. 33. ACM (2014)

16. Ernst, G.W., Ogden, W.F.: Specification of abstract data types in modula. ACM Trans. Program. Lang. Syst. **2**(4), 522–543 (1980)
17. Flon, L., Misra, J.: A unified approach to the specification and verification of abstract data types. In: Proceedings of the Specifications of Reliable Software Conference. IEEE Computer Society (1979)
18. Gehr, T., Dimitrov, D., Vechev, M.: Learning commutativity specifications. In: Kroening, D., Păsăreanu, C.S. (eds.) CAV 2015. LNCS, vol. 9206, pp. 307–323. Springer, Cham (2015). https://doi.org/10.1007/978-3-319-21690-4_18
19. Herlihy, M., Koskinen, E.: Transactional boosting: a methodology for highly concurrent transactional objects. In: Proceedings of the 13th ACM SIGPLAN Symposium on Principles and Practice of Parallel Programming (PPoPP 2008) (2008)
20. Hoare, C.A.R.: Proof of correctness of data representations. In: Broy, M., Denert, E. (eds.) Software Pioneers, pp. 385–396. Springer, New York (2002). https://doi.org/10.1007/978-3-642-59412-0_24
21. Hu, Y., Barrett, C., Goldberg, B.: Theory and algorithms for the generation and validation of speculative loop optimizations. In: Proceedings of the 2nd IEEE International Conference on Software Engineering and Formal Methods (SEFM 2004), pp. 281–289. IEEE Computer Society, September 2004
22. Kim, D., Rinard, M.C.: Verification of semantic commutativity conditions and inverse operations on linked data structures. In: Proceedings of the 32nd ACM SIGPLAN Conference on Programming Language Design and Implementation, PLDI 2011, pp. 528–541. ACM (2011)
23. Koskinen, E., Parkinson, M.J.: The push/pull model of transactions. In: ACM SIGPLAN Conference on Programming Language Design and Implementation, PLDI 2015, Portland, OR, USA, June 2015 (2015)
24. Koskinen, E., Parkinson, M.J., Herlihy, M.: Coarse-grained transactions. In: Hermenegildo, M.V., Palsberg, J. (eds.) Proceedings of the 37th ACM SIGPLAN-SIGACT Symposium on Principles of Programming Languages, POPL 2010, pp. 19–30. ACM (2010)
25. Kulkarni, M., Nguyen, D., Prountzos, D., Sui, X., Pingali, K.: Exploiting the commutativity lattice. In: Proceedings of the 32nd ACM SIGPLAN Conference on Programming Language Design and Implementation, PLDI 2011, pp. 542–555. ACM (2011)
26. Leino, K.R.M.: Specifying and verifying programs in Spec#. In: Virbitskaite, I., Voronkov, A. (eds.) PSI 2006. LNCS, vol. 4378, p. 20. Springer, Heidelberg (2007). https://doi.org/10.1007/978-3-540-70881-0_3
27. Lipton, R.J.: Reduction: a method of proving properties of parallel programs. Commun. ACM **18**(12), 717–721 (1975)
28. Meyer, B.: Applying "design by contract". IEEE Comput. **25**(10), 40–51 (1992)
29. Ni, Y., Menon, V., Adl-Tabatabai, A., Hosking, A.L., Hudson, R.L., Moss, J.E.B., Saha, B., Shpeisman, T.: Open nesting in software transactional memory. In: Proceedings of the 12th ACM SIGPLAN Symposium on Principles and Practice of Parallel Programming, PPOPP 2007, pp. 68–78. ACM (2007)
30. Rinard, M.C., Diniz, P.C.: Commutativity analysis: a new analysis technique for parallelizing compilers. ACM Trans. Program. Lang. Syst. (TOPLAS) **19**(6), 942–991 (1997)
31. Sergey, I., Hobor, A.: A concurrent perspective on smart contracts. In: Brenner, M., Rohloff, K., Bonneau, J., Miller, A., Ryan, P.Y.A., Teague, V., Bracciali, A., Sala, M., Pintore, F., Jakobsson, M. (eds.) FC 2017. LNCS, vol. 10323, pp. 478–493. Springer, Cham (2017). https://doi.org/10.1007/978-3-319-70278-0_30

32. Solar-Lezama, A., Jones, C.G., Bodík, R.: Sketching concurrent data structures. In: Proceedings of the ACM SIGPLAN 2008 Conference on Programming Language Design and Implementation PLDI 2008, pp. 136–148 (2008)
33. Tripp, O., Manevich, R., Field, J., Sagiv, M.: JAUNS: exploiting parallelism via hindsight. In: Proceedings of the 33rd ACM SIGPLAN Conference on Programming Language Design and Implementation, PLDI 2012, pp. 145–156. ACM, New York (2012)
34. Tripp, O., Yorsh, G., Field, J., Sagiv, M.: HAWKEYE: effective discovery of dataflow impediments to parallelization. In: Proceedings of the 26th Annual ACM SIGPLAN Conference on Object-Oriented Programming, Systems, Languages, and Applications, OOPSLA 2011, pp. 207–224 (2011)
35. Vechev, M.T., Yahav, E.: Deriving linearizable fine-grained concurrent objects. In: Proceedings of the ACM SIGPLAN 2008 Conference on Programming Language Design and Implementation, pp. 125–135 (2008)
36. Vechev, M.T., Yahav, E., Yorsh, G.: Abstraction-guided synthesis of synchronization. In: Proceedings of the 37th ACM SIGPLAN-SIGACT Symposium on Principles of Programming Languages, POPL 2010, pp. 327–338 (2010)
37. Wang, C., Yang, Z., Kahlon, V., Gupta, A.: Peephole partial order reduction. In: Ramakrishnan, C.R., Rehof, J. (eds.) TACAS 2008. LNCS, vol. 4963, pp. 382–396. Springer, Heidelberg (2008). https://doi.org/10.1007/978-3-540-78800-3_29

Bit-Vector Model Counting Using Statistical Estimation

Seonmo Kim([✉]) and Stephen McCamant([✉])

University of Minnesota, Minneapolis, MN 55455, USA
{smkim,mccamant}@cs.umn.edu

Abstract. Approximate model counting for bit-vector SMT formulas (generalizing #SAT) has many applications such as probabilistic inference and quantitative information-flow security, but it is computationally difficult. Adding random parity constraints (XOR streamlining) and then checking satisfiability is an effective approximation technique, but it requires a prior hypothesis about the model count to produce useful results. We propose an approach inspired by statistical estimation to continually refine a probabilistic estimate of the model count for a formula, so that each XOR-streamlined query yields as much information as possible. We implement this approach, with an approximate probability model, as a wrapper around an off-the-shelf SMT solver or SAT solver. Experimental results show that the implementation is faster than the most similar previous approaches which used simpler refinement strategies. The technique also lets us model count formulas over floating-point constraints, which we demonstrate with an application to a vulnerability in differential privacy mechanisms.

Keywords: Model counting · Bit-vectors · Floating point · #SAT
Randomized algorithms

1 Introduction

Model counting is the task of determining the number of satisfying assignments of a given formula. Model counting for Boolean formulas, #SAT, is a standard model-counting problem, and it is a complete problem for the complexity class #P in the same way that SAT is complete for NP. #P is believed to be a much harder complexity class than NP, and exact #SAT solving is also practically much less scalable than SAT solving. #SAT solving can be implemented as a generalization of the DPLL algorithm [17]. and a number of systems such as Relsat [4], CDP [6], Cachet [38], sharpSAT [41], DSHARP [35] and countAntom [9] have demonstrated various optimization techniques. However, not surprisingly given the problem's theoretical hardness, such systems often perform poorly when formulas are large and/or have complex constraints.

Since many applications do not depend on the model count being exact, it is natural to consider approximation algorithms that can give an estimate of

D. Beyer and M. Huisman (Eds.): TACAS 2018, LNCS 10805, pp. 133–151, 2018.
https://doi.org/10.1007/978-3-319-89960-2_8

a model count with a probabilistic range and confidence. Some approximate model counters include ApproxCount [43], SampleCount [24], MiniCount [31], ApproxMC [12], ApproxMC-p [30] and ApproxMC2 [13]. In this paper we build on the approximation technique of XOR streamlining [25], which reduces the number of solutions of a formula by adding randomly-chosen XOR (parity) constraints. In expectation, adding one constraint reduces the model count by a factor of 2, and k independent constraints reduce the model count by 2^k. If a formula with extra constraints has $n > 0$ solutions, the original formula likely had about $n \cdot 2^k$. If the model count after constraints is small, it can be found with a few satisfiability queries, so XOR streamlining reduces approximate model counting to satisfiability. However to have an automated system, we need an approach to choose a value of k when the model count is not known in advance.

One application of approximate model counting is measuring the amount of information revealed by computer programs. For a deterministic computation, we say that the *influence* [36] is the base-two log of the number of distinct outputs that can be produced by varying the inputs, a measure of the information flow from inputs to outputs. Influence computation is related to model counting, but formulas arising from software are more naturally expressed as SMT (satisfiability modulo theories) formulas over bit-vectors than as plain CNF, and one wants to count values only of output variables instead of all variables. The theory of arithmetic and other common operations on bounded-size bit-vectors has the same theoretical expressiveness as SAT, since richer operations can be expanded ("bit-blasted") into circuits. But bit-vector SMT is much more convenient for expressing the computations performed by software, and SMT solvers incorporate additional optimizations. We build a system for this generalized version of the problem which takes as input an SMT formula with one bit-vector variable designated as the output, and a specification of the desired precision.

Our algorithm takes a statistical estimation approach. It maintains a probability distribution that reflects an estimate of possible influence values, using a particle filter consisting of weighted samples from the distribution. Intuitively the mean of the distribution corresponds to our tool's best estimate, while the standard deviation becomes smaller as its confidence grows. At each step, we refine this estimate by adding k XOR constraints to the input formula, and then enumerating solutions under those constraints, up to a maximum of c solutions (we call this enumeration process an *exhaust-up-to-c* query [36]). At a particular step, we choose k and c based on our previous estimate (prior), and then use the query result to update the estimate for the next step (posterior). The update from the query reweights the particle filter points according to a probability model of how many values are excluded by XOR constraints. We use a simple binomial-distribution model which would be exact if each XOR constraint were fully independent. Because this model is not exact, a technique based only on it does not provide probabilistic soundness, even though it performs well practically. So we also give a variant of our technique which does produce a sound bound, at the expense of requiring more queries to meet a given precision goal.

We implement our algorithm in a tool SearchMC that wraps either a bit-vector SMT solver compatible with the SMT-LIB 2 standard or a SAT solver, and report experimental results. SearchMC can be used to count solutions with respect to a subset of the variables in a formula, such as the outputs of a computation, the capability that Klebanov et al. call projected model counting [30], and Val et al. call subset model counting [42]. In our case the variables not counted need not be of bit-vector type. For instance this makes SearchMC to our knowledge the first tool that can be used to count models of constraints over floating-point numbers (counting the floating-point bit patterns individually, as contrasted with computing the measure of a subset of $\mathbb{R}^n$ [7,15]). We demonstrate the use of this capability with an application to a security problem that arises in differential privacy mechanisms because of the limited precision of floating-point values.

Compared to ApproxMC2 [13] and ApproxMC-p [30], concurrently-developed approximate #SAT tools also based on XOR streamlining, our technique gives results more quickly for the same requested confidence levels.

In summary, the key attributes of our approach are as follows:

- Our approximate counting approach gives a two-sided bound with user-specified confidence.
- Our tool inherits the expressiveness and optimizations of SMT solvers.
- Our tool gives a probabilistically sound estimate if requested, or can give a result more quickly if empirical precision is sufficient.

2 Background

XOR Streamlining. The main idea of XOR streamlining [25] is to add randomly chosen XOR constraints to a given input formula and feed the augmented formula to a satisfiability solver. One random XOR constraint will reduce the expected number of solutions in half. Consequently, if the formula is still satisfiable after the addition of s XOR constraints, the original formula likely has at least 2^s models. If not, the formula likely has at most 2^s models. Thus we can obtain a lower bound or an upper bound with this approach. There are some crucial parameters to determine the bounds and the probability of the bounds and they need to be carefully chosen in order to obtain good bounds. However, early systems [25] did not provide an algorithm to choose the parameters.

Influence. Newsome *et al.* [36] introduced the terminology of "influence" for a specific application of model counting in quantitative information-flow measurement. This idea can capture the control of input variables over an output variable and distinguish true attacks and false positives in a scenario of malicious input to a network service. The influence of input variables over an output variable is the $\log_2$ of the number of possible output values.

Exhaust-up-to-c Query. Newsome *et al.* also introduced the terminology of an "exhaust-up-to-c query", which repeats a satisfiability query up to some number c of solutions, or until there are no satisfying values left. This is a good approach to find a model count if the number of solution is small.

Particle Filter. A particle filter [19] is an approach to the statistical estimation of a hidden state from noisy observations, in which a probability distribution over the state is represented non-parametrically by a collection of weighted samples referred to as particles. The weights evolve over time according to observations; they tend to become unbalanced, which is corrected by a resampling process which selects new particles with balanced weights. A particle filtering algorithm with periodic resampling takes the following form:

1. Sample a number of particles from a prior distribution.
2. Evaluate the importance weights for each particle and normalize the weights.
3. Resample particles (with replacement) according to the weights.
4. The posterior distribution represented by the resampled particles becomes the prior distribution to next round and go to step 2.

3 Design

This section describes the approach and algorithms used by SearchMC. It is implemented as a wrapper around an off-the-self bit-vector satisfiability solver that supports the SMT-LIB2 format [3]. It takes as input an SMT-LIB2 formula in a quantifier-free theory that includes bit-vectors (QF_BV, or an extension like QF_AUFBV or QF_FPBV) in which one bit-vector is designated as the output, i.e. the bits over which solutions should be counted. (For ease of comparison with #SAT solvers, SearchMC also has a mode that takes a Boolean formula in CNF, with a list of CNF variables designated as the output.) SearchMC repeatedly queries the SMT solver with variations of the supplied input which add XOR constraints and/or "blocking" constraints that exclude previously-found solutions; based on the results of these queries, it estimates the total number of values of the output bit-vector for which the formula has a satisfying assignment.

SearchMC chooses fruitful queries by keeping a running estimate of possible values of the model count. We model the influence ($\log_2$ of model count) as if it were a continuous quantity, and represent the estimate as a probability distribution over possible influence values. In each iteration we use the current estimate to choose a query, and then update the estimate based on the query's results. (At a given update, the most recent previous distribution is called the *prior*, and the new updated one is called the *posterior*.) As the algorithm runs, the confidence in the estimate goes up, and the best estimate changes less from query to query as it converges on the correct result. Each counting query SearchMC makes is parameterized by k, the number of random XOR constraints to add, and c, the maximum number of solutions to count. The result of the query is a number of satisfying assignments between 0 and c inclusive, where a result that stops at c means the real total is at least c. Generally a low result leads to the next estimate being lower than the current one and a high result leads to the estimate increasing. We will describe the process of updating the probability distribution, and then give the details of the algorithms that use it.

Updating Distribution and Confidence Interval. We here explain the idea of how we compute a posterior distribution over influence, where both the prior and posterior are represented by particles. Suppose we have a formula f with a known influence $\log_2 N$, and add k XOR random constraints to the formula. If we simulate checking the satisfiability of this augmented formula f_k for different XOR constraints, we can estimate a probability of sat/unsat on f_k. We expand this idea by applying exhaust-up-to-c approach to f_k. We count the number of satisfying assignments n up to c and generate the distributions for each number of satisfying assignments (where $n = c$ means that the number of satisfying assignments is in fact c or more). Thus under an assumption on the true influence of a formula, we can estimate the probabilities of each number of satisfying assignments based on k. By collecting these probabilities across a range of influence, we obtain a probability distribution over influence for an unknown formula assumed to have less than a maximum bits of influence. Under the idealized assumption that each XOR constraint is completely independent, adding k XOR constraints will leave each satisfying assignment alive with probability $1/2^k$. For any particular set of $n \geq 0$ satisfying assignments remaining out of an original N, the probability that exactly those n solutions will remain is the product of $1/2^k$ for each n and $1-(1/2^k)$ for each of the other $N-n$. Summing the total number of such sets with a binomial coefficient, we can approximately model the probability of exactly n solutions remaining as:

$$Pr_{=n}(N,k) = \binom{N}{n}(\frac{1}{2^k})^n(1-\frac{1}{2^k})^{N-n} \tag{1}$$

For the case when the algorithm stops looking when there might still be more solutions, we also want an expression for the probability that the number of solutions is n or more. We compute this straightforwardly as one minus the sum of the probabilities for smaller values:

$$Pr_{\geq n}(N,k) = 1 - \sum_{i=0}^{n-1} Pr_{=i}(N,k) \tag{2}$$

We use XOR constraints that contain each counted bit with probability one half, and are negated with probability one half. (This is the same family of constraints used in other recent systems [12,13,30]. Earlier work [25] suggested using constraints over exactly half of the bits, which have the same expected size, but less desirable independence properties.) Our binomial probability model is not precise in general, because these XOR constraints are 3-independent, but not r-independent for $r \geq 4$. When $N \geq 4$, some patterns among solutions (such as a set of four bitvectors whose XOR is all zeros) lead to correlations in the satisfiability of XOR constraints, and in turn to higher variance in the probability distribution without changing the expectation. This effect is relatively small, but we lack an analytic model of it, so we compensate by slightly increasing the confidence level our tool targets compared to what the user originally requested.

This probability model lets us simulate the probability of various query results as a function of the unknown formula influence. We use this model as a weighting function for each particle and resample particles based on each particle's weight value. Then, we estimate a posterior distribution from sampled particles that have all equal weights. For instance, given a prior distribution over the influence sampled at 0.1 bit intervals, we can compute a sampled posterior distribution by counting and re-normalizing just the probability weights that correspond to a given query result value n. From the estimated posterior distribution, the mean μ and the standard deviation σ are computed. Hence, the μ is our best possible answer as our algorithm iterates and σ shows how much we are close to the true answer. Sequentially, the posterior distribution will be the next round's prior distribution and for use in the very first step of the algorithm we also implement a case of the prior distribution as uniform over influence.

Next we compute a confidence interval (lower bound and upper bound) symmetrically from the mean of the posterior distribution even though the distribution is not likely to be symmetrical. There are several ways to compute the confidence interval but the difference of the results is negligible as the posterior distribution gets narrower. Therefore, we used a simple way to compute the confidence interval: a half interval from the left side of the mean and another half from the right side.

Algorithm. We present our main algorithm `SearchMC` that runs automatically and always gives an answer with a given confidence interval. The pseudocode for algorithm `SearchMC` is given as Algorithm 1. Our algorithm takes as input a formula f, a desired confidence level CL $(0 < CL < 1)$, a confidence level adjustment α $(0 \leq \alpha < 1)$, a desired range size *thres* and an initial prior distribution $InitDist$. f contains a set of bit-vector variables and bit-vector operators. We can obtain a confidence interval at a confidence level for a given mean and standard deviation. A confidence level CL is a fraction parameter specifying the probability with which the interval should contain the true answer, for example, 0.95 (95%) or 0.99 (99%). As we described above, the binomial probability model does not exactly capture the full behavior of XOR constraints, which could lead to our results being over-confident. We introduce a confidence level adjustment factor α to internally target a higher confidence level than the user requested, making it more likely that the requested confidence can be met. If $\alpha = 0$, we do not adjust the input confidence level. We have currently set the value for α empirically from $\frac{1}{2}$ to $\frac{1}{4}$. However this single factor may not ideally capture the control of the confidence level. Further investigation of the confidence gap will be future work. Our algorithm terminates when the length of our confidence interval is less than or equal to a given non-negative parameter *thres*. This parameter determines the amount of running time and there is a trade-off. If *thres* value is small, it gives a narrow confidence interval, but the running time would be longer. If the value is large, it gives a wide confidence interval, but a shorter running time. Our tool can choose any initial prior distribution $InitDist$ represented by particles. For example, a generic strategy is to start with a uniform distribution over 0 to a number of output variables. If we have a better prior bound on the true influence (for instance 64 bits), a uniform distribution from 0 to that bound will generally perform better.

Variables. There are several variables: *prior*, *post*, *width*, k, c, $nSat$, UB, LB and δ. *prior* represents a prior distribution by sampled particles with

Algorithm 1. SearchMC(f, $thres$, CL, α, $InitDist$)

```
CL ← CL + (1 − CL) × α                              ▷ Confidence level adjustment
width ← getWidth(f)                      ▷ The width of the output bit-vector of f
prior ← InitDist                                        ▷ Initial distribution
δ ← width
while δ > thres do
    c, k ← ComputeCandK(prior, width)
    nSat ← MBoundExhaustUpToC(f, width, k, c)
    post, UB, LB ← Update(prior, c, k, nSat, CL)
    δ ← UB − LB
    if k == 0 then
        output "Exact Count: ", nSat
    else
        prior ← post
        output "Lower: ", LB, "Upper: ", UB
    end if
end while
```

Algorithm 2. ComputeCandK($prior$, $width$)

```
μ, σ ← getMuSigma(prior)
c ← ⌈((2^σ + 1)/(2^σ − 1))^2⌉
k ← ⌊μ − (1/2) log_2 c⌋
if k ≤ 0 then
    c ← 2^width + 1                      ▷ In this case, c is effectively infinite
    k ← 0                                                   ▷ No constraints
end if
return c, k
```

corresponding weights. In one iteration, we obtain the updated posterior distribution *post* with resampled particles based on our probabilistic model as described above. The posterior becomes the prior distribution for the next iteration. While our algorithm is in the loop, it keeps updating *post*. *width* is the width of the output bit-vector of an input formula f, which is an initial upper bound for the influence since the influence cannot be more than the width of the output bit-vector. k is a number of random XOR constraints and c specifies the maximum number of solutions for the exhaust-up-to-c query. We obtain c and k using the `ComputeCandK` function shown as Algorithm 2 and discussed below. *nSat* is a number of solutions from the exhaust-up-to-c query. `MBoundExhaustUpToC` runs until it finds the model count exactly or c solutions from formula f with k random XOR constraints. UB and LB are variables to store an upper bound and a lower bound of the current model count approximation with a given confidence level as we describe above. δ is the distance between the upper bound and lower bound. This parameter determines whether our algorithm terminates or not. If δ is less than or equal to our input value *thres*, our algorithm terminates. If not, it runs again with updated *post* until δ reaches the desired range size *thres*. An extreme case $k = 0$ denotes that our guess is equivalent to the true model count. In this case, we print out the exact count and terminate the algorithm.

Functions. To motivate the definition of the function `ComputeCandK`, we view an exhaust-up-to-c query as analogous to measuring influence with a bounded-length "ruler." Suppose that we reduce the expected value of the model count by adding k XOR constraints to f. Then, we can use the "length-($\log_2 c$) ruler" to measure the influence starting at k and this measurement corresponds to the result of an exhaust-up-to-c query: the length-($\log_2 c$) ruler has c markings spaced logarithmically as illustrated in Fig. 1. Each iteration of the algorithm chooses a location (k) and length (c) for the ruler, and gets a noisy reading on the influence as one mark on the ruler. Over time, we want to converge on the true influence value, but we also wish to lengthen the rule so that the finer marks give more precise readings. Based on this idea, we have the `ComputeCandK` function to choose the length of and starting point of the ruler from a prior distribution. Then, we run an exhaust-up-to-c query and call `Update` to update the distribution based on the result of the query.

The pseudocode for algorithm `update` is described as Algorithm 3. A prior distribution *prior* and a posterior distribution *post* are represented as a set of sampled particles (influences). We sampled 500 particles for each `update` function call. Once we have the updated distribution, we can find out the interval of a given confidence level.

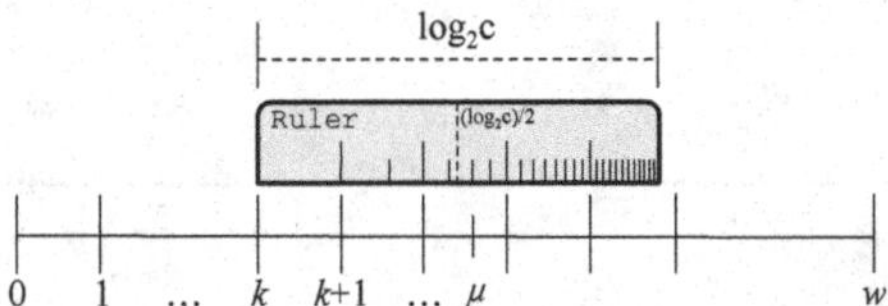

Fig. 1. Ruler intuition

Since we observe that our running σ represents how much we are close to the true answer, we use a rational function to satisfy the condition that c increases as σ decreases (i.e., we get more accurate result as c increases).

The k value denotes where to put the ruler. We want to place the ruler where the expected value of the prior distribution lies near the middle of the ruler hence our expected value is in the range of the ruler with high probability. Therefore, we subtract the half length of the ruler ($\frac{1}{2}\log_2 c$) from the expected value μ and then use the floor function to the value because k has to be an nonnegative integer value. The expected value always lies in the right-half side of the ruler by using the floor function. However, it is not essential which rounding function is used. Note that there might be a case where k becomes negative. If this happens, we set $k = 0$ and $c = \infty$, because our expected value is so small that we can run the solver exhaustively to give the exact model count. The formula for c is motivated by the intuition that the spacing between two marks near the middle of the ruler

Algorithm 3. Update(*prior*, *c*, *k*, *nSat*, *CL*)

```
for t from 1 to nParticles do
    x_t ← prior_t                    ▷ x is a list of sampled particles (influences)
    if nSat < c then                 ▷ Updating each weight of each particle
        w_t = Pr_{=nSat}(2^{x_t}, k)
    else
        w_t = Pr_{≥nSat}(2^{x_t}, k)
    end if
end for
w ← normalize()                      ▷ Normalizing the weights
post ← sample(x, w, nParticles)      ▷ Resampling based on the weights
UB, LB ← getBounds(post, CL)
return post, UB, LB
```

should be proportional to the standard deviation of the probability distribution, to ensure that a few different results of the query are possible with relatively high probability; the spacing between the two marks closest to $\frac{1}{2}\log_2 c = \log_2 \sqrt{c}$ will be about $\log_2(\sqrt{c}+\frac{1}{2}) - \log_2(\sqrt{c}-\frac{1}{2})$. Setting this equal to σ, solving for c, and taking the ceiling gives line 3 of Algorithm 2.

Probabilistic Sound Bounds. The binomial model performs well for choosing a series of queries, and it yields an estimate of the remaining uncertainty in the tool's results, but because the binomial model differs in an hard-to-quantify way from the true probability distributions, the bounds derived from it do not have any associated formal guarantee. In this section we explain how to use our tool's same query results, together with a sound bounding formula, to compute a probabilistically sound lower and upper bound on the true influence. As a trade-off, these bounds are usually not as tight as our tool's primary results.

The idea is based on Theorem 2 from Chakraborty *et al.*'s work [12], which in turn is a variant on Theorem 5 by Schmidt *et al.* [39]. For convenience we substitute our own terminology.

Lemma 1. *Let nSat be the return value from* `MBoundExhaustUpToC`. *Then,*

$$Pr\left[0 < nSat < c \text{ and } k \leq \log_2|f| \text{ and } (1+\epsilon)^{-1}|f| \leq 2^k|f_h| \leq (1+\epsilon)|f|\right] > 0.6$$

Chakraborty *et al.* use *pivot* for what we call c from an exhaust-up-to-c query and $pivot = 2\lceil 3e^{1/2}(1+\frac{1}{\epsilon})^2\rceil$. Since $0 < \epsilon < 1$, c (*pivot*) should be always greater than 40 to make the lemma true with a probability of at least 0.6. (The constant 0.6 comes from $(1-e^{-3/2})^2 \approx 0.6035$.)

In SearchMC's iterations, given c and k, we can compute ϵ value to estimate the bounds. Therefore, when c is greater than 40 from our tool's iteration, we can compute a lower and upper bound such that the true influence is within the bounds with a probability of at least 0.6.

4 Experimental Results

In this section, we present our experimental results. All our experiments were performed on a machine with an Intel Core i7 3.40 Ghz CPU and 16 GB memory. Our main algorithm is implemented with a Perl script and Update function is implemented in a C program called by the main script. Our algorithm can be applied to both SMT formulas and CNF formulas. We have tested a variety of SAT solvers and SMT solvers, and our current implementation specifically supports Cryptominisat2 [40] for CNF formulas and Z3 [18] and MathSAT5 [16] for SMT formulas. For pure bit-vector SMT formulas, our tool also supports eagerly converting the formula to CNF first and then using CNF mode. (We implement the conversion using the first phase of the STP solver [2,23] with optimizations disabled and a patch to output the SMT-to-CNF variable mapping.) Performing CNF translation eagerly gives up the benefit of some (e.g., word-level) optimizations performed by SMT solvers, but it can sometimes be profitable because it avoids repeating bit-blasting, and allows the tool to use a specialized multiple-solutions mode of Cryptominisat.

We run our algorithm with a set of DQMR (Deterministic Quick Medical Reference) benchmarks [1] and ISCAS89 benchmarks [8] converted to CNF files by TG-Pro [14] and compare the results of the benchmarks with ApproxMC2 [13] and ApproxMC-p [30]. ApproxMC2 and ApproxMC-p are state-of-the-art approximate #SAT solvers which we describe in more detail in Sect. 5. We used Cryptominisat2 as the back-end solver with all the tools for fair comparison. For the parameters for the tools, we set a 60% confidence level, a confidence level adjustment $\alpha = 0.25$ and a desired interval length of 1.7. As described above, SearchMC-sound gives correct bounds with a probability of at least 0.6. Since the desired confidence level for ApproxMC2 is $1 - \delta$, it can achieve a 60% confidence level by setting a parameter $\delta = 0.4$ which corresponds to our parameter $CL = 0.6$. Using the same confidence level for ApproxMC-p avoids an apparent mistake in the calculation of its base confidence pointed out by Biondi *et al.* [5]. The length of the interval for ApproxMC2 is computed as $\log_2(|f| \times (1+\epsilon)) - \log_2(|f| \times (1/(1+\epsilon))) = 1.7$ hence we can obtain the interval length 1.7 by setting a parameter $\epsilon = 0.8$, corresponding to our parameter $thres = 1.7$. Computing the interval for ApproxMC-p is a little different. The length of the interval for ApproxMC-p is $\log_2(|f| \times (1+\epsilon)) - \log_2(|f| \times (1-\epsilon)) = 1.7$ hence we can obtain the interval length 1.7 by setting a parameter $\epsilon = 0.53$. Note that SearchMC increases the c value of an exhaust-up-to-c query as it iterates while the corresponding ApproxMC2 and ApproxMC-p parameters are fixed as a function of ϵ (72 and 46, respectively) in this experiment. Also, we set an initial prior to be a uniform distribution over 0 to 64 bits for SearchMC. We tested 122 benchmarks (83 DQMRs and 39 ISCAS89s). All the tools were able to solve a set of 106 benchmarks (83 DQMRs and 23 ISCAS89s) within 2 h.

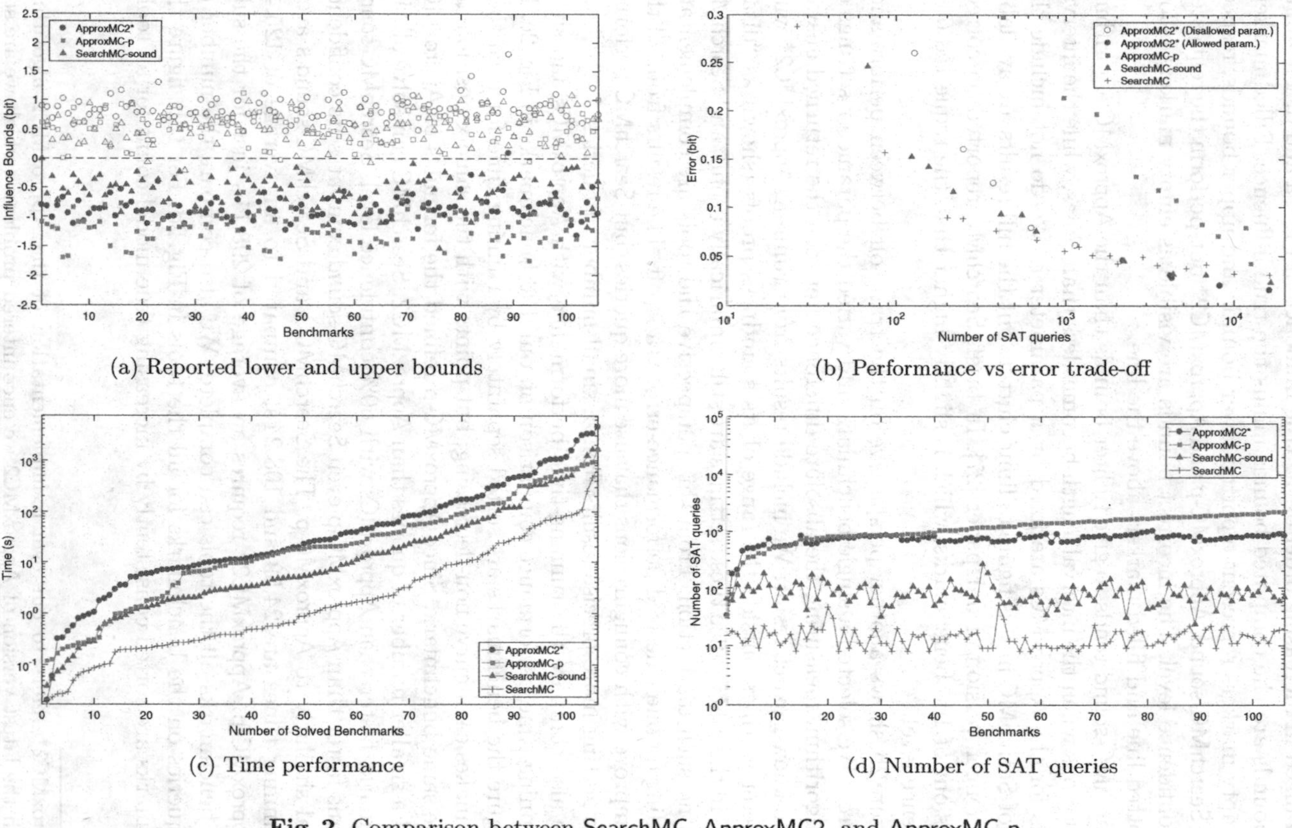

(a) Reported lower and upper bounds

(b) Performance vs error trade-off

(c) Time performance

(d) Number of SAT queries

Fig. 2. Comparison between SearchMC, ApproxMC2, and ApproxMC-p

Figure 2a compares the quality of lower bounds and upper bounds computed by SearchMC-sound, ApproxMC-p and ApproxMC2*[1]. Note that the benchmarks are arranged in increasing order of the true influence in Fig. 2a and d. The influence bounds are the computed bounds minus the true influence. Filled markers and empty markers represent reported lower bounds and upper bounds, respectively. SearchMC-sound, ApproxMC-p and ApproxMC2* out-perform the requested 60% confidence level. The incorrect bounds are visible as empty markers below the dotted line and filled markers above the line.

SearchMC-sound tends to give tighter bounds than the ApproxMC algorithms since it stops when the interval length becomes less than $thres$, while the interval lengths for the ApproxMCs are fixed by a parameter ϵ. We do not include the result of SearchMC in this figure to limit clutter, but the full results are available in the longer version of our paper [27]. In brief, SearchMC reported 65 correct bounds out of 106 benchmarks, which is slightly higher than the requested 60% confidence level.

Figure 2b shows another perspective on the trade-off between performance and error. We selected a single benchmark and varied the parameter settings of each algorithm, measuring the absolute difference between the returned answer and the known exact result. We include results from running ApproxMC2* with parameter settings outside the range of its soundness proofs (shown as "disallowed" in the plot), since these settings are still empirically useful, and SearchMC makes no such distinction. From this perspective the tools are complementary depending on one's desired performance-error trade-off. The results from all the tools improve with configurations that use more queries, but SearchMC performs best at getting more precise results from a small number of queries.

We also compare the running-time performance with ApproxMCs and show the running-time performance comparison on our 106 benchmarks in Fig. 2c. In this figure the benchmarks are sorted separately by running time for each tool, which makes each curve non-decreasing; but points with the same x position are not the same benchmark. Since ApproxMC-p refined the formulas of ApproxMC, it used a smaller number of queries than ApproxMC2. SearchMC can solve all the benchmarks faster than ApproxMCs with 60% confidence level. SearchMC-sound performs faster than ApproxMC-p even SearchMC-sound computes its confidence interval similarly to ApproxMC-p. The SearchMC's and SearchMC-sound's average running times are 24.59 and 108.24 s, compared to an average of 125.48 for ApproxMC-p. ApproxMC2* requires an average of 298.11 s just for the subset of benchmarks all the tools can complete. We also compare the number of SAT queries on the benchmarks for all the tools in Fig. 2d. For this figure the benchmarks are sorted consistently by increasing true model count for all tools.

[1] ApproxMC2* refers to our own re-implementation of the ApproxMC2 algorithm. With the latest version of ApproxMC2 we encountered problems (which we are still investigating) in which the SAT solver would sometimes fail to perform Gaussian elimination, which unfairly hurt the tool's performance. Our implementation also makes it easy to control the random seed for experiment repeatability.

Table 1. Results and performance of model counting ($\log_2$ shown) of naive Laplacian noise in IEEE floating point

Problem size	All noise			Intersection	
	Expected	SearchMC	Time	SearchMC	Time
15e7, 2^8	7.994	[7.374, 8.069]	164 s	1.000	312 s
16e7, 2^9	8.997	[8.566, 9.073]	470 s	3.322	1585 s
16e8, 2^{10}	9.999	[10.076, 10.844]	279 s	4.754	5279 s
18e8, 2^{10}	9.999	[9.675, 10.099]	583 s	1.000	1137 s
19e8, 2^{11}	10.999	[10.825, 11.404]	757 s	3.585	9848 s

The average number of SAT queries for SearchMC, SearchMC-sound ApproxMC-p and ApproxMC2* is about 14.7, 83.73, 1256.96 and 733.81 queries, respectively.

Floating Point/Differential Privacy Case Study. As an example of model counting with floating point constraints, we measure the security of a mechanism for differential privacy which can be undermined by unexpected floating-point behavior. The Laplace mechanism achieves differential privacy [22] by adding exponentially-distributed noise to a statistic to obscure its exact value. For instance, suppose we wish to release a statistic counting the number of patients in a population with a rare disease, without releasing information that confirms any single patient's status. In the worst case, an adversary might know the disease status of all patients other than the victim; for instance the attacker might know that the true count is either 10 or 11. If we add random noise from a Laplace distribution to the statistic before releasing it, we can leave the adversary relatively unsure about whether the true count was 10 or 11, while preserving the utility of an approximate result. A naive implementation of such a simple differentially private mechanism using standard floating-point techniques can be insecure because of a problem pointed out by Mironov [34]. For instance if we generate noise by dividing a random number in $[1, 2^{31}]$ by 2^{31} and taking the logarithm, the relative probability of particular floating point results will be quantized compared to the ideal probability, and many values will not be possible at all. If a particular floating point number could have been generated as $10 + noise$ but not as $11 + noise$ in our scenario, its release completely compromises the victim's privacy.

To measure this danger using model counting, we translated the standard approach for generating Laplacian noise, including an implementation of the natural logarithm, into SMT-LIB 2 floating point and bit-vector constraints. (We followed the `log` function originally by SunSoft taken from the `musl` C library, which uses integer operations to reduce the argument to $[\sqrt{2}/2, \sqrt{2})$, followed by a polynomial approximation.) A typical implementation might use double-precision floats with an 11-bit exponent and 53-bit fraction, and 32 bits of randomness, which we abbreviate "53e11, 2^{32}", but we tried a range of increasing sizes. We measured the total number of distinct values taken by $10 + noise$ as well as the size of the intersection of this set with the $11 + noise$ set.

The results and running time are shown in Table 1. (For space reasons we omit results for some smaller formats, which can be found in the extended version of the paper [27].) We ran SearchMC with a confidence level of 80%, a confidence level adjustment of 0.5 and a threshold of 1.0; the SMT solver was MathSAT 5.3.13 with settings recommended for floating-point constraints by its authors. We use one random bit to choose the sign of the noise, and the rest to choose its magnitude. The sign is irrelevant when the magnitude is 0, so the expected influence for n bits of randomness is $\log_2(2^n - 1)$. SearchMC's 80% confidence interval included the correct result in 4 out of 5 cases. The size of the intersections is small enough that SearchMC usually reports an exact result (always here). The size of the intersection is also always much less than the total set of noise values, confirming that using this algorithm and parameter setting for privacy protection would be ill-advised. The running time increases steeply as the problem size increases, which matches the conventional wisdom that reasoning about floating-point is challenging. But because floating-point SMT solving is a young area, there is future solvers may significantly improve the technique's performance.

Description of Archival Artifact. To facilitate reproduction of our experiments and future research, we have created an artifact archive containing code and data for performing the experiments described in this paper. This archive is a `zip` file containing data, instructions, source code, and binaries pre-compiled for Ubuntu 14.04 x86-64, which we have tested for compatibility with the virtual machine used during the artifact evaluation process [26]. The archive includes SearchMC itself and the modified version of STP it uses for bit-blasting, as well as scripts specific to the differential-privacy experiment, and the benchmark input files we used for performance evaluation. Information about accessing this artifact is found at the end of the paper.

5 Related Work

Exact Model Counting. Some of the earliest Boolean model counters used the DPLL algorithm [17] for counting the exact number of solutions. Birnbaum *et al.* [6] formalized this idea and introduced an algorithm for counting models of propositional formulas. Based on this idea, Relsat [4], Cachet [38] sharpSAT [43] and DSHARP [35] showed improvements by using several optimizations. The major contribution of countAntom [9] is techniques for parallelization, but it provides state-of-the-art performance even in single-threaded mode.

Phan *et al.* [37] encode a full binary search for feasible outputs in a bounded model checker. This approach is precise, but requires more than one call to the underlying solver for each feasible output. Klebanov *et al.* [29] perform exact model counting for quantitative information-flow measurement, with an approach that converts C code to a CNF formula with bounded model checking and then uses exact #SAT solving. Val *et al.* [42] integrate a symbolic execution tool more closely with a SAT solver by using techniques from SAT solving to prune the symbolic execution search space, and then perform exact model counting restricted to an output variable.

Randomized Approximate Model Counting. Randomized approximate model counting techniques perform well on many kinds of a formula for which finding single solutions is efficient. Wei and Selman [43] introduced ApproxCount which uses near-uniform sampling to estimate the true model count but it can significantly over-estimate or underestimate if the sampling is biased. SampleCount [24] improves this sampling idea and gives a lower bound with high probability by using a heuristic sampler. MiniCount [31] computes an upper bound under statistical assumptions by counting branching decisions during SAT solving. MBound [25] is an approximate model counting tool that gives probabilistic bounds on the model counts by adding randomly-chosen parity constraints as XOR streamlining. Chakraborty *et al.* [12] introduced ApproxMC, an approximate model counter for CNF formulas, which automated the choice of XOR streamlining parameters. The ApproxMC algorithm, in our terminology, starts by fixing c and a total number of iterations based on the desired precision and confidence of the results. In each iteration ApproxMC searches for an appropriate k value, adds k XOR random constraints, and then performs an exhaust-up-to-c query on the streamlined formula and multiplies the result by 2^k. It stores all the individual estimates as a multiset and computes its final estimate as the median of the values. The original ApproxMC sequentially increases k in each iteration until it finds an appropriate k value. An improved algorithm ApproxMC2 [13] uses galloping binary search and saves a starting k value between iterations to make the selection of k more efficient. Other recent systems that build on ApproxMC include SMTApproxMC [11] and ApproxMC-p [30]. ApproxMC-p implements projection (counting over only a subset of variables), which we also require.

ApproxMC2, whose initial development was concurrent with our first work on SearchMC, is the system most similar to SearchMC: its binary search for k plays a similar role to our converging μ value. However SearchMC also updates the c parameter over the course of the search, leading to fewer total queries. ApproxMC, ApproxMC2, and related systems choose the parameters of the search at the outset, and make each iteration either fully independent (ApproxMC) or dependent in a very simple way (ApproxMC2) on previous ones. These choices make it easier to prove the tool's probabilistic results are sound, but they require a conservative choice of parameters. SearchMC's approach of maintaining a probabilistic estimate at runtime means that its iterations are not at all independent: instead our approach is to extract the maximum guidance for future iterations from previous ones, to allow the search to converge more aggressively.

The runtime performance of SearchMC, like that of ApproxMC(2), is highly dependent on the behavior of SAT solvers on CNF-XOR formulas. Some roots of the difficulty of this problem have been investigated by Dudek et al. [20,21].

Non-randomized Approximate Model Counting. Non-randomized approximate model counting using techniques similar to static program analysis is generally faster than randomized approximate model counting techniques, and such systems can give good approximations for some problem classes. However, they cannot provide a precision guarantee for arbitrary problems, and it is not possible to give more effort to have more refined results.

Castro *et al.* [10] compute an upper bound on the number of bits about an input that are revealed by an error report. Meng and Smith [33] use two-bit-pattern SMT entailment queries to calculate a propositional overapproximation and count its instances with a model counter from the computer algebra system Mathematica. Luu *et al.* [32] propose a model counting technique over an expressive string constraint language.

Applications: Security and Privacy. Various applications of model counting have been proposed for security and privacy purposes. Castro *et al.* [10] use model counting and symbolic execution approaches to measure leaking private information from bug reports. They compute an upper bound on the amount of private information leaked by a bug report and allow users to decide on whether to submit the report or not. Newsome *et al.* [36] show how an untrusted input affects a program and introduce a family of techniques for measuring influence which can be applicable to x86 binaries. Biondi *et al.* [5] use CBMC and ApproxMC2 to quantify information flow on a set of benchmarks and evaluate the leakage incurred by a small instance of the Heartbleed OpenSSL bug.

6 Future Work and Conclusion

Closing the gap between the performance of SearchMC and SearchMC-sound is one natural direction for future research. On one hand, we would like to explore techniques for asserting sound probabilistic bounds which can take advantage of the results of all of SearchMC's queries. At the same time, we would like to find a model of the number of solutions remaining after XOR streamlining that is more accurate than our current binomial model, which should improve the performance of SearchMC. Another future direction made possible by the particle filter implementation is to explore different prior distributions, including unbounded ones. For instance, using a negative exponential distribution over influence as a prior would avoid the any need to estimate a maximum influence in advance, while still starting the search process with low-k queries which are typically faster to solve.

In sum, we have presented a new model counting approach SearchMC using XOR streamlining for SMT formulas with bit-vectors and other theories. We demonstrate our algorithm that adaptively maintains a probabilistic model count estimate based on the results of queries. Our tool computes a lower bound and an upper bound with a requested confidence level, and yields results more quickly than previous systems.

Data Availability Statement and Acknowledgements. An archival snapshot of the tools and datasets analyzed in this work is available in the conference `figshare` repository at https://doi.org/10.6084/m9.figshare.5928604.v1 [28]. Updates will also be available via the project's GitHub page at https://github.com/seonmokim/SearchMC. We would like to thank the anonymous conference and artifact reviewers for suggestions which have helped us to improve our system and the paper's presentation. This research is supported by the National Science Foundation under grant no. 1526319.

References

1. Bayesian-inference as model-counting benchmarks. http://www.cs.rochester.edu/users/faculty/kautz/Cachet/Model_Counting_Benchmarks/index.htm
2. STP. http://stp.github.io/
3. Barrett, C., Stump, A., Tinelli, C.: The SMT-LIB standard: Version 2.0. Technical report (2010)
4. Bayardo Jr., R.J., Schrag, R.C.: Using CSP look-back techniques to solve real-world SAT instances. In: Proceedings of AAAI, pp. 203–208 (1997)
5. Biondi, F., Enescu, M.A., Heuser, A., Legay, A., Meel, K.S., Quilbeuf, J.: Scalable approximation of quantitative information flow in programs. Verification, Model Checking, and Abstract Interpretation. LNCS, vol. 10747, pp. 71–93. Springer, Cham (2018). https://doi.org/10.1007/978-3-319-73721-8_4
6. Birnbaum, E., Lozinskii, E.L.: The good old Davis-Putnam procedure helps counting models. J. Artif. Intell. Res. (JAIR) **10**, 457–477 (1999)
7. Borges, M., Filieri, A., d'Amorim, M., Pasareanu, C.S., Visser, W.: Compositional solution space quantification for probabilistic software analysis. In: Proceedings of PLDI, pp. 123–132 (2014)
8. Brglez, F., Bryan, D., Kozminski, K.: Combinational profiles of sequential benchmark circuits. In: Proceedings of ISCAS, vol. 3, pp. 1929–1934 (1989)
9. Burchard, J., Schubert, T., Becker, B.: Laissez-Faire caching for parallel #SAT solving. In: Heule, M., Weaver, S. (eds.) SAT 2015. LNCS, vol. 9340, pp. 46–61. Springer, Cham (2015). https://doi.org/10.1007/978-3-319-24318-4_5
10. Castro, M., Costa, M., Martin, J.-P.: Better bug reporting with better privacy. In: Proceedings of ASPLOS, pp. 319–328 (2008)
11. Chakraborty, S., Meel, K.S., Mistry, R., Vardi, M.Y.: Approximate probabilistic inference via word-level counting. In: Proceedings of AAAI, pp. 3218–3224 (2016)
12. Chakraborty, S., Meel, K.S., Vardi, M.Y.: A scalable approximate model counter. In: Schulte, C. (ed.) CP 2013. LNCS, vol. 8124, pp. 200–216. Springer, Heidelberg (2013). https://doi.org/10.1007/978-3-642-40627-0_18
13. Chakraborty, S., Meel, K.S., Vardi, M.Y.: Improving approximate counting for probabilistic inference: from linear to logarithmic SAT solver calls. In: Proceedings of IJCAI, pp. 3569–3576 (2016)
14. Chen, H., Marques-Silva, J.: TG-Pro: a SAT-based ATPG system. J. Satisf. Boolean Model. Comput. **8**(1–2), 83–88 (2012)
15. Chistikov, D., Dimitrova, R., Majumdar, R.: Approximate counting in SMT and value estimation for probabilistic programs. In: Proceedings of TACAS, pp. 320–334 (2015)
16. Cimatti, A., Griggio, A., Schaafsma, B.J., Sebastiani, R.: The MathSAT5 SMT solver. In: Piterman, N., Smolka, S.A. (eds.) TACAS 2013. LNCS, vol. 7795, pp. 93–107. Springer, Heidelberg (2013). https://doi.org/10.1007/978-3-642-36742-7_7
17. Davis, M., Logemann, G., Loveland, D.: A machine program for theorem-proving. Commun. ACM **5**(7), 394–397 (1962)
18. de Moura, L., Bjørner, N.: Z3: an efficient SMT solver. In: Ramakrishnan, C.R., Rehof, J. (eds.) TACAS 2008. LNCS, vol. 4963, pp. 337–340. Springer, Heidelberg (2008). https://doi.org/10.1007/978-3-540-78800-3_24
19. Del Moral, P.: Nonlinear filtering: interacting particle solution. Markov Process. Relat. Fields **2**(4), 555–580 (1996)
20. Dudek, J., Meel, K.S., Vardi, M.Y.: Combining the k-CNF and XOR phase-transitions. In: Proceedings of IJCAI, pp. 727–734 (2016)

21. Dudek, J., Meel, K.S., Vardi, M.Y.: The hard problems are almost everywhere for random CNF-XOR formulas. In: Proceedings of IJCAI, pp. 600–606 (2017)
22. Dwork, C.: Differential privacy. In: Bugliesi, M., Preneel, B., Sassone, V., Wegener, I. (eds.) ICALP 2006. LNCS, vol. 4052, pp. 1–12. Springer, Heidelberg (2006). https://doi.org/10.1007/11787006_1
23. Ganesh, V., Dill, D.L.: A decision procedure for bit-vectors and arrays. In: Damm, W., Hermanns, H. (eds.) CAV 2007. LNCS, vol. 4590, pp. 519–531. Springer, Heidelberg (2007). https://doi.org/10.1007/978-3-540-73368-3_52
24. Gomes, C.P., Hoffmann, J., Sabharwal, A., Selman, B.: From sampling to model counting. In: Proceedings of IJCAI, pp. 2293–2299 (2007)
25. Gomes, C.P., Sabharwal, A., Selman, B.: Model counting: a new strategy for obtaining good bounds. In: Proceedings of AAAI, pp. 54–61 (2006)
26. Hartmanns, A., Wendler, P.: figshare (2018). https://doi.org/10.6084/m9.figshare.5896615
27. Kim, S., McCamant, S.: Bit-vector model counting using statistical estimation. CoRR, abs/1712.07770 (2017)
28. Kim, S., McCamant, S.: SearchMC: an approximate model counter using XOR streamlining techniques. figshare (2018). https://doi.org/10.6084/m9.figshare.5928604.v1
29. Klebanov, V., Manthey, N., Muise, C.: SAT-based analysis and quantification of information flow in programs. In: Joshi, K., Siegle, M., Stoelinga, M., D'Argenio, P.R. (eds.) QEST 2013. LNCS, vol. 8054, pp. 177–192. Springer, Heidelberg (2013). https://doi.org/10.1007/978-3-642-40196-1_16
30. Klebanov, V., Weigl, A., Weisbarth, J.: Sound probabilistic #SAT with projection. In: Workshop on QAPL (2016)
31. Kroc, L., Sabharwal, A., Selman, B.: Leveraging belief propagation, backtrack search, and statistics for model counting. In: Perron, L., Trick, M.A. (eds.) CPAIOR 2008. LNCS, vol. 5015, pp. 127–141. Springer, Heidelberg (2008). https://doi.org/10.1007/978-3-540-68155-7_12
32. Luu, L., Shinde, S., Saxena, P., Demsky, B.: A model counter for constraints over unbounded strings. In: Proceedings of PLDI, pp. 565–576 (2014)
33. Meng, Z., Smith, G.: Calculating bounds on information leakage using two-bit patterns. In: Proceedings of PLAS, pp. 1:1–1:12 (2011)
34. Mironov, I.: On significance of the least significant bits for differential privacy. In: Proceedings of CCS, pp. 650–661 (2012)
35. Muise, C., McIlraith, S.A., Beck, J.C., Hsu, E.I.: DSHARP: fast d-DNNF compilation with sharpSAT. In: Kosseim, L., Inkpen, D. (eds.) AI 2012. LNCS (LNAI), vol. 7310, pp. 356–361. Springer, Heidelberg (2012). https://doi.org/10.1007/978-3-642-30353-1_36
36. Newsome, J., McCamant, S., Song, D.: Measuring channel capacity to distinguish undue influence. In: Proceedings of PLAS, pp. 73–85 (2009)
37. Phan, Q., Malacaria, P., Tkachuk, O., Păsăreanu, C.S.: Symbolic quantitative information flow. SIGSOFT Softw. Eng. Notes **37**(6), 1–5 (2012)
38. Sang, T., Bacchus, F., Beame, P., Kautz, H.A., Pitassi, T.: Combining component caching and clause learning for effective model counting. In: Proceedings of SAT (2004)
39. Schmidt, J.P., Siegel, A., Srinivasan, A.: Chernoff-hoeffding bounds for applications with limited independence. SIAM J. Discret. Math. **8**(2), 223–250 (1995)
40. Soos, M., Nohl, K., Castelluccia, C.: Extending SAT solvers to cryptographic problems. In: Kullmann, O. (ed.) SAT 2009. LNCS, vol. 5584, pp. 244–257. Springer, Heidelberg (2009). https://doi.org/10.1007/978-3-642-02777-2_24

41. Thurley, M.: sharpSAT – counting models with advanced component caching and implicit BCP. In: Biere, A., Gomes, C.P. (eds.) SAT 2006. LNCS, vol. 4121, pp. 424–429. Springer, Heidelberg (2006). https://doi.org/10.1007/11814948_38
42. Val, C.G., Enescu, M.A., Bayless, S., Aiello, W., Hu, A.J.: Precisely measuring quantitative information flow: 10K lines of code and beyond. In: Proceeding of Euro S&P, pp. 31–46 (2016)
43. Wei, W., Selman, B.: A new approach to model counting. In: Bacchus, F., Walsh, T. (eds.) SAT 2005. LNCS, vol. 3569, pp. 324–339. Springer, Heidelberg (2005). https://doi.org/10.1007/11499107_24

Deductive Verification

Hoare Logics for Time Bounds
A Study in Meta Theory

Maximilian P. L. Haslbeck(✉) and Tobias Nipkow

Technische Universität München, Munich, Germany
haslbema@in.tum.de
http://www.in.tum.de/~haslbema
http://www.in.tum.de/~nipkow

Abstract. We study three different Hoare logics for reasoning about time bounds of imperative programs and formalize them in Isabelle/HOL: a classical Hoare like logic due to Nielson, a logic with potentials due to Carbonneaux *et al.* and a *separation logic* following work by Atkey, Chaguérand and Pottier. These logics are formally shown to be sound and complete. Verification condition generators are developed and are shown sound and complete too. We also consider variants of the systems where we abstract from multiplicative constants in the running time bounds, thus supporting a big-O style of reasoning. Finally we compare the expressive power of the three systems.

Keywords: Hoare logic · Algorithm analysis · Program verification

1 Introduction

This paper is about Hoare logics for proving upper bounds on running times and about the formalized (in a theorem prover) study of their meta theory. The paper is not about the automatic analysis of running times but about fundamental questions like soundness and completeness of logics and of verification condition generators (VCGs). The need for such a study becomes apparent when browsing the related literature (e.g. [1,6,7]): (formalized) soundness results are of course provided, but completeness of logics and VCGs is missing.

We study multiple different Hoare logics because we are interested in different aspects of the logics. One aspect is the difference between precise upper bounds and order-of-magnitude upper bounds that abstract from multiplicative constants. In the latter case we speak of "big-O style" logics.

A second aspect is modularity. We would like to combine verified results about subprograms in order to show correctness and running time for larger programs. Therefore we also study a separation logic for running time analysis.

Overall we study the meta theory of three different kinds of Hoare logics that have emerged in the literature. Our main contributions are:

M. P. L. Haslbeck—Supported by DFG GRK 1480 (PUMA) and Koselleck Grant NI 491/16-1.

D. Beyer and M. Huisman (Eds.): TACAS 2018, LNCS 10805, pp. 155–171, 2018.
https://doi.org/10.1007/978-3-319-89960-2_9

- Based on the simple imperative language IMP (Sect. 2), we formalize three logics for time bounds from the literature (Sect. 3); we show their soundness and completeness w.r.t. IMP's semantics, discuss specific weaknesses and strengths and study their interrelations (Sect. 4).
- The first logic we study is a big-O style logic due to Nielson [23] (Sect. 3.1). We improve, formalize and verify this logic and extend it with a VCG whose soundness and completeness we also verify.
- In Sect. 3.2 we formalize a quantitative Hoare logic following ideas by Carbonneaux *et al.* [4,6] and extend their work as follows: we prove completeness of the logic and design a sound and complete VCG. Additionally we extend the logic to a big-O style logic.
- Following ideas of Atkey [1] and Charguéraud and Pottier [7] we formalize a logic similar to separation logic (Sect. 3.3) for reasoning about concrete running times. We formally prove soundness and completeness.
- All proofs have been formalized in Isabelle/HOL [18,19] and are available online [9].

2 Basics

We consider the simple deterministic imperative language IMP. Its formalization is standard and can be found elsewhere [18]. IMP's commands are built up from SKIP, assignment, sequential composition, conditional and While-loop. Program states are functions from variables to values. By default c is a command and s a state. Evaluation of a boolean or arithmetic expression e in state s is denoted by $[\![e]\!]_s$.

We have defined a big-step semantics that counts the consumed time during execution: SKIP, assignment and evaluation of boolean expressions require one time unit. The precise definition of the semantics is routine. We write $(c, s) \stackrel{t}{\Rightarrow} s'$ to mean that starting command c in state s terminates after time t in state s'.

Given a pair (c, s), $\downarrow(c, s)$ means that the computation of c starting from s terminates, $\downarrow_S(c, s)$ then denotes the final state, and $\downarrow_T(c, s)$ the execution time.

3 Hoare Logics for Time Bounds

In this section we study and extend three different Hoare logics: a classical one based on [23], one using potentials [4] and one based on separation logic with time credits [1].

3.1 Nielson Style

Riis Nielson and Nielson [23] present a Hoare logic to prove the "order of magnitude of the execution time" of a program (which we call "big-O style"). They reason about triples of the form $\{P\}c\{e \Downarrow Q\}$ where P and Q are assertions and e is a time bound. The intuition is the following: if the execution of command c

is started in a state satisfying P then it terminates in a state satisfying Q after $O(e)$ time units, i.e. the execution time has order of magnitude e. Note that e is evaluated in the state before executing c.

Throughout the paper we rely on what is called a *shallow* embedding of assertions and time bounds: there is no concrete syntactic representation of assertions and time bounds but they are merely functions in HOL, our ambient logic. They map states to truth values and natural numbers.

A complication in reasoning about execution time comes from the fact that one needs to combine time bounds that refer to different points in the execution, for example when adding time bounds in a sequential composition. This difficulty can be overcome with *logical variables* that enable us to transport time bounds from the prestate to the poststate of a command. We formalize logical variables by modelling assertions as functions of two states, the state of the logical variables (typically l) and the state of the program variables (typically s).

The validity of Nielson's triples is formally defined as follows:

$$\models_1 \{P\}c\{e \Downarrow Q\} \equiv (\exists k. \forall l\ s.\ P\ l\ s \longrightarrow (\exists t\ s'.\ (c, s) \stackrel{t}{\Rightarrow} s' \wedge Q\ l\ s' \wedge t \leq k \cdot e\ s))$$

The Hoare logic below needs to generate "fresh" logical variables. Thus we need to express which logical variables are already used. This is called the *support* of an assertion. Because assertions are merely functions, the support is defined semantically:

$$\textit{support}\ Q\ \equiv\ \{x \mid \exists l_1\ l_2\ s.\ (\forall y.\ y \neq x \longrightarrow l_1\ y = l_2\ y) \wedge Q\ l_1\ s \neq Q\ l_2\ s\}$$

Our Hoare logic is shown in Fig. 1. It is largely a formalization of the system in [23, Table 10.4] but with two important changes: we have simplified rule *While* (details below) and we have replaced the consequence rule by $\textit{conseq}_K$, an adaptation of Kleymann's stronger consequence rule [15]; rules *conseq* and *const* are derived from it. Note that the latter two rules suffice for a sound and complete Hoare logic, but our proof of completeness of the VCG needs $\textit{conseq}_K$.

Now we discuss the rules in Fig. 1. Rules *Skip*, *Assign*, *If* and *conseq* are straightforward. Note that $\mathbf{1}$ is the time bound $\lambda s.1$ and $+$ is lifted to time bounds pointwise. The notation $s[a/x]$ is short for "s with x mapped to $[\![a]\!]_s$".

Now consider rule *Seq*. Given $\{P\}c_1\{e_1 \Downarrow Q\}$ and $\{Q\}c_2\{e_2 \Downarrow R\}$ one may want to conclude $\{P\}c_1; c_2\{e_1 + e_2 \Downarrow R\}$. Unfortunately, $e_1 + e_2$ does not lead to the correct result, as c_1 could have altered variables e_2 depends on. In order to adapt e_2 for the changes that occur in c_1, we use a shifted time bound e_2', and leave as a proof goal to show that the value of e_2' in the prestate is an upper bound on e_2 in the poststate of c_1. Rule *Seq* relates e_2' and e_2 through a fresh logical variable u that is equated with the value of e_2' in the prestate of c_1. The time bound e in the conclusion must be an upper bound of $e_1 + e_2'$.

In the *const* rule, the time bound can be reduced by a constant factor. Note that we split up Nielson's $\textit{cons}_e$ rule into *conseq* and *const*.

Our rule *While* is a simplification of the one in [23]. The latter is an extension with time of the "standard" While-rule for total correctness where a variable

$$\frac{}{\vdash_1 \{P\}\text{SKIP}\{\mathbf{1} \Downarrow P\}}\,\textit{Skip} \qquad \frac{}{\vdash_1 \{\lambda l\ s.\ P\ l\ (s[a/x])\}x := a\{\mathbf{1} \Downarrow P\}}\,\textit{Assign}$$

$$\frac{\vdash_1 \{\lambda l\ s.\ P\ l\ s \wedge [\![b]\!]_s\}c_1\{e \Downarrow Q\} \qquad \vdash_1 \{\lambda l\ s.\ P\ l\ s \wedge \neg[\![b]\!]_s\}c_2\{e \Downarrow Q\}}{\vdash_1 \{P\}\text{IF } b \text{ THEN } c_1 \text{ ELSE } c_2\{e + \mathbf{1} \Downarrow Q\}}\,\textit{If}$$

$$\frac{\begin{array}{c}\vdash_1 \{\lambda l\ s.\ P\ l\ s \wedge e_2'\ s = l\ u\}c_1\{e_1 \Downarrow \lambda l\ s.\ Q\ l\ s \wedge e_2\ s \le l\ u\} \qquad \vdash_1 \{Q\}c_2\{e_2 \Downarrow R\}\\ (\forall l\ s.\ P\ l\ s \Longrightarrow e_1\ s + e_2'\ s \le e\ s) \qquad u \notin \textit{support } P \qquad u \notin \textit{support } Q\end{array}}{\vdash_1 \{P\}c_1; c_2\{e \Downarrow R\}}\,\textit{Seq}$$

$$\frac{\begin{array}{c}\vdash_1 \{\lambda l\ s.\ I\ l\ s \wedge [\![b]\!]_s \wedge e'\ s = l\ u\}c\{e'' \Downarrow \lambda l\ s.\ I\ l\ s \wedge e\ s \le l\ u\}\\ (\forall l\ s.\ I\ l\ s \wedge [\![b]\!]_s \longrightarrow e\ s \ge 1 + e'\ s + e''\ s)\\ (\forall l\ s.\ I\ l\ s \wedge \neg[\![b]\!]_s \longrightarrow e\ s \ge 1) \qquad u \notin \textit{support } I\end{array}}{\vdash_1 \{I\}\text{WHILE } b \text{ DO } c\{e \Downarrow \lambda l\ s.\ I\ l\ s \wedge \neg[\![b]\!]_s\}}\,\textit{While}$$

$$\frac{\begin{array}{c}\forall l\ s.\ P'\ l\ s \longrightarrow P\ l\ s\\ \vdash_1 \{P\}c\{e \Downarrow Q\}\\ \forall l\ s'.\ Q\ l\ s' \longrightarrow Q'\ l\ s'\end{array}}{\vdash_1 \{P'\}c\{e' \Downarrow Q'\}}\,\textit{conseq} \qquad \frac{\begin{array}{c}\exists k. \forall l\ s.\ P\ l\ s \longrightarrow e\ s \le k \cdot e'\ s\\ \vdash_1 \{P\}c\{e \Downarrow Q\}\end{array}}{\vdash_1 \{P\}c\{e' \Downarrow Q\}}\,\textit{const}$$

$$\frac{\begin{array}{c}\exists k. \forall l\ s.\ P'\ l\ s \longrightarrow (e\ s \le k \cdot e'\ s \wedge (\forall s'. \exists l'.\ P\ l' s \wedge (Q\ l' s' \longrightarrow Q'\ l\ s')))\\ \vdash_1 \{P\}c\{e \Downarrow Q\}\end{array}}{\vdash_1 \{P'\}c\{e' \Downarrow Q'\}}\,\textit{conseq}_K$$

Fig. 1. Hoare logic for reasoning about order of magnitude of execution time

decreases with each loop iteration. However, once you have time, you no longer need that variable and we removed it. The key constraint in rule *While* is $e \ge 1 + e' + e''$. It can be explained by unfolding the loop once. The time e to execute the whole loop must be an upper bound for the time e'' to execute the loop body plus the time e' to execute the remaining loop iteration; the 1+ accounts for evaluation of b. The time e' to execute the remaining loop iterations is obtained from e by (intuitively) an application of rule *Seq*: in the first premise a fresh logical variable u is used to pull e back over c, resulting in e'. The rest of rule *While* is standard.

Soundness of the calculus can be shown by induction on the derivation of $\vdash_1 \{P\}c\{e \Downarrow Q\}$:

Theorem 1 (Soundness of $\vdash_1$). $\vdash_1 \{P\}c\{e \Downarrow Q\} \Longrightarrow \models_1 \{P\}c\{e \Downarrow Q\}$

Our completeness proof follows the general pattern for Hoare logics: define a weakest precondition operator *wp* and show that the triple $\{wp\ c\ Q\}c\{Q\}$ is derivable. In our setting *wp* is defined like this

$$wp\ c\ Q\ \equiv\ (\lambda l\ s.\ \exists t\ s'.\ (c, s) \overset{t}{\Rightarrow} s' \wedge Q\ l\ s')$$

and we show derivability of the following triple that also takes time into account:

Lemma 1. $\textit{finite}(\textit{support } Q) \Longrightarrow \vdash_1 \{wp\ c\ Q\}c\{\lambda s.\ \downarrow_T(c, s) \Downarrow Q\}$

As we need fresh logical variables for rules *Seq* and *While*, we assume that the set of logical variables Q depends on is finite.

It is instructive to observe that for this proof, only the Hoare rules *Skip* to *conseq* are needed. Neither *const* nor $conseq_K$ are used. Lemma 1 thus expresses that it always is possible to derive a triple with the precise execution time as a time bound. Only as a last step an abstraction of multiplicative constants and over-approximation of the time bound is necessary. This shows that for every valid triple one can first deduce a correct upper bound for the running time, only to get rid of a multiplicative constant in a final application of the *const* rule one. In the end, Lemma 1 implies completeness:

Theorem 2 (Completeness of $\vdash_1$).
$finite\ (support\ Q) \Longrightarrow\ \models_1 \{P\}c\{e \Downarrow Q\} \Longrightarrow\ \vdash_1 \{P\}c\{e \Downarrow Q\}$

In particular we can now apply the above observation about the shape of derivations of valid triples to provable ones, by soundness: in any derivation one can pull out all applications of *const* and combine them into a single one at the very root of the proof tree. We will observe the very same principle when studying the quantitative Hoare logic in Sect. 3.2.

Verification Condition Generator. Showing validity of $\{P\}c\{e \Downarrow Q\}$ now boils down to applying the correctly instantiated rules of the Hoare logic and proving their side conditions. The former is a mechanical task, which is routinely automated by a verification condition generator, while the latter is left to an automatic or interactive theorem prover.

We design a VCG that collects the side conditions for an annotated program. While for classical Hoare logic it suffices to annotate a loop with an invariant I, for reasoning about execution time we introduce two more annotations for the following reason.

Consider rule *Seq* in Fig. 1. When applying the rule to a proof goal $\vdash_1$ $\{P\}c_1; c_2\{e \Downarrow R\}$ we need to instantiate the variables P, Q, e_1, e_2, and e_2'. As for classical Hoare logic, Q is chosen to be the weakest preconditions of c_2 w.r.t. R, which can be calculated if the loops in c_2 are annotated by invariants. (Analogously for P being the weakest precondition of c_1 w.r.t. Q). Similarly, when annotating the loops in c_1 and c_2 with time bounds E, time bounds e_1 and e_2 can be constructed. Finally, e_2' can be determined if the evolution of e_2 through c_1 is known. For straight line programs, this can be deduced, only for loops a state transformer S has to be annotated. An annotated loop then has the form $\{I, S, E\}$ WHILE b DO C where I is the invariant and S and E are as above.

For our completeness proof of the VCG we also need annotations that correspond to applications of rule $conseq_K$ and record information that cannot be inferred automatically. For that purpose we introduce a new annotated command *Conseq* $\{P', Q, e'\}$ C where P', Q and e' are as in rule $conseq_K$.

We use capital letters, e.g. C, to denote annotated commands and $\overline{C}$ is the unannotated version of C stripped of all annotations.

We use three auxiliary functions *pre*, *post* and *time*. Their definitions are shown in Fig. 2.

$$
\begin{aligned}
&\mathit{pre}\ \mathrm{SKIP}\ Q = Q\\
&\mathit{pre}\ (x := a)\ Q = (\lambda l s.\ Q\ l\ (s[a/x]))\\
&\mathit{pre}\ (C_1; C_2)\ Q = \mathit{pre}\ C_1\ (\mathit{pre}\ C_2\ Q)\\
&\mathit{pre}\ (\mathit{Conseq}\ \{P', \_, \_\}\ C)\ Q = P'\\
&\mathit{pre}\ (\mathrm{IF}\ b\ \mathrm{THEN}\ C_1\ \mathrm{ELSE}\ C_2)\ Q\ l\ s =\\
&\quad \text{if } [\![b]\!]_s \text{ then } \mathit{pre}\ C_1\ Q\ l\ s \text{ else } \mathit{pre}\ C_2\ Q\ l\ s\\
&\mathit{pre}\ (\{I, \_, \_\}\ \mathrm{WHILE}\ b\ \mathrm{DO}\ C)\ Q = I
\end{aligned}
$$

$$
\begin{aligned}
&\mathit{post}\ \mathrm{SKIP}\ s = s\\
&\mathit{post}\ (x := a)\ s = s[a/x]\\
&\mathit{post}\ (C_1; C_2)\ s = \mathit{post}\ C_2\ (\mathit{post}\ C_1\ s)\\
&\mathit{post}\ (\mathit{Conseq}\ \{\_, \_, \_\}\ C) = \mathit{post}\ C\\
&\mathit{post}\ (\mathrm{IF}\ b\ \mathrm{THEN}\ C_1\ \mathrm{ELSE}\ C_2)\ s =\\
&\quad \text{if } [\![b]\!]_s \text{ then } \mathit{post}\ C_1\ s \text{ else } \mathit{post}\ C_2\ s\\
&\mathit{post}\ (\{\_, S, \_\}\ \mathrm{WHILE}\ b\ \mathrm{DO}\ C) = S
\end{aligned}
$$

$$
\begin{aligned}
&\mathit{time}\ \mathrm{SKIP}\ s = 1\\
&\mathit{time}\ (x := a)\ s = 1\\
&\mathit{time}\ (C_1; C_2)\ s = \mathit{time}\ C_1\ s + \mathit{time}\ C_2\ (\mathit{post}\ C_1\ s)\\
&\mathit{time}\ (\mathit{Conseq}\ \{\_, \_, \_\}\ C) = \mathit{time}\ C\\
&\mathit{time}\ (\mathrm{IF}\ b\ \mathrm{THEN}\ C_1\ \mathrm{ELSE}\ C_2)\ s =\\
&\quad \text{if } [\![b]\!]_s \text{ then } \mathit{time}\ C_1\ s \text{ else } \mathit{time}\ C_2\ s\\
&\mathit{time}\ (\{\_, \_, E\}\ \mathrm{WHILE}\ b\ \mathrm{DO}\ C) = E
\end{aligned}
$$

Fig. 2. Functions *pre*, *post* and *time*

The VCG reduces proving a triple $\{P\}\overline{C}\{e \Downarrow Q\}$ to checking that the annotations really are invariants, upper bounds and correct state transformers. The VCG traverses C and collects all the verification conditions for the loops into a big conjunction. The most interesting case is the loop itself:

$$
\begin{aligned}
&\mathit{vc}\ (\{I, S, E\}\ \mathrm{WHILE}\ b\ \mathrm{DO}\ C)\ Q = \mathit{vc}\ C\ I\ \wedge\\
&\quad (\forall l\ s.\ (I\ l\ s \wedge [\![b]\!]_s \longrightarrow \mathit{pre}\ C\ I\ l\ s\\
&\qquad\qquad \wedge E\ s \geq 1 + E(\mathit{post}\ C\ s) + \mathit{time}\ C\ s\\
&\qquad\qquad \wedge S\ s = S(\mathit{post}\ C\ s))\\
&\qquad \wedge (I\ l\ s \wedge \neg [\![b]\!]_s \longrightarrow Q\ l\ s \wedge E\ s \geq 1 \wedge S\ s = s))
\end{aligned}
$$

First, verification conditions are recursively generated from the loop body C and the invariant I as desired post condition. The invariant and the loop guard must imply preservation of the invariant, the recurrence inequation for the time bound and that the state transformer S obeys the fixpoint equation for loops. When exiting the loop, the post condition must hold, E has to pay for the last test of the loop guard, and S needs to be the identity.

The verification conditions for *Conseq* $\{P', Q, e'\}$ C merely check the side condition of rule conseq_K:

$$
\begin{aligned}
&\mathit{vc}\ (\mathit{Conseq}\ \{P', Q, e'\}\ C)\ Q' = \mathit{vc}\ C\ Q\ \wedge\\
&\quad \exists k.\ \forall l\ s.\ P'\ l\ s \longrightarrow \mathit{time}\ C\ s \leq k \cdot e'\ s\\
&\qquad\qquad \wedge \forall t. \exists l'.\ \mathit{pre}\ C\ Q\ l'\ s \wedge (Q\ l'\ t \longrightarrow Q'\ l\ t)
\end{aligned}
$$

The remaining equations for vc are straightforward:

$$vc \text{ SKIP } Q = True$$
$$vc\ (x := a)\ Q = True$$
$$vc\ (C_1; C_2)\ Q = (vc\ C_1\ (pre\ C_2\ Q) \wedge vc\ C_2\ Q)$$
$$vc\ (\text{IF } b \text{ THEN } C_1 \text{ ELSE } C_2)\ Q = (vc\ C_1\ Q \wedge vc\ C_2\ Q)$$

Theorem 3 (Soundness of vc**).** *Let* C *and* Q *involve only finitely many logical variables. Then* $vc\ C\ Q$ *together with* $\exists k.\forall l\ s.\ P\ l\ s \longrightarrow pre\ C\ Q\ l\ s \wedge time\ C\ s \leq k \cdot e\ s$ *imply* $\vdash_1 \{P\}\ \overline{C}\{e \Downarrow Q\}$.

That is, for proving $\vdash_1 \{P\}\ \overline{C}\{e \Downarrow Q\}$ one has to show the verification conditions, that P implies the weakest precondition (as computed by *pre*) and that the running time (as computed by *time*) is in the order of magnitude of e.

Now we come to the *raison d'être* of the stronger consequence rule $conseq_K$: the completeness proof of our VCG. The other proofs in this section only require the derived rules *conseq* and *const*. Our completeness proof of the VCG builds annotated programs that contain a *Conseq* construct for every *Seq* and *While* rule. The annotations of *Conseq* enable us to adapt the logical state; without this adaptation we failed to generate true verification conditions.

Theorem 4 (Completeness of vc**).** *If* $\vdash_1 \{P\}\ c\{e \Downarrow Q\}$ *then there is a* C *such that* $\overline{C} = c$, $vc\ C\ Q$ *is true and* $\exists k.\forall l\ s.\ P\ l\ s \longrightarrow pre\ C\ Q\ l\ s \wedge time\ C\ s \leq k \cdot e\ s$.

That is, if a triple $\vdash_1 \{P\}\ c\{e \Downarrow Q\}$ is provable then c can be annotated such that the verification conditions are true, P implies the weakest precondition (as computed by *pre*) and the running time (as computed by *time*) is in the order of magnitude of e.

Annotating loops with a correct S is troublesome, as it captures the semantics of the whole loop. Luckily S only needs to be correct for "interesting" variables, i.e. variables that occur in time bounds that need to be pulled backward through the loop body. Often these variables are not modified by a command. We implemented an optimized VCG that keeps track of which variables are of interest and requires S to be correct only on those; we also showed its soundness and completeness. Further details can be found in the formalization.

3.2 Quantitative Hoare Logic

The main idea by Carbonneaux *et al.* [4] is to generalize predicates (state $\Rightarrow \mathbb{B}$) in Hoare triples to *potentials* (state $\Rightarrow \mathbb{N}_\infty$). That is, Hoare triples are now of the form $\{P\}c\{Q\}$ where P and Q are potentials. The resulting logic does not need logical variables. We prove soundness and completeness of that logic and design a sound and complete VCG. Then we extend the logic and VCG to big-O style reasoning.

Validity of triples involving potentials is defined as follows and is a direct generalization of validity for triples involving predicates:

$$\models_2 \{P\}c\{Q\} \equiv \forall s.\ P\ s < \infty \longrightarrow (\exists t\ s'.\ (c,s) \overset{t}{\Rightarrow} s' \wedge Q\ s' < \infty \wedge P\ s \geq t + Q\ s')$$

One may interpret the refinement from $\mathbb{B}$ to $\mathbb{N}_\infty$ as follows: infinite potentials are "impossible" and thus correspond to *False*, while finite potentials correspond to *True*. In that way "$P\ s < \infty$" corresponds to "P holds in state s". Furthermore, we interpret the difference of the prepotential P and postpotential Q as an upper bound on the actual running time. Predicates can be lifted to potentials by mapping *True* to 0 and *False* to ∞. We use the $\uparrow$ symbol for that lifting: $\uparrow P\ s \equiv$ (if $P\ s$ then 0 else ∞), and similarly for boolean expressions: $\uparrow b\ s \equiv$ (if $[\![b]\!]_s$ then 0 else ∞).

$$\frac{}{\vdash_2 \{P+1\}\text{SKIP}\{P\}}\ \textit{Skip} \qquad \frac{}{\vdash_2 \{\lambda s.1 + P(s[a/x])\}x := a\{P\}}\ \textit{Assign}$$

$$\frac{\vdash_2 \{P + \uparrow b\}c_1\{Q\} \quad \vdash_2 \{P + \uparrow(\neg b)\}c_2\{Q\}}{\vdash_2 \{P+1\}\text{IF } b \text{ THEN } c_1 \text{ ELSE } c_2\{Q\}}\ \textit{If} \qquad \frac{\vdash_2 \{P\}c_1\{Q\} \quad \vdash_2 \{Q\}c_2\{R\}}{\vdash_2 \{P\}c_1; c_2\{R\}}\ \textit{Seq}$$

$$\frac{\vdash_2 \{I + \uparrow b\}c\{I+1\}}{\vdash_2 \{I+1\}\text{WHILE } b \text{ DO } c\{I + \uparrow(\neg b)\}}\ \textit{While} \qquad \frac{P' \geq P \quad \vdash_2 \{P\}c\{Q\} \quad Q \geq Q'}{\vdash_2 \{P'\}c\{Q'\}}\ \textit{conseq}$$

Fig. 3. Quantitative Hoare logic

The rules in Fig. 3 define the Hoare logic $\vdash_2$ corresponding to $\models_2$. Note that $P \geq Q$ is short for $\forall s.\ P\ s \geq Q\ s$.

Rules *Skip*, *Assign* and *If* are straightforward; the 1 time unit added to the prepotential pays for, respectively, SKIP, assignment and the evaluation of the boolean expression. The *conseq* rule also looks familiar, only that $\longrightarrow$ has been replaced by $\geq$. You can think of a bigger potential implying a smaller one; also remember that *False* corresponds to ∞.

For the *While* rule, assume one can derive that having the potential I and a true guard b before the execution of c implies a postpotential one more than the invariant I (the plus one is needed for the upcoming evaluation of the guard, which incurs cost 1), then one can conclude that, starting the loop with potential $I+1$ (again the plus one pays for the evaluation of the guard), the loop terminates with a potential equal to I and the negation of the guard holds in the final state. Although this rule resembles the *While* rule for partial correctness, the decreasing potential actually also ensures termination.

Theorem 5 (Soundness of $\vdash_2$). $\vdash_2 \{P\}c\{Q\} \Longrightarrow\ \models_2 \{P\}c\{Q\}$

For proving completeness, we generalise the *weakest precondition* to the *weakest prepotential*:

$$wp\ c\ Q\ s \equiv (\text{if } \downarrow(c,s) \text{ then } \downarrow_T(c,s) + Q(\downarrow_S(c,s)) \text{ else } \infty)$$

In fact, *wp* is also a (weakest) prepotential w.r.t. provability:

Lemma 2. $\vdash_2 \{wp\ c\ Q\}c\{Q\}$

As usual, completeness follows easily from this lemma:

Theorem 6 (Completeness of $\vdash_2$). $\models_2 \{P\}c\{Q\} \Longrightarrow \vdash_2 \{P\}c\{Q\}$

Verification Condition Generator. The simpler *Seq* rule (compared to $\vdash_1$) leads to a more compact VCG. Loops are simply annotated with invariants, which now are potentials. No *Conseq* annotations are required.

Function *pre C Q* determines the weakest prepotential of an annotated program C and postpotential Q. Its definition is by recursion on annotated commands and refines our earlier *pre* on predicates.

The VCG recursively traverses the command and collects the verification conditions at the loops (we omit the other cases of *vc*):

$$
\begin{aligned}
&vc\ (\{I\}\text{WHILE } b \text{ DO } C)\ Q = \\
&\quad I + \uparrow b \geq pre\ C\ (I + \mathbf{1})\ \wedge\ I + \uparrow(\neg b) \geq Q\ \wedge\ vc\ C\ (I + \mathbf{1})
\end{aligned}
$$

The two first conjuncts express invariant preservation and that the invariant "implies" the postcondition when exiting the loop. Soundness of the VCG is established by induction on the command.

Lemma 3 (Soundness of vc). *If we can show the verification conditions $vc\ C\ Q$ and that we have at least as much potential as the needed prepotential ($P \geq pre\ C\ Q$) then we can derive $\vdash_2 \{P\}\overline{C}\{Q\}$.*

Completeness of the VCG can be paraphrased like this: if we can derive the Hoare Triple $\vdash_2 \{P\}c\{Q\}$, we can find an annotation for c such that the verification conditions are true and P "implies" the prepotential.

Lemma 4 (Completeness of vc).
$\vdash_2 \{P\}c\{Q\} \Longrightarrow \exists C.\ \overline{C} = c \wedge vc\ C\ Q \wedge P \geq pre\ C\ Q$

Constant Factors. As for the Nielson system we can extend the quantitative Hoare logic to reason about the order of magnitude of execution time. We generalize our notion of validity from $\models_2$ to $\models_{2'}$:

$$
\models_{2'} \{P\}c\{Q\} \equiv \exists k > 0. \forall s.\ P\ s < \infty \longrightarrow \exists t\ s'. \begin{cases} (c, s) \Rightarrow t \Downarrow s' \wedge Q\ s' < \infty\ \wedge \\ k \cdot P\ s \geq t + k \cdot Q\ s' \end{cases}
$$

For intuition, assume Q is zero: then the triple is valid iff the running time t is bounded by k times the prepotential P. This amounts to O-notation.

Correspondingly we extend the set of Hoare rules $\vdash_2$ in Fig. 3 to $\vdash_{2'}$ by adding the following rule:

$$
\frac{\vdash_{2'} \{\lambda s.\ k \cdot P\ s\}c\{\lambda s.\ k \cdot Q\ s\} \qquad k > 0}{\vdash_{2'} \{P\}c\{Q\}}\, const
$$

For re-establishing soundness we can adapt the proof of Theorem 5 by catering for constants and adding one more case for rule *const*.

Theorem 7 (Soundness of $\vdash_{2'}$). $\vdash_{2'} \{P\}c\{Q\} \Longrightarrow \models_{2'} \{P\}c\{Q\}$

For the completeness proof, nothing changes. We reuse the same *wp* and the proof of $\vdash_{2'} \{wp\ c\ Q\}c\{Q\}$ is identical to that of Lemma 2 because we extended the Hoare rules, but not the command language. In particular this means that the new *const* rule is not used in this proof. The same principle as in Sect. 3.1 applies: the *const* rule is only used once at the end when showing completeness from $\vdash_{2'} \{wp\ c\ Q\}c\{Q\}$:

Theorem 8 (Completeness of $\vdash_{2'}$). $\models_{2'} \{P\}c\{Q\} \Longrightarrow \vdash_{2'} \{P\}c\{Q\}$

VCG with Constants. For the VCG we add one more annotated command *Const* $\{k\}$ C (where $k \in \mathbb{N}$, $k > 0$). It signals the application of a *const* rule. We reuse the old definitions of *pre* and *vc* but add new equations for *Const*:

$$\begin{aligned} vc\ (Const\ \{k\}\ C)\ Q\ s &= (vc\ C\ (\lambda s.\ k \cdot Q\ s) \wedge k > 0) \\ pre\ (Const\ \{k\}\ C)\ Q\ s &= ediv\ (pre\ C\ (\lambda s.\ k \cdot Q\ s)\ s)\ k \end{aligned}$$

The definition of $vc\ (Const\ \{k\}\ C)\ Q$ expresses that the execution of C must leave a potential of $k \cdot Q$ instead of just Q. The definition of $pre\ (Const\ \{k\}\ C)\ Q$ expresses that we pull back a potential of $k \cdot Q$ but that in the end we renormalize the prepotential by dividing (function *ediv*) by k. More precisely, *ediv* is integer division which rounds up for non integral results and is lifted to $\mathbb{N}_\infty$.

The soundness and completeness proofs must only be adapted marginally, only some algebraic lemmas about *ediv* are needed.

To summarize this section: we have shown how to generalize conditions to potentials, thus obtaining a compositional Hoare logic; we have extended the Hoare logic to big-O style reasoning and have adapted the calculus and proofs; we also have established sound and complete VCGs for both logics.

One drawback of the quantitative Hoare logic is that it is not modular. Imagine two independent programs c_1 and c_2 that are run one after the other. When reasoning about a subprogram c_1 we need to specify a postpotential that is then used for the following program c_2. If we change c_2, resulting in a changed time consumption, also the analysis for c_1 has do be redone. What we actually would like to do, is to reason about c_1 and c_2 locally and then combine them in a final step. Separation logic addresses this issue.

3.3 Separation Logic with Time Credits

Our last logic follows the idea by Atkey [1] to use separation logic in order to reason about the resource consumption of programs. This logic generalizes the quantitative Hoare logic.

The principle of "local reasoning" is addressed by separation logic for disjoint heap areas; Atkey [1] uses separation logic with time credits to reason about the amortised execution time of (imperative) programs.

In this section we follow his ideas and design a Hoare logic based on separation logic. As IMP does not have a heap to reason about, but we want to compare the logic to the two logics we already described, we treat the state of a program as a kind of heap: a *partial state* ps is a map from variable names to values, $dom\ ps$ is the domain of ps, we call ps_1 and ps_2 *disjoint* ($ps_1 \bot ps_2$) if their domains are, and we can add two partial states to form their disjoint union ($ps_1 + ps_2$).

We adapt evaluation of arithmetic and boolean expressions, as well as the big-step semantics (now denoted by $\Rightarrow_p$) to partial states. If all necessary variables are in the domain of the partial state ps, these new constructs coincide with their counterparts on (full) states. The new big-step semantics rule for assignment for example has an additional premise. All other rules are similar.

$$\frac{vars\ a \cup \{x\} \subseteq dom\ ps}{(x := a, ps) \stackrel{1}{\Rightarrow}_p ps(x \mapsto [\![a]\!]_{ps})} Assign$$

The new semantics admit a frame rule: we can always add disjoint partial states, without affecting the computation.

Lemma 5. $\dfrac{(c, ps_1) \stackrel{t}{\Rightarrow}_p ps_1' \qquad ps_1 \bot ps_2}{(c, ps_1 + ps_2) \stackrel{t}{\Rightarrow}_p ps_1' + ps_2}$

In that way we treat the set of variables as resources, on which separation logic can work. Additionally, as Atkey proposes, we add time credits as resources: we consider *configurations* (ps, n) which are pairs of partial states and natural numbers. Natural numbers, viewed as resources, are always disjoint and can be added; thus they form a separation algebra [2]. A pair of separation algebras is again a separation algebra. For predicates on configurations we thus have the $*$ operator from separation algebra

$$(P * Q)(ps, n) \equiv \exists ps_1\ n_1\ ps_2\ n_2. \begin{cases} ps = ps_1 + ps_2 \wedge n = n_1 + n_2 \wedge ps_1 \bot ps_2 \wedge \\ P(ps_1, n_1) \wedge Q(ps_2, n_2) \end{cases}$$

meaning that we can split up the configuration into two disjoint configurations; one satisfying P and the other satisfying Q. Our formalization builds on an existing Isabelle/HOL theory of separation algebras [14].

The validity of a Hoare triple is defined in the following way:

$$\models_3 \{P\}c\{Q\} \equiv \forall ps\ n.\ P(ps, n) \longrightarrow \exists ps'\ n'\ t. \begin{cases} (c, ps) \stackrel{t}{\Rightarrow}_p ps' \wedge \\ n = n' + t \wedge Q(ps', n') \end{cases}$$

We can now state the Hoare rules for this logic, see Fig. 4. Note that $\$n$ denotes the configuration of an empty partial state and n time resources, $(b \hookrightarrow B)\ ps$ is true, iff all variables in b are in the domain of ps and b evaluates to B in ps. Updating the partial state ps with value v for x is denoted by $ps(x \mapsto v)$.

Proving soundness and completeness follows the same lines as for the quantitative Hoare logic, only complicated by the reasoning about partial states.

$$\frac{}{\vdash \{\$1\}\text{SKIP}\{\$0\}}\,\textit{Skip}$$

$$\frac{}{\vdash \{(\lambda(ps, t).\ \{x\} \cup \textit{vars}\ a \subseteq \textit{dom}\ ps \wedge Q\ (ps(x \mapsto [\![a]\!]_{ps}), t)) * \$1\}x := a\{Q\}}\,\textit{Assign}$$

$$\frac{\vdash \{\lambda(ps, n).\ P(ps, n) \wedge (b \hookrightarrow \textit{True})\ ps\}c_1\{Q\} \quad \vdash \{\lambda(ps, n).\ P(ps, n) \wedge (b \hookrightarrow \textit{False})\ ps\}c_2\{Q\}}{\vdash \{(\lambda(ps, n).\ P(ps, n) \wedge \textit{vars}\ b \subseteq \textit{dom}\ ps) * \$1\}\text{IF}\ b\ \text{THEN}\ c_1\ \text{ELSE}\ c_2\{Q\}}\,\textit{If}$$

$$\frac{\vdash \{P\}c\{Q\}}{\vdash \{P * F\}c\{Q * F\}}\,\textit{Frame} \qquad \frac{\vdash \{P\}c_1\{Q\} \quad \vdash \{Q\}c_2\{R\}}{\vdash \{P\}c_1; c_2\{R\}}\,\textit{Seq}$$

$$\frac{\vdash \{\lambda(ps, n).\ I(ps, n) \wedge (b \hookrightarrow \textit{True})\ ps\}c\{I * \$1\}}{\vdash \{(\lambda(ps, n).\ I(ps, n) \wedge \textit{vars}\ b \subseteq \textit{dom}\ ps) * \$1\}\ \text{WHILE}\ b\ \text{DO}\ c\ \{\lambda(ps, n).\ I(ps, n) \wedge (b \hookrightarrow \textit{False})\ ps\}}\,\textit{While}$$

$$\frac{\forall ps\ n.\ P'(ps, n) \Longrightarrow P(ps, n) \quad \vdash \{P\}c\{Q\} \quad \forall ps\ n.\ Q(ps, n) \Longrightarrow Q'(ps, n)}{\vdash \{P'\}c\{Q'\}}\,\textit{conseq}$$

Fig. 4. Hoare logic with separation logic for reasoning about execution time

Theorem 9 (Soundness of $\vdash_3$). $\vdash_3 \{P\}c\{Q\} \Longrightarrow\ \models_3 \{P\}c\{Q\}$

This logic's weakest precondition is again defined as the right-hand side of the implication in the definition of validity:

$$wp\ c\ Q\ (ps, n) \equiv \exists ps'\ n'\ t.\ (c, s) \stackrel{t}{\Rightarrow}_p ps' \wedge n = n' + t \wedge\ Q\ (ps', n')$$

For completeness we first show $\vdash_3 \{wp\ c\ Q\}c\{Q\}$ by induction on the command c, and then use the definition of validity and wp to finish the proof.

Theorem 10 (Completeness of $\vdash_3$). $\models_3 \{P\}c\{Q\} \Longrightarrow\ \vdash_3 \{P\}c\{Q\}$

Big-O style. Similar to last subsection's system we extend the Hoare logic based on Separation Logic to big-O style reasoning. We again generalize our notion of validity (now $\models_{3'}$) and add a similar *const* rule to obtain the Hoare Logic $\vdash_{3'}$. Proving soundness and completeness of this new Hoare logic follows the same lines as in the subsection before. Similarly we come up with a simple VCG: somewhat unorthodoxly for separation logic, we use a backwards style, as well as we do not provide annotations for abstraction from multiplicative constants, as one final abstraction at the outer most position suffices to ensure completeness.

The approach inspired by Nielson to incorporate abstraction from multiplicative constants directly into the Hoare Logic in order to reason about the order of magnitude of the running time of programs shows weaknesses and seems to complicate matters. Our theoretical results show that it is always possible to reason about the exact running time and abstract away multiplicative constants in a last step.

4 Discussion

In this section we discuss the interrelations between the Hoare logics described in the last section.

First we can compare the expressibility of the logics. Nielson logic $\models_1$ and the quantitative Hoare logic $\models_{2'}$, both big-O style logics, are equivalent in the following sense:

Lemma 6. $\models_1 \{\lfloor P \rfloor_{\mathbb{B}}\} c \{\lambda s.\ \lfloor P\ s - Q(\downarrow_S(c, s)) \rfloor_{\mathbb{N}} \Downarrow \lfloor Q \rfloor_{\mathbb{B}}\} \Longrightarrow\ \models_{2'} \{P\} c \{Q\}$ *where* $\lfloor P \rfloor_{\mathbb{B}}\ s \equiv P\ s < \infty$ *and* $\lfloor . \rfloor_{\mathbb{N}}$ *is the coercion from* $\mathbb{N}_\infty$ *to* $\mathbb{N}$*, assuming the argument is finite.*

Validity of a triple in the quantitative Hoare logic can be reduced to validity of a transformed triple in Nielson's logic. In the other direction this is only possible for assertions P and Q that do not depend on the state of their logical variables:

Lemma 7. $\models_{2'} \{\Uparrow P + e\} c \{\Uparrow Q\} \Longrightarrow\ \models_1 \{P\} c \{e \Downarrow Q\}$ *where* $\Uparrow P\ s \equiv (\forall l. \uparrow P\ l\ s)$

The quantitative logics support amortised resource analysis. On the face of it, Nielson's logic does not, but Lemma 6 tells us that in theory it actually does. However, automatic tools for resource analysis are mainly based on the potential method, for example [5, 12].

Furthermore, as the third system based on separation logic talks about partial states, in general it cannot be simulated by any of the other systems. This can only be done for assertions that act on complete states:

Lemma 8. $\models_{2'} \{\lfloor P \rfloor\} c \{\lfloor Q \rfloor\} \Longrightarrow\ \models_{3'} \{P\} c \{Q\}$, *when* P *is only true for complete partial states, with* $\lfloor P \rfloor s \equiv \inf_{n \in \mathbb{N}} \{P(\lfloor s \rfloor, n)\}$ *and* $\lfloor s \rfloor$ *is the partial state defined everywhere and returning the same results as the total state* s*.*

On the other hand any triple in the quantitative Hoare logic $\models_{2'}$ can be embedded into the separation logic $\models_{3'}$:

Lemma 9. $\models_{3'} \{\lfloor P \rfloor\} c \{\lfloor Q \rfloor\} \Longrightarrow\ \models_{2'} \{P\} c \{Q\}$, *where* $\lfloor P \rfloor (ps, n) \equiv (\forall s.\ n \geq P \lfloor ps \rfloor^s)$ *and* $\lfloor ps \rfloor^s$ *is the extension of the partial state* ps *by the state* s *to a total state.*

Example. Let c be the IMP program that computes the discrete square root by bisection:

```
l ::= 0 ;; r::= x + 1;;  m ::= 0 ;;
(WHILE l + 1 < r DO
   m ::= (l + r) / 2;;
   (IF m * m < x THEN l ::= m ELSE r ::= m);;
   m ::= 0)
```

With the simplification that the intervals between l and r are always powers of two, we can easily show the running time to be in the order of magnitude of $1 + \log x$. Note that we can get rid of multiplicative constants, but not additive ones!

For showing $\vdash_1 \{\lambda l\ s.\ (\exists k.1 + s\ ''x'' = 2^k)\}c\{\lambda s. \log(s\ ''x'') + 1 \Downarrow \lambda l\ s.\ True)$ we provide the following annotations for the while loop: $I_1 = \lambda l\ s.\ s\ ''l'' \geq 0 \wedge (\exists k.s\ ''r'' - s\ ''l'' = 2^k)$, $E_1 = \lambda s.\ 1 + 5 \cdot \log(s\ ''r'' - s\ ''l'')$ and $S_1 = \lambda s.\ s$; then we use our optimized VCG and prove the remaining proof obligations.

For showing $\vdash_{2'} \{(\lambda s.\ \uparrow (\exists k.1 + s\ ''x'' = 2^k) + (\log(s\ ''x'') + 1)\}c\{\lambda\_.0)$, we annotate the while loop with the potential $I_{2'} = \lambda s.\ \uparrow (s\ ''l'' \geq 0 \wedge (\exists k.s\ ''r'' - s\ ''l'' = 2^k)) + 5 \cdot \log(s\ ''r'' - s\ ''l'')$.

Let us now compare the VCGs. Our VCG for Nielson's logic requires the annotation of loops with invariants I, running time bounds E and the state transformers S. In contrast, the annotations required for the VCG for the quantitative Hoare logic are uniformly potentials. In the above example, one can see that this annotated potential $I_{2'}$ exactly contains the same information as both I_1 and E_1 in the Nielson approach. The additional $1+$ in E_1 is needed, as E_1 describes the running time of the whole loop, where $I_{2'}$ describes the running time from after evaluating the loop guard. Only more practical experience can tell if it is better to work with separate I, E and S or with a combined invariant potential.

In addition our annotated commands for Nielson's system may require annotations of the form *Conseq* $\{P', Q, e'\}$, whereas for the quantitative Hoare logic we managed to reduce this to *Const* $\{k\}$ annotations. It would be desirable to reduce the *Conseq* annotations similarly.

5 Related Work

Riis Nielson [21,22] was the first to study Hoare logics for running time analysis of programs. She proved soundness and completeness of her systems (on paper) which are based on a deep embedding of her assertion language. We base our formalization on the system given in [23] where assertions are just predicates, i.e. functions. However, our inference system differs from hers in several respects and our mechanized proofs in Isabelle/HOL are completely independent. Moreover we provide a VCG and prove it sound and complete.

Possibly the first example of a resource analysis logic based on potentials is due to Hofmann and Jost [11]. The idea of generalising predicates to potentials in order to form a "quantitative Hoare logic" we borrowed from [4]: Carbonneaux *et al.* design a quantitative logic in order to reason about stack-space usage of C programs. They also formally show soundness of their logic in Coq. They employ their logic for reasoning about other resource bounds and use it as the underlying logic for an automatic tool for resource bound analysis [5,6]. In a draft version of his dissertation [3] Carbonneaux complements his tool-focused work with a theoretical treatment of an "Invariant Logic". The relation to our logics of Sect. 3.2 should be studied in more detail.

Atkey [1] proposed to use separation logic with time credits to reason about the amortised running time of programs; he formalized his logic and its soundness in Coq. Similar ideas were used by Hoffmann *et al.* [10] to prove lock-freedom of concurrent programs, and by Charguéraud and Pottier [7] to verify the amortised running time of the Union-Find data structure in Coq. Guéneau et al. [8] recently extended their framework to also obtain O results for the running time of programs. None of these works include verified VCGs.

There is also some related work that extends to probabilistic programs. Kaminski *et al.* [13] reason about the expected running time of probabilistic programs and show that their approach corresponds to Nielson's logic when restricted to deterministic algorithms. Ngo *et al.* [16] extend the idea of working with potentials to reasoning about the expected running time of probabilistic programs.

For formal treatment of program logics [17] is a good entry point. Basic concepts as well as formalizations of Hoare logics that lay the ground for our work can be found in [18].

6 Conclusion

In this paper we have studied three Hoare logics for reasoning about the running time of programs in a simple imperative language. We have formalized and verified their meta theory in Isabelle/HOL.

Further investigation is required in order to simplify the VCG for Nielson's logic and avoid the *Conseq* construct while preserving completeness of the VCG. Extending IMP with more language features is a natural next step. Adding recursive procedures should be easy (following [17]) whereas probabilistic choice (following [20]) is much more challenging and interesting. Not only is the meta theory of probabilistic programs nontrivial but even very small programs can be surprisingly hard to analyze. Although we view our work primarily as foundational, we expect that it could become a viable basis for the verification of small probabilistic programs.

Data Availability Statement and Acknowledgments. The formal proof development is available online [9]. We thank Peter Lammich for his initial help with setting up the separation logic.

References

1. Atkey, R.: Amortised resource analysis with separation logic. In: Gordon, A.D. (ed.) ESOP 2010. LNCS, vol. 6012, pp. 85–103. Springer, Heidelberg (2010). https://doi.org/10.1007/978-3-642-11957-6_6
2. Calcagno, C., O'Hearn, P.W., Yang, H.: Local action and abstract separation logic. In: Logic in Computer Science, LICS 2007, pp. 366–378. IEEE (2007)
3. Carbonneaux, Q.: Modular and certified resource-bound analyses. Ph.D. dissertation, Yale University (2017). http://cs.yale.edu/homes/qcar/diss/

4. Carbonneaux, Q., Hoffmann, J., Ramananandro, T., Shao, Z.: End-to-end verification of stack-space bounds for C programs. In: O'Boyle, M.F.P., Pingali, K. (eds.) Conference on Programming Language Design and Implementation, PLDI 2014, pp. 270–281. ACM (2014)
5. Carbonneaux, Q., Hoffmann, J., Reps, T., Shao, Z.: Automated resource analysis with Coq proof objects. In: Majumdar, R., Kunčak, V. (eds.) CAV 2017. LNCS, vol. 10427, pp. 64–85. Springer, Cham (2017). https://doi.org/10.1007/978-3-319-63390-9_4
6. Carbonneaux, Q., Hoffmann, J., Shao, Z.: Compositional certified resource bounds. In: Grove, D., Blackburn, S. (eds.) Conference on Programming Language Design and Implementation, PLDI 2015, pp. 467–478. ACM (2015)
7. Charguéraud, A., Pottier, F.: Verifying the correctness and amortized complexity of a union-find implementation in separation logic with time credits. J. Autom. Reasoning, accepted for publication
8. Guéneau, A., Charguéraud, A., Pottier, F.: A fistful of dollars: formalizing asymptotic complexity claims via deductive program verification. In: European Symposium on Programming (ESOP) (2018)
9. Haslbeck, M.P.L., Nipkow, T.: Hoare logics for time bounds. Archive of formal proofs, February 2018. https://www.isa-afp.org/entries/Hoare_Time.html. Formal proof development
10. Hoffmann, J., Marmar, M., Shao, Z.: Quantitative reasoning for proving lock-freedom. In: Logic in Computer Science, LICS 2013, pp. 124–133. IEEE (2013)
11. Hofmann, M., Jost, S.: Type-based amortised heap-space analysis. In: Sestoft, P. (ed.) ESOP 2006. LNCS, vol. 3924, pp. 22–37. Springer, Heidelberg (2006). https://doi.org/10.1007/11693024_3
12. Hofmann, M., Rodriguez, D.: Automatic type inference for amortised heap-space analysis. In: Felleisen, M., Gardner, P. (eds.) ESOP 2013. LNCS, vol. 7792, pp. 593–613. Springer, Heidelberg (2013). https://doi.org/10.1007/978-3-642-37036-6_32
13. Kaminski, B.L., Katoen, J.-P., Matheja, C., Olmedo, F.: Weakest precondition reasoning for expected run–times of probabilistic programs. In: Thiemann, P. (ed.) ESOP 2016. LNCS, vol. 9632, pp. 364–389. Springer, Heidelberg (2016). https://doi.org/10.1007/978-3-662-49498-1_15
14. Klein, G., Kolanski, R., Boyton, A.: Separation algebra. Archive of formal proofs, May 2012. http://isa-afp.org/entries/Separation_Algebra.html. Formal proof development
15. Kleymann, T.: Hoare logic and auxiliary variables. Formal Aspects Comput. **11**(5), 541–566 (1999)
16. Ngo, V.C., Carbonneaux, Q., Hoffmann, J.: Bounded expectations: resource analysis for probabilistic programs. In: Conference on Programming Language Design and Implementation, PLDI 2018 (2018)
17. Nipkow, T.: Hoare logics in Isabelle/HOL. In: Schwichtenberg, H., Steinbrüggen, R. (eds.) Proof and System-Reliability, pp. 341–367. Kluwer (2002)
18. Nipkow, T., Klein, G.: Concrete Semantics: With Isabelle/HOL. Springer, Cham (2014). https://doi.org/10.1007/978-3-319-10542-0
19. Nipkow, T., Wenzel, M., Paulson, L.C. (eds.): Isabelle/HOL—A Proof Assistant for Higher-Order Logic. LNCS, vol. 2283. Springer, Heidelberg (2002). https://doi.org/10.1007/3-540-45949-9
20. Olmedo, F., Kaminski, B.L., Katoen, J.P., Matheja, C.: Reasoning about recursive probabilistic programs. In: Logic in Computer Science, LICS 2016, pp. 672–681. ACM (2016)

21. Riis Nielson, H.: Hoare logic's for run-time analysis of programs. Ph.D. thesis, University of Edinburgh (1984)
22. Riis Nielson, H.: A Hoare-like proof system for analysing the computation time of programs. Sci. Comput. Program. **9**(2), 107–136 (1987)
23. Riis Nielson, H., Nielson, F.: Semantics with Applications: An Appetizer. Springer, New York (2007). https://doi.org/10.1007/978-1-84628-692-6

A Verified Implementation of the Bounded List Container

Raphaël Cauderlier and Mihaela Sighireanu(✉)

IRIF, University Paris Diderot and CNRS, Paris, France
{raphael.cauderlier,mihaela.sighireanu}@irif.fr

Abstract. This paper contributes to the trend of providing fully verified container libraries. We consider an implementation of the bounded doubly linked list container which manages the list in a fixed size, heap allocated array. The container provides constant time methods to update the list by adding, deleting, and changing elements, as well as cursors for list traversal and access to elements. The library is implemented in C, but we wrote the code and its specification by imitating the ones provided by GNAT for the standard library of Ada 2012. The proof of functional correctness is done using VeriFast, which provides an auto-active verification environment for Separation Logic extended with algebraic data types. The specifications proved entail the contracts of the Ada library and include new features. The verification method we used employs a precise algebraic model of the data structure and we show that it facilitates the verification and captures entirely the library contracts. This case study may be of interest for other verification platforms, thus we highlight the intricate points of its proof.

1 Introduction

Standard libraries of programming languages provide efficient implementations for common data containers. The details of these implementations are abstracted away by generic interfaces which are specified in terms of well understood mathematical structures such as sets, multisets, sequences, and partial functions. The intensive use of container libraries makes important their formal verification.

However, the functional correctness of these libraries is challenging to verify for several reasons. Firstly, their implementation is highly optimized: it employs complex data structures and manages the memory directly through pointers/references or specific memory allocators. Secondly, the specification of containers is rarely formal. Notable exceptions are, e.g., Eiffel [28] and SPARK [11]; recently, [1] provided a specification of the Ada 2012 container library. The formal specifications are very important when the library employs constructs that are out of the scope of the underlying mathematical structure. A typical example of such constructs are iterators. For example, Java iterators are generic and can exist independently of the container; Ada 2012 iterators, called cursors, are part of the container. Thirdly, the specification of the link between the low level implementation and the mathematical specification requires hybrid logics that are

D. Beyer and M. Huisman (Eds.): TACAS 2018, LNCS 10805, pp. 172–189, 2018.
https://doi.org/10.1007/978-3-319-89960-2_10

able to capture both low level and high level specifications of the container. For verification purposes, these logics shall be supported by efficient solvers.

This work focuses on the functional verification of the *bounded doubly linked lists* container, which is a GNAT implementation [12] of the doubly linked lists container in the standard library of Ada 2012 [1]. This container is currently used by client programs [2] written in SPARK [22], a subset of Ada targeted at safety- and security-critical applications. The lists have bounded capacity, fixed at the list creation, and thus avoid dynamic memory allocation during the container use. This feature is required in critical code, where it is necessary to supply formal guarantees on the maximal amount of memory used by the running code.

The container implementation is original compared with other implementations of linked lists inside arrays. It employs an array of fixed size in which it manages (i) the occupied array cells inside a doubly linked list representing the content of the container and (ii) a singly linked list of free array cells. The operations provided are classic for lists. The *amortized constant time complexity* is preserved by the implementation of insert and delete operations. The list elements are designated using (bi-directional) cursors, also used to traverse the list. In conclusion, the code of this container was designed to ensure efficiency of operations and not its verification, and therefore it provides a realistic test for the automated verification.

Thanks to the introduction of formal contracts in Ada 2012, the container has been fully specified recently based on a previous specification in Why3 by Dross et al. [11]. The specification given is "meant to facilitate the formal verification of code using this container" [12], and it is presently used to prove the clients written in SPARK. The container is specified in terms of a model representing a functional implementation of bounded vectors, also written in Ada. This kind of specification is a substitute for the algebraic data types, not supported by Ada. It has the advantage of being executable, which enables the run-time verification of the implementation. An important feature of these contracts is their completeness [27] with respect to the models considered for the container and the cursors. This aspect is a challenge for the state of the art verification tools. The formal verification of these contracts can not be done by GNATprove, the deductive verification environment for SPARK, because the code employs language constructs out of its scope.

The goal of our study is to apply on-the-shelf verification tools to prove the full functional correctness and the memory safety for this implementation, without simplifying the code or the specification. To open the case study to more verification platforms, we choose to write this library in C, because C may capture all the features of the container implementation, except the strong typing and the generic types of Ada. The C implementation mimics the Ada code. The functional specification of the C code translates the container contracts from Ada based on (i) *representation predicates* that relate heap regions with algebraic models using inductively defined predicates, (ii) algebraic lists and maps, and (iii) inductively defined predicates and functions on the algebraic models. The logic including these features is undecidable in general. Therefore, we have to help the prover to obtain push button verification. The auto-active verification [20] environments are helpful in such tasks.

The invariant properties of the implementation and the features exhibited by the specification guided us towards deductive verification platforms that support Separation Logic [31] (SL) and algebraic data types. Consequently, we choose the VeriFast [15] auto-active verification tool, which provides means for (a) the specification of representation predicates in the style introduced for SL by O'Hearn et al. [25], (b) the definition of polymorphic algebraic data types, predicates and functions, and (c) the definition of user lemmas to help verification. Using these features, we employ a verification methodology based on the refinement of the original specification. The refined specification not only captures accurately the contracts, but also eases the deductive verification process, i.e., the writing of lemmas. For example, we employ a style of writing representation predicates in SL that leads to simpler lemmas for list segment composition.

To summarize, we verified the C implementation of a bounded doubly linked list container against its functional specification. In addition, we verified the safety of memory accesses using Separation Logic. For this, we annotated the C code and we extended the library for algebraic polymorphic lists of VeriFast with new predicates and lemmas. These logic development may be used in other verification tools based on induction.

The paper begins by presenting the case study in Sect. 2. Then, we highlight in Sect. 3 the main ingredients of the verification approach used and the challenges we faced. Section 4 presents the experimental results. We compare this work with other approaches for verification of containers and complex data structures in Sect. 5.

2 Dynamic Bounded Doubly-Linked Lists

This section presents the container code and its functional specification.

2.1 Overview

Implementation: The code is written in a very simple fragment of C, which may be easily translated to most imperative programming languages. It uses records and pointers to records, dynamic memory allocation, classic accesses to record fields and array elements, basic integer type and its operations. Like in the original code, the container does not support concurrency and has been written to obtain efficient operations and not to ease the verification. The container elements are designated through *cursors*, which represent valid positions in the list; they may be moved forward and backward in the list. The container interface includes 30 operations including classic operations (creation, copy, size access, clearing and deallocation, equality test, searching) and a rich set of utilities (inserting or deleting bunches of elements at some position, searching from the end, merging lists, swapping elements or links, reversing in place, sorting).

Specification: The functional specification is *model based* [28]. Two mathematical models are used: *algebraic lists* (i.e., finite sequences) to represent the content of the list and *finite partial maps* to model the set of valid cursors (see Sect. 2.3 for details). The contracts employ operations on these mathematical models that are beyond their classic usage. For example, the test of inclusion between the set of elements of two sequences, or the test that the domain of a partial mapping has been truncated from a given value. For this reason, we enriched the library of mathematical models provided by our prover with such operations and the corresponding axiomatizations (see Sect. 3.2).

An important feature of our functional specification is the usage of *a refined abstraction* for the list to ease the proof that the operations satisfy their contracts. We introduce a *precise model* for the list, which is an algebraic list of abstract cells, storing container values together with the links between the cells. This precise model is mapped to the abstract model (sequence of values) using a catamorphic mapping [35], called `model`. Moreover, the precise model is used to compute the (abstract) model of cursors, based on a catamorphic mapping, called `positions`. The use of the precise model facilitates the verification effort for proving that implementations of operations satisfy their contracts (see Sect. 3.1).

The functional specification is complete in the sense given by [27]: the postcondition of each operation uniquely defines its result and the side effect on the model of the container and of its cursors. However, it does not check for memory overflow at the container creation.

For the syntax of specifications, we employ in the following the specification language of VeriFast, which extends the normalized specification language for C, ACSL [3], with shorthand notations and operators for Separation Logic. Therefore, we employ '`?`' to introduce existentially quantified variables, '`&*&`' for both classic conjunction and the separating one, '`|->`' for the points-to operator that defines the content (right operand) of an allocated memory cell (left operand), and `emp` for the empty heap. Algebraic lists of VeriFast have type `list` and are polymorphic; the operations on lists have classic names. The definition of new logic types (and functions) is introduced by the keyword `inductive` (resp. `fixpoint`).

2.2 List Container

List Elements: The data stored in the list container is typed by an abstract type `Element_Type`, defined as an alias to the integer type in our code. This coding is sound for the proof of the functional correctness of the container implementation because the container assumes only that values of `Element_Type` may be compared for equality.

List Cell: Also called *node* in the following, the list cell encapsulates the container element together with links to the next and previous cell in the list. A node is also an element of the array allocated for the container.

```
struct Node_Type { int prev; int next; Element_Type elem; };
```

```
inductive pnode = pnode(int, int, Element_Type);
fixpoint int pprev(pnode pn) {switch(n) {case pnode(pp, pn, pe): return pp;}}
fixpoint int pnext(pnode pn) ...
fixpoint int pelem(pnode pn) ...

predicate node(struct Node_Type* n, int capacity; pnode pn) =
  malloc_block_Node_Type(n) &*&
  n->prev|->?iprev &*& n->next|->?inext &*&
  n->elem|->?pelem &*&
  inext>=0 &*& inext<=capacity &*&
  pn==pnode(iprev, inext, pelem);

fixpoint bool is_free(pnode n) { return pprev(n)==-1; }
predicate free_node(struct Node_Type* n, int capacity; int inext) =
  node(n, capacity, ?pn) &*&
  is_free(pn)==true &*& inext==pnext(pn);

fixpoint bool is_occupied(pnode n) { return pprev(n)>=0; }
predicate occupied_node(struct Node_Type* n, int capacity; pnode pn) =
  node(n, capacity, pn) &*& is_occupied(pn)==true;

predicate bdll(struct Node_Type * tab, int capacity,
               int iprev, int ifrom, int ilast, int ito; list<pnode> m) =
  ifrom==ito ?
    (iprev==ilast &*& values==nil<pnode>)
  : (occupied_node(tab+ifrom, capacity, ?p) &*&
     pprev(p)==iprev &*&
     bdll(tab, capacity, ifrom, pnext(p), ilast, ito, ?mtl) &*&
     m==cons(p, mtl));

predicate uninit_free(struct Node_Type* tab, int capacity,
                      int ifrom, int ito; list<int> model) =
  ifrom==ito ? model==nil
  : (ifrom<ito &*& free_node(tab+ifrom, capacity, 0) &*&
     uninit_free(tab, capacity, ifrom+1, ito, ?mtl) &*&
     model==cons(ifrom, mtl));

predicate init_free(struct Node_Type* tab, int capacity,
                    int ifrom, int ito; list<int> model) =
  ifrom==ito ? model==nil
  : (ifrom>0 &*& free_node(tab+ifrom, capacity, ?inext) &*&
     init_free(tab, capacity, inext, ito, ?mtl) &*&
     model==cons(ifrom, mtl));

predicate free_nodes(struct Node_Type* tab, int cap,
                     int free, int size; list<int> fmodel) =
  free>=0 ? (init_free(tab, cap, free, 0, ?M) &*&
            fmodel==M &*& length(M)+size==cap)
  : (uninit_free(tab, cap, abs(free), cap+1, ?M) &*&
     fmodel==M &*& length(M)+size==cap);

predicate list_inv(struct List* L;
                   struct Node_Type* tab, int cap,
                   int free, list<int> free_model,
                   int head, int last, list<pnode> m) =
  malloc_block_List(L) &*&
  L->nodes|->tab &*& L->capacity|->cap &*& cap > 0 &*&
  malloc_block(tab, sizeof(struct Node_Type)*(cap+1)) &*&
  node(tab, cap, pnode(-1,0,_)) &*&
  L->first|->head &*& head>=0 &*& head<=cap &*&
  L->last|->last &*& last>=0 &*&
  bdll(tab,cap,0,head,last,0,m) &*& L->size|->length(vs) &*&
  L->free|->free &*& free<=cap &*&
  free_nodes(tab,free,length(m),cap,free_model);
```

Fig. 1. Logic definitions for the BDLL container

The values of the C type are abstracted by the ghost type `pnode`, defined at line 1 in Fig. 1, which records the values of node fields. The logic functions `pprev`, `pnext`, and `pelem` to access first, second, resp. third component of a `purenode` value.

The predicate `node` (line 6 in Fig. 1) relates a node `n` allocated in the heap with its model `pn`. The allocation property is expressed by the predefined predicate `malloc_block_Node_Type`. The values of the fields are bound to existentially quantified variables and used to build the model of the node. The predicate `node` constrains the fields `prev` and `nxt` to be indexes in an array starting at index 0 and ending at index `capacity`.

There are two kinds of nodes in the array managed by the container: nodes occupied by list elements and nodes not yet used in the list, i.e., free. Free nodes have the `prev` field at -1 and the `elem` field is irrelevant. They are specified by the predicate `free_node` (line 14 in Fig. 1), which also constraints the parameter `inext` to be equal to the value of the field `next`. Occupied nodes have the `prev` field set to a non-negative integer and the `elem` field is relevant. The predicate `occupied_node` (line 19 in Fig. 1) relates the node with its abstract model.

Acyclic Doubly Linked List: The container stores the doubly linked list (BDLL) into an array of fixed capacity, which is given at the container creation. The number of elements stored in the list can not exceed the container capacity. The nodes of the BDLL are stored starting from the index 1; index 0 plays the role of the null reference. The type of the list container is given by the following record:

```
struct List {
  int capacity; struct Node_Type* nodes; int size;
  int free; int first; int last;
};
```

The length of the list is given by the field `size`. The first and the last cells of the lists are stored at indexes `first` resp. `last`. Field `free` denotes the start of the list registering the free nodes. The operation creating the container allocates the array `nodes` and sets at free all nodes in the array. The fields denoting the size and the extreme cells of the doubly linked list are set to 0. The initialization of the `free` field is detailed in the next paragraph.

The representation predicate of the BDLL formed by the occupied nodes, `bdll`, is defined at line 22 in Fig. 1 as a doubly linked list segment starting by the node at index `ifrom`, ending by the node at index `ilast`; the starting node stores as previous node `iprev`, and the ending node stores as next node `ito`. The predicate definition is classic in Separation Logic [24], except the bound constraint on the node indexes (locations). If the source `ifrom` and target `ilast` indexes are equal, the list is empty; otherwise an occupied node is present at index `ifrom` and it is linked to the previous node and the remainder of the list. Notice the use of pointer arithmetics to access the node at index `ifrom`. The predicate `bdll` relates the heap specification with the mathematical model of the list, i.e., the sequence of abstract nodes. We employ the polymorphic algebraic type `list` available in VeriFast mathematical library and we instantiate it with

0			1 == first			2 == last			3 == -free			4		
prev	next	elem	prev	next	elem	prev	next	elem	prev	next	elem	prev	next	elem
-1	0	?	0	2	e1	1	0	e2	-1	0	?	-1	0	?

0			1 == first			2 == free			3 == last			4		
prev	next	elem	prev	next	elem	prev	next	elem	prev	next	elem	prev	next	elem
-1	0	?	0	3	e1	-1	4	?	1	0	e2	-1	0	?

Fig. 2. Two doubly linked lists of capacity 4 and length 2

the logic type `pnode`. This precise model of the list content is mapped by the inductively defined ghost function `model` to the abstract model, sequence of values of `Element_type` stored.

Acyclic List of Free Nodes: The free nodes are organized in a singly linked list, called the *free-list*. The start of this list is given by the field `free` of the type `List`. If `free` is negative, the list is built from all nodes stored between `-free` and `capacity` included; this permits a fast initialization of the free-list at the container creation. If `free` is positive, the free-list starts at index `free`, uses as successor relation the `next` field, and ends at index 0. Figure 2 illustrates the two kinds of free list. The representation predicate `uninit_free` (line 31 in Fig. 1) is used when `free` is negative. It collects in the parameter `model` the sequence of the indexes of free nodes. For the second case, we define the predicate `init_free` (line 38 in Fig. 1). The two kinds of free-list are combined in the predicate `free_nodes` (line 45 of Fig. 1) that calls the correct predicate depending on the sign of `free`. Notice that the constraints required by this predicates (the relation between container capacity, BDLL and free-list sizes) are all present in the Ada 2012 specification [12].

Representation Predicate: The invariants of the container are collected in the predicate `list_inv` (line 52 in Fig. 1) which mainly specifies that the container is allocated in the heap (predefined `malloc_block_List` predicate), and its field `tab` is also allocated as a block containing `capacity` +1 records of type `Node_Type`. The first node of this array (at address `tab`) has its `prev` and `next` fields set to −1 resp. 0. The set of remaining nodes is split between the lists specified by the `bdll` and `free_nodes` predicates due to the separating conjunction. The size of the BDLL is exactly the one of its model and stored in the field `size`.

Examples of Container Contracts: We illustrate the usage of representation predicates defined above by presenting some contracts specifying container operations. For example, the contract of the constructor is:

```
struct List* List(int capacity);
//@ requires capacity > 0;
//@ ensures list_inv(result,?t,capacity,-1,_,0,0,?m) &*& length(model(m))=0;
```

It states that the resulting container (denoted by the ghost variable `result`) is a well formed but empty bounded doubly linked list (its abstract model is the empty list) with `capacity` free nodes. As said before, the above contract (like in Ada 2012 specification), does not consider the case of memory shortage.

The contract of `is_equal` illustrates how the catamorphism `model` is used to obtain the abstract contract on the sequence of values from the precise models (given by variables `mL` and `mR` for each list parameter):

```
bool is_equal(struct List* L, struct List* R);
/*@ requires list_inv(L, ?tL, ?cL, ?fL, ?fmL, ?hL, ?lL, ?mL) &*&
            list_inv(R, ?tR, ?cR, ?fR, ?fmR, ?hR, ?lR, ?mR); @*/
/*@ ensures list_inv(L, tL, cL, fL, fmL, hL, lL, mL) &*&
           list_inv(R, tR, cR, fR, fmR, hR, lR, mR) &*&
           result == (model(mL) == model(mR)); @*/
```

The operation `clear` frees all occupied nodes. Its contract only constrains the content of the doubly linked list and leaves unspecified the free list.

```
void clear(struct List* L);
//@ requires list_inv(L,?t,?c,?f,?fm,?h,?l,?m);
//@ ensures list_inv(L,t,c,?f1,?fm1,0,0,?m1) &*& length(model(m1))=0;
```

2.3 Cursors

Following the Ada 2012 semantics [1], "a cursor designates a particular node within a list (...). A cursor keeps designating the same node (...) as long as the node is part of the container, even if the node is moved in the container. [...] If [a cursor] is not otherwise initialized, it is initialized to [...] `No_Element`." Therefore, a cursor is a record storing an *array index*. The special cursor `No_Element` is defined as a global constant storing the index 0, indeed invalid for a list node (recall that valid nodes are stored from index 1).

```
struct Cursor { int current; };
const struct Cursor No_Element = { 0 };
```

The logic type `cursor` abstracts the cursor implementation (line 1 in Fig. 3). The representation predicate for cursors, `valid_cursor_or_noelem` (line 3 in Fig. 3), checks that the cursor content, `index`, corresponds to an occupied node in the list using the precise model `m` of the BDLL (see line 13). Moreover, the predicate computes from `m` and `first`, the BDLL starting index, the segments `before` and `after`, into which the cursor `pc` splits `m`.

Given a BDLL container, the model of valid cursors for this container is defined (following Ada 2012 specification) as the finite bijection between the set of abstract cursors and the positions (from 1 to the size) in the list. We encode the mathematical type map by an association list, using the polymorphic type provided in the libraries of VeriFast. The cursor model is computed by the logic function `positions` (line 19 in Fig. 3) from the container model, the index of the first node in the BDLL, and the first position in the list.

```
inductive cursor = NoElem | Valid(int);

predicate valid_cursor_or_noelem(struct Cursor* C,
            int index, int first, list<pnode> m;
            cursor pc,
            list<pnode> before, list<pnode> after) =
  C->current|->index &*&
  pre_valid_cursor_or_noelem(index,first,vs,pc,before,after);

predicate pre_valid_cursor_or_noelem(int index, int first, list<pnode> vs;
            cursor pc, list<pnode> before, list<pnode> after) =
  pc == (index == 0 ? NoElem : Valid(index)) &*&
  index == first ?
    (before == nil &*& after == vs) :
    (vs != nil &*&
     pre_valid_cursor_or_noelem(index,pnext(head(vs)),tail(vs),pc,?bef,after) &*&
     before == cons(head(vs),bef));

fixpoint list<pair<cursor, int> > positions (list<purenode> values,
                                             int index, int position) { ... }
```

Fig. 3. Logic definitions for cursors

Notice that this manner of specifying cursor model is coherent with the sequence model of the container, because the access to the elements of a sequence is based on positions. However, this specification choice does not combine well with inductive reasoning and induces additional work for the proof (see Sect. 3). We have to enrich the inductive list model with operations using positions. For example, we define the operation `M_Element(m,p)` which returns the `p`th element of the list `m`. We also defined operations `P_Has_Key` and `P_Get` on association lists to test if an abstract cursor is in the domain of the map resp. to obtain the value to which it is bound.

An example of a contract using cursors is the operation `element`, which returns the value stored at the position in the list given by the cursor `C`:

```
Element_Type element(struct List* L, struct Cursor* C)
/*@ requires list_inv(L,?tab,?capacity,?free,?fm,?head,?last,?m) &*&
             valid_cursor_or_noelem(C,?index,head,m,?pc,?bef,?aft) &*&
             P_Has_Key(positions(m,head,1),pc)==true; @*/
/*@ ensures list_inv(L,tab,capacity,free,fm,head,last,m) &*&
            valid_cursor_or_noelem(C,index,head,m,pc,bef,aft) &*&
            result==M_Element(model(m),P_Get(positions(m,head,1),pc)); @*/
```

Contracts of functions changing the positions in the list (e.g., insert or delete) are complete with respect to the model of cursors. For example, consider the post-condition of operation `delete_first` given below, which deletes first `Count` elements of the list. It uses a conditional expression (syntax like in C) to specify two contract cases. The first case corresponds to an input container with size less than `Count`. In the second case, the container preserved its content after position `Count` (predicate `M_Range_Shifted`) and the positions of valid cursors in the new container (of model `nvs`) are shifted by `Count` (predicate `P_Positions_Shifted`) with respect to the old container.

```
void delete_first(struct List* L, int Count);
/*@ requires list_inv(L,?tab,?cap,?free,?fm,?head,?last,?m) &*&
```

```
            Count >= 0; @*/
/*@ ensures list_inv(L,tab,cap,?nfree,?nfm,?nhead,?nlast,?nm) &*&
          length(m) <= Count ? length(nm) == 0
          : length(nm) == length(m) - Count &*&
            M_Range_Shifted(model(nm),model(m),1,length(nm),Count) &*&
            P_Positions_Shifted(positions(nm,nhead,1),
                                     positions(m,head,1),1,Count); @*/
```

3 Verification Approach

We employ an auto-active verification approach [20], supported by the tool VeriFast [15]. The auto-active approach provides more automation of the verification process based on the ability given to the user to help the prover by adding annotations and lemmas and the efficient use of back-end solvers. This section highlights the methodology applied to conduct auto-active verification for this case study. This methodology is independent of the specific tool used. We also comment on the advantages and difficulties encountered with the tool used. Notice that we did not have prior experience with VeriFast.

3.1 Model-Based Specification for Verification

The contracts provided for our container are in a first order logic over sequences and maps, which employs recursive logic functions. This theory is undecidable so we have to provide lemma to help the prover to tackle verification conditions.

Usage of a precise model is the solution we found to ease the writing of lemmas. It consists in refining the abstract model used for the container specification into a model that captures more details on the container organization. The abstract model is obtained from the refined one using a catamorphic mapping. This methodology is required by the gap between the abstract model and the lower level implementation of the container.

Let us explain why this methodology leads to efficient verification in our case. Consider the specification where (i) the model for the container is the sequence of the values stored and (ii) the model for the cursors is the mapping of occupied nodes to list positions. To capture these models with the representation predicate for the heap, i.e., the predicate `bdll` defined at line 22 in Fig. 1, we have to replace the model `m` by the sequence of values `vs` and the map of cursors `mc`. The verification of iterative operations on the list requires to provide a lemma that allows to compose "well linked" list segments into a new list segment, i.e.,

```
lemma void bdll_concat(struct Node_Type * t,
              int p, int f, int l1, int n1, int l, int n)
requires bdll(t,?c,p,f,l1,n1,?vs1,?mc1) &*&
         bdll(t,c,l1,n1,l,n,?vs2,?mc2) &*& node(t+n, c, ?pn);
ensures bdll(t,c,p,f,l,n,append(vs1,vs2),
            append_maps(mc1,mc2)) &*& node(t+n, c, pn);
{ ... }
```

This lemma employs an operation `append_maps`, that concatenates two models of counters `mc1` and `mc2` such that the positions associated with counters in `mc1` are shifted by the size of the domain of `mc1`. This operation is more difficult to axiomatize than list concatenation. Moreover, all invariant proofs require to keep together the two loosely related models (sequence and map) which leads to less modular proofs. Our solution to this problem is to employ the precise model of the list segment represented by the `bdll` predicate, as has been presented in Sect. 2.2. The composition lemma for `bdll` predicate is simpler because it avoids the reasoning on the model of cursors.

The catamorphism mappings used to obtain the abstract model of the container and the model of valid cursors have good inductive definitions and enable efficient decision procedures [35]. However, these decision procedures are not available in our verification tool; this work may be a motivation to add them.

Specification of user types by representation predicates mapping them to inductive types is classical in Separation Logic. We encode the invariant of the BDLL data structure in the predicate `list_inv`. The adoption of C for the implementation keeps us away from the problems of verifying object-related properties, for example. However, this choice leads to an overburden in annotations because we have to specify that parameters of type '`struct List*`' satisfy the invariant.

Additional annotation have been supplied to axiomatize global constants (like the `No_Element` record in Fig. 1) and arrays of user-defined structures (like `nodes` in `List`).

Contract cases are intensively used in the considered GNAT library. We got around the absence of contract cases in VeriFast using conditional expressions and logic predicate and functions that relate two models (old and new). We do not observe any expressivity or performance problems with this method of encoding contracts.

3.2 Support for Specification Types

Specification of model types is done based on the mathematical models sequence (or inductive polymorphic list) and map (or inductive polymorphic association list). The VeriFast libraries including these models (mainly `list.*`) contain 9 predicates and 20 lemmas, and are not enough for the operations on models required in our specifications. We added tens of lemma and predicates. They are useful not only for the container proof but also for the verification of client programs with inductive back-end solvers. (Nowadays, these proofs are done by GNATprove by calling SMT solvers with quantifiers support.)

More problematic was the lack of support for finite maps and automation of inductive reasoning. VeriFast does not provide sets and finite maps as primitives. The encoding of cursor models by association lists renders more complex the lemmas needed on cursor models. For example, the map inclusion property is defined as follows:

```
predicate P_le<t>(list<pair<t,int> > Left, list<pair<t,int> > Right) =
    switch(Left) {
        case nil: return true;
        case cons(p, m):
            return P_Has_Key(Right, fst(p)) == true &*&
                   snd(p) == P_Get(Right, fst(p)) &*&
                   P_le(m, Right);
    };
```

This definition is not as easy to reason about as we might expect. In particular, some properties of this definition of inclusion such as reflexivity are only provable under the additional assumption that the keys are distinct.

We proved that the models of cursors fulfill the constraint `distinct_keys` (defined also in VeriFast libraries) because keys are index positions in the array used to denote separated cells.

```
lemma void positions_distinct_keys(int index, list<purenode> m, int pos)
requires bdll(?tab, ?cap, ?fst, index, ?last, ?z, m) &*& node(tab+z, cap, ?tab0);
ensures bdll(tab, cap, fst, index, last, z, m) &*& node(tab+z, cap, tab0) &*&
        distinct_keys(positions(m, index, pos)) == true;
```

Notice that these proofs are not necessary for provers with support for finite maps and sets. Although VeriFast supports as back-end solver Z3 [9], it does not use it for such theories. The inductive theories are supported by other back-end solvers, e.g., CVC4 [30] that are not connected to VeriFast.

3.3 Annotations Load

The annotations required by the proof of our library belong to two categories: (1) mandatory annotations including function contracts and predicates employed by these contracts and (2) auxiliary annotations including loop invariants, open/-close of predicates, definitions and calls of lemmas.

The prover VeriFast includes all this annotation burden, since we can not direct the prover in the usage of these annotations. VeriFast provides two mechanisms to limit the burden of the auxiliary annotations: (i) lemmas can be marked as automated which means they will be given to the backend solver on all problems, (ii) inductive predicate definitions can be automatically folded and unfolded when used with computed parameters.

We introduce few automated lemmas and call them in order to lighten the prover load. We don't observe performance problems by including all these annotations and despite the absence of modular proofs. The frame reasoning rule of Separation Logic seems to play an important role in this good behavior.

We found useful the two ways of specifying inductive predicates in VeriFast: by case on the model or by case over the aliasing of heap locations. We started with the first style, but finally chose the second to bring advantages of automatic folding and unfolding of computed predicates.

3.4 Challenges Dealt

To resume, we faced the following challenges during the verification process:

- We considered a functional specification which is already in use in client code. Therefore, we can not adapt this specification to ease the verification. Instead, we propose a method based on a refined specification based on a precise model of the container that eases the verification and allows to obtain the initial specification with minimal cost.
- The specification we received is complete with respect to the model of containers and cursors. This requires to specify logic functions and predicates that are more complex than the usual ones.
- The code has been designed to obtain efficient container implementation and does not focus on verification. Therefore, the verification task has been more difficult compared with previous work verifying functional specification of container libraries [28,39] designed with verification in mind.
- Only specifications of contracts for public operations on the container were provided. We had to annotate the code and the internal operations. This implied an additional cost in annotations because some internal operations break the data structure invariants.
- Having in mind the extension of this verification effort to other bounded container libraries (for sets or maps), we propose reusable logic libraries and suggest some improvements for the auto-active verification tool in use.

4 Verification Results

Bugs Found: We did not find spectacular bugs in the code, which is normal for a library that has been used for years. We only detected a potential arithmetic overflow in the computation of the memory to be allocated and a potential memory shortage. The last problem is in fact dealt for the SPARK clients using tools that measure the memory allocated by the program.

Complete Specifications: We also fix some minor completeness problems with the original specifications. Our verification effort leads to a complete functional specifications for all operations, including non public operations.

Specification Load: We have coded, specified, and verified 27 functions out of the 39 provided by the container library including equality and emptiness tests, clear, assign and copy, getting and setting one element, manipulating the cursors, inserting and deleting at some cursor, finding an element before and after a cursor. Most of the 12

Table 1. Statistics on the proof

File	#pred	#fix-points	#lemma	lines	
				annot	code
vflist.gh	2	8	9	234	–
vfseq.gh	14	10	34	482	–
vfmap.gh	13	9	64	1251	–
cfdlli.h	4	10	0	407	36
cfdlli.c	14	5	64	2684	506
Total	47	42	171	5058	542

remaining functions deal with sorting. The size of our development is given in Table 1. To obtain a specification close to the Ada 2012 one, we wrote two files of logic definitions for models (`vfseq.gh` and `vfmap.gh`) extending the VeriFast libraries. Additional fixpoint functions and lemmas required on VeriFast lists are written in file `vflist.gh`. The rate between source code and annotations is about 1 to 9. The required annotations (i.e., data structure invariant, pre/post conditions, and logic predicate and function used directly in them) represent a quarter of all annotations (including also loop invariants and lemmas). In Ada 2012 container, the rate between source code and contracts is already of about 1 to 3.

Verification Performance: We run VeriFast on a machine with 16 GB RAM, Intel core i5, and 2.70 GHz, installed with Linux. The back-end solver of VeriFast was redux. The verification takes 1.3 s for the full container.

5 Related Work

The verification of individual data structures has received special attention. General safety properties (i.e., absence of out of array bounds accesses, null dereferences, division by zero, arithmetic overflow) may be verified automatically with low load of annotations using *static analysis methods*, e.g. [13,17,19,21]. More complex properties like reachability of locations in the heap and shape of the data structures could also be proved with static analysis methods based on shape analysis, e.g., [4,6,10,32]. These automatic techniques have been applied to linked lists coded in arrays [34]. These methods concern limited properties and may be used in the early stages of the library development to infer internal invariant properties. Extension of fully automatic techniques to cover functional specification abstractions like sets or bags are based either on *shape analysis*, e.g., [7,14] or on logic fragments supported by SMT decision procedures [16,18,37,38]. These functional specifications capture essential mathematical properties of the data structure but do not deal with properties of iterators over them.

At the opposite end of the spectrum of verification techniques, *interactive provers* have been used to obtain detailed specifications about data structures based on powerful theories, e.g., [8,23,29], but they require expertise and great amount of proof scripting.

At the intermediate level of automation, functional verification tools have been used to tackle the verification of specific data structures (e.g., Dafny [33], GRASShoper [26], VeriFast [15], or Why3 [36]) but we are not aware of any experiment on bounded lists.

The full functional correctness of container libraries has been considered in [28,39]. They consider complex data structures in imperative and object oriented languages that require to verify special properties and may benefit from modular verification thanks to inheritance. In both cited works, a special effort has been deployed to improve the prover to call solvers for different theories or to generate verification conditions that may be dealt with efficiently. This efforts lead to a low annotation overhead, especially in [28]. We use an on-the-shelf auto-active verification tool but improve its performances by employing a refinement method which leads to more automation but a more important annotation overhead. None of these works consider the container of bounded list.

6 Conclusion

We apply auto-active verification provided by the VeriFast tool to prove the functional specifications of the bounded doubly linked list container. The implementation we consider is in C, but it mimics the GNAT library [12], which is used in SPARK client programs. The functional specification is model-based and uses sequence and map mathematical models in a specific way to model the content of the list and its valid cursors. Our main contributions are (i) the improvement of the logic libraries of VeriFast to deal with such specific models and (ii) the use of a refinement based methodology to ease the proof automation.

This case study provides a motivation for the development of inductive solvers and their connection with auto-active provers like VeriFast. This experiment is another demonstration of the known fact (see [28]) that proving functional specifications of real world containers is more difficult than proving functional specification of data structures. The support for automation of these proofs is of an utmost importance to scale the verification to a full library of containers.

Data Availability Statement and Acknowledgements. The annotated code of the library and the sources used by its proof are available in the FIGSHARE repository [5]. The file-set also includes the distribution of the VeriFast tool running in the virtual machine provided at https://doi.org/10.6084/m9.figshare.5896615.

This work has been supported by the French national research organization ANR (grant ANR-14-CE28-0018). We thank Claire Dross and Yannick Moy from AdaCore for guiding us through the Ada standard library and for supplying the latest version of its specification. We thank Samantha Dihn for the first C version of the Ada containers.

References

1. Ada Europe: Ada Reference Manual - Language and Standard Libraries, Chapter A.18.3 The Generic Package Containers. Doubly_Linked_Lists Norm ISO/IEC 8652:2012(E) (2012). http://www.adaic.org/resources/add_content/standards/12rm/html/RM-TTL.html
2. AdaCore: SPARK verification gallery. https://github.com/AdaCore/spark2014/tree/master/testsuite/gnatprove/tests
3. Baudin, P., Filliâtre, J.C., Hubert, T., Marché, C., Monate, B., Moy, Y., Prevosto, V.: ACSL: ANSI C Specification Language (preliminary design V1.2), preliminary edition, May 2008
4. Calcagno, C., Distefano, D., O'Hearn, P.W., Yang, H.: Compositional shape analysis by means of bi-abduction. J. ACM **58**(6), 26:1–26:66 (2011)
5. Cauderlier, R., Sighireanu, M.: A verified implementation of the bounded list container. In: TACAS 2018 (2018). Figshare. https://doi.org/10.6084/m9.figshare.5919145.v1

6. Chang, B.E., Rival, X.: Relational inductive shape analysis. In: Proceedings of POPL, pp. 247–260. ACM (2008)
7. Chin, W.-N., David, C., Nguyen, H.H., Qin, S.: Automated verification of shape, size and bag properties via user-defined predicates in separation logic. Sci. Comput. Program. **77**(9), 1006–1036 (2012). The Programming Languages track at the 24th ACM Symposium on Applied Computing (SAC 2009)
8. Chlipala, A., Malecha, J.G., Morrisett, G., Shinnar, A., Wisnesky, R.: Effective interactive proofs for higher-order imperative programs. In: Proceedings of ICFP, pp. 79–90. ACM (2009)
9. de Moura, L.M., Bjørner, N.: Z3: an efficient SMT solver. In: Ramakrishnan, C.R., Rehof, J. (eds.) TACAS 2008. LNCS, vol. 4963, pp. 337–340. Springer, Heidelberg (2008). https://doi.org/10.1007/978-3-540-78800-3_24
10. Drăgoi, C., Enea, C., Sighireanu, M.: Local shape analysis for overlaid data structures. In: Logozzo, F., Fähndrich, M. (eds.) SAS 2013. LNCS, vol. 7935, pp. 150–171. Springer, Heidelberg (2013). https://doi.org/10.1007/978-3-642-38856-9_10
11. Dross, C., Filliâtre, J.-C., Moy, Y.: Correct code containing containers. In: Gogolla, M., Wolff, B. (eds.) TAP 2011. LNCS, vol. 6706, pp. 102–118. Springer, Heidelberg (2011). https://doi.org/10.1007/978-3-642-21768-5_9
12. GNU Fundation: GNAT library components in gcc 7.1. https://sourceware.org/svn/gcc/tags/gcc_7_1_0_release/gcc/ada/ files `a-cfdlli.ad*`
13. Halbwachs, N., Péron, M.: Discovering properties about arrays in simple programs. In: Proceedings of PLDI, pp. 339–348. ACM (2008)
14. Itzhaky, S., Bjørner, N., Reps, T., Sagiv, M., Thakur, A.: Property-directed shape analysis. In: Biere, A., Bloem, R. (eds.) CAV 2014. LNCS, vol. 8559, pp. 35–51. Springer, Cham (2014). https://doi.org/10.1007/978-3-319-08867-9_3
15. Jacobs, B., Smans, J., Piessens, F.: A quick tour of the VeriFast program verifier. In: Ueda, K. (ed.) APLAS 2010. LNCS, vol. 6461, pp. 304–311. Springer, Heidelberg (2010). https://doi.org/10.1007/978-3-642-17164-2_21
16. Jacobs, S., Kuncak, V.: Towards complete reasoning about axiomatic specifications. In: Jhala, R., Schmidt, D. (eds.) VMCAI 2011. LNCS, vol. 6538, pp. 278–293. Springer, Heidelberg (2011). https://doi.org/10.1007/978-3-642-18275-4_20
17. Kirchner, F., Kosmatov, N., Prevosto, V., Signoles, J., Yakobowski, B.: Frama-C: a software analysis perspective. FAC **27**(3), 573–609 (2015)
18. Kuncak, V., Piskac, R., Suter, P., Wies, T.: Building a calculus of data structures. In: Barthe, G., Hermenegildo, M. (eds.) VMCAI 2010. LNCS, vol. 5944, pp. 26–44. Springer, Heidelberg (2010). https://doi.org/10.1007/978-3-642-11319-2_6
19. Laviron, V., Logozzo, F.: SubPolyhedra: a family of numerical abstract domains for the (more) scalable inference of linear inequalities. STTT **13**(6), 585–601 (2011)
20. Leino, K.R.M., Moskal, M.: Usable auto-active verification (2010). http://www.fm.csl.sri.com
21. Liu, J., Rival, X.: Abstraction of arrays based on non contiguous partitions. In: D'Souza, D., Lal, A., Larsen, K.G. (eds.) VMCAI 2015. LNCS, vol. 8931, pp. 282–299. Springer, Heidelberg (2015). https://doi.org/10.1007/978-3-662-46081-8_16
22. McCormick, J.W., Chapin, P.C.: Building High Integrity Applications with SPARK. Cambridge University Press, Cambridge (2015)
23. Nanevski, A., Morrisett, G., Shinnar, A., Govereau, P., Birkedal, L.: Ynot: dependent types for imperative programs. In: Proceeding of ICFP, pp. 229–240. ACM (2008)
24. O'Hearn, P.W., Reynolds, J.C., Yang, H.: Local reasoning about programs that alter data structures. In: Fribourg, L. (ed.) CSL 2001. LNCS, vol. 2142, pp. 1–19. Springer, Heidelberg (2001). https://doi.org/10.1007/3-540-44802-0_1

25. O'Hearn, P.W., Yang, H., Reynolds, J.C.: Separation and information hiding. In: Proceedings of POPL, pp. 268–280. ACM (2004)
26. Piskac, R., Wies, T., Zufferey, D.: Automating Separation logic with trees and data. In: Biere, A., Bloem, R. (eds.) CAV 2014. LNCS, vol. 8559, pp. 711–728. Springer, Cham (2014). https://doi.org/10.1007/978-3-319-08867-9_47
27. Polikarpova, N., Furia, C.A., Meyer, B.: Specifying reusable components. In: Leavens, G.T., O'Hearn, P.W., Rajamani, S.K. (eds.) VSTTE 2010. LNCS, vol. 6217, pp. 127–141. Springer, Heidelberg (2010). https://doi.org/10.1007/978-3-642-15057-9_9
28. Polikarpova, N., Tschannen, J., Furia, C.A.: A fully verified container library. In: Bjørner, N., de Boer, F. (eds.) FM 2015. LNCS, vol. 9109, pp. 414–434. Springer, Cham (2015). https://doi.org/10.1007/978-3-319-19249-9_26
29. Pottier, F.: Verifying a hash table and its iterators in higher-order separation logic. In: Proceedings of CPP, pp. 3–16. ACM (2017)
30. Reynolds, A., Kuncak, V.: Induction for SMT solvers. In: D'Souza, D., Lal, A., Larsen, K.G. (eds.) VMCAI 2015. LNCS, vol. 8931, pp. 80–98. Springer, Heidelberg (2015). https://doi.org/10.1007/978-3-662-46081-8_5
31. Reynolds, J.C.: Separation logic: a logic for shared mutable data structures. In: Proceedings of LICS, pp. 55–74. IEEE (2002)
32. Rinetzky, N., Sagiv, M., Yahav, E.: Interprocedural shape analysis for cutpoint-free programs. In: Hankin, C., Siveroni, I. (eds.) SAS 2005. LNCS, vol. 3672, pp. 284–302. Springer, Heidelberg (2005). https://doi.org/10.1007/11547662_20
33. Rustan, K., Leino, M.: Main Microsoft research Dafny web page. http://research.microsoft.com/en-us/projects/dafny
34. Sotin, P., Rival, X.: Hierarchical shape abstraction of dynamic structures in static blocks. In: Jhala, R., Igarashi, A. (eds.) APLAS 2012. LNCS, vol. 7705, pp. 131–147. Springer, Heidelberg (2012). https://doi.org/10.1007/978-3-642-35182-2_10
35. Suter, P., Dotta, M., Kuncak, V.: Decision procedures for algebraic data types with abstractions. In: Proceedings of POPL, pp. 199–210. ACM (2010)
36. Why3-Team: Why3 verification gallery. http://toccata.lri.fr/gallery/
37. Wies, T., Muñiz, M., Kuncak, V.: An efficient decision procedure for imperative tree data structures. In: Bjørner, N., Sofronie-Stokkermans, V. (eds.) CADE 2011. LNCS (LNAI), vol. 6803, pp. 476–491. Springer, Heidelberg (2011). https://doi.org/10.1007/978-3-642-22438-6_36
38. Wies, T., Muñiz, M., Kuncak, V.: Deciding functional lists with sublist sets. In: Joshi, R., Müller, P., Podelski, A. (eds.) VSTTE 2012. LNCS, vol. 7152, pp. 66–81. Springer, Heidelberg (2012). https://doi.org/10.1007/978-3-642-27705-4_6
39. Zee, K., Kuncak, V., Rinard, M.C.: Full functional verification of linked data structures. In: Proceedings of PLDI, pp. 349–361. ACM (2008)

Automating Deductive Verification for Weak-Memory Programs

Alexander J. Summers(✉) and Peter Müller(✉)

Department of Computer Science,
ETH Zurich, Zurich, Switzerland
{alexander.summers,peter.mueller}@inf.ethz.ch

Abstract. Writing correct programs for weak memory models such as the C11 memory model is challenging because of the weak consistency guarantees these models provide. The first program logics for the verification of such programs have recently been proposed, but their usage has been limited thus far to manual proofs. Automating proofs in these logics via first-order solvers is non-trivial, due to features such as higher-order assertions, modalities and rich permission resources.

In this paper, we provide the first encoding of a weak memory program logic using existing deductive verification tools. Our work enables, for the first time, the (unbounded) verification of C11 programs at the level of abstraction provided by the program logics; the only necessary user interaction is in the form of specifications written in the program logic.

We tackle three recent program logics: Relaxed Separation Logic and two forms of Fenced Separation Logic, and show how these can be encoded using the Viper verification infrastructure. In doing so, we illustrate several novel encoding techniques which could be employed for other logics. Our work is implemented, and has been evaluated on examples from existing papers as well as the Facebook open-source Folly library.

1 Introduction

Reasoning about programs running on weak memory is challenging because weak memory models admit executions that are not sequentially consistent, that is, cannot be explained by a sequential interleaving of concurrent threads. Moreover, weak-memory programs employ a range of operations to access memory, which require dedicated reasoning techniques. These operations include fences as well as read and write accesses with varying degrees of synchronisation.

Some of these challenges are addressed by the first program logics for weak-memory programs, in particular, Relaxed Separation Logic (RSL) [38], GPS [36], Fenced Separation Logic (FSL) [17], and FSL++ [18]. These logics apply to interesting classes of C11 programs, but their tool support has been limited to

D. Beyer and M. Huisman (Eds.): TACAS 2018, LNCS 10805, pp. 190–209, 2018.
https://doi.org/10.1007/978-3-319-89960-2_11

$$s ::= l := \mathtt{alloc}_{\mathtt{na}}() \mid l := \mathtt{alloc}_{\rho}(\mathcal{Q}) \mid [l]_{\sigma} := e \mid x := [l]_{\sigma}$$
$$\mid \mathtt{fence}_{\mathtt{acq}} \mid \mathtt{fence}_{\mathtt{rel}}(A) \mid x := \mathtt{CAS}_{\tau}(l, e_1, e_2)$$
$$\textit{where } \rho \in \{\mathtt{acq}, \mathtt{RMW}\}, \quad \sigma ::= \mathtt{na} \mid \tau, \quad \tau \in \{\mathtt{acq}, \mathtt{rel}, \mathtt{rel\_acq}, \mathtt{rlx}\}$$

Fig. 1. Syntax for memory accesses. na indicates a non-atomic operation; τ indicates an atomic access mode (as defined in C11), discussed in later sections. ρ, and assertions A and invariants $\mathcal{Q}$ are program annotations, needed as input for our encoding. Expressions e include boolean and arithmetic operations, but no heap accesses. We assume that source programs are type-checked.

embeddings in Coq. Verification based on these embeddings requires substantial user interaction, which is an obstacle to applying and evaluating these logics.

In this paper, we present a novel approach to automating deductive verification for weak memory programs. We encode large fractions of RSL, FSL, and FSL++ (collectively referred to as *the RSL logics*) into the intermediate verification language Viper [27], and use the existing Viper verification backends to reason automatically about the encoded programs. This encoding reduces all concurrency and weak-memory features as well as logical features such as higher-order assertions and custom modalities to a much simpler sequential logic.

Defining an encoding into Viper is much more lightweight than developing a dedicated verifier from scratch, since we can reuse the existing automation for a variety of advanced program reasoning features. Compared to an embedding into an interactive theorem prover such as Coq, our approach leads to a significantly higher degree of automation than that typically achieved through tactics. Moreover, it allows users to interact with the verifier on the abstraction level of source code and annotations, without exposing the underlying formalism. Verification in Coq can provide foundational guarantees, whereas in our approach, errors in the encoding or bugs in the verifier could potentially invalidate verification results. We mitigate the former risk by a soundness argument for our encoding and the latter by the use of a mature verification system. We are convinced that both approaches are necessary: foundational verification is ideal for meta-theory development and application areas such as safety-critical systems, whereas our approach is well-suited for prototyping and evaluating logics, and for making a verification technique applicable by a wider user base.

The contributions of this paper are: (1) The first automated deductive verification approach for weak-memory logics. We demonstrate the effectiveness of this approach on examples from the literature, which are available online [3]. (2) An encoding of large fractions of RSL, FSL, and FSL++ into Viper. Various aspects of this encoding (such as the treatment of higher-order features and modalities, as well as the overall proof search strategy) are generic and can be reused to encode other advanced separation logics. (3) A prototype implementation, which is available online [4].

Related Work. The existing weak-memory logics RSL [38], GPS [36], FSL [17], and FSL++ [18] have been formalized in Coq and used to verify small examples.

$$A ::= e \mid l \overset{k}{\mapsto} e \mid A_1 * A_2 \mid e \Rightarrow A \mid (e\ ?\ A_1 : A_2)$$
$$\mid \mathsf{Uninit}(l) \mid \mathsf{Acq}(l, \mathcal{Q}) \mid \mathsf{Rel}(l, \mathcal{Q}) \mid \mathsf{Init}(l) \mid \triangle A \mid \nabla A \mid \mathsf{RMWAcq}(l, \mathcal{Q})$$

Fig. 2. Assertion syntax of the RSL logics. The top row of constructs are standard for separation logics; those in the second row are specific to the RSL logics, and explained throughout the paper. Invariants $\mathcal{Q}$ are *functions* from values to assertions (cf. Sect. 3).

The proofs were constructed mostly manually, whereas our approach automates most of the proof steps. As shown in our evaluation, our approach reduces the overhead by more than an order of magnitude. The degree of automation in Coq could be increased through logic-specific tactics (e.g. [13,32]), whereas our approach benefits from Viper's automation for the intermediate language, which is independent of the encoded logic.

Jacobs [20] proposed a program logic for the TSO memory model that has been encoded in VeriFast [21]. This encoding requires a substantial amount of annotations, whereas our approach provides a higher degree of automation and handles the more complex C11 memory model.

Weak-memory reasoning has been addressed using techniques based on model-checking (e.g. [5,6,11]) and static analyses (e.g. [7,16]). These approaches are fully automatic, but do not analyse code modularly, which is e.g. important for verifying libraries independently from their clients. Deductive verification enables compositional proofs by requiring specifications at function boundaries. Such specifications can express precise information about the (unbounded) behaviour of a program's constituent parts.

Automating logics via encodings into intermediate verification languages is a proven approach, as witnessed by the many existing verifiers (e.g. [14,15,24,25]) which target Boogie [8] or Why3 [9]. Our work is the first that applies this approach to logics for weak-memory concurrency. Our encoding benefits from Viper's native support for separation-logic-style reasoning and several advanced features such as quantified permissions and permission introspection [26,27], which are not available in other intermediate verification languages.

Outline. The next four sections present our encoding for the core features of the C11 memory model: we discuss non-atomic locations in Sect. 2, release-acquire accesses in Sect. 3, fences in Sect. 4, and compare-and-swap in Sect. 5. We discuss soundness and completeness of our encoding in Sect. 6 and evaluate our approach in Sect. 7. Section 8 concludes. Further details of our encoding and examples are available in our accompanying technical report (hereafter, TR) [35]. A prototype implementation of our encoding (with all examples) is available as an artifact [4].

2 Non-atomic Locations

We present our encoding for a small imperative programming language similar to the languages supported by the RSL logics. C11 supports *non-atomic*

$$\dfrac{}{\vdash \{\mathsf{true}\}\ l := \mathtt{alloc}_{\mathsf{na}}()\ \{\mathsf{Uninit}(l)\}} \qquad \dfrac{}{\vdash \{l \overset{1}{\mapsto} \_ \vee \mathsf{Uninit}(l)\}\ [l]_{\mathsf{na}} := e\ \{l \overset{1}{\mapsto} e\}}$$

$$\dfrac{}{\vdash \{l \overset{k}{\mapsto} e\}\ x := [l]_{\mathsf{na}}\ \{x = e * l \overset{k}{\mapsto} e\}} \qquad (l \overset{k}{\mapsto} e\ *\ l \overset{k'}{\mapsto} e') \Leftrightarrow (e = e' * l \overset{k+k'}{\mapsto} e)$$

Fig. 3. Adapted RSL rules for non-atomics. Read access requires a non-zero permission. Write access requires either write permission or that the location is uninitialised. The underscore _ stands for an arbitrary value.

memory accesses and different forms of *atomic* accesses. The access operations are summarised in Fig. 1. We adopt the common simplifying assumption [36,38] that memory locations are partitioned into those accessed only via non-atomic accesses (*non-atomic locations*), and those accessed only via C11 atomics (*atomic locations*). Read and write statements are parameterised by a mode σ, which is either na (non-atomic) or one of the atomic access modes τ. We focus on non-atomic accesses in this section and discuss atomics in subsequent sections.

RSL Proof Rules. Non-atomic memory accesses come with no synchronisation guarantees; programmers need to ensure that all accesses to non-atomic locations are data-race free. The RSL logics enforce this requirement using standard separation logic [28,31]. We show the syntax of assertions in Fig. 2, which will be explained throughout the paper. A *points-to assertion* $l \overset{k}{\mapsto} e$ denotes a transferable *resource*, providing permission to access the location l, and expressing that l has been initialised and its current value is e. Here, k is a fraction $0 < k \leq 1$; $k = 1$ denotes the *full* (or exclusive) permission to read and write location l, whereas $0 < k < 1$ provides (non-exclusive) read access [12]. Points-to resources can be split and recombined, but never duplicated or forged; when transferring such a resource to another thread it is removed from the current one, avoiding data races by construction. The RSL assertion $\mathsf{Uninit}(l)$ expresses exclusive access to a location l that has been allocated, but not yet initialised; l may be written to but not read from. The main proof rules for non-atomic locations, adapted from RSL [38], are shown in Fig. 3.

Encoding. The Viper intermediate verification language [27] supports an assertion language based on Implicit Dynamic Frames [33], a program logic related to separation logic [29], but which separates permissions from value information. Viper is object-based; the only memory locations are field locations $e.f$ (in which e is a reference, and f a field name). Permissions to access these heap locations are described by *accessibility predicates* of the form **acc(**$e.f$**,** k**)**, where k is a fraction as for points-to predicates above (k defaults to 1). Assertions that do not contain accessibility predicates are called *pure*. Unlike in separation logics, heap locations may be read in pure assertions.

We model C-like memory locations l using a field val of a Viper reference l. Consequently, a separation logic assertion $l \overset{k}{\mapsto} e$ is represented in Viper as `acc(l.val, k) && l.val == e`. We assume that memory locations have type int,

```
field val: Int
field init: Bool

⟦Uninit(l)⟧ ⇝ acc(l.val) && acc(l.init) && !l.init
⟦l ↦^k e⟧ ⇝ acc(l.val, k) && acc(l.init, k) && l.val == ⟦e⟧ && l.init

⟦l := alloc_na()⟧ ⇝ l := new(); inhale ⟦Uninit(l)⟧
⟦x := [l]_na⟧ ⇝ assert l.init; x := l.val
⟦[l]_na := e⟧ ⇝ l.val := ⟦e⟧; l.init := true
```

Fig. 4. Viper encoding of the RSL assertions and the rules for non-atomic memory accesses from Fig. 3.

but a generalisation is trivial. Viper's conjunction && treats permissions like a separating conjunction, requiring the sum of the permissions in each conjunct, and acts as logical conjunction for pure assertions (just as $*$ in separation logic).

Viper provides two key statements for encoding proof rules: **inhale** A *adds* the permissions denoted by the assertion A to the current state, and *assumes* pure assertions in A. This can be used to model gaining new resources, e.g., acquiring a lock in the source program. Dually, **exhale** A checks that the current state satisfies A (otherwise a verification error occurs), and *removes* the permissions that A denotes; the values of any locations to which no permission remains are *havoced* (assigned arbitrary values). For example, when forking a new thread, its precondition is exhaled to transfer the necessary resources from the forking thread. Inhale and exhale statements can be seen as the permission-aware analogues of the assume and assert statements of first-order verification languages [25].

The encoding of the rules for non-atomics from Fig. 3 is presented in Fig. 4. $\llbracket A \rrbracket \rightsquigarrow \ldots$ denotes the encoding of an RSL assertion A as a Viper assertion, and analogously $\llbracket s \rrbracket \rightsquigarrow \ldots$ for source-level statements s.

The first two lines show background declarations. The assertion encodings follow the explanations above. Allocation is modelled by obtaining a fresh reference (via **new**()) and inhaling permissions to its val and init fields; assuming !l.init reflects that the location is not yet initialised. Viper implicitly checks the necessary permissions for field accesses (verification fails otherwise). Hence, the translation of a non-atomic read only needs to check that the read location is initialised before obtaining its value. Analogously, the translation of a non-atomic write only stores the value and records that the location is now initialised.

Note that Viper's implicit permission checks are both necessary and sufficient to encode the RSL rules in Fig. 3. In particular, the assertions $l \overset{1}{\mapsto} \_$ and Uninit(l) both provide the permissions to write to location l. By including **acc**(l.val) in the encoding of both assertions, we avoid the disjunction of the RSL rule.

Like the RSL logics, our approach requires programmers to annotate their code with access modes for locations (as part of the alloc statement), and specifications such as pre and postconditions for methods and threads. Given these inputs, Viper constructs the proof automatically. In particular, it automatically

$$\mathcal{Q}_1 \equiv (\mathcal{V} \neq 0 \Rightarrow a \overset{1}{\mapsto} 42) \qquad \mathcal{Q}_2 \equiv (\mathcal{V} \neq 0 \Rightarrow b \overset{1}{\mapsto} 7)$$

$$\begin{array}{c}
\{\mathsf{true}\} \\
a := \mathtt{alloc}_{\mathtt{na}}();\ b := \mathtt{alloc}_{\mathtt{na}}();\ l := \mathtt{alloc}_{\mathtt{acq}}(\mathcal{Q}_1 * \mathcal{Q}_2);\ [l]_{\mathtt{rel}} := 0 \\
\left.\begin{array}{l}
\{\mathsf{Acq}(l, \mathcal{Q}_1) * \mathsf{Init}(l)\} \\
\mathtt{while}([l]_{\mathtt{acq}} == 0); \\
x := [a]_{\mathtt{na}} \\
[a]_{\mathtt{na}} := x + 1 \\
\{\mathsf{true} * a \overset{1}{\mapsto} 43\}
\end{array}\right\| \left.\begin{array}{l}
\{\mathsf{Uninit}(a) * \mathsf{Uninit}(b) * \mathsf{Rel}(l, \mathcal{Q}_1 * \mathcal{Q}_2)\} \\
[a]_{\mathtt{na}} := 42 \\
[b]_{\mathtt{na}} := 7 \\
[l]_{\mathtt{rel}} := 1 \\
\{\mathsf{true} * \mathsf{Init}(l)\}
\end{array}\right\| \begin{array}{l}
\{\mathsf{Acq}(l, \mathcal{Q}_2) * \mathsf{Init}(l)\} \\
\mathtt{while}([l]_{\mathtt{acq}} == 0); \\
y := [b]_{\mathtt{na}} \\
[b]_{\mathtt{na}} := y + 1 \\
\{\mathsf{true} * b \overset{1}{\mapsto} 8\}
\end{array} \\
\{\mathsf{true} * a \overset{1}{\mapsto} 43 * b \overset{1}{\mapsto} 8 * \mathsf{Init}(l)\}
\end{array}$$

Fig. 5. An example illustrating "message passing" of non-atomic ownership, using release acquire atomics (inspired by an example from [17]). Annotations are shown in blue. This example corresponds to `RelAcqDblMsgPassSplit` in our evaluation (Sect. 7).

proves entailments, and splits and combines fractional permissions (hence, the equivalence in Fig. 3 need not be encoded). Automation can be increased further by inferring some of the required assertions, but this is orthogonal to the encoding presented in this paper.

3 Release-Acquire Atomics

The simplest form of C11 atomic memory accesses are *release write* and *acquire read* operations. They can be used to synchronise the transfer of ownership of (and information about) other, non-atomic locations, using a *message passing idiom*, illustrated by the example in Fig. 5. This program allocates two non-atomic locations a and b, and an atomic location l (initialised to 0), which is used to synchronise the three threads that are spawned afterwards. The middle thread makes changes to the non-atomics a and b, and then signals completion via a release write of 1 to l; conceptually, it gives up ownership of the non-atomic locations via this signal. The other threads loop attempting to acquire-read a non-zero value from l. Once they do, they each gain ownership of one non-atomic location via the acquire read of 1 and access that location. The release write and acquire reads of value 1 enforce *ordering constraints* on the non-atomic accesses, preventing the left and right threads from racing with the middle one.

RSL Proof Rules. The RSL logics capture message-passing idioms by associating a *location invariant* $\mathcal{Q}$ with each atomic location. Such an invariant is a function from values to assertions; we represent such functions as assertions with a distinguished variable symbol $\mathcal{V}$ as parameter. Location invariants prescribe the intended ownership that a thread obtains when performing an acquire read of value $\mathcal{V}$ from the location, and that must correspondingly be given up by a thread performing a release write. The main proof rules [38] are shown in Fig. 6.

When allocating an atomic location for release/acquire accesses (first proof rule), a location invariant $\mathcal{Q}$ must be chosen (as an annotation on the allocation). The assertions $\mathsf{Rel}(l, \mathcal{Q})$ and $\mathsf{Acq}(l, \mathcal{Q})$ record the invariant to be used

$$\frac{}{\vdash \{\mathsf{true}\}\ l := \mathtt{alloc}_{\mathsf{acq}}(\mathcal{Q})\ \{\mathsf{Rel}(l,\mathcal{Q}) * \mathsf{Acq}(l,\mathcal{Q})\}}$$

$$\frac{}{\vdash \{\mathcal{Q}(e) * \mathsf{Rel}(l,\mathcal{Q})\}\ [l]_{\mathtt{rel}} := e\ \{\mathsf{Init}(l) * \mathsf{Rel}(l,\mathcal{Q})\}}$$

$$\frac{}{\vdash \{\mathsf{Init}(l) * \mathsf{Acq}(l,\mathcal{Q})\}\ x := [l]_{\mathsf{acq}}\ \{\mathcal{Q}[x/\mathcal{V}] * \mathsf{Acq}(l,(\mathcal{V} \neq x \Rightarrow \mathcal{Q}))\}}$$

$$\mathsf{Init}(l) \Leftrightarrow \mathsf{Init}(l) * \mathsf{Init}(l) \qquad \mathsf{Rel}(l,\mathcal{Q}) \Leftrightarrow \mathsf{Rel}(l,\mathcal{Q}) * \mathsf{Rel}(l,\mathcal{Q})$$

$$\mathsf{Acq}(l,\mathcal{Q}_1 * \mathcal{Q}_2) \Leftrightarrow \mathsf{Acq}(l,\mathcal{Q}_1) * \mathsf{Acq}(l,\mathcal{Q}_2) \qquad \mathcal{Q}_1 \models \mathcal{Q}_2 \Rightarrow \mathsf{Acq}(l,\mathcal{Q}_1) \models \mathsf{Acq}(l,\mathcal{Q}_2)$$

Fig. 6. Adapted RSL rules for release-acquire atomics.

with subsequent release writes and acquire reads. To perform a release write of value e (second rule), a thread must hold the $\mathsf{Rel}(l,\mathcal{Q})$ assertion and *give up* the assertion $\mathcal{Q}[e/\mathcal{V}]$. For example, the line $[l]_{\mathtt{rel}} := 1$ in Fig. 5 causes the middle thread to give up ownership of both non-atomic locations a and b. The assertion $\mathsf{Init}(l)$ represents that atomic location l is initialised; both $\mathsf{Init}(l)$ and $\mathsf{Rel}(l,\mathcal{Q})$ are *duplicable* assertions; once obtained, they can be passed to multiple threads.

Multiple acquire reads might read the value written by a single release write operation; RSL prevents ownership of the transferred resources from being obtained (unsoundly) by multiple readers in two ways. First, $\mathsf{Acq}(l,\mathcal{Q})$ assertions cannot be duplicated, only split by partitioning the invariant $\mathcal{Q}$ into disjoint parts. For example, in Fig. 5, $\mathsf{Acq}(l,\mathcal{Q}_1)$ is given to the left thread, and $\mathsf{Acq}(l,\mathcal{Q}_2)$ to the right. Second, the rule for acquire reads adjusts the invariant in the Acq assertion such that subsequent reads of the same value will not obtain any ownership.

Encoding. A key challenge for encoding the above proof rules is that Rel and Acq are parameterised by the invariant $\mathcal{Q}$; higher-order assertions are not directly supported in Viper. However, for a given program, only finitely many such parameterisations will be required, which allows us to apply defunctionalisation [30], as follows. Given an annotated program, we assign a unique *index* to each syntactically-occurring invariant $\mathcal{Q}$ (in particular, in allocation statements, and as parameters to Rel and Acq assertions in specifications). Furthermore, we assign unique indices to all *immediate conjuncts* of these invariants. We write *indices* for the set of indices used. For each i in *indices*, we write *inv*(i) for the invariant which i indexes. For an invariant $\mathcal{Q}$, we write $\langle\mathcal{Q}\rangle$ for its index, and $\langle\!\langle\mathcal{Q}\rangle\!\rangle$ for the set of indices assigned to its immediate conjuncts.

Our encoding of the RSL rules from Fig. 6 is summarised in Fig. 7. To encode duplicable assertions such as $\mathsf{Init}(l)$, we make use of Viper's *wildcard permissions* [27], which represent unknown positive permission amounts. When exhaled, these amounts are chosen such that the amount exhaled will be *strictly smaller* than the amount held (verification fails if no permission is held) [19]. So after inhaling an $\mathsf{Init}(l)$ assertion (that is, a **`wildcard`** permission), it is possible to exhale two **`wildcard`** permissions, corresponding to two $\mathsf{Init}(l)$ assertions. Note that for atomic locations, we only use the `init` field's permissions, not its value.

```
field rel: Int
field acq: Bool
predicate AcqConjunct(l: Ref, idx: Int)

function valsRead(l: Ref, i: Int): Set[Int]
  requires AcqConjunct(l, i)

define SomeRel(l)  acc(l.rel, wildcard)
define SomeAcq(l)  acc(l.acq, wildcard) && l.acq == true

⟦Init(l)⟧ ⇝ acc(l.init, wildcard)
⟦Rel(l, Q)⟧ ⇝ SomeRel(l) && l.rel == ⟨Q⟩
⟦Acq(l, Q)⟧ ⇝ SomeAcq(l) && (foreach i in ⟪Q⟫:
  AcqConjunct(l, i) && valsRead(l, i) == Set[Int]() end)

⟦l := alloc_acq(Q)⟧ ⇝ l := new(); inhale ⟦Rel(l, Q)⟧ && ⟦Acq(l, Q)⟧

⟦[l]_rel := e⟧ ⇝ assert SomeRel(l);
  foreach i in indices do
    if (i == l.rel) { exhale inv(i)[e/V] }
  end
  inhale Init(l)

⟦x := [l]_acq⟧ ⇝ assert Init(l) && SomeAcq(l); x := havoc(); // unknown Int
  foreach i in indices do
    if (perm(AcqConjunct(l, i)) == 1 && !(x in valsRead(l, i))) {
      inhale inv(i)[x/V]
      tmpSet := valsRead(l, i)
      exhale AcqConjunct(l, i)
      inhale AcqConjunct(l, i) && valsRead(l,i) == tmpSet union Set(x)
    }
  end
```

Fig. 7. Viper encoding of the RSL rules for release-acquire atomics from Fig. 6. The operations in italics (e.g. *foreach*) are expanded statically in our encoding into conjunctions or statement sequences. The value of the `acq` field will be explained in Sect. 5.

We represent a $\mathsf{Rel}(l, \_)$ assertion for *some* invariant via a **`wildcard`** permission to a `rel` field; this is represented via the `SomeRel(l)` macro[1], and is used as the precondition for a release write (we must hold *some* Rel assertion, according to Fig. 6). The specific invariant associated with the location l is represented by storing its index as the *value* of the `rel` field; when encoding a release write, we branch on this value to exhale the appropriate assertion.

Analogously to Rel, we represent an Acq assertion for *some* invariant using a **`wildcard`** permission (the `SomeAcq` macro), which is the precondition for executing an acquire read. However, to support splitting, we represent the invariant in a more fine-grained way, by recording individual conjuncts separately. Each conjunct i of the invariant is modelled as an abstract *predicate* instance `AcqConjunct(`l`, `i`)`, which can be inhaled and exhaled individually. This encoding handles the common case that invariants are split along top-level conjuncts, as

[1] Viper macros can be defined for assertions or statements, and are syntactically expanded (and their arguments substituted) on use.

in Fig. 5. More complex splits can be supported through additional annotations: see App. C of the TR [35].

A release write is encoded by checking that some Rel assertion is held, and then exhaling the associated invariant for the value written. Moreover, it records that the location is initialised. The RSL rule for acquire reads adjusts the Acq invariant by obliterating the assertion for the value read. Instead of directly representing the adjusted invariant (which would complicate our numbering scheme), we track the set of values read as state in our encoding. We complement each `AcqConjunct` predicate instance with an (uninterpreted) Viper function **`valsRead(`**l**`,`** i**`)`**, returning a set of indices[2]).

An acquire read checks that the location is initialised and that we have *some* Acq assertion for the location. It assigns an unknown value to the lhs variable x, which is subsequently constrained by the invariant associated with the Acq assertion as follows: We check for each index whether we both currently hold an `AcqConjunct` predicate for that index[3], and if so, have not previously read the value x from that conjunct of our invariant. If these checks succeed, we inhale the indexed invariant for x, and then include x in the values read.

The encoding presented so far allows us to automatically verify annotated C11 programs using release writes and acquire reads (e.g., the program of Fig. 5) without any custom proof strategies [3]. In particular, we can support the higher-order Acq and Rel assertions through defunctionalisation and enable the splitting of invariants through a suitable representation.

4 Relaxed Memory Accesses and Fences

In contrast to release-acquire accesses, C11's *relaxed* atomic accesses provide no synchronisation: threads may observe reorderings of relaxed accesses and other memory operations. Correspondingly, RSL's proof rules for relaxed atomics provide weak guarantees, and do not support ownership transfer. Memory fence instructions can eliminate this problem. Intuitively, a *release fence* together with a subsequent relaxed write allows a thread to transfer away ownership of resources, similarly to a release write. Dually, an *acquire fence* together with a prior relaxed read allows a thread to obtain ownership of resources, similarly to an acquire read. This reasoning is justified by the ordering guarantees of the C11 model [17].

FSL Proof Rules. FSL and FSL++ provide proof rules for fences (see Fig. 8). They use *modalities* $\triangle$ ("up") and $\triangledown$ ("down") to represent resources that are transferred through relaxed accesses and fences. An assertion $\triangle A$ represents a resource A which has been prepared, via a release fence, to be transferred by a relaxed write operation; dually, $\triangledown A$ represents resources A obtained via a relaxed

[2] Viper's heap-dependent functions are mathematical functions of their parameters and the resources stated in their preconditions (here, **`AcqConjunct(`**l**`,`**i**`)`**) [27,34].

[3] A **`perm`** expression yields the permission fraction held for a field or predicate instance.

$$\frac{}{\{A\}\ \mathtt{fence_{rel}}\ \{\triangle A\}} \qquad \frac{}{\{\nabla A\}\ \mathtt{fence_{acq}}\ \{A\}}$$

$$\frac{}{\{\triangle \mathcal{Q}(e) * \mathsf{Rel}(l,\mathcal{Q})\}\ [l]_{\mathtt{rlx}} := e\ \{\mathsf{Init}(l) * \mathsf{Rel}(l,\mathcal{Q})\}}$$

$$\frac{}{\{\mathsf{Init}(l) * \mathsf{Acq}(l,\mathcal{Q})\}\ x := [l]_{\mathtt{rlx}}\ \{\nabla \mathcal{Q}[x/\mathcal{V}] * \mathsf{Acq}(l, \mathcal{V} \neq x \Rightarrow \mathcal{Q})\}}$$

$$(A_1 \Rightarrow A_2) \Leftrightarrow (\triangle A_1 \Rightarrow \triangle A_2) \Leftrightarrow (\nabla A_1 \Rightarrow \nabla A_2)$$

$\nabla(A_1 * A_2) \equiv (\nabla A_1) * (\nabla A_2)$ *and analogously for* $\triangle$ *and other binary connectives*

Fig. 8. Adapted FSL rules for relaxed atomics and fences.

$$\mathcal{Q}_1 \equiv (\mathcal{V} \neq 0 \Rightarrow a \overset{1}{\mapsto} 42) \qquad \mathcal{Q}_2 \equiv (\mathcal{V} \neq 0 \Rightarrow b \overset{1}{\mapsto} 7)$$

$\{\mathsf{true}\}$

$a := \mathtt{alloc_{na}}();\ b := \mathtt{alloc_{na}}();\ l := \mathtt{alloc_{acq}}(\mathcal{Q}_1 * \mathcal{Q}_2);\ [l]_{\mathtt{rel}} := 0$

$\{\mathsf{Acq}(l,\mathcal{Q}_1) * \mathsf{Init}(l)\}$	$\{\mathsf{Uninit}(a) * \mathsf{Uninit}(b) * \mathsf{Rel}(x,\mathcal{Q}_1 * \mathcal{Q}_2)\}$	$\{\mathsf{Acq}(l,\mathcal{Q}_2) * \mathsf{Init}(l)\}$
$\mathtt{while}([l]_{\mathtt{rlx}} == 0);$	$[a]_{\mathtt{na}} := 42;$	$\mathtt{while}([l]_{\mathtt{rlx}} == 0);$
$\mathtt{fence_{acq}};$	$[b]_{\mathtt{na}} := 7;$	$\mathtt{fence_{acq}};$
$x := [a]_{\mathtt{na}}$	$\mathtt{fence_{rel}}(a \overset{1}{\mapsto} 42 * b \overset{1}{\mapsto} 7);$	$y := [b]_{\mathtt{na}};$
$[a]_{\mathtt{na}} := x + 1$	$[l]_{\mathtt{rlx}} := 1;$	$[b]_{\mathtt{na}} := y + 1$
$\{\mathsf{true} * a \overset{1}{\mapsto} 43\}$	$\{\mathsf{true} * \mathsf{Init}(l)\}$	$\{\mathsf{true} * b \overset{1}{\mapsto} 8\}$

$\{\mathsf{true} * a \overset{1}{\mapsto} 43 * b \overset{1}{\mapsto} 8\}$

Fig. 9. A variant of the message-passing example of Fig. 5, combining relaxed memory accesses and fences to achieve ownership transfer. The example is also a variant of Fig. 2 of the FSL paper [17], which is included in our evaluation (`FencesDblMsgPass`) in Sect. 7.

read, which may not be made use of until an acquire fence is encountered. The proof rule for relaxed write is identical to that for a release write (cf. Fig. 6), except that the assertion to be transferred away must be under the $\triangle$ modality; this can be achieved by the rule for release fences. The rule for a relaxed read is the same as that for acquire reads, except that the gained assertion is under the ∇ modality. The modality can be removed by a subsequent acquire fence. Finally, assertions may be rewritten under modalities, and both modalities distribute over all other logical connectives.

Figure 9 shows an example program, which is a variant of the message-passing example from Fig. 5. Comparing the left-hand one of the three parallel threads, a relaxed read is used in the spin loop; after the loop, this thread will hold the assertion $\nabla a \overset{1}{\mapsto} 42$. The subsequent $\mathtt{fence_{acq}}$ statement allows the modality to be removed, allowing the non-atomic location a to be accessed. Dually, the middle thread employs a $\mathtt{fence_{rel}}$ statement to place the ownership of the non-atomic locations under the $\triangle$ modality, in preparation for the relaxed write to l.

Encoding. The main challenge in encoding the FSL rules for fences is how to represent the two new modalities. Since these modalities guard assertions which cannot be currently used or combined with modality-free assertions, we

```
domain threeHeaps {
  function up(x: Ref) : Ref;    function upInv(x: Ref) : Ref;
  function down(x: Ref) : Ref;  function downInv(x: Ref) : Ref;
  function heap(x: Ref) : Int;  // identifies which heap a Ref is from
  axiom { forall r:Ref :: upInv(up(r)) == r &&
    (heap(r) == 0 ==> heap(up(r)) == 1 }
  axiom { forall r:Ref :: up(upInv(r)) == r &&
    (heap(r) == 1 ==> heap(upInv(r)) == 0 }
  axiom { forall r:Ref :: downInv(down(r)) == r &&
    (heap(r) == 0 ==> heap(down(r)) == -1 }
  axiom { forall r:Ref :: down(downInv(r)) == r &&
    (heap(r) == -1 ==> heap(downInv(r)) == 0 }
}
```

$\llbracket \triangle A \rrbracket \rightsquigarrow \lceil \llbracket A \rrbracket \rceil^{up} \qquad \llbracket \nabla A \rrbracket \rightsquigarrow \lceil \llbracket A \rrbracket \rceil^{down}$

$\llbracket [l]_{\mathtt{rlx}} := e \rrbracket \rightsquigarrow$ ... *encoded as for release writes (Fig. 7) except using* $\lceil inv(i) \rceil^{up}$ *in place of* $inv(i)$

$\llbracket x := [l]_{\mathtt{rlx}} \rrbracket \rightsquigarrow$ ... *encoded as for acquire reads (Fig. 7) except using* $\lceil inv(i) \rceil^{down}$ *in place of* $inv(i)$

$\llbracket \mathtt{fence_{rel}}(A) \rrbracket \rightsquigarrow$ **exhale** $\llbracket A \rrbracket$; **inhale** $\lceil \llbracket A \rrbracket \rceil^{up}$

```
[[fence_acq]] ~> var rs : Set[Ref];  rs := havoc() // unknown set of Refs
  assume forall r: Ref :: r in rs <==> perm(down(r).val) > none
  inhale forall r: Ref :: r in rs ==> acc(r.val, perm(down(r).val))
  assume forall r: Ref :: r in rs ==> r.val == down(r).val
  exhale forall r: Ref :: r in rs ==> acc(down(r).val, perm(down(r).val))
  // analogously for each other field, predicate (in place of val)
```

Fig. 10. Viper encoding of the FSL rules for relaxed atomics and memory fences from Fig. 8. We omit triggers for the quantifiers for simplicity, but see [3].

model them using two *additional heaps* to represent the assertions under each modality. The program heap (along with associated permissions) is a built-in notion in Viper, and so we cannot directly employ three heaps. Therefore, we construct the additional "up" and "down" heaps, by axiomatising bijective mappings up and down between a real program reference and its counterparts in these heaps. That is, technically our encoding represents each source location through three references in Viper's heap (rather than one reference in three heaps). Assertions $\triangle A$ are then represented by replacing *all references* r in the encoded assertion A with their counterpart up(r). We write $\lceil A \rceil^{up}$ for the transformation which performs this replacement. For example, $\lceil$**acc**(x.val) && x.val == 4$\rceil^{up} \rightsquigarrow$ **acc**(up(x).val) && up(x).val == 4. We write $\lceil A \rceil^{down}$ for the analogous transformation for the down function.

The extension of our encoding is shown in Fig. 10. We employ a Viper *domain* to introduce and axiomatise the mathematical functions for our up and down mappings. By axiomatising inverses for these mappings, we guarantee bijectivity. Bijectivity allows Viper to conclude that (dis)equalities and other information is preserved under these mappings. Consequently, we do not have to explicitly encode the last two rules of Fig. 8; they are reduced to standard assertion manipulations in our encoding. An additional heap function labels references with an integer identifying the heap to which they belong (0 for real references, -1 and

1 for their "down" and "up" counterparts); this labelling provides the verifiers with the (important) information that these notional heaps are disjoint.

Our handling of relaxed reads and writes is almost identical to that of acquire reads and release writes in Fig. 7; this similarity comes from the proof rules, which only require that the modalities be inserted for the invariant. Our encoding for release fences requires an annotation in the source program to indicate which assertion to prepare for release by placing it under the $\triangle$ modality.

Our encoding for acquire fences does *not* require any annotations. *Any* assertion under the $\triangledown$ modality can (and should) be converted to its corresponding version without the modality because $\triangledown A$ is strictly less-useful than A itself. To encode this conversion, we find *all* permissions currently held in the down heap, and transfer these permissions and the values of the corresponding locations over to the real heap. These steps are encoded for each field and predicate separately; Fig. 10 shows the steps for the `val` field. We first define a set `rs` to be precisely the set of all references `r` to which *some* permission to `down(r).val` is currently held, i.e., **`perm(down(r).val) > none`**. For each such reference, we **`inhale`** exactly the same amount of permission to the corresponding `r.val` location, equate the heap values, and then remove the permission to the down locations.

With our encoding based on multiple heaps, reasoning about assertions under modalities inherits all of Viper's native automation for permission and heap reasoning. We will reuse this idea for a different purpose in the following section.

5 Compare and Swap

C11 includes atomic *read-modify-write* operations, commonly used to implement high-level synchronisation primitives such as locks. FSL++ [18] provides proof rules for *compare-and-swap* (CAS) operations. An atomic compare and swap $\mathsf{CAS}_\tau(l, e, e')$ reads and returns the value of location l; if the value read is equal to e, it also writes the value e' (otherwise we say that the CAS *fails*).

FSL++ Proof Rules. FSL++ provides an assertion $\mathsf{RMWAcq}(l, \mathcal{Q})$, which is similar to $\mathsf{Acq}(l, \mathcal{Q})$, but is used for CAS operations instead of acquire reads. A successful CAS *both* obtains ownership of an assertion via its read operation and gives up ownership of an assertion via its write operation.

FSL++ does not support general combinations of atomic reads and CAS operations on the same location; the way of reading must be chosen at allocation via the annotation ρ on the allocation statement (see Fig. 1). In contrast to the Acq assertions used for atomic reads, RMWAcq assertions can be freely duplicated and their invariants need not be adjusted for a successful CAS: when using only CAS operations, each value read from a location corresponds to a different write.

Our presentation of the relevant proof rules is shown in Fig. 11. Allocating a location with annotation `RMW` provides a Rel and a RMWAcq assertion, such that the location can be used for release writes and CAS operations.

For the CAS operation, we present a single, general proof rule instead of four rules for the different combinations of access modes in FSL++. The rule requires that l is initialised (since its value is read), Rel and RMWAcq assertions, and an

$$\overline{\{\mathsf{true}\}\ l := \mathtt{alloc}_{\mathsf{RMW}}(\mathcal{Q})\ \{\mathsf{Rel}(l,\mathcal{Q}) * \mathsf{RMWAcq}(l,\mathcal{Q})\}}$$

$$\frac{\begin{array}{ll} x \notin FV(P) & \\ x \notin FV(e) & P' \equiv \begin{cases} P & \textit{if } \tau \in \{\mathtt{rel}, \mathtt{rel\_acq}\} \\ \Delta P & \textit{otherwise} \end{cases} \\ \mathcal{Q}[e/\mathcal{V}] \models A * T & \\ P * T \models \mathcal{Q}[e'/\mathcal{V}] & A' \equiv \begin{cases} A & \textit{if } \tau \in \{\mathtt{acq}, \mathtt{rel\_acq}\} \\ \nabla A & \textit{otherwise} \end{cases} \end{array}}{\left\{ \begin{array}{l} \mathsf{Init}(l) * \mathsf{Rel}(l,\mathcal{Q}) * \\ \mathsf{RMWAcq}(l,\mathcal{Q}) * P' \end{array} \right\} x := \mathsf{CAS}_\tau(l,e,e') \left\{ \begin{array}{l} (x = e \ ?\ A' : P') * \mathsf{Init}(l) * \\ \mathsf{Rel}(l,\mathcal{Q}) * \mathsf{RMWAcq}(l,\mathcal{Q}) \end{array} \right\}}$$

$$\mathsf{RMWAcq}(l,\mathcal{Q}) \quad \Leftrightarrow \quad \mathsf{RMWAcq}(l,\mathcal{Q}) * \mathsf{RMWAcq}(l,\mathcal{Q})$$

Fig. 11. Adapted FSL++ rules for compare and swap operations. FV yields the free variables of an assertion.

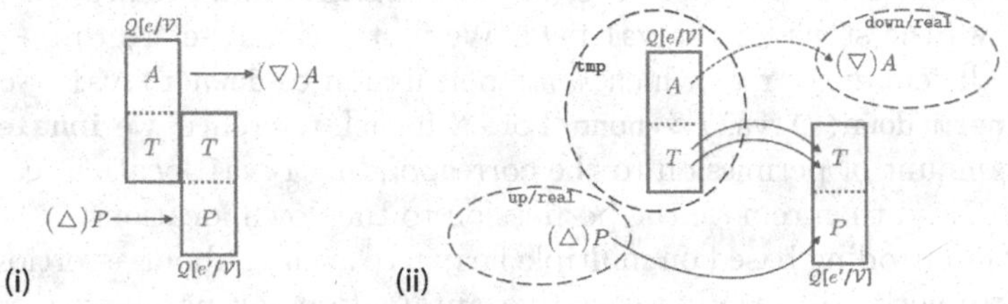

Fig. 12. An illustration of (i) the proof rule for CAS operations and (ii) our Viper encoding; the dashed regions denote the relevant heaps employed in the encoding.

assertion P' that provides the resources needed for a successful CAS. If the CAS fails (that is, $x \neq e$), its precondition is preserved.

If the CAS succeeds, it has read value e and written value e'. Assuming for now that the access mode τ permits ownership transfer, the thread has acquired $\mathcal{Q}[e/\mathcal{V}]$ and released $\mathcal{Q}[e'/\mathcal{V}]$. As illustrated in Fig. 12(i), these assertions may overlap. Let T denote the assertion characterising the overlap; then assertion A denotes $\mathcal{Q}[e/\mathcal{V}]$ without the overlap, and P denotes $\mathcal{Q}[e'/\mathcal{V}]$ without the overlap. The net effect of a successful CAS is then to acquire A and to release P, while T remains with the location invariant across the CAS. Automating the choice of T, A, and P is one of the main challenges of encoding this rule. Finally, if the access mode τ does not permit ownership transfer (that is, fences are needed to perform the transfer), A and P are put under the appropriate modalities.

Encoding. Our encoding of CAS operations uses several techniques presented in earlier sections: see App. E of the TR [35] for details. We represent RMWAcq assertions analogously to our encoding of Acq assertions (see Sect. 3). We use the value of field `acq` (cf. Fig. 7) to distinguish holding some RMWAcq assertion from some Acq assertion. Since RMWAcq assertions are duplicable (cf. Fig. 11), we employ **`wildcard`** permissions for the corresponding `AcqConjunct` predicates.

Our encoding of the proof rule for CAS operations is somewhat involved; we give a high-level description here, and relegate the details to App. E of the TR.

We focus on the more-interesting case of a successful CAS here. The key challenge is how to select assertion T to satisfy the premises of the rule. Maximising this overlap is desirable in practice since this reduces the resources to be transferred, and which must interact in some cases with the modalities. Our Viper encoding indirectly *computes* this largest-possible T as follows (see Fig. 12(ii) for an illustration).

We introduce yet another heap ("tmp") in which we inhale the invariant $\mathcal{Q}[e/\mathcal{V}]$ for the value read. Now, we exhale the invariant $\mathcal{Q}[e'/\mathcal{V}]$ for the value written, but adapt the assertions as follows: for each permission in the invariant, we take *the maximum possible* amount from our "tmp" heap; these permissions correspond to T. Any remainder is taken from the current heap (either the real or the "up" heap, depending on τ); these correspond to P. Any permissions remaining in the "tmp" heap after this exhale correspond to the assertion A and are moved (in a way similar to our $\texttt{fence}_{\texttt{acq}}$ encoding in Fig. 10) to either the real or "down" heap (depending on τ).

This combination of techniques results in an automatic support for the proof rule for CAS statements. This completes the core of our Viper encoding, which now handles the complete set of memory access constructs from Fig. 1.

6 Soundness and Completeness

We give a brief overview of the soundness argument for our encoding here, and also discuss where it can be incomplete compared with a manual proof effort; further details are included in App. F of the TR [35].

Soundness. Soundness means that if the Viper encoding of a program and its specification verifies, then there exists a proof of the program and specification using the RSL logics. We can show this property in two main steps. First, we show that the states before and after each encoded statement in the Viper program satisfy several invariants. For example, we never hold permissions to a non-atomic reference's `val` field but not its `init` field. Second, we reproduce a Hoare-style proof outline in the RSL logics. For this purpose, we define a mapping from *states* of the Viper program back to RSL *assertions* and show two properties: (1) When we map the initial and final states of an encoded program statement to RSL assertions, we obtain a provable Hoare triple. (2) Any automatic entailment reasoning performed by Viper coincides with entailments sound in the RSL logics. These two facts together imply that our technique will only verify (encoded) properties for which a proof exists in the RSL logics; i.e. our technique is sound.

Completeness. Completeness means that all programs provable in the RSL logics can be verified via their encoding into Viper. By systematically analysing each rule of these logics, we identify three sources of incompleteness of our encoding: (1) It does not allow one to strengthen the invariant in a Rel assertion;

strengthening the requirement on writing does not allow more programs to be verified [37]. (2) For a $\mathtt{fence}_{\mathtt{acq}}$, our encoding removes *all* assertions from under a $\triangledown$ modality. As explained in Sect. 4, the ability to choose *not* to remove the modality is not useful in practice. (3) The ghost state employed in FSL++ can be defined over a *custom permission structure* (partial commutative monoid), which is not possible in Viper. This is the only incompleteness of our encoding arising in practice; we will discuss an example in Sect. 7.

7 Examples and Evaluation

We evaluated our work with a prototype front-end tool [4], and some additional experiments directly at the Viper level [3]. Our front-end tool accepts a simple input language for C11 programs, closely modelled on the syntax of the RSL logics. It supports all features described in this paper, with the exception of invariant rewriting (*cf.* App. C of the TR [35]) and ghost state (App. D of the TR), which will be simple extensions. We encoded examples which require these features, additional theories, or custom permission structures manually into Viper, to simulate what an extended version of our prototype will be able to achieve.

Our encoding supports several extra features which we used in our experiments but mention only briefly here: (1) We support the FSL++ rules for *ghost state*: see App. D of the TR. (2) Our encoding handles common spin loop patterns without requiring loop invariant annotations. (3) We support fetch-update instructions (e.g. atomic increments) natively, modelled as a CAS which never fails.

Examples. We took examples from the RSL [38] and FSL [17] papers, along with variants in which we seeded errors, to check that verification fails as expected (and in comparable time). We also encoded the Rust reference-counting (ARC) library [1], which is the main example from FSL++ [18]. The proof there employs a custom permission structure, which is not yet supported by Viper. However, following the suggestion of one of the authors [37], we were able to fully verify two variants of the example, in which some access modes are strengthened, making the code slightly less efficient but enabling a proof using a simpler permission model. For these variants, we required *counting permissions* [10], which we expressed with additional background definitions (see [3] for details, and App. B of the TR [35] for the code). Finally, we tackled seven core functions of a reader-writer-spinlock from the Facebook Folly library [2]. We were able to verify five of them directly. The other two employ code idioms which seem to be beyond the scope of the RSL logics, at least without sophisticated ghost state. For both functions, we also wrote and verified alternative implementations. The Rust and Facebook examples demonstrate a key advantage of building on top of Viper; both require support for extra theories (counting permissions as well as modulo and bitwise arithmetic), which we were able to encode easily.

Performance. We measured the verification times on an Intel Core i7-4770 CPU (3.40 GHz, 16 Gb RAM) running Windows 10 Pro and report the average

Program	Prototype support	Size (LOC, funcs,loops)	Time (s)	Specs PP	Specs LI	Other Annot.	Coq Annot.
RSLSpinLock	✓	7,3,2	10.83	3	1	1	120 [38]
RSLLockNoSpin	✓	6,3,1	10.33	3	0	1	84 [22]
RSLLockNoSpin_err	✓	6,3,1	9.74	3	0	1	n/a
RelAcqMsgPass	✓	15,3,1	10.46	3	0	1	99 [38]
RelAcqMsgPass_err	✓	15,3,1	9.57	3	0	1	n/a
RelAcqDblMsgPassSplit	✓	21,4,2	10.84	4	0	1	n/a
RelAcqDblMsgPassSplit_err	✓	21,4,2	9.86	4	0	1	n/a
CASModesTest	✓	23,3,2	18.05	3	0	2	n/a
CASModesTest_err	✓	24,3,2	17.50	3	0	2	n/a
FencesDblMsgPass	✓	27,4,2	12.32	4	0	3	n/a
FencesDblMsgPass_err	✓	27,4,2	10.73	4	0	3	n/a
FencesDblMsgPassSplit	✓	24,4,2	12.61	4	0	2	n/a
FencesDblMsgPassSplit_err	✓	24,4,2	11.53	4	0	2	n/a
FencesDblMsgPassAcqRewrite		24,4,2	15.75	4	0	3	n/a
RustARCOriginal_err		10,4,0	37.53	4	0	2	654 [18]
RustARCStronger		10,4,0	31.86	4	0	2	n/a
RelAcqRustARCStronger		9,4,0	15.75	4	0	2	n/a
FollyRWSpinlock_err		24,7,2	28.21	7	2	0	n/a
FollyRWSpinlockStronger		26,7,3	21.93	7	3	0	n/a

Fig. 13. The results of our evaluation. Examples including `_err` are expected to generate errors; those with `Stronger` are variants of the original code with less-efficient atomics and a correspondingly different proof. "Time" reports the verification time in seconds, including the generation of the Viper code. Under "Size", we measure lines of code, number of distinct functions/threads, and number of loops. Under "Specs", "PP" stands for the necessary pairs of pre and post-conditions; "LI" stands for loop invariants required. "Other Annot." counts any other annotations needed. For examples that have been verified in Coq, we report the number of manual proof steps (in addition to pre-post pairs) and provide a reference to the proof.

of 5 runs. For those examples supported by our front-end, the times include the generation of the Viper code. As shown in Fig. 13, verification times are reasonable (generally around 10 s, and always under a 40 s).

Automation. Each function (and thread) must be annotated with an appropriate pre and post-condition, as is standard for modular verification. In addition, some of our examples require loop invariants and other annotations (e.g. on allocation statements). Critically, the number of such annotations is very low. In particular, our annotation overhead is between one and two orders of magnitude lower than the overhead of existing mechanised proofs (using the Coq formalisations for [18,38] and a recent encoding [22] of RSL into Iris [23]). Such ratios are consistent with other recent Coq-mechanised proofs based on separation logic (e.g. [39]), which suggests that the strong soundness guarantees provided by Coq have a high cost when *applying* the logics. By contrast, once the specifications are provided, our approach is almost entirely automatic.

8 Conclusions and Future Work

We have presented the first encoding of modern program logics for weak memory models into an automated deductive program verifier. The encoding enables programs (with suitable annotations) to be verified automatically by existing back-end tools. We have implemented a front-end verifier and demonstrated that our encoding can be used to verify weak-memory programs efficiently and with low annotation overhead. As future work, we plan to tackle other weak-memory logics such as GPS [36]. Building practical tools that implement such advanced formalisms will provide feedback that inspires further improvements of the logics.

Data Availability Statement and Acknowledgements. The artifact accompanying our submission is available in the TACAS figshare repository [4] at https://doi.org/10.6084/m9.figshare.5900233.v1.
We are grateful to Viktor Vafeiadis and Marko Doko for many explanations of the RSL logics and helpful discussions about our encoding. We thank Christiane Goltz for her work on the prototype tool, and Malte Schwerhoff for implementing additional features. We thank Marco Eilers for his assistance with the online appendix, and Arshavir Ter-Gabrielyan for automating our artifact assembly for various operating systems. We also thank Andrei Dan, Lucas Brutschy and Malte Schwerhoff for feedback on earlier versions of this manuscript.

References

1. ARC (Atomic Reference Counting) Rust library. https://doc.rust-lang.org/std/sync/struct.Arc.html
2. Facebook Folly reader-writer spinlock implementation. https://github.com/facebook/folly/blob/master/folly/RWSpinLock.h
3. Online appendix of Viper-encoded examples. http://viper.ethz.ch/onlineappendix-rsl-encoding/
4. RSL to Viper front-end. figshare. https://doi.org/10.6084/m9.figshare.5900233.v1
5. Abdulla, P.A., Atig, M.F., Bouajjani, A., Ngo, T.P.: The benefits of duality in verifying concurrent programs under TSO. CoRR, abs/1701.08682 (2017)
6. Abdulla, P.A., Atig, M.F., Jonsson, B., Leonardsson, C.: Stateless model checking for POWER. In: Chaudhuri, S., Farzan, A. (eds.) CAV 2016, Part II. LNCS, vol. 9780, pp. 134–156. Springer, Cham (2016). https://doi.org/10.1007/978-3-319-41540-6_8
7. Alglave, J., Cousot, P.: Ogre and pythia: an invariance proof method for weak consistency models. In: POPL 2017, pp. 3–18. ACM, New York (2017)
8. Barnett, M., Chang, B.-Y.E., DeLine, R., Jacobs, B., Leino, K.R.M.: Boogie: a modular reusable verifier for object-oriented programs. In: de Boer, F.S., Bonsangue, M.M., Graf, S., de Roever, W.-P. (eds.) FMCO 2005. LNCS, vol. 4111, pp. 364–387. Springer, Heidelberg (2006). https://doi.org/10.1007/11804192_17
9. Bobot, F., Filliâtre, J.-C., Marché, C., Paskevich, A.: Why3: Shepherd your herd of provers. In: Boogie 2011: First International Workshop on Intermediate Verification Languages, Wrocław, Poland, pp. 53–64, August 2011
10. Bornat, R., Calcagno, C., O'Hearn, P., Parkinson, M.: Permission accounting in separation logic. In: Proceedings of POPL 2005, pp. 259–270. ACM, New York (2005)

11. Bouajjani, A., Derevenetc, E., Meyer, R.: Checking and enforcing robustness against TSO. In: Felleisen, M., Gardner, P. (eds.) ESOP 2013. LNCS, vol. 7792, pp. 533–553. Springer, Heidelberg (2013). https://doi.org/10.1007/978-3-642-37036-6_29
12. Boyland, J.: Checking interference with fractional permissions. In: Cousot, R. (ed.) SAS 2003. LNCS, vol. 2694, pp. 55–72. Springer, Heidelberg (2003). https://doi.org/10.1007/3-540-44898-5_4
13. Chlipala, A.: Mostly-automated verification of low-level programs in computational separation logic. In: Proceedings of the 32nd ACM SIGPLAN Conference on Programming Language Design and Implementation, PLDI 2011, pp. 234–245. ACM, New York (2011)
14. Cohen, E., Dahlweid, M., Hillebrand, M., Leinenbach, D., Moskal, M., Santen, T., Schulte, W., Tobies, S.: VCC: a practical system for verifying concurrent C. In: Berghofer, S., Nipkow, T., Urban, C., Wenzel, M. (eds.) TPHOLs 2009. LNCS, vol. 5674, pp. 23–42. Springer, Heidelberg (2009). https://doi.org/10.1007/978-3-642-03359-9_2
15. Cuoq, P., Kirchner, F., Kosmatov, N., Prevosto, V., Signoles, J., Yakobowski, B.: Frama-C. In: Eleftherakis, G., Hinchey, M., Holcombe, M. (eds.) SEFM 2012. LNCS, vol. 7504, pp. 233–247. Springer, Heidelberg (2012). https://doi.org/10.1007/978-3-642-33826-7_16
16. Dan, A., Meshman, Y., Vechev, M., Yahav, E.: Effective abstractions for verification under relaxed memory models. In: D'Souza, D., Lal, A., Larsen, K.G. (eds.) VMCAI 2015. LNCS, vol. 8931, pp. 449–466. Springer, Heidelberg (2015). https://doi.org/10.1007/978-3-662-46081-8_25
17. Doko, M., Vafeiadis, V.: A program logic for C11 memory fences. In: Jobstmann, B., Leino, K.R.M. (eds.) VMCAI 2016. LNCS, vol. 9583, pp. 413–430. Springer, Heidelberg (2016). https://doi.org/10.1007/978-3-662-49122-5_20
18. Doko, M., Vafeiadis, V.: Tackling real-life relaxed concurrency with FSL++. In: Yang, H. (ed.) ESOP 2017. LNCS, vol. 10201, pp. 448–475. Springer, Heidelberg (2017). https://doi.org/10.1007/978-3-662-54434-1_17
19. Heule, S., Leino, K.R.M., Müller, P., Summers, A.J.: Abstract read permissions: fractional permissions without the fractions. In: Giacobazzi, R., Berdine, J., Mastroeni, I. (eds.) VMCAI 2013. LNCS, vol. 7737, pp. 315–334. Springer, Heidelberg (2013). https://doi.org/10.1007/978-3-642-35873-9_20
20. Jacobs, B.: Verifying TSO programs. CW Reports CW660, Department of Computer Science, KU Leuven, May 2014
21. Jacobs, B., Smans, J., Piessens, F.: A quick tour of the VeriFast program verifier. In: Ueda, K. (ed.) APLAS 2010. LNCS, vol. 6461, pp. 304–311. Springer, Heidelberg (2010). https://doi.org/10.1007/978-3-642-17164-2_21
22. Kaiser, J.-O., Dang, H.-H., Dreyer, D., Lahav, O., Vafeiadis, V.: Strong Logic for weak memory: reasoning about release-acquire consistency in Iris. In: ECOOP 2017, vol. 74. LIPIcs, pp. 17:1–17:29. Schloss Dagstuhl-Leibniz (2017)
23. Krebbers, R., Jung, R., Bizjak, A., Jourdan, J.-H., Dreyer, D., Birkedal, L.: The essence of higher-order concurrent separation logic. In: Yang, H. (ed.) ESOP 2017. LNCS, vol. 10201, pp. 696–723. Springer, Heidelberg (2017). https://doi.org/10.1007/978-3-662-54434-1_26
24. Leino, K.R.M.: Dafny: an automatic program verifier for functional correctness. In: Clarke, E.M., Voronkov, A. (eds.) LPAR 2010. LNCS (LNAI), vol. 6355, pp. 348–370. Springer, Heidelberg (2010). https://doi.org/10.1007/978-3-642-17511-4_20

25. Leino, K.R.M., Müller, P.: A basis for verifying multi-threaded programs. In: Castagna, G. (ed.) ESOP 2009. LNCS, vol. 5502, pp. 378–393. Springer, Heidelberg (2009). https://doi.org/10.1007/978-3-642-00590-9_27
26. Müller, P., Schwerhoff, M., Summers, A.J.: Automatic verification of iterated separating conjunctions using symbolic execution. In: Chaudhuri, S., Farzan, A. (eds.) CAV 2016. LNCS, vol. 9779, pp. 405–425. Springer, Cham (2016). https://doi.org/10.1007/978-3-319-41528-4_22
27. Müller, P., Schwerhoff, M., Summers, A.J.: Viper: a verification infrastructure for permission-based reasoning. In: Jobstmann, B., Leino, K.R.M. (eds.) VMCAI 2016. LNCS, vol. 9583, pp. 41–62. Springer, Heidelberg (2016). https://doi.org/10.1007/978-3-662-49122-5_2
28. O'Hearn, P., Reynolds, J., Yang, H.: Local reasoning about programs that alter data structures. In: Fribourg, L. (ed.) CSL 2001. LNCS, vol. 2142, pp. 1–19. Springer, Heidelberg (2001). https://doi.org/10.1007/3-540-44802-0_1
29. Parkinson, M.J., Summers, A.J.: The relationship between separation logic and implicit dynamic frames. Logical Methods Comput. Sci. **8**(3:01), 1–54 (2012)
30. Reynolds, J.C.: Definitional interpreters for higher-order programming languages. In: ACM Annual Conference, vol. 2, ACM 1972, pp. 717–740. ACM (1972)
31. Reynolds, J.C.: Separation logic: a logic for shared mutable data structures. In: LICS. IEEE Computer Society Press (2002)
32. Sergey, I., Nanevski, A., Banerjee, A.: Mechanized verification of fine-grained concurrent programs. In: Proceedings of PLDI 2015, pp. 77–87. ACM, New York (2015)
33. Smans, J., Jacobs, B., Piessens, F.: Implicit dynamic frames. ACM Trans. Program. Lang. Syst. **34**(1), 2:1–2:58 (2012)
34. Summers, A.J., Drossopoulou, S.: A formal semantics for isorecursive and equirecursive state abstractions. In: Castagna, G. (ed.) ECOOP 2013. LNCS, vol. 7920, pp. 129–153. Springer, Heidelberg (2013). https://doi.org/10.1007/978-3-642-39038-8_6
35. Summers, A.J., Müller, P.: Automating deductive verification for weak-memory programs (extended version). arXiv:1703.06368 (2018)
36. Turon, A., Vafeiadis, V., Dreyer, D.: GPS: navigating weak memory with ghosts, protocols, and separation. In: OOPSLA, pp. 691–707. ACM (2014)
37. Vafeiadis, V.: Personal communication, December 2016
38. Vafeiadis, V., Narayan, C.: Relaxed separation logic: a program logic for C11 concurrency. In: OOPSLA, pp. 867–884. ACM (2013)
39. Xu, F., Fu, M., Feng, X., Zhang, X., Zhang, H., Li, Z.: A practical verification framework for preemptive OS kernels. In: Chaudhuri, S., Farzan, A. (eds.) CAV 2016, Part II. LNCS, vol. 9780, pp. 59–79. Springer, Cham (2016). https://doi.org/10.1007/978-3-319-41540-6_4

Software Verification and Optimisation

Property Checking Array Programs Using Loop Shrinking

Shrawan Kumar[1(✉)], Amitabha Sanyal[2], R. Venkatesh[1], and Punit Shah[1]

[1] Tata Consultancy Services Ltd., Pune, India
{shrawan.kumar,r.venky,shah.punit}@tcs.com
[2] Department of CSE, IIT Bombay, Mumbai 400076, India
as@cse.iitb.ac.in

Abstract. Most verification tools find it difficult to prove properties of programs containing loops that process arrays of large or unknown size. These methods either fail to abstract the array at the right granularity and are therefore limited in precision or scalability, or they attempt to synthesize an appropriate invariant that is quantified over the elements of the array, a task known to be difficult. In this paper, we present a different approach based on a notion called *loop shrinkability*, in which an array processing loop is transformed to a loop of much smaller bound that processes only a few non-deterministically chosen elements of the array. The result is a finite state program with a drastically reduced state space that can be analyzed by bounded model checkers. We show that the proposed transformation is an over-approximation, i.e. if the transformed program is correct, so is the original. In addition, when applicable, the method is impervious to the size or existence of the bound of the array. As an assessment of usefulness, we tested a tool based on our method on the *ArraysReach* category of SV-COMP 2017 benchmarks. After excluding programs with feature not handled by our tool, we could successfully verify 87 of the 93 remaining programs.

1 Introduction

An array processing loop is a common occurrence in programs, and an assurance of reliability often requires the program developer to prove properties that are quantified over the elements of the array being processed. This is, in general, difficult because such programs have huge, at times infinite state space. So while static analysis techniques like array smashing and partitioning [4,5,11,14,16,17] fail due to abstractions that are too coarse, attempts with bounded model checkers or theorem provers that are equipped with array theories [3,8,9,15,18,22,23] tend to fail for lack of scalability or their inability to synthesize the right quantified invariants.

In certain situations, the decidability of property checking of finite state programs can be used to prove properties of infinite state space programs. Consider a program P and a property ψ that can be transformed to an abstract finite state program P' and a property ψ', such that if the property ψ' holds in P'

D. Beyer and M. Huisman (Eds.): TACAS 2018, LNCS 10805, pp. 213–231, 2018.
https://doi.org/10.1007/978-3-319-89960-2_12

```
1  #define N 7
2  main()
3  {
4    int i, m;
5    int a[N]={8,4,6,2,11,2,2};
6    m = a[0];
7    i=0;
8    while(i < N)
9    {
10     if(m >= a[i]-1)
11       m = a[i];
12     i++;
13   }
14   assert ∀j∈[0..N−1].(m≤a[j]);
15 }
```

(a) Concrete program

```
#define N 7
main() {
  int i, m, a[N]={8,4,6,2,11,2,2};
  unsigned li, it[2];
  m = a[0]; i=0;
  it[0]=nondet(); it[1]=nondet();
  assume(1 <= it[0] && it[0]<it[1]);
  for (li=0; li < 2 ; li++) {
    i = it[li] - 1;
    if (!(i < N)) break;
    if(m >= a[i]-1) m = a[i];
    i++;
  }
  assume(li==2);
  assert ∀t∈it.(m≤a[t−1]);
}
```

(b) Abstract program

Fig. 1. Loop shrinking abstraction illustration

then the property ψ holds in P. Then P' can be analyzed for ψ' to show that ψ holds in P. In this paper we present such a transformation for programs which process arrays in loops. The property ψ is usually a $\forall$ or a $\exists$ property over elements of the array, but can also be a property over scalar variables modified in the loop. The transformation replaces the loop that manipulates an array of possibly large or even unknown size with a smaller loop that operates only on a few non-deterministically chosen elements of the array.

As an example, consider the program in Fig. 1(a). The loop in the program purportedly computes in a variable `m`, the minimum element, denoted min, of an array `a`. However, due to a programmer error at line 10 (`a[i]-1` instead of `a[i]`), the program actually computes the last value in the longest subsequence $\mathtt{a}[i_1], \mathtt{a}[i_2], \ldots, \mathtt{a}[i_p]$ of the array, such that $\mathtt{a}[i_1] = min$, and for any two consecutive elements $\mathtt{a}[i_k]$ and $\mathtt{a}[i_{k+1}]$ of the subsequence, $\mathtt{a}[i_{k+1}] \leq \mathtt{a}[i_k] + 1$.[1] Notice that for ease of exposition, we have used a $\forall$ to express universal quantification; in reality, a loop will be used instead. The property holds for the example because the longest subsequence of the array with the stated properties is $\{2, 2, 2\}$, and the last element happens to be the same as min. However, the assertion will fail if, for example, the last two elements of the array are changed to 3 and 5, so that the longest subsequence is now $\{2, 3\}$.

Abstraction based verifiers as well as bounded model checkers fail to verify this program when the array size is increased to 1000. For example, CBMC 5.8 [8] reports "out of memory", when run with an unwinding count of 20. Abstraction based verifiers like SATABS 3.2 [9] and CPAchecker 1.6 [3] keep on iterating in their abstraction refinement cycle in search of an appropriate loop invariant, until they run out of memory. Therefore, it is worthwhile to look for an abstraction

[1] There is a unique such subsequence for any array.

of the property checking problem for array processing loops that can be verified by a bounded model checker (BMC).

Observe that in this program, the assertion will hold if and only if, after the last index containing the minimum value min, no other index in a contains the value $min + 1$. This can be conservatively checked by examining for each pair of array indices, say k and $k + j$, $j > 0$, whether $\texttt{a}[k + j] = \texttt{a}[k] + 1$. The computation is effected by selecting a pair of indices non-deterministically and executing in sequence the loop body with the loop index i first instantiated to k and then to $k+j$. The resulting value of m can then be checked for the condition $\texttt{m} \leq \texttt{a}[k] \wedge \texttt{m} \leq \texttt{a}[k + j]$. As we shall see later, it is helpful to think in terms of iteration numbers instead of array indices; the correspondence between the two for the present example is that the value at index i of the array is accessed at iteration number $i + 1$.

In other words, we compute m for every pair of iterations of the loop, and check if m satisfies the property for the chosen iterations. For example, the value of m computed for the iterations numbered 2 and 3 of the loop is 4, and the property restricted to these two iterations, $\texttt{m} \leq \texttt{a}[1] \wedge \texttt{m} \leq \texttt{a}[2]$, is satisfied. On the other hand, if we change the last two elements to 3 and 5 then the property fails for the original program. However, we can now find a pair of iterations, namely 4 and 6, such that value of m calculated on the basis of just these two iterations will be 3, and it will not satisfy the corresponding property $\texttt{m} \leq \texttt{a}[3] \wedge \texttt{m} \leq \texttt{a}[5]$, since $\texttt{a}[3]$ is 2. In summary, if executing the loop for every sequence of two iterations $[i_1, i_2]$, $i_2 > i_1$, establishes the property restricted to these iterations, then the property will also hold for the entire loop. Read contrapositively, if the given program does not satisfy the assertion, then there must be a sequence of two iterations for which the property will not hold. This is true irrespective of the size or the contents of the array in the program. Loops which exhibit this feature for iteration sequences of length k (k is 2 in this example) will be called *shrinkable loops with a shrink-factor* k.

We create a second program, shown in Fig. 1(b), that over-approximates the behaviour of the original with respect to the property being checked. The `while` loop is substituted with a loop that executes the non-deterministically chosen iteration sequence stored in the two-element array `it`. The `while` loop in the original program, schematically denoted as `while` (C) B, is replaced by a `for` loop that is equivalent to the unrolled program fragment `i=it[0]-1;if(`C`){`B`;i=it[1]-1;if(`C`)`B`}`. We call this `for` loop (or its unrolled equivalent) the *residual loop* for the iteration sequence `it`. The `break` statement ensures that the chosen iteration numbers do not result in an out-of-bounds access of the array, and the `assume` statement ensures that exactly two iterations are chosen. Similarly, the given property is also substituted by a *residual property* quantified over array indexes corresponding to the same chosen iteration sequence. CBMC is able to verify the property on this transformed program, as the original loop, even with a changed bound of 1000, is now reduced to only two iterations. We call this method *property checking by loop shrinking*. Needless to say, the method can only be applied to a program if its shrinkability and shrink-factor are known. We develop a method to determine both using a BMC.

Thus the central idea, demonstrated in the rest of the paper, is that over-approximation using shrinkability is an effective technique to verify properties of programs that iterate over arrays of large or unknown size. Specifically, our contributions are:

1. We introduce and formalize a concept called *shrinkability* for loops that process arrays. We show formally that a shrinkable loop with shrink-factor k can be over-approximated by a loop that executes only k non-deterministically chosen iterations.
2. We provide an algorithm to find the shrink-factor k for which the loop is shrinkable.
3. We describe an implementation of the proposed abstraction.
4. We report experimental results showing the effectiveness of the technique on SV-COMP 2017 [2] benchmarks in the *ArraysReach* category.

2 Background

We shall present our ideas in the context of imperative programs that consist of assignment statements, conditional statements, while loops, and function calls. We assume that conditional expressions have no side effects. We restrict ourselves to goto-less programs with single-entry single-exit loops. This makes for an easier formal treatment of our method without losing expressibility.

Let *Var* be the set of variables in a program P and *Val* be the set of possible values which the variables in *Var* can take. A *program state* is a valuation of the variables in *Var* that is consistent with their declared types. It is represented by a map $\sigma : Var \rightarrow Val$. $\sigma(v)$ denotes the value of v in the program state σ.

Property checking will be expressed in a formalism called a *Hoare triple* and denoted as $\{\varphi\}P\{\psi\}$. Here φ and ψ are first order formulas representing sets of states, and P is a program. A Hoare triple is said to be *valid* if and only if starting from an initial state satisfying φ, the execution of P terminates in a final state that satisfies ψ. In this paper we shall only consider programs that are deterministic and guaranteed to terminate. A fact that we shall make use of is that in the special case when φ represents a single program state σ. Since our programs are deterministic, ψ also will be a unique single state. Therefore, the invalidity of $\{\sigma\}P\{\psi\}$ is equivalent to the validity of $\{\sigma\}P\{\neg\psi\}$.

An *iteration sequence* is a strictly ascending sequence of numbers, representing iteration counts. Iterations of a loop are counted starting from 1. The notation $i : T$ will represent a sequence whose first element is i and the sequence comprising the rest of the elements is T. Given sequences U and T, we shall use $U \sqsubset T$ to mean that U is a strict subsequence of T. Further, we shall write $\mathcal{P}_k(T)$ to denote the set of all k-sized subsequences of a sequence T. For example, if $T = [1, 2, 5]$ then $\mathcal{P}_2(T) = \{[1, 2], [2, 5], [1, 5]\}$.

Loop acceleration [19] is a commonly used technique for finding loop invariants. It captures the effect of a loop through closed-form expressions that give the value of variables at the beginning of an iteration in terms of the initial state and the iteration count. Variables whose values can be expressed in this manner are called *accelerable*. For example, in the program of Fig. 1, the value of the variable `i` in the beginning of an iteration j is expressible as j-1. We assume that we have available tools [12] to identify accelerable variables and their corresponding accelerating expressions. While our approach does not require us to identify all accelerable variables, the precision of the result does depend on the identification of as many accelerable variables as possible.

Our technique makes good use of bounded model checkers (BMCs). Industrial strength BMCs exist [8] and are widely used to detect property violations in safety critical software. Given a program P and a property ψ, a BMC searches for a counterexample to ψ in executions of P whose length is bounded by some integer n. If it finds a counterexample to ψ within the bound, then it reports the program as being unsafe. However, if it does not find a counter example within the given bound, then the program cannot be regarded as either being safe or unsafe. BMCs are, therefore, very effective in finding bugs but not in proving properties.

3 Programs and Properties of Interest

We focus on programs that process arrays in loops that we assume always terminate. The property to be checked is encoded in a fragment of code that follows the array processing loop. If the property is expressed as a loop, we denote it in our discussion as a universally or existentially quantified formula over the elements of the array. As an illustration, the property checked in the motivating example is $\forall j.0 \leq j < N \implies m \leq a[j]$. Similarly, the program `min2` of Fig. 3 checks for the property $\exists j.0 \leq j < S \wedge min = a[j]$. In particular, we consider program fragments R ; Q ; ψ, in which R is a simple loop possibly manipulating arrays, Q is a loop free (possibly empty) sequence of statements and ψ is the property to be checked. We call R ; Q as an *array processing loop.* In addition, we assume R has an upper bound on number of iterations which can be computed through static analysis [10]. The property ψ is assumed to have at most one quantifier. We assume that the array-processing loop and the loop which checks the property have the same number of iterations. Finally, since the quantified variable ranges over a finite domain (iteration counts of a finite loop), it is useful to think of ψ as a set of quantifier-free formulas, connected by conjunction in the case of $\forall$ and disjunction in the case of $\exists$.

```
i=1;
if (i < N) {
  if (m >= a[i]-1) m = a[i];
  i++;
} else
   goto loop_exit;
```

```
i=3;
if (i< N) {
  if (m >= a[i]-1) m = a[i];
  i++;
} else goto loop_exit;
loop_exit: ;
```

Fig. 2. Residual loop for iteration sequence [2,4] for the program in Fig. 1

3.1 Residual Loop and Residual Property

Consider a program P consisting of an array processing loop $L \equiv$ `while(C){B}Q` followed by code that checks the property ψ. Let $T = [j_1, j_2, ..., j_n]$ be an arbitrary iteration sequence of the loop. We define the *residual loop* for the iteration sequence T, denoted as L_T, as the statements $\{S_{j_1}; S_{j_2}; \ldots S_{j_n};$ `loop_exit:Q`$\}$, where each S_{j_r} is $\{A_{j_r}$; `if(C)`$\{B\}$; `else goto loop_exit;`$\}$. Here A_{j_r} is the sequence of statements assigning to each accelerable variable the corresponding expression defining its value at the beginning of iteration j_r. Obviously, for $T = j : T'$ with T' being nonempty, $L_T = S_j; L_{T'}$. As an illustration, the code fragment in Fig. 2 is the residual loop for the iteration sequence [2,4] for the program in Fig. 1(a). If the loop iterates for a maximum of N times, then $[1, 2, ..., N]$ will be called the *complete iteration sequence* of the loop. It is obvious that, the residual loop $L_{[1,2,...,N]}$ represents an unrolling of L and the two are semantically equivalent. Similarly, for the iteration sequence $T = [j_1, j_2, ..., j_m]$ and the property ψ, we define the residual property ψ_T as a conjunction or disjunction of a set of clauses $\{\psi_{j_1}, \psi_{j_2}, \ldots, \psi_{j_m}\}$.

Let us represent the set of initial states at the beginning of the loop L as φ. Then the set of states at the beginning of an iteration numbered i would be given by $sp(S_1; S_2; ...S_{i-1}, \varphi)$, the strongest post-condition of $S_1; S_2; ...S_{i-1}$ wrt φ. However, we sometimes have to estimate these set of states in the context of an arbitrary iteration sequence T that contains iteration i and in which the sequence of iterations preceding i is not exactly known. Therefore, instead of the earlier exact calculation, we over-approximate the set of states at the beginning of iteration i, denoted φ_i, through the recurrences $\varphi_1 = \varphi$, and $\varphi_i = sp(S_{i-1}, \varphi_{i-1}) \cup \varphi_{i-1}$. The additional term φ_{i-1} in the union accounts for the possibility that the iteration $i-1$ may not precede i in T, and therefore the set of states at the beginning of i should also include the states at the beginning of $i-1$.

```
int i, min, a[S];
min = a[0]; i=1;
while (i< S) {
  if (a[i] < min) min = a[i];
  i++;
}
assert ∃j∈[0..S−1].(a[j]==min);
```

(a) Program min2

```
int i, m, a[S];
m = a[0]; i=0;
while(i < S){
  if(m >= a[i]-1) m = a[i];
  i++;
}
assert ∀j∈[0..S−1].(m≤a[j]+d);
```

(b) Program lmin

Fig. 3. Examples showing property loops

4 Shrinkability of Loops

We now characterize the conditions under which the behaviour of an array-processing loop L with respect to a property ψ can be over-approximated by a residual loop L_U with respect to the corresponding residual property ψ_U, where the iteration sequence U consists of fewer (non-deterministically chosen) iterations than the iterations in the original program, i.e. $U \sqsubset [1, 2, \ldots, N]$.

Definition 1. *(Shrinkable loops) Consider a program consisting of a loop L and a property ψ to be checked. Let T represent the complete sequence of iterations of the loop. The loop is said to be shrinkable with respect to ψ and with a shrink-factor k, $0 < k < |T|$, if and only if, starting from any state $\sigma \in \varphi$, the loop L satisfies ψ whenever the residual loops L_U of each k-length subsequence U of T satisfy the corresponding residual property ψ_U. Formally:*

$$\forall \sigma \in \varphi : ((\forall U \in \mathcal{P}_k(T) : \{\sigma\}L_U\{\psi_U\}) \implies \{\sigma\}L\{\psi\}) \tag{1}$$

It will often be useful to read the formal description above in a contrapositive manner, i.e. starting from a state in φ, if the loop L fails to satisfy ψ, then the failure is also witnessed by a k-length sequence U whose residual loop L_U also fails to satisfy the corresponding residual property ψ_U. Note that executions of both L and L_U begin with the same state in φ.

A shrinkable loop with a shrink-factor k will be called *k-shrinkable*. If we know that a loop is k-shrinkable, we can construct an abstract program that non-deterministically chooses an iteration sequence of size k, runs the residual loop and then checks the corresponding residual property. If the residual property holds, then shrinkability guarantees the correctness of the original program. However, a counter-example in the abstract program does not necessarily imply a violation of the property in the original program, except in situations described below.

In the absence of loop-carried dependences [1], the values assigned to variables that are not accelerable, in any iteration are independent of the values assigned in any other iteration. In addition, consider the case when the array elements accessed in ith iteration of the array-processing loop are also asserted in ψ_i. In this situation, if the original program P violates the property ψ, in particular the clause, say ψ_i, then the program consisting of the residual loop $L_{[\,i\,]}$, constructed on the basis of the only iteration i, will also violate the residual clause $\psi_{[\,i\,]}$. Thus a loop without loop-carried dependences is 1-shrinkable. More significantly, if the property being tested for such programs is universal, the converse is also true, i.e. if the residual loop corresponding to a sequence consisting of a single iteration violates its residual property, then the original program will also not satisfy its specified property.

Note that according to Definition 1, if a program P satisfies its property ψ, then the loop constituting the program is k-shrinkable for any shrink-factor $k > 0$. Similarly, a loop with a bound of m iterations is trivially m-shrinkable. Obviously, if the shrink-factor is small, then the abstract program with a smaller length iteration sequence loads the verifier to a lesser extent and thus offers greater chances of verifier returning with an answer. Therefore, we are interested in finding shrink-factors that are much smaller than the loop bound.

However, finding out whether a loop is shrinkable is difficult as we illustrate through an example. Consider the two programs `min2` and `lmin` in Fig. 3 which are similar in structure and in the nature of what they compute. The program `min2` computes the minimum of the array and is correct with respect to the asserted property. Thus the loop in the program is k-shrinkable for all k from 1 to `S`. The second program `lmin` is similar to our motivating example with a property that asserts that the final value of `m` does not exceed any array element by more than a value d. The reader can verify that this property does not hold for $d < \mathtt{S} - 1$.[2] It turns out that the loop in `lmin` is shrinkable with a shrink-factor $k = d + 2$. This illustrates the difficulty of analytically finding whether a given loop is shrinkable, and based on the development in rest of this section, we shall suggest an empirical method in Sect. 5.

4.1 Identifying Shrinkable Loops

While Definition 1 lays down the consequences of a loop being shrinkable, it does not provide a convenient method to decide whether a loop is shrinkable and find the shrink-factor. To get around this problem, we first extend the notion of shrinkability from loops to arbitrary iteration sequences. We then identify the conditions under which the shrinkability of smaller iteration sequences (that are checked explicitly) would imply the shrinkability of larger iteration sequences and eventually of the entire loop.

Definition 2. *(Shrinkable iteration sequence) Consider a program consisting of a loop L and a property ψ to be checked. Let T be an iteration sequence, and let j be the first iteration in T. The sequence T is k-shrinkable with respect to ψ, $0 < k < |T|$, if and only if, starting from every state $\sigma \in \varphi_j$, the residual loop L_T satisfies the residual property ψ_T whenever the residual loops L_U of each k-length subsequences U of T satisfy the corresponding residual property ψ_U. Formally:*

$$\forall \sigma \in \varphi_j : ((\forall U \in \mathcal{P}_k(T) : \{\sigma\}L_U\{\psi_U\}) \implies \{\sigma\}L_T\{\psi_T\}) \tag{2}$$

The only difference between the notion of shrinkability of a loop and an iteration sequence is the starting state σ, which, in this case, is from the set φ_j. Recall that φ_j is an over-approximation of the set of states at the beginning of iteration j in the residual loop of any iteration sequence that contains j. As in the case of loops, by k-shrinkable sequence we shall mean a shrinkable sequence with shrink-factor k. It is obvious that, if the sequence consisting of all iterations of a loop is k-shrinkable then the loop itself is k-shrinkable.

As an illustration of an iteration sequence that is not shrinkable, consider the program `lmin` in Fig. 3(b) with $d = 0$. Consider the array `a` with its initial two elements as $\{0, 1\}$ and the iteration sequence $T = [1, 2]$. The residual loop of T computes $\mathtt{m} = 1$ for which the residual property ψ_T does not hold ($\mathtt{m} > \mathtt{a[0]}$). However, the residual loop for every 1-length sequence satisfies its residual property, and thus T is not 1-shrinkable. Also notice that when $d = 0$, the program is the same as the motivating example in Fig. 1 except for array initialisation. Thus, from the observations in Sect. 1, every iteration sequence of length 3 is 2-shrinkable.

[2] Observe that, starting with the second element of the array, if the value of each element exceeds the value of the previous element by 1, then `m` will exceed the first element by $\mathtt{S} - 1$.

4.2 Conditions Guaranteeing Shrinkability of Loops

We are interested in a method which guarantees that a loop is shrinkable by examining iteration sequences up to a given length. More specifically, we are interested in a pair of numbers n and a k, such that the k-shrinkability of all sequences of length between $k+1$ and n would imply the k-shrinkability of any sequence longer than n—in particular, the complete sequence of iterations comprising the loop. If we can identify the conditions under which we can find such a pair, then our strategy would be to establish the k-shrinkability of sequences up to n empirically, and the k-shrinkability of all iteration sequences with lengths greater than n will follow.

Since empirical verification of k-shrinkability for all subsequences of length between $k+1$ and n would be costly, we shall consider the case where $n = k+1$, i.e. we shall empirically find a k such that all $k+1$ length iteration sequences are k-shrinkable. The identified conditions will then ensure the k-shrinkability of sequences larger than $k+1$. Notice that the generalization from $k+1$ to larger sequences does not happen unconditionally. As an example, consider the program `lmin` in Fig. 3(b). For `d=2`, all the iteration sequences of size 3 are 2-shrinkable but not all sequences of size 4 are 2-shrinkable.

To derive the required conditions, let us examine what it takes to ensure the k-shrinkability of a sequence of length $k+2$, given the k-shrinkability of all sequences of length $k+1$. For simplicity of exposition, we shall limit ourselves to conjunctive properties. The treatment for disjunctive properties is very similar, and we shall merely touch upon it later in this section.

Consider an iteration sequence T of size $k+2$, represented as $j : T'$. Obviously, T' being of size $k+1$, is k-shrinkable. Taking a contrapositive view of the condition for shrinkability, assume that starting from σ, the residual property ψ_T is violated for the program L_T i.e. $\{\sigma\}L_T\{\neg\psi_T\}$ is true. Given that all sequences of length $k+1$ are k-shrinkable, it suffices to find a subsequence $T'' \sqsubset T$ of length $k+1$ such that $\{\sigma\}L_{T''}\{\neg\psi_{T''}\}$ is true. k-shrinkability will then ensure that there is a k-length subsequence $U \sqsubset T'' \sqsubset T$ such that $\{\sigma\}L_U\{\neg\psi_U\}$. Let the state after the iteration j in the sequence be σ'. Clearly $\{\sigma'\}L_{T'}\{\neg\psi_{[j]} \vee \neg\psi_{T'}\}$ is true.

1. Consider the case when $\psi_{T'}$ is violated. Since T' is k-shrinkable, it is possible to find a k-length subsequence U within T' such that starting from σ', ψ_U would be violated after L_U. Now consider the iteration sequence $T'' = j : U$. Clearly, starting from σ, $\psi_{T''}$ would be violated after executing $L_{T''}$, and thus the $k+1$-length sequence that we want is T''.
2. Now suppose that ψ_T is violated only because the clause $\psi_{[j]}$ is violated. There are two subcases to be considered. In the first, assume that the violation of $\psi_{[j]}$ also shows up in the state after iteration $k+1$. In this case the T'' that we want is the $(k+1)$-length prefix of T.
3. The interesting case is when the violation of ψ_T is solely because of $\psi_{[j]}$, and this violation of $\psi_{[j]}$ does not show up in the state after iteration $k+1$. In this case, the definition of shrinkability, in its current form, does not enable

us to produce the required sequence T''. To remedy this, notice that for the subsequence T', there is an iteration in the past, namely j, whose clause $\psi_{[j]}$ has been violated. If we revise the definition of k-shrinkability of iteration sequences (Definition 2) to ensure that this violation also shows up at the end of some k-length subsequence U' of T', then we are done. The required $k+1$-length subsequence T'' in this case would be $j : U'$ for which $\{\sigma\}L_{T''}\{\neg\psi_{T''}\}$ would be satisfied.

We call the modification introduced above as *past-preservation*. The revised definition of shrinkability that includes past-preservation is presented below.

Definition 3. *(Shrinkable iteration sequence, revised) Consider a program consisting of a loop L and a property ψ to be checked. Let T be an iteration sequence, and let j be the first iteration in T. In addition, let i stand for any iteration before j. The sequence T is k-shrinkable with respect to a property ψ, $0 < k < |T|$, if and only if, starting from every state $\sigma \in \varphi_j$ the residual loop L_T satisfies $\psi_T \wedge \psi_{[i]}$ whenever the residual loops L_U of each k-length subsequences U of T satisfy the corresponding property $\psi_U \wedge \psi_{[i]}$. In other words:*

$$\forall \sigma \in \varphi_j, \forall 0 \le i < j : ((\forall U \in \mathcal{P}_k(T) : \{\sigma\}L_U\{\psi_U \wedge \psi_{[i]}\}) \implies \{\sigma\}L_T\{\psi_T \wedge \psi_{[i]}\}) \quad (3)$$

A contrapositive reading of the revised condition for shrinkability of T says that if an execution of L_T with initial state σ results in a violation of its residual property ψ_T or the clause $\psi_{[i]}$ corresponding to a past iteration i, then there exists a k-length subsequence U of T such that execution of L_U with the same initial state also violates ψ_U or $\psi_{[i]}$. Henceforth we will consider this to be the definition of shrinkability of iteration sequences.

As a technical point, notice that we include 0 as a possible value of a past iteration. Otherwise, any sequence that starts with iteration 1, would have an empty set of past iterations and the condition of k-shrinkability would be vacuously true for the sequence. We therefore include 0 as a past-iteration and define $\psi_{[0]}$ to be *true*. A pleasing consequence of this is when the iteration sequence consists of all the iterations of a loop, the revised definition that includes past-preservation also coincides with the definition of shrinkability of loops (Definition 1).

Consider the example `lmin` in Fig. 3(b) with $\mathtt{S} = 5$ and $d = 1$. Not all sequences of length two are 1-shrinkable by the revised definition. To see this, consider the case of an array `a` as $\{2, 1, 2, 3, 4\}$. Let T be [4,5] and take past iteration i as 1. Let `m` be 2 in a state σ. Then $\psi_{[1]} = \mathtt{m} \le \mathtt{a[0]} + 1 \equiv \mathtt{m} \le 3$. Clearly, starting from state σ, for the residual loops of size 1 subsequences U, i.e. [4] and [5], the resulting `m` will be 3 and 2 respectively and $\psi_{[1]} \wedge \psi_U$ is satisfied. But starting from the same state σ, the residual loop L_T, will produce $\mathtt{m} = 4$, and therefore $\psi_{[1]} \wedge \psi_T$ is not satisfied. On the other hand, it is easy to see that, for the same d, all the sequences of size 4 are 3-shrinkable.

We now formally prove the result that we have been working towards: For a loop to be k-shrinkable, it is enough if every iteration sequence of size $k+1$ is k-shrinkable. Our method of determining shrinkable and the shrink-factor will make use of this important result.

Theorem 1. *An array processing loop is k-shrinkable with respect to a property ψ, if every iteration sequence of size $k+1$ is k-shrinkable with respect to ψ.*

Proof. To show that the loop is k-shrinkable, it is enough to show that the complete iteration sequence of the loop is k-shrinkable according to Definition 3. However, we shall show a stronger condition that all sequences of size greater than k are k-shrinkable. The proof is by induction on the length n of an iteration sequence T of the loop. For the base case $n = k+1$, the k-shrinkability of T is a given in the statement of the theorem. Now let n be greater than $k+1$ and assume as the induction hypothesis that every sequence of length less than n is k-shrinkable. Let $T = j : T'$. As usual, we take a contrapositive view of the shrinkability condition and assume that for some past iteration i of T, starting from a state $\sigma \in \varphi_j$, the property $\psi_{[i]} \wedge \psi_T$ fails after executing L_T i.e. $\{\sigma\}L_T\{\neg\psi_{[i]} \vee \neg\psi_T\}$ is true. We show that there exists a k-sized subsequence $U \sqsubset T$ such that $\{\sigma\}L_U\{\neg\psi_{[i]} \vee \neg\psi_U\}$ is true.

Since $L_T = S_j; L_{T'}$ and $\psi_T = \psi_{[j]} \wedge \psi_{T'}$, we have $\{\sigma\}S_j; L_{T'}\{\neg\psi_{[i]} \vee \neg\psi_{[j]} \vee \neg\psi_{T'}\}$. Assume that starting with σ, the state reached after executing S_j, the loop body for the iteration j, is σ_1, i.e. $\{\sigma\}S_j\{\sigma_1\}$. We then have $\{\sigma_1\}L_{T'}\{\neg\psi_{[i]} \vee \neg\psi_{T'}\} \bigvee \{\sigma_1\}L_{T'}\{\neg\psi_{[j]} \vee \neg\psi_{T'}\}$. We show the existence of the desired U by assuming that the first disjunct is true. Since i and j are both past iterations for T', the proof in the case in which only the second disjunct is true is similar. Assume that the first iteration of T' is j'. Obviously $\sigma_1 \in \varphi_{j'}$. Since T' is k-shrinkable, we must have a k-sized subsequence $U' \sqsubset T'$ such that $\{\sigma_1\}L_{U'}\{\neg\psi_{[i]} \vee \neg\psi_{U'}\}$ is true. It follows that $\{\sigma\}S_j; L_{U'}\{\neg\psi_{[i]} \vee \neg\psi_{U'}\}$ and therefore $\{\sigma\}S_j; L_{U'}\{\neg\psi_{[i]} \vee \neg\psi_{[j]} \vee \neg\psi_{U'}\}$ are also true. Let T'' be $j : U'$. Obviously, $T'' \sqsubset T$. Since the size of T'' is $k+1$, T'' is k-shrinkable by the induction hypothesis and therefore there exists a k-sized subsequence $U \sqsubset T'' \sqsubset T$ such that $\{\sigma\}L_U\{\neg\psi_{[i]} \vee \neg\psi_U\}$ holds. ∎

For a disjunctive property ψ, the definition (3) of sequence shrinkability, changes as follows:

$$\forall\sigma \in \varphi_j, \forall 0 \leq i < j : ((\exists U \in \mathcal{P}_k(T) : \{\sigma\}L_U\{\psi_U \vee \psi_{[i]}\}) \implies \{\sigma\}L_T\{\psi_T \vee \psi_{[i]}\}) \quad (4)$$

Theorem 1 applies to disjunctive properties as well, and the proof is similar.

5 Determining Shrinkability and Property Checking

We now show how Theorem 1 can be used to empirically determine whether a given loop is shrinkable and also find the corresponding shrink-factor. Starting with 1, we repeatedly construct the program shown in Fig. 4 for successive values of `k`, the candidate shrink-factor, and feed it to a bounded model checker for verification. If the program is verified to be correct for some value of `k`, then Theorem 1 guarantees that the loop in the given program is `k`-shrinkable. The constructed program depends on `k`, the loop L and the property to be verified, ψ. The process stops when we either find a `k` for which the loop is shrinkable (success), or we reach a predefined limit l that is dependent on the available time and computing resources (failure). As we shall see in Sect. 6, the shrink-factors for shrinkable loops are usually small. This is a favourable situation, since programs with a smaller shrink-factors are relatively easier to verify than programs with larger shrink-factors.

5.1 Checking Shrinkability of an Iteration Sequence

Recall that according to Theorem 1, a loop is k-shrinkable, if every iteration sequence of length $k+1$ is k shrinkable. In addition, with our assumption that the loop has a statically computable upper bound of number of iterations, the number of such iteration sequences will be finite. Given a candidate `k`, the procedure `check_loop` in Fig. 4 non-deterministically chooses an iteration sequence T of length `k+1`, and attempts to verify that T is `k`-shrinkable. This is done in the procedure `check_iter_seq`, which encodes the criterion for sequence shrinkability, as given by Definition 3. The construction shown applies to conjunctive properties; disjunctive properties can be handled in a similar manner.

```
check_loop(k)
{
  choose an arbitrary
    iteration-sequence
    T of size k+1
  check_iter_seq(T);
}
```

(a) Checking loop shrinkability

```
1  check_iter_seq(T)
2  {
3    j = head(T); i = nondet();
4    assume(0 <= i < j);
5    X_initial= nondet(); c = true;
6    for each k sized U⊏T {
7      X = X_initial; L_U; c=ψ(i)∧ψ_U
8      if (!c) break;
9    }
10   X = X_initial ; L_T; r=ψ(i)∧ψ_T
11   assert(c⟹r);
12 }
```

(b) Checking sequence shrinkability

Fig. 4. Program construction for determining shrinkability. Note that `X` and `X_initial` are vectors of variables, and `nondet()`, accordingly, generates a vector of values.

Assume that the given program consists of an array processing loop L of the form `while`$(C)\{B\};Q$ followed by the assertion assert(ψ). Let `X` denote the vector of variables which *may be* modified (by resolving dereferences, if any, using a safe points-to-analysis) in the loop body B. Recall that the implication in the criterion for shrinkability is required to hold for all states in φ_j, where j is the head of sequence T. The states in φ_j are over-approximated by assigning non-deterministic values to `X` (through `X_initial`). Thus our process of determining shrinkability is conservative and a future extension to this work would be a static analysis to obtain a better approximation of φ_j.

The loop in lines 6–9 checks the antecedent $(\forall U \in \mathcal{P}_k(T).\{\sigma\}L_U\{\psi_U \wedge \psi_{[i]}\})$ in the implication in the shrinkability condition (Definition 3), and stores the result in `c`. This loop executes a maximum of $k + 1$ times, the number of subsequences of T of size k. Line 10 checks the consequent $\{\sigma\}L_T\{\psi_T \wedge \psi_{[i]}\}$ of the same implication, and stores it in `r`. Finally line 11 checks the condition for shrinkability, given by the implication `c` $\Rightarrow$ `r` itself. Observe that the residual loop for each subsequence U and the residual loop for the sequence T are all evaluated in the same state denoted by the values of the variables in `X_initial`. It is clear that the program shown in Fig. 4 can be automatically constructed for any given k, L, and ψ.

The fact that shrinkable loops usually have a low shrink-factor has two consequences for the procedure to determine shrinkability: (i) it allows us to keep the number l till which a program is tested for shrinkability at a low value without the fear of missing out many shrinkable programs, and (ii) since the `for` loop in lines 6–9 has a bound of $k + 1$, and k is smaller than l, the shrinkability testing procedure is fairly efficient.

5.2 Property Checking for Shrinkable Loops

Once we discover that the loop of a program is k-shrinkable, we construct an abstract program that consists of a program fragment to non-deterministically choose a k-sized iteration sequence T, a residual loop L_T, and a residual property ψ_T. The abstract program is submitted to a BMC for verification. The motivating example of Fig. 1 illustrates the nature of the abstract program, and it is easy to generalize and automate the process of abstraction to arbitrary programs that are within the scope of our method.

Since the quantified property is also encoded as a loop, the residual property can also be constructed as a residual of this loop. Consider a program with a loop L for which the residual has to be constructed with respect to a k-length iteration sequence. Assume that the maximum iteration count of the loop is m. Let $a[e]$ be an arbitrary expression involving an array a of size n. Also assume that the index expression e is accelerable and is of the form $f(i)$, where $i \in [1..m]$ represents a particular loop iteration, and f is the acceleration function. The abstract program non-deterministically chooses a k-length iteration sequence, whose elements are in the range $[1..m]$. The iteration sequence is concretely represented as an array. A loop iterates over all the values of the iteration sequence. The expression $a[e]$ in the loop body is replaced by the corresponding accelerable expression $a[f(i)]$.

To make this clearer, consider the example in Fig. 5(a). Assume that the size `p` of the array is more than $(\texttt{n}+1)/2$. The loop initializes the array element `a[t]` with the value `2*t`. Assume that the loop is `k`-shrinkable for some property. The maximum iteration count m for the loop is $(\texttt{n} + 1)/2$. The code in Fig. 5(b), written in a C-like notation, is an abstract description of the residual loop. The call to `init` initializes the array `T` with a non-deterministically chosen `k`-length iteration sequence. The C-style comment indicates the constraints on the chosen iteration sequence `T`. The conditions `1` $\leq$ `T[`l`-1]` $<$ `T[`l`]` and `0` $\leq$ `2*(T[`l`]-1)` $<$ `n` together ensure that the iteration sequence consists of increasing values in the range $[1 \ldots m]$, and the condition `T[`l`]-1` $<$ `p` ensures that the chosen values do not cause an out-of-bounds access of the array. The `for` loop covering lines 7 to 11 iterates over the elements in `T`. Inside the loop body, `i` and `j` are computed through acceleration functions applied to the iteration numbers picked from `T`.

In practice, the constraints on the values in `T` would be enforced programmatically, and this is shown in Fig. 5(c). Here an increasing sequence of values are chosen, and the constraint that the chosen values are in the range $[1..m]$ is enforced through the the conditional `break`. Similarly, the constraint that the index of `a` does not exceed its bound is enforced through the `assume` at line 8. Finally, `assume(l==k)` ensures that the residual indeed iterates `k` times and does not break out of the loop earlier.

Our method can also be used when the program consists of a cascaded series of simple loops that can be coalesced into one simple loop. To elaborate, let the program be $\{Q_1; R_1; Q_2; R_2; Q_3; R_3\}$, where the Q_is are loop-free statements and the R_is are simple loops of the form `while` (C_i) $\{B_i\}$. Our method can handle such a program, if it can be transformed to a semantically equivalent program Q; `while` (C) $\{B_1; B_2; B_3\}$ for some loop-free statements, Q, and condition C. Even this simple strategy enabled us to verify 50 of the 81 programs with non-nested multiple loops in the SV-COMP 2017 benchmark suite. However, our method, in its present form, cannot handle nested loops.

```
1  int a[p];
2  int i=0,t=0;
3  while(i < n)
4  {
5    a[t] = i;
6    i+=2; t++;
7  }
```

(a) Given program

```
1  int a[p],i=0,t=0,T[k];
2  init(T) ;
3  //∀l∈1..k-1.
4  // 1≤T[l-1]<T[l]
5  // 0≤2*(T[l]-1)<n
6  // T[l]-1<p
7  for j in T {
8    i = (j-1)*2;
9    t = j-1; a[t]=i;
10   i+=2; t++;
11 }
```

(b) Abstract description of residual

```
1  int a[p], T[k], l, i=0, t=0;
2  init(T) ;
3  //∀l∈1..k-1. 1≤T[l-1]<T[l]
4  for (l=0;l<k;l++) {
5    j = T[l]; i = (j-1)*2;
6    t = j-1;
7    if (!(i < n)) break;
8    a[assume(0<=t<p),t] = i;
9    i+=2; t++;
10 }
11 assume(l==k);
```

(c) Residual as generated by the tool

Fig. 5. Example illustrating the residual of a shrinkable loop. Program in (b) is an abstract description of the residual, presented for ease of explanation

6 Implementation and Measurements

The proposed abstraction has been implemented in a tool called *VeriAbs* [7]. Within the scope of our method, i.e. a single loop followed by the property to be checked, the tool supports most C constructs including pointers, structure, arrays, heaps and non-recursive function calls. It uses LABMC [12] to discover index expressions that can be accelerated and CBMC 5.8 as the bounded model checker to determine shrinkability of the loop and to check the residual property on the abstracted program. If a loop is not found shrinkable within a candidate shrink-factor of 5, we report the shrinkability of the loop to be unknown. Given a program with a shrinkable loop, if the verification of the corresponding abstract program succeeds on the residual property, the tool declares the original program to be correct with respect to the given property. On the other hand, if the verification of the abstract program fails and the loop in the program has no loop-carried dependencies, the original program is declared to be incorrect. Otherwise the tool indicates its inability to decide on the correctness of the program.

6.1 Experiments

An early version of the tool *VeriAbs* competed in the SV-COMP 2017 verification competition [2], where it ranked third amongst the 17 participating tools in the *ArraysReach* category. We have re-run the current version on the same benchmark. We ran the experiment on a machine with two i7-4600U cores @2.70 GHz and 8 GB RAM. *ArraysReach* consisted of 135 programs, of which 95 are correct and the remaining 40 incorrect with respect to their properties. Table (a) of Fig. 6 categorizes these programs. 42 of the 135 programs were beyond the scope of *VeriAbs* because they either contained nested loops (12 programs) or contained multiple loops which were not collapsible (30 programs). Out of the remaining 93 programs, 89 programs were 1-shrinkable, 2 were 2-shrinkable, and while our tool could not find the shrinkability of the remaining 2 programs, we manually found those to be non-shrinkable.

Figure 6(b) gives the verification results of the 91 shrinkable programs. All correct programs except one were verified successfully. Moreover, none of the 26 incorrect programs were declared to be correct, demonstrating the soundness of our tool. 23 of these 26 incorrect programs also had no loop carried dependency, and thus the tool could rightly declare these as being incorrect. For the remaining 3 programs our tool remained indecisive. The timing data shows the average time taken in verifying each program. As expected, the bulk of time is taken in determining shrinkability, as the BMC has to verify $O(k^2)$ residual programs to determine that the shrink-factor is k, while property checking of the abstract program involves a loop with just k iterations. Given the limits of the machine configuration, the timings are reasonable.

Programs	True	False	Total
With nested loops	5	7	12
With non-collapsible multiple loops	24	6	30
Shrinkable	65	26	91
Shrinkability unknown	1	1	2
Total	95	40	135

(a) Programs categories

Results on shrinkable programs	#Cases	Average time per program (in seconds)	
		Checking shrinkability	Total
Property declared correct	64	30.60	39.68
Property declared incorrect	23	10.72	19.73
Unable to decide	4	227.26	236.06
Total	91	34.22	43.27

(b) Property verification results

Fig. 6. Experimental results for SV-COMP 2017 ArraysReach benchmarks

An interesting property of *Veriabs* is that, while it is limited by its ability to deal only with shrinkable loops, once a loop is discovered to be shrinkable, the method is impervious to either the existence or the size of loop bounds—increasing the loop bound does not cause an otherwise verifiable program to timeout. Comparison with the two tools that fared better than *VeriAbs* in the competition, namely *ceagle* [24] and *smack* [6], reveals interesting information. We selected four correct programs, one from each of the following categories, array copy, array initialisation, two index copying and finding minimum, of the test suite, and increased the array size considerably (from 100000 to 10000000). While both tools succeeded on the programs with the original array sizes, *smack* started timing out after the increase and *ceagle* either crashed or declared the programs to be incorrect. We surmise that the two tools are based on bounded model checking without any abstraction. In this respect, our tool performs better than these two tools that were placed ahead of ours in the competition.

7 Related Work

The various approaches to handle arrays have their roots in the types of static analyses used for property verification, namely: abstract interpretation, predicate abstraction, bounded model checking and theorem proving.

In abstract interpretation, arrays are handled using *array smashing*, *array expansion* and *array slicing*. In array smashing, all elements of an array are clubbed as a single anonymous element, with writes treated as weak updates. As a result it is imprecise. It cannot be used, for example, to verify the motivating example. In array expansion, array elements are explicated as a collection of scalar variables, and the resulting programs have fewer number of weak updates than array smashing. However, it works well only for small-sized arrays. A mix of smashing and expansion has been used in [4,5] to prove that the program does not perform executions with undefined behaviours such as out-of-bounds array accesses. In array slicing, the idea is to track partitions of arrays based upon some criteria inferred from programs [11,16,17]. Each partition is treated as an independent smashed element. The approach is further refined in [14] to introduce the notion of *fluid updates*, where a write operation may result in a strong update of one partition of the array and weak update of other partitions. In contrast to these approaches, our abstraction is based not only on the program but also on the associated property. By declaring an array-processing loop as k-shrinkable, we guarantee that an erroneous behaviour of the program with respect to the property can indeed be replayed on some k elements of the array.

Methods based on predicate abstraction go through several rounds of counterexample guided abstraction refinement (CEGAR). In each round a suitable invariant is searched based on the counter-example using *Craig interpolants* [21]. Tools like SATABS [9] and CPAchecker [3] are based on this technique. To handle arrays, the approach relies on finding appropriate quantified loop invariants. However generating interpolants for scalar programs is by itself a hard problem. With the inclusion of arrays, which require universally quantified interpolants, the problem becomes even harder [20,22]. Our method, in contrast, does not rely on the ability to find invariants. Instead, we find a bound on the number of loop iterations, and, in turn, the number of array elements that have to be accessed in a run of abstract program.

Theorem proving based methods generate a set of constraints, typically Horn clauses. The clauses relate invariants at various program points and the invariants are predicates over arrays. The constraints are then fed to a solver in order to find a model. However, these methods also face the same difficulty of synthesizing quantified invariants over arrays. A technique, called *k-distinguished cell abstraction*, addresses this problem by abstracting the array to only k elements. A 1-distinguished cell abstraction, for example, abstracts a predicate $P(a)$ involving an array a by $P'(i, a_i)$, where i and a_i are scalars. The relation between the two predicates is that $P'(i, a_i)$ holds whenever $P(a)$ holds and the value of $a[i]$ is a_i. The resulting constraints are easier to solve using a back end solver such as Z3 [13]. This technique and its variants appear in [22,23] and in [15], where the term *skolem constants* is used instead of distinguished cells. We experimented with VAPHOR, a tool based on [23]. By way of comparison, we present two examples, one with a $\exists$ property and the other with a $\forall$ property. The first program computes the minimum of an array and asserts that the minimum is the same as some element in the array. The second program copies all but 1 elements from one large array to another. It then asserts that the copied elements are pairwise equal. While our tool could verify both examples, VAPHOR declared the first program to be incorrect with 1 and 2 distinguished cell abstraction and timed out on the second program.

A method that is properly subsumed by our method is [18]. This uses only one distinguished element called a *witness element*, and transforms a program to a loop free scalar program. This program is model-checked using a BMC. This approach works well on what authors call *full array processing loops* and such loops are a proper subset of our 1-shrinkable loops.

8 Conclusion

We have proposed a fully automatic approach for property checking over array processing programs using loop shrinking. The approach enables us to verify properties over large or even unbounded loops by converting them to loops with a small finite bound. Towards this, we have defined a notion called shrinkability of a loop, and showed that arrays processed by k-shrinkable loops can be abstracted using only k elements. The abstracted program can then be checked using any bounded model checker as back-end. An important contribution of our method is an automated method to find out the required bound k. Although there are approaches that are based on abstracting an array by fewer elements, none of these provide a way to find out the number of elements that are sufficient to reason about the array. Our experiments have shown that the approach is powerful enough to handle a variety of array processing programs. As future work, we want to add a suitable refinement step to address false positives and extend our method to support nested loops and multi-dimensional arrays.

References

1. Allen, R., Kennedy, K.: Automatic translation of fortran programs to vector form. ACM Trans. Program. Lang. Syst. **9**(4), 491–542 (1987)
2. Beyer, D.: SV-COMP 2017–6th International Conference on Software Verification (2017). https://sv-comp.sosy-lab.org
3. Beyer, D., Keremoglu, M.E.: CPAchecker: a tool for configurable software verification. In: Gopalakrishnan, G., Qadeer, S. (eds.) CAV 2011. LNCS, vol. 6806, pp. 184–190. Springer, Heidelberg (2011). https://doi.org/10.1007/978-3-642-22110-1_16
4. Blanchet, B., Cousot, P., Cousot, R., Feret, J., Mauborgne, L., Miné, A., Monniaux, D., Rival, X.: Design and implementation of a special-purpose static program analyzer for safety-critical real-time embedded software. In: Mogensen, T.Æ., Schmidt, D.A., Sudborough, I.H. (eds.) The Essence of Computation. LNCS, vol. 2566, pp. 85–108. Springer, Heidelberg (2002). https://doi.org/10.1007/3-540-36377-7_5
5. Blanchet, B., Cousot, P., Cousot, R., Feret, J., Mauborgne, L., Miné, A., Monniaux, D., Rival, X.: A static analyzer for large safety-critical software. In: Proceedings of the PLDI 2003, pp. 196–207. ACM, New York (2003)
6. Carter, M., He, S., Whitaker, J., Rakamarić, Z., Emmi, M.: Smack software verification toolchain. In: Proceedings of the 38th International Conference on Software Engineering Companion, ICSE 2016, pp. 589–592. ACM, New York (2016)
7. Chimdyalwar, B., Darke, P., Chauhan, A., Shah, P., Kumar, S., Venkatesh, R.: VeriAbs: verification by abstraction (competition contribution). In: Legay, A., Margaria, T. (eds.) TACAS 2017, Part II. LNCS, vol. 10206, pp. 404–408. Springer, Heidelberg (2017). https://doi.org/10.1007/978-3-662-54580-5_32
8. Clarke, E., Kroening, D., Lerda, F.: A tool for checking ANSI-C programs. In: Jensen, K., Podelski, A. (eds.) TACAS 2004. LNCS, vol. 2988, pp. 168–176. Springer, Heidelberg (2004). https://doi.org/10.1007/978-3-540-24730-2_15
9. Clarke, E., Kroening, D., Sharygina, N., Yorav, K.: SATABS: SAT-based predicate abstraction for ANSI-C. In: Halbwachs, N., Zuck, L.D. (eds.) TACAS 2005. LNCS, vol. 3440, pp. 570–574. Springer, Heidelberg (2005). https://doi.org/10.1007/978-3-540-31980-1_40
10. Cousot, P., Cousot, R.: Abstract interpretation: a unified lattice model for static analysis of programs by construction or approximation of fixpoints. In: POPL 1977: Proceedings of the 4th ACM SIGACT-SIGPLAN Symposium on Principles of Programming Languages, pp. 238–252. ACM, New York (1977)
11. Cousot, P., Cousot, R., Logozzo, F.: A parametric segmentation functor for fully automatic and scalable array content analysis. In: SIGPLAN Not, vol. 46, no. 1, pp. 105–118, January 2011
12. Darke, P., Chimdyalwar, B., Venkatesh, R., Shrotri, U., Metta, R.: Over-approximating loops to prove properties using bounded model checking. In: Proceedings of the DATE 2015, pp. 1407–1412. EDA Consortium, San Jose (2015)
13. de Moura, L., Bjørner, N.: Z3: an efficient SMT solver. In: Ramakrishnan, C.R., Rehof, J. (eds.) TACAS 2008. LNCS, vol. 4963, pp. 337–340. Springer, Heidelberg (2008). https://doi.org/10.1007/978-3-540-78800-3_24
14. Dillig, I., Dillig, T., Aiken, A.: Fluid updates: beyond strong vs. weak updates. In: Gordon, A.D. (ed.) ESOP 2010. LNCS, vol. 6012, pp. 246–266. Springer, Heidelberg (2010). https://doi.org/10.1007/978-3-642-11957-6_14
15. Flanagan, C., Qadeer, S.: Predicate abstraction for software verification. In: Proceedings of the POPL 2002, pp. 191–202. ACM, New York (2002)

16. Gopan, D., Reps, T., Sagiv, M.: A framework for numeric analysis of array operations. In: SIGPLAN Not. vol. 40, no. 1, pp. 338–350, January 2005
17. Halbwachs, N., Péron, M.: Discovering properties about arrays in simple programs. In: SIGPLAN Not, vol. 43, no. 6, pp. 339–348, June 2008
18. Jana, A., Khedker, U.P., Datar, A., Venkatesh, R., Niyas, C.: Scaling bounded model checking by transforming programs with arrays. In: Hermenegildo, M.V., Lopez-Garcia, P. (eds.) LOPSTR 2016. LNCS, vol. 10184, pp. 275–292. Springer, Cham (2017). https://doi.org/10.1007/978-3-319-63139-4_16
19. Jeannet, B., Schrammel, P., Sankaranarayanan, S.: Abstract acceleration of general linear loops. In: Proceedings of POPL 2014, pp. 529–540. ACM, New York (2014)
20. Jhala, R., McMillan, K.L.: Array abstractions from proofs. In: Damm, W., Hermanns, H. (eds.) CAV 2007. LNCS, vol. 4590, pp. 193–206. Springer, Heidelberg (2007). https://doi.org/10.1007/978-3-540-73368-3_23
21. McMillan, K.L.: Applications of Craig interpolants in model checking. In: Halbwachs, N., Zuck, L.D. (eds.) TACAS 2005. LNCS, vol. 3440, pp. 1–12. Springer, Heidelberg (2005). https://doi.org/10.1007/978-3-540-31980-1_1
22. Monniaux, D., Alberti, F.: A simple abstraction of arrays and maps by program translation. In: Blazy, S., Jensen, T. (eds.) SAS 2015. LNCS, vol. 9291, pp. 217–234. Springer, Heidelberg (2015). https://doi.org/10.1007/978-3-662-48288-9_13
23. Monniaux, D., Gonnord, L.: Cell morphing: from array programs to array-free Horn clauses. In: Rival, X. (ed.) SAS 2016. LNCS, vol. 9837, pp. 361–382. Springer, Heidelberg (2016). https://doi.org/10.1007/978-3-662-53413-7_18
24. Wang, D.: Tool ceagle (2017). http://sts.thss.tsinghua.edu.cn/ceagle

Invariant Synthesis for Incomplete Verification Engines

Daniel Neider[1(✉)], Pranav Garg[2], P. Madhusudan[3], Shambwaditya Saha[3], and Daejun Park[3]

[1] Max Planck Institute for Software Systems, Kaiserslautern, Germany
neider@mpi-sws.org
[2] Amazon India, Bangalore, India
[3] University of Illinois at Urbana-Champaign, Champaign, IL, USA

Abstract. We propose a framework for synthesizing inductive invariants for incomplete verification engines, which soundly reduce logical problems in undecidable theories to decidable theories. Our framework is based on the counter-example guided inductive synthesis principle (CEGIS) and allows verification engines to communicate *non-provability information* to guide invariant synthesis. We show precisely how the verification engine can compute such non-provability information and how to build effective learning algorithms when invariants are expressed as Boolean combinations of a fixed set of predicates. Moreover, we evaluate our framework in two verification settings, one in which verification engines need to handle quantified formulas and one in which verification engines have to reason about heap properties expressed in an expressive but undecidable separation logic. Our experiments show that our invariant synthesis framework based on non-provability information can both effectively synthesize inductive invariants and adequately strengthen contracts across a large suite of programs.

1 Introduction

The paradigm of *deductive verification* [15,22] combines manual annotations and semi-automated theorem proving to prove programs correct. Programmers annotate code they develop with contracts and inductive invariants, and use high-level directives to an underlying, mostly-automated logic engine to verify their programs correct. Several mature tools have emerged that support such verification, in particular tools based on the intermediate verification language Boogie [3] and the SMT solver Z3 [34] (e.g., Vcc [8] and Dafny [29]).

Viewed through the lens of deductive verification, the primary challenges in automating verification are two-fold. First, even when strong annotations in terms of contracts and inductive invariants are given, the validity problem for the resulting verification conditions is often undecidable (e.g., in reasoning about the heap, reasoning with quantified logics, and reasoning with non-linear arithmetic). Second, the synthesis of loop invariants and strengthenings of contracts that

D. Beyer and M. Huisman (Eds.): TACAS 2018, LNCS 10805, pp. 232–250, 2018.
https://doi.org/10.1007/978-3-319-89960-2_13

prove a program correct needs to be automated so as to lift this burden currently borne by the programmer.

A standard technique to solve the first problem (i.e., intractability of validity checking of verifications conditions) is to build automated, sound but incomplete verification engines for validating verification conditions, thus skirting the undecidability barrier. Several such techniques exist; for instance, for reasoning with quantified formulas, tactics such as model-based quantifier instantiation [19] are effective in practice, and they are known to be complete in certain settings [30]. In the realm of heap verification, the so-called *natural proof method* explicitly aims to provide automated and sound but incomplete methods for checking validity of verification conditions with specifications in separation logic [7,30,39,41].

Turning to the second problem of invariant generation, several techniques have emerged that can synthesize invariants automatically when validation of verification conditions fall in decidable classes. Prominent among these are interpolation [32] and IC3/PDR [4,12]. Moreover, a class of counter-example guided inductive synthesis (CEGIS) methods have emerged recently, including the ICE learning model [17] for which various instantiations exist [17,18,27,43]. The key feature of the latter methods is a program-agnostic, data-driven learner that learns invariants in tandem with a verification engine that provides concrete program configurations as counterexamples to incorrect invariants.

Although classical invariant synthesis techniques, such as Houdini [14], are sometimes used with incomplete verification engines, to the best of our knowledge there is no fundamental argument as to why this should work in general. In fact, we are not aware of any systematic technique for synthesizing invariants when the underlying verification problem falls in an undecidable theory. When verification is undecidable and the engine resorts to sound but incomplete heuristics to check validity of verification conditions, it is unclear how to extend interpolation/IC3/PDR techniques to this setting. Data-driven learning of invariants is also hard to extend since the verification engine typically cannot generate a concrete model for the negation of verification conditions when verification fails. Hence, it cannot produce the concrete configurations that the learner needs.

The main contribution of this paper is a general, learning-based invariant synthesis framework that learns invariants using non-provability information provided by verification engines. Intuitively, when a conjectured invariant results in verification conditions that cannot be proven, the idea is that the verification engine must return information that generalizes the reason for non-provability, hence pruning the space of future conjectured invariants.

Our framework assumes a verification engine for an undecidable theory $\mathcal{U}$ that reduces verification conditions to a decidable theory $\mathcal{D}$ (e.g., using heuristics such as bounded quantifier instantiation to remove universal quantifiers, function unfolding to remove recursive definitions, and so on) that permits producing models for satisfiable formulas. The translation is assumed to be conservative in the sense that if the translated formula in $\mathcal{D}$ is valid, then we are assured that the original verification condition is $\mathcal{U}$-valid. If the verification condition is found to be not $\mathcal{D}$-valid (i.e., its negation is satisfiable), on the other hand, our framework describes how to extract non-provability information from the $\mathcal{D}$-model. This information is encoded as conjunctions and disjunctions in a Boolean theory $\mathcal{B}$, called *conjunctive/disjunctive non-provability information (CD-NPI)*, and communicated back to the learner. To complete our framework, we show how the formula-driven problem of learning expressions from CD-NPI constraints can be reduced to the data-driven ICE model. This reduction allows us to use a host of existing ICE learning algorithms and results in a robust invariant synthesis framework that guarantees to synthesize a provable invariant if one exists.

However, our CD-NPI learning framework has non-trivial requirements on the verification engine, and building or adapting appropriate engines is not straightforward. To show that our framework is indeed applicable and effective in practice, our second contribution is an application of our technique to the verification of dynamically manipulated data-structures against rich logics that combine properties of structure, separation, arithmetic, and data. More precisely, we show how *natural proof verification engines* [30,39], which are sound but incomplete verification engines that translate a powerful undecidable separation logic called DRYAD to decidable logics, can be fit into our framework. Moreover, we implement a prototype of such a verification engine on top of the program verifer Boogie [3] and demonstrate that this prototype is able to fully automatically verify a large suite of benchmarks, containing standard algorithms for manipulating singly and doubly linked lists, sorted lists, as well as balanced and sorted trees. Automatically synthesizing invariants for this suite of heap-manipulating programs against an expressive separation logic is very challenging, and we do not know of any other technique that can automatically prove all of them. Thus, we have to leave a comparison to other approaches for future work.

In addition to verifying heap properties, we successfully applied our framework to the verification of programs against specifications with universal quantification, which occur, for instance, when defining recursive properties. Details can be found in an extended version of this paper [35], which also contains further material (e.g., proofs) that had to be omitted due to space constraints.

To the best of our knowledge, our technique is the first to systematically address the problem of invariant synthesis for incomplete verification engines that work by soundly reducing undecidable logics to decidable ones. We believe our experimental results provide the first evidence of the tractability of this important problem.

Related Work

Techniques for invariant synthesis include abstract interpretation [10], interpolation [32], IC3 [4], predicate abstraction [2], abductive inference [11], as well as synthesis algorithms that rely on constraint solving [9,20,21]. Complementing them are data-driven invariant synthesis techniques based on learning, such as Daikon [13] that learn likely invariants, and HOUDINI [14] and ICE [17] that learn inductive invariants. The latter typically requires a teacher that can generate counter-examples if the conjectured invariant is not adequate or inductive. Classically, this is possible only when the verification conditions of the program fall in decidable logics. In this paper, we investigate data-driven invariant synthesis for incomplete verification engines and show that the problem can be reduced to ICE learning if the learning algorithm learns from non-provability information and produces hypotheses in a class that is restricted to positive Boolean formulas over a fixed set of predicates. Data-driven synthesis of invariants has regained recent interest [16,17,27,37,38,43–47] and our work addresses an important problem of synthesizing invariants for programs whose verification conditions fall in undecidable fragments.

Our application to learning invariants for heap-manipulating programs builds upon DRYAD [39,41], and the natural proof technique line of work for heap verification developed by Qiu et al. Techniques, similar to DRYAD, for automated reasoning of dynamically manipulated data structure programs have also been proposed in [6,7]. However, unlike our current work, none of these works synthesize heap invariants. Given invariant annotations in their respective logics, they provide procedures to validate if the verification conditions are valid. There has also been a lot of work on synthesizing invariants for separation logic using shape analysis [5,28,42]. However, most of them are tailored for memory safety and shallow properties rather than rich properties that check full functional correctness of data structures. Interpolation has also been suggested recently to synthesize invariants involving a combination of data and shape properties [1]. It is, however, not clear how the technique can be applied to a more complicated heap structure, such as an AVL tree, where shape and data properties are not cleanly separated but are intricately connected. Recent work also includes synthesizing heap invariants in the logic from [23] by extending IC3 [24,25].

In this work, our learning algorithm synthesizes invariants over a fixed set of predicates. When all programs belong to a specific class, such as the class of programs manipulating data structures, these predicates can be uniformly chosen using templates. Investigating automated ways for discovering candidate predicates is a very interesting future direction. Related work in this direction includes recent works [37,38].

2 An Invariant Synthesis Framework for Incomplete Verification Engines

In this section, we develop our framework for synthesizing inductive invariants for incomplete verification engines, using a counter-example guided inductive synthesis approach. We do this in the setting where the hypothesis space consists of formulas that are Boolean combinations of a fixed set of predicates $\mathcal{P}$, which need not be finite for the general framework—when developing concrete learning algorithms later, we will assume $\mathcal{P}$ is a finite set of predicates. For the rest of this section, let us fix a program P that is annotated with assertions (and possibly with some partial annotations describing pre-conditions, post-conditions, and

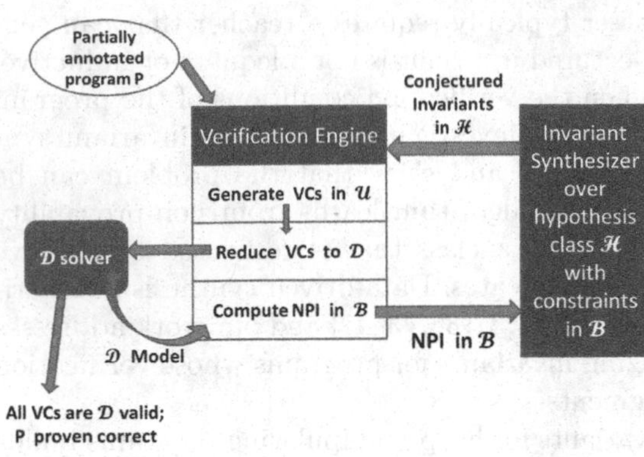

$\mathcal{H}$ – The hypothesis class of invariants
$\mathcal{U}$ – The underlying theory of the program; undecidable
$\mathcal{D}$ – The theory that the verification engine soundly reduces verification conditions to; decidable and can produce models
$\mathcal{B}$ – The theory of propositional logic that the verification engine uses to communicate to the invariant synthesis engine

Fig. 1. A non-provability information (NPI) framework for invariant synthesis

assertions). Moreover, we refer to a formula α being weaker (or stronger) than β in a logic $\mathcal{L}$, and by this we mean that $\vdash_{\mathcal{L}} \beta \Rightarrow \alpha$ (or $\vdash_{\mathcal{L}} \alpha \Rightarrow \beta$), respectively, where $\vdash_{\mathcal{L}} \varphi$ means that φ is valid in $\mathcal{L}$.

Figure 1 depicts our general framework of invariant synthesis when verification is undecidable. We fix several parameters for our verification effort. First, let us assume a uniform signature for logic, in terms of constant symbols, relation symbols, functions, and types. We will, for simplicity of exposition, use the same syntactic logic for the various logics $\mathcal{U}$, $\mathcal{D}$, $\mathcal{B}$ in our framework as well as for the logic $\mathcal{H}$ used to express invariants.

Let us fix $\mathcal{U}$ as the underlying theory that is ideally needed for validating the verification conditions that arise for the program; we presume validity of formulas in $\mathcal{U}$ is undecidable. Since $\mathcal{U}$ is an undecidable theory, the engine will resort to sound approximations (e.g., using bounded quantifier instantiations using mechanisms such as triggers [33], bounded unfolding of recursive functions, or natural proofs [30,39]) to reduce this logical task to a *decidable* theory $\mathcal{D}$. This reduction is assumed to be sound in the sense that if the resulting formulas in $\mathcal{D}$ are valid, then the verification conditions are valid in $\mathcal{U}$ as well. If a formula is found *not valid* in $\mathcal{D}$, then we require that the logic solver for $\mathcal{D}$ returns a model for the negation of the formula.[1] Note that this model may not be a model for the negation of the formula in $\mathcal{U}$.

Moreover, we fix a hypothesis class $\mathcal{H}$ for invariants consisting of *positive* Boolean combination of predicates in a fixed set of predicates $\mathcal{P}$. Note that restricting to *positive* formulas over $\mathcal{P}$ is not a restriction, as one can always add negations of predicates to $\mathcal{P}$, thus effectively synthesizing any Boolean combination of predicates. The restriction to positive Boolean formulas is in fact desirable, as it allows restricting invariants to *not* negate certain predicates,

[1] Note that our framework requires model construction in the theory $\mathcal{D}$. Hence, incomplete logic solvers for $\mathcal{U}$ that simply time out after some time threshold or search for a proof of a particular kind and give up otherwise are not suitable candidates.

which is useful when predicates have intuitionistic definitions (as several recursive definitions of heap properties do).

The invariant synthesis proceeds in rounds, where in each round the synthesizer proposes invariants in $\mathcal{H}$. The verification engine generates verification conditions in accordance to these invariants in the underlying theory $\mathcal{U}$. It then proceeds to translate them into the decidable theory $\mathcal{D}$, and gives them to a solver that decides validity in the theory $\mathcal{D}$. If the verification conditions are found to be $\mathcal{D}$-valid, then by virtue of the fact that the verification engine reduced VCs in a sound fashion to $\mathcal{D}$, we are done proving the program P.

However, if the formula is found not to be $\mathcal{D}$-valid, the solver returns a $\mathcal{D}$-model for the negation of the formula. The verification engine then extracts from this model certain *non-provability information (NPI)*, expressed as Boolean formulas in a Boolean theory $\mathcal{B}$, that captures more general reasons why the verification failed (the rest of this section is devoted to developing this notion of non-provability information). This non-provability information is communicated to the synthesizer, which then proceeds to synthesize a new conjecture invariant that satisfies the non-provability constraints provided in all previous rounds.

In order for the verification engine to extract meaningful non-provability information, we make the following natural assumption, called *normality*, which essentially states that the engine can do at least some minimal Boolean reasoning (if a Hoare triple is not provable, then Boolean weakenings of the precondition and Boolean strengthening of the post-condition must also be unprovable):

Definition 1. *A verification engine is* normal *if it satisfies two properties:*

1. *if the engine cannot prove the validity of the Hoare triple* $\{\alpha\}s\{\gamma\}$ *and* $\vdash_{\mathcal{B}} \delta \Rightarrow \gamma$*, then it cannot prove the validity of the Hoare triple* $\{\alpha\}s\{\delta\}$*; and*
2. *if the engine cannot prove the validity of the Hoare triple* $\{\gamma\}s\{\beta\}$ *and* $\vdash_{\mathcal{B}} \gamma \Rightarrow \delta$*, then it cannot prove the validity of the Hoare triple* $\{\delta\}s\{\beta\}$*.*

The remainder of this section is now structured as follows. In Sect. 2.1, we first develop an appropriate language to communicate non-provability constraints, which allow the learner to appropriately weaken or strengthen a future hypothesis. It turns out that *pure conjunctions* and *pure disjunctions* over $\mathcal{P}$, which we term *CD-NPI constraints* (conjunctive/disjunctive non-provability information constraints), are sufficient for this purpose. We also describe concretely how the verification engine can extract this non-provability information from $\mathcal{D}$-models that witness that negations of VCs are satisfiable. Then, in Sect. 2.2, we show how to build learners for CD-NPI constraints by reducing this learning problem to another, well-studied learning framework for invariants called ICE learning. Section 2.3 argues the soundness of our framework and guarantees of convergence.

2.1 Conjunctive/Disjunctive Non-provability Information

We assume that the underlying decidable theory $\mathcal{D}$ is stronger than propositional theory $\mathcal{B}$, meaning that every valid statement in $\mathcal{B}$ is valid in $\mathcal{D}$ as well.

The reader may want to keep the following as a running example where $\mathcal{D}$ is the decidable theory of uninterpreted functions and linear arithmetic, say. In this setting, a formula is $\mathcal{B}$-valid if, when treating atomic formulas as Boolean variables, the formula is propositionally valid. For instance, $f(x) = y \Rightarrow f(f(x)) = f(y)$ will not be $\mathcal{B}$-valid though it is $\mathcal{D}$-valid, while $f(x) = y \vee \neg(f(x) = y)$ is $\mathcal{B}$-valid.

To formally define CD-NPI constraints and their extraction from a failed verification attempt, let us first introduce the following notation. For any $\mathcal{U}$-formula φ, let $approx(\varphi)$ denote the $\mathcal{D}$-formula that the verification engine generates such that the $\mathcal{D}$-validity of $approx(\varphi)$ implies the $\mathcal{U}$-validity of φ. Moreover, for any Hoare triple $\{\alpha\}s\{\beta\}$, let $VC(\{\alpha\}s\{\beta\})$ denote the verification condition corresponding to the Hoare triple that the verification engine generates.

Let us now assume, for the sake of a simpler exposition, that the program has a single annotation hole A where we need to synthesize an inductive invariant and prove the program correct. Further, suppose the learner conjectures an annotation γ as an inductive invariant for the annotation hole A, and the verification engine fails to prove the verification condition corresponding to a Hoare triple $\{\alpha\}s\{\beta\}$, where either α, β, or both could involve the synthesized annotation. This means that the negation of $approx(VC(\{\alpha\}s\{\gamma\}))$ is $\mathcal{D}$-satisfiable and the verification engine needs to extract non-provability information from a model of it. To this end, we assume that every program snippet s has been augmented with a set of ghost variables $g_1, \dots, g_n$ that track the predicates $p_1, \dots, p_n$ mentioned in the invariant (i.e., these ghost variables are assigned the values of the predicates). The valuation $\boldsymbol{v} = \langle v_1, \dots, v_n \rangle$ of the ghost variables in the model before the execution of s and the valuation $\boldsymbol{v}' = \langle v_1', \dots, v_n' \rangle$ after the execution of s can then be used to derive non-provability information, as we describe shortly.

The type of non-provability information the verification engine extracts depends on where the annotation appears in a Hoare triple $\{\alpha\}s\{\beta\}$. More specifically, the synthesized annotation might appear in α, in β, or in both. We now handle all three cases individually.

- Assume the verification of a Hoare triple of the form $\{\alpha\}s\{\gamma\}$ fails (i.e., the verification engine cannot prove a verification condition where the pre-condition α is a user-supplied annotation and the post-condition is the synthesized annotation γ). Then, $approx(VC(\{\alpha\}s\{\gamma\}))$ is not $\mathcal{D}$-valid, and the decision procedure for $\mathcal{D}$ would generate a model for its negation.
  Since γ is a positive Boolean combination, the reason why $\boldsymbol{v}'$ does not satisfy γ is due to the variables mapped to *false* by $\boldsymbol{v}'$, as any valuation extending this will not satisfy γ. Intuitively, this means that the $\mathcal{D}$-solver is not able to prove the predicates in $P_{false} = \{p_i \mid v_i' = false\}$. In other words, $\{\alpha\}s\{\bigvee P_{false}\}$ is unprovable (a witness to this fact is the model of the negation of $approx(VC(\{\alpha\}s\{\gamma\}))$ from which the values $\boldsymbol{v}'$ are derived). Note that any invariant γ' that is stronger than $\bigvee P_{false}$ will result in an unprovable VC due to the verification engine being normal. Consequently we can choose $\chi = \bigvee P_{false}$ as the weakening constraint, demanding that future invariants should not be stronger than χ.

The verification engine now communicates χ to the synthesizer, asking it never to conjecture in future rounds invariants γ'' that are stronger than χ (i.e., such that $\not\vdash_{\mathcal{B}} \gamma'' \Rightarrow \chi$).

- The next case is when a Hoare triple of the form $\{\gamma\}s\{\beta\}$ fails to be proven (i.e., the verification engine cannot prove a verification condition where the post-condition β is a user-supplied annotation and the pre-condition is the synthesized annotation γ). Using similar arguments as above, the *conjunction* $\eta = \bigwedge\{p_i \mid v_i = \mathit{true}\}$ of the predicates mapped to *true* by $\boldsymbol{v}$ in the corresponding $\mathcal{D}$-model gives a stronger precondition η such that $\{\eta\}s\{\alpha\}$ is not provable. Hence, η is a valid *strengthening* constraint. The verification engine now communicates η to the synthesizer, asking it never to conjecture in future rounds invariants γ'' that are weaker than η (i.e., such that $\not\vdash_{\mathcal{B}} \eta \Rightarrow \gamma''$).
- Finally, consider the case when the Hoare triple is of the form $\{\gamma\}s\{\gamma\}$ and fails to be proven (i.e., the verification engine cannot prove a verification condition where the pre- and post-condition is the synthesized annotation γ). In this case, the verification engine can offer advice on how γ can be strengthened *or* weakened to avoid this model. Analogous to the two cases above, the verification engine extracts a pair of formulas (η, χ), called an *inductivity constraint*, based on the variables mapped to *true* by $\boldsymbol{v}$ and to *false* by $\boldsymbol{v}'$. The meaning of such a constraint is that the invariant synthesizer must conjecture in future rounds invariants γ'' such that either $\not\vdash_{\mathcal{B}} \eta \Rightarrow \gamma''$ or $\not\vdash_{\mathcal{B}} \gamma'' \Rightarrow \chi$ holds.

This leads to the following scheme, where γ denotes the conjectured invariant:

- When a Hoare triple of the form $\{\alpha\}s\{\gamma\}$ fails, the verification engine returns the $\mathcal{B}$-formula $\bigvee_{i \mid v_i' = \mathit{false}} p_i$ as a weakening constraint.
- When a Hoare triple of the form $\{\gamma\}s\{\beta\}$ fails, the verification engine returns the $\mathcal{B}$-formula $\bigwedge_{i \mid v_i = \mathit{true}} p_i$ as a strengthening constraint.
- When a Hoare triple of the form $\{\gamma\}s\{\gamma\}$ fails, the verification engine returns the pair $(\bigwedge_{i \mid v_i = \mathit{true}} p_i, \bigvee_{i \mid v_i' = \mathit{false}} p_i)$ of $\mathcal{B}$-formulas as an inductivity constraint.

It is not hard to verify that the above formulas are proper strengthening and weakening constraints, in the sense that *any* inductive invariant must satisfy these constraints. This motivates the following form of non-provability information.

Definition 2 (CD-NPI Samples). *Let $\mathcal{P}$ be a set of predicates. A* CD-NPI sample *(short for* conjunction-disjunction-NPI sample*) is a triple $\mathfrak{S} = (W, S, I)$ consisting of*

- *a finite set W of disjunctions over $\mathcal{P}$ (weakening constraints);*
- *a finite set S of conjunctions over $\mathcal{P}$ (strengthening constraints); and*
- *a finite set I of pairs, where the first element is a conjunction and the second is a disjunction over $\mathcal{P}$ (inductivity constraints).*

An annotation γ *is* consistent *with a CD-NPI sample* $\mathfrak{S} = (W, S, I)$ *if* $\not\vdash_{\mathcal{B}} \gamma \Rightarrow \chi$ *for each* $\chi \in W$, $\not\vdash_{\mathcal{B}} \eta \Rightarrow \gamma$ *for each* $\eta \in S$, *and* $\not\vdash_{\mathcal{B}} \eta \Rightarrow \gamma$ *or* $\not\vdash_{\mathcal{B}} \gamma \Rightarrow \chi$ *for each* $(\eta, \chi) \in I$.

A CD-NPI learner is an effective procedure that synthesizes, given an CD-NPI sample, an annotation γ consistent with the sample. In our framework, the process of proposing candidate annotations and checking them repeats until the learner proposes a valid annotation or it detects that no valid annotation exists (e.g., if the class of candidate annotations is finite and all annotations are exhausted). We comment on using an CD-NPI learner in this iterative fashion below.

2.2 Building CD-NPI Learners

Let us now turn to the problem of building efficient learning algorithms for CD-NPI constraints. To this end, we assume that the set of predicates $\mathcal{P}$ is finite.

Roughly speaking, the CD-NPI learning problem is to synthesize annotations that are positive Boolean combinations of predicates in $\mathcal{P}$ and that are consistent with given CD-NPI samples. Though this is a learning problem where samples are *formulas*, in this section we will reduce CD-NPI learning to a learning problem from *data*. In particular, we will show that CD-NPI learning reduces to the ICE learning framework for learning positive Boolean formulas. The latter is a well-studied framework, and the reduction allows us to use efficient learning algorithms developed for ICE learning in order to build CD-NPI learners.

We now first recap the ICE-learning framework and then reduce CD-NPI learning to ICE learning. Finally, we briefly sketch how the popular HOUDINI algorithm can be seen as an ICE learning algorithm, which, in turn, allows us to use HOUDINI as an CD-NPI learning algorithm.

The ICE Learning Framework. Although the ICE learning framework [17] is a general framework for learning inductive invariants, we consider here the case of learning Boolean formulas. To this end, let us fix a set B of Boolean variables, and let $\mathcal{H}$ be a subclass of positive Boolean formulas over B, called the hypothesis class, which specifies the admissible solutions to the learning task.

The objective of the (passive) ICE learning algorithm is to learn a formula in $\mathcal{H}$ from a sample of positive examples, negative examples, and implication examples. More formally, if $\mathcal{V}$ is the set of valuations $v \colon B \rightarrow \{\mathit{true}, \mathit{false}\}$ (mapping variables in B to true or false), then an *ICE sample* is a triple $\mathcal{S} = (S_+, S_-, S_\Rightarrow)$ where $S_+ \subseteq \mathcal{V}$ is a set of *positive examples*, $S_- \subseteq \mathcal{V}$ is a set of *negative examples*, and $S_\Rightarrow \subseteq \mathcal{V} \times \mathcal{V}$ is a set of *implications*. Note that positive and negative examples are *concrete* valuations of the variables B, and the implication examples are pairs of such concrete valuations.

A formula φ is said to be *consistent with an ICE sample* $\mathcal{S}$ if it satisfies the following three conditions:[2] $v \models \varphi$ for each $v \in S_+$, $v \not\models \varphi$ for each $v \in S_-$, and $v_1 \models \varphi$ implies $v_2 \models \varphi$, for each $(v_1, v_2) \in S_\Rightarrow$.

[2] In the following, $\models$ denotes the usual satisfaction relation.

In algorithmic learning theory, one distinguishes between *passive learning* and *iterative learning*. The former refers to a learning setting in which a learning algorithm is confronted with a finite set of data and has to learn a concept that is consistent with this data. Using our terminology, the *passive ICE learning problem* for a hypothesis class $\mathcal{H}$ is then *"given an ICE sample $\mathcal{S}$, find a formula in $\mathcal{H}$ that is consistent with $\mathcal{S}$"*. Recall that we here require the learner to learn positive Boolean formulas, which is slightly stricter than the original definition [17].

Iterative learning, on the other hand, is the iteration of passive learning where new data is added to the sample from one iteration to the next. In a verification context, this new data is generated by the verification engine in response to incorrect annotations and used to guide the learning algorithm towards an annotation that is adequate to prove the program. To reduce our learning framework to ICE learning, it is therefore sufficient to reduce the (passive) CD-NPI learning problem described above to the passive ICE learning problem.

Reduction of Passive CD-NPI Learning to Passive ICE Learning. Let $\mathcal{H}$ be a subclass of positive Boolean formulas. We reduce the CD-NPI learning problem for $\mathcal{H}$ to the ICE learning problem for $\mathcal{H}$. The main idea is to (a) treat each predicate $p \in \mathcal{P}$ as a Boolean variable for the purpose of ICE learning and (b) to translate a CD-NPI sample $\mathfrak{S}$ into an *equi-consistent* ICE sample $\mathcal{S}_{\mathfrak{S}}$, meaning that a positive Boolean formula is consistent with $\mathfrak{S}$ if and only if it is consistent with $\mathcal{S}_{\mathfrak{S}}$. Then, learning a consistent formula in the CD-NPI framework for the hypothesis class $\mathcal{H}$ reduces to learning consistent formulas in $\mathcal{H}$ in the ICE learning framework.

The following lemma will help translate between the two frameworks. Its proof is straightforward, and follows from the fact that for any *positive* formula α, if a valuation v sets a larger subset of propositions to true than v' does and $v' \models \alpha$, then $v \models \alpha$ as well.

Lemma 1. *Let v be a valuation of $\mathcal{P}$ and α be a positive Boolean formula over $\mathcal{P}$. Then, the following holds:*

- *$v \models \alpha$ if and only if $\vdash_{\mathcal{B}} (\bigwedge_{p \mid v(p)=true} p) \Rightarrow \alpha$ (and, therefore, $v \not\models \alpha$ if and only if $\not\vdash_{\mathcal{B}} (\bigwedge_{p \mid v(p)=true} p) \Rightarrow \alpha$).*
- *$v \models \alpha$ if and only if $\not\vdash_{\mathcal{B}} \alpha \Rightarrow (\bigvee_{p \mid v(p)=false} p)$.*

This motivates our translation, which relies on two functions, d and c. The function d translates a disjunction $\bigvee J$, where $J \subseteq \mathcal{P}$ is a subset of propositions, into the valuation $d(\bigvee J) = v$ with $v(p) = false$ if and only if $p \in J$. The function c translates a conjunction $\bigwedge J$, where $J \subseteq \mathcal{P}$, into the valuation $c(\bigwedge J) = v$ with $v(p) = true$ if and only if $p \in J$. By substituting v in Lemma 1 with $c(\bigwedge J)$ and $d(\bigvee J)$, respectively, one immediately obtains the following.

Lemma 2. *Let $J \subseteq \mathcal{P}$ and α be a positive Boolean formula over $\mathcal{P}$. Then, the following holds:(a) $c(\bigwedge J) \not\models \alpha$ if and only if $\not\vdash_{\mathcal{B}} \bigwedge J \Rightarrow \alpha$, and (b) $d(\bigvee J) \models \alpha$ if and only if $\not\vdash_{\mathcal{B}} \alpha \Rightarrow \bigvee J$.*

Based on the functions c and d, the translation of a CD-NPI sample into an equi-consistent ICE sample is as follows.

Definition 3. *Given a CD-NPI sample* $\mathfrak{S} = (W, S, I)$*, the ICE sample* $\mathcal{S}_{\mathfrak{S}} = (S_+, S_-, S_\Rightarrow)$ *is defined by* $S_+ = \{d(\bigvee J) \mid \bigvee J \in W\}$*,* $S_- = \{c(\bigwedge J) \mid \bigwedge J \in S\}$*, and* $S_\Rightarrow = \{(c(\bigwedge J_1), d(\bigvee J_2)) \mid (\bigwedge J_1, \bigvee J_2) \in I\}$.

By virtue of the lemma above, we can now establish the correctness of the reduction from the CD-NPI learning problem to the ICE learning problem (a proof can be found in our extended paper [35]).

Theorem 1. *Let* $\mathfrak{S} = (W, S, I)$ *be a CD-NPI sample,* $\mathcal{S}_{\mathfrak{S}} = (S_+, S_-, S_\Rightarrow)$ *the ICE sample as in Definition 3,* γ *a positive Boolean formula over* $\mathcal{P}$*. Then,* γ *is consistent with* $\mathfrak{S}$ *if and only if* γ *is consistent with* $\mathcal{S}_{\mathfrak{S}}$.

ICE Learners for Boolean Formulas. The reduction above allows us to use any ICE learning algorithm in the literature that synthesizes positive Boolean formulas. As we mentioned earlier, we can add the negations of predicates as first-class predicates, and hence synthesize invariants over the class of all Boolean combinations of a finite set of predicates as well.

The problem of passive ICE learning for one round, synthesizing a formula that satisfies the ICE sample, can usually be achieved efficiently and in a variety of ways. However, the crucial aspect is not the complexity of learning in one round, but the *number* of rounds it takes to converge to an adequate invariant that proves the program correct. When the set $\mathcal{P}$ of candidate predicates is large (hundreds in our experiments), since the number of Boolean formulas over $\mathcal{P}$ is doubly exponential in $n = |\mathcal{P}|$, building an effective learner is not easy. However, there is one class of formulas that are particularly amenable to efficient ICE learning—learning *conjunctions of predicates over* $\mathcal{P}$. In this case, there are ICE learning algorithms that promise learning the invariant (provided one exists expressible as a conjunct over $\mathcal{P}$) in $n + 1$ rounds. Note that this learning is essentially finding an invariant in a hypothesis class $\mathcal{H}$ of size 2^n in $n+1$ rounds.

HOUDINI [14] is such a learning algorithm for conjunctive formulas. Though it is typically seen as a particular way to synthesize invariants, it is a prime example of an ICE learner for conjuncts, as described in the work by Garg et al. [17]. In fact, Houdini is similar to the classical PAC learning algorithm for conjunctions [26], but extended to the ICE model. The time HOUDINI spends in each round is *polynomial* and in an iterative setting, is guaranteed to converge in at most $n+1$ rounds or report that no conjunctive invariant over $\mathcal{P}$ exists. We use this ICE learner to build a CD-NPI learner for conjunctions.

2.3 Main Result

To state the main result of this paper, let us assume that the set $\mathcal{P}$ of predicates is finite. We comment on the case of infinitely many predicates below.

Theorem 2. *Assume a normal verification engine for a program P to be given. Moreover, let $\mathcal{P}$ be a finite set of predicates over the variables in P and $\mathcal{H}$ a hypothesis class consisting of positive Boolean combinations of predicates in $\mathcal{P}$. If there exists an annotation in $\mathcal{H}$ that the verification engine can use to prove P correct, then the CD-NPI framework described in Sect. 2.1 is guaranteed to converge to such an annotation in finite time.*

The proof of Theorem 2 can be found in our extended paper [35]. Under certain realistic assumptions on the CD-NPI learning algorithm, Theorem 2 remains true even if the number of predicates is infinite. An example of such an assumption is that the learning algorithm always conjectures a smallest consistent annotation with respect to some fixed total order on $\mathcal{H}$. In this case, one can show that such a learner will at some point have proposed all inadequate annotation up to the smallest annotation the verification engine can use to prove the program correct. It will then conjecture this annotation in the next iteration.

3 Application: Learning Invariants that Aid Natural Proofs for Heap Reasoning

We now develop an instantiation of our learning framework for verification engines based on natural proofs for heap reasoning [39,41].

Background: Natural Proofs and Dryad DRYAD [39,41] is a dialect of separation logic that allows expressing second order properties using recursive functions and predicates. DRYAD has a few restrictions, such as disallowing negations inside recursive definitions and in sub-formulas connected by spatial conjunctions (see [39]). DRYAD is expressive enough to state a variety of data-structures (singly and doubly linked lists, sorted lists, binary search trees, AVL trees, max-heaps, treaps), recursive definitions over them that map to numbers (length, height, etc.), as well as data stored within the heap (the multiset of keys stored in lists, trees, etc.).

The technique of using natural proofs [39,41] is a sound but incomplete strategy for deciding satisfiability of DRYAD formulas. The first step the natural proof verifier performs is to convert all predicates and functions in a DRYAD-annotated program to *classical logic*. This translation introduces *heaplets* (modeled as sets of locations) explicitly in the logic. Furthermore, it introduces assertions that demand that the accesses of each method are contained in the heaplet implicitly defined by its precondition (taking into account newly allocated or freed nodes), and that at the end of the program, the modified heaplet precisely matches the implicit heaplet defined by the post-condition.

The second step the natural proof verifier does is to perform *transformations* on the program and translate it to BOOGIE [14], an intermediate verification language that handles proof obligations using automatic theorem provers (typically SMT solvers). VCDRYAD extends VCC [8] to perform several natural proof transformations on heap-manipulating C programs that essentially perform three tasks: (a) abstract all recursive definitions on the heap using uninterpreted functions but introduce finite-depth unfoldings of recursive definitions at every place in the code where locations are dereferenced, (b) model heaplets and other sets using a decidable theory of maps, (c) insert *frame reasoning* explicitly in the code that allows the verifier to derive that certain properties continue to hold across a heap update (or function call) using the heaplet that is modified.

The resulting program is a BOOGIE program with no recursive definitions, where all verification conditions are in decidable logics, and where the logic engine can return models when formulas are satisfiable. The program can be verified if supplied with correct inductive loop-invariants and adequate pre/post conditions. We refer the reader to [39,41] for more details.

Learning Heap Invariants. We have implemented a prototype[3] that consists of the entire VCDryad pipeline, which takes C programs annotated in DRYAD and converts them to BOOGIE programs via the natural proof transformations described above. We then apply our transformation to the ICE learning framework and pair BOOGIE with an invariant synthesis engine that learns invariants over the space of conjuncts over a finite set of predicates; we describe below how these predicates are generated. After these transformations, BOOGIE satisfies the requirements on verification engines of our framework.

Given the DRYAD definitions of data structures, we automatically generate a set $\mathcal{P}$ of *predicates*, which serve as the basic building blocks of our invariants. The predicates are generated from generic templates, which are instantiated using all combinations of program variables that occur in the program being verified. We refer the reader to our extended paper [35] for a full description.

The templates define a fairly exhaustive set of predicates. These predicates include properties of the store (equality of pointer variables, equality and inequalities between integer variables, etc.), shape properties (singly and doubly linked lists and list segments, sorted lists, trees, BST, AVL, treaps, etc.), and recursive definitions that map data structures to numbers (keys/data stored in a structure, lengths of lists and list segments, height of trees) involving arithmetic relationships and set relationships. In addition, there are also predicates describing heaplets of various structures, involving set operations, disjointness, and equalities. The structures and predicates are extensible, of course.

The predicates are grouped into three categories, roughly in increasing complexity. Category 1 predicates involve shape-related properties, Category 2 involves properties related to the keys stored in the data-structure, and Category 3 predicates involve size-predicates on datastructures (lengths of lists and heights of trees). Given a program to verify and its annotations, we choose the category of predicates depending on whether the specification refers to shape only, shapes and keys, or shapes, keys, and sizes (choosing a category includes the predicates of lower category as well). Then, predicates are automatically

[3] This prototype as well as the benchmarks used to reproduce the results presented below are publicly available on figshare [36].

generated by instantiating the templates with all (combinations of) program variables; this allows us to control the size of the set of predicates used.

Evaluation. We have evaluated our prototype on ten benchmark suits (82 routines in total) that contain standard algorithms on dynamic data structures, such as searching, inserting, or deleting items in lists and trees. These benchmarks were taken from the following sources: (1) GNU C Library(glibc) singly/sorted linked lists, (2) GNU C Library(glibc) doubly linked lists, (3) OpenBSD SysQueue, (4) GRASSHOPPER [40] singly linked lists, (5) GRASSHOPPER [40] doubly linked lists, (6) GRASSHOPPER [40] sorted linked lists, (7) VCDRYAD [39] sorted linked lists, (8) VCDRYAD [39] binary search trees, AVL trees, and treaps, (9) AFWP [23] singly/sorted linked lists, and (10) ExpressOS [31] MemoryRegion. The specifications for these programs are generally checks for their full functional correctness, such as preserving or altering shapes of data structures, inserting or deleting keys, filtering or finding elements, and sortedness of elements. The specifications hence involve separation logic with arithmetic as well as recursive definitions that compute numbers (like lengths and heights), data-aggregating recursive functions (such as multisets of keys stored in data-structures), and complex combinations of these properties (e.g., to specify binary search trees, AVL trees and treaps). All programs are annotated in DRYAD, and checking validity of the resulting verification conditions is undecidable.

From these benchmark suites, we first picked all programs that contained iterative loops, *erased* the user-provided loop invariants, and used our framework to synthesize an adequate inductive invariant. We also selected some programs that were purely recursive, where the contract for the function had been strengthened to make the verification succeed. We *weakened* these contracts to only state the specification (typically by removing formulas in the post-conditions of recursively called functions) and introduced annotation holes instead. The goal was to synthesize strengthenings of these contracts that allow proving the program correct. We also chose five straight-line programs, deleted their post-conditions, and evaluated whether we can learn post-conditions for them. Since our conjunctive learner learns the strongest invariant expressible as a conjunct, we can use our framework to synthesize post-conditions as well.

After removing annotations from the benchmarks, we automatically inserted appropriate predicates over which to build invariants and contracts as described above. For all benchmark suits, conjunctions of these predicates were sufficient to prove the program correct.

Experimental Results. We performed all experiments in a virtual machine running Ubuntu 16.04.1 on a single core of an Intel Core i7-7820 HK 2.9 GHz CPU with 2 GB memory. The box plots in Fig. 2 summarize the results of this empirical evaluation aggregated by benchmark suite, specifically the time required to verify the programs, the number of automatically inserted base predicates, and the number of iterations in the learning process (see our extended paper [35] for full details). Each box in the diagrams shows the lower and upper

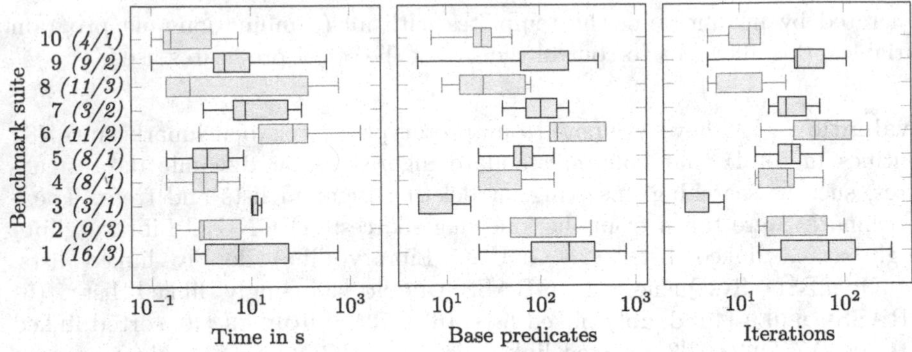

Fig. 2. Experimental evaluation of our prototype. The numbers in italic brackets shows the total number or programs in the suite (first number) and the maximum predicate category used (second number).

quartile (left and right border of the box, respectively), the median (line within the box), as well as the minimum and maximum (left and right whisker, respectively).

Our prototype was successful in learning invariants and contracts for all 82 benchmarks. The fact that the median time for a great majority of benchmark suits is less than 10 s shows that our technique is extremely effective in finding inductive DRYAD invariants. We observe that despite many examples having hundreds of base predicates, which suggests a worst-case complexity of hundreds of iterations, the learner was able to learn with much fewer iterations and the number of predicates in the final invariant is small. This shows that non-provability information provides much more information than the worst-case suggests.

To the best of our knowledge, our prototype is the only tool currently able of fully automatically verifying this challenging benchmark set. We must emphasize, however, that there are subsets of our benchmarks that can be solved by reformulating verification in decidable fragments of separation logic studied—we refer the reader to the related work in Sect. 1 for a survey of such work. Our goal in this evaluation, however, is not to compete with other, mature tools on a subset of benchmarks, but to measure the efficacy of our proposed CD-NPI based invariant synthesis framework on the whole benchmark set.

4 Conclusions and Future Work

We have presented a learning-based framework for invariant synthesis in the presence of sound but incomplete verification engines. To prove that our technique is effective in practice, we have implemented a prototype, based on the natural proofs verification engine, and demonstrated that this prototype can verify a large set of heap-manipulating programs against specifications expressed in an expressive and undecidable dialect of separation logic. We are not aware of any other technique that can handle this extremely challenging benchmark suite.

Several future research directions are interesting. First, the framework we have developed is based on CEGIS where the invariant synthesizer synthesizes invariants using non-provability information but does not directly work on the program's structure. It would be interesting to extend white-box invariant generation techniques such as interpolation/IC3/PDR, working using $\mathcal{D}$ (or $\mathcal{B}$) abstractions of the program directly in order to synthesize invariants for them. Second, in the NPI learning framework we have put forth, it would be interesting to change the underlying logic of communication $\mathcal{B}$ to a richer logic, say the theory of arithmetic and uninterpreted functions; the challenge here would be to extract non-provability information from the models to the richer theory, and pairing them with synthesis engines that synthesize expressions against constraints in $\mathcal{B}$. Finally, we think invariant learning should also include *experience* gained in verifying other programs in the past, both manually and automatically. A learning algorithm that combines logic-based synthesis with experience and priors gained from repositories of verified programs can be more effective.

Data Availability Statement and Acknowledgments. The prototype developed in this project as well as the benchmarks used to produce the results presented in this work are available in the figshare repository at https://doi.org/10.6084/m9.figshare.5928094.v1.

This material is based upon work supported by the National Science Foundation under Grants #1138994, and #1527395.

References

1. Albargouthi, A., Berdine, J., Cook, B., Kincaid, Z.: Spatial interpolants. In: Vitek, J. (ed.) ESOP 2015. LNCS, vol. 9032, pp. 634–660. Springer, Heidelberg (2015). https://doi.org/10.1007/978-3-662-46669-8_26
2. Ball, T., Majumdar, R., Millstein, T.D., Rajamani, S.K.: Automatic predicate abstraction of C programs. In: PLDI 2001, pp. 203–213 (2001)
3. Barnett, M., Chang, B.-Y.E., DeLine, R., Jacobs, B., Leino, K.R.M.: Boogie: a modular reusable verifier for object-oriented programs. In: de Boer, F.S., Bonsangue, M.M., Graf, S., de Roever, W.-P. (eds.) FMCO 2005. LNCS, vol. 4111, pp. 364–387. Springer, Heidelberg (2006). https://doi.org/10.1007/11804192_17
4. Bradley, A.R.: SAT-based model checking without unrolling. In: Jhala, R., Schmidt, D. (eds.) VMCAI 2011. LNCS, vol. 6538, pp. 70–87. Springer, Heidelberg (2011). https://doi.org/10.1007/978-3-642-18275-4_7
5. Calcagno, C., Distefano, D., O'Hearn, P.W., Yang, H.: Compositional shape analysis by means of bi-abduction. J. ACM **58**(6), 26 (2011)
6. Chin, W.N., David, C., Nguyen, H.H., Qin, S.: Automated verification of shape, size and bag properties via user-defined predicates in separation logic. Sci. Comput. Program. **77**(9), 1006–1036 (2012)
7. Chu, D., Jaffar, J., Trinh, M.: Automatic induction proofs of data-structures in imperative programs. In: PLDI 2015, pp. 457–466. ACM (2015)
8. Cohen, E., Dahlweid, M., Hillebrand, M., Leinenbach, D., Moskal, M., Santen, T., Schulte, W., Tobies, S.: VCC: a practical system for verifying concurrent C. In: Berghofer, S., Nipkow, T., Urban, C., Wenzel, M. (eds.) TPHOLs 2009. LNCS, vol. 5674, pp. 23–42. Springer, Heidelberg (2009). https://doi.org/10.1007/978-3-642-03359-9_2

9. Colón, M.A., Sankaranarayanan, S., Sipma, H.B.: Linear invariant generation using non-linear constraint solving. In: Hunt, W.A., Somenzi, F. (eds.) CAV 2003. LNCS, vol. 2725, pp. 420–432. Springer, Heidelberg (2003). https://doi.org/10.1007/978-3-540-45069-6_39
10. Cousot, P., Cousot, R.: Abstract interpretation: a unified lattice model for static analysis of programs by construction or approximation of fixpoints. In: POPL 1977, pp. 238–252. ACM Press (1977)
11. Dillig, I., Dillig, T., Li, B., McMillan, K.L.: Inductive invariant generation via abductive inference. In: OOPSLA 2013, pp. 443–456 (2013)
12. Een, N., Mishchenko, A., Brayton, R.: Efficient implementation of property directed reachability. In: FMCAD 2011, pp. 125–134. FMCAD Inc (2011)
13. Ernst, M.D., Czeisler, A., Griswold, W.G., Notkin, D.: Quickly detecting relevant program invariants. In: ICSE 2000, pp. 449–458. ACM Press (2000)
14. Flanagan, C., Leino, K.R.M.: Houdini, an annotation assistant for ESC/Java. In: Oliveira, J.N., Zave, P. (eds.) FME 2001. LNCS, vol. 2021, pp. 500–517. Springer, Heidelberg (2001). https://doi.org/10.1007/3-540-45251-6_29
15. Floyd, R.W.: Assigning meanings to programs. In: Schwartz, J.T. (ed.) Proceedings of a Symposium on Applied Mathematics. Mathematical Aspects of Computer Science, vol. 19, pp. 19–31. American Mathematical Society (1967)
16. Garg, P., Löding, C., Madhusudan, P., Neider, D.: Learning universally quantified invariants of linear data structures. In: Sharygina, N., Veith, H. (eds.) CAV 2013. LNCS, vol. 8044, pp. 813–829. Springer, Heidelberg (2013). https://doi.org/10.1007/978-3-642-39799-8_57
17. Garg, P., Löding, C., Madhusudan, P., Neider, D.: ICE: a robust framework for learning invariants. In: Biere, A., Bloem, R. (eds.) CAV 2014. LNCS, vol. 8559, pp. 69–87. Springer, Cham (2014). https://doi.org/10.1007/978-3-319-08867-9_5
18. Garg, P., Madhusudan, P., Neider, D., Roth, D.: Learning invariants using decision trees and implication counterexamples. In: POPL 2016, pp. 499–512 (2016)
19. Ge, Y., de Moura, L.: Complete instantiation for quantified formulas in satisfiabiliby modulo theories. In: Bouajjani, A., Maler, O. (eds.) CAV 2009. LNCS, vol. 5643, pp. 306–320. Springer, Heidelberg (2009). https://doi.org/10.1007/978-3-642-02658-4_25
20. Gulwani, S., Srivastava, S., Venkatesan, R.: Program analysis as constraint solving. In: PLDI 2008, pp. 281–292. ACM (2008)
21. Gupta, A., Rybalchenko, A.: InvGen: an efficient invariant generator. In: Bouajjani, A., Maler, O. (eds.) CAV 2009. LNCS, vol. 5643, pp. 634–640. Springer, Heidelberg (2009). https://doi.org/10.1007/978-3-642-02658-4_48
22. Hoare, C.A.R.: An axiomatic basis for computer programming. Commun. ACM **12**(10), 576–580 (1969)
23. Itzhaky, S., Banerjee, A., Immerman, N., Nanevski, A., Sagiv, M.: Effectively-propositional reasoning about reachability in linked data structures. In: Sharygina, N., Veith, H. (eds.) CAV 2013. LNCS, vol. 8044, pp. 756–772. Springer, Heidelberg (2013). https://doi.org/10.1007/978-3-642-39799-8_53
24. Itzhaky, S., Bjørner, N., Reps, T., Sagiv, M., Thakur, A.: Property-directed shape analysis. In: Biere, A., Bloem, R. (eds.) CAV 2014. LNCS, vol. 8559, pp. 35–51. Springer, Cham (2014). https://doi.org/10.1007/978-3-319-08867-9_3
25. Karbyshev, A., Bjørner, N., Itzhaky, S., Rinetzky, N., Shoham, S.: Property-directed inference of universal invariants or proving their absence. In: Kroening, D., Păsăreanu, C.S. (eds.) CAV 2015. LNCS, vol. 9206, pp. 583–602. Springer, Cham (2015). https://doi.org/10.1007/978-3-319-21690-4_40

26. Kearns, M.J., Vazirani, U.V.: An Introduction to Computational Learning Theory. MIT Press, Cambridge (1994)
27. Krishna, S., Puhrsch, C., Wies, T.: Learning invariants using decision trees. CoRR abs/1501.04725 (2015)
28. Le, Q.L., Gherghina, C., Qin, S., Chin, W.-N.: Shape analysis via second-order bi-abduction. In: Biere, A., Bloem, R. (eds.) CAV 2014. LNCS, vol. 8559, pp. 52–68. Springer, Cham (2014). https://doi.org/10.1007/978-3-319-08867-9_4
29. Leino, K.R.M.: Dafny: an automatic program verifier for functional correctness. In: Clarke, E.M., Voronkov, A. (eds.) LPAR 2010. LNCS (LNAI), vol. 6355, pp. 348–370. Springer, Heidelberg (2010). https://doi.org/10.1007/978-3-642-17511-4_20
30. Löding, C., Madhusudan, P., Peña, L.: Foundations for natural proofs and quantifier instantiation. PACMPL **2**(POPL), 10:1–10:30 (2018). http://doi.acm.org/10.1145/3158098
31. Mai, H., Pek, E., Xue, H., King, S.T., Madhusudan, P.: Verifying security invariants in expressos. In: ASPLOS 2013, pp. 293–304. ACM (2013)
32. McMillan, K.L.: Interpolation and SAT-based model checking. In: Hunt, W.A., Somenzi, F. (eds.) CAV 2003. LNCS, vol. 2725, pp. 1–13. Springer, Heidelberg (2003). https://doi.org/10.1007/978-3-540-45069-6_1
33. de Moura, L., Bjørner, N.: Efficient E-matching for SMT solvers. In: Pfenning, F. (ed.) CADE 2007. LNCS (LNAI), vol. 4603, pp. 183–198. Springer, Heidelberg (2007). https://doi.org/10.1007/978-3-540-73595-3_13
34. de Moura, L., Bjørner, N.: Z3: an efficient SMT solver. In: Ramakrishnan, C.R., Rehof, J. (eds.) TACAS 2008. LNCS, vol. 4963, pp. 337–340. Springer, Heidelberg (2008). https://doi.org/10.1007/978-3-540-78800-3_24
35. Neider, D., Garg, P., Madhusudan, P., Saha, S., Park, D.: Invariant synthesis for incomplete verification engines. CoRR abs/1712.05581 (2017). https://arxiv.org/abs/1712.05581
36. Neider, D., Garg, P., Madhusudan, P., Saha, S., Park, D.: Prototype and benchmarks for "invariant synthesis for incomplete verification engines", February 2018. https://doi.org/10.6084/m9.figshare.5928094.v1
37. Padhi, S., Sharma, R., Millstein, T.D.: Data-driven precondition inference with learned features. In: PLDI 2016, pp. 42–56 (2016)
38. Pavlinovic, Z., Lal, A., Sharma, R.: Inferring annotations for device drivers from verification histories. In: ASE 2016, pp. 450–460 (2016)
39. Pek, E., Qiu, X., Madhusudan, P.: Natural proofs for data structure manipulation in C using separation logic. In: PLDI 2014, p. 46. ACM (2014)
40. Piskac, R., Wies, T., Zufferey, D.: Automating separation logic using SMT. In: Sharygina, N., Veith, H. (eds.) CAV 2013. LNCS, vol. 8044, pp. 773–789. Springer, Heidelberg (2013). https://doi.org/10.1007/978-3-642-39799-8_54
41. Qiu, X., Garg, P., Stefanescu, A., Madhusudan, P.: Natural proofs for structure, data, and separation. In: PLDI 2013, pp. 231–242. ACM (2013)
42. Sagiv, M., Reps, T., Wilhelm, R.: Parametric shape analysis via 3-valued logic. In: POPL 1999, pp. 105–118. ACM (1999)
43. Sharma, R., Aiken, A.: From invariant checking to invariant inference using randomized search. In: Biere, A., Bloem, R. (eds.) CAV 2014. LNCS, vol. 8559, pp. 88–105. Springer, Cham (2014). https://doi.org/10.1007/978-3-319-08867-9_6
44. Sharma, R., Gupta, S., Hariharan, B., Aiken, A., Liang, P., Nori, A.V.: A data driven approach for algebraic loop invariants. In: Felleisen, M., Gardner, P. (eds.) ESOP 2013. LNCS, vol. 7792, pp. 574–592. Springer, Heidelberg (2013). https://doi.org/10.1007/978-3-642-37036-6_31

45. Sharma, R., Gupta, S., Hariharan, B., Aiken, A., Nori, A.V.: Verification as learning geometric concepts. In: Logozzo, F., Fähndrich, M. (eds.) SAS 2013. LNCS, vol. 7935, pp. 388–411. Springer, Heidelberg (2013). https://doi.org/10.1007/978-3-642-38856-9_21
46. Sharma, R., Nori, A.V., Aiken, A.: Interpolants as classifiers. In: Madhusudan, P., Seshia, S.A. (eds.) CAV 2012. LNCS, vol. 7358, pp. 71–87. Springer, Heidelberg (2012). https://doi.org/10.1007/978-3-642-31424-7_11
47. Zhu, H., Nori, A.V., Jagannathan, S.: Learning refinement types. In: ICFP 2015, pp. 400–411. ACM (2015)

Accelerating Syntax-Guided Invariant Synthesis

Grigory Fedyukovich[1](✉) and Rastislav Bodík[2]

[1] Princeton University, Princeton, USA
grigoryf@cs.princeton.edu
[2] University of Washington, Seattle, USA
bodik@cs.washington.edu

Abstract. We present a fast algorithm for syntax-guided synthesis of inductive invariants which combines enumerative learning with inductive-subset extraction, leverages counterexamples-to-induction and interpolation-based bounded proofs. It is a variant of a recently proposed probabilistic method, called FreqHorn, which is however less dependent on heuristics than its predecessor. We present an evaluation of the new algorithm on a large set of benchmarks and show that it exhibits a more predictable behavior than its predecessor, and it is competitive to the state-of-the-art invariant synthesizers based on Property Directed Reachability.

1 Introduction

Syntax-guided techniques [1] recently earned significant success in the field of synthesis of inductive invariants [13] for a given program and a given safety specification. Invariants are needed to represent over-approximations of the set of reachable program states, such that from their empty intersection with the set of error states one could conclude that the program is safe. While searching for invariants, it is intuitive to collect various statistics from the syntactical constructions, which appear in the program's source code, and use them as a guidance.

This work continues the track of FreqHorn, a completely automatic approach for (1) construction of the formal grammar based on the symbolic program encoding, and (2) probabilistic search through the candidate formulas belonging to that grammar. FreqHorn utilizes an SMT solver for checking inductiveness of each generated formula and iteratively constructs a suitable invariant based on the successful attempts (those formulas are called lemmas). Since based on a finite number of expressions, the formal grammar is sufficiently small, and thus the candidate formulas can be enumerated relatively quickly. We distinguish two types of candidates: (1) formulas directly extracted from the program's encoding (called *seeds*) and (2) formulas which are syntactically close to seeds (called *mutants*).

The conceptual novelty of FreqHorn is believed to be in the combined use of seeds and mutants, but the original paper [13] is largely silent on the

D. Beyer and M. Huisman (Eds.): TACAS 2018, LNCS 10805, pp. 251–269, 2018.
https://doi.org/10.1007/978-3-319-89960-2_14

matter. Furthermore, it turns a blind eye to some algorithmic and practical details which are required for making the approach actually efficient. Among the downsides are (1) the treatment of all syntactic expressions equally and ignorance to whether the candidates have any relevance to the given safety specification; and (2) inability to predict a more-or-less appropriate order of candidates to be sampled and checked.

Luckily, elements of the Property Directed Reachability (PDR) [4,10] can be adapted in various stages of FreqHorn's workflow and can mitigate the downsides of the original algorithm. In particular, we propose to check candidates in batches, and we show that in practice it helps discovering larger amounts of lemmas. Additionally, we propose to keep a history of counterexamples-to-induction (CTI) which blocked FreqHorn from learning a lemma. With some periodicity, our new algorithm checks if there is a CTI which is invalidated by the currently learned lemmas, and this triggers the re-check of that failed lemma.

Last but not least, we integrate our new algorithm with the classic techniques based on Bounded Model Checking [3]. We propose to compute additional candidates by Craig interpolation [6] from proofs of bounded safety. We show that it is often sufficient to obtain some fixed amount of candidates from interpolants in the beginning of the synthesis process, and further to *bootstrap* the initial set of learned lemmas by the inductive subset extracted from the combination of the syntactic seeds and interpolants. In contrast to the entirely randomized workflow of the original version of FreqHorn, the behavior of our revised implementation at the bootstrapping is predictable. The randomized search is used by the new algorithm only for discovering mutants; and in our experiments, it was required in about one third of cases only.

To sum up, the paper contributes to the previous knowledge in the following main respects:

- A new revision and a new implementation of the FreqHorn algorithm which is split into the bootstrapping and the sampling stages. In the first stage, it deterministically exploits seeds only. In the second stage, it keeps generating and checking only mutants, and it is by design nondeterministic.
- In the bootstrapping stage, interpolation-based proofs of bounded safety that replenish the set of seeds by the candidates that likely reflect the nature of the error unreachability and consequently affect the grammar-based generation of mutants.
- In the sampling stage, the routine to extract inductive subsets which mitigates the effect of an unpredictably chosen sampling order.
- A more accurate strategy for the search space pruning and an efficient counterexample-guided approach to give some failed candidates a second chance.

The rest of the paper is structured as follows. In Sect. 2, we briefly formulate the inductive synthesis problem, and in Sect. 3 we sketch the basic FreqHorn algorithm that attempts to solve it. With the help of techniques from Sect. 4, in Sect. 5 the FreqHorn algorithm gets augmented and reformulated. In Sect. 6, we show the experimental evidence that it indeed outperforms its predecessor and is competitive to state-of-the-art. Finally, the related work, conclusion, and acknowledgments complete the paper in Sects. 7 and 8.

2 Background and Notation

A first-order theory $\mathcal{T}$ consists of a signature Σ, which gathers variables, function and predicate symbols, and a set *Expr* of Σ-formulas. Formula $\varphi \in \mathit{Expr}$ is called $\mathcal{T}$-satisfiable if there exists an interpretation m of each element (i.e., a variable, a function or a predicate symbol), under which φ evaluates to $\top$ (denoted $m \models \varphi$); otherwise φ is called $\mathcal{T}$-unsatisfiable (denoted $\varphi \implies \bot$). The Satisfiability Modulo Theory (SMT) problem [8] for a given theory $\mathcal{T}$ and a formula φ aims at determining whether φ is $\mathcal{T}$-satisfiable. In this work, we formulate the tasks arising in program verification by encoding them to the SMT problems.

Definition 1. *A* transition system *P is a tuple $\langle V \cup V', \mathit{Init}, \mathit{Tr}\rangle$, where V' is a primed copy of a set of variables V; Init and Tr are $\mathcal{T}$-encodings of respectively the* initial states *and the* transition relation.

We view *programs* as *transition systems* and throughout the paper use both terms interchangeably. *Verification task* is a pair $\langle P, \mathit{Bad}\rangle$, where $P = \langle V \cup V', \mathit{Init}, \mathit{Tr}\rangle$ is a program, and *Bad* is a $\mathcal{T}$-encoding the *error states.* A verification task has a solution if the set of error states is unreachable. A solution to the verification task is represented by a *safe inductive invariant,* a formula that covers every initial state, is closed under the transition relation, and does not cover any of the error states.

Definition 2. *Let $P = \langle V \cup V', \mathit{Init}, \mathit{Tr}\rangle$; a formula Inv is a* safe inductive invariant *if the following conditions (respectively called an initiation, a consecution, and a safety) hold:*

$$\mathit{Init}(V) \implies \mathit{Inv}(V) \tag{1}$$

$$\mathit{Inv}(V) \wedge \mathit{Tr}(V, V') \implies \mathit{Inv}(V') \tag{2}$$

$$\mathit{Inv}(V) \wedge \mathit{Bad}(V) \implies \bot \tag{3}$$

To simplify reading, in the rest of the paper *safe inductive invariants* are referred to as just *invariants.* We assume that an invariant *Inv* has the form of conjunction, i.e., $\mathit{Inv} = \ell_0 \wedge \ldots \wedge \ell_n$, and each ℓ_i is called a *lemma.*

The validity of each implication (1) and (2) is equivalent to the unsatisfiability of the negation of the corresponding formula. Suppose, a formula *Inv* makes (1) valid, but does not make (2) valid. Thus, there exists an interpretation m satisfying $\mathit{Inv}(V) \wedge \mathit{Tr}(V, V') \wedge \neg\mathit{Inv}(V')$, to which we refer to as a *counterexample-to-induction* (CTI).

Example 1. The loop in program in Fig. 1a iterates `N` times, and in each iteration it nondeterministically picks a value `M`, adds it to `x` (conditionally) and to `c`,

```
int x, k, c = 0;
int N = NONDET();
while (c < N) {
  int M = NONDET();
  if (k mod 2 == 0)
    x = x + M;
  c = c + M;
  k = x + c;
}
assert (x ≥ N);
```

(a)

$x = 0$
$c = 0$
$k = 0$
$c < N$
$k \texttt{ mod } 2 = 0$
$k = x + c$
$c \geq N$
$x \geq N$

(b)

$$\begin{aligned}
\alpha &::= 1 \mid -1\\
\beta &::= 0 \mid 2\\
\gamma &::= x \mid y \mid k \mid N\\
\delta &::= \alpha \cdot \gamma + \ldots + \alpha \cdot \gamma \mid \gamma \texttt{ mod } \beta\\
\mathit{cand} &::= \delta = \beta \mid \delta > \beta \mid \delta \geq \beta
\end{aligned}$$

(c)

$$\begin{cases}
x = 0 \wedge k = 0 \wedge c = 0 \implies \boldsymbol{Inv}(x, k, c, N)\\
\boldsymbol{Inv}(x, k, c, N) \wedge c < N \wedge x' = \texttt{ite } (k \texttt{ mod } 2 = 0, x + M, x) \wedge\\
\qquad c' = c + M \wedge k' = x' + c' \implies \boldsymbol{Inv}(x', k', c', N)\\
\boldsymbol{Inv}(x, k, c, N) \wedge c \geq N \wedge \neg(x \geq N) \implies \bot
\end{cases}$$

(d)

Fig. 1. Loopy program **(a)**, its encoding **(d)**, subexpressions extracted from the encoding **(b)**, and grammar that generalizes the subexpressions **(c)**.

and assigns the sum of `x` and `c` to `k`. We wish to prove that after the loop terminates, `x` $\geq$ `N`. An invariant for the program is defined non-uniquely, e.g., both the conjunction ($k \texttt{ mod } 2 = 0 \wedge x = c$) and conjunction ($k = x + c \wedge x \geq c$) are the solutions for this verification task. □

3 Syntax-Guided Invariant Synthesis

In this work, we aim at discovering invariants in an enumerative way, i.e., by guessing a candidate formula, substituting it for conditions (1), (2), and (3), and checking their validity. Here we present a moderately reformulated and simplified view of an algorithm recently proposed in [13].[1] The pseudocode of the algorithm, called FreqHorn, is shown in Algorithm 1. The key insight behind the algorithm is the automatic construction of a grammar G (line 2) based on a

[1] The original description [13] focuses on the probabilistic routines. In the interest of this work, we do not discuss them here but restrict our attention on describing and exemplifying the pre-processing steps.

Algorithm 1. FreqHorn: Sampling inductive invariants, **cf.** [13].

Input: $\langle P, \mathit{Bad}\rangle$: verification task, where $P = \langle V \cup V', \mathit{Init}, \mathit{Tr}\rangle$
Output: $\mathit{Lemmas} \subseteq 2^{\mathit{Expr}}$

1 $\mathit{Seeds} \leftarrow$ getSubExprs($\mathit{Init}, \mathit{Tr}, \mathit{Bad}$);
2 $G \leftarrow$ getGrammarAndDistributions(Seeds);
3 $\mathit{Lemmas} \leftarrow \varnothing$;
4 **while** $\mathit{Bad}(V) \wedge \bigwedge_{\ell \in \mathit{Lemmas}} \ell(V) \not\Longrightarrow \bot$ **do**
5 $\quad \mathit{cand} \leftarrow$ sample(G);
6 $\quad \mathit{res} \leftarrow (\mathit{Init}(V) \Longrightarrow \mathit{cand}(V)) \wedge (\mathit{cand}(V) \wedge \bigwedge_{\ell \in \mathit{Lemmas}} \ell(V) \wedge \mathit{Tr}(V, V') \Longrightarrow \mathit{cand}(V'))$;
7 $\quad$ **if** res **then**
8 $\quad\quad \mathit{Lemmas} \leftarrow \mathit{Lemmas} \cup \{\mathit{cand}\}$;
9 $\quad G \leftarrow$ adjust($G, \mathit{cand}, \mathit{res}$);

fixed set *Seeds* of expressions obtained by traversing parse trees of *Init*, *Tr*, and *Bad* (line 1).

To create G from *Seeds*, we drop all expressions that contain variables from both, V and V', and deprime all variables in the remaining expressions. Then, we normalize elements of *Seeds* to have the form of equalities, inequalities, or disjunctions of equalities and inequalities. Finally, formulas are rewritten, such that all terms are moved to the left side, and the subtraction, $<$, and $\leq$ are rewritten respectively as the addition, $>$, and $\geq$.

The algorithm uses G for generating the candidate formulas (line 5) and populates the set of lemmas until their conjunction is an invariant. The algorithm learns from each positive and negative attempt (line 9). That is, G gets adjusted, such that the candidate (and some of its close relatives) is not going to be sampled in any of the following iterations.

Example 2. The verification condition for the program in Fig. 1a is represented by three implications in Fig. 1d. They are syntactically split into the set *Seeds* of expressions over V, elements of which used to contain only primed or only unprimed variables (shown in Fig. 1b). In particular, equalities $x' = x + M$ and $c' = c + M$ are excluded from *Seeds*, and equality $k' = x' + c'$ is rewritten to $k = x + c$. The grammar containing the normalized expressions from *Seeds* is shown in Fig. 1c. It is easy to see that all lemmas consisting in both invariants from Example 1, $(k \,\mathtt{mod}\, 2 = 0 \wedge x = c)$ and $(k = x + c \wedge x \geq c)$, can be generated by applying the grammar's production rules recursively. □

Definition 3. *Each formula contained in set Seeds, which is used for constructing grammar G (in line 2), is called a* seed. *Formula cand produced by G is called a* mutant *if* $\mathit{cand} \notin \mathit{Seeds}$.

The main downside of Algorithm 1 is that it is hard to choose a sampling order for each individual lemma at the final invariant. Suppose, $cand = (x = c)$ is sampled and checked in the first iteration of Algorithm 1. Consequently, condition (2) is not fulfilled, and it is witnessed by the following CTI: $[x \leftarrow 0; k \leftarrow 1; c \leftarrow 0; N \leftarrow 10; x' \leftarrow 0; k' \leftarrow 7; c \leftarrow 7; M \leftarrow 7]$. The grammar is then adjusted, such that $x = c$ (and some syntactically relevant, stronger or equivalent formulas, e.g. $-x = -c$) do not belong to the grammar anymore.

Suppose, in the second iteration of Algorithm 1, $cand = (k \,\texttt{mod}\, 2 = 0)$. It passes checks (1) and (2), gets inserted to set *Lemmas*, and thus it is going to be taken into account in the following iterations (see implications in lines 4 and 6). The grammar is then adjusted again, such that $k \,\texttt{mod}\, 2 = 0$ (and some weaker or equivalent formulas, e.g. $k \,\texttt{mod}\, 2 \geq 0$) do not belong to the grammar anymore. Note that if in the third iteration $cand = (x = c)$ was sampled again, the algorithm would terminate. However, it is impossible since the sampling grammar was adjusted after both negative and positive attempts.

The opposite sampling order (i.e., $cand = (k \,\texttt{mod}\, 2 = 0)$ first, and $cand = (x = c)$ then) would lead to a faster convergence of the algorithm. Since it is hard to decide which order to choose, the production rules are equipped with probability distributions that allow both orders under certain probabilities. In this paper, we propose to use a strategy which is less dependent on an order – to check candidates in batches – and we describe it in Sect. 5 in more detail.

4 Old Friends Are Best

In this section, we rehash two ideas widely used in symbolic model checking that can be adapted to accelerate syntax-guided invariant synthesis.

4.1 Interpolation-Based Proofs of Bounded Safety

Bounded Model Checking (BMC) [3] is a formal technique, primarily used for bug finding. Given a transition system $\langle V \cup V', \mathit{Init}, \mathit{Tr} \rangle$, set of error states *Bad*, and a non-negative integer number k, the *BMC task* is to check if there exists a path of length k ending in an error state. The idea is to unroll *Tr* k times, conjoin it with *Init* and with the negation of *Bad*, and to check the satisfiability of the resulting formula (called a BMC formula):

$$\mathit{Init}(V) \wedge \underbrace{\mathit{Tr}(V, V') \wedge \mathit{Tr}(V', V'') \wedge \ldots \wedge \mathit{Tr}(V^{(k-1)}, V^{(k)})}_{k} \wedge \mathit{Bad}(V^{(k)})$$

Algorithm 2. BMCITP: Obtaining bounded proofs, **cf.** [24, 25].

Input: $\langle P, Bad \rangle$: verification task, where $P = \langle V \cup V', Init, Tr \rangle$, k: bound
Output: $proof \subseteq 2^{Expr}$

1 $unr \leftarrow \top$;
2 **for** $(i \leftarrow k;\ i > 0;\ i \leftarrow i - 1)$ **do**
3 $\quad unr \leftarrow unr \wedge Tr(V^{(i-1)}, V^{(i)})$;
4 $\quad$ **if** $unr \wedge Bad(V^{(k)}) \implies \bot$ **then**
5 $\quad\quad proof \leftarrow$ GETITP$(unr, Bad(V^{(k)}))$;
6 $\quad\quad$ **return**;
7 $unr \leftarrow unr \wedge Bad(V^{(k)})$;
8 **if** $Init(V^{(0)}) \wedge unr \implies \bot$ **then**
9 $\quad proof \leftarrow$ GETITP$(Init(V^{(0)}), unr)$;

Here, each $V^{(i)}$ is a fresh copy of V. Each satisfying assignment to the BMC formula represents a counterexample of length k. Otherwise, if the formula is unsatisfiable, then no counterexample of length k exists.

Lemma 1. *If a BMC formula for program P and some k is satisfiable then no invariant exists.*

A proof of *bounded safety* is an over-approximation I of the set of initial states, such that any path of length k, that starts in a state satisfying I, does not end in a state satisfying *Bad*. Extraction of proofs is typically done with the help of Craig interpolation [6].

Definition 4. *Given two formulas A and B, such that $A \wedge B \implies \bot$, an interpolant I is a formula satisfying three conditions: (1) $A \implies I$, (2) $I \wedge B \implies \bot$, and (3) I is expressed over the common alphabet to A and B.*

For an invocation of a procedure of generating an interpolant I for A and B and splitting it to a set of conjunction-free clauses (i.e., $I = \ell_0 \wedge \cdots \wedge \ell_n$), we write $\{\ell_i\} \leftarrow$ GETITP(A, B). Algorithm 2 shows an algorithm to generate interpolation-based proofs of bounded safety for BMC formulas. It iteratively unrolls the transition relation and applies the interpolation to the entire BMC formula. In addition, in spirit of Lazy Annotation [25], while decrementing i, the algorithm applies a backward reasoning and checks if an error state is reachable by $(k - i)$ steps from an empty state (line 4). It triggers the interpolation to be applied to smaller formulas, and in some cases fastens the proof search (line 5).

Example 3. Let the program in Fig. 1a is unrolled 0 times, then its BMC formula is constructed as follows: $\underbrace{x = 0 \wedge k = 0 \wedge c = 0}_{Init} \wedge \underbrace{c \geq N \wedge \neg(x \geq N)}_{Bad}$. It is unsatisfiable, and since interpolants are not unique, function GETITP$(Init, Bad)$ could return $proof_1 = \{x \geq 0, c \leq 0\}$, $proof_2 = \{x = c\}$, or $proof_3 = \{x \geq c\}$. □

Algorithm 3. HOUDINI: Calculating an inductive subset, **cf.** [14] and keeping counterexamples-to-induction.

Input: $P = \langle V \cup V', \mathit{Init}, \mathit{Tr} \rangle$: program; $\mathit{Cands} \subseteq 2^{\mathit{Expr}}$;
$\mathit{CTI} \subseteq 2^{V \to \mathbb{R}}$; CTImap: $\mathit{CTI} \to 2^{\mathit{Expr}}$

Output: inductive $\mathit{Cands} \subseteq 2^{\mathit{Expr}}$; updated CTI and CTImap

1 **while** $\bigwedge_{\mathit{cand}' \in \mathit{Cands}} \mathit{cand}'(V) \wedge \mathit{Tr}(V, V') \not\Rightarrow \bigwedge_{\mathit{cand}' \in \mathit{Cands}} \mathit{cand}'(V')$ **do**

2   **for** $\mathit{cand} \in \mathit{Cands}$ **do**

3   **if** $\exists \pi$, s.t. $\pi \models (\bigwedge_{\mathit{cand}' \in \mathit{Cands}} \mathit{cand}'(V) \wedge \mathit{Tr}(V, V') \wedge \neg \mathit{cand}(V'))$ **then**

4             $\mathit{Cands} \leftarrow \mathit{Cands} \setminus \{\mathit{cand}\}$;

5             $\mathit{CTI} \leftarrow \mathit{CTI} \cup \{\pi|_V\}$;

6             $\mathit{CTImap}(\pi|_V) \leftarrow \mathit{CTImap}(\pi|_V) \cup \mathit{cand}$;

4.2 Inductive Subset Extraction

When checking the consecution of a set of candidate formulas "*one-by-one*" (i.e., like in Algorithm 1), the order of checks is crucial, and the chance to miss some important lemma is high. It can be overcome by checking all candidate formulas at once, identifying which ones brake the validity of implication (2), removing them from the set, and repeating the "*all-at-once*" check. Algorithm 3 shows a simple implementation of this iterative algorithm, which is extensively used in PDR and also known as HOUDINI [14], Note that HOUDINI is only meaningful for the candidate formulas which are already implied by the initial states.

Example 4. Conjunction of formulas from set *Seeds* in Fig. 1b is unsatisfiable, and its minimal unsatisfiable core is $c < N \wedge c \geq N$. Thus, Algorithm 3 would immediately return the entire set *Seeds*. Let a set *Cands* be constructed from *Seeds* by removing all elements, for which condition (1) does not hold. Conjunction of the elements in *Cands* is satisfiable: $\{x = 0, c = 0, k = 0, k \bmod 2 = 0, k = x + c\}$. Applying Algorithm 3 to *Cands* gives the inductive subset $\{k \bmod 2 = 0, k = x + c\}$. □

Note that we extended Algorithm 3 with a routine to extract a counterexample-to-induction π for each element dropped from *Cands* (lines 3–6). We restrict each π to only assignments to variables from V (denoted $\pi|_V$) and group all non-inductive formulas from *Cands* by the particular π that killed them. This routine is important for optimizing the syntax-guided invariant synthesis algorithm, and it is discussed in more detail in Sect. 5.

5 Reconsidering Syntax-Guided Invariant Synthesis

The lesson we learned when running the FREQHORN algorithm is that the program encoding gives many hints on how the shape of lemmas should look like.

However, the encoding itself can barely give any information about the sampling order. Our main idea to revise the FreqHorn algorithm is to treat seeds and mutants separately. Indeed, as we have seen in Example 2, both seeds and mutants are needed for constructing an invariant, but seeds do *not* actually need to be re-sampled – these candidates are ready to be checked prior to any sampling.

5.1 Overview

We present a new revision of the FreqHorn algorithm which is split into two main stages, the *bootstrapping* and the *sampling*. In the first stage, it exploits only seeds. The idea is to terminate this stage as quickly as possible and to populate the set of lemmas with (preferably, the maximal) inductive subset of seeds. If this subset is not enough for an invariant, the algorithm should proceed to the next stage, in which it should keep generating and checking only mutants.

The pseudocode of the new FreqHorn's revision is shown in Algorithm 4. In the bootstrapping, the algorithm relies on Algorithm 2 to replenish the set of seeds by semantically-meaningful candidates, and in the sampling stage, it relies on Algorithm 3 to mitigate the effect of an unpredictably chosen sampling order. Another algorithmic advantage against Algorithm 1 (to be explained in Sect. 5.2) lies in a more accurate strategy for the search space pruning and the efficient counterexample-guided method to give some failed candidates a *second chance*.

The algorithm takes as input a verification task and values of important configuration parameters N, M, and K (to be explained further). Like Algorithm 1, it starts with obtaining a set of expressions *Seeds* from *Init*, *Tr*, and *Bad* (line 1). Then, *Seeds* gets merged with sets of formulas obtained by Craig interpolation from proofs of bounded safety for a range of bounds $0, \ldots, N$. Note that if there is a counterexample of length $k < N$ discoverable by the BMC engine then an invariant does not exist (recall Lemma 1), and Algorithm 4 terminates (line 5).

The bootstrapping ends when the merged set *Seeds* is taken as input by Algorithm 3, and it extracts an inductive subset (line 19). However, prior to it, the algorithm checks the initiation condition for all elements of the merged set, and the set is filtered accordingly (lines 15–18).

Algorithm 4. FreqHorn-2: Sampling inductive invariants with Houdini, bmcItp, and the second-chance candidates.

Input: $\langle P, Bad\rangle$: verification task, where $P = \langle V \cup V', Init, Tr\rangle$; N, M, K: knobs
Output: $Lemmas \subseteq 2^{Expr}$

```
Seeds ← getSubExprs(Init, Tr, Bad);
for (k ← 0; k < N; k ← k + 1) do
    proof ← bmcItp(⟨P, Bad⟩, k);
    if proof = ∅ then
        return;
    else
        Seeds ← Seeds ∪ proof;
G ← getGrammarAndDistributions(Seeds);
CTI, CTImap ← ∅;
#learned ← 0;
Cands ← Seeds;
while Bad(V) ∧ ⋀_{ℓ∈Lemmas} ℓ(V) ⇏ ⊥ do
    while |Cands| < M do
        Cands ← Cands ∪ {sample(G)};
    for cand ∈ Cands do
        if Init(V) ⇏ cand(V) then
            G ← adjust(G, cand, false);
            Cands ← Cands \ {cand};
    ⟨Lemmas', CTI, CTImap⟩ ← Houdini(P, Cands ∪ Lemmas, CTI, CTImap);
    for ℓ' ∈ Lemmas' \ Lemmas do
        G ← adjust(G, ℓ', true);
    NewLemmas = {ℓ' | ℓ' ∈ Lemmas', s.t. ⋀_{ℓ∈Lemmas} ⇏ ℓ'};
    #learned ← #learned + |NewLemmas|;
    Lemmas = Lemmas ∪ NewLemmas;
    Cands ← ∅;
    if #learned > K then
        #learned ← 0;
        for m ∈ CTI do
            if m ⊭ ⋀_{ℓ∈Lemmas} ℓ(V) then
                CTI ← CTI \ m;
                Cands ← Cands ∪ CTImap(m);
```

Example 5. Let set *Seeds* be as in Fig. 1b, and set *Cands* be constructed from *Seeds* by removing all elements, for which condition (1) does not hold. Assume that a proof of bounded safety for $k = 0$ is $\{x = c\}$ (as one of the options in Example 3). Applying Algorithm 3 to $Cands \cup \{x = c\}$, we get the inductive subset $\{k \bmod 2 = 0, k = x + c, x = c\}$. Since the conjunction of these lemmas is an invariant, the algorithm terminates just after the bootstrapping. □

Checking the candidate formulas in batches is an important improvement over Algorithm 1. This way, the algorithm becomes less dependent of the heuristics for prioritizing the search-space traversal. The size of the batch M is configurable, and if the size of set *Cands* is less than M, then the set gets additional mutants (lines 13–14). Mutants are sampled from the grammar, which is powered by both, the program's encoding (similar to Algorithm 1) and the proofs of bounded safety (new in Algorithm 4). This enlarges the search space for the further mutants.

If the initial batch of candidates still misses some lemmas necessary for an invariant, then Algorithm 4 proceeds to a new iteration. In particular, the extracted inductive subset gets merged with the set of lemmas (line 24), and the assembly of a new batch of candidates starts from scratch (line 25).

Example 6. Assume that a proof of bounded safety is $proof_1 = \{x \geq 0, c \leq 0\}$ (as in Example 3). However, the initiation condition is fulfilled for none of the elements of $proof_1$, so none of them contains in the set of formulas *Cands* taken as input by Algorithm 3. Thus, $proof_1$ does not bring any additional value to the set of seeds, and (contrary to the case in Example 5) the algorithm does not terminate after the bootstrapping. Instead, it proceeds to sampling fresh mutants. □

Theorem 1. *If Algorithm 4 terminates, then either an actual bug is found (line 5), or an invariant is synthesized (after the while-loop).*

5.2 Learning Strategy

A substantial distinction between the FreqHorn's revisions is how they react to the positive and negative attempts. In Algorithm 1, the search space gets adjusted after each individual check (recall the example after Definition 3). The grammar adjustments are performed by changing the probabilities assigned to the production rules. In addition to zeroing the probability of sampling a candidate *cand* itself, after each positive check, Algorithm 1 zeroes the probabilities of sampling some formulas which are weaker than *cand*, and after each negative check – the probabilities of sampling some formulas which are stronger than *cand* (see [13] for more details).

In contrast, Algorithm 4 reacts just to the failed candidates after the initiation check (line 17) and to the successful candidates after the consecution check (line 21). Otherwise, if the consecution check failed for a candidate *cand* (inside Algorithm 3), Algorithm 4 does not disqualify *cand* from being checked again in the future, and this is done by keeping *cand* locally and periodically seeking an opportunity to give *cand* a *second chance*.

To efficiently exploit the second-chance candidates, we rely on the extension of Algorithm 3 by the routine to extract counterexamples-to-induction. That is, for each failed *cand* there exists $m \in CTI$ that killed it. To maintain this information, every application of Algorithm 3 updates the map *CTImap* from *CTI* to failed candidates. In Algorithm 4, it remains to periodically check whether some m is eliminated (line 29), and it would increase chances of all candidates killed by m (line 31) to succeed the consecution check in the next iteration. On the other hand, if some m still models the conjunction of learned lemmas then it is guaranteed that candidates in $CTImap(m)$ will fail the consecution check again.

Finally, to ensure that the CTI-check happens not too often, we run it only when at least K new lemmas are learned. To make this happen, Algorithm 4 performs a redundancy check (line 22) for all lemmas ℓ that have passed the initiation and the consecution checks: ℓ gets learned only when the conjunction of all lemmas learned so far does not imply ℓ. Obviously, when no new lemmas (after the redundancy check) are added, it does not make sense to run the CTI-check since all CTIs are still valid.

5.3 Optimizations

The following tricks are omitted from the algorithm's pseudocode to simplify reading, but they are important for the algorithm's efficiency.

- As a consequence of calculating frequencies, in the original FreqHorn algorithm, seeds were given priorities, but mutants were considered with a relatively small probability. In contrast, the new FreqHorn's revision forces seeds to be checked in the bootstrapping. So while doing sampling, it gives priorities to mutants, and for that it ignores frequencies.
- The initiation checks (lines 15–18) for proofs of bounded safety are omitted since by definition of interpolant (Definition 4) they are already fulfilled. The initiation checks for the second-chance candidates are omitted as well.
- In case a candidate fails the consecution check, and it is queued for a second chance, it is still possible that Algorithm 4 samples it again in the next iterations. Re-sampling is avoided by additional adjustments to the probabilities of the sampling grammar in line 6 of Algorithm 3.
- Algorithm 3 could be optimized if solved *with assumptions*. However, in our experience, it may lead to dropping more candidates than needed. Ideas for getting a maximal inductive subset from [23] could be applied here as well.
- For getting proofs of bounded safety for various bounds, an incremental SMT solver could be used. That is, it could reuse parts of a BMC formula for bound k to encode the BMC formula for bound $k+1$. Potentially, other tricks (e.g., [5,30]) could also be applied here. Finally, interpolation could be replaced by the weakest precondition computation.

6 Evaluation

We implemented FreqHorn-2 on top of our prior implementation FreqHorn[2]. The tool takes as input a verification task in a form of linear constrained Horn

[2] The source code and benchmarks are available at https://github.com/grigoryfedyukovich/aeval/tree/rnd.

clauses (CHC), automatically performs its unrolling, searches for counterexamples, generates proofs of bounded safety, and performs the HOUDINI-style extraction of inductive subsets. All the symbolic reasoning is performed by the Z3 SMT solver [7].

We evaluated FREQHORN-2 on various safe and buggy programs taken from SVCOMP[3] and literature (e.g., [9,15]). Since most of benchmarks, proposed by [9], appeared to be solvable during the bootstrapping of FREQHORN-2 (more details in Sect. 6.1) within (fractions of) seconds, we crafted additional harder benchmarks by ourselves.

All the programs were encoded using the theories of linear (LIA) and nonlinear integer arithmetic (NIA). We did run FREQHORN-2 on unsafe instances for the testing purposes only. It was able to detect a counterexample, but since no invariant exists in these cases, we do not discuss this experience here.

6.1 The Bootstrapping Experiment

In total, we considered **171** safe programs. For **103** of them, the seeds, generated by breaking the symbolic encoding to pieces, did already contain all lemmas needed for invariants. However, when we checked the seeds one-by-one, we revealed invariants for only 63, but using the inductive subset extraction helped revealing all 103. Each set of seeds contained in average 9 formulas.

For our BMC implementation, we considered bounds 1, 2, and 3. Generated interpolants already contained all lemmas for invariants for **70** programs.[4] Each set of bounded proofs contained in average 2 formulas. In all these cases, the output of Algorithm 2 was taken as input by Algorithm 3, and the final safety check was performed afterwards. Our most promising results were achieved while running Algorithm 3 for the merged sets of seeds and proofs of bounded safety (i.e., both sets as in the two prior runs together). The merged sets already contained all lemmas for invariants for **114** programs.

This experiment lets us to conclude that *the bootstrapping is exceptionally important* for accelerating syntax-guided invariant synthesis. In contrast to FREQHORN's fully randomized workflow, FREQHORN-2's behavior at the bootstrapping is predictable. FREQHORN-2 uses the randomized search only to discover mutants, and in our experiments, it was required only in 57 out of 171 cases.

6.2 Overall Statistics

Since technically FREQHORN-2 is a CHC-solver, we compared it against other CHC-solvers, namely μZ [17,22] and SPACER3 [22]. All the tools were provided with the same CHC-encodings of verification problems (and thus, the results do not directly depend on a process of encoding a C-program to a CHC-file). Both μZ and SPACER3 are PDR-based, and despite the latter is faster than the

[3] Software Verification Competition, http://sv-comp.sosy-lab.org/, `loop-*` categories.

[4] Currently interpolation in FREQHORN-2 is limited to LIA, so we had to skip interpolation for 17 benchmarks over NIA.

Table 1. Exact timings.

Benchmark	FreqHorn_2	FreqHorn	μZ	Spacer
abdu_01	ϵ	1.27	ϵ	ϵ
abdu_04	ϵ	8.64	ϵ	ϵ
bouncy_three	6.87	6.76	ϵ	ϵ
bouncy_two	2.74	2.41	∞	∞
cegar1	ϵ	2.18	ϵ	ϵ
cggmp_iter_1	3.09	8.73	ϵ	ϵ
cggmp_iter_2	10.50	24.92	ϵ	ϵ
cggmp_iter_3	18.80	55.86	ϵ	ϵ
const_div_1	ϵ	2.61	ϵ	ϵ
const_div_2	ϵ	1.40	ϵ	ϵ
const_div_3	∞	∞	21.31	∞
const_mod_3	ϵ	∞	ϵ	ϵ
count_by_2_modif	3.28	10.98	∞	∞
count_by_2	2.80	1.62	∞	∞
countud	3.60	15.96	∞	ϵ
css2003	ϵ	9.59	ϵ	ϵ
dillig02	10.91	35.48	ϵ	ϵ
dillig03	ϵ	ϵ	∞	∞
dillig05	4.74	2.04	∞	∞
dillig07	1.93	2.58	ϵ	ϵ
dillig08	ϵ	1.26	∞	ϵ
dillig10	2.28	2.72	ϵ	ϵ
dillig13_1	∞	∞	ϵ	ϵ
dillig13	∞	∞	ϵ	ϵ
dillig14	1.90	6.98	ϵ	ϵ
dillig15	3.28	3.61	∞	ϵ
dillig16	20.14	15.35	∞	ϵ
dillig20_1	ϵ	1.65	ϵ	ϵ
dillig20_2	ϵ	4.97	ϵ	ϵ
dillig20_3	34.51	4.53	ϵ	ϵ
dillig21	ϵ	4.06	7.5	3.98
dillig22_2	ϵ	8.59	ϵ	ϵ
dillig22_3	29.77	15.43	ϵ	ϵ
dillig22_4	9.99	15.20	ϵ	ϵ
dillig22_5	14.12	12.02	ϵ	ϵ
dillig22_6	25.88	13.75	∞	ϵ
dillig22	ϵ	7.25	ϵ	ϵ
dillig37	1.48	1.67	ϵ	ϵ
dillig41	ϵ	1.41	∞	∞
dillig42_1	23.88	∞	ϵ	ϵ
dillig42	52.13	∞	ϵ	ϵ
dillig44_1	ϵ	∞	ϵ	ϵ
dillig44	ϵ	∞	ϵ	ϵ
dillig46	6.20	4.86	ϵ	ϵ
ex7	2.28	8.93	ϵ	ϵ
exact_iters_1	26.55	35.58	ϵ	ϵ
exact_iters_2	∞	22.76	∞	∞
exact_iters_3	23.96	26.60	∞	∞
exact_iters_4	∞	29.19	ϵ	ϵ
fig3	ϵ	21.82	ϵ	ϵ
formula22	ϵ	11.34	ϵ	ϵ
formula25	ϵ	1.12	ϵ	ϵ
formula27	ϵ	20.31	ϵ	ϵ
gcd_2	2.15	1.84	ϵ	ϵ
gcd_3	2.40	3.58	ϵ	ϵ
gj2007	∞	∞	∞	ϵ
half_true_modif	∞	58.15	ϵ	ϵ
half_true_orig	35.58	45.00	ϵ	ϵ
hhk2008	6.60	28.46	ϵ	ϵ
menlo_park_term_simpl_1	ϵ	1.39	∞	15.84
menlo_park_term_simpl_2	12.29	58.36	∞	∞
n_c11	ϵ	∞	ϵ	ϵ
nonlin_div	26.00	∞	∞	∞
nonlin_factorial	ϵ	∞	∞	∞
nonlin_minus_1	ϵ	1.78	∞	∞

Benchmark	FreqHorn_2	FreqHorn	μZ	Spacer
nonlin_minus_2	ϵ	2.60	∞	∞
nonlin_mod_1	5.78	16.13	∞	∞
nonlin_mod_2	∞	18.46	∞	∞
nonlin_mod_mult	ϵ	ϵ	∞	∞
nonlin_mult_1	ϵ	ϵ	∞	∞
nonlin_mult_2	ϵ	2.28	∞	∞
nonlin_mult_3	ϵ	2.86	∞	∞
nonlin_mult_4	ϵ	2.48	∞	∞
nonlin_mult_5	∞	3.22	∞	∞
nonlin_mult_6	ϵ	3.27	∞	∞
nonlin_power	ϵ	∞	ϵ	ϵ
nonlin_square	ϵ	ϵ	∞	∞
nonterm_01	ϵ	ϵ	∞	ϵ
phases1	∞	10.81	∞	∞
s_disj_ite_01	8.77	5.43	ϵ	ϵ
s_disj_ite_02	3.98	5.98	ϵ	ϵ
s_disj_ite_03	13.15	2.71	ϵ	∞
s_disj_ite_04	7.01	4.13	ϵ	ϵ
s_disj_ite_05	4.64	∞	18.66	40.38
s_disj_ite_06	6.43	∞	ϵ	ϵ
s_mutants_01	ϵ	ϵ	∞	∞
s_mutants_02	ϵ	2.40	∞	∞
s_mutants_03	ϵ	ϵ	∞	∞
s_mutants_05	7.86	1.90	∞	∞
s_mutants_06	ϵ	ϵ	∞	∞
s_mutants_07	1.63	1.75	ϵ	ϵ
s_mutants_09	ϵ	3.41	ϵ	ϵ
s_mutants_11	ϵ	1.86	4.72	ϵ
s_mutants_12	ϵ	4.09	ϵ	ϵ
s_mutants_13	ϵ	10.42	ϵ	ϵ
s_mutants_14	ϵ	11.47	ϵ	ϵ
s_mutants_15	ϵ	14.50	ϵ	ϵ
s_mutants_16	14.38	∞	∞	∞
s_mutants_17	14.56	5.83	∞	∞
s_mutants_18	39.85	∞	ϵ	ϵ
s_mutants_19	ϵ	1.31	1.44	ϵ
s_mutants_20	41.15	36.47	∞	∞
s_mutants_21	∞	24.68	∞	∞
s_mutants_22	14.82	16.52	∞	∞
s_mutants_23	1.61	1.11	∞	∞
s_mutants_24	1.58	2.81	∞	ϵ
s_seeds_04	ϵ	∞	20.49	ϵ
s_seeds_05	ϵ	ϵ	∞	ϵ
s_seeds_06	ϵ	1.78	ϵ	∞
s_seeds_10	ϵ	∞	ϵ	ϵ
s_triv_01	ϵ	1.33	ϵ	ϵ
s_triv_07	ϵ	1.15	ϵ	ϵ
s_triv_08	ϵ	∞	ϵ	ϵ
s_triv_09	ϵ	∞	ϵ	ϵ
s_triv_11	ϵ	∞	ϵ	ϵ
s_triv_12	ϵ	∞	ϵ	ϵ
s_triv_14	ϵ	ϵ	∞	ϵ
s_triv_16	ϵ	∞	ϵ	ϵ
s_triv_17	ϵ	∞	ϵ	ϵ
sn_1024	6.14	14.64	24.83	7.12
sn_2048	25.91	26.11	∞	30.87
sn_4096	7.57	∞	∞	∞
sn_8192	11.82	41.01	∞	∞
three_dots_moving_1	ϵ	58.48	10.28	ϵ
three_dots_moving_2	ϵ	∞	ϵ	ϵ
three_dots_moving_3	ϵ	∞	ϵ	ϵ
trex3	ϵ	8.23	ϵ	ϵ
yz_plus_minus	4.35	∞	∞	∞

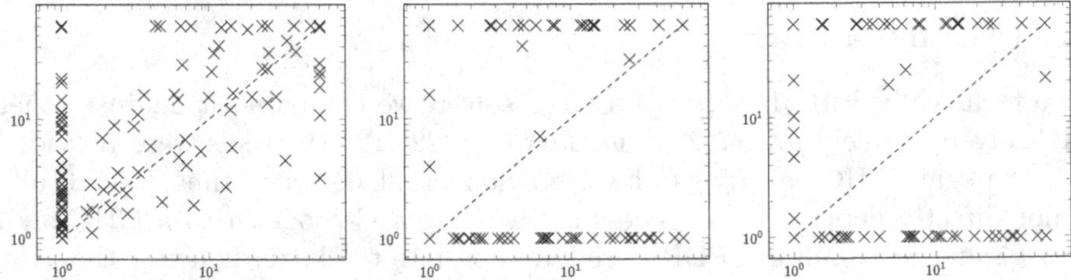

Fig. 2. FreqHorn-2 vs respectively FreqHorn, Spacer3, and μZ.

former and can solve more benchmarks, there are 26 instances, for which the former outperforms the latter.

Table 1 shows the precise running times of FreqHorn-2, FreqHorn, μZ, and Spacer3. To simplify reading, we removed non-representative "*noise*"-runs which took less that 1 s or exceeded a timeout of 60 s by all tools. In the table, ϵ denotes an insignificant amount of time ($\leq$1 s), and ∞ denotes the timeout. The numbers of FreqHorn and FreqHorn-2 are the means of three individual runs. In total, the table contains **128** instances. Additionally, Fig. 2 shows three scatter plots comparing running times of FreqHorn-2 vs FreqHorn, μZ, and Spacer3 respectively. Each point in a plot represents a pair of the FreqHorn-2 run (x-axis) and the competing tool run (y-axis).

FreqHorn-2 outperformed its predecessor in **90** out of 128 cases. We witnessed the speedup up to **233X**, and in average FreqHorn-2 was *four times* faster than FreqHorn. In **40** cases FreqHorn-2 outperformed Spacer3, and in 38 cases Spacer3 outperformed FreqHorn-2. In **51** cases FreqHorn-2 outperformed μZ, and in 34 cases μZ outperformed FreqHorn-2. Unfortunately, FreqHorn-2 still has some performance anomalies, which we believe are connected to the often blind grammar-construction mechanism, inability to generate large disjunctions, and possible inefficiencies of the black-box interpolation engine.

7 Related Work

In this work we exploit a range of techniques originated from symbolic model checking, and in particular from IC3/PDR [4,10], e.g., the idea of keeping CTIs and analyzing them to push previously considered lemmas [29]. Various strategies could be applied for making the lemma pushing more or less eager, i.e., as soon as a newly-added lemma invalidates some CTI. In some IC3 implementations (e.g., [16]), eager pushing does not pay off, but avoiding to push certain lemmas during the regular pushing stage of IC3 results in an improvement. Since we do not have many lemmas, eager pushing also pays off.

The idea of applying Houdini to extract invariants from proofs of bounded safety was fundamental for the first version of Spacer [23]. They, however, keep obtaining proofs along the entire verification process. In contrast, we use proofs mainly for the bootstrapping, while the remaining progress of the algorithm is entirely dictated by the success of sampling.

Most of the successful verification tools today use various combinations of different techniques. In particular, approaches [2,28] use invariants from abstract interpretation to force convergence of k-induction. Recently, k-induction was benefitted from lemmas obtained from PDR [21]. A promising idea to exploit the data from traces [12,15] while creating and manipulating the candidates for invariants could also be used in our syntax-guided approach: at least we could add more constants to the grammar. However we are currently unaware of a strategy to find meaningful constants and to avoid over-population of the grammar by too many constants. Our preliminary experiments resulted so far in the performance decrease.

Techniques for automatic construction of grammars were applied outside of formal verification, but in the domains of security analysis and dynamic test generation [18,19]. Indeed, mutations of the input data for some program can in fact be used as new input data and therefore can increase the testing coverage.

Finally, syntax-guided techniques [1] keep being used in program synthesis more frequently than in the inductive invariant synthesis. For instance, in applications [11,20,26,27] a formal grammar is additionally provided, and it is considered a part of specification. In contrast, in our application, the verification condition contains the encoding of the entire program and the safety specification, which together are enough for construction of formal grammars completely automatically. This is in fact the main driving idea behind FreqHorn, and it leaves us a spacious room for its further adaptations, e.g., in proving and disproving program termination, automated repair of software regressions, and security analysis.

8 Conclusion

We have presented the new revision of the FreqHorn algorithm to synthesize safe inductive invariants based on syntactic features of the source code and the proofs of bounded safety. The new algorithm contains the deterministic bootstrapping stage and the nondeterministic sampling stage, which make it more predictable than its predecessor, allows converging more frequently and in average four times faster. Similarly to most of the state-of-the-art verification techniques, our approach enjoys a tight integration with well renowned formal methods and should be treated as an example of successful interchange of ideas across application domains.

Acknowledgments. It is hard to underestimate the value of discussions with Alexander Ivrii, Arie Gurfinkel, Michael W. Whalen, and other attendees of the International Conference on Formal Methods in Computer-Aided Design (FMCAD 2017) which gave rise to many interesting ideas and inspired this work.

References

1. Alur, R., Bodík, R., Juniwal, G., Martin, M.M.K., Raghothaman, M., Seshia, S.A., Singh, R., Solar-Lezama, A., Torlak, E., Udupa, A.: Syntax-guided synthesis. In: FMCAD, pp. 1–17. IEEE (2013)
2. Beyer, D., Dangl, M., Wendler, P.: Boosting k-induction with continuously-refined invariants. In: Kroening, D., Păsăreanu, C.S. (eds.) CAV 2015. LNCS, vol. 9206, pp. 622–640. Springer, Cham (2015). https://doi.org/10.1007/978-3-319-21690-4_42
3. Biere, A., Cimatti, A., Clarke, E., Zhu, Y.: Symbolic model checking without BDDs. In: Cleaveland, W.R. (ed.) TACAS 1999. LNCS, vol. 1579, pp. 193–207. Springer, Heidelberg (1999). https://doi.org/10.1007/3-540-49059-0_14
4. Bradley, A.R.: SAT-based model checking without unrolling. In: Jhala, R., Schmidt, D. (eds.) VMCAI 2011. LNCS, vol. 6538, pp. 70–87. Springer, Heidelberg (2011). https://doi.org/10.1007/978-3-642-18275-4_7

5. Cabodi, G., Camurati, P., Palena, M., Pasini, P., Vendraminetto, D.: Interpolation-based learning as a mean to speed-up bounded model checking (short paper). In: Cimatti, A., Sirjani, M. (eds.) SEFM 2017. LNCS, vol. 10469, pp. 382–387. Springer, Cham (2017). https://doi.org/10.1007/978-3-319-66197-1_25
6. Craig, W.: Three uses of the Herbrand-Gentzen theorem in relating model theory and proof theory. J. Symbolic Logic, 269–285 (1957)
7. de Moura, L., Bjørner, N.: Z3: an efficient SMT solver. In: Ramakrishnan, C.R., Rehof, J. (eds.) TACAS 2008. LNCS, vol. 4963, pp. 337–340. Springer, Heidelberg (2008). https://doi.org/10.1007/978-3-540-78800-3_24
8. Detlefs, D., Nelson, G., Saxe, J.B.: Simplify: a theorem prover for program checking. J. ACM **52**(3), 365–473 (2005)
9. Dillig, I., Dillig, T., Li, B., McMillan, K.L.: Inductive invariant generation via abductive inference. In: OOPSLA, pp. 443–456. ACM (2013)
10. Eén, N., Mishchenko, A., Brayton, R.K.: Efficient implementation of property directed reachability. In: FMCAD, pp. 125–134. IEEE (2011)
11. Fedyukovich, G., Ahmad, M.B.S., Bodík, R.: Gradual synthesis for static parallelization of single-pass array-processing programs. In: PLDI, pp. 572–585. ACM (2017)
12. Fedyukovich, G., D'Iddio, A.C., Hyvärinen, A.E.J., Sharygina, N.: Symbolic detection of assertion dependencies for bounded model checking. In: Egyed, A., Schaefer, I. (eds.) FASE 2015. LNCS, vol. 9033, pp. 186–201. Springer, Heidelberg (2015). https://doi.org/10.1007/978-3-662-46675-9_13
13. Fedyukovich, G., Kaufman, S., Bodík, R.: Sampling invariants from frequency distributions. In: FMCAD, pp. 100–107. IEEE (2017)
14. Flanagan, C., Leino, K.R.M.: Houdini, an annotation assistant for ESC/Java. In: Oliveira, J.N., Zave, P. (eds.) FME 2001. LNCS, vol. 2021, pp. 500–517. Springer, Heidelberg (2001). https://doi.org/10.1007/3-540-45251-6_29
15. Garg, P., Neider, D., Madhusudan, P., Roth, D.: Learning invariants using decision trees and implication counterexamples. In: POPL, pp. 499–512. ACM (2016)
16. Gurfinkel, A., Ivrii, A.: Pushing to the top. In: FMCAD, pp. 65–72. IEEE (2015)
17. Hoder, K., Bjørner, N.: Generalized property directed reachability. In: Cimatti, A., Sebastiani, R. (eds.) SAT 2012. LNCS, vol. 7317, pp. 157–171. Springer, Heidelberg (2012). https://doi.org/10.1007/978-3-642-31612-8_13
18. Höschele, M., Zeller, A.: Mining input grammars from dynamic taints. In: ASE, pp. 720–725. ACM (2016)
19. Höschele, M., Zeller, A.: Mining input grammars with AUTOGRAM. In: ICSE - Companion Volume, pp. 31–34. IEEE Computer Society (2017)
20. Inala, J.P., Polikarpova, N., Qiu, X., Lerner, B.S., Solar-Lezama, A.: Synthesis of recursive ADT transformations from reusable templates. In: Legay, A., Margaria, T. (eds.) TACAS 2017. LNCS, vol. 10205, pp. 247–263. Springer, Heidelberg (2017). https://doi.org/10.1007/978-3-662-54577-5_14
21. Jovanovic, D., Dutertre, B.: Property-directed k-induction. In: FMCAD, pp. 85–92. IEEE (2016)
22. Komuravelli, A., Gurfinkel, A., Chaki, S.: SMT-based model checking for recursive programs. In: Biere, A., Bloem, R. (eds.) CAV 2014. LNCS, vol. 8559, pp. 17–34. Springer, Cham (2014). https://doi.org/10.1007/978-3-319-08867-9_2. https://bitbucket.org/spacer/code/branch/spacer3
23. Komuravelli, A., Gurfinkel, A., Chaki, S., Clarke, E.M.: Automatic abstraction in SMT-based unbounded software model checking. In: Sharygina, N., Veith, H. (eds.) CAV 2013. LNCS, vol. 8044, pp. 846–862. Springer, Heidelberg (2013). https://doi.org/10.1007/978-3-642-39799-8_59

24. McMillan, K.L.: Interpolation and SAT-based model checking. In: Hunt, W.A., Somenzi, F. (eds.) CAV 2003. LNCS, vol. 2725, pp. 1–13. Springer, Heidelberg (2003). https://doi.org/10.1007/978-3-540-45069-6_1
25. McMillan, K.L.: Lazy annotation revisited. In: Biere, A., Bloem, R. (eds.) CAV 2014. LNCS, vol. 8559, pp. 243–259. Springer, Cham (2014). https://doi.org/10.1007/978-3-319-08867-9_16
26. Phothilimthana, P.M., Jelvis, T., Shah, R., Totla, N., Chasins, S., Bodík, R.: Chlorophyll: synthesis-aided compiler for low-power spatial architectures. In: PLDI, pp. 396–407. ACM (2014)
27. Pu, Y., Bodík, R., Srivastava, S.: Synthesis of first-order dynamic programming algorithms. In: OOPSLA, pp. 83–98. ACM (2011)
28. Roux, P., Delmas, R., Garoche, P.: SMT-AI: an abstract interpreter as oracle for k-induction. Electr. Notes Theor. Comput. Sci. **267**(2), 55–68 (2010)
29. Suda, M.: Triggered clause pushing for IC3. CoRR, abs/1307.4966 (2013)
30. Vizel, Y., Gurfinkel, A., Malik, S.: Fast interpolating BMC. In: Kroening, D., Păsăreanu, C.S. (eds.) CAV 2015. LNCS, vol. 9206, pp. 641–657. Springer, Cham (2015). https://doi.org/10.1007/978-3-319-21690-4_43

Daisy - Framework for Analysis and Optimization of Numerical Programs (Tool Paper)

Eva Darulova[1](✉), Anastasiia Izycheva[2], Fariha Nasir[3], Fabian Ritter[3], Heiko Becker[1], and Robert Bastian[1]

[1] MPI-SWS, Saarbrücken, Germany
{eva,hbecker,robert}@mpi-sws.org
[2] Technische Universität München, Munich, Germany
izycheva@in.tum.de
[3] Saarland University, Saarbrücken, Germany
fnasir@mpi-sws.org, fabian.ritter@cs.uni-saarland.de

Abstract. Automated techniques for analysis and optimization of finite-precision computations have recently garnered significant interest. Most of these were, however, developed independently. As a consequence, reuse and combination of the techniques is challenging and much of the underlying building blocks have been re-implemented several times, including in our own tools. This paper presents a new framework, called Daisy, which provides in a single tool the main building blocks for accuracy analysis of floating-point and fixed-point computations which have emerged from recent related work. Together with its modular structure and optimization methods, Daisy allows developers to easily recombine, explore and develop new techniques. Daisy's input language, a subset of Scala, and its limited dependencies make it furthermore user-friendly and portable.

1 Introduction

Floating-point or fixed-point computations are an integral part of many embedded and scientific computing applications, as are the roundoff errors they introduce. They expose an interesting tradeoff between efficiency and accuracy: the more precision we choose, the closer the results will be to the ideal real arithmetic, but the more costly the computation becomes. Unfortunately, the unintuitive and complex nature of finite-precision arithmetic makes manual optimization infeasible such that automated tool support is indispensable.

This has been recognized previously and several tools for the analysis and optimization of finite-precision computations have been developed. For instance, the tools Fluctuat [22], Rosa [14], Gappa [17], FPTaylor [41], Real2Float [31] and PRECiSA [34] automatically provide sound error bounds on floating-point

D. Beyer and M. Huisman (Eds.): TACAS 2018, LNCS 10805, pp. 270–287, 2018.
https://doi.org/10.1007/978-3-319-89960-2_15

(and some also on fixed-point) roundoff errors. Such a static error analysis is a pre-requisite for any optimization technique providing rigorous results, such as recent ones which choose a mixed-precision assignment [10] or an error-minimizing rewriting of the non-associative finite-precision arithmetic [15,37].

Many of these techniques are complementary. The static analysis techniques have different strengths, weaknesses, and accuracy/efficiency tradeoffs, and optimization techniques should ideally be combined for best results [16]. However, today's techniques are mostly developed independently, resulting in re-implementations and making re-combination and re-use challenging and time-consuming.

In this paper, we present the framework Daisy for the analysis and optimization of finite-precision computations. In contrast to previous work, we have developed Daisy from the ground up to be modular, and thus easily extensible. Daisy is being actively developed and currently already provides many of today's state-of-the-art techniques — all in one tool. In particular, it provides dataflow- as well as optimization-based sound roundoff error analysis, support for mixed-precision and transcendental functions, rewriting optimization, interfaces to several SMT solvers and code generation in Scala and C. Daisy furthermore supports both floating-point and fixed-point arithmetic (whenever the techniques do), making it generally applicable to both scientific computing and embedded applications.

Daisy is aimed at tool developers as well as non-expert users. To make it user-friendly, we adopt the input format of Rosa, which is a real-valued functional domain-specific language in Scala. Unlike other tools today, which have custom input formats [41] or use prefix notation [12], Daisy's input is easily human readable[1] and natural to use.

Daisy is itself written in the Scala programming language [35] and has limited and optional dependencies, making it portable and easy to install. Daisy's main design goals are code readability and extensibility, and not necessarily performance. We demonstrate with our experiments that roundoff errors computed by Daisy are nonetheless competitive with state-of-the-art tools with reasonable running times.

Daisy has replaced Rosa for our own development, and we are happy to report that simple extensions (e.g. adding support for fused multiply-add operations) were integrated quickly by MSc students previously unfamiliar with the tool.

Contributions. We present the new tool Daisy which *integrates* several techniques for sound analysis and optimization of finite-precision computations:

- static dataflow analysis for finite-precision roundoff errors [14] with mixed-precision support and additional support for the dReal SMT solver [21],
- FPTaylor's optimization-based absolute error analysis [41],
- transcendental function support, for dataflow analysis following [13],
- interval subdivision, used by Fluctuat [22] to obtain tighter error bounds,
- rewriting optimization based on genetic programming [15].

[1] We realize a preference for prefix or infix notation is personal.

We show in Sect. 5 that results computed by Daisy are competitive. The code is available open-source at https://github.com/malyzajko/daisy.

We focus primarily on *sound* verification techniques. The goal of this effort is not to develop the next even more accurate technique, rather to consolidate existing ones and to provide a solid basis for further research. Other efforts related to Daisy, which have been described elsewhere and which we do not focus on here are the generation and checking of formal certificates [4], relative error computation [26], and mixed-precision tuning [16].

2 User's Guide: An Overview of Daisy

We first introduce Daisy's functionality from a user's perspective, before reviewing background in roundoff error analysis (Sect. 3) and then describing the developer's view and the internals of Daisy (Sect. 4).

Installation. Daisy is set up with the simple build tool (sbt) [30], which takes care of installing all Scala-related dependencies fully automatically. This basic setup was successfully tested on Linux, macOS and Windows. Some of Daisy's functionality requires additional libraries, which are also straight-forward to install: the Z3 and dReal SMT-solvers [19,21], and the MPFR arbitrary-precision library [20]. Z3 works on all platforms, we have tested MPFR on Linux and Mac, and dReal on Linux.

Input Specification Language. The input to Daisy is a source program written in a real-valued specification language; Fig. 1 shows an example nonlinear embedded controller [15]. The specification language is not executable (as real-valued computation is infeasible), but it is a proper subset of Scala. The `Real` data type is implemented with Scala's dedicated support for numerical types.

Each input program consists of a number of functions which are handled by Daisy separately. In the function's precondition (the `require` clause), the user

```
import daisy.lang._; import Real._;

object RigidBody {
  def rigidBody(x1: Real, x2: Real, x3: Real): Real = {
    require(-15.0 <= x1 && x1 <= 15 && -15.0 <= x2 && x2 <= 15.0 &&
      -15.0 <= x3 && x3 <= 15 && x1 +/- 1e-5)

      -x1*x2 - 2*x2*x3 - x1 - x3

  } ensuring(res => res +/- 1.75e-13)
}
```

Fig. 1. Example input program

provides the ranges of all input variables[2]. In addition, Daisy allows to specify an initial error (beyond only roundoff) on input variables with the notation `x1 +/- 1e-5` as well as additional (non-interval) constraints, e.g. `x1 * x2 <= 100`.

The function body consists of a numerical expression with possibly local variable declarations. Daisy supports arithmetic ($+, -, *, /, \sqrt{}$), the standard transcendental functions (sin, cos, tan, log, exp) as well as fused multiply-add (FMA). Daisy currently does not support conditionals and loops; we discuss the challenges and possible future avenues in Sect. 6. The (optional) postcondition in the **`ensuring`** clause specifies the result's required accuracy in terms of worst-case absolute roundoff error. For our controller, this information may be for instance determined from the specification of the system's sensors or the analysis of the controller's stability [32].

Main Functionality. The main mode of interaction with Daisy is through a command-line interface. Here we review Daisy's main features through the most commonly used command-line options. Brackets denote a choice and curly braces optional parameters. For more options and more fine-grained settings, run `--help`.

The main feature of Daisy is the analysis of finite-precision roundoff errors. For this, Daisy provides several methods:

```
--analysis=[dataflow:opt:relative] {--subdiv}
```

Daisy supports forward dataflow analysis (as implemented in Rosa, Fluctuat and Gappa) and an optimization-based analysis (as implemented in FPTaylor and Real2Float). These methods compute absolute error bounds, and whenever a relative error can be computed, it is also reported. Daisy also supports a dedicated relative error computation [26] which is often more accurate, but also more expensive. All methods can be combined with interval subdivision, which can provide tighter error bounds at the expense of larger running times. We explain these analyses in more detail in Sect. 3.

Accuracy and correspondingly cost of both dataflow and optimization-based analysis can be adjusted by choosing the method which is used to bound ranges:

```
--rangeMethod=[interval:affine:smt] {--solver=[z3, dReal]}
```

With the `smt` option, the user can select between currently two SMT solvers, which have to be installed separately. For dataflow analysis, one can also select the method for bounding errors: `--errorMethod=[interval, affine]`.

Daisy performs roundoff error analysis by default w.r.t. to uniform double floating-point precision, but it also supports various other floating-point and fixed-point precisions:

```
--precision=[Fixed8:Fixed16:Fixed32:Float16:Float32:Float64:Quad:QuadDouble]
```

[2] The magnitude of roundoff errors depends on the magnitude of all intermediate expressions; in general, with unbounded ranges, roundoff errors are also unbounded.

Mixed-precision, i.e. choosing different precisions for different variables, is supported by providing a mapping from variables to precisions in a separate file (`--mixed-precision=file`).

Finite-precision arithmetic is not associative, i.e. different rewritings, even though they are equivalent under a real-valued semantics, will exhibit different roundoff errors. The `--rewrite` optimization [15] uses genetic search to find a rewriting for which it can show the smallest roundoff error.

Daisy prints the analysis result to the terminal. If a postcondition is specified, but the computed error does not satisfy it, Daisy also prints a warning. Optionally, the user can also choose to generate executable code (`--codegen`) in Scala or C, which is especially useful for fixed-point arithmetic, as Daisy's code generator includes all necessary bit shifts.

Static analysis computes a sound over-approximation of roundoff errors, but an under-approximation can also be useful, e.g. to estimate how big the over-approximation of static analysis is. This is provided by the `--dynamic` analysis in Daisy which runs a program in the finite precision of interest and a higher-precision version side-by-side. For this, the MPFR library is required.

Online Interface. We also provide an online interface for Daisy, which allows one to quickly try it out, although it does not yet support all the options: daisy.mpi-sws.org, see the screenshot in Fig. 2.

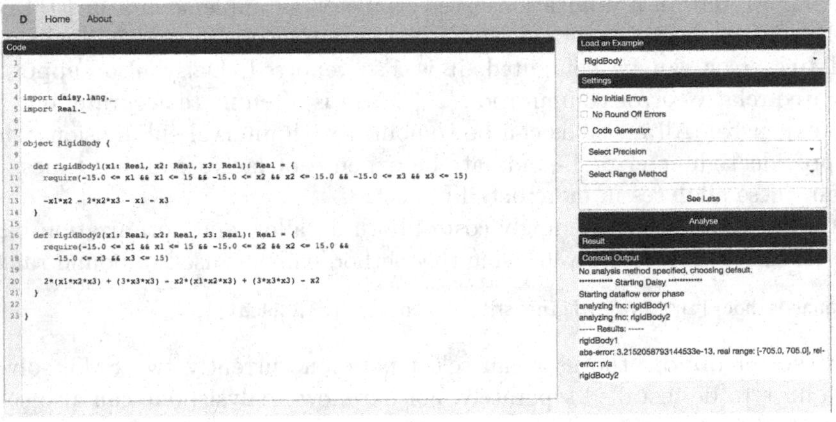

Fig. 2. Screenshot of Daisy's online interface

3 Theoretical Foundations

Before describing the inner architecture of Daisy, we review necessary background on finite-precision arithmetic and static analysis of their roundoff errors.

Floating-Point Arithmetic. One of the most commonly used finite-precision representations is floating-point arithmetic, which is standardized by IEEE754 [24]. The standard defines several precisions as well as rounding operators; here we will consider the most commonly used ones, i.e. single and double precision with operations in rounding-to-nearest mode. Then, arithmetic operations satisfy the following abstraction:

$$x \circ_{fl} y = (x \circ y)(1 + e) + d\ , \quad |e| \leq \epsilon_m, |d| \leq \delta_m \tag{1}$$

where $\circ \in +, -, *, /$ and $\circ_{fl}$ denotes the respective floating-point version. Square root follows similarly, and unary minus does not introduce roundoff errors. The machine epsilon ϵ_m bounds the maximum relative error for so-called normal values. Roundoff errors of subnormal values, which provide gradual underflow, are expressed as an absolute error, bounded by δ_m. $\epsilon_m = 2^{-24}, \delta_m = 2^{-150}$ and $\epsilon_m = 2^{-53}, \delta_m = 2^{-1075}$ for single and double precision, respectively.

Higher precisions are usually implemented in software libraries on top of standard double floating-point precision [2]. Daisy supports quad and quad-double precision, where we assume $\epsilon_m = 2^{-113}$ and $\epsilon_m = 2^{-211}$, respectively. Depending on the library, δ_m may or may not be defined, and Daisy can be adjusted accordingly.

Static analyses usually use this abstraction of floating-point arithmetic, as bit-precise reasoning does not scale, and furthermore is unsuitable for computing roundoff errors w.r.t. continuous real-valued semantics (note that Eq. 1 is also real-valued). The abstraction furthermore only holds in the absence of not-a-number special values (NaN) and infinities. Daisy's static analysis detects such cases automatically and reports them as errors.

Fixed-Point Arithmetic. Floating-point arithmetic requires dedicated support, either in hardware or software, and depending on the application this support may be too costly. An alternative is fixed-point arithmetic which can be implemented with integers only, but which in return requires that the radix point alignments are precomputed at compile time. While no standard exists, fixed-point values are usually represented by bit vectors with an integer and a fractional part, separated by an implicit radix point. At runtime, the alignments are then performed by bit-shift operations. These shift operations can also be handled by special language extensions for fixed-point arithmetic [25]. For more details see [1], whose fixed-point semantics we follow. We use truncation as the rounding mode for arithmetic operations. The absolute roundoff error at each operation is determined by the fixed-point format, i.e. the (implicit) number of fractional bits available, which in turn can be computed from the range of possible values at that operation.

Range Arithmetic. The magnitude of floating-point and fixed-point roundoff errors depends on the magnitudes of possible values. Thus, in order to accurately bound roundoff errors, any static analysis first needs to be able to bound the ranges of all (intermediate) expressions accurately, i.e. tightly. Different range arithmetics have been developed and each has a different accuracy/efficiency tradeoff. Daisy supports interval [33] and affine arithmetic [18] as well as a more accurate, but also more expensive, combination of interval arithmetic and SMT [14].

Interval arithmetic (IA) [33] is an efficient choice for range estimation, which computes a bounding interval for each basic operation $\circ \in \{+, -, *, /\}$ as

$$[x_0, x_1] \circ [y_0, y_1] = [\min(x \circ y), \max(x \circ y)], \text{ where } x \in [x_0, x_1], y \in [y_0, y_1]$$

and analogously for square root. Interval arithmetic cannot track correlations between variables (e.g. $x - x \neq [0, 0]$), and thus can introduce significant over-approximations of the true ranges, especially when the computations are longer.

Affine arithmetic (AA) [18] tracks *linear* correlations by representing possible values of variables as affine forms:

$$\hat{x} = x_0 + \sum_{i=1}^{n} x_i \epsilon_i, \quad \text{where } \epsilon_i \in [-1, 1]$$

where x_0 denotes the central value (of the represented interval) and each *noise term* $x_i \epsilon_i$ denotes a deviation from this central value. The range represented by an affine form is computed as $[\hat{x}] = [x_0 - rad(\hat{x}), x_0 + rad(\hat{x})]$, $rad(\hat{x}) = \sum_{i=1}^{n} |x_i|$. Linear operations are performed term-wise and are computed exactly, whereas nonlinear ones need to be approximated and thus introduce over-approximations. Overall, AA can produce tighter ranges in practice (though not universally). In particular, AA is often beneficial when the individual noise terms (x_i's) are small, e.g. when they track roundoff errors.

The over-approximation due to nonlinear arithmetic can be mitigated [14] by refining ranges computed by IA with a binary search in combination with a SMT solver which supports nonlinear arithmetic such as Z3 [19] or dReal [21].

Static Analysis for Roundoff Error Estimation. The worst-case absolute roundoff error that most static analyses approximate is:

$$\max_{x \in [a,b]} |f(x) - \tilde{f}(\tilde{x})| \tag{2}$$

where $[a, b]$ is the range for x given in the precondition, and f and x are a mathematical real-valued arithmetic expression and variable, respectively, and $\tilde{f}$ and $\tilde{x}$ their finite-precision counterparts. This definition extends to multivariate f component-wise.

An automated and general estimation of relative errors ($\frac{|f(x) - \tilde{f}(\tilde{x})|}{|f(x)|}$), though it may be more desirable, presents a significant challenge today. For instance, when the range of $f(x)$ includes zero, relative errors are not well defined and this is often the case in practice. For a more thorough discussion, we refer the reader to [26]; the technique is also implemented within Daisy.

For bounding absolute errors, two main approaches exist today, which we review in the following.

Dataflow Analysis. One may think that just evaluating a program in interval arithmetic and interpreting the width of the resulting interval as the error bound would be sufficient. While this is certainly a sound approach, it computes too pessimistic error bounds in general. This is especially true if we consider relatively large ranges on inputs; we cannot distinguish which part of the interval width is due to the input interval or due to accumulated roundoff errors.

Thus, dataflow analysis computes roundoff error bounds in two steps, recursively over the abstract syntax tree (AST) of the arithmetic expression:

1. *range analysis* computes sound range bounds (for real semantics),
2. *error analysis* propagates errors from subexpressions and computes the new worst-case roundoffs using the previously computed ranges.

In practice, these two steps can be performed in a single pass over the AST. A side effect of this separation is that it provides us with a modular approach: we can choose different range arithmetics with different accuracy/efficiency tradeoffs for ranges and errors (and possibly for different parts of a program).

The main challenge of dataflow analysis is to minimize over-approximations due to nonlinear arithmetic (linear arithmetic can be handled well with AA). Previous tools chose different strategies. For instance, Rosa [14] employs the combination of interval arithmetic with a non-linear SMT-solver, which we described earlier. Fluctuat [22], which uses AA for both bounding the ranges as well as the errors, uses interval subdivision. In Fluctuat, the user can designate up to two variables whose input ranges will be subdivided into intervals of equal width. The analysis is performed separately for each and the overall error is then the maximum error over all subintervals. Interval subdivision increases the runtime of the analysis, especially for multivariate functions, and the choice of which variables to subdivide and by how much is usually not straight-forward.

Optimization-based Analysis. FPTaylor [41], Real2Float [31] and PRECiSA [34], unlike Daisy, Rosa, Gappa and Fluctuat, formulate the roundoff error bounds computation as an optimization problem, where the absolute error expression from Eq. 2 is to be maximized, subject to interval constraints on its parameters. Due to the discrete nature of floating-point arithmetic, FPTaylor optimizes the continuous, real-valued abstraction from Eq. 1. However, this expression is still too complex and features too many variables for optimization procedures in practice.

FPTaylor introduces the Symbolic Taylor approach, where the objective function is simplified using a first order Taylor approximation with respect to e and d (the variables representing roundoff errors at each arithmetic operation). To solve the optimization problem, FPTaylor uses a rigorous branch-and-bound procedure.

4 Developer's Guide: Daisy's Internals

This section provides more details on Daisy's architecture and explains some of our design decisions. Daisy is written in the Scala programming language which provides a strong type system as well as a large collection of (parallel) libraries. While Scala supports both imperative and functional programming styles, we have written Daisy functionally as much as possible, which we found to be beneficial to ensuring correctness and readability of code.

4.1 Input Language and Frontend

Daisy's input language is implemented as a domain-specific language in Scala, and Daisy's frontend calls the Scala compiler which performs parsing and type-checking. While designing our own simple input format and parser would be certainly more efficient in terms of Daisy's running time (and could be done in the future), we have deliberately chosen not to do this. An existing programming language provides clear semantics and feels natural to users. Using the Scala compiler furthermore helps to ensure that Daisy parses the program correctly, for instance that it indeed conforms e.g. to Scala's typing rules. Furthermore, extending the input language is usually straight-forward.

The other major design decision was to make the input program real-valued. This explicitly specifies the baseline against which roundoff errors should be computed, but it also makes it easy for the user to explore different options. For instance, changing the precision only requires changing a flag, whereas a finite-precision input program (like FPTaylor's or Fluctuat's) requires editing the source code.

Mixed-precision is also supported respecting Scala semantics and is thus transparent. The user may annotate variables, including local ones, with different precisions. To specify the precision of every individual operation, the program can be transformed into three-address form (Daisy can do this automatically), and then each arithmetic operation can be annotated via the corresponding variable.

Daisy currently does not support data structures such as arrays or lists in its input language, mainly because the static analysis of these is largely orthogonal to the analysis of the actual computation and we believe that standard strategies like unrolling computations over array elements or abstracting the array as a single variable can be employed.

4.2 Modular Architecture

Daisy is built up in a modular way by implementing its functionality in phases, which can be combined. See the overview in Fig. 3. Each phase takes as input and returns as output a `Program` and a `Context`, and can modify both. For instance, rewriting transforms the program and roundoff error analysis adds the analysis information to the context. This information is then re-used by later phases, for instance the analysis information is used to generate fixed-point arithmetic programs in the code generation phase. This modularity allows, for instance, the rewriting optimization phase to be combined with any other roundoff error analysis.

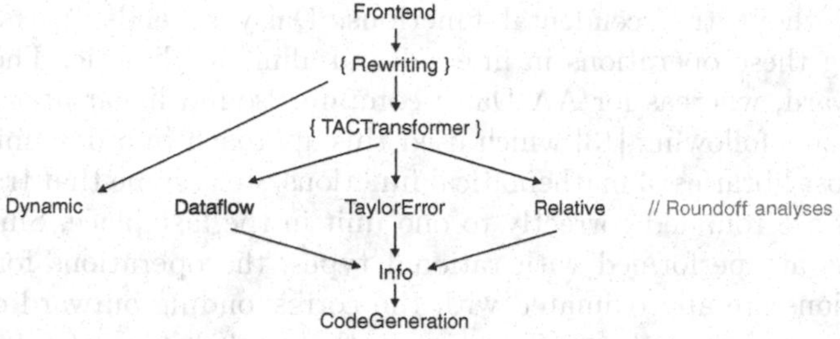

Fig. 3. Overview of Daisy's phases. Phases in curly braces are optional.

In addition to the modular architecture, Daisy's main functionality is provided as a set of library tools, which allows for further reuse across different phases. It could also be used as a separate library in other tools. Here we highlight the main functionality provided:

- `Rational` provides an implementation of rational numbers based on Java's BigInteger library. Rationals are used throughout Daisy for computations in order to avoid internal roundoff errors which could affect soundness.
- `MPFRFloat` is an interface to GNU's MPFR arbitrary precision library [20].
- `Interval` and `AffineForm` provide implementations of interval and affine arithmetic. Daisy uses no external libraries for these in order to facilitate extensions and integration.
- `SMTRange` implements Rosa's combination of interval arithmetic with an SMT solver [14] for improved range bounds. Daisy uses the scala-smtlib library[3] to interface with the Z3 and dReal SMT solvers. Other solvers can be added with little effort, provided they support the SMT-LIB standard [3].
- `RoundoffEvaluators` implement dataflow roundoff error analysis. The analysis is parametric in the range method used, and due to its implementation as a library function can be easily used in different contexts.
- `Taylor` provides methods for computing and simplifying partial derivatives.
- `GeneticSearch` provides a generic implementation of a (simple) genetic search, which is currently used for the rewriting optimization.

The fixed-point precision class in Daisy supports any bitlength (i.e. only the frontend has a limited selection) and floating-point types can be straightforwardly added by specifying the corresponding machine epsilon and representable range.

4.3 Implementation Details

Here we provide details about Daisy's implementation of previous techniques. The dataflow analysis approach, e.g. in Rosa, only considered arithmetic

[3] https://github.com/regb/scala-smtlib.

operations without transcendental functions. Daisy extends this support by implementing these operations in interval and affine arithmetic. The former is straight-forward, whereas for AA Daisy computes sound linear approximations of the functions, following [13] which used this approach in a dynamic analysis. Following most libraries of mathematical functions, we assume that transcendental functions are rounded correctly to one unit in the last place. Since internal computations are performed with rational types, the operations for transcendental functions are approximated with the corresponding outward or upwards rounding to ensure soundness. To support the combination of interval arithmetic and SMT, we integrate the dReal solver in Daisy, which provides support for transcendental functions. Although dReal is only δ-complete, this does not affect Daisy's soundness as the algorithm relies on UNSAT answers, which are always sound in dReal.

Interval subdivision can be an effective tool to reduce overapproximations in static analysis results, which is why Daisy offers it for all its analyses. Daisy subdivides every input variable range into a fixed number of subintervals (the number can be controlled by the user) and takes the cartesian product. The analysis is then performed separately for each set of subintervals. This clearly increases the running time, but is also trivially parallelizable.

Daisy also includes an initial implementation of FPTaylor's optimization-based static analysis. The major difference is that Daisy does not use a branch-and-bound algorithm for solving the optimization problem, but relies on the already existing range analyses. We would like to include a proper optimization solver in the future; currently custom interfaces have been an obstacle.

5 Experimental Evaluation

We have experimentally evaluated Daisy's roundoff error analysis on a number of finite-precision verification benchmarks taken from related work [15,16,31,41]. Benchmarks marked with a superscript ^{T} contain transcendental functions. The goal of this evaluation is twofold. First, Daisy should be able to compute reasonably tight error bounds in a reasonable amount of time to be useful. Secondly, exploiting the fact that Daisy implements several different analysis methods within a single tool allows us to provide a direct comparison of their tradeoffs.

We compare Daisy with FPTaylor, which has been shown previously to provide tight error bounds [41]. It furthermore implements the optimization-based approach, which we re-implement in Daisy (in an albeit preliminary version). We do not compare against tools which employ dataflow static analysis, as Daisy's analyses essentially subsume those.

Comparison with FPTaylor. We first compare roundoff errors computed by Daisy with different methods against errors computed by FPTaylor (version from 20 Sept 2017) in Table 1. All errors are computed for uniform double floating-point precision, assuming roundoff errors on inputs. We abbreviate the settings used in Daisy by e.g. IA - AA, where IA and AA specify the methods used

Table 1. Roundoff errors for uniform 64-bit double precision by dynamic analysis, FPTaylor and Daisy (subset of benchmarks).

			Daisy							
Benchmark	Dynamic	FPTaylor	IA - AA	Z3 - AA	Z3 - IA	dReal - AA	AA-AA+sub	opt - Z3	%	Z3-AA+rw
bspline0	2.84e-17	1.07e-16	1.62e-16	1.62e-16	1.62e-16	1.62e-16	1.62e-16	1.19e-16	1.11	1.62e-16
bspline1	1.74e-16	3.59e-16	7.96e-16	7.03e-16	8.14e-16	7.03e-16	5.17e-16	6.51e-16	1.44	4.81e-16
doppler	7.04e-14	1.22e-13	4.19e-13	4.19e-13	4.36e-13	4.19e-13	2.61e-13	1.72e-13	1.41	1.72e-13
himmilbeau	5.27e-13	1.00e-12	2.33e-12	1.00e-12	1.00e-12	1.00e-12	1.00e-12	1.42e-12	1.00	1.01e-12
invertedPend.	2.43e-14	3.21e-14	3.67e-14	3.67e-14	3.67e-14	3.67e-14	3.67e-14	4.44e-14	1.14	2.43e-14
kepler0	4.02e-14	5.85e-14	1.04e-13	9.06e-14	1.14e-13	9.20e-14	7.88e-14	1.15e-13	1.35	5.70e-14
kepler1	1.27e-13	1.96e-13	4.82e-13	3.97e-13	4.81e-13	3.97e-13	3.30e-13	4.92e-13	1.68	2.89e-13
kepler2	5.21e-13	1.47e-12	2.47e-12	2.25e-12	2.69e-12	2.25e-12	1.93e-12	2.28e-12	1.31	1.73e-12
rigidBody1	2.00e-13	2.95e-13	3.22e-13	3.22e-13	3.22e-13	3.22e-13	3.22e-13	5.08e-13	1.09	2.24e-13
rigidBody2	2.03e-11	3.61e-11	3.65e-11	3.65e-11	3.65e-11	3.65e-11	3.65e-11	6.48e-11	1.01	2.91e-11
sine	2.76e-16	4.44e-16	1.13e-15	6.95e-16	7.41e-16	6.95e-16	6.49e-16	6.54e-16	1.46	5.91e-16
sineOrder3	3.38e-16	5.94e-16	1.45e-15	1.23e-15	1.34e-15	1.23e-15	1.02e-15	8.00e-16	1.35	1.22e-15
sqroot	2.35e-13	2.81e-13	3.13e-13	3.09e-13	3.21e-13	3.09e-13	2.97e-13	3.97e-13	1.06	2.89e-13
train4 out1	1.33e-10	3.39e-10	4.28e-10	4.28e-10	4.28e-10	4.28e-10	3.99e-10	5.21e-10	1.18	3.34e-10
train4 state9	5.93e-15	8.12e-15	8.66e-15	8.66e-15	8.66e-15	8.66e-15	8.66e-15	1.20e-14	1.07	3.33e-15
turbine1	6.78e-15	1.67e-14	9.49e-14	8.87e-14	9.14e-14	8.87e-14	4.26e-14	2.80e-14	1.68	8.68e-14
turbine2	1.06e-14	2.00e-14	1.39e-13	1.23e-13	1.29e-13	1.23e-13	4.35e-14	3.67e-14	1.84	1.19e-13
turbine3	4.38e-15	9.57e-15	7.07e-14	6.27e-14	6.55e-14	6.27e-14	1.96e-14	1.65e-14	1.72	5.98e-14
jetEngine	5.24e-12	8.75e-12	-	1.15e-08	1.16e-08	1.15e-08	3.64e-08	2.20e-11	2.51	1.12e-08
pendulum1^T	3.31e-16	3.47e-16	4.61e-16	4.61e-16	4.61e-16	4.61e-16	4.61e-16	4.67e-16	1.33	4.61e-16
pendulum2^T	8.88e-16	9.15e-16	9.42e-16	9.42e-16	9.42e-16	9.42e-16	9.37e-16	1.16e-15	1.02	9.41e-16
analysis1^T	1.41e-16	1.95e-16	1.67e-15	1.67e-15	1.67e-15	1.30e-15	1.61e-15	1.92e-15	6.67	1.67e-15
analysis2^T	4.40e-16	5.49e-16	6.08e-14	6.08e-14	6.28e-14	3.11e-15	3.84e-15	1.28e-13	5.66	6.08e-14
logExp^T	1.29e-15	1.99e-15	3.33e-12	3.33e-12	3.33e-12	3.33e-12	2.18e-13	3.31e-12	109.55	3.33e-12
sphere^T	4.47e-15	8.18e-15	1.20e-14	1.20e-14	1.20e-14	1.20e-14	3.22e-14	1.63e-14	1.47	1.17e-14

Table 2. Execution times of FPTaylor and Daisy for different settings

Benchmark	FPTaylor	Z3 - AA	AA-AA (sub)	opt - Z3
bspline	2 s 884 ms	4 s 450 ms	2 s 190 ms	3 s 320 ms
doppler	1 s 465 ms	3 s 221 ms	2 s 657 ms	2 s 939 ms
himmilbeau	660 ms	3 s 545 ms	1 s 975 ms	2 s 760 ms
invertedPend.	14 s 69 ms	3 s 109 ms	2 s 31 ms	2 s 570 ms
kepler	18 s 629 ms	40 s 627 ms	3 s 160 ms	21 s 893 ms
rigidBody	1 s 430 ms	6 s 31 ms	2 s 206 ms	4 s 118 ms
sine	1 s 580 ms	4 s 49 ms	2 s 179 ms	3 s 114 ms
sqrt	7 s 381 ms	4 s 92 ms	1 s 884 ms	2 s 988 ms
traincar	27 s 846 ms	22 s 670 ms	7s 452 ms	15 s 61 ms
turbine	2 s 452 ms	7 s 93 ms	3 s 951 ms	5 s 522 ms
jetEngine	1 s 434 ms	35 s 267 ms	3 s 583 ms	19 s 425 ms
transcendental	34 s 547 ms	2 s 770 ms	2s 959 ms	2 s 865 ms

for computing the ranges and errors, respectively. 'sub' means subdivision, 'rw' rewriting and 'opt' denotes the optimization-based approach. We underline the lowest roundoff errors computed among the different Daisy settings (without rewriting). The column marked '%' denotes the factor by which the lowest error computed by Daisy differs from FPTaylor's computed error.

FPTaylor supports different backend solvers; we have performed experiments with the internal branch-and-bound and the Gelpia solver, but observed only minor differences. We thus report results for the Gelpia solver. We furthermore chose the lowest verbosity level in both FPTaylor and Daisy to reduce the execution time. Table 1 also shows an underapproximation of roundoff errors computed using Daisy's dynamic analysis which provides an idea of the tightness of roundoff errors.

Table 2 shows the corresponding execution times of the tools. Execution times are average real time measured by the bash `time` command. We have performed all experiments on a Linux desktop computer with an Intel Xeon 3.30 GHz processor and 32 GB RAM, with Scala version 2.11.11.

The focus when implementing Daisy was to provide a solid framework with modular and clear code, not to improve roundoff error bounds. Nonetheless, Daisy's roundoff error bounds are mostly competitive with FPTaylor's, with the notable exception of the jetEngine benchmark (additionally, interval arithmetic fails to bound the divisor away from zero).

Overall we observe that using an SMT solver for tightening ranges is helpful, but interval subdivision is preferable. Furthermore, using affine arithmetic for bounding errors is preferable over interval arithmetic. Finally, rewriting can often improve roundoff error bounds significantly.

Our optimization-based analysis is not yet quite as good as FPTaylor's, but acceptable for a first re-implementation. We suspect the difference is mainly due to the fact that Daisy does not use a dedicated optimization procedure, which we hope to include in the future.

Execution times of FPTaylor and Daisy are comparable. It should be noted that the times are end-to-end, and in particular for Daisy this includes the Scala compiler frontend, which takes a constant 1.3 s (irrespective of input). Clearly, with a hand-written parser this could be improved, but we do not consider this as critical. Furthermore, Daisy performs overflow checks at every intermediate subexpression; it is unclear whether FPTaylor does this as well.

Table 1 seems to suggest that one should use FPTaylor's optimization-based approach for bounding roundoff errors. We include dataflow analysis in Daisy nonetheless for several reasons. First, dataflow analysis computes overflow checks without extra cost. Secondly, the optimization-based approach is only applicable when errors can be specified as relative errors, which is not the case for instance for fixed-point arithmetic, which is important for many embedded applications.

Fixed-Point vs Floating-Point. In Table 3 we use Daisy to compare roundoff errors for 32-bit fixed-point and 32-bit floating-point arithmetic, with and without rewriting. For this comparison, we use the dataflow analysis, as the optimization-based approach is not applicable to fixed-point arithmetic. Not surprisingly, the results confirm that (at least for our examples with limited ranges) fixed-point arithmetic can provide better accuracy for the same bitlength, and furthermore that rewriting can improve the error bounds further.

6 Related Work

We have already mentioned the directly related techniques and tools Gappa, Fluctuat, Rosa, FPTaylor, Real2Float and PRECiSA throughout the paper. Except for Fluctuat and Rosa, these tools also provide either a proof script or a certificate for the correctness (of certain parts) of the analysis, which can be independently checked in a theorem prover. Certificate generation and checking for Daisy has been described in a separate paper [4].

Daisy currently handles straight-line arithmetic expressions, i.e. it does not handle conditionals and loops. Abstract interpretation of floating-point programs handles conditionals by joins, however, for roundoff error analysis this approach is not sufficient. The real-valued and finite-precision computations can diverge and a simple join does not capture this 'discontinuity error'. Programs with loops are challenging, because roundoff errors in general grow with each loop iteration and thus a nontrivial fixpoint does not exist in general (loop unrolling can however be applied). Widening operators compute non-trivial bounds only for very special cases where roundoff errors decrease with each loop iteration. These challenges have been (partially) addressed [16,23], and we plan to include those techniques in Daisy in the future. Nonetheless, conditionals and loops remain open problems.

Sound techniques have also been applied for both the range and the error analysis for bitwidth optimization of fixed-point arithmetic, for instance

Table 3. Roundoff errors for 32-bit floating-point and fixed-point arithmetic.

Benchmark	Z3 - AA float 32	Z3 - AA fixed 32	Z3 - AA + rewriting float 32	Z3 - AA + rewriting fixed 32
bspline0	8.69e-8	2.28e-9	8.69e-8	2.28e-9
bspline1	3.77e-7	7.86e-9	2.58e-7	6.00e-9
doppler	2.25e-4	3.52e-6	9.26e-5	1.45e-6
himmilbeau	5.37e-4	8.84e-6	6.85e-4	1.13e-5
invertedPendulum	1.97e-5	3.54e-7	1.30e-5	2.03e-7
kepler0	4.87e-5	7.60e-7	3.06e-5	4.78e-7
kepler1	2.13e-4	3.33e-6	1.76e-4	2.76e-6
kepler2	1.21e-3	1.88e-5	8.85e-4	1.38e-5
rigidBody1	1.73e-4	3.12e-6	1.20e-4	2.30e-6
rigidBody2	1.96e-2	3.13e-4	1.56e-2	2.51e-4
sine	3.73e-7	7.14e-9	3.17e-7	6.68e-9
sineOrder3	6.58e-7	1.31e-8	6.54e-7	1.39e-8
sqroot	1.66e-4	8.00e-6	1.60e-4	7.68e-6
train4 out1	2.30e-1	4.14e-3	1.79e-1	3.34e-3
train4 state9	4.65e-6	1.45e-7	1.79e-6	1.03e-7
turbine1	4.76e-5	1.05e-6	4.66e-5	1.04e-6
turbine2	6.61e-5	1.19e-6	6.40e-5	1.16e-6
turbine3	3.37e-5	7.42e-7	3.21e-5	7.17e-7
jetEngine	6.22	1.00e-1	1.44e-1	2.46e-3

in [28,29,36,38] and Lee et. al. [29] provide a nice overview of static and dynamic techniques.

Dynamic analysis can be used to find inputs which cause large roundoff errors, e.g. running a higher-precision floating-point program alongside the original one [5] or with a guided search to find inputs which maximize errors [11]. In comparison, Daisy's dynamic analysis is a straight-forward approach, and some more advanced techniques could be integrated as well.

Optimization techniques targeting accuracy of floating-point computations, like rewriting [37] or mixed-precision tuning [10] include some form of roundoff error analysis, and any of the above approaches, including Daisy's, can be potentially used as a building block.

More broadly related are abstract interpretation-based static analyses, which are sound w.r.t. floating-point arithmetic [6,9,27]. These techniques can prove the absence of runtime errors, such as division-by-zero, but cannot quantify roundoff errors. Floating-point arithmetic has also been formalized in theorem provers and entire numerical programs have been proven correct and accurate within these [7,39]. Most of these formal verification efforts are, however, to a large part manual. Floating-point arithmetic has also been formalized in an

SMT-lib [40] theory and SMT solvers exist which include floating-point decision procedures [8,19]. These are, however, not suitable for roundoff error quantification, as a combination with the theory of reals would be necessary which does not exist today.

7 Conclusion

We have presented the framework Daisy which integrates several state-of-the-art techniques for the analysis and optimization of finite-precision programs. It is actively being developed, improved and extended and we believe that it can serve as a useful building block in future optimization techniques.

References

1. Anta, A., Majumdar, R., Saha, I., Tabuada, P.: Automatic verification of control system implementations. In: EMSOFT (2010)
2. Bailey, D.H., Hida, Y., Li, X.S., Thompson, B.: C++/Fortran-90 double-double and quad-double package. Technical report (2015)
3. Barrett, C., Fontaine, P., Tinelli, C.: The SMT-LIB Standard: Version 2.6. Technical report, University of Iowa (2017). www.SMT-LIB.org
4. Becker, H., Darulova, E., Myreen, M.O.: A verified certificate checker for floating-point error bounds. Technical report (2017). arXiv:1707.02115
5. Benz, F., Hildebrandt, A., Hack, S.: A dynamic program analysis to find floating-point accuracy problems. In: PLDI (2012)
6. Blanchet, B., Cousot, P., Cousot, R., Feret, J., Mauborgne, L., Miné, A., Monniaux, D., Rival, X.: A static analyzer for large safety-critical software. In: PLDI (2003)
7. Boldo, S., Clément, F., Filliâtre, J.-C., Mayero, M., Melquiond, G., Weis, P.: Wave equation numerical resolution: a comprehensive mechanized proof of a C program. J. Autom. Reason. **50**(4), 423–456 (2013)
8. Brain, M., D'Silva, V., Griggio, A., Haller, L., Kroening, D.: Deciding floating-point logic with abstract conflict driven clause learning. Form. Methods Syst. Des. **45**(2), 213–245 (2013)
9. Chen, L., Miné, A., Cousot, P.: A sound floating-point polyhedra abstract domain. In: Ramalingam, G. (ed.) APLAS 2008. LNCS, vol. 5356, pp. 3–18. Springer, Heidelberg (2008). https://doi.org/10.1007/978-3-540-89330-1_2
10. Chiang, W.-F., Gopalakrishnan, G., Rakamaric, Z., Briggs, I., Baranowski, M.S., Solovyev, A.: Rigorous floating-point mixed precision tuning. In: POPL (2017)
11. Chiang, W.-F., Gopalakrishnan, G., Rakamaric, Z., Solovyev, A.: Efficient search for inputs causing high floating-point errors. In: PPoPP (2014)
12. Damouche, N., Martel, M., Panchekha, P., Qiu, C., Sanchez-Stern, A., Tatlock, Z.: Toward a standard benchmark format and suite for floating-point analysis. In: Bogomolov, S., Martel, M., Prabhakar, P. (eds.) NSV 2016. LNCS, vol. 10152, pp. 63–77. Springer, Cham (2017). https://doi.org/10.1007/978-3-319-54292-8_6
13. Darulova, E., Kuncak, V.: Trustworthy numerical computation in scala. In: OOPSLA (2011)
14. Darulova, E., Kuncak, V.: Sound compilation of reals. In: POPL (2014)
15. Darulova, E., Kuncak, V., Majumdar, R., Saha, I.: Synthesis of fixed-point programs. In: EMSOFT (2013)

16. Darulova, E., Sharma, S., Horn, E.: Sound mixed-precision optimization with rewriting. Technical report (2017). arXiv:1707.02118
17. Daumas, M., Melquiond, G.: Certification of bounds on expressions involving rounded operators. ACM Trans. Math. Softw. **37**(1), 2:1–2:20 (2010)
18. de Figueiredo, L.H., Stolfi, J.: Affine arithmetic: concepts and applications. Numer. Algorithms **37**(1), 147–158 (2004)
19. de Moura, L., Bjørner, N.: Z3: an efficient SMT solver. In: Ramakrishnan, C.R., Rehof, J. (eds.) TACAS 2008. LNCS, vol. 4963, pp. 337–340. Springer, Heidelberg (2008). https://doi.org/10.1007/978-3-540-78800-3_24
20. Fousse, L., Hanrot, G., Lefèvre, V., Pélissier, P., Zimmermann, P.: MPFR: a multiple-precision binary floating-point library with correct rounding. ACM Trans. Math. Softw. **33**(2) (2007)
21. Gao, S., Kong, S., Clarke, E.M.: dReal: an SMT solver for nonlinear theories over the reals. In: Bonacina, M.P. (ed.) CADE 2013. LNCS (LNAI), vol. 7898, pp. 208–214. Springer, Heidelberg (2013). https://doi.org/10.1007/978-3-642-38574-2_14
22. Goubault, E., Putot, S.: Static analysis of finite precision computations. In: Jhala, R., Schmidt, D. (eds.) VMCAI 2011. LNCS, vol. 6538, pp. 232–247. Springer, Heidelberg (2011). https://doi.org/10.1007/978-3-642-18275-4_17
23. Goubault, E., Putot, S.: Robustness analysis of finite precision implementations. In: Shan, C. (ed.) APLAS 2013. LNCS, vol. 8301, pp. 50–57. Springer, Cham (2013). https://doi.org/10.1007/978-3-319-03542-0_4
24. Computer Society IEEE. IEEE Standard for Floating-Point Arithmetic. IEEE Std 754–2008 (2008)
25. ISO/IEC. Programming languages — C — Extensions to support embedded processors. Technical report ISO/IEC TR 18037 (2008)
26. Izycheva, A., Darulova, E.: On sound relative error bounds for floating-point arithmetic. In: FMCAD (2017)
27. Jeannet, B., Miné, A.: Apron: a library of numerical abstract domains for static analysis. In: Bouajjani, A., Maler, O. (eds.) CAV 2009. LNCS, vol. 5643, pp. 661–667. Springer, Heidelberg (2009). https://doi.org/10.1007/978-3-642-02658-4_52
28. Kinsman, A.B., Nicolici, N.: Finite precision bit-width allocation using SAT-modulo theory. In: DATE (2009)
29. Lee, D.U., Gaffar, A.A., Cheung, R.C.C., Mencer, O., Luk, W., Constantinides, G.A.: Accuracy-guaranteed bit-width optimization. Trans. Comp.-Aided Des. Integ. Cir. Sys. **25**(10), 1990–2000 (2006)
30. Lightbend. sbt - The interactive build tool (2017). http://www.scala-sbt.org/
31. Magron, V., Constantinides, G., Donaldson, A.: Certified roundoff error bounds using semidefinite programming. ACM Trans. Math. Softw. **43**(4) (2017)
32. Majumdar, R., Saha, I., Zamani, M.: Synthesis of minimal-error control software. In: EMSOFT (2012)
33. Moore, R.E.: Interval Analysis. Prentice-Hall, Englewood Cliffs (1966)
34. Moscato, M., Titolo, L., Dutle, A., Muñoz, C.A.: Automatic estimation of verified floating-point round-off errors via static analysis. In: Tonetta, S., Schoitsch, E., Bitsch, F. (eds.) SAFECOMP 2017. LNCS, vol. 10488, pp. 213–229. Springer, Cham (2017). https://doi.org/10.1007/978-3-319-66266-4_14
35. Odersky, M., Spoon, L., Venners, B.: Programming in Scala: A Comprehensive Step-by-Step Guide. Artima Incorporation (2008)
36. Osborne, W.G., Cheung, R.C.C., Coutinho, J., Luk, W., Mencer, O.: Automatic accuracy-guaranteed bit-width optimization for fixed and floating-point systems. In: Field Programmable Logic and Applications, pp. 617–620 (2007)

37. Panchekha, P., Sanchez-Stern, A., Wilcox, J.R., Tatlock, Z.: Automatically improving accuracy for floating point expressions. In: PLDI (2015)
38. Pang, Y., Radecka, K., Zilic, Z.: An efficient hybrid engine to perform range analysis and allocate integer bit-widths for arithmetic circuits. In: ASPDAC (2011)
39. Ramananandro, T., Mountcastle, P., Meister, B., Lethin, R.: A unified Coq framework for verifying C programs with floating-point computations. In: CPP (2016)
40. Rümmer, P., Wahl, T.: An SMT-LIB theory of binary floating-point arithmetic. In: SMT (2010)
41. Solovyev, A., Jacobsen, C., Rakamarić, Z., Gopalakrishnan, G.: Rigorous estimation of floating-point round-off errors with symbolic Taylor expansions. In: Bjørner, N., de Boer, F. (eds.) FM 2015. LNCS, vol. 9109, pp. 532–550. Springer, Cham (2015). https://doi.org/10.1007/978-3-319-19249-9_33

Model Checking

Oink: An Implementation and Evaluation of Modern Parity Game Solvers

Tom van Dijk(✉)

Formal Models and Verification, Johannes Kepler University, Linz, Austria
tom.vandijk@jku.at

Abstract. Parity games have important practical applications in formal verification and synthesis, especially to solve the model-checking problem of the modal mu-calculus. They are also interesting from the theory perspective, as they are widely believed to admit a polynomial solution, but so far no such algorithm is known. In recent years, a number of new algorithms and improvements to existing algorithms have been proposed. We implement a new and easy to extend tool Oink, which is a high-performance implementation of modern parity game algorithms. We further present a comprehensive empirical evaluation of modern parity game algorithms and solvers, both on real world benchmarks and randomly generated games. Our experiments show that our new tool Oink outperforms the current state-of-the-art.

1 Introduction

Parity games are turn-based games played on a finite graph. Two players *Odd* and *Even* play an infinite game by moving a token along the edges of the graph. Each vertex is labeled with a natural number *priority* and the winner of the game is determined by the parity of the highest priority that is encountered infinitely often. Player Odd wins if this parity is odd; otherwise, player Even wins.

Parity games are interesting both for their practical applications and for complexity theoretic reasons. Their study has been motivated by their relation to many problems in formal verification and synthesis that can be reduced to the problem of solving parity games, as parity games capture the expressive power of nested least and greatest fixpoint operators [17]. In particular, deciding the winner of a parity game is polynomial-time equivalent to checking non-emptiness of non-deterministic parity tree automata [33], and to the explicit model-checking problem of the modal μ-calculus [14,15,23,32].

Parity games are interesting in complexity theory, as the problem of determining the winner of a parity game is known to lie in UP ∩ co-UP [26], as well as in NP ∩ co-NP [15]. This problem is therefore unlikely to be NP-complete and it is widely believed that a polynomial solution may exist. Despite much effort, no such algorithm has yet been found.

T. van Dijk—Supported by FWF, NFN Grant S11408-N23 (RiSE).

D. Beyer and M. Huisman (Eds.): TACAS 2018, LNCS 10805, pp. 291–308, 2018.
https://doi.org/10.1007/978-3-319-89960-2_16

Motivated by recent publications with both novel approaches and improvements to known algorithms, we implement a number of modern solvers in our new tool **Oink**, which aims to provide a high-performance implementation of parity game solvers. Oink is designed as a library that integrates with other tools and can easily be extended. We use Oink to provide a modern empirical evaluation of parity game solvers based on both real world benchmarks and randomly generated games.

In past publications new and improved algorithms are often tested against the implementation of Zielonka's algorithm in the PGSolver tool [19]. However, various recent publications [1,34,40] suggest that much better performance can be obtained. We combine a number of improvements from the literature [34,40,41] and propose additional optimizations. We show that our implementation of Zielonka's algorithm outperforms PGSolver by several orders of magnitude.

We describe Oink in Sect. 3 and provide accessible descriptions of the implemented state-of-the-art algorithms in Sects. 4–7. We implement the *strategy improvement* algorithm (Sect. 4), both the *small progress measures* and the recently proposed *quasi-polynomial progress measures* algorithms (Sect. 5), the well-known *Zielonka* algorithm (Sect. 6) as well as a number of related algorithms from the *priority promotion* family (Sect. 7). We also propose an alternative multi-core implementation of strategy improvement.

2 Preliminaries

Parity games are two-player turn-based infinite-duration games over a finite directed graph $G = (V, E)$, where every vertex belongs to exactly one of two players called player *Even* and player *Odd*, and where every vertex is assigned a natural number called the *priority*. Starting from some initial vertex, a play of both players is an infinite path in G where the owner of each vertex determines the next move. The winner of such an infinite play is determined by the parity of the highest priority that occurs infinitely often along the play.

More formally, a parity game ∂ is a tuple $(V_{\Diamond}, V_{\Box}, E, \mathsf{pr})$ where $V = V_{\Diamond} \cup V_{\Box}$ is a set of vertices partitioned into the sets $V_{\Diamond}$ controlled by player *Even* and $V_{\Box}$ controlled by player *Odd*, and $E \subseteq V \times V$ is a total relation describing all possible moves, i.e., every vertex has at least one successor. We also write $E(u)$ for all successors of u and $u \rightarrow v$ for $v \in E(u)$. The function $\mathsf{pr}\colon V \rightarrow \{0, 1, \ldots, d\}$ assigns to each vertex a *priority*, where d is the highest priority in the game.

We write $\mathsf{pr}(v)$ for the priority of a vertex v and $\mathsf{pr}(V)$ for the highest priority of a set of vertices V and $\mathsf{pr}(\partial)$ for the highest priority in the game ∂. Furthermore, we write $\mathsf{pr}^{-1}(i)$ for all vertices with the priority i. A *path* $\pi = v_0 v_1 \ldots$ is a sequence of vertices consistent with E, i.e., $v_i \rightarrow v_{i+1}$ for all successive vertices. A *play* is an infinite path. We write $\mathsf{pr}(\pi)$ for the highest priority in π is π is finite, or the highest priority that occurs infinitely often if π is infinite. Player Even wins a play π if $\mathsf{pr}(\pi)$ is even; player Odd wins if $\mathsf{pr}(\pi)$ is odd.

A *strategy* $\sigma\colon V \rightarrow V$ is a partial function that assigns to each vertex in its domain a single successor in E, i.e., $\sigma \subseteq E$. We typically refer to *a strategy of player* α to restrict σ to all vertices controlled by player α. A player wins a vertex if they have a strategy such that all plays consistent with this strategy are winning for the player. A fundamental result for parity games is that they are memoryless determined [13], i.e., each vertex is winning for exactly one player, and both players have a strategy for each of their winning vertices.

Algorithms for solving parity games frequently employ (variations of) *attractor computation.* Given a set of vertices A, the attractor of A for a player α represents those vertices that α can force the play toward. We write $Attr_{\alpha}^{\partial}(A)$ to attract vertices in ∂ to A as player α, i.e.,

$$\mu Z \,.\, A \cup \{\, v \in V_\alpha \mid E(v) \cap Z \neq \emptyset \,\} \cup \{\, v \in V_{\overline{\alpha}} \mid E(v) \subseteq Z \,\}$$

Informally, we compute the α-attractor of A by iteratively adding vertices to A of α that have a successor in A and of $\overline{\alpha}$ that have no successors outside A.

2.1 Solvers

We briefly introduce several approaches to solving parity games. These approaches can be roughly divided into two categories.

First, several algorithms iteratively perform local updates to vertices until a fixed point is reached. Each vertex is equipped with some measure which records the best game either player knows that they can play from that vertex so far. By updating measures based on the successors, they play the game backwards. The final measures indicate the winning player of each vertex and typically a winning strategy for one or both players. The *strategy improvement* algorithm (Sect. 4) and the *progress measures* algorithms (Sect. 5) fall into this category.

Second, several algorithms employ attractor computation to partition the game into regions that share a certain property. This partition is refined until the winners of some or all vertices can be identified, as well as the strategy for the winning player(s). The *recursive Zielonka* algorithm (Sect. 6) and the recently proposed *priority promotion* algorithms (Sect. 7) fall into this category.

2.2 Empirical Evaluation

Our goal in the empirical study is three-fold. *First*, we aim to compare modern algorithms and treat them fairly. We therefore need to establish that our implementation is competitive with existing work. *Second*, we compare the algorithms that are implemented in Oink directly. *Third*, as two algorithms have a parallel implementation, we also study the obtained parallel speedup and the parallel overhead when going from a sequential to a multi-core implementation.

We use the parity game benchmarks from model checking and equivalence checking proposed by Keiren [31] that are publicly available online. This is a total of 313 model checking and 216 equivalence checking games. We also consider different classes of random games, in part because the literature on parity games tends to favor studying the behavior of algorithms on random games. We include three classes of self-loop-free random games generated using PGSolver with a fixed number of vertices:

- low out-degree random games (`randomgame N N 1 2 x`)
  $N \in \{ 100, 200, 500, 1000, 2000, 5000, 10000, 20000 \}$
- fully random games (`randomgame N N 1 N x`)
  $N \in \{ 100, 500, 1000, 2000, 4000 \}$
- low-degree steady games (`steadygame N 1 4 1 4`)
  $N \in \{ 100, 200, 500, 1000, 2000, 5000, 10000, 20000 \}$

We generate 20 games for each parameter N, in total 420 random games. We include low-degree games, since the solvers may behave differently on games where all vertices have few edges.

We present the evaluation in two ways. We compare runtimes of algorithms and penalize algorithms that do not finish on time (with a timeout of 15 min) by a factor 2× (PAR2), i.e., we assume that their runtime is 2× the timeout. This may still be quite optimistic. Compared to a timeout of 10 min, only few more games could be solved in 15 min. We also generate so-called *cactus plots* (often used to compare solvers in the SAT community) that show that a solver solved X models within Y seconds individually.

All experimental scripts and log files are available online via http://www.github.com/trolando/oink-experiments. The experiments were performed on a cluster of Dell PowerEdge M610 servers with two Xeon E5520 processors and 24 GB internal memory each. The tools were compiled with gcc 5.4.0.

3 Oink

We study modern parity game algorithms using our research tool named **Oink**. Oink is written in C++ and is publicly available under a permissive license via https://www.github.com/trolando/oink. Oink is easy to extend, as new solvers subclass the `Solver` class and only require a few extra lines in `solvers.cpp`.

Apart from implementing the full solvers described below, Oink also implements several preprocessors similar to other parity game solvers. We base our choices mainly on the practical considerations and observations by Friedmann and Lange [19] and by Verver [41]. We always reorder the vertices by priority and renumber the priorities from 0 to eliminate gaps (not the same as compression). The former is beneficial for the attractor-based algorithms in Sects. 6 and 7. The latter may reduce the amount of memory required for the measures-based algorithms in Sects. 4 and 5.

The following preprocessors are optional. Oink can perform priority inflation and priority compression, as described in [19]. We implement self-loop solving and winner-controlled winning cycle detection, as proposed in [41]. Winner-controlled winning cycle detection is a prerequisite for the strategy improvement algorithm of Sect. 4 but is optional for the other algorithms. We trivially solve games with only a single parity. Finally, we also implement SCC decomposition, which repeatedly solves a bottom SCC of the game until the full game is solved.

The correctness of an algorithm does not imply that implementations are correct. Although a formal proof of the implementations would be preferred, we also implement a fast solution verifier and verify all obtained solutions.

4 Strategy Improvement

Strategy improvement is a technique where each player iteratively improves their strategies until they are optimal. Strategy improvement algorithms were first explored for parity games by Jurdziński and Vöge [42] and have been subsequently improved in [7,16,20,35,38]. Recently, parallel implementations have been studied for the GPU [17,24,36]. Fearnley [17] also implements their parallel algorithm for multi-core CPUs. Our treatment in this section is mostly based on [17,35].

In the strategy improvement algorithm, player Even has a strategy σ and player Odd has a strategy τ for all their vertices. They improve their strategies until a fixed point is reached, at which point the game is solved. Instead of choosing a successor, player Even may also end the play. In the specific algorithm here, player Even delays selecting a strategy for a vertex until there is a favorable continuation. As σ and τ cover all vertices, they induce a fixed path from each vertex. This path is either infinite (a play) or ends at a vertex of player Even. The strategy is evaluated by computing a valuation for each vertex based on the current paths. Strategies are improved by choosing the most favorable successor.

The valuation used in e.g. [17,35] assigns to (infinite) plays the value $\top$ and to (finite) paths a function $L(p)$ that records for each priority p how often it occurs in the path. To determine the best move for each player, a total order $\sqsubset$ compares valuations as follows. For non-$\top$ valuations L_1 and L_2, $L_1 \sqsubset L_2$ iff there exists a highest priority z that is different in L_1 and L_2, i.e., $z = \max\{\, z \mid L_1(z) \neq L_2(z) \,\}$, and either $L_1(z) < L_2(z)$ if z is even, or $L_1(z) > L_2(z)$ if z is odd. Furthermore, $L \sqsubset \top$ for any $L \neq \top$. If $L_1 \sqsubset L_2$, then L_2 is more favorable for player Even and L_1 is more favorable for player Odd.

Intuitively, player Even likes plays where higher even priorities occur more often. Furthermore, player Even will end the play unless the highest priority in the continuation is even. Thus infinite paths are won by player Even and the valuation $\top$ represents this. Player Even will always play to $\top$ and player Odd will always try to avoid $\top$. This assumes that no winner-controlled winning cycles exist where player Odd wins, which can be guaranteed using a preprocessing step that removes these cycles.

For every strategy σ of player Even, a so-called *best response* τ of player Odd minimizes the valuation of each position. Player Even always plays against this best response. In each iteration, after player Odd computes their best response, player Even computes all *switchable edges* based on the current valuation L and the current strategy σ. An edge (u, v) is *switchable* if $L_v \sqsupset L_{\sigma(u)}$. Not all switchable edges need to be selected for the improved strategy, but as argued in [17], the *greedy all-switches* rule that simply selects the best edge (maximal in $\sqsubset$) for every position performs well in practice.

There are different methods to compute the best response of player Odd. We refer again to [17] for a more in-depth discussion. Player Odd can compute their best response by repeatedly switching all *Odd-switchable* edges, i.e., edges (u, v) s.t. $L_v \sqsubset L_{\tau(u)}$ and L_v is minimal in $\sqsubset$ of all successors of u.

```
1  def strategy-improvement:
2      σ ← (V₀ ↦ ⊥), τ ← random strategy for Odd
3      repeat
4          repeat
5              compute-valuations(V, σ ∪ τ, L)
6              τ ← τ[S_Odd] where S_Odd = All_Odd(⊇, τ, L)
7          until S_Odd = ∅
8          mark-won({v ∈ V: L_v = ⊤})
9          σ ← σ[S_Even] where S_Even = All_Even(⊇, σ, L)
10     until S_Even = ∅
11     return (W₀, W₁, σ, τ) where W₀ ← {v ∈ V: L_v = ⊤}, W₁ ← V \ W₀
```

Algorithm 1. The strategy improvement algorithm.

```
def backwards-update(v, into, L):
    for u ∈ into(v) :
        L_u ← L_v[pr(u) ↦ L_v(pr(u)) + 1]
        spawn compute-valuation(u, σ, L)
    sync all
def compute-valuations(V, σ, L):
    parallel for v ∈ V : L_v ← ⊤ ; into(v) ← ∅
    parallel for v ∈ V | σ(v) ≠ ⊥ : add v to into(σ(v))
    parallel for v ∈ V | σ(v) = ⊥ :
        L_v ← 0 [pr(v) ↦ 1]
        backwards-update(v, into, L)
```

Algorithm 2. Computing valuations in parallel.

The players thus improve their strategies as in Algorithm 1, where All_{Odd} and All_{Even} compute all switchable edges as described above. The initial strategy for player Even is to always end the play. Player Odd computes their best response, starting from a random τ initially. Player Even then improves their strategy once. They improve their strategies until a fixed point is reached. Then all vertices with valuation $\top$ are won by player Even with strategy σ and all other vertices are won by player Odd with strategy τ [17]. We extend the algorithm given in [17] at line 8 by marking vertices with valuation $\top$ after player Odd computes their best response as "won". We no longer need to consider them for All_{Odd} and All_{Even} as player Odd was unable to break the infinite play and thus they are won by Even.

The valuations can be computed in different ways. Fearnley implements a parallel algorithm that uses list ranking in two steps. The first step computes an Euler tour of the game restricted to chosen strategies σ and τ resulting in a list. The second step uses a three-step parallel reduction algorithm to sum all values of the list. The list is divided into sublists which are each summed independently in the first sweep, all subresults are then propagated in the second sweep and then the final values are computed in the third sweep. See further [17].

We propose an alternative parallel algorithm to compute the valuation. We start from each Even vertex where the path ends and perform updates along a recursive backwards search, processing predecessors in parallel using task parallelism. Any vertex that is not visited has valuation $\top$. See Algorithm 2. This algorithm is implemented in Oink using the high-performance work-stealing framework Lace [12]. When updating the valuations in L, we first sweep twice over all vertices to initialize L for each vertex to $\top$ and to add all vertices to $\mathtt{into}(v)$ that have their strategy to v. We also implement computing switchable edges in parallel via a straight-forward binary reduction using Lace.

Table 1. Runtimes in sec. (PAR2) and number of timeouts (15 min) of the three solvers PGSolver (`pgsi`), the solver by Fearnley [17] with sequential (`parsi-seq`) and multi-core variants, and Oink with sequential (`psi`) and multi-core variants.

	Model checking		Equiv checking		Random games		Total	
psi-8	**694**	0	**1078**	0	**315**	0	**2087**	0
psi	860	0	3262	0	480	0	4603	0
psi-1	1190	0	4090	0	487	0	5767	0
parsi-seq	1471	0	4199	0	1534	0	7204	0
parsi-8	2501	1	2908	0	56529	27	61938	28
parsi-1	4200	1	13867	6	71280	39	89347	46
pgsi	167596	88	95407	49	58839	27	321842	164

Empirical Evaluation. We compare the performance of Oink with the sequential and parallel solvers (1 or 8 threads) by Fearnley [17] and the "optstratimprov" solver in PGSolver. We disable optional preprocessing in all solvers. We only consider games without winner-controlled winning cycles, which are 289 model checking, 182 equivalence checking and 279 random games, in total 750 games.

See Table 1. We observe that PGSolver is vastly outperformed by Oink and the sequential solver of Fearnley. PGSolver timed out for 160 games, whereas `psi` and `parsi-seq` only timed out for 1 and 5 models, respectively. We observe similar parallel speedup for the parallel solvers, although Fearnley's solver has more overhead from sequential to parallel with 1 thread. This might be due to the extra work to produce the Euler tour and to perform list ranking. The speedup we obtain with Oink is not very impressive, but the vast majority of the games are solved within 1 s already. Furthermore, `psi` and `parsi-seq` are fairly close in performance. This is not a surprise, as their implementations are similar; the main difference is that Fearnley uses a forward search and we use a backward search. Hence, Oink is faster, but not by a large margin. Finally, we remark that Fearnley reports excellent results for list ranking on GPUs, whereas our algorithm is designed for a multi-core architecture.

5 Progress Measures

Progress measures is a technique that assigns to each vertex a monotonically increasing *measure*. The measure of each vertex is *lifted* based on the measures of its successors. By lifting vertices, players Even and Odd essentially play the game backwards. The measure represents a statistic of the most optimal play so far from the vertex, without storing the plays explicitly.

While progress measures have been used elsewhere, they were introduced for parity games by Jurdziński [27]. Several improvements to the original algorithm are due to Verver [41] and Gazda and Willemse [22]. A number of parallel implementations have been proposed for the Playstation 3 [6], for multi-core architectures [25,37] and for GPUs [8,24]. Furthermore, Chatterjee et al. proposed an implementation using BDDs [10]. Different types of progress measures were introduced after the recent breakthrough of a quasi-polynomial time algorithm due to Calude et al. [9], which resulted in the progress measures algorithms by Jurdziński et al. [28] and by Fearnley et al. [18]. This section studies small progress measures [27] and quasi-polynomial progress measures [18].

5.1 Small Progress Measures

The original small progress measures algorithm is due to Jurdziński [27]. We rely on the operational interpretation by Gazda and Willemse [22] and propose the *cap-and-carryover* mechanism to further understand the algorithm.

Progress measures record how favorable the game is for one of the players. W.l.o.g. we assume *even* progress measures. Given the highest priority d, define $\mathbb{M}^{\diamond} \subseteq \mathbb{N}^d \cup \{\top\}$ to be the largest set containing $\top$ ($\top \notin \mathbb{N}^d$) and only those d-tuples with 0 (denoted as _) on *odd* positions. An even progress measure $m \in \mathbb{N}^d$ essentially records for a vertex v how often each even priority p is encountered along the most optimal play (starting at v) so far, until a higher priority is encountered, i.e., until p no longer dominates. Such a prefix of the play is called a p-dominated stretch. Suppose that the sequence of priorities for a given play π is $\underline{00}10\underline{2}1\underline{2}0\underline{2}321\underline{4}2\underline{6}5\underline{6}201$, then $m = \{\,2\_3\_1\_2\,\}$, since the play starts with a 0-dominated stretch containing two 0s, with a 2-dominated stretch containing three 2s, with a 4-dominated stretch containing one 4, and with a 6-dominated stretch containing two 6s. Furthermore, the special measure $\top$ represents that the vertex can be won by player Even.

A total order $\sqsubset$ compares measures as follows. For non-$\top$ measures m_1 and m_2, $m_1 \sqsubset m_2$ iff there exists a highest priority $z = \max\{\, z \mid m_1(z) \neq m_2(z) \,\}$ and $m_1(z) < m_2(z)$. Furthermore, $m \sqsubset \top$ for all $m \neq \top$. We define a derived ordering $\sqsubset_p$ by restricting z to priorities $\geq p$. Examples:

$$\{1\_1\_1\} \sqsubset_0 \{0\_0\_2\}$$
$$\{3\_2\_1\} \sqsubset_0 \{0\_3\_1\}$$
$$\{1\_2\_1\} \sqsubseteq_1 \{0\_2\_1\}$$
$$\{3\_3\_1\} \sqsubseteq_4 \{0\_0\_1\}$$

To compute the progress measure for vertex v when playing to vertex w, given current measures $\rho\colon V \to \mathbb{M}^\diamond$, we define $\mathrm{Prog}(\rho, v, w)$ as follows:

$$\mathrm{Prog}(\rho, v, w) := \begin{cases} \min\{\, m \in \mathbb{M}^\diamond \mid m \sqsupset_{\mathsf{pr}(v)} \rho(w) \,\} & \mathsf{pr}(v) \text{ is even} \\ \min\{\, m \in \mathbb{M}^\diamond \mid m \sqsupseteq_{\mathsf{pr}(v)} \rho(w) \,\} & \mathsf{pr}(v) \text{ is odd} \end{cases}$$

Prog computes the measure of the play obtained by playing from v to the play recorded in $\rho(w)$. By choosing the lowest measure m according to $\sqsupseteq_{\mathsf{pr}(v)}$, we ensure that all $m(p)$ for $p < \mathsf{pr}(v)$ are set to 0. The inequality is strict for even priorities $\mathsf{pr}(v)$ to ensure that $m(\mathsf{pr}(v))$ increases.

Player Even wants to achieve the highest measure, whereas player Odd wants to achieve the lowest measure. We define $\mathrm{Lift}(\rho, v)$ as follows:

$$\mathrm{Lift}(\rho, v) = \begin{cases} \rho\,[\,v \mapsto \max\{\,\rho(v), \max\{\,\mathrm{Prog}(\rho, v, w) \mid v \to w\,\}\,\}\,] & \text{if } v \in V_\Diamond \\ \rho\,[\,v \mapsto \max\{\,\rho(v), \min\{\,\mathrm{Prog}(\rho, v, w) \mid v \to w\,\}\,\}\,] & \text{if } v \in V_\Box \end{cases}$$

By definition, the Lift operation increases measures monotonically. For the specific algorithm described here, we also observe that $\mathrm{Prog}(\rho, v, w) \sqsupseteq_{\mathsf{pr}(v)} \rho(w)$ and therefore Lift would even monotonically increase ρ without taking the maximum of the current measure and the best updated successor measure in a lifting procedure that starts with $\rho = V \mapsto 0$.

If we iteratively lift vertices from $\rho = V \mapsto 0$ using Lift, eventually some vertex may have a measure m such that $m(p)$ for some p is higher than the number of vertices with priority p, i.e., $m(p) > |V_p|$. In this case, we know that m represents a play that visits at least one vertex with priority p twice and thus contains a cycle dominated by p. Furthermore, player Odd cannot escape from this cycle unless by playing to a higher losing priority. This follows from the fact that if player Odd could escape from the cycle, then it would not lift to this measure. The option to play to the higher losing priority is not considered because a measure to a higher priority is $\sqsupset$ a measure that records a cycle.

We need a mechanism to let player Odd play to the next higher priority if it is forced into a cycle. However, we cannot let just any vertex play to a higher priority when its measure records a cycle, since some other vertex may escape to a lower higher priority. Therefore we need a mechanism that finds the lowest escape for player Odd. Small progress measures achieves this using a *cap-and-carryover* mechanism. $\mathbb{M}^\diamond$ is restricted such that values for each even priority p may not be higher than $|V_p|$. When this cap is reached, Prog will naturally find a next higher m by increasing the value of higher priorities and eventually reach $\top$. For example, if we have two vertices of priority 2 and two vertices of priority 4 in a game and there is a self-loop of priority 2, measures increase as follows: $\{0\_2\_0\}$, $\{0\_0\_1\}$, $\{0\_1\_1\}$, $\{0\_2\_1\}$, $\{0\_0\_2\}$, $\{0\_1\_2\}$, $\{0\_2\_2\}$, $\top$.

Thus all vertices involved in a cycle will find their measures slowly rising until the measure of some vertex controlled by Odd becomes equal to the measure when playing to a vertex that is not rising. This is the lowest escape. If no such escape is found, then the measures rise until $\top$ and these vertices are won by player Even. The slowly increasing measures no longer follow the operational interpretation described above, but can be understood as player Odd looking for the lowest escape.

We refer to [27] for the proof that the fixed point of applying the above lifting operation solves the parity game, such that vertices with measure $\top$ are won by player Even and all other vertices are won by player Odd with a strategy that chooses the successor for which $\text{Prog}(\rho, v, w)$ is the lowest.

We implement three known improvements. Improvements 2 and 3 are also implemented by PGSolver [19].

1. When a vertex with some even priority p is raised to $\top$, the cap of p may be lowered. The reason is that if a play records priority p $|V_p|$ times, it either contains a vertex now won by player Even or a cycle of priority p [41].
2. Small progress measures only computes the strategy for player Odd according to measures for player Even. We compute both *even* and *odd* measures simultaneously to compute the strategy for both players.
3. In addition, we occasionally halt the lifting procedure to perform an attractor computation for player Even to the set of *even*-liftable vertices. Any vertices not in this set are won by player Odd. We can immediately lift these vertices to $\top$ in the *odd* measures. We perform this analysis also for *odd*-liftable measures to potentially lift vertices to $\top$ in the *even* measures.

5.2 Quasi-polynomial Progress Measures

Different types of progress measures were introduced after the recent breakthrough of a quasi-polynomial time algorithm due to Calude et al. [9], which resulted in the progress measures algorithms by Jurdziński et al. [28] and by Fearnley et al. [18]. We only briefly and informally describe the idea of [18]. (Even) measures are k-tuples $M\colon (\mathbb{N}\cup\{\bot\})^k\cup\{\top\}$, which record that the optimal play consists of consecutive stretches that are dominated by vertices with even priority. For example, in the path $1\underline{2}131\underline{4}23\underline{2}15\underline{6}3\underline{2}1\underline{2}$, all vertices are dominated by each pair of underlined vertices of even priority. k is such that there are fewer than 2^k vertices with even priority in the game. An 8-tuple $\{\,2\;2\;4\;\bot\;5\;\bot\;6\;\bot\,\}$ denotes a game with consecutive stretches of 1, 2, 4, 16 and 64 even vertices, where the first dominating vertex has priority $M(i)$ and may actually be *odd* instead of even. If the first dominating vertex has an odd priority, then player Even must reach a higher priority before continuing to build a play where they have more dominating even vertices than are in the game. If player Even can visit more dominating even vertices than are in the game, then at least one of these is visited twice and therefore player Even knows that they can win and lifts to $\top$.

5.3 Empirical Evaluation

We compare our implementation of small progress measures and quasi-polynomial progress measures to the small progress measures implementation of

Table 2. Runtimes in sec. (PAR2) and number of timeouts (15 min) of PGSolver (`pgspm`), pbespgsolve (`pbesspm`) and the implementations `spm` and `qpt` in Oink.

	Model checking		Equiv checking		Random games		Total	
spm	**3637**	1	**7035**	0	168271	93	**178944**	94
qpt	122549	64	65310	31	**66303**	35	254162	130
pbesspm	38397	20	52422	27	183742	101	274561	148
pgspm	88800	45	59885	30	320666	171	469351	246

pbespgsolve that comes with the mCRL2 model checker [11,41] and the implementation of small progress measures in PGSolver [19]. Unfortunately, the solver used in [18] contains proprietary source code and cannot be compiled and compared. For this comparison, we disabled optional preprocessing, i.e., removing self-loops, winner-controlled winning cycles and solving single-parity games.

See Table 2. Although Fearnley et al. [18] say that the QPT solver is mainly interesting for the theoretical result rather than practical performance, we observe that `qpt` outperforms the other solvers for random games. Oink is faster than PGSolver, especially for model checking and equivalence checking.

6 Zielonka's Recursive Algorithm

The algorithm by Zielonka [43] is a recursive solver that despite its relatively bad theoretical complexity is known to outperform other algorithms in practice [19]. Furthermore, tight bounds are known for various classes of games [21].

Zielonka's recursive algorithm is based on attractor computation. At each step, given current subgame $\Game$, the algorithm removes the attractor $A := \mathsf{Attr}^{\Game}_{\alpha}(\mathsf{pr}^{-1}(\mathsf{pr}(\Game)))$, i.e., all vertices attracted to the current highest vertices of priority $p := \mathsf{pr}(\Game)$ for player $\alpha = p \bmod 2$, and recursively computes the winning regions $(W_{\Diamond}, W_{\Box})$ of the remaining subgame $\Game \setminus A$. If the opponent $\overline{\alpha}$ can attract vertices in A to $W_{\overline{\alpha}}$, then $\overline{\alpha}$ wins $W'_{\overline{\alpha}} := \mathsf{Attr}^{\Game}_{\overline{\alpha}}(W_{\overline{\alpha}})$ and the solution for the remainder $\Game \setminus W'_{\overline{\alpha}}$ is computed recursively. Otherwise, α wins A and no further recursion is necessary. The strategies for both players are trivially obtained during attractor computation and by assigning to winning p-vertices in A any strategy to vertices in $W_{\alpha} \cup A$.

Zielonka's original algorithm has been extended and improved over the years. In his thesis, Verver [41] improves the partitioning of the game after computing A by extending A with the attractors of the next highest vertices if they are of the same parity. The original algorithm always recomputes the solution of $\Game \setminus W'_{\overline{\alpha}}$ if $W_{\overline{\alpha}}$ is nonempty, even if no vertices are attracted to $W_{\overline{\alpha}}$. Liu et al. propose that this is not necessary [34]. See Algorithm 3 for the recursive algorithm with these modifications. Other extensions that we do not consider here are the subexponential algorithm [29] and the big steps algorithm [39] that have been reported to perform slower than ordinary Zielonka [19]. Also, variations using BDDs have been proposed [2,30].

1 **def** `zielonka`($\Game$):
2   **if** $\Game = \emptyset$ **: return** $\emptyset, \emptyset$
3     $\alpha \leftarrow \mathsf{pr}(\Game) \bmod 2$
4     $A \leftarrow$ `attr`$(\Game, \alpha)$
5     $W_\Diamond, W_\Box \leftarrow$ `zielonka`$(\Game \setminus A)$
6     $W'_{\overline{\alpha}} \leftarrow \mathrm{Attr}^{\Game}_{\overline{\alpha}}(W_{\overline{\alpha}})$
7   **if** $W'_{\overline{\alpha}} = W_{\overline{\alpha}}$ **:**
8         $W_\alpha \leftarrow W_\alpha \cup A$
9   **else:**
10         $W_\Diamond, W_\Box \leftarrow$ `zielonka`$(\Game \setminus W'_{\overline{\alpha}})$
11         $W_{\overline{\alpha}} \leftarrow W_{\overline{\alpha}} \cup W'_{\overline{\alpha}}$
12   **return** $W_\Diamond, W_\Box$
13 **def** `attr`$(\Game, \alpha)$:
14     $A \leftarrow \emptyset$
15   **while** $\mathsf{pr}(\Game \setminus A) =_2 \alpha$ **:** $A \leftarrow A \cup \mathrm{Attr}^{\Game \setminus A}_{\alpha}(\mathsf{pr}^{-1}(\mathsf{pr}(\Game \setminus A)))$
16   **return** A

Algorithm 3. The recursive Zielonka algorithm.

Although the implementation of the recursive algorithm in PGsolver [19] is typically used for comparisons in the literature, improved implementations have been proposed by Verver [41], Di Stasio et al. [40], Liu et al. [34], and Arcucci et al. [1]. Verver suggests to record the number of remaining "escaping" edges for each vertex during attractor computation, to reduce the complexity of attractor computation at the cost of an extra integer per vertex. Di Stasio et al. avoid creating copies of the game for recursive operations by recording which vertices are removed in a special array. Recently, Arcucci et al. extended the implementation in [40] with a multi-core implementation of attractor computation [1].

The implementation in Oink is based upon the ideas described above. Furthermore, we improve the implementation using the following techniques.

- Instead of creating copies of the "removed" array [40] for each recursive step, we use a single "region" array that stores for each vertex that it is attracted by the rth call to `attr`. This value is initially $\bot$ for all vertices and is reset to $\bot$ for vertices in $\Game \setminus W'_{\overline{\alpha}}$ (line 10). We record the initial r at each depth and thus derive that all vertices with a value $\geq r$ or $\bot$ are part of the subgame.
- As a preprocessing step, we order all vertices by priority. We can then quickly obtain the highest vertex of each subgame.
- We eliminate the recursion using a stack.
- We implement an alternative lock-free attractor, relying on the work-stealing library Lace [12] that provides fine-grained load balancing.

In the interest of space, we cannot describe the multi-core attractor in-depth. This implementation is fairly straightforward. We implement the attractor recursively where the work-stealing framework runs the recursive operations in parallel. Like typical lock-free algorithms, we rely on the `compare-and-swap` operation

Table 3. Runtimes in sec. (PAR2) and number of timeouts (15 min) of the four solvers PGSolver (`pgzlk`), SPGSolver (`spg`), pbespgsolve (`pbeszlk`) and Oink (sequential `zlk`, multi-core `zlk-1` and `zlk-8`, unoptimized `uzlk`).

	Model checking		Equiv checking		Random games		Total	
zlk-8	94	0	415	0	11	0	**521**	0
zlk	88	0	472	0	**6**	0	566	0
zlk-1	97	0	512	0	7	0	616	0
uzlk	89	0	472	0	69	0	630	0
pbeszlk	64	0	513	0	338	0	915	0
spg-seq	**58**	0	**198**	0	694	0	950	0
spg-mc	389	0	1451	0	72608	37	74447	37
pgzlk	65905	33	68013	36	41629	14	175547	83

to implement safe communication between threads. The attractor uses this operation when manipulating the number of escaping edges and to "claim" a vertex by setting its value in the region array from $\bot$ to r.

Empirical Evaluation. We compare our implementation of Zielonka's recursive algorithm with and without the optimizations of Algorithm 3 to PGSolver, to Verver's implementation pbespgsolve [11,41] and to SPGSolver [1,40]. Unfortunately, the Java version of SPGSolver (all three variations) suffers from severe performance degradation for unknown reasons. They also provide a C++ implementation in their online repository, which we used instead. The multi-core version of the SPGSolver tool relies on `async` tasks provided by C++11. Similar to the previous sections, we disable the optional preprocessors that solve single parity games, remove self-loops and solve winner-controlled winning cycles.

See Table 3. The results show that the implementation in Oink outperforms PGSolver by several orders of magnitude on all benchmark types. PGSolver timed out for 83 of all 949 games. The solvers `spg-seq` and `pbeszlk` are faster than Oink on the model checking and equivalence checking games, but are significantly outperformed on random games. We also observe severe performance degradation for `spg-mc` on random games. It appears that our parallel implementation of Zielonka's algorithm also does not scale well. Finally, there seems to be no significant difference between the optimized and unoptimized versions of Zielonka's algorithm, except for random games.

7 Priority Promotion

In recent work, a new family of algorithms has been proposed based on *priority promotion* [5]. Priority promotion starts with a similar decomposition of the game as Zielonka's recursive algorithm. Priority promotion is based on the insight that a recursive decomposition based on attractor computation leads to regions

Table 4. Runtimes in sec. (PAR2) and number of timeouts (15 min) of the five priority promotion solvers in Oink.

	Model checking		Equiv checking		Random games		Total	
ppp	**81**	0	**382**	0	**12**	0	**475**	0
pp	82	0	**382**	0	**12**	0	476	0
rr	**81**	0	385	0	**12**	0	477	0
dp	84	0	389	0	15	0	488	0
rrdp	83	0	394	0	14	0	491	0

with a specific property related to the highest priority in the region, called its *measure* p. This property is that all plays that stay in the region are won by the player who wins the highest priority p, denoted by player α. The other player $\overline{\alpha}$ has three options. They either lose the game by staying in the region, or they can leave the region by playing to an α-region of higher measure, or they can leave the region to a lower region of either player via a vertex with priority p. The goal of α is to find "closed" α-regions, where $\overline{\alpha}$ cannot escape to lower regions. The result is a region where player $\overline{\alpha}$ either loses, or leaves the region to a higher α-region which may or may not be closed. The measure of the closed α-region is then "promoted" to the measure of the lowest higher region to which $\overline{\alpha}$ can escape and the attractor-based decomposition is recomputed for all lower regions. The promoted region may now attract from regions with a measure between its original measure and its promoted measure, thus requiring recomputing the decomposition. When player $\overline{\alpha}$ cannot escape from an α-region to a higher α-region, player α is the winner of all vertices in the region.

Priority promotion was proposed in [5] and improved in [3,4]. The original PP algorithm [5] forgets all progress ("resets") in lower regions after promotion. The PP+ algorithm [3] only resets lower regions of player $\overline{\alpha}$. The RR algorithm [4] only resets *some* lower regions of player $\overline{\alpha}$. The DP algorithm [3] uses a heuristic to delay certain promotions to avoid resets. We implement all four algorithms and also combine the DP algorithm, which is based on PP+, with the RR algorithm.

Empirical Evaluation. We compare our implementation of five variations of priority promotion in Oink. As we do not compare with other solvers, we enable the optional preprocessors that solve single parity games, remove self-loops and solve winner-controlled winning cycles.

See Table 4. Overall, we see that the simplest solver pp performs just as good as the more complex solvers. The motivation for the variations is based on crafted families that require an exponential number of promotions. The pp solver may be most vulnerable to these crafted families, but on practical games and random games there is no significant difference.

8 Conclusions

See Table 5 for a comparison of the five main sequential algorithms in Oink, including the preprocessing that removes winner-controlled winning cycles, self-loops and solves single parity games. The results show that the `zlk` and the pp solvers have similar performance and outperform the other solvers. See also Fig. 1 for a cactus plot of these five solvers.

Priority promotion is a powerful and attractive idea, as promoting closed α-regions is similar to *cap-and-carryover* in small progress measures. Attractor computation finds such regions directly whereas value iteration algorithms may require many iterations. We confirm the observations in [5] that the algorithm has a good performance but it is not faster than Zielonka's algorithm.

In this work, we studied modern parity game algorithms using a new tool named **Oink**. Oink is publicly available via https://www.github.com/trolando/oink. We implemented a number of modern algorithms and provided a comprehensive description of these algorithms, introducing *cap-and-carryover* to understand small progress measures. We proposed improvements to strategy improvement and to Zielonka's algorithm. We presented an empirical evaluation of Oink, comparing its performance with state-of-the-art solvers, especially the popular PGSolver tool. The results demonstrate that Oink is competitive with other

Table 5. Runtimes in sec. (PAR2) and number of timeouts (15 min) of the sequential implementations of the five solvers in Oink described in this paper.

	Model checking		Equiv checking		Random games		Total	
pp	82	0	**382**	0	12	0	**476**	0
zlk	**78**	0	393	0	**10**	0	481	0
psi	231	0	2440	0	689	0	3359	0
spm	1007	0	3079	0	156885	87	160971	87
qpt	59559	31	60728	31	62104	33	182391	95

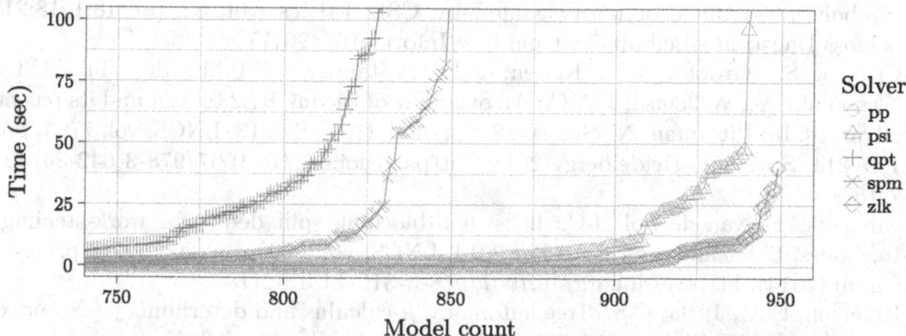

Fig. 1. A cactus plot of five sequential solvers implemented in Oink. The plot shows how many games are (individually) solved within a certain amount of time.

implementations and in fact outperforms PGSolver for all algorithms, especially Zielonka's recursive algorithm. This result is particularly interesting considering that many publications compare the performance of novel ideas to Zielonka's algorithm in PGSolver.

Acknowledgements. We thank Tim Willemse and John Fearnley for their helpful comments and Jaco van de Pol for the use of their computer cluster.

References

1. Arcucci, R., Marotta, U., Murano, A., Sorrentino, L.: Parallel parity games: a multicore attractor for the Zielonka recursive algorithm. In: ICCS, Procedia Computer Science, vol. 108, pp. 525–534. Elsevier (2017)
2. Bakera, M., Edelkamp, S., Kissmann, P., Renner, C.D.: Solving μ-calculus parity games by symbolic planning. In: Peled, D.A., Wooldridge, M.J. (eds.) MoChArt 2008. LNCS (LNAI), vol. 5348, pp. 15–33. Springer, Heidelberg (2009). https://doi.org/10.1007/978-3-642-00431-5_2
3. Benerecetti, M., Dell'Erba, D., Mogavero, F.: A delayed promotion policy for parity games. In: GandALF 2016. EPTCS, vol. 226, pp. 30–45 (2016)
4. Benerecetti, M., Dell'Erba, D., Mogavero, F.: Improving priority promotion for parity games. In: Bloem, R., Arbel, E. (eds.) HVC 2016. LNCS, vol. 10028, pp. 117–133. Springer, Cham (2016). https://doi.org/10.1007/978-3-319-49052-6_8
5. Benerecetti, M., Dell'Erba, D., Mogavero, F.: Solving parity games via priority promotion. In: Chaudhuri, S., Farzan, A. (eds.) CAV 2016. LNCS, vol. 9780, pp. 270–290. Springer, Cham (2016). https://doi.org/10.1007/978-3-319-41540-6_15
6. van der Berg, F.: Solving parity games on the playstation 3. In: Twente Student Conference (2010)
7. Björklund, H., Vorobyov, S.G.: A combinatorial strongly subexponential strategy improvement algorithm for mean payoff games. Discret. Appl. Math. **155**(2), 210–229 (2007)
8. Bootsma, P.: Speeding up the small progress measures algorithm for parity games using the GPU. Master's thesis, Eindhoven University of Technology (2013)
9. Calude, C.S., Jain, S., Khoussainov, B., Li, W., Stephan, F.: Deciding parity games in quasipolynomial time. In: STOC, pp. 252–263. ACM (2017)
10. Chatterjee, K., Dvorák, W., Henzinger, M., Loitzenbauer, V.: Improved set-based symbolic algorithms for parity games. In: CSL, LIPIcs, vol. 82, pp. 18:1–18:21. Schloss Dagstuhl - Leibniz-Zentrum fuer Informatik (2017)
11. Cranen, S., Groote, J.F., Keiren, J.J.A., Stappers, F.P.M., de Vink, E.P., Wesselink, W., Willemse, T.A.C.: An overview of the mCRL2 toolset and its recent advances. In: Piterman, N., Smolka, S.A. (eds.) TACAS 2013. LNCS, vol. 7795, pp. 199–213. Springer, Heidelberg (2013). https://doi.org/10.1007/978-3-642-36742-7_15
12. van Dijk, T., van de Pol, J.C.: Lace: non-blocking split deque for work-stealing. In: Lopes, L., et al. (eds.) Euro-Par 2014. LNCS, vol. 8806, pp. 206–217. Springer, Cham (2014). https://doi.org/10.1007/978-3-319-14313-2_18
13. Emerson, E.A., Jutla, C.S.: Tree automata, μ-calculus and determinacy (extended abstract). In: FOCS, pp. 368–377. IEEE Computer Society (1991)
14. Emerson, E.A., Jutla, C.S., Sistla, A.P.: On model-checking for fragments of μ-calculus. In: Courcoubetis, C. (ed.) CAV 1993. LNCS, vol. 697, pp. 385–396. Springer, Heidelberg (1993). https://doi.org/10.1007/3-540-56922-7_32

15. Emerson, E.A., Jutla, C.S., Sistla, A.P.: On model checking for the μ-calculus and its fragments. Theor. Comput. Sci. **258**(1–2), 491–522 (2001)
16. Fearnley, J.: Non-oblivious strategy improvement. In: Clarke, E.M., Voronkov, A. (eds.) LPAR 2010. LNCS (LNAI), vol. 6355, pp. 212–230. Springer, Heidelberg (2010). https://doi.org/10.1007/978-3-642-17511-4_13
17. Fearnley, J.: Efficient parallel strategy improvement for parity games. In: Majumdar, R., Kunčak, V. (eds.) CAV 2017. LNCS, vol. 10427, pp. 137–154. Springer, Cham (2017). https://doi.org/10.1007/978-3-319-63390-9_8
18. Fearnley, J., Jain, S., Schewe, S., Stephan, F., Wojtczak, D.: An ordered approach to solving parity games in quasi polynomial time and quasi linear space. In: SPIN, pp. 112–121. ACM (2017)
19. Friedmann, O., Lange, M.: Solving parity games in practice. In: Liu, Z., Ravn, A.P. (eds.) ATVA 2009. LNCS, vol. 5799, pp. 182–196. Springer, Heidelberg (2009). https://doi.org/10.1007/978-3-642-04761-9_15
20. Friedmann, O., Lange, M.: Local strategy improvement for parity game solving. In: GandALF. EPTCS, vol. 25, pp. 118–131 (2010)
21. Gazda, M., Willemse, T.A.C.: Zielonka's recursive algorithm: dull, weak and solitaire games and tighter bounds. In: GandALF. EPTCS, vol. 119, pp. 7–20 (2013)
22. Gazda, M., Willemse, T.A.C.: Improvement in small progress measures. In: GandALF. EPTCS, vol. 193, pp. 158–171 (2015)
23. Grädel, E., Thomas, W., Wilke, T. (eds.): Automata Logics, and Infinite Games: A Guide to Current Research. LNCS, vol. 2500. Springer, Heidelberg (2002). https://doi.org/10.1007/3-540-36387-4
24. Hoffmann, P., Luttenberger, M.: Solving parity games on the GPU. In: Van Hung, D., Ogawa, M. (eds.) ATVA 2013. LNCS, vol. 8172, pp. 455–459. Springer, Cham (2013). https://doi.org/10.1007/978-3-319-02444-8_34
25. Huth, M., Kuo, J.H.-P., Piterman, N.: Concurrent small progress measures. In: Eder, K., Lourenço, J., Shehory, O. (eds.) HVC 2011. LNCS, vol. 7261, pp. 130–144. Springer, Heidelberg (2012). https://doi.org/10.1007/978-3-642-34188-5_13
26. Jurdzinski, M.: Deciding the winner in parity games is in UP $\cap$ co-UP. Inf. Process. Lett. **68**(3), 119–124 (1998)
27. Jurdziński, M.: Small progress measures for solving parity games. In: Reichel, H., Tison, S. (eds.) STACS 2000. LNCS, vol. 1770, pp. 290–301. Springer, Heidelberg (2000). https://doi.org/10.1007/3-540-46541-3_24
28. Jurdzinski, M., Lazic, R.: Succinct progress measures for solving parity games. In: LICS, pp. 1–9. IEEE Computer Society (2017)
29. Jurdzinski, M., Paterson, M., Zwick, U.: A deterministic subexponential algorithm for solving parity games. SIAM J. Comput. **38**(4), 1519–1532 (2008)
30. Kant, G., van de Pol, J.: Generating and solving symbolic parity games. In: GRAPHITE. EPTCS, vol. 159, pp. 2–14 (2014)
31. Keiren, J.J.A.: Benchmarks for parity games. In: Dastani, M., Sirjani, M. (eds.) FSEN 2015. LNCS, vol. 9392, pp. 127–142. Springer, Cham (2015). https://doi.org/10.1007/978-3-319-24644-4_9
32. Kozen, D.: Results on the propositional mu-calculus. Theor. Comput. Sci. **27**, 333–354 (1983)
33. Kupferman, O., Vardi, M.Y.: Weak alternating automata and tree automata emptiness. In: STOC, pp. 224–233. ACM (1998)
34. Liu, Y., Duan, Z., Tian, C.: An improved recursive algorithm for parity games. In: TASE, pp. 154–161. IEEE Computer Society (2014)
35. Luttenberger, M.: Strategy iteration using non-deterministic strategies for solving parity games. CoRR abs/0806.2923 (2008)

36. Meyer, P.J., Luttenberger, M.: Solving mean-payoff games on the GPU. In: Artho, C., Legay, A., Peled, D. (eds.) ATVA 2016. LNCS, vol. 9938, pp. 262–267. Springer, Cham (2016). https://doi.org/10.1007/978-3-319-46520-3_17
37. van de Pol, J., Weber, M.: A multi-core solver for parity games. Electr. Notes Theor. Comput. Sci. **220**(2), 19–34 (2008)
38. Schewe, S.: An optimal strategy improvement algorithm for solving parity and payoff games. In: Kaminski, M., Martini, S. (eds.) CSL 2008. LNCS, vol. 5213, pp. 369–384. Springer, Heidelberg (2008). https://doi.org/10.1007/978-3-540-87531-4_27
39. Schewe, S.: Solving parity games in big steps. J. Comput. Syst. Sci. **84**, 243–262 (2017)
40. Di Stasio, A., Murano, A., Prignano, V., Sorrentino, L.: Solving parity games in scala. In: Lanese, I., Madelaine, E. (eds.) FACS 2014. LNCS, vol. 8997, pp. 145–161. Springer, Cham (2015). https://doi.org/10.1007/978-3-319-15317-9_9
41. Verver, M.: Practical improvements to parity game solving. Master's thesis, University of Twente (2013)
42. Vöge, J., Jurdziński, M.: A discrete strategy improvement algorithm for solving parity games. In: Emerson, E.A., Sistla, A.P. (eds.) CAV 2000. LNCS, vol. 1855, pp. 202–215. Springer, Heidelberg (2000). https://doi.org/10.1007/10722167_18
43. Zielonka, W.: Infinite games on finitely coloured graphs with applications to automata on infinite trees. Theor. Comput. Sci. **200**(1–2), 135–183 (1998)

More Scalable LTL Model Checking via Discovering Design-Space Dependencies (D^3)

Rohit Dureja(✉) and Kristin Yvonne Rozier

Iowa State University, Ames, USA
{dureja,kyrozier}@iastate.edu

Abstract. Modern system design often requires comparing several models over a large design space. Different models arise out of a need to weigh different design choices, to check core capabilities of versions with varying features, or to analyze a future version against previous ones. Model checking can compare different models; however, applying model checking off-the-shelf may not scale due to the large size of the design space for today's complex systems. We exploit relationships between different models of the same (or related) systems to optimize the model-checking search. Our algorithm, D^3, preprocesses the design space and checks fewer model-checking instances, e.g., using NUXMV. It automatically prunes the search space by reducing both the number of models to check, and the number of LTL properties that need to be checked for each model in order to provide the complete model-checking verdict for every individual model-property pair. We formalize heuristics that improve the performance of D^3. We demonstrate the scalability of D^3 by extensive experimental evaluation, e.g., by checking 1,620 real-life models for NASA's NextGen air traffic control system. Compared to checking each model-property pair individually, D^3 is up to 9.4× faster.

1 Introduction

In the early phases of design, there are frequently many different models of the system under development [2,23,29] constituting a *design space*. We may need to evaluate different design choices, to check core capabilities of system versions with varying feature-levels, or to analyze a future version against previous ones in the product line. The models may differ in their assumptions, implementations, and configurations. We can use model checking to aid system development via a thorough comparison of the set of system models against a set of properties representing requirements. Model checking, in combination with related techniques like fault-tree analysis, can provide an effective comparative analysis [23,29]. The classical approach checks each model one-by-one, as a set of independent model-checking runs. For large and complex design spaces, performance can be inefficient or even fail to scale to handle the combinatorial size of the design

Thanks to NSF CAREER Award CNS-1552934 for supporting this work.

D. Beyer and M. Huisman (Eds.): TACAS 2018, LNCS 10805, pp. 309–327, 2018.
https://doi.org/10.1007/978-3-319-89960-2_17

space. Nevertheless, the classical approach remains the most widely used method in industry [3,23,25,29,30]. Algorithms for family-based model checking [11,13] mitigate this problem but their efficiency and applicability still depends on the use of custom model checkers to deal with model families.

We assume that each model in the design space can be parameterized over a finite set of parametric inputs that enable/disable individual assumptions, implementations, or behaviors. It might be the case that for any pair of models the assumptions are dependent, their implementations contradict each other, or they have the same behavior. Since the different models of the same system are related, it is possible to exploit the known relationships between them, if they exist, to optimize the model checking search. These relationships can exist in two ways: relationships between the models, and relationships between the properties checked for each model.

We present an algorithm that automatically prunes and dynamically orders the model-checking search space by exploiting inter-model relationships. The algorithm, Discover Design-Space Dependencies (D^3), reduces both the number of models to check, and the number of LTL properties that need to be checked for each model. Rather than using a custom model checker, D^3 works with any off-the-shelf checker. This allows practitioners to use state-of-the-art, optimized model-checking algorithms, and to choose their preferred model checker, which enables adoption of our method by practitioners who already use model checking with minimum change in their verification workflow. We reason about a set of system models by introducing the notion of a *Combinatorial Transition System* (CTS). Each individual model, or *instance*, can be derived from the CTS by configuring it with a set of parameters. Each transition in the CTS is enabled/disabled by the parameters. We model check each instance of the CTS against sets of properties. We assume the properties are in Linear Temporal Logic (LTL) and are independent of the choice of parameters, though not all properties may apply to all instances. D^3 preprocesses the CTS to find relationships between parameters and minimizes the number of instances that need to be checked to produce results for the whole set. It uses LTL satisfiability checking [33] to determine the dependencies between pairs of LTL properties, then reduces the number of properties that are checked for each instance. D^3 returns results for every model-property pair in the design space, aiming to compose these results from a reduced series of model-checking runs compared to the classical approach of checking every model-property pair. We demonstrate the industrial scalability of D^3 using a set of 1,620 real-life, publicly-available SMV-language benchmark models with LTL specifications; these model NASA's NextGen air traffic control system [8,23,29]. We also evaluate the property-dependence analysis separately on real-life models of Boeing AIR 6110 Wheel Braking System [3] to evaluate D^3 in multi-property verification workflows.

Related Work. One striking contrast between D^3 and related work is that D^3 is a preprocessing algorithm, does not require custom modeling, and works with any off-the-shelf LTL model checker. Parameter synthesis [9] can generate the many models in a design space that can be analyzed by D^3; however existing parameter synthesis techniques require custom modeling of a system. We take the easier path of reasoning over an already-restricted set of models of interest to system designers. D^3 efficiently compares any set of models rather than finding all models that meet the requirements. Several parameter synthesis approaches designed for parametric Markov models [15,16,24,31] use PRISM and compute the region of parameters for which the model satisfies a given probabilistic property (PCTL or PLTL); D^3 is an LTL-based algorithm. Parameter synthesis of a parametric Markov model with non-probabilistic transitions can generate the many models that D^3 can analyze. In multi-objective model checking [1,21,22,28], given a Markov decision process and a set of LTL properties, the algorithms find a controller strategy such that the Markov process satisfies all properties with some set probability. Differently from multi-objective model checking, which generates "trade-off" Pareto curves, D^3 gives a boolean result. The parameterized model checking problem (PCMP) [20] deals with infinite families of homogeneous processes in a system; in our case, the models are finite and heterogeneous. Specialized model-set checking algorithms [18] can check the reduced set of D^3 processed models.

In multi-property model checking, multiple properties are checked on the same system. Existing approaches simplify the task by algorithm modifications [4,7], SAT-solver modifications [26,27], and property grouping [5,6]. The inter-property dependence analysis of D^3 can be used in multi-property checking. We compare D^3 against the *affinity* [6] based approach to property grouping.

Product line verification techniques, e.g., with Software Product Lines (SPL), also verify parametric models describing large design spaces. We borrow the notion of an *instance*, from SPL literature [32,34]. An extension to NuSMV in [13] performs symbolic model checking of feature-oriented CTL. The symbolic analysis is extended to the explicit case and support for feature-oriented LTL in [11,12]. The work most closely related to ours is [17] where product line verification is done without a family-based model checker. D^3 outputs model-checking results for every model-property pair in the design space (e.g. all parameter configurations) without dependence on any *feature* whereas in SPL verification using an off-the-shelf checker, if a property fails then it isn't possible to know which models *do* satisfy the property [14,17].

Contributions. The preprocessing algorithm presented is an important stepping stone to smarter algorithms for checking large design spaces. Our contributions are summarized as follows:

1. A fully automated, general, and scalable algorithm for checking design spaces; it can be applied to LTL model checking problems without major modifications to the system designers' verification workflow.
2. Modification to the general model-checking procedure of sequentially checking properties against a model to a dynamic procedure; the next property to check is chosen to maximize the number of yet-to-be-checked properties for which the result can be determined from inter-property dependencies.
3. Comparison of our novel inter-property dependence analysis to existing work in multi-property verification workflows [6].

4. Extensive experimental analysis using real-life benchmarks; all reproducibility artifacts and source code are publicly available.

2 Preliminaries

Definition 1. A *labeled transition system* (LTS) is a system model of the form $M = (\Sigma, S, s_0, L, \delta)$ where,

1. Σ is a finite alphabet, or set of atomic propositions,
2. S is a finite set of states,
3. $s_0 \in S$ is an initial state,
4. $L : S \to 2^{\Sigma}$ is a labeling function that maps each state to the set of atomic propositions that hold in it, and
5. $\delta : S \to S$ is the transition function.

A computation path, or *run* of LTS M is a sequence of states $\pi = s_0 \to s_1 \to \ldots \to s_n$ over the word $w = L(s_0), L(s_1), \ldots, L(s_n)$ such that $s_i \in S$ for $0 \leq i \leq n$, and $(s_i, s_{i+1}) \in \delta$ for $0 \leq i < n$. Given a LTL property φ and a LTS M, M *models* φ, denoted $M \models \varphi$, iff φ holds in all possible computation paths of M.

Definition 2. A *parameter* P_i is a variable with the following properties.

1. The *domain* of P_i, denoted $[\![P_i]\!]$, is a finite set of possible assignments to P_i.
2. Parameter P_i is *set* by assigning a single value from $[\![P_i]\!]$, i.e. $P_i = d_{P_i} \in [\![P_i]\!]$. A non-assigned parameter is considered *unset.*
3. Parameter setting is static, i.e., it does not change during a run of the system.

Let P be a finite set of parameters. $|P|$ denotes the number of parameters. For each $P_i \in P$, $|P_i|$ denotes the size of the domain of P_i. Let $Form(P)$ denote the set of all Boolean formulas over P generated using the BNF grammar $\varphi ::= \top \mid P_i == \mathrm{D}$ and $\mathrm{D} ::= P_{i_1} \mid P_{i_2} \mid \ldots \mid P_{i_n}$; for each $P_i \in P$, $n = |P_i|$, and $[\![P_i]\!] = \{P_{i_1}, P_{i_2}, \ldots, P_{i_n}\}$. Therefore, $Form(P)$ contains $\top$ and equality constraints over parameters in P.

Definition 3. A *combinatorial transition system* (CTS) is a combinatorial system model $M_P = (\Sigma, S, s_0, L, \delta, P, L_P)$, such that $(\Sigma, S, s_0, L, \delta)$ is a LTS and

1. P is a finite set of parameters to the system, and
2. $L_P : \delta \to Form(P)$ is function labeling transitions with a guard condition.

We limit the guard condition over a transition to $\top$ or an equality constraint over a single parameter for simpler expressiveness and formalization. However, there can be multiple transitions between any two states with different guards. A transition is *enabled* if its guard condition evaluates to true, otherwise, it is *disabled.* A label of $\top$ implies the transition is always enabled. A *possible run* of a CTS is a sequence of states $\pi_P = s_0 \xrightarrow{\nu_1} s_1 \xrightarrow{\nu_2} \ldots \xrightarrow{\nu_n} s_n$ over the word $w = L(s_0), L(s_1), \ldots, L(s_n)$ such that $s_i \in S$ for $0 \leq i \leq n$, $\nu_i \in Form(P)$ for $0 < i \leq n$, and $(s_i, s_{i+1}) \in \delta$ and $(s_i, s_{i+1}, \nu_{i+1}) \in L_P$ for $0 \leq i < n$, i.e., there is transition from s_i to s_{i+1} with guard condition ν_{i+1}. A *prefix* α of a possible run $\pi_P = \alpha \xrightarrow{\nu_i} \ldots \xrightarrow{\nu_n} s_n$ is also a possible run.

Example 1. A Boolean parameter has domain $\{true, false\}$. Figure 1 shows a CTS with Boolean parameters $P = \{P_1, P_2, P_3\}$. For brevity, guard condition $P_i == true$ is written as P_i, while $P_i == false$ is written as $\neg P_i$. A transition with label P_1 is enabled if P_1 is set to *true*. Similarly, a label of $\neg P_3$ implies the transition is enabled if P_3 is set to *false*.

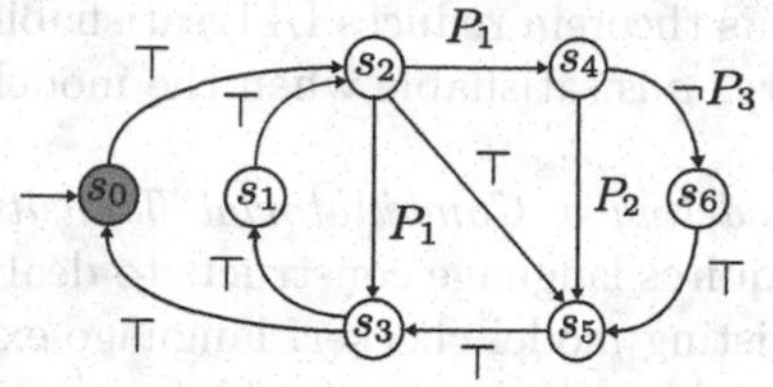

Fig. 1. An example of a combinatorial transition system M_P with parameters $P = \{P_1, P_2, P_3\}$.

Definition 4. A *parameter configuration* c for a set of parameters P is a k-tuple $(d_{P_1}, d_{P_2}, \ldots, d_{P_k})$, for $k = |P|$, that sets each parameter in P, i.e., for every $1 \leq i \leq k$, $P_i = d_{P_i}$ and $d_{P_i} \in [\![P_i]\!]$ is a setting. The set of all possible configurations $\mathbb{C}$ over P is equal to $P_1 \times P_2 \times \ldots \times P_k$ where $\times$ denotes the cross product. The setting for P_i in configuration c is denoted by $c(P_i)$.

A *configured run* of a CTS M_P over a configuration c, or c-run, is a sequence of states $\pi_{P(c)} = s_0 \xrightarrow{\nu_1} s_1 \xrightarrow{\nu_2} \ldots \xrightarrow{\nu_n} s_n$ such that $\pi_{P(c)}$ is a possible run, and $c \vdash \nu_i$ for $0 < i \leq n$, where $\vdash$ denotes propositional logic satisfaction of the guard condition ν_i under parameter configuration c. Given a CTS M_P and a parameter configuration c, a state t is *reachable* iff there exists a c-run such that $s_n = t$, denoted $s_0 \xrightarrow[c]{*} t$, i.e., t can be reached in zero or more transitions. A transition with guard ν is *reachable* iff $(s_j, s_{j+1}, \nu) \in L_P$, $(s_j, s_{j+1}) \in \delta$, and $s_0 \xrightarrow[c]{*} s_j$.

Definition 5. An *instance* of a CTS $M_P = (\Sigma, S, s_0, L, \delta, P, L_P)$ for parameter configuration c is a LTS $M_{P(c)} = (\Sigma, S, s_0, L, \delta')$ where $\delta' = \{t \in \delta \mid c \vdash L_P(t)\}$.

Given a LTL property φ and a CTS $M_P = (\Sigma, S, s_0, L, \delta, P, L_P)$, the *model checking problem* for M_P is to find all parameter configurations $c \in \mathbb{C}$ over P such that φ holds in all c-runs of M_P, or all computation paths of LTS $M_{P(c)}$.

Definition 6. Given a CTS M_P with parameters P_i, P_j, and a parameter configuration c, P_j is *dependent on* P_i, denoted $P_j \leadsto_c P_i$, iff

- In all possible runs with a transition guard over P_j, a transition with guard over P_i appears before a transition with guard over P_j, and
- In all configured runs, the setting for P_i in c makes transitions with guard conditions over P_j unreachable.

Example 1. In Fig. 1, if P_1 is set to false, execution never reaches the transition labeled $\neg P_3$. Therefore, if configuration $c = (false, true, true)$ then $P_3 \leadsto_c P_1$.

Definition 7. A *universal model* U is a LTS that generates all possible computations paths over its atomic propositions.

Theorem 1 (LTL Satisfiability). [33] Given a LTL property φ and a universal model U, φ is satisfiable if and only if $U \not\models \neg\varphi$.

This theorem reduces LTL satisfiability checking to LTL model checking. Therefore, φ is satisfiable when the model checker finds a counterexample.[1]

Modeling a Combinatorial Transition System. Efficient modeling of a CTS requires language constructs to deal with parameters. Since our goal is to use an existing model checker, language extensions are outside the scope of this work. An alternative way to add parameters to any system description is by utilizing the C preprocessor (`cpp`). Given a set of parameters P, and a combinatorial model M_P, each run of the preprocessor with a configuration $c \in \mathbb{C}$ generates an instance $M_{P(c)}$. Figure 2 demonstrates generating a CTS from two related SMV models. Model 1 and Model 2 differ in the initial configuration of the parameter. The corresponding CTS replaces the parameter initiation with the `PARAMETER_CONF` preprocessor directive. The `cpp` is run on the CTS model with `#define PARAMETER_CONF 0`, and `#define PARAMETER_CONF 1` to generate the two models.

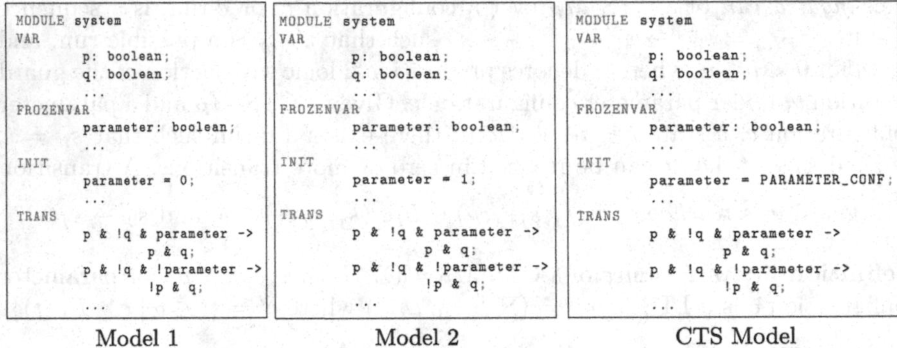
MODULE system
VAR
p: boolean;
q: boolean;
...
FROZENVAR
parameter: boolean;
...
INIT
parameter = 0;
...
TRANS
p & !q & parameter ->
p & q;
p & !q & !parameter ->
!p & q;
...
MODULE system
VAR
p: boolean;
q: boolean;
...
FROZENVAR
parameter: boolean;
...
INIT
parameter = 1;
...
TRANS
p & !q & parameter ->
p & q;
p & !q & !parameter ->
!p & q;
...
MODULE system
VAR
p: boolean;
q: boolean;
...
FROZENVAR
parameter: boolean;
...
INIT
parameter = PARAMETER_CONF;
...
TRANS
p & !q & parameter ->
p & q;
p & !q & !parameter ->
!p & q;
...
Model 1
Model 2
CTS Model

Fig. 2. Model 1 and Model 2 written in the SMV language can be combined to form a CTS model with the use of `PARAMETER_CONF` preprocessor directive.

3 Discovering Design-Space Dependencies

In this section we describe D^3. Our approach speeds up model checking of combinatorial transitions systems by preprocessing of the input instances; it therefore increases efficiency of both BDD-based and SAT-based model checkers. The problem reduction is along two dimensions: number of instances, and number of properties.

[1]This is why we do not consider CTL; CTL satisfiability is EXPTIME-complete and cannot be accomplished via linear time CTL model checking.

3.1 Reduction Along the Number of Instances

Given a set of parameters P, a combinatorial transition system M_P, and a property φ, M_P is model checked by sending, for all parameter configuration $c \in \mathbb{C}$, instance $M_{P(c)}$ to the LTS model checker, along with the property φ. The output is aggregated for $|\mathbb{C}|$ runs of the model checker, and all parameter configurations c, such that $M_{P(c)} \models \varphi$ are returned. In principle, parameters can be encoded as state variables, and the parametric model can be posed as one big model-checking obligation, however there are caveats.

1. State space explosion before any useful results are obtained.
2. Counterexample generated from one run of the model checker gives a single undesirable configuration.

Our goal is to make the classical approach of individual-model checking more scalable as the design space grows by intelligently integrating possible dependencies between parameter configurations.

Lemma 1. *Given a CTS $M_P = (\Sigma, S, s_0, L, \delta, P, L_P)$ with parameters $A, B \in P$, if $B \leadsto_c A$ for some parameter configuration c, then there does not exist any possible run of M_P with prefix $\alpha = s_0 \xrightarrow{*} s_i \xrightarrow{\nu_B} s_j \xrightarrow{*} s_k \xrightarrow{\nu_A} s_l$, where ν_A and ν_B are guards over A and B, resp., and $s_i, s_j, s_k, s_l \in S$, i.e., a transition with guard over B does not appear before a transition with guard over A.*

As a corollary to Lemma 1, there also do not exist possible runs with transition guards only over B (and no other $P_i \in P$). Therefore, given a CTS M_P with states $s_i, s_j, s_k, s_l \in S$ and parameters $A, B \in P$, if $B \leadsto_c A$ for some parameter configuration c, then all possible runs of M_P have one of the following prefixes:

1. $s_0 \xrightarrow{*} s_i \xrightarrow{\nu_A} s_j \xrightarrow{*} s_k \xrightarrow{\nu_B} s_l$ (guard over A before guard over B)
2. $s_0 \xrightarrow{*} s_i \xrightarrow{\nu_A} s_j \xrightarrow{*} s_k \xrightarrow{\nu_A} s_l$ (guards only over A)
3. $s_0 \xrightarrow{*} s_i \xrightarrow{*} s_j \xrightarrow{*} s_k \xrightarrow{*} s_l$ (guards neither over A nor B)

Similarly, if $A \leadsto_c B$ for some parameter configuration c, then all possible runs of M_P have one of the following prefixes:

1. $s_0 \xrightarrow{*} s_i \xrightarrow{\nu_B} s_j \xrightarrow{*} s_k \xrightarrow{\nu_A} s_l$ (guard over B before guard over A)
2. $s_0 \xrightarrow{*} s_i \xrightarrow{\nu_B} s_j \xrightarrow{*} s_k \xrightarrow{\nu_B} s_l$ (guards only over B)
3. $s_0 \xrightarrow{*} s_i \xrightarrow{*} s_j \xrightarrow{*} s_k \xrightarrow{*} s_l$ (guards neither over A nor B)

Therefore, when A and B are not dependent, there is no possible run with transition guards over both A and B. Note that for a CTS M_P with $A, B \in P$, if A and B are dependent, then either $A \leadsto_c B$ or $B \leadsto_c A$ but not both for any configuration c. We only show formalization for $B \leadsto_c A$; $A \leadsto_c B$ follows directly.

Theorem 2 (Redundant Instance). *Given a CTS $M_P = (\Sigma, S, s_0, L, \delta, P, L_P)$ with parameters $A, B \in P$ such that $B \leadsto_c A$ for some configuration c, and a LTL property φ, there exist configurations $c_1, c_2, \ldots c_k \in \mathbb{C}$ for $k = |B|$ such that*

```
function FINDUP (M_P, ĉ)
Input: M_P = CTS (Σ, S, s_o, L, δ, P, L_P)
       ĉ = partial configuration
Output: P_u = unset parameter queue
if all parameters are set in ĉ : return ∅
   # initially P_u is empty.
traverse M_P # depth-first traversal
   if t ∈ δ̂ is reachable and
              L_P(t) is undefined :
      # L_P(t) is undefined when its parameter
      is NOT set in partial configuration ĉ.
   enqueue (p : L_P(t) is guard over p) in P_u
return P_u
```

(a) FINDUP **algorithm to find unset parameters in a partially configured CTS.**

```
configuration set Ĉ # initially empty
function GENPC (M_P, P_u, ĉ)
Input: M_P = CTS (Σ, S, s_o, L, δ, P, L_P)
   P_u = unset parameter queue
   ĉ = partial config # initially empty
while P_u not empty :
  p = dequeue element from P_u
     # iterate on possible assignments to p
  for each p_d in ⟦p⟧ :
    set parameter p to p_d in ĉ
      # get unset parameters
    P_u = FINDUP(M_P, ĉ)
    if P_u is empty : # all parameters set
      add ĉ to Ĉ and return
    else: # set unset parameters
      GENPC(M_P, P_u, ĉ)
```

(b) GENPC **algorithm to generate parameter configurations to be checked.**

Fig. 3. Algorithms for reduction along the number of instances

- $c_i(A) = c(A)$ *for* $0 < i \leq k$, *and*
- $c_i(B) = d_{B_i} \in [\![B]\!]$ *for* $0 < i \leq k$ *and* $[\![B]\!] = \{d_{B_1}, d_{B_2}, \ldots, d_{B_k}\}$

For such configurations $M_{P(c_1)} \models \varphi \equiv M_{P(c_2)} \models \varphi \equiv \ldots \equiv M_{P(c_k)} \models \varphi$.

Theorem 2 allows us to reduce the number of model checker runs by exploiting redundancy between instances. The question that needs to be answered is how to find dependent parameters? A *partial parameter configuration*, $\hat{c}$, is a parameter configuration in which not all parameters have been set. Given a CTS $M_P = (\Sigma, S, s_0, L, \delta, P, L_P)$, for a transition $t \in \delta$, such that $L_P(t) = \nu$, the guard ν is

- *defined*, if its corresponding parameter is set in $\hat{c}$, and
- *undefined*, otherwise.

A defined guard evaluates to true when $\hat{c} \vdash L_P(t)$, or false when $\hat{c} \not\vdash L_P(t)$. Algorithm FINDUP (**Find U**nset **P**arameters) in Fig. 3(a) solves the dual problem of finding independent parameters. It takes as input a CTS M_P and a partial parameter configuration $\hat{c}$, and returns unset parameters for which guard conditions are undefined and their corresponding transitions are reachable. It traverses (depth-first) the CTS starting from a node for the initial state s_0. During traversal, an edge (transition) $t = (s_i, s_j)$ connects two nodes (states) $s_i, s_j \in S$ if $t \in \delta$ and $\hat{c} \vdash L_P(t)$. The edge is disconnected if $t \notin \delta$ or $\hat{c} \not\vdash L_P(t)$. Since M_P is defined relationally in the annotated SMV language with preprocessor directives (Sect. 2), in the worst case, FINDUP takes polynomial time in the number of symbolic states and transitions. From an implementation point of view, FINDUP invokes the cpp for parameter settings in $\hat{c}$ on the input model, and parses the output for unset parameters.

Lemma 2. FINDUP *returns unset parameters* $P_i \in P$ *for all reachable transitions* $t \in \delta$ *such that guard* $L_P(t)$ *is a guard over* P_i, *and is undefined.*

Algorithm GENPC (**Gen**erate **P**arameter **C**onfigurations) in Fig. 3(b) uses FINDUP as a subroutine to recursively find parameter configurations that need to be checked. It takes as input a CTS M_P, queue of unset parameters P_u, and a partial parameter configuration $\hat{c}$. Initially, $\hat{c}$ contains no set parameters and P_u =FINDUP(M_P, $\hat{c}$). Upon termination of GENPC, $\hat{\mathbb{C}}$ contains the set of partial parameter configurations that need to be checked. On every iteration, GENPC picks a parameter p from P_u, assigns it a value from its domain $[\![p]\!]$ in $\hat{c}$, and uses FINDUP to find unset parameters in CTS M_P. If the returned unset parameter queue is empty, $\hat{c}$ added to $\hat{\mathbb{C}}$. Otherwise, GENPC is called again with the new unset parameter queue.

Theorem 3 (GenPC is sound). *Given a CTS M_P with parameters $A, B \in P$, if there exists a partial configuration $\hat{c} \in \hat{\mathbb{C}}$ with $\hat{c}(A) = d_{A_n} \in [\![A]\!]$ and B unset, then there exist configurations $c_1, c_2, \ldots c_k \in \mathbb{C}$ for $k = |B|$ such that*

- *$c_i(A) = \hat{c}(A)$ for $0 < i \leq k$, and*
- *$c_i(B) = d_{B_i} \in [\![B]\!]$ for $0 < i \leq k$ and $[\![B]\!] = \{d_{B_1}, d_{B_2}, \ldots, d_{B_k}\}$*

for which $B \rightsquigarrow_{c_i} A$.

Theorem 4 (GenPC is complete). *Given a CTS M_P with parameters $A, B \in P$, if there exist configurations $c_1, c_2, \ldots c_k \in \mathbb{C}$ for $k = |B|$ such that*

- *$c_i(A) = d_{A_n}$ for $0 < i \leq k$ and $d_{A_n} \in [\![A]\!]$, and*
- *$c_i(B) = d_{B_i} \in [\![B]\!]$ for $0 < i \leq k$ and $[\![B]\!] = \{d_{B_1}, d_{B_2}, \ldots, d_{B_k}\}$*

for which $B \rightsquigarrow_{c_i} A$, then there exists a partial configuration $\hat{c} \in \hat{\mathbb{C}}$ with $\hat{c}(A) = d_{A_n}$ and B unset.

GENPC returns partial configurations $\hat{c} \in \hat{\mathbb{C}}$ over parameters. A partial configuration $\hat{c}$ is converted to a parameter configuration c by setting the unset parameters in $\hat{c}$ to an arbitrary value from their domain. Note that this operation is safe since the arbitrarily set parameters are not reachable in the instance $M_{P(c)}$. As a result of this operation, $\hat{\mathbb{C}}$ contains configurations c that have all parameters set to a value from their domain.

Theorem 5 (Minimality). *The minimal set of parameter configurations is $\hat{\mathbb{C}}$.*

3.2 Reduction Along the Number of Properties

In model checking, properties describe the intended behavior of the system. Usually, properties are iteratively refined to express the designer's intentions. For small systems, it can be manually determined if two properties are dependent on one another. However, practically determining property dependence for large and complex systems requires automation. Given a set of properties $\mathcal{P}$, and LTS M, an off-the-shelf model checker is called $N = |\mathcal{P}|$ times.

In order to check all properties in $\mathcal{P}$, a straightforward possibility is to generate a grouped property φ_g given by the conjunction of all properties $\varphi_i \in \mathcal{P}$, i.e., $\varphi_g = \bigwedge_i \varphi_i$. However, the straightforward approach may not scale [6] due to

1. State-space explosion due to orthogonal cone-of-influences of properties.
2. Need for additional analysis of individual properties one-by-one in order to discriminate failed ones and generate individual counterexamples.
3. Computational cost of verifying grouped properties in one run can be significantly higher than verifying individual properties in a series of runs.

Our goal is to minimize the number of properties checked by intelligently using dependencies between LTL properties. For two LTL properties φ_1 and φ_2 *dependence* can be characterized in four ways: $(\varphi_1 \rightarrow \varphi_2)$, $(\varphi_1 \rightarrow \neg\varphi_2)$, $(\neg\varphi_1 \rightarrow \varphi_2)$, and $(\neg\varphi_1 \rightarrow \neg\varphi_2)$. Theorem 6 allows us to find dependencies automatically.

Theorem 6 (Property Dependence). For two LTL properties φ_1 and φ_2 dependence can be established by model checking with universal model U.

The dependencies learned as a result of Theorem 6 have implications on the verification workflow. For instance, if $\varphi_1 \rightarrow \varphi_2$ is valid, then for a model M, if $M \models \varphi_1$ then $M \models \varphi_2$. Of particular interest are $(\varphi_1 \rightarrow \varphi_2)$, $(\neg\varphi_1 \rightarrow \varphi_2)$, and $(\neg\varphi_1 \rightarrow \neg\varphi_2)$ because they allow use of previous counterexamples (for $(\varphi_1 \rightarrow \neg\varphi_2)$, even if φ_1 is *true*, there is no counterexample to prove that φ_2 is *false*).

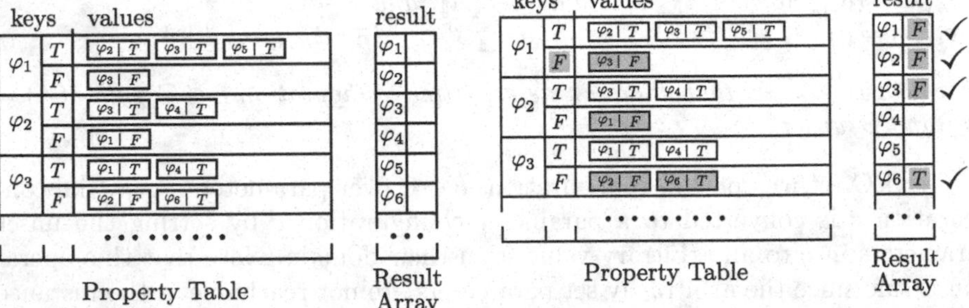

(a) Initial layout of the property table.

(b) Results that can be determined based on knowing φ_1 does not hold in model M.

Fig. 4. Property table to store dependence between every LTL property pair in set $\mathcal{P}$. Each row entry in the table is a $(key, value)$ pair. Multiple entries with the same *key* have been merged in a single row. E.g., if $\varphi_1 \rightarrow \varphi_2$, the table contains a row $(\varphi_1 : T, \varphi_2 : T)$ implying that if φ_1 holds for model M then φ_2 also holds.

The pairwise property dependencies are stored in a property table as shown in Fig. 4(a). Each row in the table is a $(key, value)$ pair. For LTL properties φ_1, φ_2, and φ_3 in $\mathcal{P}$, if $(\varphi_1 \rightarrow \varphi_2)$ is valid, then the table contains a row $(\varphi_1 : T, \varphi_2 : T)$ implying that if φ_1 holds for a model M then φ_2 also holds. Similarly, for $(\neg\varphi_3 \rightarrow \neg\varphi_2)$ the table entry $(\varphi_3 : F, \varphi_2 : F)$ implies that if φ_3 doesn't hold for M then φ_2 doesn't hold. Algorithm CHECKRP (**Check R**educed **P**roperties) in Fig. 5 takes as input a LTS M, a set of LTL properties $\mathcal{P}$, and a property table T over $\mathcal{P}$. CHECKRP selects an unchecked LTL property φ, checks whether φ holds in M, and stores the outcome. Based on the outcome, it uses the property table to determine checking results for all dependent properties and stores them. For example, in Fig. 4(b), if $M \not\models \varphi_1$, then $M \not\models \varphi_3$, $M \not\models \varphi_2$, and $M \models \varphi_6$. The LTL property to check is selected using two heuristics.

```
array results  # initially empty
function CHECKRP (M, P, T)
Input: M = LTS (Σ, S, s0, L, δ)
       P = set of LTL properties
       D = property table
while unchecked properties remain :
  φ = get unchecked property
  outcome = MODELCHECK(M, φ)
      # outcome = T if M ⊨ φ, else F
  set S = {(φ : outcome)}
  while S is not empty :
    (p : result) = pop element from S
    results[ p ] = result  # update result
    S = S ∪ unchecked properties
             dependent on (p : result) in D
return
```

Fig. 5. CHECKRP algorithm to check LTL properties against a model.

```
function D³ (M_P, P)
Input: M_P = CTS (Σ, S, s0, L, δ, P, L_P)
       P = set of LTL properties
configuration set Ĉ  # initially empty
parameter queue P_u = FINDUP(M_P, _)
Ĉ = GENPC(M_P, P_u, _)  # See § 3.1
   # generate property table, see § 3.2
property table D  # initially empty
for every property pair (φ1, φ2) in P :
  check if φ1 and φ2 are dependent
  add entry to D
  # check configured instances
for each c in Ĉ :
  generate instance M_P(c)  # See § 2
  array results  # initially empty
  CHECKRP(M_P(c), P, D)  # See § 3.2
  return results
```

Fig. 6. Discovering design-space dependencies (D^3) algorithm.

H1: Maximum Dependence. The tabular layout of property dependencies is used to calculate the number of dependencies for each property. The unchecked LTL property with the most right-hand side entries is selected. If $\mathcal{U} \subseteq \mathcal{P}$ are unchecked properties in table D, the next LTL property to check is then

$$\varphi \in \mathcal{U} : count(\varphi) = max(\{count(\psi) \mid \forall \psi \in \mathcal{U}\})$$

where $count(x) = |D[x:T] \cup D[x:F]|$ returns the number of dependencies for a LTL property in table D, and $max(S)$ returns the largest element from S.

H2: Property Grouping. Most model-checking techniques are computationally sensitive to the cone-of-influence (COI) size. Grouping properties based on overlap between their COI can speed up checking. Property *affinity* [5,6] based on *Jaccard Index* can compare the similarity between COI. For two LTL properties φ_i and φ_j, let V_i and V_j, respectively, denote the variables in their COI with respect to a model M. The affinity α_{ij} for φ_i and φ_j is given by

$$\alpha_{ij} = \frac{|V_i \cap V_j|}{|V_i| + |V_j| - |V_i \cap V_j|}$$

If α_{ij} is larger than a given threshold, then properties φ_i and φ_j are grouped together. The model M is then checked against $\varphi_i \wedge \varphi_j$. If verification fails, then φ_i and φ_j are checked individually against model M.

4 Experimental Analysis

Our revised model checking procedure D^3 is shown in Fig. 6. D^3 takes as input a CTS M_P and a set of LTL properties $\mathcal{P}$. It uses GENPC to find the parameter configurations that need to be checked. It then generates a property table to store dependencies between LTL properties. Lastly, CHECKRP checks each instance against properties in $\mathcal{P}$. Results are collated for every model-property pair.

4.1 Benchmarks

We evaluated D^3 on two benchmarks derived from real-world case studies.

(1) *Air Traffic Controller (ATC) Models:* are a set of 1,620 real-world models representing different possible designs for NASA's NextGen air traffic control (ATC) system. In previous work, this set of models were generated from a contract-based, parameterized NUXMV model; individual-model checking enabled their comparative analysis with respect to a set of requirements for the system [23]. In the formulation of [23], the checking problem for each model is split in to five phases.[2] In each phase, all 1,620 models are checked. For our analysis and to gain better understanding of the experimental results, we categories the phases based on the property verification results (UNSAT if property holds for the model, and SAT if it does not). Each of the 1,620 models can be seen as instances of a CTS with seven parameters. Each of the 1620 instances is checked against a total of 191 LTL properties. The original NUXMV code additionally uses OCRA [10] for compositional modeling, though we do not rely on its features when using the generated model-set.

(2) *Boeing Wheel Braking System (WBS) Models:* are a set of seven real-world NUXMV models representing possible designs for the Boeing AIR 6110 wheel braking system [3]. Each model in the set is checked against ~200 LTL properties. However, the seven models are not generated from a CTS. We evaluate D^3 against this benchmark to evaluate performance on multi-property verification workflows, and compare with existing work on property grouping [6].

4.2 Experiment Setup

D^3 is implemented as a preprocessing script in ~2,000 lines of Python code. We model check using NUXMV 1.1.1 with the IC3-based back-end. All experiments

[2] For a detailed explanation we refer the reader to [23].

Table 1. Timing results of 1,620 models for each phase using individual-model checking, and D^3. For individual-model checking, **Time** indicates model checking time, whereas, for D^3, **Time** indicates preprocessing time + model checking time.

Phase	Property mix	Properties	Model checking time (in hours)		Speedup	Overall speedup
		Total (median)	Individual	D^3		
I	UNSAT	25 (24)	6.02	4.02	1.5×	4.5×
II	UNSAT	29 (19)	12.76	5.17	2.5×	
III	UNSAT	29 (1)	139.79	14.80	9.4×	
IV	SAT+UNSAT	54 (43)	24.81	14.25	1.7×	1.8×
V	SAT+UNSAT	54 (44)	31.15	16.03	1.9×	
Total		191	214.53	54.27	4.0×	-

were performed on Iowa State University's Condo Cluster comprising of nodes having two 2.6Ghz 8-core Intel E5-2640 processors, 128 GB memory, and running Enterprise Linux 7.3. Each model checking run has dedicated access to a node, which guarantees that no resource conflict with other jobs will occur.

4.3 Experimental Results

(1) *Air Traffic Controller (ATC) Models.* All possible models are generated by running the C preprocessor (`cpp`) on the annotated composite SMV model representing the CTS. Table 1 summarizes the results for complete verification of the ATC design space: 191 LTL properties for each of 1,620 models.

Compared to individual model checking, wherein every model-property pair is checked one-by-one, verification of the ATC design space using D^3 is 4.0× faster. It reduces the 1,620 models in the design space to 1,028 models. D^3 takes roughly three hours to find dependencies between LTL properties for all phases. Dependencies established are local to each model-checking phase and are computed only once per phase. The number of reduced LTL properties checked for each model in a phase vary; we use CHECKRP with the Maximum Dependence heuristic (H1). Although the logical dependencies are global for each phase, the property verification results vary for different models. In phases containing UNSAT properties, speedup achieved by D^3 varies between 1.5× to 9.4×; since all properties are true for the model, only $(\varphi_1 : T \to \varphi_2 : T)$ dependencies in the property table are used. A median of one property is checked per model in phase III. For phases IV and V, D^3's performance is consistent as shown in Fig. 7.

Interesting Observation. D^3 requires a minimum number of models to be faster than individual-model checking. When the design space is small, individually checking the models is faster than verifying using D^3. This is due to the fact that D^3 requires an initial set-up time. The number of models after which D^3 is faster is called the "*crossover point*". For the benchmark, the crossover happens after ~120 models. As the number of models, and the relationships between them increase, the time speedup due to D^3 also increases.

Overall. From the initial problem of checking 1,620 models against 191 LTL properties, D^3 checks 1,028 models with a median of 129 properties per model (45% reduction of design space). Once D^3 terminates, the model-checking results for each model are compared using the data analysis technique of [23].

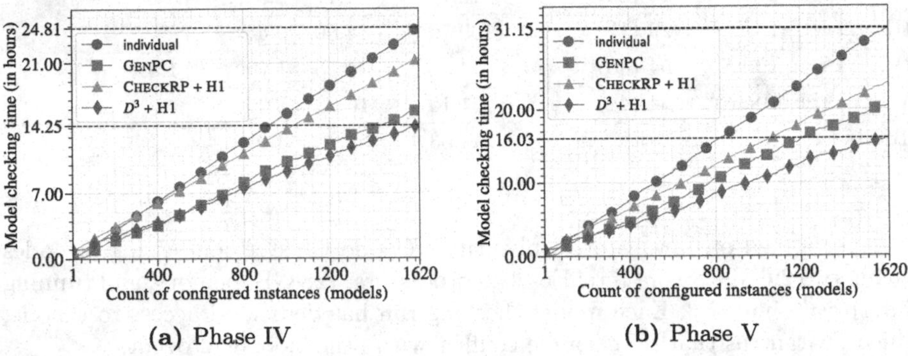

(a) Phase IV **(b)** Phase V

Fig. 7. Cumulative time for checking each model for all properties one-by-one (individual), checking reduced instances for all properties (GenPC), checking all models for reduced properties (CheckRP + H1), and checking reduced instances for reduced properties (D^3 + H1). D^3 outperforms individual-model checking in all phases.

(2) *Boeing Wheel Braking System (WBS) Models.* LTL Properties for each of the seven models are checked using four algorithms:

i. Single: properties are checked one-by-one against the model,
ii. CheckRP: properties are checked using inter-property dependencies,
iii. CheckRP + Maximum Dependence (H1): unchecked property with the maximum dependent properties as per inter-property dependencies is checked,
iv. CheckRP + Property Affinity (H2): properties are pairwise grouped and the unchecked pair with the maximum dependent properties is checked.

Figure 8 summarizes the results. On every call to the model checker, a single or grouped LTL property is checked. CheckRP is successful in reducing the number of checker runs by using inter-property dependencies. The Maximal Dependences (H1) and Property Grouping (H2) heuristics improve the performance of CheckRP, the former more than the latter. The timing results for each algorithm is shown in Table 2.

Analysis. For H2, we limited our experiments to pairwise groupings, however, larger groupings may be possible (trade-off required between property interdependencies and groupings). It took ~50 min to establish dependence between properties for a model, which is much higher than checking them one-by-one without using CheckRP. This brings us back to the question of estimating a *crossover point*. However, as the number of models increase for the same set of properties, CheckRP will start reaping benefits. Nevertheless, CheckRP is suited for multi-property verification in large design spaces.

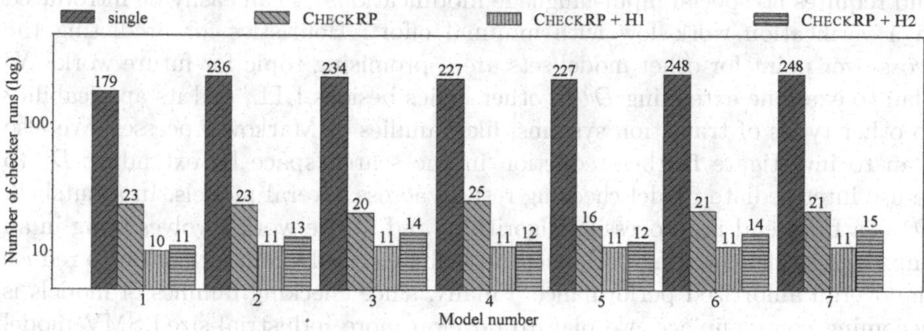

Fig. 8. Number of calls made to the model checker to verify all properties in the set for a model. Every call to the checker verifies one property: single or grouped. For CheckRP, multiple property results are determined (based on inter-property dependencies) on every checker run. Heuristics H1 and H2 improve performance of CheckRP.

Table 2. Timing results (in seconds) for performance of D^3's inter-property dependence analysis. A property: single or grouped, is verified on each checker run. Overall time indicates the total time to verify all properties for a model.

Model	Single		CheckRP		CheckRP+H1		CheckRP+H2	
	Overall time	Checker	Overall time	Checker runs	Overall time	Checker runs	Overall time	Checker runs
1	17.81	179	2.92	23	1.28	10	2.05	11
2	64.37	236	9.35	23	3.94	11	5.67	13
3	54.22	234	7.11	20	3.40	11	4.97	14
4	53.18	227	9.71	25	3.41	11	5.89	12
5	61.02	227	6.86	16	4.01	11	5.58	12
6	68.24	248	8.34	21	3.93	11	5.34	14
7	58.40	248	7.74	21	3.39	11	5.98	15

5 Conclusions and Future Work

We present an algorithm, D^3, to increase the efficiency of LTL model checking for large design spaces. It is successful in reducing the number of models that need to be verified, and also the properties verified for each model. In contrast to software product line model checking techniques using an off-the-shelf checker, D^3 returns the model-checking results for all models, and for all properties. D^3 is general and extensible; it can be combined with optimized checking algorithms implemented in off-the-shelf model checkers. We demonstrate the practical scalability of D^3 on a real-life benchmark models. We calculate a crossover point as a crucial measure of when D^3 can be used to speed up checking. D^3 is fully automated and requires no special input-language modifications; it can easily be introduced in a verification work-flow with minimal effort. Heuristics for predicting the cross-over point for other model sets are a promising topic for future work. We plan to examine extending D^3 to other logics besides LTL, and its applicability to other types of transition systems, like families of Markov processes. We also plan to investigate further reduction in the search space by extending D^3 to re-use intermediate model checking results across several models. In a nutshell, D^3 is a front-end preprocessing algorithm, and future work involves tying in an improved model checking back-end and utilizing available information to reduce the overall amortized performance. Finally, since checking families of models is becoming commonplace, we plan to develop more industrial-sized SMV model sets and make them publicly available as research benchmarks.

6 Supporting Artifact

The artifact for reproducibility of our experiments [19] is publicly available under the MIT License, and supports all reported results of Sect. 4. It includes

1. *Benchmarks:* NASA's NextGen Air Traffic Control System [23] and Boeing's Wheel Braking System [3] (Sect. 4.1).
2. *Scripts:* Python scripts to run D^3 on the two benchmarks (Fig. 6).
3. *Datasets:* Ready-to-use datasets generated during our analysis (Sect. 4.3)

The artifact supports the following usage scenarios.

1. Verify the benchmarks using both individual-model checking and model checking with D^3, or run the complete experimental analysis to reproduce the results reported in Tables 1 and 2.
2. Study and evaluate the benchmarks and source code for D^3, sub-algorithms (GenPC and CheckRP), and heuristics (H1 and H2).
3. Introduce extensions to D^3 and experiment with new heuristics.

Please refer to the README files in the artifact for further information. Every README inside a directory details the directory structure, usage of contained files with respect to the evaluation, and step-by-step instructions on how to the use the contained scripts to regenerate the experimental analysis.

Data Availability Statement. The benchmarks evaluated, source code, and data-sets generated during our experimental analysis are available in the Springer/ Figshare repository: https://doi.org/10.6084/m9.figshare.5913013.v1. Theorem proofs and extended results are available on the paper's accompanying website: http://temporallogic.org/research/TACAS18/.

References

1. Baier, C., Dubslaff, C., Klüppelholz, S., Daum, M., Klein, J., Märcker, S., Wunderlich, S.: Probabilistic model checking and non-standard multi-objective reasoning. In: Gnesi, S., Rensink, A. (eds.) FASE 2014. LNCS, vol. 8411, pp. 1–16. Springer, Heidelberg (2014). https://doi.org/10.1007/978-3-642-54804-8_1
2. Bauer, C., Lagadec, K., Bès, C., Mongeau, M.: Flight control system architecture optimization for fly-by-wire airliners. J. Guidance, Control Dyn. **30**(4), 1023–1029 (2007)
3. Bozzano, M., Cimatti, A., Fernandes Pires, A., Jones, D., Kimberly, G., Petri, T., Robinson, R., Tonetta, S.: Formal design and safety analysis of AIR6110 wheel brake system. In: Kroening, D., Păsăreanu, C.S. (eds.) CAV 2015, Part I. LNCS, vol. 9206, pp. 518–535. Springer, Cham (2015). https://doi.org/10.1007/978-3-319-21690-4_36
4. Cabodi, G., Camurati, P., Garcia, L., Murciano, M., Nocco, S., Quer, S.: Speeding up model checking by exploiting explicit and hidden verification constraints. In: DATE (2009)
5. Cabodi, G., Camurati, P.E., Loiacono, C., Palena, M., Pasini, P., Patti, D., Quer, S.: To split or to group: from divide-and-conquer to sub-task sharing for verifying multiple properties in model checking. Int. J. Softw. Tools Technol. Transfer (2017). https://doi.org/10.1007/s10009-017-0451-8
6. Cabodi, G., Nocco, S.: Optimized model checking of multiple properties. In: DATE (2011)
7. Cabodi, G., Garcia, L.A., Murciano, M., Nocco, S., Quer, S.: Partitioning interpolant-based verification for effective unbounded model checking. TCAD **29**(3), 382–395 (2010)
8. Cavada, R., et al.: The NUXMV symbolic model checker. In: Biere, A., Bloem, R. (eds.) CAV 2014. LNCS, vol. 8559, pp. 334–342. Springer, Cham (2014). https://doi.org/10.1007/978-3-319-08867-9_22
9. Cimatti, A., Griggio, A., Mover, S., Tonetta, S.: Parameter synthesis with IC3. In: FMCAD (2013)
10. Cimatti, A., Dorigatti, M., Tonetta, S.: OCRA: A tool for checking the refinement of temporal contracts. In: ASE (2013)
11. Classen, A., Cordy, M., Heymans, P., Legay, A., Schobbens, P.Y.: Model checking software product lines with SNIP. JSTTT **14**(5), 589–612 (2012)
12. Classen, A., Cordy, M., Schobbens, P.Y., Heymans, P., Legay, A., Raskin, J.F.: Featured transition systems: foundations for verifying variability-intensive systems and their application to LTL model checking. TSE **39**(8), 1069–1089 (2013)
13. Classen, A., Heymans, P., Schobbens, P.Y., Legay, A.: Symbolic model checking of software product lines. In: ICSE (2011)
14. Classen, A., Heymans, P., Schobbens, P.Y., Legay, A., Raskin, J.F.: Model checking lots of systems: efficient verification of temporal properties in software product lines. In: ICSE (2010)
15. Dehnert, C., Junges, S., Jansen, N., Corzilius, F., Volk, M., Bruintjes, H., Katoen, J.-P., Ábrahám, E.: PROPhESY: a PRObabilistic ParamEter SYnthesis tool. In: Kroening, D., Păsăreanu, C.S. (eds.) CAV 2015, Part I. LNCS, vol. 9206, pp. 214–231. Springer, Cham (2015). https://doi.org/10.1007/978-3-319-21690-4_13
16. Dehnert, C., Junges, S., Jansen, N., Corzilius, F., Volk, M., Bruintjes, H., Katoen, J.P., Ábrahám, E.: Parameter synthesis for probabilistic systems. In: MBMV (2016)

17. Dimovski, A.S., Al-Sibahi, A.S., Brabrand, C., Wąsowski, A.: Family-based model checking without a family-based model checker. In: Fischer, B., Geldenhuys, J. (eds.) SPIN 2015. LNCS, vol. 9232, pp. 282–299. Springer, Cham (2015). https://doi.org/10.1007/978-3-319-23404-5_18
18. Dureja, R., Rozier, K.Y.: FuseIC3: an algorithm for checking large design spaces. In: FMCAD (2017)
19. Dureja, R., Rozier, K.Y.: More Scalable LTL Model Checking via Discovering Design-Space Dependencies (Artifact) (2018). https://doi.org/10.6084/m9.figshare.5913013.v1
20. Emerson, E.A., Kahlon, V.: Reducing model checking of the many to the few. In: McAllester, D. (ed.) CADE 2000. LNCS (LNAI), vol. 1831, pp. 236–254. Springer, Heidelberg (2000). https://doi.org/10.1007/10721959_19
21. Etessami, K., Kwiatkowska, M., Vardi, M.Y., Yannakakis, M.: Multi-objective model checking of markov decision processes. In: Grumberg, O., Huth, M. (eds.) TACAS 2007. LNCS, vol. 4424, pp. 50–65. Springer, Heidelberg (2007). https://doi.org/10.1007/978-3-540-71209-1_6
22. Forejt, V., Kwiatkowska, M., Norman, G., Parker, D., Qu, H.: Quantitative multi-objective verification for probabilistic systems. In: Abdulla, P.A., Leino, K.R.M. (eds.) TACAS 2011. LNCS, vol. 6605, pp. 112–127. Springer, Heidelberg (2011). https://doi.org/10.1007/978-3-642-19835-9_11
23. Gario, M., Cimatti, A., Mattarei, C., Tonetta, S., Rozier, K.Y.: Model checking at scale: automated air traffic control design space exploration. In: Chaudhuri, S., Farzan, A. (eds.) CAV 2016, Part II. LNCS, vol. 9780, pp. 3–22. Springer, Cham (2016). https://doi.org/10.1007/978-3-319-41540-6_1
24. Hahn, E.M., Han, T., Zhang, L.: Synthesis for PCTL in parametric markov decision processes. In: Bobaru, M., Havelund, K., Holzmann, G.J., Joshi, R. (eds.) NFM 2011. LNCS, vol. 6617, pp. 146–161. Springer, Heidelberg (2011). https://doi.org/10.1007/978-3-642-20398-5_12
25. James, P., Moller, F., Nguyen, H.N., Roggenbach, M., Schneider, S., Treharne, H.: On modelling and verifying railway interlockings: tracking train lengths. Sci. Comput. Program. **96**(3), 315–336 (2014)
26. Khasidashvili, Z., Nadel, A.: Implicative simultaneous satisfiability and applications. In: Eder, K., Lourenço, J., Shehory, O. (eds.) HVC 2011. LNCS, vol. 7261, pp. 66–79. Springer, Heidelberg (2012). https://doi.org/10.1007/978-3-642-34188-5_9
27. Khasidashvili, Z., Nadel, A., Palti, A., Hanna, Z.: Simultaneous SAT-based model checking of safety properties. In: Ur, S., Bin, E., Wolfsthal, Y. (eds.) HVC 2005. LNCS, vol. 3875, pp. 56–75. Springer, Heidelberg (2006). https://doi.org/10.1007/11678779_5
28. Kwiatkowska, M., Norman, G., Parker, D., Qu, H.: Compositional probabilistic verification through multi-objective model checking. Inf. Comput. **232**, 38–65 (2013)
29. Mattarei, C., Cimatti, A., Gario, M., Tonetta, S., Rozier, K.Y.: Comparing different functional allocations in automated air traffic control design. In: FMCAD (2015)
30. Moller, F., Nguyen, H.N., Roggenbach, M., Schneider, S., Treharne, H.: Defining and model checking abstractions of complex railway models using CSP||B. In: Biere, A., Nahir, A., Vos, T. (eds.) HVC 2012. LNCS, vol. 7857, pp. 193–208. Springer, Heidelberg (2013). https://doi.org/10.1007/978-3-642-39611-3_20
31. Quatmann, T., Dehnert, C., Jansen, N., Junges, S., Katoen, J.-P.: Parameter synthesis for Markov models: faster than ever. In: Artho, C., Legay, A., Peled, D. (eds.) ATVA 2016. LNCS, vol. 9938, pp. 50–67. Springer, Cham (2016). https://doi.org/10.1007/978-3-319-46520-3_4

32. Rosenmüller, M., Siegmund, N.: Automating the configuration of multi software product lines. VaMoS **10**, 123–130 (2010)
33. Rozier, K.Y., Vardi, M.Y.: LTL satisfiability checking. In: Bošnački, D., Edelkamp, S. (eds.) SPIN 2007. LNCS, vol. 4595, pp. 149–167. Springer, Heidelberg (2007). https://doi.org/10.1007/978-3-540-73370-6_11
34. Schirmeier, H., Spinczyk, O.: Challenges in software product line composition. In: HICSS. IEEE (2009)

Generation of Minimum Tree-Like Witnesses for Existential CTL

Chuan Jiang(✉) and Gianfranco Ciardo

Department of Computer Science,
Iowa State University, Ames, IA 50011, USA
{cjiang,ciardo}@iastate.edu

Abstract. An advantage of model checking is its ability to generate witnesses or counterexamples. Approaches exist to generate small or minimum witnesses for simple unnested formulas, but no existing method guarantees minimality for general nested ones. Here, we give a definition of witness size, use edge-valued decision diagrams to recursively compute the minimum witness size for each subformula, and describe a general approach to build minimum tree-like witnesses for existential CTL. Experimental results show that for some models, our approach is able to generate minimum witnesses while the traditional approach is not.

1 Introduction

Model checking is an automated technique to rigorously establish the correctness of a system by exploring its computation graph, explicitly or symbolically. Instead of merely answering "yes" or "no", model checkers may be able to return a witness or counterexample to verify satisfaction or violation of a specification. Since witnesses and counterexamples provide important debugging information and may be inspected by engineers, smaller ones are always preferable.

Computation Tree Logic (CTL) is widely used to express temporal properties due to its simple yet expressive semantics. Although much work has been published on witness or counterexample generation [8,11,14], to the best of our knowledge, no existing method guarantees their minimality for a general CTL formula with nested temporal quantifiers. Clarke et al. [7] showed that the general form of a counterexample to a universal CTL formula is tree-like; of course, for CTL, counterexample generation for a universal formula can be converted to witness generation for an existential formula, thus we choose to limit our discussion to witness generation for the existential fragment of CTL. The use of backward exploration to verify **EX**, **EF**, and **EU** properties inherently guarantees minimality of their linear witnesses, while a minimum lasso-shaped **EG** witness can be generated by computing transitive closures, for example using the saturation algorithm [17]. However, these approaches do not extend to general tree-like witnesses, i.e., local minimality does not imply global minimality.

By recursively computing local fixpoints, the saturation algorithm [3] has clear advantages over traditional symbolic breadth-first approaches for state-space generation. It has also been applied to the computation of minimum **EF** [4]

D. Beyer and M. Huisman (Eds.): TACAS 2018, LNCS 10805, pp. 328–343, 2018.
https://doi.org/10.1007/978-3-319-89960-2_18

and **EG** [17] witnesses. Here, we extend these ideas into a global approach to build minimum witnesses for arbitrary existential CTL formulas.

Our paper is organized as follows. Section 2 summarizes background on CTL, decision diagrams, and symbolic CTL model checking. Section 3 defines the witness size and formalizes the computation of its minimum. Section 4 proposes saturation-based algorithms to symbolically encode minimum witness sizes for each existential temporal operator, needed to obtain an overall minimum witness size. Section 5 describes how to generate a witness from the computed witness size functions. Section 6 presents experimental results, Sect. 7 comments on our definition of witness size, and Sect. 8 concludes and outlines future work.

2 Background

We denote sets using calligraphic letters (e.g., $\mathcal{A}$, $\mathcal{B}$, $\mathcal{C}$), except for the booleans $\mathbb{B} = \{0,1\}$, the natural numbers $\mathbb{N} = \{0,1,2...\}$, and $\mathbb{N}_\infty = \mathbb{N} \cup \{\infty\}$.

2.1 Kripke Structures, CTL, and Witnesses

A Kripke structure is a tuple $(\mathcal{S}, \mathcal{S}_{init}, \mathcal{N}, \mathcal{A}, \mathcal{L})$, where $\mathcal{S}$ is the state space, $\mathcal{S}_{init} \subseteq \mathcal{S}$ are the initial states, $\mathcal{N} : \mathcal{S} \to 2^{\mathcal{S}}$ is the next-state function, $\mathcal{A}$ is a set of atomic propositions, and $\mathcal{L} : \mathcal{S} \to 2^{\mathcal{A}}$ is a labeling that gives the atomic propositions holding in each state (subject to *true* $\in \mathcal{A}$ holding in every state).

We assume $\mathcal{S}$ to be the product $\mathcal{S}_1 \times \cdots \times \mathcal{S}_L$ of L finite state spaces, i.e., each *global* state $\mathbf{i} \in \mathcal{S}$ is a tuple $(i_1, ..., i_L)$, where $i_k \in \mathcal{S}_k$ is the *local* state for the kth submodel. We also assume $\mathcal{N}$ to be disjunctively partitioned according to a set $\mathcal{E}$ of *asynchronous* events, i.e., $\mathcal{N} = \bigcup_{e \in \mathcal{E}} \mathcal{N}_e$ and, for each $e \in \mathcal{E}$, $\mathcal{N}_e : \mathcal{S} \to 2^{\mathcal{S}}$. $\mathcal{N}_e(\mathbf{i})$ contains the states that can be nondeterministically reached in one step when event e occurs in state $\mathbf{i}$. Correspondingly, we let $\mathcal{N}_e^{-1}$ denote the previous-state function, i.e., $\mathcal{N}_e^{-1}(\mathbf{j}) = \{\mathbf{i} : \mathbf{j} \in \mathcal{N}_e(\mathbf{i})\}$, the set of states that can reach $\mathbf{j}$ in one step through the occurrence of event e, and we let $\mathcal{N}^{-1} = \bigcup_{e \in \mathcal{E}} \mathcal{N}_e^{-1}$.

Let $\mathcal{P}(\mathbf{i})$ be the set of paths starting at $\mathbf{i} \in \mathcal{S}$, i.e., finite sequences $(\mathbf{i}_0, \mathbf{i}_1, ..., \mathbf{i}_n)$ for $n \geq 0$, or infinite sequences $(\mathbf{i}_0, \mathbf{i}_1, ...)$, where $\mathbf{i}_0 = \mathbf{i}$ and $\mathbf{i}_m \in \mathcal{N}(\mathbf{i}_{m-1})$ for all applicable m. Let $\mathcal{C}(\mathbf{i}) \subseteq \mathcal{P}(\mathbf{i})$ be the set of cycles starting at $\mathbf{i}$, i.e., finite paths $(\mathbf{i}_0, \mathbf{i}_1, ..., \mathbf{i}_n)$ with $n > 0$ and $\mathbf{i}_0 = \mathbf{i}_n = \mathbf{i}$.

We consider ECTL, the existential fragment of the temporal logic CTL [6], where formulas have syntax (ϕ and ρ are formulas, a is an atomic proposition):

$$\phi ::= a \mid \neg a \mid \phi \wedge \rho \mid \phi \vee \rho \mid \mathbf{EX}\phi \mid \mathbf{E}\phi\mathbf{U}\rho \mid \mathbf{EG}\phi,$$

and the conditions for state $\mathbf{i}$ to satisfy formula ϕ, written $\mathbf{i} \models \phi$, are as follows:

$$\begin{array}{ll}
\mathbf{i} \models a & \Leftrightarrow a \in \mathcal{L}(\mathbf{i}) \\
\mathbf{i} \models \neg a & \Leftrightarrow a \notin \mathcal{L}(\mathbf{i}) \\
\mathbf{i} \models \phi \wedge \rho & \Leftrightarrow \mathbf{i} \models \phi \text{ and } \mathbf{i} \models \rho \\
\mathbf{i} \models \phi \vee \rho & \Leftrightarrow \mathbf{i} \models \phi \text{ or } \mathbf{i} \models \rho \\
\mathbf{i} \models \mathbf{EX}\phi & \Leftrightarrow \exists (\mathbf{i}_0, \mathbf{i}_1) \in \mathcal{P}(\mathbf{i}), \mathbf{i}_1 \models \phi \\
\mathbf{i} \models \mathbf{E}\phi\mathbf{U}\rho & \Leftrightarrow \exists (\mathbf{i}_0, \mathbf{i}_1, ..., \mathbf{i}_n) \in \mathcal{P}(\mathbf{i}), n \geq 0, \mathbf{i}_n \models \rho \wedge \forall m \in \{0, ..., n-1\}, \mathbf{i}_m \models \phi \\
\mathbf{i} \models \mathbf{EG}\phi & \Leftrightarrow \exists (\mathbf{i}_0, \mathbf{i}_1, ...) \in \mathcal{P}(\mathbf{i}), \forall m \geq 0, \mathbf{i}_m \models \phi
\end{array}$$

(formula $\mathbf{EF}\phi$ is just a shorthand for $\mathbf{E}\mathit{true}\mathbf{U}\phi$, so we do not discuss it separately).

Since the state space $\mathcal{S}$ is finite, all infinite paths contain a cycle. Thus, path $(\mathbf{i}_0, \mathbf{i}_1, ...)$ demonstrating $\mathbf{i} \models \mathbf{EG}\phi$ must have a finite prefix $(\mathbf{i}_0, ..., \mathbf{i}_m, ..., \mathbf{i}_n)$, for some $m \geq 0$ and $n > m$, where $\mathbf{i}_m = \mathbf{i}_n$, that is, it is a "lasso" formed by merging (on state $\mathbf{i}_m$) a possibly empty "handle" $(\mathbf{i}_0, ..., \mathbf{i}_m)$ and a "cycle" $(\mathbf{i}_m, ..., \mathbf{i}_n)$.

We focus on witness generation, i.e., the computation of "tree-like" subgraphs demonstrating how a state satisfies an ECTL formula. This also serves to generate counterexamples for ACTL, the universal fragment of CTL, since a counterexample to $\mathbf{AX}\phi$, $\mathbf{AG}\phi$, or $\mathbf{A}[\phi\mathbf{U}\rho]$ is a witness to $\mathbf{EX}(\neg\phi)$, $\mathbf{EF}(\neg\phi)$, or $\mathbf{E}[\neg\rho\mathbf{U}(\neg\phi \wedge \neg\rho)] \vee \mathbf{EG}(\neg\rho)$, respectively (where the negation $\neg$ can be "pushed down" to atomic propositions), i.e., the negation of an ACTL formula is an ECTL formula.

2.2 Decision Diagrams

We encode sets and relations symbolically with (ordered) *multiway decision diagrams* (MDDs) [10]. An L-level MDD over $\mathcal{S} = \mathcal{S}_1 \times \cdots \times \mathcal{S}_L$ is an acyclic directed edge-labeled level graph with *terminal* nodes 0 and 1, at level 0, while each *nonterminal* node p is at some level $p.lvl = k \in \{1, ..., L\}$, and, for $i_k \in \mathcal{S}_k$, has an outgoing edge labeled with i_k and pointing to a child $p[i_k]$ at level $p[i_k].lvl < k$.

MDD node p at level k encodes function $f_p : \mathcal{S} \to \mathbb{B}$, recursively defined by $f_p(i_1, ..., i_L) = f_{p[i_k]}(i_1, ..., i_L)$, with base case $f_p(i_1, ..., i_L) = p$ when $k = 0$. Interpreting f_p as an indicator function, p encodes set $\mathcal{X}_p = \{\mathbf{i} : f_p(\mathbf{i}) = 1\} \subseteq \mathcal{S}$. To encode relations over $\mathcal{S}$, we use $2L$-level MDDs over $(\mathcal{S}_1 \times \mathcal{S}_1) \times \cdots \times (\mathcal{S}_L \times \mathcal{S}_L)$, where the first set in each pair corresponds to a "*from*", or "*unprimed*", local state and the second set corresponds to a "*to*", or "*primed*", local state.

We use instead (ordered) *additive edge-valued MDDs*, (EV$^+$MDDs) [4] to encode partial integer-valued functions. An EV$^+$MDD is an acyclic directed edge-labeled and edge-valued level graph with terminal node Ω, at level 0, while each nonterminal node p is at some level $p.lvl = k \in \{1, ..., L\}$, and, for $i_k \in \mathcal{S}_k$, has an outgoing edge with label i_k, pointing to a child $p[i_k].c$ at a level $p[i_k].c.lvl < k$, and value $p[i_k].v \in \mathbb{N}_\infty$. We write $p[i_k] = \langle p[i_k].v, p[i_k].c \rangle$.

EV$^+$MDD node p at level k encodes function $f_p : \mathcal{S} \to \mathbb{N}_\infty$ recursively defined by $f_p(i_1, ..., i_L) = p[i_k].v + f_{p[i_k].c}(i_1, ..., i_L)$, with base case $f_\Omega(i_1, ..., i_L) = 0$.

For efficiency, we restrict ourselves to *canonical* forms of decision diagrams, where each function that can be encoded by a given class of decision diagrams has a unique representation in that class. All such forms forbid *duplicate nodes*: if $p.lvl = q.lvl = k > 0$ and $\forall i_k \in \mathcal{S}_k, p[i_k] = q[i_k]$, then $p = q$. For ease of exposition, we only consider the *quasi-reduced* form in this paper, achieved by forbidding *skipped levels*: all roots (nodes without parent nodes) are at level L and, if $p.lvl = k$, then all p's children are at level $k - 1$. For EV$^+$MDDs, in addition, we require *normalized nodes*: each nonterminal node must have at least one edge with value 0 and all edges with value ∞ must point to Ω. This means that the minimum value of the function encoded by any node is 0, but we can encode any partial function $g : \mathcal{S} \to \mathbb{N}_\infty$ with a "root edge" $\langle \sigma, p \rangle$, where σ is the minimum value assumed by g, while p at level L satisfies $f_p = g - \sigma$.

```
Min(EV+MDD ⟨α,p⟩, EV+MDD ⟨β,q⟩)
1: if α = ∞ or β = ∞ then return ⟨∞, Ω⟩
2: k ← p.lvl                          ▷ we assume quasi-reduced rule, thus p.lvl = q.lvl
3: if k = 0 then return ⟨min{α, β}, Ω⟩                       ▷ terminal case, p = q = Ω
4: if MinGet(p,q,α−β,u) then return ⟨min{α,β},u⟩ ▷ Min(p,q,α−β)=⟨min(α,β),u⟩
5: u ← EVMDDNode(k)                    ▷ create a new EV+MDD node at level k
6: for each i ∈ S_k do          ▷ recursively compute the children of the result node
7:     u[i] ← Min(⟨α + p[i].v, p[i].c⟩, ⟨β + q[i].v, q[i].c⟩)
8: ⟨μ, u⟩ ← Normalize(u)   ▷ subtract μ to u's edge values so that the minimum is 0
9:                      ▷ ...unless they are all ∞, in which case ⟨μ, u⟩ = ⟨∞, Ω⟩
10: MinPut(p, q, α − β, u)                                  ▷ memoize the result
11: return ⟨μ, u⟩
```

Fig. 1. Algorithm to compute the element-wise minimum of two functions.

However, our algorithms are actually implemented using the more efficient *fully-identity-reduced* form for $2L$-level MDDs and EV$^+$MDDs (indicated MDD2 and EV$^+$MDD2 in our algorithms, respectively) [5]. This form allows us to exploit independence of events from local states: given $e \in \mathcal{E}$, let $Top(e) = k$ if e affects or depends on the kth local state but not the lth one, for any $l > k$. In the following, we then define $\mathcal{N}_k = \bigcup_{e:Top(e)=k} \mathcal{N}_e$.

Procedure *Min* in Fig. 1 shows the classic recursive manipulation of decision diagrams. Given functions $f, g : \mathcal{S} \to \mathbb{N}_\infty$, let $Min_{f,g} : \mathcal{S} \to \mathbb{N}_\infty$ be their element-wise minimum: for $\mathbf{i} \in \mathcal{S}$, $Min_{f,g}(\mathbf{i}) = \min\{f(\mathbf{i}), g(\mathbf{i})\}$. Given two EV$^+$MDDs $\langle\alpha, p\rangle$ and $\langle\beta, q\rangle$ encoding f and g, procedure *Min* returns the EV$^+$MDD encoding $Min_{f,g}$. As the EV$^+$MDDs are quasi-reduced, $p.lvl = q.lvl$ unless $\alpha = \infty$ or $\beta = \infty$.

Procedure *Normalize* (line 8) normalizes a node u by subtracting the minimum edge value μ from all its edge values, so that at least one is 0, stores the normalized u in the unique table (if not already there), and returns $\langle\mu, u\rangle$.

Throughout this paper, procedures *XxxGet* (line 4) or *XxxPut* (line 10) are queries to or insertions into compute tables (or "caches"), commonly used in decision diagrams operations to avoid re-computation. The structure of the hash key and returned value may of course depend on the specific operation *Xxx*.

2.3 Symbolic CTL Algorithms

McMillan proposed symbolic CTL model checking based on binary decision diagrams (BDDs) [12]. Given the BDDs encoding the set of states satisfying ϕ and ρ, algorithms to compute the BDD encoding the set of states satisfying $\mathbf{EX}\phi$, $\mathbf{E}\phi\mathbf{U}\rho$, and $\mathbf{EG}\phi$ suffice, since all CTL formulas can be expressed using these three CTL operators, plus the standard logical operations of negation, conjunction, and disjunction. Using MDDs instead of BDDs is a relatively obvious extension.

Clarke et al. [8] proposed the first symbolic approach to CTL witness generation. Considering first unnested CTL formulas, a witness for $\mathbf{EX}a$ can be generated by one image computation, and is by definition minimum since all witnesses have size two. Using a symbolic breadth-first search, witness generation for $\mathsf{E}a\mathsf{U}b$ also guarantees minimality, while minimality is more difficult to satisfy for $\mathsf{EG}a$, where a witness is a path from an initial state to a cycle, such that all states along that path and on the cycle satisfy a. In other words, a state $\mathbf{i}$ satisfying $\mathsf{EG}a$ must have a successor also satisfying $\mathsf{EG}a$; thus, we can incrementally build a path of states satisfying $\mathsf{EG}a$, which must finally lead to a state already on the path, closing the cycle and resulting in a witness. A witness generation algorithm for (weakly fair) **EG** was proposed in [8] based on this idea. Since $\mathbf{i}$ might have multiple successors satisfying $\mathsf{EG}a$, the algorithm is nondeterministic and the size of the witness depends on the state chosen at each step. While the algorithm uses a symbolic encoding, the approach is largely explicit, as it follows a single specific path. Decision diagrams help by efficiently encoding all states satisfying **EG**, but offer no help at all when deciding which of the states in $\mathcal{N}(\mathbf{i})$ satisfying **EG** should be chosen next, to continue the path from $\mathbf{i}$.

Witness generation for arbitrarily nested CTL formulas is much harder. Of course, we cannot exhibit witnesses for universal formulas, only counterexamples, thus the presence of both existential and universal (non-negated) quantifiers in a CTL formula ϕ means that we can neither provide a witness (in case ϕ holds) nor a counterexample (in case ϕ does not hold). The most general approach to date is by Clarke et al. [7] for general (nested) ACTL formulas, which proposed algorithms to generate tree-like counterexamples, or witnesses for general (nested) ECTL formulas. However, their work did not address minimality.

3 Defining the Minimum Witness Size

We focus on the generation of *minimum* witnesses for general (nested) ECTL formulas. As discussed by Clarke et al. [7], these witnesses are finite tree-like Kripke structures and complete for ECTL. To discuss their size, we unfold these witnesses, i.e., the same state may appear multiple times and each appearance contributes to the count defining the size of the witness. For example, consider the (portion of a) Kripke structure shown in Fig. 2(a), satisfying formula $\mathsf{E}(\mathsf{EG}a)\mathsf{U}b$ (state are identified by numbers and the atomic propositions holding in each state are listed close to it). An unfolded tree-like witness for this formula is shown in Fig. 2(b), where state 5's self-loop is repeated three times, once for each of the states 1, 2, and 3, since we need to show that each of them satisfies $\mathsf{EG}a$ (for clarity, a cycle is represented as a linear path along which the first and the last states are the same; dashed nodes represent the states closing cycles). Another way to think of this witness is that the first states of paths $[\![1,5,\overline{5}]\!]$, $[\![2,5,\overline{5}]\!]$, and $[\![3,5,\overline{5}]\!]$, each satisfying the inner formula $\phi' = \mathsf{EG}a$, are "glued" onto the first three states of path $[\![1,2,3,4]\!]$, satisfying the outermost formula $\mathsf{E}\phi'\mathsf{U}\phi''$, as is the first (and only) state of path $[\![4]\!]$, satisfying the (atomic) inner formula $\phi'' = b$. We write $\overline{5}$ for the last state of the **EG** witnesses to stress that state 5 does not need to have its witness repeated, since it is just closing the cycle. We define the *size* of a witness as the number of nodes in the resulting tree-like graph. Thus, a witness for a is path $[\![1]\!]$, of size 1, a witness for $\mathsf{EX}a$

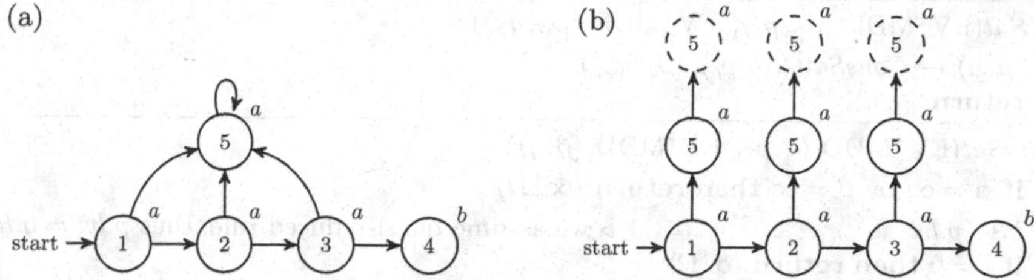

Fig. 2. A Kripke structure satisfying $\mathsf{E}(\mathsf{EG}a)\mathsf{U}b$ and its tree-like witness.

is path $[\![1,2]\!]$, of size 2, a witness for $\mathsf{E}a\mathsf{U}b$ is path $[\![1,2,3,4]\!]$, of size 4, and a witness to $\mathsf{E}(\mathsf{EG}a)\mathsf{U}b$ is the three-like graph $[\![[\![1,5,\overline{5}]\!],[\![2,5,\overline{5}]\!],[\![3,5,\overline{5}]\!],4]\!]$, of size 10. For conjunction, we need additional path notation: a witness for $\mathsf{EX}a \wedge \mathsf{E}a\mathsf{U}b$ is a tree-like graph $[\![[\![1,5]\!]\lozenge[\![1,2,3,4]\!]]\!]$, of size 5, where the separator $\lozenge$ indicates that the tree-like graphs to its left and its right are to be merged on their root.

We recursively define function $\pi_\phi : \mathcal{S} \to \mathbb{N}_\infty$ describing the minimum witness size for an ECTL formula ϕ starting from a state $\mathbf{i} \in \mathcal{S}$ as follows:

$\pi_a(\mathbf{i}) \quad = \text{if } \mathbf{i} \models a\text{: } 1\text{, else: } \infty$

$\pi_{\neg a}(\mathbf{i}) \quad = \text{if } \mathbf{i} \models a\text{: } \infty\text{, else: } 1$

$\pi_{\phi\wedge\rho}(\mathbf{i}) = \pi_\phi(\mathbf{i}) + \pi_\rho(\mathbf{i}) - 1$ (the "-1" avoids double-counting state $\mathbf{i}$)

$\pi_{\phi\vee\rho}(\mathbf{i}) = min\{\pi_\phi(\mathbf{i}), \pi_\rho(\mathbf{i})\}$

$\pi_{\mathsf{EX}\phi}(\mathbf{i}) = min\{\pi_\phi(\mathbf{j}) : \forall \mathbf{j} \in \mathcal{N}(\mathbf{i})\} + 1$

$\pi_{\mathsf{E}\phi\mathsf{U}\rho}(\mathbf{i}) = \text{if } \mathbf{i} \models \mathsf{E}\phi\mathsf{U}\rho\text{: } min\{\pi_\rho(\mathbf{i}), \pi_\phi(\mathbf{i}) + min\{\pi_{\mathsf{E}\phi\mathsf{U}\rho}(\mathbf{j}) : \forall \mathbf{j} \in \mathcal{N}(\mathbf{i})\}\}\text{, else: } \infty$

$\pi_{\mathsf{EG}\phi}(\mathbf{i}) = \text{if } \mathbf{i} \models \mathsf{EG}\phi\text{: } min\{\chi_\phi(\mathbf{i}), \pi_\phi(\mathbf{i}) + min\{\pi_{\mathsf{EG}\phi}(\mathbf{j}) : \forall \mathbf{j} \in \mathcal{N}(\mathbf{i})\}\}\text{, else: } \infty$

$\chi_\phi(\mathbf{i}) \quad = \text{if } \mathcal{C}(\mathbf{i}) \neq \emptyset\text{: } min\{\sum_{i=1}^{n} \pi_\phi(\mathbf{i}_i) : \forall (\mathbf{i}_0, \mathbf{i}_1, ..., \mathbf{i}_n) \in \mathcal{C}(\mathbf{i})\} + 1\text{, else: } \infty$

where $\mathcal{C}(\mathbf{i})$ is the set of cycles starting at $\mathbf{i}$, and $\chi_\phi(\mathbf{i})$ is the minimum witness size among cycles satisfying $\mathsf{EG}\phi$ and starting at $\mathbf{i}$. In the sum for $\chi_\phi(\mathbf{i})$, we exclude $\pi_\phi(\mathbf{i}_0)$ and add 1 because state $\mathbf{i} = \mathbf{i}_0 = \mathbf{i}_n$ starting and ending the cycle appears twice, but we should not count the witness for $\mathbf{i} \models \phi$ twice.

4 Computing the Minimum Witness Size

The first and most complex step to generate a minimum tree-like witness for an arbitrary ECTL formula ϕ^* is to build: (1) for each subformula ϕ of ϕ^*, starting from the innermost atomic propositions, an EV$^+$MDD encoding the size $\pi_\phi(\mathbf{i})$ of a minimum witness for ϕ starting from each state $\mathbf{i}$, and (2) for each subformula $\mathsf{EG}\phi$ of ϕ^*, an EV$^+$MDD2 encoding the size, $TC_\phi(\mathbf{i},\mathbf{j})$, of a minimum witness for a path of states satisfying ϕ from each state $\mathbf{i}$ to each state $\mathbf{j}$.

We present algorithms to compute the minimum witness size for **EU** and **EG**, while we omit the simpler ones for logical operators, **EX**, and atomic propositions.

$\mathit{EUSat}(\text{EV}^+\text{MDD } \langle\alpha_\rho, p_\rho\rangle,\ \text{EV}^+\text{MDD } \langle\beta_\phi, q_\phi\rangle)$

$\langle\mu, u\rangle \leftarrow \mathit{ConsSat}(\langle\alpha_\rho, p_\rho\rangle, \langle\beta_\phi, q_\phi\rangle)$

return $\langle\mu, u\rangle$

$\mathit{ConsSat}(\text{EV}^+\text{MDD } \langle\alpha, p\rangle,\ \text{EV}^+\text{MDD } \langle\beta, q\rangle)$

if $\alpha = \infty$ **or** $\beta = \infty$ **then return** $\langle\infty, \Omega\rangle$

$k \leftarrow p.\mathit{lvl}$ ▷ we assume quasi-reduced rule, thus $p.\mathit{lvl} = q.\mathit{lvl}$

if $l = 0$ **then return** $\langle\alpha, \Omega\rangle$

if $\mathit{ConsSatGet}(p, \langle\beta,q\rangle, \langle\gamma,u\rangle)$ **then return** $\langle\alpha+\gamma, u\rangle$ ▷ $\mathit{ConsSat}(\langle 0,p\rangle, \langle\beta,q\rangle) = \langle\gamma,u\rangle$

$u \leftarrow \mathit{EVMDDNode}(k)$

for each $i \in \mathcal{S}_k$ **do**

> **if** $q[i].v = \infty$ **then** $u[i] \leftarrow p[i]$
>
> **else** $u[i] \leftarrow \mathit{ConsSat}(p[i], \langle\beta + q[i].v, q[i].c\rangle)$

repeat

> **for each** $i, j \in \mathcal{S}_k$ **do**
>
> > $\langle\tau, t\rangle \leftarrow \mathit{ConsRelProdSat}(\langle\alpha + u[i].v, u[i].c\rangle, \langle\beta + q[j].v, q[j].c\rangle, \mathcal{N}_k^{-1}[i][j])$
> >
> > $u[j] \leftarrow \mathit{Min}(u[j], \langle\tau, t\rangle)$

until u does not change

$\langle\mu, u\rangle \leftarrow \mathit{Normalize}(u)$

$\mathit{ConsSatPut}(p, \langle\beta, q\rangle, \langle\mu - \alpha, u\rangle)$ ▷ memoize the result

return $\langle\mu, u\rangle$

$\mathit{ConsRelProdSat}(\text{EV}^+\text{MDD } \langle\alpha, p\rangle,\ \text{EV}^+\text{MDD } \langle\beta, q\rangle,\ \text{MDD2 } r)$

if $\alpha = \infty$ **or** $\beta = \infty$ **or** $r = 0$ **then return** $\langle\infty, \Omega\rangle$

$k \leftarrow p.\mathit{lvl}$ ▷ we assume quasi-reduced rule, thus $p.\mathit{lvl} = q.\mathit{lvl}$

if $l = 0$ **then return** $\langle\alpha + \beta, \Omega\rangle$

if $\mathit{ConsRelProdSatGet}(p, \langle\beta, q\rangle, r, \langle\gamma, u\rangle)$ **then return** $\langle\alpha + \gamma, u\rangle$

$u \leftarrow \mathit{EVMDDNode}(k)$

for each $i, j \in \mathcal{S}_k$ **do**

> $\langle\tau, t\rangle \leftarrow \mathit{ConsRelProdSat}(\langle\alpha + p[i].v, p[i].c\rangle, \langle\beta + q[j].v, q[j].c\rangle, r[i][j])$
>
> $u[j] \leftarrow \mathit{Min}(u[j], \langle\tau, t\rangle)$

$\langle\mu, u\rangle \leftarrow \mathit{Normalize}(u)$

$\langle\mu, u\rangle \leftarrow \mathit{ConsSat}(\langle\mu, u\rangle, \langle\beta, q\rangle)$

$\mathit{ConsRelProdSatPut}(p, \langle\beta, q\rangle, r, \langle\mu - \alpha, u\rangle)$ ▷ memoize the result

return $\langle\mu, u\rangle$

Fig. 3. Algorithm to compute the minimum witness size for **EU** formulas.

4.1 Computing the Minimum Witness Size for EU Formulas

In [15], we introduced a "constrained" variant of saturation that restricts exploration to states satisfying a given property. Instead of applying "after-the-fact" intersections, this approach employs a "check-and-fire" policy, firing an event only when the next states to be obtained satisfy the given property, through an on-the-fly check. Now, we further extend this idea to take into account the sizes of subwitnesses demonstrating the satisfaction of subformulas.

EUSat in Fig. 3 is the top-level procedure to compute $\pi_{\mathsf{E}\phi\mathsf{U}\rho}$, given $\langle \alpha_\rho, p_\rho \rangle$ encoding π_ρ and $\langle \beta_\phi, q_\phi \rangle$ encoding π_ϕ (both obtained by computing the minimum witness size function of subformulas). *ConsSat* computes a fixpoint for the subfunction encoded by $\langle \alpha, p \rangle$, under constraint $\langle \beta, q \rangle$, w.r.t. events affecting variables up to p's level. *ConsRelProdSat* first recursively computes the $\langle \beta, q \rangle$-constrained relational product of $\langle \alpha, p \rangle$ and r (specifically, it serves as a constrained version of the pre-image operation since we use the previous-state function), then it saturates the resulting node to ensure that it reaches a local fixpoint.

When exploring the pre-image of state $\mathbf{i}$, we compute, for each predecessor $\mathbf{j} \in \mathcal{N}(\mathbf{i})$, the sum of $\pi_\rho(\mathbf{j})$ and the value currently associated to $\mathbf{i}$ (line 3 in *ConsRelProdSat*), and use it to reduce the value associated to $\mathbf{j}$, if smaller (line 12 in *ConsSat* and line 8 in *ConsRelProdSat*). Upon reaching a fixpoint, we have the size of the minimum tree-like $\mathsf{E}\phi\mathsf{U}\rho$ witness for each state $\mathbf{i}$ (∞ if $\mathbf{i} \not\models \mathsf{E}\phi\mathsf{U}\rho$).

The hash-key for the cache entries of *ConsSat* and *ConsRelProdSat* consists of two nodes, p and q, plus the value β attached to the edge for q, representing the constraint. Storing the *difference* $\alpha - \beta$, as done for *Min*, would be incorrect because saturation computes local fixpoints and thus may fire an event multiple times in one call, and α just serves as an offset to all the values in the final function, while, for each individual state, it does not affect whether the new value obtained from one firing is smaller than the currently associated value. In other words, if it is known that $ConsSat(\langle 0, p \rangle, \langle \beta, q \rangle) = \langle \gamma, u \rangle$, then we can conclude that $ConsSat(\langle \alpha, p \rangle, \langle \beta, q \rangle) = \langle \alpha + \gamma, u \rangle$, for any $\alpha > 0$.

4.2 Computing the Minimum Witness Size for EG Formulas

A witness of $\mathsf{EG}p$ is a lasso-shaped infinite path consisting of a finite prefix leading to a cycle [1]. Thus, two steps are needed to compute a minimum tree-like witness for $\mathsf{EG}\phi$: (1) identify all states in cycles of states satisfying ϕ, and their minimum witness size; (2) starting from these states, explore the model backward to find all states satisfying $\mathsf{EG}p$, and their minimum witness size. This second step is essentially an EU computation, thus we focus on the first step.

Given a graph, the transitive closure (TC) describes the reachability between any pair of nodes. Computing TCs was deemed infeasible for large models [13], but recent attempts using saturation to compute TCs symbolically have been successful [16, 17]. We generalize this approach so that, for $\mathsf{EG}\phi$, the size of a minimum ϕ witness for each state in a ϕ cycle contributes to the cycle size.

We compute function $TC_\phi : \mathcal{S} \times \mathcal{S} \to \mathbb{N}_\infty$ s.t. $TC_\phi(\mathbf{i}, \mathbf{j})$ is the minimum size of any path $\mathbf{i}, \mathbf{i}_1, \cdots, \mathbf{j}$, computed as $\pi_\phi(\mathbf{i}_1) + \cdots + \pi_\phi(\mathbf{j})$, or ∞ if no such path exists. We do not include $\pi_\phi(\mathbf{i})$ because we compute TC_ϕ to obtain the minimum witness size of cycles, $\chi_\phi(\mathbf{i}) = TC_\phi(\mathbf{i}, \mathbf{i}) + 1$, and $\pi_\phi(\mathbf{i})$ should not be added twice.

The procedure to compute TC_ϕ is analogous to a symbolic implementation of Dijkstra's algorithm in a weighted graph. We initialize the function

$$\lambda_\phi(\mathbf{i}_1, \mathbf{i}_2) = \begin{cases} \pi_\phi(\mathbf{i}_2) & \text{if } \mathbf{i}_2 \in \mathcal{N}(\mathbf{i}_1), \mathbf{i}_1 \models \phi, \text{ and } \mathbf{i}_2 \models \phi \\ \infty & \text{otherwise} \end{cases}$$

and repeat the following computation until reaching a fixpoint:

$$\lambda_\phi(\mathbf{i}_1,\mathbf{i}_2) = \min\{\lambda_\phi(\mathbf{i}_1,\mathbf{i}_2), \min\{\lambda_\phi(\mathbf{i}_1,\mathbf{i}) + \pi_\phi(\mathbf{i}_2) : \forall \mathbf{i} \in \mathcal{N}^{-1}(\mathbf{i}_2)\}\}.$$

This iteration never increases the value of λ_ϕ, thus it terminates, and when it does the resulting fixpoint is TC_ϕ. Procedures *TCSat* and *TCRelProdSat* in Fig. 4 are similar to *ConsSat* and *ConsRelProdSat* in Fig. 3, except that they apply saturation to an EV$^+$MDD2. *TCMin* (line 14 in *TCSat*, line 11 in *TCRelProdSat*) is an implementation of *Min* over pairs of states: for each $\mathbf{i},\mathbf{j} \in \mathcal{S}$, $TCMin_{f,g}(\mathbf{i},\mathbf{j}) = \min\{f(\mathbf{i},\mathbf{j}), g(\mathbf{i},\mathbf{j})\}$.

Finally, we compute $\pi_{\mathsf{EG}\phi}$ with procedure *EGSat*, where $\langle\beta_\phi, q_\phi\rangle$ encodes π_ϕ. *BuildLambda* (line 1) builds an EV$^+$MDD2 encoding function λ_ϕ, to initialize the computation of TC_ϕ. *ExtractCycles* (line 2) returns an EV+MDD encoding $\chi_\phi(\mathbf{i})$ by extracting elements $TC_\phi(\mathbf{i},\mathbf{i})$ from TC_ϕ, for $\mathbf{i} \in \mathcal{S}$, and adding 1 to them.

5 Generating a Minimum Tree-Like Witness

Recall that, if function f is encoded as an EV$^+$MDD, one can retrieve $MinVal(f)$, the minimum value of f, in constant time (as the value labeling the edge pointing to the root node) and $MinState(f)$, a state achieving that minimum value, in time proportional to the number of levels L (follow a path of 0-valued edges from the root to Ω). Evaluating $f(\mathbf{i})$ for a given state $\mathbf{i}$ also requires just L steps.

To obtain a minimum overall witness recursively, we start from an initial state $\mathbf{i}^*$ with a minimum witness for ϕ^*. This state can be found by building an EV$^+$MDD encoding the function $f_{init} : \mathcal{S} \rightarrow \{0, \infty\}$ evaluating to 0 iff $\mathbf{i} \in \mathcal{S}_{init}$, and then the EV$^+$MDD encoding $\pi_{\phi^*\wedge init}$, the elementwise maximum of f_{init} and π_{ϕ^*} (i.e., the restriction of the minimum witness size for ϕ^* to the initial states). If $MinVal(\pi_{\phi^*\wedge init}) = \infty$, no initial state satisfies ϕ^*, thus no witness exists. Otherwise, there is a minimum witness of size $MinVal(\pi_{\phi^*\wedge init})$ starting from an initial state $\mathbf{i}^* = MinState(\pi_{\phi^*\wedge init})$, and the call $MinWit(\mathbf{i}^*, \phi^*, \pi_{\phi^*}(\mathbf{i}^*))$ (see Fig. 5) will recursively generate one such minimum witness.

6 Experimental Results

We implemented both our EV$^+$MDD-based approach to generate minimum tree-like witnesses (MinWit) and the traditional MDD-aided BFS approach [7] to generate (not necessarily minimum) tree-like witnesses (Wit) in our model checker SMART [2]. Then we ran them on a benchmark suite consisting of nine Petri net models from the 2017 Model Checking Contest (https://mcc.lip6.fr/2017/). All models have one or more scaling parameters affecting the number of states and state-to-state transitions, thus the model size and complexity. To generate tree-like witnesses, we define an ECTL formula that the model satisfies (the specific formula is listed in the results presented in Table 1). The datasets we utilized are available in the figshare repository [9].

```
EGSat(EV⁺MDD ⟨β_ϕ, q_ϕ⟩)
⟨τ, t⟩ ← TCSat(BuildLambda(⟨β_ϕ, q_ϕ⟩), ⟨β_ϕ, q_ϕ⟩)
⟨μ, u⟩ ← ConsSat(ExtractCycles(⟨τ, t⟩), ⟨β_ϕ, q_ϕ⟩)
return ⟨μ, u⟩
```

```
TCSat(EV⁺MDD2 ⟨α, p⟩, EV⁺MDD ⟨β, q⟩)
if α = ∞ or β = ∞ then return ⟨∞, Ω⟩
k ← p.lvl                          ▷ we assume quasi-reduced rule, thus p.lvl = q.lvl
if k = 0 then return ⟨α, Ω⟩
if TCSatGet(p,⟨β,q⟩,⟨γ,u⟩) then return ⟨α+γ,u⟩     ▷ TCSat(⟨0,p⟩,⟨β,q⟩)=⟨γ,u⟩
u ← EVMDD2Node(k)
for each i, j ∈ S_k do
    u[i].c[j] ← TCSat(⟨α + p[i].v + p[i].c[j].v, p[i].c[j].c⟩, ⟨β + q[j].v, q[j].c⟩)
for each i ∈ S_k do
    w ← EVMDD2Node(prime(k))
    repeat
        for each j, j' ∈ S_k do
            ⟨α', u'⟩ ← ⟨α + u[i].v + u[i].c[j].v, u[i].c[j].c⟩
            ⟨τ, t⟩ ← TCRelProdSat(⟨α', u'⟩, ⟨β + q[j'].v, q[j'].c⟩, N_k[j][j'])
            w[j'] ← TCMin(w[j'], ⟨τ, t⟩)
    until w does not change
    u[i] ← Normalize(w)
⟨μ, u⟩ ← Normalize(u)
TCSatPut(p, ⟨β, q⟩, ⟨μ − α, u⟩)                              ▷ memoize the result
return ⟨μ, u⟩
```

```
TCRelProdSat(EV⁺MDD2 ⟨α, p⟩, EV⁺MDD ⟨β, q⟩, MDD2 r)
if α = ∞ or β = ∞ or r = 0 then return ⟨∞, Ω⟩
k ← p.lvl                          ▷ we assume quasi-reduced rule, thus p.lvl = q.lvl
if k = 0 then return ⟨α + β, Ω⟩
if TCRelProdSatGet(p, ⟨β, q⟩, r, ⟨γ, u⟩) then return ⟨α + γ, u⟩
u ← EVMDD2Node(k)
for each i ∈ S_k do
    w ← EVMDD2Node(prime(k))
    for each j, j' ∈ S_k do
        ⟨α', p'⟩ ← ⟨α + p[i].v + p[i].c[j].v, p[i].c[j].c⟩
        ⟨τ, t⟩ ← TCRelProdSat(⟨α', p'⟩, ⟨β + q[j'].v, q[j'].c⟩, r[j][j'])
        w[j'] ← TCMin(w[j'], ⟨τ, t⟩)
    u[i] ← Normalize(w)
⟨μ, u⟩ ← Normalize(u)
⟨μ, u⟩ ← TCSat(⟨μ, u⟩, ⟨β, q⟩)
TCRelProdSatPut(p, ⟨β, q⟩, r, ⟨μ − α, u⟩)                    ▷ memoize the result
return ⟨μ, u⟩
```

Fig. 4. Algorithm to compute the minimum witness size for **EG** formulas.

MinWit(*state* $\mathbf{i}$, *ECTLformula* ϕ, *size* n)

if $\phi \in \mathcal{A}$ **then return** $\mathbf{i}$ ▷ $n = 1$, ϕ is an atomic proposition

if $\phi = \phi' \wedge \rho'$ **then** ▷ $n = \pi_{\phi'}(\mathbf{i}) + \pi_{\phi'}(\mathbf{j}) - 1$

  return $[\![MinWit(\mathbf{i}, \phi', \pi_{\phi'}(\mathbf{i}))]\!] \Diamond [\![MinWit(\mathbf{i}, \rho', \pi_{\rho'}(\mathbf{i}))]\!]$

if $\phi = \phi' \vee \rho'$ **then** ▷ $n = \min\{\pi_{\phi'}(\mathbf{i}), \pi_{\rho'}(\mathbf{i})\}$

  if $n = \pi_{\phi'}(\mathbf{i})$ **then return** $[\![MinWit(\mathbf{i}, \phi', \pi_{\phi'}(\mathbf{i}))]\!]$

  else return $[\![MinWit(\mathbf{i}, \rho', \pi_{\rho'}(\mathbf{i}))]\!]$

if $\phi = \mathsf{EX}\phi'$ **then**

  choose $\mathbf{j} \in \mathcal{N}(\mathbf{i})$ s.t. $\pi_{\phi'}(\mathbf{j}) = n - 1$ ▷ there exists at least one such $\mathbf{j}$

  return $\mathbf{i}, [\![MinWit(\mathbf{j}, \phi', n - 1)]\!]$

if $\phi = \mathsf{E}\phi'\mathsf{U}\rho'$ **then**

  if $\pi_{\rho'}(\mathbf{i}) = n$ **then** ▷ a minimum witness for $\mathbf{i} \models \rho'$ works for $\mathbf{i} \models \mathsf{E}\phi'\mathsf{U}\rho'$

    return $[\![MinWit(\mathbf{i}, \rho', n)]\!]$

  else ▷ no witness for $\mathbf{i} \models \rho'$ is minimum for $\mathbf{i} \models \mathsf{E}\phi'\mathsf{U}\rho'$

    choose $\mathbf{j} \in \mathcal{N}(\mathbf{i})$ s.t. $\pi_{\phi'}(\mathbf{j}) = n - \pi_{\phi'}(\mathbf{i})$ ▷ there exists at least one such $\mathbf{j}$

    return $[\![MinWit(\mathbf{i}, \phi', \pi_{\phi'}(\mathbf{i}))]\!], MinWit(\mathbf{j}, \phi, n - \pi_{\phi'}(\mathbf{i}))$

if $\phi = \mathsf{EG}\phi'$ **then**

  if $TC_{\phi'}(\mathbf{i},\mathbf{i}) = n - 1$ **then** ▷ a minimum cycle witness for $\mathbf{i}$ works for $\mathbf{i} \models \mathsf{EG}\phi'$

    return $CloseCycle(\mathbf{i}, \mathbf{i}, \phi', n - 1)$

  else ▷ $\mathbf{i}$ is on the handle of a lasso for a minimum witness for $\mathbf{i} \models \mathsf{EG}\phi'$

    choose $\mathbf{j} \in \mathcal{N}(\mathbf{i})$ s.t. $\pi_{\phi}(\mathbf{j}) = n - \pi_{\phi'}(\mathbf{i})$ ▷ there exists at least one such $\mathbf{j}$

    return $[\![MinWit(\mathbf{i}, \phi', \pi_{\phi'}(\mathbf{i}))]\!], MinWit(\mathbf{j}, \phi, n - \pi_{\phi'}(\mathbf{i}))$

CloseCycle(*state* $\mathbf{j}$, *state* $\mathbf{i}$, *ECTLformula* ϕ, *size* n)

if $\pi_{\phi}(\mathbf{i}) = n$ **then** ▷ it must be that $\mathbf{i} \in \mathcal{N}(\mathbf{j})$, close the cycle with $\bar{\mathbf{i}}$

  return $[\![MinWit(\mathbf{j}, \phi, \pi_{\phi}(\mathbf{j}))]\!], \bar{\mathbf{i}}$

else

  choose $\mathbf{k} \in \mathcal{N}(\mathbf{j})$ s.t. $TC_{\phi}(\mathbf{k}, \mathbf{i}) = n - \pi_{\phi}(\mathbf{k})$ ▷ there exists at least one such $\mathbf{k}$

  return $[\![MinWit(\mathbf{j}, \phi, \pi_{\phi}(\mathbf{j}))]\!], CloseCycle(\mathbf{k}, \mathbf{i}, \phi, n - \pi_{\phi}(\mathbf{k}))$

Fig. 5. Algorithm to generate a minimum tree-like witness.

For MinWit, we run each model instance with a timeout of one hour, and report the runtime, the peak memory consumption, and the size of the minimum witness. For Wit, we run each instance 100 times and report the total runtime, the peak memory consumption, and the minimum, average and maximum size among the all the generated witnesses. The minimum witness size is in bold when Wit did not manage to generate a minimum witness in any of the 100 runs. Obviously, the choice of $R = 100$ runs is arbitrary: the larger R is, the more likely Wit is to generate smaller witnesses, possibly a minimum one, but, on the other hand, the overall time Wit spends for witness generation is roughly proportional to R. Fundamentally, however, we have no easy way to know if the smallest witness generated by Wit is a minimum one, regardless of how large R is, while MinWit guarantees minimality.

A few observations are in order. First, it is not surprising that MinWit is sometimes orders of magnitude slower and requires more memory than Wit.

Table 1. Performance comparison of MinWit and Wit.

Model (parms)	#States	#Trans	Time (s)		Memory (MB)		Size			
			MinWit	Wit	MinWit	Wit	MinWit	Wit		
								min	avg	max
$\mathsf{EG}(\mathsf{EF}((Section\_2 = 1) \wedge (Section\_3 = 1)))$										
CircularTrain(12)	$2.0 \cdot 10^2$	$5.0 \cdot 10^2$	0.4	0.0	20.6	4.8	**25**	32	71	275
CircularTrain(24)	$8.7 \cdot 10^4$	$4.1 \cdot 10^5$	2244.9	4.6	2924.5	11.8	**37**	91	404	889
$\mathsf{E}(\mathsf{EF}(ERKPP > 5)\ \mathsf{U}\ \mathsf{EG}(RKIPP\_RP > 5))$										
ERK(20)	$1.7 \cdot 10^6$	$1.6 \cdot 10^7$	93.9	3.8	591.0	6.5	**129**	258	313	391
ERK(22)	$2.8 \cdot 10^6$	$2.7 \cdot 10^7$	224.1	4.4	932.1	6.9	**129**	246	314	393
ERK(25)	$5.7 \cdot 10^6$	$5.4 \cdot 10^7$	793.4	5.0	1800.6	8.0	**129**	256	315	397
$\mathsf{EF}((P1 = 3) \wedge \mathsf{EG}((P1 > P2) \wedge (P2 > P3)))$										
FMS(5)	$2.9 \cdot 10^6$	$3.2 \cdot 10^7$	0.6	2.7	21.0	7.6	13	13	48	193
FMS(8)	$2.5 \cdot 10^8$	$3.6 \cdot 10^9$	31.6	17.5	447.6	13.7	22	22	51	201
FMS(10)	$2.5 \cdot 10^9$	$4.1 \cdot 10^{10}$	458.9	30.6	1510.1	23.5	28	28	54	217
$\mathsf{EF}((P1 < P2) \wedge \mathsf{EG}(P1 = P4))$										
Kanban(20)	$8.1 \cdot 10^{11}$	$1.1 \cdot 10^{13}$	18.4	1530.3	269.6	289.0	10	10	10	11
Kanban(22)	$2.1 \cdot 10^{12}$	$2.9 \cdot 10^{13}$	28.6	2297.8	395.9	410.4	10	10	10	11
Kanban(25)	$7.7 \cdot 10^{12}$	$1.1 \cdot 10^{14}$	53.9	4224.4	691.6	707.9	10	10	10	11
$\mathsf{E}(\mathsf{EF}(Phase1 < Phase2)\ \mathsf{U}\ (Phase2 > Phase3))$										
MAPK(8)	$6.1 \cdot 10^6$	$7.9 \cdot 10^7$	14.0	2.0	353.0	6.1	**70**	126	126	126
MAPK(12)	$3.2 \cdot 10^8$	$5.0 \cdot 10^9$	1881.4	6.2	1764.2	8.7	**109**	204	204	204
$\mathsf{EF}((Think\_1 = 0) \wedge \mathsf{EG}(Eat\_1 = 0))$										
Philosophers(20)	$3.5 \cdot 10^9$	$5.4 \cdot 10^{10}$	1.3	2.1	52.4	9.2	5	5	8	22
Philosophers(50)	$7.2 \cdot 10^{23}$	$2.8 \cdot 10^{25}$	44.9	10.8	763.5	29.1	5	5	7	20
Philosophers(100)	$5.2 \cdot 10^{47}$	$4.0 \cdot 10^{49}$	timeout	52.1	–	94.0	–	5	7	28
$\mathsf{E}(\mathsf{EF}(P\_client\_ack\_1 = 1)\ \mathsf{U}\ ((P\_server\_ack\_1 = 1) \wedge (P\_server\_ack\_2 = 1)))$										
SimpleLoadBal(2)	$8.3 \cdot 10^2$	$3.4 \cdot 10^3$	0.1	0.8	9.0	5.9	23	23	32	44
SimpleLoadBal(5)	$1.2 \cdot 10^5$	$7.5 \cdot 10^5$	37.6	19.2	1032.6	41.0	**23**	26	69	80
$\mathsf{E}(\mathsf{EF}(TaskOnDisk < CPUUnit)\ \mathsf{U}\ (CPUUnit < DiskControllerUnit))$										
SmallOS(64,32)	$9.1 \cdot 10^6$	$6.8 \cdot 10^7$	17.5	1987.7	374.6	401.6	**662**	694	1189	1552
SmallOS(128,64)	$2.6 \cdot 10^8$	$2.0 \cdot 10^9$	294.4	53522.2	3228.4	1850.0	**2342**	2430	4698	5920
$\mathsf{EF}(\mathsf{EG}(Undress < InBath))$										
SwimmingPool(1)	$9.0 \cdot 10^4$	$4.5 \cdot 10^5$	109.7	4.7	1334.9	6.6	16	16	24	43
SwimmingPool(2)	$3.4 \cdot 10^6$	$2.0 \cdot 10^7$	timeout	39.1	–	22.3	–	16	24	53

Building EV$^+$MDDs or EV$^+$MDD2s encoding both states and size information is much more expensive than the image computations on MDDs used to just run the model checking phase, as Wit does. However, this is offset by a minimality guarantee. Interestingly, there are cases where MinWit completes with a runtime and memory consumption comparable to a single run of Wit (e.g., Kanban) or even faster (e.g., SmallOS). We give credit to the saturation algorithm for its efficient locality-exploiting exploration.

Second, for models where small, simple witnesses exist, Wit may be able to generate a minimum witness. Since the backward exploration guarantees the local minimality of subwitnesses for **EX**, **EF** and **EU** segments, such greedy strategy may result in a global minimum witness, determined by the structure of the model. But this occurrence cannot be guaranteed, regardless of whether we use 100 runs or 10,000 runs, so that, even when WIT happens to generate a minimum witness, users do not know that this is indeed the case.

Third, for models where only large, complex witnesses exist, generating a minimum witness is almost impossible for WIT, while the witness from MINWIT can be only 40% as large as the smallest one generated by WIT (e.g., Circular-Train with $N = 24$). Additionally, WIT's greedy strategy may trap itself into a local optimum. For example, the ECTL formula used for model MAPK does not contain **EG**, and the minimum, average, and maximum witness sizes generated by WIT are equal, implying that WIT is unaware of other possibilities when it chooses branching states. Adopting a probabilistic non-optimal strategy like simulated annealing may alleviate this problem, but it still would not provide guarantees and would likely require many more runs.

The main limitation of MINWIT is that, since computing the minimum witness size function is computationally intensive, long runtimes and large amounts of memory are required as the model complexity scales up. However, engineers usually debug models with small scaling parameters first, perhaps running model checking tools overnight, thus, the resource requirement of MINWIT may often be acceptable in practice. In real-world applications, we believe that MINWIT and WIT can complement each other. WIT generates a large number of witnesses in a short time, but if all the witnesses are complex, MINWIT can be run to find a smaller, easier-to-inspect one. Conversely, if MINWIT fails to generate a minimum witness due to time or memory limitation, WIT can be run to obtain not-necessarily-minimum ones by running it repeatedly, as many times as one can afford. The best approach, given enough resources and in the presence of critical deadlines, may well be to run both methods in parallel, so that we can be sure to have a minimum witness if MINWIT completes, but we have at least some witnesses from WIT, if MINWIT fails to complete in time.

7 A Comment About Our Definition of Witness Size

In Sect. 3, we defined the witness size as "the number of appearances of states in the unfolded tree-like witness". An alternative definition could have been "the number of distinct states in the unfolded tree-like witness". However, a state may appear multiple times for different purposes in a witness. For example, the witness for $\mathbf{EF}(a \wedge \mathbf{EG}b)$ in Fig. 6 contains state 2 twice, one in $[\![3, 2, \overline{3}]\!]$ to verify for the **EG** fragment, the other in $[\![1, 2, 3]\!]$ to verify the **EF** fragment. Considering each appearance separately makes each subpath independently verifiable, while merging states that appear multiple times and counting only distinct states loses this information. Admittedly, our definition of witness size also enables our approach to obtain minimum witnesses, while we do not know a practical algorithm that can derive minimum witnesses according to a definition of size where common paths and states appearing multiple times are counted without repetition.

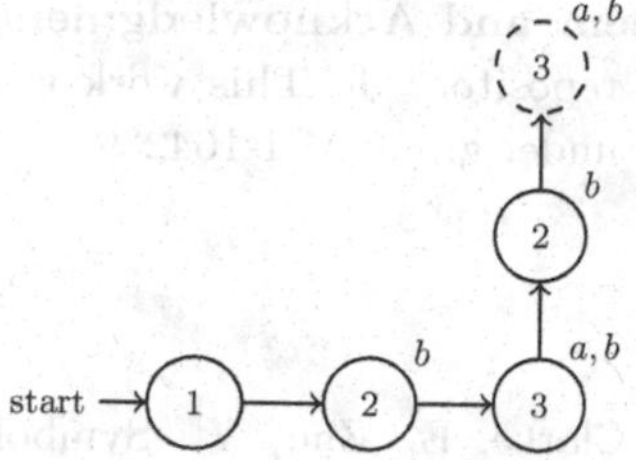

Fig. 6. A witness for $\mathbf{EF}(a \wedge \mathbf{EG}b)$.

Of course, after obtaining a minimum witness according to our definition, we could attempt to merge shared portions among subpaths that demonstrate the same property, but doing so would not generally result in minimum witnesses according to this alternative view of witness size.

8 Conclusions

We presented a definition of witness size and an approach to compute minimum tree-like witnesses for ECTL formulas, based on edge-valued decision diagrams to capture a global view of witness size. Experimental results demonstrate that our approach is able to generate minimum witnesses (with a guarantee that it is doing so) for some models, while the traditional approach is not. While the runtime and memory requirements of our approach tend to be higher, sometimes they are comparable to that of the traditional approach.

There are several directions for future work to improve this approach itself or extend its applicability. One interesting possibility is to selectively employ our approach or the traditional approach for different subformulas; this would not guarantee witness minimality, but could generate smaller witness than with the traditional approach alone, while being faster than using our approach alone. Especially for **EG** formulas, the traditional approach has no global view about the size of witnesses it generates, while, for formulas where the minimum witness size from each state varies widely, the EV$^+$MDDs and EV$^+$MDD2s built by our method tend to be large and costly to compute. Thus, heuristics that consider both the structure of the model and of the formula are needed.

Finally, our approach could be further extended by generalizing the concept of "size" to "weight". Specifically, by assigning a weight to each state, engineers could convey their preference to model checkers, which would then tend to generate witnesses containing the desired states and subpaths, instead of just counting the number of states in the witness. The algorithmic difference in doing so would be negligible, the only additional cost could be a potential growth in the size of the corresponding EV$^+$MDDs and EV$^+$MDD2s, as the functions being encoded might have less sharing of nodes.

Data Availability Statement and Acknowledgments. The datasets we utilized are available in the figshare repository [9]. This work was supported in part by the National Science Foundation under grant ACI-1642397.

References

1. Biere, A., Cimatti, A., Clarke, E., Zhu, Y.: Symbolic model checking without BDDs. In: Cleaveland, W.R. (ed.) TACAS 1999. LNCS, vol. 1579, pp. 193–207. Springer, Heidelberg (1999). https://doi.org/10.1007/3-540-49059-0_14
2. Ciardo, G., Jones, R.L., Miner, A.S., Siminiceanu, R.: Logical and stochastic modeling with SMART. Perf. Eval. **63**, 578–608 (2006)
3. Ciardo, G., Marmorstein, R., Siminiceanu, R.: The saturation algorithm for symbolic state space exploration. Software Tools for Technology Transfer **8**(1), 4–25 (2006)
4. Ciardo, G., Siminiceanu, R.: Using edge-valued decision diagrams for symbolic generation of shortest paths. In: Aagaard, M.D., O'Leary, J.W. (eds.) FMCAD 2002. LNCS, vol. 2517, pp. 256–273. Springer, Heidelberg (2002). https://doi.org/10.1007/3-540-36126-X_16
5. Ciardo, G., Yu, A.J.: Saturation-based symbolic reachability analysis using conjunctive and disjunctive partitioning. In: Borrione, D., Paul, W. (eds.) CHARME 2005. LNCS, vol. 3725, pp. 146–161. Springer, Heidelberg (2005). https://doi.org/10.1007/11560548_13
6. Clarke, E.M., Emerson, E.A.: Design and synthesis of synchronization skeletons using branching time temporal logic. In: Kozen, D. (ed.) Logic of Programs 1981. LNCS, vol. 131, pp. 52–71. Springer, Heidelberg (1982). https://doi.org/10.1007/BFb0025774
7. Clarke, E., Jha, S., Lu, Y., Veith, H.: Tree-like counterexamples in model checking. In: Proceedings of the LICS, pp. 19–29. IEEE Computer Society Press (2002)
8. Clarke, E.M., Grumberg, O., McMillan, K., Zhao, X.: Efficient generation of counterexamples and witnesses in symbolic model checking. In: 32nd Design Automation Conference (DAC 1995), pp. 427–432 (1995)
9. Jiang, C., Ciardo, G.: Generation of minimum tree-like witnesses for existential CTL. Figshare (2018). https://doi.org/10.6084/m9.figshare.5926555.v1
10. Kam, T., Villa, T., Brayton, R.K., Sangiovanni-Vincentelli, A.: Multi-valued decision diagrams: theory and applications. Multiple-Valued Logic **4**(1–2), 9–62 (1998)
11. Kashyap, S., Garg, V.K.: Producing short counterexamples using "crucial events". In: Gupta, A., Malik, S. (eds.) CAV 2008. LNCS, vol. 5123, pp. 491–503. Springer, Heidelberg (2008). https://doi.org/10.1007/978-3-540-70545-1_47
12. McMillan, K.L.: Symbolic model checking: an approach to the state explosion problem. Ph.D. thesis, School of Computer Science, Carnegie Mellon University, May 1992. CMU-CS-92-131
13. Ravi, K., Bloem, R., Somenzi, F.: A comparative study of symbolic algorithms for the computation of fair cycles. In: Hunt, W.A., Johnson, S.D. (eds.) FMCAD 2000. LNCS, vol. 1954, pp. 162–179. Springer, Heidelberg (2000). https://doi.org/10.1007/3-540-40922-X_10
14. Tan, J., Avrunin, G.S., Clarke, L.A., Zilberstein, S., Leue, S.: Heuristic-guided counterexample search in FLAVERS. In: Proceedings of the SIGSOFT, pp. 201–210. ACM (2004)

15. Zhao, Y., Ciardo, G.: Symbolic CTL model checking of asynchronous systems using constrained saturation. In: Liu, Z., Ravn, A.P. (eds.) ATVA 2009. LNCS, vol. 5799, pp. 368–381. Springer, Heidelberg (2009). https://doi.org/10.1007/978-3-642-04761-9_27
16. Zhao, Y., Ciardo, G.: Symbolic computation of strongly connected components using saturation. In: Proceedings of the 2nd NASA Formal Methods Symposium (NFM 2010), NASA/CP-2010-216215, pp. 201–211. NASA (2010)
17. Zhao, Y., Jin, X., Ciardo, G.: A symbolic algorithm for shortest EG witness generation. In: Proceedings of the TASE, pp. 68–75. IEEE Computer Society Press (2011)

From Natural Projection to Partial Model Checking and Back

Gabriele Costa[1(✉)], David Basin[2], Chiara Bodei[3], Pierpaolo Degano[3], and Letterio Galletta[3]

[1] DIBRIS, Università degli Studi di Genova, Genoa, Italy
gabriele.costa@unige.it

[2] Department of Computer Science, ETH Zurich, Zürich, Switzerland
basin@inf.ethz.ch

[3] Dipartimento di Informatica, Università di Pisa, Pisa, Italy
{chiara,degano,galletta}@di.unipi.it

Abstract. Specification decomposition is a theoretically interesting and practically relevant problem for which two approaches were independently developed by the control theory and verification communities: *natural projection* and *partial model checking*. In this paper we show that, under reasonable assumptions, natural projection reduces to partial model checking and, when cast in a common setting, the two are equivalent. Aside from their theoretical interest, our results build a bridge whereby the control theory community can reuse algorithms and results developed by the verification community. In addition, we present an algorithm and a tool for the partial model checking of finite-state automata that can be used as an alternative to natural projection.

1 Introduction

System verification requires comparing a system's behavior against a specification. When the system consists of several components, we can distinguish between *local* and *global* specifications. A local specification applies to a single component, whereas a global specification should hold for the entire system. Since these specifications are needed to reason at different levels of abstraction, both of them are often present.

Ideally, we would like to freely pass from local to global specifications and vice versa. Most specification formalisms natively support specification composition. Logical conjunction, set intersection, and the synchronous product of automata are all examples of operators for composing specifications. Unfortunately, the same does not hold for specification decomposition: obtaining local specifications from a global one is, in general, extremely complex, as illustrated below.

G. Costa and L. Galletta—The current address of the authors is IMT Lucca.

D. Beyer and M. Huisman (Eds.): TACAS 2018, LNCS 10805, pp. 344–361, 2018.
https://doi.org/10.1007/978-3-319-89960-2_19

Example 1. Consider the classical submodule construction problem (SCP) [27]: given a system and a global specification, find a submodule whose composition with the system leads to a global behavior conformant to the global specification. For instance, imagine that we aim to control the usage of a buffer of size n, where two agents, A and B, can insert and remove items. Now assume that A's behavior is to "insert one item when the buffer is empty and delete one item when it is full", while B's behavior is unknown. If we want to prevent buffer overflow and underflow, some questions arise about B. For example, are there compatible behaviors for B? Is there a *most general* one? How could we effectively compute it? These questions require decomposing the buffer overflow/underflow specification so that it only refers to B, while exploiting the known structure of A. □

Over the past decades, researchers have investigated methods for decomposing specifications. Interestingly, different communities have tackled this problem independently, each considering specification formalisms and assumptions appropriate for their application context. In particular, important results were obtained in two distinct fields: *control theory* and *formal verification.*

In control theory, *natural projection* [33] is used for simplifying systems built from multiple components, modeled as automata. It is often applied component-wise to synthesize local controllers from a global specification of asynchronous *discrete-event system* [9], namely the *controller synthesis problem* (CSP). Briefly, local controllers guarantee that the global specification is not violated by interacting only with a single component of a system. The local controllers can be used to implement distributed control systems [34,35] by composing them in parallel with other sub-systems.

In the formal verification community, *partial model checking* [1] was proposed as a technique for mitigating the state explosion problem when verifying large systems built from many parallel processes. Partial model checking tackles this problem by decomposing a specification, given as a formula of the μ-calculus [22], using a *quotienting* operator, thereby supporting the analysis of the individual processes independently. Quotienting carries out a partial evaluation of a specification while *preserving the model checking problem.* Thus, a system built by composing two modules satisfies a specification if and only if one of the modules

Table 1. Summary of existing results on natural projection and partial model checking. Notice that the algorithm in [32] runs in PTIME on a specific class of discrete-event systems.

	Natural Projection	Partial MC
Spec. Lang.	FSA [19,31]	μ-calculus [1,3]
Theory	FSA [19,31]	LTS [1,3]
Complexity	EXPTIME [14,32]	EXPTIME [1,3]
Tools	TCT [13], IDES3 [30], DESTool [28]	mCRL2 [18], CADP [23], MuDiv [2]

satisfies the specification after quotienting against the other [1]. This may reduce the problem size, resulting in smaller models and hence faster verification.

Table 1 summarizes some relevant facts about the two approaches and we refer the reader to Sect. 5 for a more detailed analysis. Since natural projection and partial model checking apply to different formalisms, they cannot be directly compared without defining a common framework (see below). For instance, a relevant question is comparing how specifications grow under the two approaches. Although it is known that both may lead to exponential growth (see [3,21,32]), these results apply in one case to finite-state automata (FSAs) and in the other case to μ-calculus formulae.

Over the past few years, there has been a substantial cross-fertilization between the two research communities [12]. For instance, methods for synthesizing controllers using partial model checking are given in [6,25]. The authors of [15,17] propose similar techniques, but they use fragments of the μ-calculus and CTL*, respectively.

We follow here the suggestion of Ehlers et al. [12], who advocate formally connecting these two approaches so as to make them interchangeable. In their words:

> "Such a formal bridge should be a source of inspiration for new lines of investigation that will leverage the power of the synthesis techniques that have been developed in these two areas. [...] It would be worthwhile to develop case studies that would allow a detailed comparison of these two frameworks in terms of plant and specification modeling, computational complexity of synthesis, and implementation of derived supervisor/ controller."

As for the first remark, we show that, under reasonable assumptions, natural projection reduces to partial model checking and, when cast in a common setting, they are equivalent. To this end, we first define a common theoretical framework for both. In particular, we slightly extend both the notion of natural projection and the semantics of the μ-calculus in terms of the satisfying traces. These extensions allow us to apply natural projection to the language denoted by a specification. In addition, we extend the main property of the quotienting operator by showing that it corresponds to the natural projection of the language denoted by the specification, and vice versa (Theorem 4).

We provide additional results that contribute to the detailed comparison referred to in the second remark. Namely we define a new algorithm for partial model checking directly on LTSs (rather than on the μ-calculus). We prove our algorithm correct with respect to the traditional quotienting rules and we show it runs in polynomial time, like the algorithms based on natural projection. We have implemented this algorithm in a tool, which is available online [11]. Along with the tool, we developed several case studies illustrating its application to the synthesis of both submodules and local controllers.

Structure of the paper. Section 2 presents our unified theoretical framework for natural projection and partial model checking. Section 3 contains our main theoretical results, in particular Theorem 4 on the equivalence of quotienting and natural projection. In Sect. 4 we introduce a novel quotienting algorithm, discuss its properties, and apply it to our running example. In Sect. 5 we briefly survey the related literature and in Sect. 6 we draw conclusions. The formal proofs together with the correctness and the complexity of our algorithm, and our experimental results are available at https://github.com/SCPTeam/pests/blob/master/proofs_and_experiments.pdf.

2 A General Framework

In this section we cast both natural projection and partial model checking in a common framework. We start with a running example: a scenario inspired by [10,33], which is an instance of Example 1.

Example 2 (Running example). A drone package delivery (DPD) system relies on unmanned aerial vehicles (UAVs) to transport goods within a given area. Drones interact with docking stations where they can pick up (action u) or deposit (action d) an item. These actions are only observable to the docking station. Additional interactions are represented by the two control actions s (for synchronize) and t (for terminate). An action t takes place when UAVs are requested to leave the station, e.g., due to a maintenance operation, while s is used for the global synchronization of both the docking station and UAVs.

Figure 1 depicts a transition system that encodes the specification of an n-position buffer $P(n)$ handled by a docking station. Intuitively, UAVs cannot perform d actions when the buffer is full (state p_n) and u actions when the buffer is empty (state p_0). Since synchronization actions s and t are immaterial, they label self-loops. □

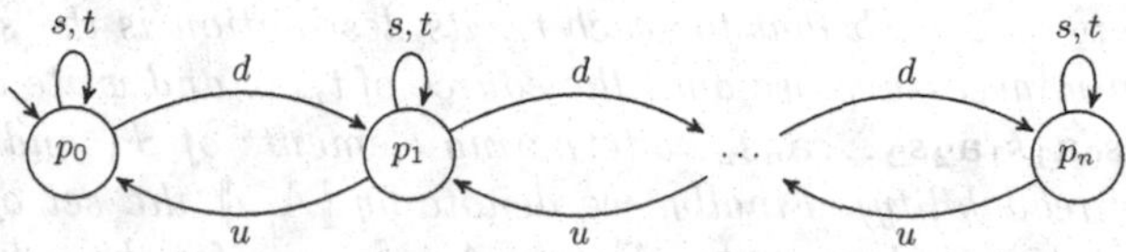

Fig. 1. An n-positions buffer specification $P(n)$.

2.1 Language Semantics Versus State Semantics

Natural projection is commonly defined over (sets of) *words* [33]. Words are finite sequences of actions, i.e., symbols labeling each transition between two states of a finite-state automaton (FSA). The language of an FSA is the set of all words that label a sequence of transitions from an initial state to some distinguished state, like a final or marking state. We call the function $\mathcal{L}$ that maps each FSA to the corresponding *language semantics*. Given a system T and a specification S, both FSAs, then T is said to satisfy S whenever $\mathcal{L}(T) \subseteq \mathcal{L}(S)$.

For partial model checking, the specification S is defined by a formula of the μ-calculus. In this case, the standard interpretation is given by a *state semantics*, i.e., a function that given a system T and a formula Φ returns the set of states of T that satisfy Φ. Usually, T is given as a labeled transition system (LTS). An LTS is similar to an FSA, but with a weaker notion of acceptance, where all states are final. A set of evaluation rules formalizes whether a state satisfies a formula or not. Given an LTS T and a μ-calculus formula Φ, we say that T satisfies Φ whenever its initial state does.

The language semantics of temporal logics is strictly less expressive than the state-based one [16]. A similar fact holds for FSA and regular expressions [5]. Here we use a semantics from which both the state-based and the language semantics can be obtained.

2.2 Operational Model and Natural Projection

We now generalize slightly the existing approaches based on partial model checking and on supervisory control theory used for locally verifying global properties of discrete event systems. We then constructively prove that the two approaches are equally expressive so that techniques from one can be transferred to the other. To this end, we consider models expressed as (finite) labeled transition systems, which describe the behavior of discrete systems. In particular, we restrict ourselves here to deterministic transition systems.

Definition 1. *A (deterministic) labeled transition system (LTS) is a tuple $A = (S_A, \Sigma_A, \rightarrow_A, \imath_A)$ where S_A is a finite set of states (with $\imath_A$ the initial state), Σ_A is a finite set of action labels, and $\rightarrow_A : S_A \times \Sigma_A \rightarrow S_A$ is the transition function. We write $t = s \xrightarrow{a} s'$ to denote a* transition, *whenever $\rightarrow_A (a, s) = s'$, and we call s the* source *state, a the* action *label, and s' the* destination *state.*

A trace *$\sigma \in \mathcal{T}$ of an LTS A is either a single state s or a sequence of transitions $t_1 \cdot t_2 \cdot \ldots$ such that for each t_i, its destination is the source of t_{i+1} (if any). When unnecessary, we omit the source of t_{i+1}, and write a trace as the sequence $\sigma = s_0\mathbf{a_1}s_1\mathbf{a_2}s_2 \ldots \mathbf{a_n}s_n$, alternating elements of S_A and Σ_A (written in boldface for readability). Finally, we denote by $[\![A, s]\!]$ the set of traces of A starting from state s and we write $[\![A]\!]$ for $[\![A, \imath_A]\!]$, i.e., for those traces starting from the initial state $\imath_A$.* □

Example 3. Consider again our running example. Figure 2 depicts the LTSs A and B. A models an UAV that deposits (d) two items in the buffer and performs a synchronization action (s). Optionally, A can also leave the docking station (t). In contrast, B repeatedly picks an item and synchronizes. Both A and B may also leave the docking station (t). Notice that the traces $[\![A]\!]$ starting from the initial state of A are $[\![A]\!] = \{q_0, q_0\mathbf{d}q_1, q_0\mathbf{t}q_3, q_0\mathbf{d}q_1\mathbf{d}q_2, q_0\mathbf{d}q_1\mathbf{d}q_2\mathbf{s}q_0, \ldots\}$. In contrast, the traces starting from the initial state of B are

$$[\![B]\!] = \{r_0, r_0\mathbf{u}r_1, r_0\mathbf{t}r_2, r_0\mathbf{u}r_1\mathbf{s}r_0, r_0\mathbf{u}r_1\mathbf{s}r_0\mathbf{u}r_1, \ldots\}.$$ □

Typically, a system, or *plant* in control theory terms, consists of multiple interacting components running in parallel. Below we rephrase the synchronous product of [33]. Intuitively, when two LTSs are put in parallel, each proceeds asynchronously, except on those actions they share, upon which they synchronize.

Definition 2. *Given two LTSs A and B such that $\Sigma_A \cap \Sigma_B = \Gamma$, the* synchronous product *of A and B is $A \parallel B = (S_A \times S_B, \Sigma_A \cup \Sigma_B, \rightarrow_{A\parallel B}, \langle \imath_A, \imath_B \rangle)$, where $\rightarrow_{A\parallel B}$ is as follows:*

$$\begin{aligned}
\langle s_A, s_B \rangle &\xrightarrow{a}_{A\parallel B} \langle s'_A, s_B \rangle \text{ if } s_A \xrightarrow{a}_A s'_A \text{ and } a \in \Sigma_A \setminus \Gamma \\
\langle s_A, s_B \rangle &\xrightarrow{b}_{A\parallel B} \langle s_A, s'_B \rangle \text{ if } s_B \xrightarrow{b}_B s'_B \text{ and } b \in \Sigma_B \setminus \Gamma \\
\langle s_A, s_B \rangle &\xrightarrow{\gamma}_{A\parallel B} \langle s'_A, s'_B \rangle \text{ if } s_A \xrightarrow{\gamma}_A s'_A, s_B \xrightarrow{\gamma}_A s'_B, \text{ and } \gamma \in \Gamma.
\end{aligned}$$

□

Example 4. Consider again the LTSs A and B of Fig. 2. Their synchronous product $A \parallel B$ (with $\Gamma = \{s, t\}$) is depicted in Fig. 3. □

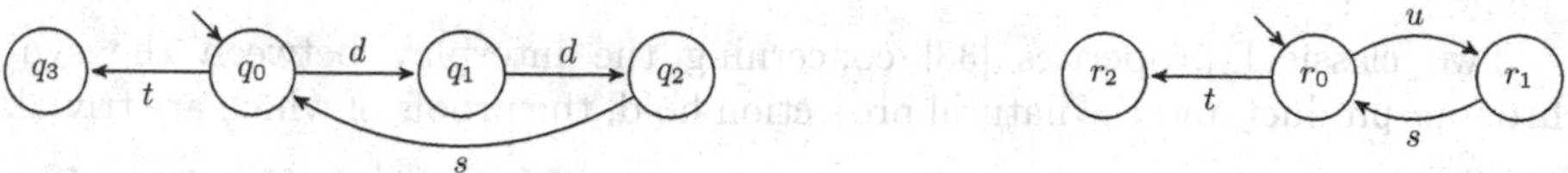

Fig. 2. From left to right, two UAVs adding to (A) and removing from (B) the buffer.

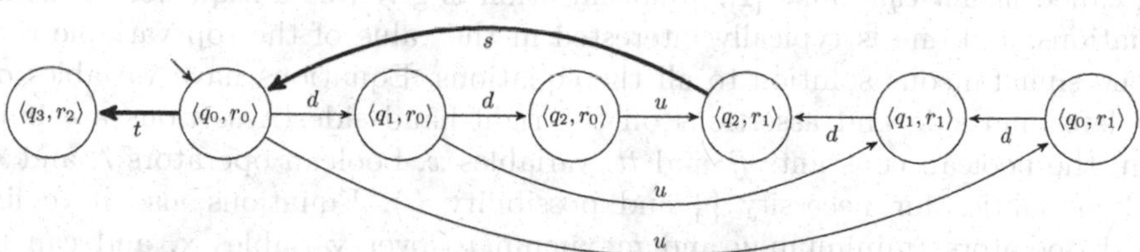

Fig. 3. Synchronous product $A \parallel B$ where bold transitions denote synchronous moves.

Next, we generalize the natural projection on languages, which is a kind of inverse operation of the synchronous product of two LTSs. Given a computation of $A \parallel B$, the natural projection extracts the relevant trace of one of the LTSs, including the synchronized transitions (see the second case below). Note that, unlike the definition given, for example in [33], our definition returns a sequence of transitions, including both states and actions. We also define the inverse projection in the expected way.

Definition 3. *For LTSs A and B with $\Gamma = \Sigma_A \cap \Sigma_B$, the* natural projection on A *of a trace σ, in symbols $P_A(\sigma)$, is defined as follows:*

$$\begin{aligned} &P_A(\langle s_A, s_B\rangle) &&= s_A && \\ &P_A(\langle s_A, s_B\rangle \xrightarrow{a}_{A\|B} \langle s'_A, s'_B\rangle \cdot \sigma) &&= s_A \xrightarrow{a}_A s'_A \cdot P_A(\sigma) && \text{if } a \in \Sigma_A \\ &P_A(\langle s_A, s_B\rangle \xrightarrow{b}_{A\|B} \langle s_A, s'_B\rangle \cdot \sigma) &&= P_A(\sigma) && \text{if } b \in \Sigma_B \setminus \Gamma. \end{aligned}$$

Natural projection on second component B is analogously defined. We extend the natural projection to sets of traces in the usual way: $P_A(T) = \{P_A(\sigma) \mid \sigma \in T\}$.

The inverse projection *of a trace σ over an LTS $A \parallel B$, in symbols $P_A^{-1}(\sigma)$, is defined as $P_A^{-1}(\sigma) = \{\sigma' \mid P_A(\sigma') = \sigma\}$. Its extension to sets is $P_A^{-1}(T) = \bigcup_{\sigma \in T} P_A^{-1}(\sigma)$.* □

Example 5. Consider the two traces $\sigma_1 = \langle q_0, r_0\rangle \mathbf{d} \langle q_1, r_0\rangle \mathbf{u} \langle q_1, r_1\rangle \mathbf{d} \langle q_2, r_1\rangle \mathbf{s} \langle q_0, r_0\rangle$ and $\sigma_2 = \langle q_0, r_0\rangle \mathbf{u} \langle q_0, r_1\rangle \mathbf{d} \langle q_1, r_1\rangle \mathbf{d} \langle q_2, r_1\rangle \mathbf{s} \langle q_0, r_0\rangle$. We have that the projections $P_A(\sigma_1) = P_A(\sigma_2) = q_0 \mathbf{d} q_1 \mathbf{d} q_2 \mathbf{s} q_0 \in [\![A]\!]$, and $\sigma_1, \sigma_2 \in P_B^{-1}(q_0 \mathbf{d} q_1 \mathbf{d} q_2 \mathbf{s} q_0)$. Also notice that all the traces of the form $(\langle q_0, r_0\rangle \mathbf{d})^* \sigma_1$ belong to $P_B^{-1}(q_0 \mathbf{d} q_1 \mathbf{d} q_2 \mathbf{s} q_0)$. □

Two classical properties [33] concerning the interplay between the synchronous product and the natural projection hold, the proofs of which are trivial.

Fact 1. $P_A([\![A \parallel B]\!]) \subseteq [\![A]\!]$ *and* $[\![A \parallel B]\!] = P_B^{-1}([\![A]\!]) \cap P_A^{-1}([\![B]\!])$.

2.3 Equational μ-calculus and Partial Model Checking

Below, we recall the variant of μ-calculus commonly used in partial model checking called *modal equations* [1]. A specification is given as a sequence of modal equations, and one is typically interested in the value of the top variable that is the simultaneous solution to all the equations. Equations have variables on the left-hand side and assertions on the right-hand side. Assertions are built from the boolean constants *ff* and *tt*, variables x, boolean operators $\wedge$ and $\vee$, and modalities for necessity $[\cdot]$ and possibility $\langle\cdot\rangle$. Equations also have fixpoint operators (minimum μ and maximum ν) over variables x, and can be organized in equation systems.

Definition 4 (Syntax of the μ-calculus). *Given a set of variables $x \in X$ and an alphabet of actions $a \in \Sigma$,* assertions *$\varphi, \varphi' \in \mathcal{A}$ are given by the syntax:*

$$\varphi ::= ff \mid tt \mid x \mid \varphi \wedge \varphi' \mid \varphi \vee \varphi' \mid [a]\varphi \mid \langle a\rangle\varphi.$$

An equation *is $x =_\pi \varphi$, where $\pi \in \{\mu, \nu\}$, μ denotes a minimum fixed point equation, and ν a maximum one. An* equation system *Φ is a possibly empty sequence (ϵ) of equations, where each variable x occurs in the left-hand side of at most a single equation. Thus Φ is given by*

$$\Phi ::= x =_\pi \varphi; \Phi \mid \epsilon.$$

A top assertion *$\Phi \downarrow x$ projects the simultaneous solution of an equation system Φ onto the top variable x.* □

We define the semantics of modal equations in terms of the traces of an LTS by extending the usual state semantics of [1] as follows. First, given an assertion φ, its state semantics $\|\varphi\|_\rho$ is given by the set of states of an LTS that satisfy φ in the context ρ, where the function ρ assigns meaning to variables. The boolean connectives are interpreted as intersection and union. The possibility modality $\|\langle a\rangle\varphi\|_\rho$ (respectively, the necessity modality $\|[a]\varphi\|_\rho$) denotes the states for which some (respectively, all) of their outgoing transitions labeled by a lead to states that satisfy φ. For more details on μ-calculus see [8,22].

Definition 5 (Semantics of the μ-calculus [1]**).** *Let A be an LTS, and $\rho : X \to 2^{S_A}$ be an* environment *that maps variables to sets of A's states. Given an assertion φ, the* state semantics *of φ is the mapping $\|\cdot\| : \mathcal{A} \to (X \to 2^{S_A}) \to 2^{S_A}$ inductively defined as follows.*

$$\|\mathit{ff}\|_\rho = \emptyset \qquad \|tt\|_\rho = S_A \qquad \|x\|_\rho = \rho(x)$$
$$\|\varphi \wedge \varphi'\|_\rho = \|\varphi\|_\rho \cap \|\varphi'\|_\rho \quad \|[a]\varphi\|_\rho = \{s \in S_A \mid \forall s'.s \xrightarrow{a}_A s' \Rightarrow s' \in \|\varphi\|_\rho\}$$
$$\|\varphi \vee \varphi'\|_\rho = \|\varphi\|_\rho \cup \|\varphi'\|_\rho \quad \|\langle a\rangle\varphi\|_\rho = \{s \in S_A \mid \exists s'.s \xrightarrow{a}_A s' \wedge s' \in \|\varphi\|_\rho\}$$

We extend the state semantics from assertions to equation systems. First we introduce some auxiliary notation. The empty mapping is represented by $[\,]$, $[x \mapsto U]$ is the environment where U is assigned to x, and $\rho \circ \rho'$ is the mapping obtained by composing ρ and ρ'. Given a function $f(U)$ on the powerset of S_A, let $\pi U.f(U)$ be the corresponding fixed-point. We now define the semantics of equation systems by:

$$\begin{aligned} \|\epsilon\|_\rho &= [\,] \\ \|x =_\pi \varphi; \Phi\|_\rho &= R(U^*) \quad \textit{where } U^* = \pi U.\|\varphi\|_{\rho \circ R(U)} \\ & \qquad\qquad\quad \textit{and } R(U) = [x \mapsto U] \circ \|\Phi\|_{\rho \circ [x \mapsto U]}. \end{aligned}$$

Finally, for top assertions, let $\|\Phi \downarrow x\|$ be a shorthand for $\|\Phi\|_{[\,]}(x)$. □

Note that whenever we apply function composition $\circ$, its arguments have disjoint domains. Next, we present the trace semantics: a trace starting from a state s satisfies φ if s does.

Definition 6. *Given an LTS A, an environment ρ, and a state $s \in S_A$, the* trace semantics *of an assertion φ is a function $\langle\!\langle\cdot\rangle\!\rangle : \mathcal{A} \to S_A \to (X \to 2^{S_A}) \to \mathcal{T}$, which we also extend to equation systems, defined as follows.*

$$\langle\!\langle\varphi\rangle\!\rangle^s_\rho = \begin{cases} [\![A, s]\!] \text{ if } s \in \|\varphi\|_\rho \\ \emptyset \text{ otherwise} \end{cases} \qquad \langle\!\langle\Phi\rangle\!\rangle_\rho = \lambda x. \bigcup_{s \in \|\Phi\|_\rho(x)} [\![A, s]\!].$$

We write $\langle\!\langle\Phi \downarrow x\rangle\!\rangle$ in place of $\langle\!\langle\Phi\rangle\!\rangle_{[\,]}(x)$. □

Example 6. Consider $\Phi \downarrow x$ where $\Phi = \{x =_\mu [d]y \wedge \langle u\rangle tt; y =_\nu \langle d\rangle x \vee \langle s\rangle x\}$. We compute $\|\Phi \downarrow x\|$ with respect to $A \parallel B$. $\|\Phi \downarrow x\| = U^* = \mu U.F(U)$, where $F(U) = \|[d]y \wedge \langle u\rangle tt\|_{[x \mapsto U, y \mapsto G(U)]}$ and $G(U) = \nu U'.\|\langle d\rangle x \vee \langle s\rangle x\|_{[x \mapsto U, y \mapsto U']} =$

$\|\langle d\rangle x \vee \langle s\rangle x\|_{[x\mapsto U]}$ (since y does not occur in the assertion). Following the Knaster-Tarski theorem, we compute $U^* = \bigcup^n F^n(\emptyset)$:

1. $G(\emptyset) = \|\langle d\rangle x \vee \langle s\rangle x\|_{[x\mapsto\emptyset]} = \emptyset$ and $U^1 = F(\emptyset) = \|[d]y \wedge \langle u\rangle tt\|_{[x\mapsto\emptyset, y\mapsto\emptyset]} = \{\langle q_2, r_0\rangle\}$ (i.e., the only state that admits u but not d).
2. $G(\{\langle q_2, r_0\rangle\}) = \|\langle d\rangle x \vee \langle s\rangle x\|_{[x\mapsto\{\langle q_2,r_0\rangle\}]} = \{\langle q_1, r_0\rangle\}$ (since $\langle q_1, r_0\rangle \xrightarrow{d} \langle q_2, r_0\rangle$) and $U^2 = F(\{\langle q_2, r_0\rangle\}) = \|[d]y \wedge \langle u\rangle tt\|_{[x\mapsto\{\langle q_2,r_0\rangle\}, y\mapsto\{\langle q_1,r_0\rangle\}]} = \{\langle q_0, r_0\rangle, \langle q_2, r_0\rangle\}$.
3. $G(U^2) = \|\langle d\rangle x \vee \langle s\rangle x\|_{[x\mapsto\{\langle q_0,r_0\rangle,\langle q_2,r_0\rangle\}]} = \{\langle q_1, r_0\rangle, \langle q_2, r_1\rangle\}$ and $U^3 = F(U^2) = \|[d]y \wedge \langle u\rangle tt\|_{[x\mapsto U^2, y\mapsto G(U^2)]} = \{\langle q_0, r_0\rangle, \langle q_2, r_0\rangle\}$.

Since $U^2 = U^3$, we have obtained the fixed point U^*. Finally, we can compute $\langle\!\langle \Phi\downarrow x\rangle\!\rangle$, which amounts to $[\![A, \langle q_0, r_0\rangle]\!] \cup [\![A, \langle q_2, r_0\rangle]\!]$. □

We now define when an LTS satisfies an equation system. Recall that $[\![A]\!]$ stands for $[\![A, \imath_A]\!]$.

Definition 7. *An LTS A satisfies a top assertion $\Phi\downarrow x$, in symbols $A \models_s \Phi\downarrow x$, if and only if $\imath_A \in \|\Phi\downarrow x\|$. Moreover, let $A \models_\sigma \Phi\downarrow x$ if and only if $[\![A]\!] \subseteq \langle\!\langle \Phi\downarrow x\rangle\!\rangle$.* □

The following fact relates the notion of satisfiability defined in terms of state semantics ($\models_s$) with the one based on trace semantics ($\models_\sigma$); its proof is immediate by Definition 6.

Fact 2. *$A \models_s \Phi\downarrow x$ if and only if $A \models_\sigma \Phi\downarrow x$.*

As previously mentioned, partial model checking is based on the *quotienting* operation $/\!\!/$. Roughly, the idea is to specialize the specification of a composed system on a particular component. Below, we define the *quotienting* operation [1] on the LTS $A \parallel B$. Quotienting reduces $A \parallel B \models_s \Phi$ to solving $B \models_s \Phi\downarrow x /\!\!/_B A$. Note that each equation of the system Φ gives rise to a system of equations, one for each state s_i of A, all of the same kind, minimum or maximum (thus forming a π-*block* [3]). This is done by introducing a fresh variable x_{s_i} for each state s_i. Intuitively, the equation $x_{s_i} =_\pi \varphi /\!\!/_{\Sigma_B} s_i$ represents the requirements on B when A is in state s_i. Since the occurrence of the variables on the right-hand side depends on the A's transitions, $\Phi\downarrow x /\!\!/_B A$ embeds the behavior of A.

Definition 8. *Given a top assertion $\Phi \downarrow x$, we define the quotienting of the assertion on an LTS A with respect to an alphabet Σ_B as follows.*

$$\Phi\downarrow x /\!\!/_{\Sigma_B} A = (\Phi /\!\!/_{\Sigma_B} A)\downarrow x_{\imath_A}, \text{ where}$$

$$\epsilon /\!\!/_{\Sigma_B} A = \epsilon \qquad (x =_\pi \varphi; \Phi) /\!\!/_{\Sigma_B} A = \begin{cases} x_{s_1} =_\pi \varphi /\!\!/_{\Sigma_B} s_1 \\ \vdots \\ x_{s_n} =_\pi \varphi /\!\!/_{\Sigma_B} s_n \end{cases} ;\ \Phi /\!\!/_{\Sigma_B} A \quad (\forall\, s_i \in S_A)$$

$$x /\!\!/_{\Sigma_B} s = x_s \qquad tt /\!\!/_{\Sigma_B} s = tt \qquad ff /\!\!/_{\Sigma_B} s = ff$$

$$\varphi \vee \varphi' /\!\!/_{\Sigma_B} s = \varphi /\!\!/_{\Sigma_B} s \vee \varphi' /\!\!/_{\Sigma_B} s \qquad \varphi \wedge \varphi' /\!\!/_{\Sigma_B} s = \varphi /\!\!/_{\Sigma_B} s \wedge \varphi' /\!\!/_{\Sigma_B} s$$

$$\begin{array}{lll} (\langle a \rangle \varphi) /\!\!/_{\Sigma_B} s = \bigvee_{s \xrightarrow{a} s'} \varphi /\!\!/_{\Sigma_B} s' & ([a]\varphi) /\!\!/_{\Sigma_B} s = \bigwedge_{s \xrightarrow{a} s'} \varphi /\!\!/_{\Sigma_B} s' & \text{if } a \in \Sigma_A \setminus \Gamma \\ (\langle b \rangle \varphi) /\!\!/_{\Sigma_B} s = \langle b \rangle (\varphi /\!\!/_{\Sigma_B} s) & ([b]\varphi) /\!\!/_{\Sigma_B} s = [b](\varphi /\!\!/_{\Sigma_B} s) & \text{if } b \in \Sigma_B \setminus \Gamma \\ (\langle \gamma \rangle \varphi) /\!\!/_{\Sigma_B} s = \bigvee_{s \xrightarrow{\gamma} s'} \langle \gamma \rangle (\varphi /\!\!/_{\Sigma_B} s') & ([\gamma]\varphi) /\!\!/_{\Sigma_B} s = \bigwedge_{s \xrightarrow{\gamma} s'} [\gamma](\varphi /\!\!/_{\Sigma_B} s') & \text{if } \gamma \in \Gamma. \end{array}$$

□

Example 7. Consider the top assertion $\Phi \downarrow x$ of Example 6 and the LTSs A and B of Example 3. Quotienting $\Phi \downarrow x$ against B, we obtain $\Phi /\!\!/_{\Sigma_A} B \downarrow x_{r_0}$ where

$$\Phi /\!\!/_{\Sigma_A} B = \begin{cases} x_{r_0} =_\mu [d] y_{r_0} \wedge tt \\ x_{r_1} =_\mu [d] y_{r_1} \wedge ff \\ x_{r_2} =_\mu [d] y_{r_2} \wedge ff \\ y_{r_0} =_\nu \langle d \rangle x_{r_0} \vee ff \\ y_{r_1} =_\nu \langle d \rangle x_{r_1} \vee \langle s \rangle x_{r_0} \\ y_{r_2} =_\nu \langle d \rangle x_{r_2} \vee ff \end{cases} = \begin{cases} x_{r_0} =_\mu [d] y_{r_0} \\ x_{r_1} =_\mu ff \\ x_{r_2} =_\mu ff \\ y_{r_0} =_\nu \langle d \rangle x_{r_0} \\ y_{r_1} =_\nu \langle d \rangle x_{r_1} \vee \langle s \rangle x_{r_0} \\ y_{r_2} =_\nu \langle d \rangle x_{r_2} \end{cases} = \begin{cases} x_{r_0} =_\mu [d] y_{r_0} \\ y_{r_0} =_\nu \langle d \rangle x_{r_0}. \end{cases}$$

The leftmost equations are obtained by applying the rules of Definition 8. Then we simplify on the right-hand sides. Finally we reduce the number of equations by removing those unreachable from the top variable x_{r_0}. For a detailed description of our simplification strategies we refer the reader to [3]. By proceeding as in Example 6, we obtain $\{q_0, q_2, q_3\}$ as the fixpoint. □

3 Unifying the Logical and the Operational Approaches

In this section we prove the equivalence between natural projection and partial model checking (Theorem 4). To start, we introduce an auxiliary definition that roughly acts as a quotienting of an environment ρ. Below, we will write $\bigoplus_{i \in I} \rho_i$ for the finite composition of functions ρ_i over the elements of an index set I.

Definition 9. *Given a synchronous product* $A \parallel B$*, we define* $\Delta_B(\cdot) : (X \to 2^{S_A \times S_B}) \to (X_{S_A} \to 2^{S_B})$ *as*

$$\Delta_B(\rho) = \bigoplus_{x \in Dom(\rho)} \bigoplus_{s_A \in S_A} [x_{s_A} \mapsto U_B^x(s_A)], \text{ where } U_B^x(s_A) = \{s_B \mid \langle s_A, s_B \rangle \in \rho(x)\}.$$

□

A technical lemma follows. Intuitively, quotienting an assertion (and an environment) preserves the semantics, i.e., a state $\langle s_A, s_B \rangle$ satisfies φ if and only if s_B satisfies the quotient of φ on B. Indeed, the following statement can be rewritten as $\|\varphi /\!\!/_{\Sigma_B} s_A\|_{\Delta_B(\rho)} = \{s_B \mid \langle s_A, s_B \rangle \in \|\varphi\|_\rho\}$.

Lemma 1. *For all* A, B, ρ *and* φ *on* $A \parallel B$, $\langle s_A, s_B \rangle \in \|\varphi\|_\rho \iff s_B \in \|\varphi /\!\!/_{\Sigma_B} s_A\|_{\Delta_B(\rho)}$.

We next extend Lemma 1 to a system of equations, providing an alternative view of quotienting an assertion on a component of a synchronous product.

Lemma 2. *For all* A, B, ρ *and* Φ *on* $A \parallel B$, $\Delta_B(\|\Phi\|_\rho) = \|\Phi /\!\!/_{\Sigma_B} A\|_{\Delta_B(\rho)}$.

The following corollary is immediate (recall that x_{s_A} is the variable corresponding to the quotient of x on s_A).

Corollary 1. *For all* A, B, ρ, x *and* Φ *on* $A \parallel B$,

$$\langle s_A, s_B \rangle \in \|\Phi\|_\rho(x) \Longleftrightarrow s_B \in \|\Phi /\!\!/_{\Sigma_B} A\|_{\Delta_B(\rho)}(x_{s_A}).$$

We next establish the correspondence between quotienting and natural projection.

Theorem 3. *For all* A, B, x *and* Φ *on* $A \parallel B$, $\langle\!\langle \Phi \downarrow x /\!\!/_{\Sigma_B} A \rangle\!\rangle = P_B(\langle\!\langle \Phi \downarrow x \rangle\!\rangle)$.

The following theorem states that the synchronous product of two LTSs satisfies a global equation system if and only if its components satisfy their quotients, i.e., their local assertions.

Theorem 4. *For all* A, B, x *and* Φ *on* $A \parallel B$,

$$A \parallel B \models_\varsigma \Phi \downarrow x \qquad (\varsigma \in \{s, \sigma\})$$

if and only if any of the following equivalent statements holds:
1. $A \models_\varsigma \Phi \downarrow x /\!\!/_{\Sigma_A} B$ *2.* $B \models_\varsigma \Phi \downarrow x /\!\!/_{\Sigma_B} A$
3. $A \models_\sigma P_A(\langle\!\langle \Phi \downarrow x \rangle\!\rangle)$ *4.* $B \models_\sigma P_B(\langle\!\langle \Phi \downarrow x \rangle\!\rangle)$.

4 Quotienting Finite-State Systems

In this section we present an algorithm for quotienting a finite-state system defined as an LTS. Afterwards, we prove its correctness with respect to the standard quotienting operator and we study its complexity. Finally, we apply it to our working example to address three problems: verification, submodule construction, and controller synthesis.

4.1 Quotienting Algorithm

Our algorithm consists of two procedures that are applied sequentially. The first, called `quotient` (Table 2), builds a non-deterministic transition system from two LTSs, i.e., a specification P and an agent A. Moreover, it takes as an argument the alphabet of actions of the new transition system. Non-deterministic transition systems have a distinguished label λ, and serve as an intermediate representation. The states of the resulting transition system include all the pairs of states of P and A, except for those that denote a violation of P (line 1). The transition relation (line 3) is defined using the quotienting rules from Sect. 2. Also, note that the relation $\rightarrow$ is restricted to the states of S (denoted $\rightarrow_S$).

The second procedure, called `unify` (given in Table 3) translates a non-deterministic transition system back to an LTS. Using closures over λ, `unify` groups states of the transition system. This process is similar to the standard subset construction algorithm [19], except that we put an $a \in \Sigma_B \setminus \Gamma$ transition between two groups Q and M only if (i) M is the intersection of the λ-closures of the states reachable from Q with an a transition and (ii) all the states of Q admit at least an a transition leading to a state of M ($\wedge$-`move`). Procedure `unify` works as follows. Starting from the λ-closure of B's initial state (line 1) it repeats a partition generation cycle (lines 4–13). Each cycle removes an element Q from the set S of the partitions to be processed. Then, for all the actions in $\Sigma_B \setminus \{\lambda\}$, a partition M is computed by $\wedge$-`move` (line 7). If the partition is nonempty, a new transition is added from Q to M (line 9). Also, if M is a freshly generated partition, i.e., $M \notin R$, it is added to both S and R (line 10). The procedure terminates when no new partitions are generated.

Table 2. The quotienting algorithm.

Begin proc quotient
  input P = $<S_P,\ \Sigma_P,\ \rightarrow_P,\ i_P>$
  input A = $<S_A,\ \Sigma_A,\ \rightarrow_A,\ i_A>$
  input Σ_B

$S := (S_P \times S_A) \setminus \bigcup_{a \in \Sigma_A} \{(s_P, r_A) \mid s_P \not\xrightarrow{a}_P \wedge r_A \xrightarrow{a}_A\}$

$i := (i_P, i_A)$

$$\rightarrow\ := \bigcup_{s_P} \begin{cases} \bigcup_{a \in \Sigma_A \setminus \Gamma} \{((s_P, r_A), \lambda, (s'_P, r'_A)) \mid s_P \xrightarrow{a}_P s'_P \wedge r_A \xrightarrow{a}_A r'_A\} \\ \bigcup_{a \in \Sigma_B \setminus \Gamma} \{((s_P, r_A), a, (s'_P, r_A)) \mid s_P \xrightarrow{a}_P s'_P\} \\ \bigcup_{a \in \Gamma} \{((s_P, r_A), a, (s'_P, r'_A)) \mid s_P \xrightarrow{a}_P s'_P \wedge r_A \xrightarrow{a}_A r'_A\} \end{cases}$$

B := $<S,\ \Sigma_B,\ \rightarrow_S,\ i>$

output unify(B)

End proc

Our quotienting algorithm is correct with respect to the quotienting operator and runs in PTIME. Intuitively, we avoid an exponential blow-up in our contribution (in contrast to Table 1) since we only consider deterministic transition systems. Notice that a determinization step for non-deterministic transition systems is exponential in the worst case.

4.2 Prototype and Application to the Running Example

We implemented the algorithm presented above as part of a tool suite for the partial evaluation of finite state models called the *partial evaluator of simple transition systems* (PESTS).[1] We applied the prototype to some case studies,

[1] The tools in our library work on FSA.

Table 3. The unification algorithm.

```
Begin proc unify
  input B = <S_B , Σ_B , →_B , i_B>

  I := λ-close({i_B})
  R, S := {I}
  → := ∅
  while S ≠ ∅ do
    Q := pick&remove(S)
    for each a ∈ Σ_B \ {λ}
      M := Λ-move(Q, a)
      if M ≠ ∅ then
        → := → ∪ {(Q, a, M)}
        if M ∉ R then S := S ∪ {M}; R := R ∪ {M} end if
      end if
    end for
  end while
  output <R, Σ_B \ {λ}, →, I>
end proc
```

```
Begin proc Λ-move
  input Q
  input a

  M := λ-close( ⋂_{q∈Q} {q' | q -a->_B q'})
  output M
end proc
```

including a real world one based on a flexible manufacturing system.[2] For the sake of presentation we only show here the application to the running example. In particular, we leverage our algorithm to address three different problems: (*i*) reducing the verification of a parallel composition to that of a single component, (*ii*) synthesizing a submodule that respects a global specification (SCP), and (*iii*) synthesizing a controller for a given component (CSP).

Verification. Here we want to check whether $A \parallel B \not\models_s P(2)$. To do this we follow the approach of [1], i.e., we start by quotienting the specification $P(2)$ against A (see Fig. 2). The result is a two-state specification P' having a single transition labeled with t. Clearly $B \not\models_s P'$ and a counterexample is the trace $\sigma = \mathbf{r_0}u\mathbf{r_1}s\mathbf{r_0}t\mathbf{r_2}$, as $\sigma \in [\![B]\!]$ while $\sigma \notin [\![P']\!]$. As a consequence $A \parallel B \not\models_s P$. Intuitively, this is because after the two d actions, A performs a single s, which is insufficient to delimit a "safety zone" for actions u by B (which might occur too late, e.g., after another d by A). Thus, P' does not allow an s that might permit A to carry out the third d move before a u action.

Fixing the example. Given to the previous reasoning, we cannot synthesize meaningful submodules and controllers starting from A. To fix our example, we therefore replace A with A', as depicted in Fig. 4. A' resembles A but has an extra state q_4 that enables a second s transition. Intuitively, it represents the "safety zone" just described.

SCP. We now apply the quotienting algorithm to A' in the case of buffer sizes 2 and 3 to construct the submodules that comply with $P(2)$ and $P(3)$, respectively.

[2] *FlexFact* http://www.rt.eei.uni-erlangen.de/FGdes/productionline.html.

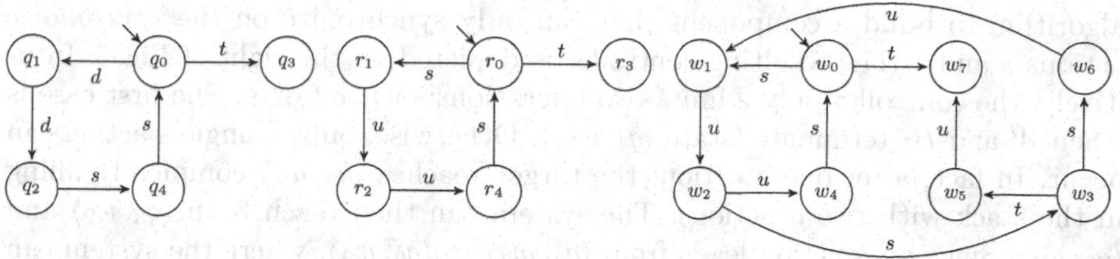

Fig. 4. Graphical representation of A', B_2 and B_3 (from left to right).

Thus, we set $\Sigma_B = \{u, s, t\}$. In this way, the quotienting algorithm generates a component that not only synchronizes through actions s and t, but also performs actions u autonomously. The resulting agents B_2 and B_3 appear in Fig. 4.

The agent B_2 synchronizes on the first s transition of A' to ensure that both the d actions have been performed. Afterwards, the buffer must be cleared (two u actions) before synchronizing again on s (thereby permitting A' to cycle). Synchronizing on t is also possible. In this case, no further modifications of the buffer happen.

With a buffer of size 3, the agent B_3 is more complex. Intuitively, A' can perform its two d actions only when the buffer contains at most one item. Thus, B_3 has two loops. The inner loop (passing through the states $w_0\, w_1\, w_2\, w_4$) is analogous to that of B_2 (where two u actions are performed in sequence) and, if completed, it empties the buffer. Moreover, the specification includes an external loop ($w_2\, w_3\, w_6\, w_1$) that removes two elements from the full buffer of size 3. As expected, the two cycles can be combined. Finally, notice that the action t can occur under two conditions: if the buffer contains no items (w_0) or exactly 1 item (w_3). In the second case, a final u action (w_5) can occur.

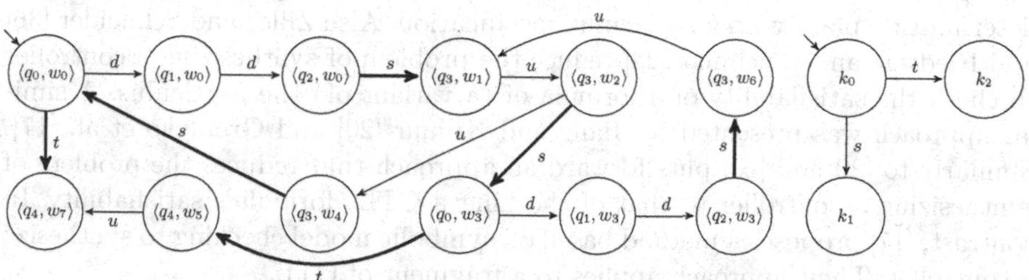

Fig. 5. Graphical representation of $A' \parallel B_3$ and C (from left to right).

CSP. We consider now the problem of synthesizing a controller for $A' \parallel B_3$ (see Fig. 5). In particular, we want a controller to enforce $P(2)$ on it.[3] To generate the controller, we run the quotienting algorithm with $\Sigma_B = \{s, t\}$, i.e., we force the

[3] Notice that $A' \parallel B_3$ does not comply with $P(2)$ as B_3 was synthesized from $P(3)$.

algorithm to build a component that can only synchronize on the *controllable* actions s and t. The resulting controller is depicted on the right of Fig. 5. Intuitively, the controller only admits two operations: either t or s. The first case is when A' and B_3 terminate (state $\langle q_4, w_7\rangle$). Otherwise, only a single s action can occur. In fact, after one s action, the target reaches $\langle q_3, w_1\rangle$ completely filling in the stack with two d actions. The system can then reach both $\langle q_3, w_2\rangle$ and $\langle q_3, w_4\rangle$. Since an s action leads from $\langle q_3, w_2\rangle$ to $\langle q_0, w_3\rangle$, where the system can perform other two d transitions, it is not allowed.

5 Related Work

Natural projection is mostly used by the community working on control theory and discrete-event systems. In the 1980s, the seminal works by Wonham et al. (e.g., [34,35]) exploited natural projection-based algorithms for synthesizing both local and global controllers. Along this line of research, other authors proposed extensions and refinements, relying on natural projection (e.g., see [13,14,24,32]).

Partial model checking has been successfully applied to the synthesis of controllers. Given an automaton representing a plant and a μ-calculus formula, Basu and Kumar [6] compute the quotient of the specification with respect to the plant. The satisfiability of the resulting formula is checked using a tableau that also returns a valid model yielding the controller. Their tableau works similarly to our quotienting algorithm, but applies to a more specific setting, as they are interested in generating controllers. In contrast, Martinelli and Matteucci [26] use partial model checking to generate a control process for a partially unspecified system in order to guarantee the compliance against a μ-calculus formula. The generated controller takes the form of an edit automaton [7].

Some authors proposed techniques based on the formal verification of temporal logics for addressing CSP. Arnold et al. [4] were among the first to control a deterministic plant with a μ-calculus specification. Also Ziller and Schneider [36] and Riedwge and Pinchinat [29] reduce the problem of synthesizing a controller to check the satisfiability of a formula of (a variant of) the μ-calculus. A similar approach was presented by Jiang and Kumar [20] and Gromyko et al. [17]. Similarly to [29,36], [20] puts forward an approach that reduces the problem of synthesizing a controller to that of checking a CTL* formula's satisfiability. In contrast, [17] proposes a method based on symbolic model checking to synthesize a controller. Their approach applies to a fragment of CTL.

6 Conclusion

Our work goes in the same direction of [12] and provides results that build a new bridge between supervisory control theory and formal verification. In particular, we have formally established the relationship between partial model checking and natural projection by reducing natural projection to partial model checking and proving them equivalent under common assumptions. This equivalence helps explain why some authors use partial model checking and others use natural projection to synthesize controllers. We have also developed a working prototype that we haven applied to our running example and to a realistic case study.

Besides establishing an interesting and novel connection, our work also opens new directions for investigation. Since natural projection is related to language theory in general, there could be other application fields where partial model checking can be used as an alternative. The original formulation of partial model checking applies to the μ-calculus, while our quotienting algorithm works on LTSs. To the best of our knowledge, no quotienting algorithms exist for formalisms with a different expressive power, such as LTL or CTL.

Data Availability Statement and Acknowledgments. All the experiments and artifacts generated during the current study are available in the github repository: https://doi.org/10.6084/m9.figshare.5918707.v1.

This work was partially supported by SNSF funded project IZK0Z2_168370 "Enforceable Security Policies in Fog Computing" and by CINI Cybersecurity National Laboratory within the project FilieraSicura: Securing the Supply Chain of Domestic Critical Infrastructures from Cyber Attacks (www.filierasicura.it) funded by CISCO Systems Inc. and Leonardo SpA.

References

1. Andersen, H.R.: Partial model checking (extended abstract). In: Proceedings of Tenth Annual IEEE Symposium on Logic in Computer Science, pp. 398–407. IEEE Computer Society Press (1995)
2. Andersen, H.R., Lind-Nielsen, J.: MuDiv: a tool for partial model checking. Demo Presentation at CONCUR (1996)
3. Andersen, H.R., Lind-Nielsen, J.: Partial model checking of modal equations: a survey. Int. J. Softw. Tools Technol. Transf. **2**(3), 242–259 (1999)
4. Arnold, A., Vincent, A., Walukiewicz, I.: Games for synthesis of controllers with partial observation. Theor. Comput. Sci. **1**(303), 7–34 (2003)
5. Baeten, J.C.M., Luttik, B., Muller, T., Van Tilburg, P.: Expressiveness modulo bisimilarity of regular expressions with parallel composition. Mathe. Struct. Comput. Sci. **26**, 933–968 (2016)
6. Basu, S., Kumar, R.: Quotient-based approach to control of nondeterministic discrete-event systems with μ-calculus specification (2006). http://home.eng.iastate.edu/~rkumar/PUBS/acc06-muctrl.pdf
7. Bauer, L., Ligatti, J., Walker, D.: More enforceable security policies. In: Foundations of Computer Security, Copenhagen, Denmark, July 2002
8. Bradfield, J., Stirling, C.: Modal Mu-calculi. In: Handbook of Modal Logic, vol. 3. Elsevier Science (2006)
9. Cassandras, C.G., Lafortune, S.: Introduction to Discrete Event Systems. Kluwer, Boston (1999)
10. Open Fog Consortium: Out of the Fog: Use Case Scenarios. Supply Chain, High-Scale Drone Package Delivery, July 2016. https://www.openfogconsortium.org/wp-content/uploads/OpenFog-Transportation-Drone-Delivery-Use-Case.pdf. Accessed Jan 2017

11. Costa, G., Basin, D., Bodei, C., Degano, P., Galletta, L.: Pests: Partial evaluator of simple transition systems. GitHub, February 2018. https://github.com/SCPTeam/pests, https://doi.org/10.6084/m9.figshare.5918707.v1
12. Ehlers, R., Lafortune, S., Tripakis, S., Vardi, M.: Bridging the gap between supervisory control and reactive synthesis: case of full observation and centralized control. IFAC Proc. Volumes **47**(2), 222–227 (2014)
13. Feng, L., Wonham, W.M.: TCT: a computation tool for supervisory control synthesis. In: Proceedings of 2006 8th International Workshop on Discrete Event Systems, pp. 388–389 (2006)
14. Feng, L., Wonham, W.M.: On the computation of natural observers in discrete-event systems. Discret. Event Dyn. Syst. **20**(1), 63–102 (2010)
15. Feuillade, G., Pinchinat, S.: Modal specifications for the control theory of discrete event systems. Discret. Event Dyn. Syst. **17**(2), 211–232 (2007)
16. Giacobazzi, R., Ranzato, F.: States vs. traces in model checking by abstract interpretation. In: Hermenegildo, M.V., Puebla, G. (eds.) SAS 2002. LNCS, vol. 2477, pp. 461–476. Springer, Heidelberg (2002). https://doi.org/10.1007/3-540-45789-5_32
17. Gromyko, A., Pistore, M., Traverso, P.: A tool for controller synthesis via symbolic model checking. In: 8th International Workshop on Discrete Event Systems, pp. 475–476, July 2006
18. Groote, J.F., Mousavi, M.R.: Modeling and Analysis of Communicating Systems. The MIT Press, Cambridge (2014)
19. Hopcroft, J.E., Motwani, R., Ullman, J.D.: Introduction to Automata Theory, Languages, and Computation, 3rd edn. Addison-Wesley Longman Publishing Co., Inc., Boston (2006)
20. Jiang, S., Kumar, R.: Supervisory control of discrete event systems with ctl* temporal logic specifications. SIAM J. Control Optim. **44**(6), 2079–2103 (2006)
21. Jirásková, G., Masopust, T.: On a structural property in the state complexity of projected regular languages. Theoret. Comput. Sci. **449**, 93–105 (2012)
22. Kozen, D.: Results on the propositional mu-calculus. Theor. Comput. Sci. **27**, 333–354 (1983)
23. Lang, F., Mateescu, R.: Partial model checking using networks of labelled transition systems and boolean equation systems. In: Flanagan, C., König, B. (eds.) TACAS 2012. LNCS, vol. 7214, pp. 141–156. Springer, Heidelberg (2012). https://doi.org/10.1007/978-3-642-28756-5_11
24. Lin, F., Wonham, W.M.: Decentralized supervisory control of discrete-event systems. Inf. Sci. **44**(3), 199–224 (1988)
25. Martinelli, F., Matteucci, I.: Synthesis of local controller programs for enforcing global security properties. In: 3rd International Conference on Availability, Reliability and Security (ARES), pp. 1120–1127, March 2008
26. Martinelli, F., Matteucci, I.: A framework for automatic generation of security controller. Softw. Test. Verif. Reliab. **22**(8), 563–582 (2012)
27. Merlin, P., Bochmann, G.V.: On the construction of submodule specifications and communication protocols. ACM Trans. Program. Lang. Syst. (TOPLAS) **5**(1), 1–25 (1983)
28. Moor, T., Schmidt, K., Perk, S.: libFAUDES – an open source C++ library for discrete event systems. In: 9th International Workshop on Discrete Event Systems, pp. 125–130, May 2008
29. Riedweg, S., Pinchinat, S.: Quantified Mu-calculus for control synthesis. In: Rovan, B., Vojtáš, P. (eds.) MFCS 2003. LNCS, vol. 2747, pp. 642–651. Springer, Heidelberg (2003). https://doi.org/10.1007/978-3-540-45138-9_58

30. Rudie, K., Grigorov, L.: Integrated Discrete-Event Systems (IDES), Department of Electrical and Computer Engineering, Queen's University in Kingston, ON, Canada. https://qshare.queensu.ca/Users01/rudie/www/software.html. Accessed Feb 2017
31. Su, R., Wonham, W.M.: Global and local consistencies in distributed fault diagnosis for discrete-event systems. IEEE Trans. Autom. Control **50**(12), 1923–1935 (2005)
32. Wong, K.C.: On the complexity of projections of discrete-event systems. In: Proceedings of IEEE Workshop on Discrete Event Systems, pp. 201–208 (1998)
33. Wonham, W.M.: Supervisory control of discrete-event systems, Department of Electrical and Computer Engineering. University of Toronto, ON, Canada. http://www.control.toronto.edu/DES. Accessed Feb 2017
34. Wonham, W.M., Ramadge, P.J.: On the supremal controllable sublanguage of a given language. In: Proceedings of the 23rd IEEE Conference on Decision and Control, pp. 1073–1080, December 1984
35. Wonham, W.M., Ramadge, P.J.: Modular supervisory control of discrete-event systems. Math. Control Signals Syst. **1**(1), 13–30 (1988)
36. Ziller, R., Schneider, K.: Combining supervisor synthesis and model checking. ACM Trans. Embed. Comput. Syst. **4**(2), 331–362 (2005)

Machine Learning

ICE-Based Refinement Type Discovery for Higher-Order Functional Programs

Adrien Champion[1(✉)], Tomoya Chiba[1], Naoki Kobayashi[1], and Ryosuke Sato[2]

[1] The University of Tokyo, Tokyo, Japan
adrien.champion@email.com
[2] Kyushu University, Fukuoka, Japan

Abstract. We propose a method for automatically finding refinement types of higher-order function programs. Our method is an extension of the ICE framework of Garg *et al.* for finding invariants. In addition to the usual positive and negative samples in machine learning, their ICE framework uses *implication constraints*, which consist of pairs (x, y) such that if x satisfies an invariant, so does y. From these constraints, ICE infers *inductive* invariants effectively. We observe that the implication constraints in the original ICE framework are not suitable for finding invariants of recursive functions with multiple function calls. We thus generalize the implication constraints to those of the form $(\{x_1, \dots, x_k\}, y)$, which means that if all of $x_1, \dots, x_k$ satisfy an invariant, so does y. We extend their algorithms for inferring likely invariants from samples, verifying the inferred invariants, and generating new samples. We have implemented our method and confirmed its effectiveness through experiments.

1 Introduction

Higher-order functional program verification is an interesting but challenging problem. Over the past two decades, several approaches have been proposed: refinement types with manual annotations [10,31], liquid types [23], and reduction to higher-order recursion schemes [24]. These approaches face the same problem found in imperative and synchronous data-flow program verification: the need for predicates describing how loops and components behave for the verification and/or abstraction method to work in practice [9,12,17]. This paper proposes to address this issue by combining refinement types with the recent machine-learning-based, invariant discovery framework ICE from [11,12].

Consider for instance a function `f` from integers to integers such that if its input `n` is less than or equal to 101, then its output is 91, otherwise it is $\mathtt{n} - 10$. (This is the case of the `mc_91` function on Fig. 1.) Then our objective is to automatically discover, by using an *adaptation* of ICE, the refinement type

$$\mathtt{f} : \{n : \mathrm{int} \mid \mathit{true}\} \rightarrow \{r : \mathrm{int} \mid (n > 101 \wedge r = n - 10) \vee r = 91\}.$$

D. Beyer and M. Huisman (Eds.): TACAS 2018, LNCS 10805, pp. 365–384, 2018.
https://doi.org/10.1007/978-3-319-89960-2_20

That is, function f accepts any integer n that satisfies *true* as input, and yields an integer r equal to $n-10$ when $n > 101$, and equal to 91 otherwise. The traditional ICE framework is not appropriate for our use-case. We briefly summarize it below, and then discuss how this approach needs to be extended for the purpose of functional program verification.

Brief Review of the ICE *Framework.* Let $\mathscr{S}$ be a transition system $\langle\ \vec{s}, \mathcal{I}(\vec{s}), \mathcal{T}(\vec{s}, \vec{s}')\ \rangle$, with $\vec{s}$ its vector of state variables, $\mathcal{I}(\vec{s})$ its initial predicate, and $\mathcal{T}(\vec{s}, \vec{s}')$ the transition relation between consecutive states. Suppose we wish to prove that $\mathcal{P}(\vec{s})$ is an invariant, i.e., that a property $\mathcal{P}(\vec{s})$ holds for any state $\vec{s}$ reachable from an initial state. Then it suffices to find a predicate $Inv(\vec{s})$ that satisfies the following conditions.

$$\mathcal{I}(\vec{s}) \models Inv(\vec{s}) \tag{1}$$

$$Inv(\vec{s}) \models \mathcal{P}(\vec{s}) \tag{2}$$

$$Inv(\vec{s}) \wedge \mathcal{T}(\vec{s}, \vec{s}') \models Inv(\vec{s}') \tag{3}$$

The predicate $Inv(\vec{s})$ is an invariant that is *inductive* in that it is preserved by the transition relation, as guaranteed by (3). We call such an $Inv(\vec{s})$ a *strengthening inductive invariant* for $\mathcal{P}(\vec{s})$. It serves as a *certificate* that $\mathcal{P}(\vec{s})$ is a (plain) invariant. Given a candidate for $Inv(\vec{s})$, the conditions (1)–(3) can be checked by an SMT [3] solver. In the rest of this section, "invariant" will always mean "strengthening inductive invariant".

The ICE framework is a machine-learning-based method combining a *learner* that incrementally produces candidate invariants, and a *teacher* that checks whether the candidates are such that (1), (2) and (3) hold. If a given candidate is not an invariant, the teacher produces *learning data* as follows, so that the learner can produce a better candidate. Given a candidate $C_k(\vec{s})$, the teacher checks whether (1) holds — using an SMT solver for instance. If it does not, a concrete state $\vec{e}$ is extracted and will be given to the learner as an *example*: the next candidate C_{k+1} should be such that $C_{k+1}(\vec{e})$ holds. Conversely, if (2) does not hold, a concrete state $\vec{c}$ is extracted and will be given as a *counterexample*: the next candidate should be such that $C_{k+1}(\vec{c})$ does not hold.

Unlike traditional machine-learning approaches, in ICE the teacher also extracts learning data from (3) when it does not hold. It takes the form of a pair of (consecutive) concrete states $(\vec{i}, \vec{i}')$, and is called an *implication constraint*: the next candidate should be such that $C_{k+1}(\vec{i}) \Rightarrow C_{k+1}(\vec{i}')$. Implication constraints are crucial for the learner to discover inductive invariants, as they let it know why its current candidate failed the induction check. The ICE framework does not specify how the learner generates candidates, but this is typically done by building a *classifier* consistent with the learning data, in the form of a decision tree—discussed further in Sect. 3.

Refinement Type Inference as a Predicate Synthesis Problem. We now discuss why the original ICE framework is ill-suited for functional program verification.

```
let rec mc_91 n = if n > 100 then n - 10
                  else let tmp = mc_91 (n + 11) in mc_91 tmp
let main m =
  let res = mc_91 m in if m ≤ 101 then assert (res = 91)
```

Fig. 1. McCarthy's 91 function.

Consider McCarthy's 91 function from Fig. 1. To prove this program correct in a refinement type setting, it is enough to find some refinement type

$$\{n : \text{int} \mid \rho_1(n)\} \rightarrow \{r : \text{int} \mid \rho_2(n,r)\}$$

for mc_91, where ρ_1 and ρ_2 are such

$$\rho_1(n) \wedge n > 100 \wedge r = n - 10 \models \rho_2(n,r) \quad (4)$$
$$\rho_1(n) \wedge n \leq 100 \models \rho_1(n+11) \quad (5)$$
$$\rho_1(n) \wedge n \leq 100 \wedge \rho_2(n+11, \mathit{tmp}) \models \rho_1(\mathit{tmp}) \quad (6)$$
$$\rho_1(n) \wedge n \leq 100 \wedge \rho_2(n+11, \mathit{tmp}) \wedge \rho_2(\mathit{tmp}, r) \models \rho_2(n,r) \quad (7)$$
$$\mathit{true} \models \rho_1(m) \quad (8)$$
$$m \leq 101 \wedge \rho_2(m, \mathit{res}) \models \mathit{res} = 91 \quad (9)$$

We can observe some similarities between the Horn clauses above and (1)–(3). The constraints (8) and (9) respectively correspond to the constraints (1) and (2) on initial states and the property to be proved, whereas the constraints (4)–(7) correspond to the induction constraint (3). This observation motivates us to reuse the ICE framework for refinement type inference.

There are, however, two obstacles in adapting the ICE framework to refinement type inference. First, we must infer not one but several mutually-dependent predicates. Second, and more importantly, we need to generalize the notion of implication constraint because of the nested recursive calls found in functional programs. To illustrate, let us assume that we realized that mc_91's precondition is $\rho_1(n) = \mathit{true}$. Then the third constraint from the `else` branch is

$$n \leq 100 \wedge \rho_2(n+11, \mathit{tmp}) \wedge \rho_2(\mathit{tmp}, r) \models \rho_2(n,r).$$

Contrary to the ones found in the original ICE framework, this Horn clause is *non-linear*: it has more than one application of the same predicate (ρ_2, here) in its antecedents. Now, assuming we have a candidate for which this constraint is falsifiable, the implication constraint should have form $(\{(n_1,r_1), (n_2,r_2)\}, (n,r))$, which means that the next candidate C should be such that $C(n_1,r_1) \wedge C(n_2,r_2) \Rightarrow C(n,r)$. This is because there are two occurrences of ρ_2 on the left-hand side of the implication.

The need to infer more than one predicate and support non-linear Horn clauses is not specific to higher-order functional program verification. After all, McCarthy's 91 function is first-order and is occasionally mentioned in first-order imperative program verification papers [5]. SV-COMP [4], the main (imperative) software verification competition features *3247 Horn clause problems in its linear arithmetic track* (https://github.com/sosy-lab/sv-benchmarks/tree/master/clauses/LIA), 54 of which contain non-linear Horn clauses. In our context of higher-order functional program verification the ratio is much higher, with 63 of our 164 OCaml [20] programs yielding non-linear Horn clauses.

The main contribution of this paper is to address the two issues aforementioned and propose a modified ICE framework suitable for higher-order program verification in particular. While adapting machine-learning techniques to higher-order program verification has been done before [34, 35], transposing implication constraints to this context is, to the best of our knowledge, new work. We have implemented our approach as a program verifier for a subset of OCaml and report on our experiments.

The rest of the paper is organized as follows. Section 2 introduces our target language and describes verification condition generation and simplification. The modified ICE framework is discussed in Sect. 3. We report on our implementation and experiments of the approach in Sect. 4, and discuss related work in Sect. 5 before concluding in Sect. 6.

2 Target Language and Verification Conditions

In this section, we first introduce the target language of our refinement type inference method. We then introduce a refinement type system and associated verification conditions (i.e., sufficient conditions for the typability of a given program).

2.1 Language

The target of the method is a simply-typed, call-by-value, higher-order functional language with recursion. Its syntax is given by:

$$\begin{aligned} D \text{ (programs)} &::= \{f_1(\widetilde{z_1}) = e_1, \ldots, f_n(\widetilde{z_n}) = e_n\} \\ e \text{ (expressions)} &::= n \mid x \mid \oplus\{a_1 \Rightarrow e_1, \ldots, a_n \Rightarrow e_n\} \mid \texttt{fail} \\ &\quad\mid \texttt{let}\ x = * \ \texttt{in}\ e \mid \texttt{let}\ x = a\ \texttt{in}\ e \mid \texttt{let}\ x = y z\ \texttt{in}\ e \\ a \text{ (arith. expressions)} &::= n \mid x \mid op(a_1, a_2) \qquad v \text{ (values)} ::= n \mid f_i\, \widetilde{v} \\ \tau \text{ (simple types)} &::= \texttt{int} \mid \tau_1 \rightarrow \tau_2 \end{aligned}$$

We use the meta-variables $x, y, \ldots, f, g, \ldots$ for variables. We write $\widetilde{\cdot}$ for a sequence; for example, we write $\widetilde{x}$ for a sequence of variables. For the sake of simplicity, we consider only integers as base values. We represent booleans using integers, and treat 0 as false and non-zero values as true. We sometimes write *true* for 1 and *false* for 0.

We briefly explain programs and expressions; the formal semantics is given in the longer version [7]. We use let-normal-form-style for simplicity. A program

D is a set of mutually recursive function definitions $f(\widetilde{z}) = e$. The expression $\oplus\{a_i \Rightarrow e_i\}_{1\le i\le n}$ evaluates e_i non-deterministically if the value of a_i is non-zero, which can be also used to generate non-deterministic booleans/integers. We also write $(a_1 \Rightarrow e_1) \oplus \cdots \oplus (a_n \Rightarrow e_n)$ for $\oplus\{a_i \Rightarrow e_i\}_{1\le i\le n}$, and write $\texttt{if}\ a\ \texttt{then}\ e_1\ \texttt{else}\ e_2$ for $(a \Rightarrow e_1) \oplus (\neg a \Rightarrow e_2)$. The expression $\texttt{let}\ x = *\ \texttt{in}\ e$ generates an integer, then binds x to it, and evaluates e. The expression $\texttt{let}\ x = a\ \texttt{in}\ e$ ($\texttt{let}\ x = yz\ \texttt{in}\ e$, resp.) binds x to the value of a (yz, resp.), and then evaluates e. The expression fail aborts the program. An assert expression $\texttt{assert}(a)$ can be represented as $\texttt{if}\ a\ \texttt{then}\ 0\ \texttt{else}\ \texttt{fail}$. In the definition of values, function application $f_i\,\widetilde{v}$ must be partial, i.e., the length $|\widetilde{v}|$ of arguments $\widetilde{v}$ must be smaller than $|\widetilde{x_i}|$, where $(f_i(\widetilde{x_i}) = e_i) \in D$.

We assume that a program is well-typed under the standard simple type system. We also assume that every function in D has a non-zero arity, the body of each function definition has the integer type, and D contains a distinguished function symbol $\texttt{main} \in \{f_1,\dots,f_n\}$ whose simple type is $\texttt{int} \to \texttt{int}$.

The goal of our verification is to find an invariant (represented in the form of refinement types) of the program that is sufficient to verify that, for every integer n, $\texttt{main}\ n$ does not fail (i.e., is not reduced to fail).

2.2 Refinement Type System

We present a refinement type system for the target language. The syntax of refinement types is given by:

$$T(\text{refinement types}) ::= \{x : \texttt{int} \mid a\} \mid (x : T_1) \to T_2.$$

The refinement type $\{x : \texttt{int} \mid a\}$ denotes the set of integers that satisfy a, *i.e.*, the value of a is non-zero. For example, $\{x : \texttt{int} \mid x \ge 0\}$ represents natural numbers. The type $(x : T_1) \to T_2$ denotes the set of functions that take an argument x of type T_1 and return a value of type T_2. Here, note that x may occur in T_2. We write int for $\{x : \texttt{int} \mid \mathit{true}\}$, and $T_1 \to T_2$ for $(x : T_1) \to T_2$ when x does not occur in T_2. By abuse of notation, we sometimes (as in Sect. 1) write $\{x : \texttt{int} \mid a\} \to T$ for $(x : \{x : \texttt{int} \mid a\}) \to T$.

A judgment $\Gamma \vdash t : T$ means that term t has refinement type T under refinement type environment Γ, which is a sequence of refinement type bindings and guard predicates: $\Gamma ::= \emptyset \mid \Gamma, x{:}T \mid \Gamma, a$. Here, $x{:}T$ means that x has refinement type T, and a means that a holds. Figure 2 shows the typing rules, which are the standard ones.

The type system is sound in the sense that if $\vdash D : \Gamma$ holds for some Γ, then $\texttt{main}\ n$ does not fail for any integer n. We omit to prove this type system sound as it is a rather standard system [23,28,29]. The type system is, however, incomplete: there are programs that never fail but are not typable in the refinement type system. Implicit parameters are required to make the type system complete [30].

$$\frac{}{\Gamma \vdash n : \{x : \mathrm{int} \mid x = n\}}\ (\text{T-Const}) \qquad \frac{\Gamma(x) = T}{\Gamma \vdash x : T}\ (\text{T-Var}) \qquad \frac{[\![\Gamma]\!] \models \mathit{false}}{\Gamma \vdash \mathbf{fail} : T}\ (\text{T-Fail})$$

$$\frac{\Gamma, a_i \vdash e_i : T \quad \text{for each } i \in \{1, \dots, n\}}{\Gamma \vdash \oplus\{a_1 \Rightarrow e_1, \dots, a_n \Rightarrow e_n\} : T}\ (\text{T-Branch}) \qquad \frac{\Gamma, x : \mathrm{int} \vdash e : T}{\Gamma \vdash \mathbf{let}\ x = *\ \mathbf{in}\ e : T}\ (\text{T-Rand})$$

$$\frac{\Gamma, x : \{y : \mathrm{int} \mid y = a\} \vdash e : T}{\Gamma \vdash \mathbf{let}\ x = a\ \mathbf{in}\ e : [a/x]T}\ (\text{T-AExp}) \qquad \frac{\Gamma \vdash t : T' \quad \Gamma \vdash_s T' <: T}{\Gamma \vdash t : T}\ (\text{T-Sub})$$

$$\frac{[\![\Gamma]\!], a_1 \models a_2}{\Gamma \vdash_s \{x : \mathrm{int} \mid a_1\} <: \{x : \mathrm{int} \mid a_2\}}\ (\text{S-Int}) \qquad \frac{\Gamma \vdash_s T_{21} <: T_{11} \quad \Gamma, x : T_{21} \vdash_s T_{12} <: T_{22}}{\Gamma \vdash_s (x : T_{11}) \to T_{12} <: (x : T_{21}) \to T_{22}}\ (\text{S-Fun})$$

$$\frac{\Gamma \vdash y : (z : T_1) \to T_2 \quad \Gamma \vdash z : T_1 \quad \Gamma, x : T_2 \vdash e : T}{\Gamma \vdash \mathbf{let}\ x = yz\ \mathbf{in}\ e : T}\ (\text{T-App})$$

$$\frac{\begin{array}{c}\Gamma(\mathrm{main}) = (x : \mathrm{int}) \to \mathrm{int} \\ x_1 : T_1, \dots, x_k : T_k \vdash t : T \text{ for each } f : (x_1 : T_1) \to \cdots \to (x_k : T_k) \to T \in \Gamma \quad \text{where } f(x_1, \dots, x_k) = t \in D\end{array}}{\vdash D : \Gamma}\ (\text{T-Prog})$$

$$[\![\emptyset]\!] = \mathit{true}, \quad [\![\Gamma, x : \{y : \mathrm{int} \mid a\}]\!] = [\![\Gamma]\!] \wedge [x/y]a, \quad [\![\Gamma, a]\!] = [\![\Gamma]\!] \wedge a, \quad [\![\Gamma, x : (y : T_1) \to T_2]\!] = [\![\Gamma]\!]$$

Fig. 2. Typing rules of refinement type system

2.3 Verification Conditions

Our goal has now been reduced to finding Γ such that $\vdash D : \Gamma$, if such Γ exists. To this end, we first infer simple types for the target program by using the Hindley-Milner type inference algorithm. From the simple types, we construct the refinement type templates by adding predicate variables, and then generate the verification conditions, *i.e.*, constraints on the predicate variables that describe a sufficient condition for $\vdash D : \Gamma$. The construction of the verification conditions is also rather standard [23,28,29], hence we do not discuss it here—see [7]. We note that the verification conditions can be normalized to a set of Horn clauses [5].

Example 1. Consider the following program and its associated simple types:

```
let incr n = n + 1 in let twice f x = f (f x) in
let main m = assert (twice incr m > m)
```

$$\mathtt{main} : \mathtt{int} \to \mathtt{int}, \quad \mathtt{incr} : \mathtt{int} \to \mathtt{int}, \quad \mathtt{twice} : (\mathtt{int} \to \mathtt{int}) \to \mathtt{int} \to \mathtt{int}$$

By assigning a unique predicate variable to each integer type, we can obtain the following refinement type templates.

$$\mathtt{main} : \mathtt{int} \to \mathtt{int}, \qquad \mathtt{incr} : \{n : \mathtt{int} \mid \rho_1(n')\} \to \{k : \mathtt{int} \mid \rho_2(n, k)\},$$
$$\mathtt{twice} : (\{y : \mathtt{int} \mid \rho_1'(y)\} \to \{z : \mathtt{int} \mid \rho_2'(y, z)\}) \to \{x : \mathtt{int} \mid \rho_3'(x)\} \to \{r : \mathtt{int} \mid \rho_4'(x, r)\}.$$

We then extract the following verification conditions from the body of the program:

$$\begin{array}{lll} \rho_1(n) \models \rho_2(n, n+1) & \rho_3'(x) \models \rho_1'(x) & \rho_3'(x) \wedge \rho_2'(x, z_1) \models \rho_1'(z_1) \\ \rho_3'(x) \wedge \rho_2'(x, z_1) \wedge \rho_2'(z_1, z_2) \models \rho_4'(x, z_2) & & \rho_1'(n) \models \rho_1(n) \\ \mathit{true} \models \rho_3'(m) & \rho_4'(m, r) \models r > m & \rho_1'(y) \wedge \rho_2(y, z) \models \rho_2'(y, z). \end{array}$$

2.4 Simplifying Verification Conditions

The number of unknown predicates to infer is critical to the efficiency of our algorithm in Sect. 3, because the algorithm succeeds only when the learner comes up with correct solutions for *all* the unknown predicates. We discuss here a couple of techniques to reduce the number of unknown predicates.

The first one takes place at the level of Horn clauses and is not limited to refinement type inference over functional programs. Suppose that some predicate ρ occurs in the clauses $\varphi \models \rho$ and $C[\rho] \models \varphi'$, where $C[\rho]$ is a formula having only positive occurrences of ρ, and ρ does not occur in φ, φ', nor any other clauses of the verification condition. Then, we can replace the two clauses above with $C[\varphi] \models \varphi'$ and $\rho \equiv \varphi$. For example, recall the `incr/twice` from the example above. The predicate ρ_1 occurs only in the clauses $\rho'_1(n) \models \rho_1(n)$ and $\rho_1(n) \models \rho_2(n, n+1)$. Thus, we can replace them with $\rho'_1(n) \models \rho_2(n, n+1)$ and $\rho_1(n) \equiv \rho'_1(n)$. In this manner we can reduce the number of unknown predicate variables. This optimization itself is not specific to our context of functional program verification; similar (and more sophisticated) techniques are also discussed in [5]. We found this optimization particularly useful in our context, because the standard verification condition generation for higher-order functional programs introduces too many predicate variables.

The other optimization is specific to our context of refinement type inference. Suppose that the simple type of a function f is $\texttt{int} \to \texttt{int}$. Then, in general, we prepare the refinement type template $\{x : \texttt{int} \mid \rho_1(x)\} \to \{r : \texttt{int} \mid \rho_2(x, r)\}$. If the evaluation of $f(n)$ does not fail for any integer n, however, then the above refinement type is equivalent to $\{x : \texttt{int} \mid \mathit{true}\} \to \{r : \texttt{int} \mid \rho_1(x) \Rightarrow \rho_2(x, r)\}$. Thus, the simpler template $(x : \texttt{int}) \to \{r : \texttt{int} \mid \rho_3(x, r)\}$ suffices, with $\rho_3(x, r)$ corresponding to $\rho_1(x) \Rightarrow \rho_2(x, r)$. For instance, in the `mc_91` example from Sect. 1, it is obvious that $\texttt{mc\_91}(n)$ never fails as its body contains no assertions and contains only calls to itself. Thus, we can actually set $\rho_1(n)$ to *true*.

In practice we use effect analysis [22] to check whether a function can fail. To this end, we extend simple types to effect types defined by: $\sigma ::= \texttt{int} \mid \sigma_1 \xrightarrow{\xi} \sigma_2$, where ξ is either an empty effect ϵ, or a failure $\texttt{f}$. The type $\sigma_1 \xrightarrow{\xi} \sigma_2$ describes functions that take an argument of type σ_1 and return a value of type σ_2, but with a possible side effect of ξ. We can infer these effect types using a standard effect inference algorithm [22]. A function with effect type $\texttt{int} \xrightarrow{\epsilon} \sigma$ takes an integer as input and returns a value of σ without effect, i.e., without failure. For this type, we then use the simpler refinement type template $\{x : \texttt{int} \mid \mathit{true}\} \to \cdots$ instead of $\{x : \texttt{int} \mid \rho(x)\} \to \cdots$. For example, since `mc_91` has effect type $\texttt{int} \xrightarrow{\epsilon} \texttt{int}$, we assign the template $(x : \texttt{int}) \to \{r : \texttt{int} \mid \rho(x, r)\}$ for the refinement type of `mc_91`.

3 Modified Ice Framework

This section discusses our modified ICE framework tackling the predicate synthesis problem extracted from the input functional program as detailed in Sect. 2.

Algorithm 1. Teacher supervising the learning process.

Input: set of verification conditions VC over predicates $\rho_1, \ldots, \rho_n$ from Sect. 2
Result: concrete predicates for $\rho_1, \ldots, \rho_n$ for which $\bigwedge VC$ is valid

1 $(\mathcal{P}, \mathcal{N}, \mathcal{I}) = (\emptyset, \emptyset, \emptyset)$;
2 $(P_1, \ldots, P_n) = \mathit{learn}(\mathtt{quals}, \mathcal{P}, \mathcal{N}, \mathcal{I})$; (see Algorithm 2)
3 **while** $\bigwedge VC(P_1, \ldots, P_n)$ *is falsifiable* **do**
4 $\quad (\mathcal{P}', \mathcal{N}', \mathcal{I}') = \mathit{extract\_data}(VC, P_1, \ldots, P_n)$; (discussed in Sect. 3.1)
5 $\quad (\mathcal{P}, \mathcal{N}, \mathcal{I}) = (\mathcal{P} \cup \mathcal{P}', \mathcal{N} \cup \mathcal{N}', \mathcal{I} \cup \mathcal{I}')$;
6 $\quad (P_1, \ldots, P_n) = \mathit{learn}(\mathtt{quals}, \mathcal{P}, \mathcal{N}, \mathcal{I})$; (see Algorithm 2)
7 $(P_1, \ldots, P_n)$

Algorithm 1 details how the teacher supervises the learning process. Following the original ICE approach, teacher and learner only communicate by exchanging guesses for the predicates (from the latter to the former) and positive ($\mathcal{P}$), negative ($\mathcal{N}$) and implication ($\mathcal{I}$) data—from the former to the latter. These three sets of learning data are incrementally populated as long as the verification conditions are falsifiable, as discussed below.

3.1 Teacher

We now describe our modified version of the ICE teacher that, given some candidate predicates for $\Pi = \{\rho_1, \ldots, \rho_n\}$, returns learning data if the verification conditions instantiated on the candidates are falsifiable. Since there are several predicates to discover, the positive, negative and implication learning data (concrete values) will always be annotated with the predicate(s) concerned.

Now, all the constraints from the verification condition set VC have one of the following shapes, reminiscent of the original ICE's (1)–(3) from Sect. 1:

$$\alpha_1 \wedge \ldots \wedge \alpha_m \wedge C \models \alpha_{m+1} \tag{10}$$

$$\alpha_1 \wedge \ldots \wedge \alpha_m \wedge C \models \mathit{false} \qquad m \geq 1 \tag{11}$$

where each $\alpha_1, \ldots, \alpha_{m+1}$ is an application of one of the $\rho_1, \ldots, \rho_n$ to variables of the program, and C is a concrete formula ranging over the variables of the program. In the following, we write $\rho(\alpha_i)$ for the predicate α_i is an application of. To illustrate, recall constraint (7) of the example from Fig. 1:

$$\underbrace{\rho_1(n)}_{\alpha_1} \wedge \underbrace{\rho_2(n+11, \mathit{tmp})}_{\alpha_2} \wedge \underbrace{\rho_2(\mathit{tmp}, r)}_{\alpha_3} \wedge \underbrace{n \leq 100}_{C} \models \underbrace{\rho_2(n, r)}_{\alpha_4}.$$

It has the same shape as (10), with $\rho(\alpha_1) = \rho_1$ and $\rho(\alpha_2) = \rho(\alpha_3) = \rho(\alpha_4) = \rho_2$.

Given some guesses $P_1, \ldots, P_n$ for the predicates $\rho_1, \ldots, \rho_n$, the teacher can check whether $VC(P_1, \ldots, P_n)$ is falsifiable using an SMT solver. If it is, then function *extract_data* (Algorithm 1 line 4) extracts new learning data as follows.

If a verification condition with shape (10) and $m = 0$ can be falsified, then we extract some values $\widetilde{x}$ from the model produced by the solver. This constitutes a *positive example* $(\rho(\alpha_1), \widetilde{x})$ since $\rho(\alpha_1)$ should evaluate to *true* for $\widetilde{x}$. From a counterexample model for a verification condition of the form (11), we extract a *negative constraint* $\{\ (\rho(\alpha_1), \widetilde{x}_1),\ \ldots,\ (\rho(\alpha_m), \widetilde{x}_m)\ \}$. It means that *at least one* of the $(\rho(\alpha_i), \widetilde{x}_i)$ should be such that $\rho(\alpha_i)(\widetilde{x}_i)$ evaluates to *false*. Last, an *implication constraint* comes from a counterexample model for a verification condition of shape (10) with $m > 0$ and is a pair

$$(\ \{\ (\rho(\alpha_1), \widetilde{x}_1),\ \ldots,\ (\rho(\alpha_m), \widetilde{x}_m)\ \},\quad (\rho(\alpha_{m+1}), \widetilde{x}_{m+1})\ ).$$

Similarly to the original ICE implication constraints, this constraint means that if $\rho(\alpha_1)(\widetilde{x}_1) \wedge \ldots \wedge \rho(\alpha_m)(\widetilde{x}_m)$ evaluates to *true*, then so should $\rho(\alpha_{m+1})(\widetilde{x}_{m+1})$.

Remark 1. Note that negative examples and implication constraints in the original ICE framework are special cases of the negative constraints and implication constraints above. A negative example of the original ICE is just a singleton set $\{(\rho(\alpha_1), \widetilde{x}_1)\}$, and an implication constraint of ICE is a special case of the implication constraint where $m = 1$. Due to the generalization of learning data, negative constraints also contain unclassified data (unless they are singletons).

3.2 Learner

We now describe the learning part of our approach, which is an adaptation of the decision tree construction procedure from the original ICE framework [12]. The main difference is that the unclassified data can also contain values from negative constraints, as explained in Remark 1. This impacts decision tree construction as we now need to make sure the negative constraints are respected, in addition to checking that the implication constraints hold. Also, we adapted the qualifier selection heuristic (discussed in Sect. 3.3) to fit our context.

The learner first prepares a finite set of atomic formulas called *qualifiers*, and then tries to find solutions for Horn clauses as Boolean combinations of qualifiers, by running Algorithm 2. We first explain Algorithm 2; we discuss how the qualifiers are obtained in Sect. 3.4.

Algorithm 2 first classifies data—pairs of the form $(\rho, \widetilde{x})$ — to *true*, *false*, and *unknown*. It then calls `build_tree` (Algorithm 3) for each unknown predicate ρ, to construct a decision tree that encodes a candidate solution for ρ. A *tree* T is defined by $T := \mathit{Node}(q, T_+, T_-) \mid \mathit{Leaf}(b)$ where b is a boolean. The formula it corresponds to is given by function f, defined inductively by

$$f(\ \mathit{Node}(q, T_+, T_-)\ ) = (\ q \wedge f(T_+)\ ) \vee (\ \neg q \wedge f(T_-)\ ) \quad \text{and} \quad f(\ \mathit{Leaf}(b)\ ) = b.$$

Algorithm 3 shows the decision tree construction process for a given $\rho \in \Pi$. It chooses qualifiers splitting the learning data until there is no negative (positive) data left and the unclassified data can be classified as positive (negative). The main difference with the tree construction from the original ICE framework is

Algorithm 2. learn(quals, $\mathcal{P}$, global $\mathcal{N}$, global $\mathcal{I}$)

Result: concrete predicates for $\{\rho_1, \ldots, \rho_n\} = \Pi$ consistent with the learning data

```
global class = (
    { (ρ, x̃) ↦ true | ∃e ∈ 𝒫, (ρ, x̃) ∈ e } ∪ { (ρ, x̃) ↦ false | {(ρ, x̃)} ∈ 𝒩 }
);
foreach (ρ, x̃) appearing in the elements of ℐ and 𝒩 do
    if class(ρ, x̃) is undefined then class(ρ, x̃) ← unknown
{ ρ ↦ build_tree(
      ρ, quals(ρ), {x̃ | class(ρ, x̃)}, {x̃ | ¬class(ρ, x̃)}, {x̃ | class(ρ, x̃) = unknown}
) }
```

Algorithm 3. build_tree(ρ, Q, P, N, U)

Input: Predicate variable ρ, qualifiers Q, positive (P), negative (N) and unclassified (U) projected learning data.

```
if N = ∅ ∧ can_be_pos(U, class) then
    foreach u ∈ U do class(ρ, u) ← true ;
    Leaf(true)
else if P = ∅ ∧ can_be_neg(U, class) then
    foreach u ∈ U do class(ρ, u) ← false ;
    Leaf(false)
else
    choose q in Q that best divides the data
    (P+, N+, U+) = data x̃ from (P, N, U) such that q(x̃) ;
    (P−, N−, U−) = data x̃ from (P, N, U) such that ¬q(x̃) ;
    T+ = build_tree(ρ, Q \ q, P+, N+, U+,) ;
    T− = build_tree(ρ, Q \ q, P−, N−, U−,) ;
    Node(q, T+, T−)
```

that the classification checks now take into account the negative constraints introduced earlier. Qualifier selection is discussed separately in Sect. 3.3.

Function can_be_pos checks whether all the unclassified data can be classified as positive. This consists in making sure that negative and implication constraints are verified or contain unclassified data—meaning future choices are able to (and will) verify the constraints. Given unclassified data U, constraint sets $\mathcal{N}$ and $\mathcal{I}$, and classifier mapping class, can_be_pos checks that the following conditions hold for every $u \in U$:

$$\forall N \in \mathcal{N},\ \ (\rho, u) \in N \quad \Rightarrow \exists (\rho', n) \in N \setminus \{(\rho, u') | u' \in U\},\ \texttt{class}(\rho', n) \simeq \mathit{false}$$

$$\forall (\mathit{LHS}, \mathit{rhs}) \in \mathcal{I},\ (\rho, u) \in \mathit{LHS} \quad \Rightarrow \begin{cases} \texttt{class}(\mathit{rhs}) \simeq \mathit{true} \\ \vee\ \exists (\rho', l) \in \mathit{LHS} \setminus \{(\rho, u') | u' \in U\}, \\ \qquad \texttt{class}(\rho', l) \simeq \mathit{false} \end{cases}$$

where $\texttt{class}(n) \simeq b$ means that $\texttt{class}(n)$ is *unknown* or equal to b. Conversely, function can_be_neg checks that all the unclassified data can be classified as negative:

$$\forall u \in U, \forall (\mathit{LHS}, \mathit{rhs}) \in \mathcal{I},\quad (\rho, u) = \mathit{rhs} \ \Rightarrow\ \exists (\rho', l) \in \mathit{LHS},\ \texttt{class}(\rho', l) \simeq \mathit{false}.$$

While we did not specify the order in which the trees are constructed (Algorithm 2 line 8), it can impact performance greatly because the classification choices influence later runs of `build_tree`. Hence, it is better to treat the elements of Π that have the least amount of unclassified data first. Doing so directs the choices of the qualifier q (Algorithm 3 line 8, discussed below) on as much classified data as possible. The data is then split (lines 9 and 10) using q: more classified data thus means more informed splits, leading to more relevant classifications of unclassified data in the terminal cases of the decision tree construction.

3.3 Qualifier Selection in Algorithm 3

We now discuss how to choose qualifier $q \in Q$ on line 8 in Algorithm 3. The choice of the qualifier q used to split the learning data $D = (P, N, U)$ in $D_q = (P_q, N_q, U_q)$ and $D_{\neg q} = (P_{\neg q}, N_{\neg q}, U_{\neg q})$ is crucial. In [12], the authors introduce two heuristics based on the notion of *Shannon Entropy* ε:

$$\varepsilon(D) = -\frac{|P|}{|P|+|N|}\log_2\frac{|P|}{|P|+|N|} - \frac{|N|}{|P|+|N|}\log_2\frac{|N|}{|P|+|N|} \tag{12}$$

which yields a value between 0 and 1. This entropy rates the ratio of positive and negative examples: it gets close to 1 when $|P|$ and $|N|$ are close. A small entropy is preferred as it indicates that the data contains significantly more of one than the other. The *information gain* γ of a split is

$$\gamma(D, q) = \varepsilon(D) - \left(\frac{|D_q|\varepsilon(D_q)}{\lfloor D \rceil} + \frac{|D_{\neg q}|\varepsilon(D_{\neg q})}{\lfloor D \rceil} \right) \tag{13}$$

where $\lfloor D = (P, N, U) \rceil = |P| + |N|$. A high information gain means q separates the positive examples from the negative ones. Note that the information gain ignores unclassified data, a shortcoming the ICE framework [12] addresses by proposing two qualifier selection heuristics. The first subtracts a penalty to the information gain. It penalizes qualifiers separating data coming from the same implication constraint—called *cutting the implication*. The second heuristic changes the definition of entropy by introducing a function approximating the probability that a non-classified example will eventually be classified as positive. We present here our adaptation of this second heuristic, as it is much more natural to transfer to our use-case.

The idea is to create a function *Pr* that approximates the probability that some values from the projected learning data $D = (P, N, U)$ end up classified as positive. More precisely, $Pr(v)$ approximates the ratio between the number of *legal* (constraint-abiding) classifications in which v is classified positively and the number of all legal classifications. Computing this ratio for the whole data is impractical: it falls in the *counting problems* class and it is $\#P$-complete [2]. The approximation we propose uses the following notion of *degree*:

$$Degree(v) = \sum_{(\widetilde{x}, v) \in \mathcal{I}} \frac{1}{1+|\widetilde{x}|} - \sum_{(\widetilde{x}, y) \in \mathcal{I}, v \in \widetilde{x}} \frac{1}{1+|\widetilde{x}|} - \sum_{\widetilde{x} \in \mathcal{N}, v \in \widetilde{x}} \frac{1}{|\widetilde{x}|}$$

The three terms appearing in function *Degree* are based on the following remarks. Let v be some value in the projected learning data. If $(\widetilde{x}, v) \in \mathcal{I}$, there is only one classification for $\widetilde{x}$ to force v to be true: the classification where all the elements of $\widetilde{x}$ are classified positively. More elements in $\widetilde{x}$ generally mean more legal classifications where one of them is false and v need not be true: $Pr(v)$ should be higher if $\widetilde{x}$ has few elements. If v appears in the antecedents of a constraint $(\widetilde{x}, y)$, then $Pr(v)$ should be lower. Still, if $\widetilde{x}$ has many elements it means v is less constrained. There are statistically more classifications in which v is true without triggering the implication, and thus more legal classifications where v is true. Last, if v appears in a negative constraint $\widetilde{x}$ then it is less likely to be true. Again, a bigger $\widetilde{x}$ means v is less constrained, since there are statistically more legal classifications where v is true.

Our Pr function compresses the degree between 0 and 1, and we define a new multi-predicate-friendly entropy function ε to compute the information gain:

$$Pr(D) = \frac{\sum_{v \in D} Pr(v)}{|P|+|N|+|U|} \quad Pr(v) = \begin{cases} 1 & \text{if } v \in \mathcal{P} \\ 0 & \text{if } v \in \mathcal{N} \\ \dfrac{1}{2} + \dfrac{\arctan Degree(v)}{\pi} & \text{otherwise} \end{cases}$$

$$\varepsilon(D) = -Pr(D)\log_2 Pr(D) \;-\; (1 - Pr(D))\log_2(1 - Pr(D))$$

Note that it can happen that none of the qualifiers can split the data, *i.e.* there is no qualifier left or they all have an information gain of 0. In this case we synthesize qualifiers that we know will split the data as described in the next subsection.

3.4 Mining and Synthesizing Qualifiers

We now discuss how to prepare the set Q of qualifiers used in Algorithm 3. The learner in both the original ICE approach and our modified version spend a lot of time evaluating qualifiers. Having too many of them slows down the learning process considerably, while not considering enough of them reduces the expressiveness of the candidates. The compromise we propose is to *(i)* mine for (few) qualifiers from the clauses, and *(ii)* synthesize (possibly many) qualifiers when needed, driven by the data we need to split.

To mine for qualifiers, for every clause C and for every predicate application of the form $\rho(\widetilde{v})$ in C, we add every boolean atom a in C as a qualifier for ρ as long as all the free variables of a are in $\widetilde{v}$. All the other qualifiers are synthesized during the analysis.

Based on our experience, we have chosen the following synthesis strategy. With $v_1, \ldots, v_n$ the formal inputs of ρ, for all $(x_1, \ldots, x_n) \in P \cup N \cup U$, we generate the set of new qualifiers

$$\begin{array}{l} \{ \quad v_i \diamond x_i \quad \mid 1 \leq i \leq n, \quad \diamond \in \{\leq, \geq\} \} \\ \cup \{ v_i + v_j \diamond x_i + x_j \mid 1 \leq i < j \leq n, \ \diamond \in \{\leq, \geq\} \} \\ \cup \{ v_i - v_j \diamond x_i - x_j \mid 1 \leq i < j \leq n, \ \diamond \in \{\leq, \geq\} \} \end{array}$$

Adding these qualifiers allows to split the data on these (strict, when negated) inequalities, and encode (dis)equalities by combining them in the decision tree. Also, notice that when no qualifier can split the data we have in general *small* P, N and U sets, and the number of new qualifiers is quite tractable. The learning process is an iterative one where relatively few new samples are added at each step, compared to the set of all samples. Since we could split the samples from the previous iteration, it is very often the case that P, N and U contain mostly new samples. Last, our approach shares the limitation of the original ICE: it will not succeed if a particular relation between the variables is needed to conclude, but no qualifier of the right shape is ever mined for or synthesized.

4 Experimental Evaluation

Let us now briefly present our implementation before reporting on our experimental evaluation. Our implementation consists of two parts. RType is a frontend (written in OCaml) generating Horn clauses from programs written in a subset of OCaml as discussed in Sect. 2. It relies on an external Horn clause solver for actually solving the clauses, and post-processes the solution (if any) to yield refinement types for the original program. HoIce[1], written in Rust [1], is one such Horn clause solver and implements the modified ICE framework presented in this paper. All experiments in this section use RType `v1.0` and HoIce `v1.0`. Under the hood, HoIce relies on the Z3[2] SMT solver [21] for satisfiability checks. In the following experiments, RType uses HoIce as the Horn clause solver.

Note that the input OCaml programs are not annotated: the Horn clauses correspond to the verification conditions encoding the fact that the input program cannot falsify its assertion(s). RType supports a subset of OCaml including (mutually) recursive functions and integers, without algebraic data types. Our benchmark suite of 162 programs[3] includes the programs from [24,34] in the fragment RType supports, along with programs automatically generated by the termination verification tool from [18], and 10 new benchmarks written by ourselves. We only considered programs that are safe since RType is not refutation-sound. All the experiments presented in this section ran on a machine running Ubuntu (Xeon E5-2680v3, 64 GB of RAM) with a timeout of 100 s. The number between parentheses in the keys of the graphs is the number of benchmarks solved. We begin by evaluating the optimizations discussed in Sect. 2, followed by a comparison against automated verification tools for OCaml programs. Last, we evaluate our predicate synthesis engine against other Horn-clause-level solvers.

[1] Hosted at https://github.com/hopv/r_type and https://github.com/hopv/hoice.
[2] The revision of Z3 in all the experiments is the latest at the time of writing: 5bc4c98.
[3] Hosted at https://github.com/hopv/benchmarks.

4.1 Evaluation of the Optimizations

Figure 3a shows our evaluation of the effect analysis (**EA**) and clause reduction (**Red**) simplifications discussed in Sect. 2. It is clear that both effect analysis and Horn reduction speedup the learning process significantly. They work especially well together and can reduce drastically the number of predicates on relatively big synthesis problems, as shown on Fig. 3c.

The 11 programs that we fail to verify show inherent limitations of our approach. Two of them require an invariant of the form $x + y \geq z$. Our current compromise for qualifier mining and synthesis (in Sect. 3.3) does not consider such qualifiers unless they appear explicitly in the program. We are currently investigating how to alter our qualifier synthesis approach to raise its expressiveness with a reasonable impact on performance. The remaining nine programs are not typable with refinement types, meaning the verification conditions generated by RType are actually unsatisfiable. An extension of the type system is required to prove these programs correct [30].

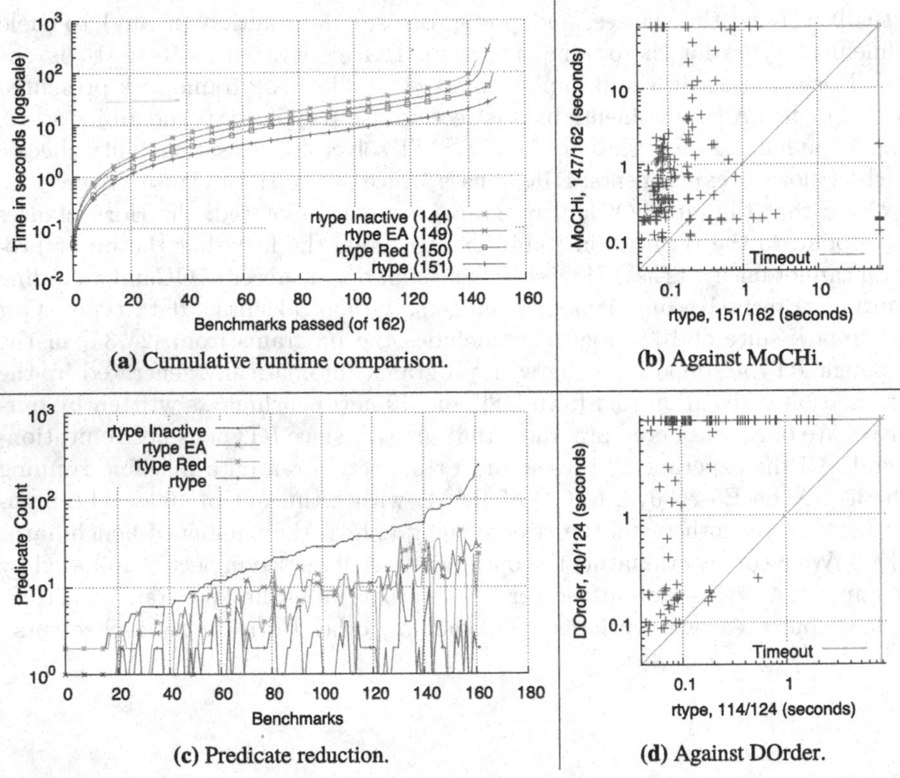

Fig. 3. Evaluation: verification of OCaml programs.

4.2 Comparison with Other OCaml Program Verifiers

The first tool we compare RType to is the higher-order program verifier MoCHi from [24] (Fig. 3b). MoCHi infers intersection types, which makes it more expressive than RType. The nine programs that MoCHi proves but RType cannot verify are the (refinement-)untypable ones discussed above. While this shows a clear advantage of intersection types over our approach in terms of expressiveness, the rest of the experiments make it clear that, when applicable, RType outperforms MoCHi on a significant part of our benchmarks.

We also evaluated our implementation against DOrder from [34,35]. This comparison is interesting as DOrder also uses machine-learning to infer refinement types, but does not support implication constraints. DOrder compensates by conducting test runs of the program on random inputs to gather better positive data. It supports a different subset of OCaml than RType though, and after removing the programs it does not support, 124 programs are left. The results are on Fig. 3d, and show that RType overwhelmingly outperforms DOrder. This is consistent with the results reported for the original ICE framework: the benefit gained by considering implication constraints is huge.

These results show that, despite its limitations, our approach is competitive and often outperforms other state-of-the-art automated verification tools for OCaml programs.

4.3 Horn-Clause-Level Evaluation

Last, we compare our Horn clause solver HoIce to other solvers (Fig. 4): Spacer [16], Duality [19], Z3's PDR [13], and Eldarica [14]. The first three are implemented in Z3 (C++) while Eldarica is implemented in Scala. The benchmarks are the Horn clauses encoding the safety of the 162 programs aforementioned with additional two programs, omitted in the previous evaluation as they are unsafe.

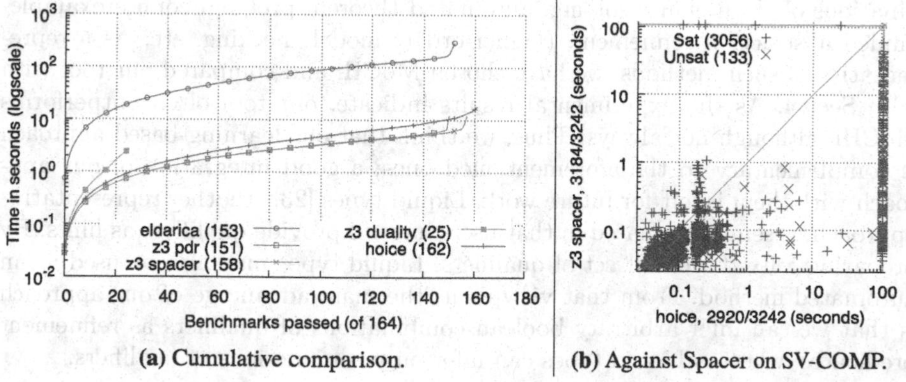

Fig. 4. Comparison with Horn clause solvers.

HoIce solves the most benchmarks at 162.[4] The fastest tool overall is Z3's Spacer which solves slightly fewer benchmarks. The two timeouts for HoIce come from the programs discussed above for which HoIce does not have the appropriate qualifiers to conclude. Because it mixes IC3 [6] with interpolation, Spacer infers the right predicates quite quickly. Thus, in our use-case, our approach is competitive with state-of-the-art Horn clause solvers in terms of speed, in addition to being more precise. We also include a comparison on the SV-COMP with Spacer on Fig. 4b. HoIce is generally competitive, but timeouts on a significant part of the benchmarks. Quite a few of them are unsatisfiable; the ICE framework is not made to be efficient at proving unstatisfiability. The rest of the timeouts require qualifiers we do not mine for nor synthesizes, showing that some more work is needed on this aspect of the approach.

In our experience, it is often the case that HoIce's models are significantly simpler than those of Spacer's and PDR's (as illustrated in [7]). Note that simpler models can be interesting if the Horn clause solver is placed inside a CEGAR loop such as the one in MoCHi [24], which is a perspective we want to explore in future work.

5 Related Work

There has been a lot of work on sampling-based approaches to program invariant discoveries during the last decade [11,12,25–27,33–35]. Among others, most closely related to this paper are Garg et al.'s ICE framework [11,12] (which this paper extends) and Zhu et al.'s refinement type inference methods [33–35]. To the best of our knowledge, Zhu et al. [33–35] were the first to apply a sampling-based approach to refinement type inference for higher-order functional programs. They did not, however, consider implication constraints. As discussed in Sect. 4, their tool fails to verify some programs due to the lack of implication constraints.

There are other automated/semi-automated methods for verification of higher-order functional programs [15,23,28–30,32,34,35], based on some combinations of Horn clause solving, automated theorem proving, counterexample-guided abstraction refinement, (higher-order) model checking, etc. As a representative of such methods, we have chosen MoCHi and compared our tool with it in Sect. 4. As the experimental results indicate, our tool often outperforms MoCHi, although not always. Thus, we think that our learning-based approach is complementary to the aforementioned ones; a good integration of our approach with them is left for future work. Liquid types [23], another representative approach, is semi-automated in that users have to provide qualifiers as hints. By preparing a fixed, default set of qualifiers, Liquid types may also be used as an automated method. From that viewpoint, the main advantage of our approach is that we can infer arbitrary boolean combinations of qualifiers as refinement predicates, whereas Liquid types can infer only conjunctions of qualifiers.

[4] This is consistent with the OCaml results: 151 sat results, 9 unsat from programs RType cannot verify, and 2 unsat from unsafe programs.

6 Conclusion

In this paper we proposed an adaptation of the machine-learning-based, invariant discovery framework ICE to refinement type inference. The main challenge was that implication constraints and negative examples were ill-suited for solving Horn clauses of the form $\rho(\widetilde{x_1}) \wedge \cdots \wedge \rho(\widetilde{x_n}) \wedge \ldots \models \rho(\widetilde{x})$, which tend to appear often in our context of functional program verification because of nested recursive calls.

We addressed this issue by generalizing ICE's notion of implication constraint. For similar reasons, we also adapted negative *examples* by turning them into negative *constraints*. This means that, unlike the original ICE framework, our learner might have to make classification choices to respect the negative learning data. We have introduced a modified version of the ICE framework accounting for these adaptations, and have implemented it, along with optimizations based on effect analysis. Our evaluation on a representative set of programs show that it is competitive with state of the art OCaml model-checkers and Horn clause solvers.

Data Availability Statement and Acknowledgments. We would like to thank He Zhu for his help in benchmarking DOrder, and the reviewers for their constructive feedback. This work was supported by JSPS KAKENHI Grant Number JP15H05706.

The benchmarks analyzed and the datasets generated during the current study are available in the figshare repository:

https://doi.org/10.6084/m9.figshare.5902390.v1

This artifact [8] contains all the benchmarks and tools, as well as scripts allowing to re-generate the data and plots discussed in Sect. 4. The only exception is DOrder, for reasons discussed in the artifact. Consistently with the TACAS 2018 Artifact Evaluation guidelines, all binaries are provided for Ubuntu 64 bits. Please refer to the README in the artifact for more information.

References

1. The Rust language. https://www.rust-lang.org/en-US/
2. Arora, S., Barak, B.: Computational Complexity - A Modern Approach. Cambridge University Press, Cambridge (2009)
3. Barrett, C.W., Sebastiani, R., Seshia, S.A., Tinelli, C.: Satisfiability modulo theories. In: Handbook of Satisfiability, Frontiers in Artificial Intelligence and Applications, vol. 185, pp. 825–885. IOS Press (2009)
4. Beyer, D.: Competition on software verification. In: Flanagan, C., König, B. (eds.) TACAS 2012. LNCS, vol. 7214, pp. 504–524. Springer, Heidelberg (2012). https://doi.org/10.1007/978-3-642-28756-5_38
5. Bjørner, N., Gurfinkel, A., McMillan, K., Rybalchenko, A.: Horn clause solvers for program verification. In: Beklemishev, L.D., Blass, A., Dershowitz, N., Finkbeiner, B., Schulte, W. (eds.) Fields of Logic and Computation II. LNCS, vol. 9300, pp. 24–51. Springer, Cham (2015). https://doi.org/10.1007/978-3-319-23534-9_2

6. Bradley, A.R.: SAT-based model checking without unrolling. In: Jhala, R., Schmidt, D. (eds.) VMCAI 2011. LNCS, vol. 6538, pp. 70–87. Springer, Heidelberg (2011). https://doi.org/10.1007/978-3-642-18275-4_7
7. Champion, A., Chiba, T., Kobayashi, N., Sato, R.: ICE-based refinement type discovery for higher-order functional programs. http://www-kb.is.s.u-tokyo.ac.jp/~koba/papers/tacas18-long.pdf. A longer version
8. Champion, A., Chiba, T., Kobayashi, N., Sato, R.: ICE-based refinement type discovery for higher-order functional programs. figshare. https://doi.org/10.6084/m9.figshare.5902390.v1
9. Champion, A., Mebsout, A., Sticksel, C., Tinelli, C.: The KIND 2 model checker. In: Chaudhuri, S., Farzan, A. (eds.) CAV 2016. LNCS, vol. 9780, pp. 510–517. Springer, Cham (2016). https://doi.org/10.1007/978-3-319-41540-6_29
10. Freeman, T.S., Pfenning, F.: Refinement types for ML. In: Proceedings of PLDI 1991, pp. 268–277. ACM (1991)
11. Garg, P., Löding, C., Madhusudan, P., Neider, D.: ICE: A robust framework for learning invariants. In: Biere, A., Bloem, R. (eds.) CAV 2014. LNCS, vol. 8559, pp. 69–87. Springer, Cham (2014). https://doi.org/10.1007/978-3-319-08867-9_5
12. Garg, P., Neider, D., Madhusudan, P., Roth, D.: Learning invariants using decision trees and implication counterexamples. In: Proceedings of POPL 2016, pp. 499–512. ACM (2016)
13. Hoder, K., Bjørner, N.: Generalized property directed reachability. In: Cimatti, A., Sebastiani, R. (eds.) SAT 2012. LNCS, vol. 7317, pp. 157–171. Springer, Heidelberg (2012). https://doi.org/10.1007/978-3-642-31612-8_13
14. Hojjat, H., Konečný, F., Garnier, F., Iosif, R., Kuncak, V., Rümmer, P.: A verification toolkit for numerical transition systems. In: Giannakopoulou, D., Méry, D. (eds.) FM 2012. LNCS, vol. 7436, pp. 247–251. Springer, Heidelberg (2012). https://doi.org/10.1007/978-3-642-32759-9_21
15. Jhala, R., Majumdar, R., Rybalchenko, A.: HMC: verifying functional programs using abstract interpreters. In: Gopalakrishnan, G., Qadeer, S. (eds.) CAV 2011. LNCS, vol. 6806, pp. 470–485. Springer, Heidelberg (2011). https://doi.org/10.1007/978-3-642-22110-1_38
16. Komuravelli, A., Gurfinkel, A., Chaki, S.: SMT-based model checking for recursive programs. Form. Methods Syst. Des. **48**(3), 175–205 (2016)
17. Kovács, L., Voronkov, A.: Finding loop invariants for programs over arrays using a theorem prover. In: Chechik, M., Wirsing, M. (eds.) FASE 2009. LNCS, vol. 5503, pp. 470–485. Springer, Heidelberg (2009). https://doi.org/10.1007/978-3-642-00593-0_33
18. Kuwahara, T., Terauchi, T., Unno, H., Kobayashi, N.: Automatic termination verification for higher-order functional programs. In: Shao, Z. (ed.) ESOP 2014. LNCS, vol. 8410, pp. 392–411. Springer, Heidelberg (2014). https://doi.org/10.1007/978-3-642-54833-8_21
19. McMillan, K., Rybalchenko, A.: Computing relational fixed points using interpolation. Technical report, January 2013
20. Minsky, Y.: OCaml for the masses. ACM Queue **9**(9), 43 (2011)
21. de Moura, L., Bjørner, N.: Z3: an efficient SMT solver. In: Ramakrishnan, C.R., Rehof, J. (eds.) TACAS 2008. LNCS, vol. 4963, pp. 337–340. Springer, Heidelberg (2008). https://doi.org/10.1007/978-3-540-78800-3_24
22. Nielson, F., Nielson, H.R., Hankin, C.: Principles of Program Analysis. Springer, Heiedelberg (1999). https://doi.org/10.1007/978-3-662-03811-6

23. Rondon, P.M., Kawaguchi, M., Jhala, R.: Liquid types. In: Proceedings of PLDI 2008, pp. 159–169. ACM (2008)
24. Sato, R., Unno, H., Kobayashi, N.: Towards a scalable software model checker for higher-order programs. In: Proceedings of PEPM 2013, pp. 53–62. ACM (2013)
25. Sharma, R., Aiken, A.: From invariant checking to invariant inference using randomized search. In: Biere, A., Bloem, R. (eds.) CAV 2014. LNCS, vol. 8559, pp. 88–105. Springer, Cham (2014). https://doi.org/10.1007/978-3-319-08867-9_6
26. Sharma, R., Gupta, S., Hariharan, B., Aiken, A., Liang, P., Nori, A.V.: A data driven approach for algebraic loop invariants. In: Felleisen, M., Gardner, P. (eds.) ESOP 2013. LNCS, vol. 7792, pp. 574–592. Springer, Heidelberg (2013). https://doi.org/10.1007/978-3-642-37036-6_31
27. Sharma, R., Gupta, S., Hariharan, B., Aiken, A., Nori, A.V.: Verification as learning geometric concepts. In: Logozzo, F., Fähndrich, M. (eds.) SAS 2013. LNCS, vol. 7935, pp. 388–411. Springer, Heidelberg (2013). https://doi.org/10.1007/978-3-642-38856-9_21
28. Terauchi, T.: Dependent types from counterexamples. In: Proceedings of POPL, pp. 119–130. ACM (2010)
29. Unno, H., Kobayashi, N.: Dependent type inference with interpolants. In: Proceedings of PPDP 2009, pp. 277–288. ACM (2009)
30. Unno, H., Terauchi, T., Kobayashi, N.: Automating relatively complete verification of higher-order functional programs. In: Proceedings of POPL 2013, pp. 75–86. ACM (2013)
31. Xi, H., Pfenning, F.: Dependent types in practical programming. In: Proceedings of POPL 1999, pp. 214–227. ACM (1999)
32. Zhu, H., Jagannathan, S.: Compositional and lightweight dependent type inference for ML. In: Giacobazzi, R., Berdine, J., Mastroeni, I. (eds.) VMCAI 2013. LNCS, vol. 7737, pp. 295–314. Springer, Heidelberg (2013). https://doi.org/10.1007/978-3-642-35873-9_19
33. Zhu, H., Nori, A.V., Jagannathan, S.: Dependent array type inference from tests. In: D'Souza, D., Lal, A., Larsen, K.G. (eds.) VMCAI 2015. LNCS, vol. 8931, pp. 412–430. Springer, Heidelberg (2015). https://doi.org/10.1007/978-3-662-46081-8_23
34. Zhu, H., Nori, A.V., Jagannathan, S.: Learning refinement types. In: Proceedings of ICFP 2015, pp. 400–411. ACM (2015)
35. Zhu, H., Petri, G., Jagannathan, S.: Automatically learning shape specifications. In: Proceedings of PLDI 2016, pp. 491–507. ACM (2016)

cc
BY

Strategy Representation by Decision Trees in Reactive Synthesis

Tomáš Brázdil[1], Krishnendu Chatterjee[2], Jan Křetínský[3](✉), and Viktor Toman[2]

[1] Masaryk University, Brno, Czech Republic
[2] Institute of Science and Technology Austria, Klosterneuburg, Austria
[3] Technical University of Munich, Munich, Germany
jan.kretinsky@tum.de

Abstract. Graph games played by two players over finite-state graphs are central in many problems in computer science. In particular, graph games with ω-regular winning conditions, specified as parity objectives, which can express properties such as safety, liveness, fairness, are the basic framework for verification and synthesis of reactive systems. The decisions for a player at various states of the graph game are represented as strategies. While the algorithmic problem for solving graph games with parity objectives has been widely studied, the most prominent data-structure for strategy representation in graph games has been binary decision diagrams (BDDs). However, due to the bit-level representation, BDDs do not retain the inherent flavor of the decisions of strategies, and are notoriously hard to minimize to obtain succinct representation. In this work we propose decision trees for strategy representation in graph games. Decision trees retain the flavor of decisions of strategies and allow entropy-based minimization to obtain succinct trees. However, decision trees work in settings (e.g., probabilistic models) where errors are allowed, and overfitting of data is typically avoided. In contrast, for strategies in graph games no error is allowed, and the decision tree must represent the entire strategy. We develop new techniques to extend decision trees to overcome the above obstacles, while retaining the entropy-based techniques to obtain succinct trees. We have implemented our techniques to extend the existing decision tree solvers. We present experimental results for problems in reactive synthesis to show that decision trees provide a much more efficient data-structure for strategy representation as compared to BDDs.

1 Introduction

Graph Games. We consider nonterminating two-player graph games played on finite-state graphs. The vertices of the graph are partitioned into states controlled by the two players, namely, player 1 and player 2, respectively. In each round the state changes according to a transition chosen by the player controlling the current state. Thus, the outcome of the game being played for an infinite

D. Beyer and M. Huisman (Eds.): TACAS 2018, LNCS 10805, pp. 385–407, 2018.
https://doi.org/10.1007/978-3-319-89960-2_21

number of rounds, is an infinite path through the graph, which is called a play. An objective for a player specifies whether the resulting play is either winning or losing. We consider zero-sum games where the objectives of the players are complementary. A strategy for a player is a recipe to specify the choice of the transitions for states controlled by the player. Given an objective, a winning strategy for a player from a state ensures the objective irrespective of the strategy of the opponent.

Games and Synthesis. These games play a central role in several areas of computer science. One important application arises when the vertices and edges of a graph represent the states and transitions of a reactive system, and the two players represent controllable versus uncontrollable decisions during the execution of the system. The *synthesis* problem for reactive systems asks for the construction of a winning strategy in the corresponding graph game. This problem was first posed independently by Church [17] and Büchi [14], and has been extensively studied [15,28,37,45]. Other than applications in synthesis of discrete-event and reactive systems [43,46], game-theoretic formulations play a crucial role in modeling [1,21], refinement [30], verification [3,20], testing [5], compatibility checking [19], and many other applications. In all the above applications, the objectives are ω-regular, and the ω-regular sets of infinite paths provide an important and robust paradigm for reactive-system specifications [36,50].

Parity Games. Graph games with parity objectives are relevant in reactive synthesis, since all common specifications for reactive systems are expressed as ω-regular objectives that can be transformed to parity objectives. In particular, a convenient specification formalism in reactive synthesis is LTL (linear-time temporal logic). The LTL synthesis problem asks, given a specification over input and output variables in LTL, whether there is a strategy for the output sequences to ensure the specification irrespective of the behavior of the input sequences. The conversion of LTL to non-deterministic Büchi automata, and non-deterministic Büchi automata to deterministic parity automata, gives rise to a parity game to solve the LTL synthesis problem. Formally, the algorithmic problem asks for a given graph game with a parity objective and a starting state, whether player 1 has a winning strategy. This problem is central in verification and synthesis. While it is a major open problem whether the problem can be solved in polynomial time, it has been widely studied in the literature [16,48,52].

Strategy Representation. In graph games, the strategies are the most important objects as they represent the witness to winning of a player. For example, winning strategies represent controllers in the controller synthesis problem. Hence all parity-games solvers produce the winning strategies as their output. While the algorithmic problem of solving parity games has received huge attention, quite surprisingly, data-structures for representation of strategies have received little attention. While the data-structures for strategies could be relevant in particular algorithms for parity games (e.g., strategy-iteration algorithm), our focus is very different than improving such algorithms. Our main focus is the representation of the strategies themselves, which are the main output of the parity-games solvers, and hence our strategy representation serves as post-processing of the output of the solvers. The standard data-structure for representing strategies is binary decision diagrams (BDDs) [2,13] and it is used as follows: a strategy is interpreted as a lookup table of pairs that specifies for every controlled state of the player the transition to choose, and then the lookup table is represented as a binary decision diagram (BDD).

Strategies as BDDs. The desired properties of data-structures for strategies are as follows: (a) *succinctness*, i.e., small strategies are desirable, since strategies correspond to controllers, and smaller strategies represent efficient controllers that are required in resource-constrained environments such as embedded systems; (b) *explanatory*, i.e., the representation explains the decisions of the strategies. In this work we consider different data-structure for representation of strategies in graph games. The key drawbacks of BDDs to represent strategies in graph games are as follows. First, the size of BDDs crucially depends on the variable ordering. The variable ordering problem is notoriously difficult: the optimal variable ordering problem is NP-complete, and for large dimensions no heuristics are known to work well. Second, due to the fact that strategies have to be input to the BDD construction as Boolean formulae, the representation though succinct, does not retain the inherent important choice features of the decisions of the strategies (for an illustration see Example 2).

Strategies as Decision Trees. In this work, we propose to use *decision trees*, i.e. [38], for strategy representation in graph games. A decision tree is a structure similar to a BDD, but with nodes labelled by various predicates over the system's variables. In the basic algorithm for decision trees, the tree is constructed using an unfolding procedure where the branching for the decision making is done in order to maximize the information gain at each step.

The key advantages of decision trees over BDDs are as follows:

- The first two advantages are conceptual. First, while in BDDs, a level corresponds to one variable, in decision trees, a predicate can appear at different levels and different predicates can appear at the same level. This allows for more flexibility in the representation. Second, decision trees utilize various predicates over the given features in order to make decisions, and ignore all the unimportant features. Thus they retain the inherent flavor of the decisions of the strategies.
- The other important advantage is algorithmic. Since the data-structure is based on information gain, sophisticated algorithms based on entropy exist for their construction. These algorithms result in a succinct representation, whereas for BDDs there is no good algorithmic approach for variable reordering.

Key Challenges. While there are several advantages of decision trees, and decision trees have been extensively studied in the machine learning community, there are several key challenges and obstacles for representation of strategies in graph games by decision trees.

– First, decision trees have been mainly used in the probabilistic setting. In such settings, research from the machine learning community has developed techniques to show that decision trees can be effectively pruned to obtain succinct trees, while allowing small error probabilities. However, in the context of graph games, no error is allowed in the strategic choices.
– Second, decision trees have been used in the machine learning community in classification, where an important aspect is to ensure that there is no overfitting of the training data. In contrast, in the context of graph games, the decision tree must fit the entire representation of the strategies.

While for probabilistic models such as Markov decision processes (MDPs), decision trees can be used as a blackbox [9], in the setting of graph games their use is much more challenging. In summary, in previous settings where decision trees are used small error rates are allowed in favor of succinctness, and overfitting is not permitted, whereas in our setting no error is allowed, and the complete fitting of the tree has to be ensured. The basic algorithm for decision-tree learning (called ID3 algorithm [38,44]) suffers from the curse of dimensionality, and the error allowance is used to handle the dimensionality. Hence we need to develop new techniques for strategy learning with decision trees in graph games.

Our Techniques. We present a new technique for learning strategies with decision trees based on *look-ahead.* In the basic algorithm for decision trees, at each step of the unfolding, the algorithm proceeds as long as there is any information gain. However, suppose for no possible branching there is any information gain. This represents the situation where the local (i.e., one-step based) decision making fails to achieve information gain. We extend this process so that look-ahead is allowed, i.e., we consider possible information gain with multiple steps. The look-ahead along with complete unfolding ensure that there is no error in the strategy representation. While the look-ahead approach provides a systematic principle to obtain precise strategy representation, it is computationally expensive, and we present heuristics used together with look-ahead for computational efficiency and succinctness of strategy representation.

Implementation and Experimental Results. Since in our setting existing decision tree solvers cannot be used as a blackbox, we extended the existing solvers with our techniques mentioned above. We have then applied our implementation to compare decision trees and BDDs for representation of strategies for problems in reactive synthesis. First, we compared our approach against BDDs for two classical examples of reactive synthesis from SYNTCOMP benchmarks [32]. Second, we considered randomly generated LTL formulae, and the graph games obtained for the realizability of such formulae. In both the above experiments the decision trees represent the winning strategies much more efficiently as compared to BDDs.

Related Work. Previous non-explicit representation of strategies for verification or synthesis purposes typically used BDDs [51] or automata [39,41] and do not explain the decisions by the current valuation of variables. *Decision trees* have been used a lot in the area of machine learning as a classifier that naturally explains a decision [38]. They have also been considered for approximate representation of values in states and thus implicitly for an approximate representation of *strategies*, for the model of Markov decision processes (MDPs) in [7,8]. Recently, in the context of verification, this approach has been modified to capture strategies guaranteed to be ε-optimal, for MDPs [9] and partially observable MDPs [10]. Learning a compact decision tree representation of an MDP strategy was also investigated in [35] for the case of body sensor networks. Besides, decision trees are becoming more popular in verification and programming languages in general, for instance, they are used to capture program invariants [27,34]. To the best of our knowledge, decision trees were only used in the context of (possibly probabilistic) systems with only a single player. Our decision-tree approach is thus the first in the game setting with two players that is required in reactive synthesis.

Summary. To summarize, our main contributions are:

1. We propose decision trees as data-structure for strategy representation in graph games.
2. The representation of strategies with decision trees poses many obstacles, as in contrast to the probabilistic setting no error is allowed in games. We present techniques that overcome these obstacles while still retaining the algorithmic advantages (such as entropy-based methods) of decision trees to obtain succinct decision trees.
3. We extend existing decision tree solvers with our techniques and present experimental results to demonstrate the effectiveness of our approach in reactive synthesis.

Further details and proofs can be found in [12].

2 Graph Games and Strategies

Graph Games. A *graph game* consists of a tuple $G = \langle S, S_1, S_2, A_1, A_2, \delta\rangle$, where:

- S is a finite set of states partitioned into player 1 states S_1 and player 2 states S_2;
- A_1 (resp., A_2) is the set of actions for player 1 (resp., player 2); and
- $\delta\colon (S_1 \times A_1) \cup (S_2 \times A_2) \to S$ is the transition function that given a player 1 state and a player 1 action, or a player 2 state and a player 2 action, gives the successor state.

Plays. A *play* is an infinite sequence of state-action pairs $\langle s_0 a_0 s_1 a_1 \ldots\rangle$ such that for all $j \geq 0$ we have that if $s_j \in S_i$ for $i \in \{1, 2\}$, then $a_j \in A_i$ and $\delta(s_j, a_j) = s_{j+1}$. We denote by $\mathsf{Plays}(G)$ the set of all plays of a graph game G.

Strategies. A strategy is a recipe for a player to choose actions to extend finite prefixes of plays. Formally, a strategy π for player 1 is a function $\pi\colon S^{\star} \cdot S_1 \to A_1$

that given a finite sequence of visited states chooses the next action. The definitions for player 2 strategies γ are analogous. We denote by $\Pi(G)$ and $\Gamma(G)$ the set of all strategies for player 1 and player 2 in graph game G, respectively. Given strategies $\pi \in \Pi(G)$ and $\gamma \in \Gamma(G)$, and a starting state s in G, there is a unique play $\varrho(s, \pi, \gamma) = \langle s_0 a_0 s_1 a_1 \ldots \rangle$ such that $s_0 = s$ and for all $j \geq 0$ if $s_j \in S_1$ (resp., $s_j \in S_2$) then $a_j = \pi(\langle s_0 s_1 \ldots s_j \rangle)$ (resp., $a_j = \gamma(\langle s_0 s_1 \ldots s_j \rangle)$). A *memoryless* strategy is a strategy that does not depend on the finite prefix of the play but only on the current state, i.e., functions $\pi \colon S_1 \to A_1$ and $\gamma \colon S_2 \to A_2$.

Objectives. An *objective* for a graph game G is a set $\varphi \subseteq \mathsf{Plays}(G)$. We consider the following objectives:

- *Reachability and safety objectives.* A reachability objective is defined by a set $T \subseteq S$ of target states, and the objective requires that a state in T is visited at least once. Formally, $\mathsf{Reach}(F) = \{\langle s_0 a_0 s_1 a_1 \ldots \rangle \in \mathsf{Plays}(G) \mid \exists i : s_i \in T\}$. The dual of reachability objectives are safety objectives, defined by a set $F \subseteq S$ of safe states, and the objective requires that only states in F are visited. Formally, $\mathsf{Safe}(F) = \{\langle s_0 a_0 s_1 a_1 \ldots \rangle \in \mathsf{Plays}(G) \mid \forall i : s_i \in F\}$.
- *Parity objectives.* For an infinite play ϱ we denote by $\mathsf{Inf}(\varrho)$ the set of states that occur infinitely often in ϱ. Let $p \colon S \to \mathbb{N}$ be a *priority function.* The *parity* objective $\mathsf{Parity}(p) = \{\varrho \in \mathsf{Plays}(G) \mid \min\{p(s) \mid s \in \mathsf{Inf}(\varrho)\}$ is even $\}$ requires that the minimum of the priorities of the states visited infinitely often be even.

Winning Region and Strategies. Given a game graph G and an objective φ, a *winning* strategy π from state s for player 1 is a strategy such that for all strategies $\gamma \in \Gamma(G)$ we have $\varrho(s, \pi, \gamma) \in \varphi$. Analogously, a winning strategy γ for player 2 from s ensures that for all strategies $\pi \in \Pi(G)$ we have $\varrho(s, \pi, \gamma) \notin \varphi$. The *winning region* $W_1(G, \varphi)$ (resp., $W_2(G, \overline{\varphi})$) for player 1 (resp., player 2) is the set of states such that player 1 (resp., player 2) has a winning strategy. A fundamental result for graph games with parity objectives shows that the winning regions form a partition of the state space, and if there is a winning strategy for a player, then there is a memoryless winning strategy [25].

LTL Synthesis and Objectives. Reachability and safety objectives are the most basic objectives to specify properties of reactive systems. Most properties that arise in practice for analysis of reactive systems are ω-regular objectives. A convenient logical framework to express ω-regular objectives is the LTL (linear-time temporal logic) framework. The problem of synthesis from specifications, in particular, LTL synthesis has received huge attention [18]. LTL objectives can be translated to parity automata, and the synthesis problem reduces to solving games with parity objectives.

In reactive synthesis it is natural to consider games where the state space is defined by a set of variables, and the game is played by input and output player who choose the respective input and output signals. We describe such games below that easily correspond to graph games.

I/O Games with Variables. Consider a finite set $X = \{x_1, x_2, \ldots, x_n\}$ of variables from a finite domain; for simplicity, we consider Boolean variables only. A *valuation* is an assignment to each variable, in our case 2^X denotes the set of all valuations. Let X be partitioned into input signals, output signals, and state variables, i.e., $X = I \uplus O \uplus V$. Consider the alphabet $\mathcal{I} = 2^I$ (resp., $\mathcal{O} = 2^O$) where each letter represents a subset of the input (resp., output) signals and the alphabet $\mathcal{V} = 2^V$ where each letter represents a subset of state variables. The input/output choices affect the valuation of the variables, which is given by the next-step valuation function $\Delta\colon \mathcal{V} \times \mathcal{I} \times \mathcal{O} \to \mathcal{V}$. Consider a game played as follows: at every round the input player chooses a set of input signals (i.e., a letter from $\mathcal{I}$), and given the input choice the output player chooses a set of output signals (i.e., a letter from $\mathcal{O}$). The above game can be represented as a graph game $\langle S, S_1, S_2, A_1, A_2, \delta\rangle$ as follows:

- $S = \mathcal{V} \cup (\mathcal{V} \times \mathcal{I})$;
- player 1 represents the input player and $S_1 = \mathcal{V}$; player 2 represents the output player and $S_2 = \mathcal{V} \times \mathcal{I}$;
- $A_1 = \mathcal{I}$ and $A_2 = \mathcal{O}$; and
- given a valuation $v \in \mathcal{V}$ and $a_1 \in A_1$ we have $\delta(v, a_1) = (v, a_1)$, and for $a_2 \in A_2$ we have $\delta((v, a_1), a_2) = \Delta(v, a_1, a_2)$.

In this paper, we use decision trees to represent memoryless strategies in such graph games, where states are represented as vectors of Boolean values. In Sect. 5 we show how such games arise from various sources (AIGER specifications [31], LTL synthesis) and why it is sufficient to consider memoryless strategies only.

3 Decision Trees and Decision Tree Learning

In this section we recall decision trees and learning decision trees. A key application domain of games on graphs is reactive synthesis (such as safety synthesis from SYNTCOMP benchmarks as well as LTL synthesis) and our comparison for strategy representation is against BDDs. BDDs are particularly suitable for states and actions represented as bitvectors. Hence for a fair comparison against BDDs, we consider a simple version of decision trees over bitvectors, though decision trees and their corresponding methods can be naturally extended to richer domains (such as vectors of integers as used in [9]).

Decision Trees. A *decision tree* over $\{0,1\}^d$ is a tuple $\mathcal{T} = (T, \rho, \theta)$ where T is a finite rooted binary (ordered) tree with a set of inner nodes N and a set of leaves L, ρ assigns to every inner node a number of $\{1, \ldots, d\}$, and θ assigns to every leaf a value *YES* or *NO*.

The language $\mathcal{L}(\mathcal{T}) \subseteq \{0,1\}^d$ of the tree is defined as follows. For a vector $\boldsymbol{x} = (x_1, \ldots, x_d) \in \{0,1\}^d$, we find a path p from the root to a leaf such that for each inner node n on the path, $\boldsymbol{x}(\rho(n)) = 0$ iff the first child of n is on p. Denote the leaf on this particular path by ℓ. Then $\boldsymbol{x}$ is in the language $\mathcal{L}(\mathcal{T})$ of $\mathcal{T}$ iff $\theta(\ell) = \textit{YES}$.

Example 1. Consider dimension $d = 3$. The language of the tree depicted in Fig. 1 can be described by the following regular expression $\{0,1\}^2 \cdot 0 + \{0,1\} \cdot 1 \cdot 1$. Intuitively, the root node represents the predicate of the third value, the other inner node represents the predicate of the second value. For each inner node, the first and second children correspond to the cases where the value at the position specified by the predicate of the inner node is 0 and 1, respectively. We supply the edge labels to depict the tree clearly. The leftmost leaf corresponds to the subset of $\{0,1\}^3$ where the third value is 0, the rightmost leaf corresponds to the subset of $\{0,1\}^3$ where the third value is 1 and the second value is 1.

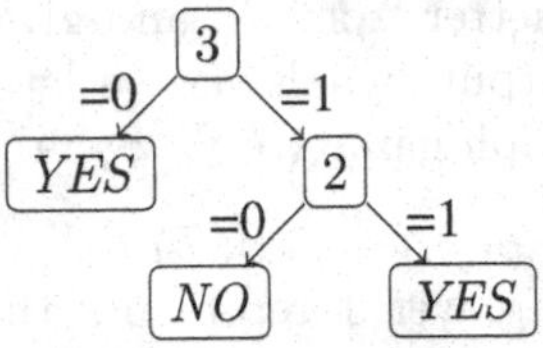

Standard DT Learning. We describe the standard process of binary classification using decision trees (see Algorithm 1). Given a *training set* $\mathit{Train} \subseteq \{0,1\}^d$, partitioned into two subsets *Good* and *Bad*, the process of learning according to the algorithm ID3 [38,44] computes a decision tree $\mathcal{T}$ that assigns *YES* to all elements of *Good* and *NO* to all elements of *Bad*. In the algorithm, a leaf $\ell \subseteq \{0,1\}^d$ is *mixed* if ℓ has a non-empty intersection with both *Good* and *Bad*. To split a leaf ℓ on $\mathit{bit} \in \{1,\ldots,d\}$ means that ℓ becomes an internal node with the two new leaves ℓ_0 and ℓ_1 as its children. Then, the leaf ℓ_0 contains the samples of ℓ where the value in the position *bit* equals 0, and the leaf ℓ_1 contains the rest of the samples of ℓ, since these have the value in the position *bit* equal to 1. The *entropy* of a node is defined as

Fig. 1. A decision tree over $\{0,1\}^3$

$$H(\ell) = -\frac{|\ell \cap Good|}{|\ell|} log_2 \frac{|\ell \cap Good|}{|\ell|} - \frac{|\ell \cap Bad|}{|\ell|} log_2 \frac{|\ell \cap Bad|}{|\ell|}.$$

An *information gain* of a given $\mathit{bit} \in \{1,\ldots,d\}$ (and thus also of the split into ℓ_0 and ℓ_1) is defined by

$$H(\ell) - \frac{|\ell_0|}{|\ell|} H(\ell_0) - \frac{|\ell_1|}{|\ell|} H(\ell_1) \qquad (1)$$

where ℓ_0 is the set of all $\boldsymbol{x} = (x_1,\ldots,x_d) \in \ell \subseteq \{0,1\}^d$ with $x_{bit} = 0$ and $\ell_1 = \ell \setminus \ell_0$. Finally, given $\ell \subseteq \{0,1\}^d$ we define

$$maxclass(\ell) = \begin{cases} YES & |\ell \cap Good| \geq |\ell \cap Bad| \\ NO & \text{otherwise.} \end{cases}$$

Intuitively, the splitting on the component with the highest gain splits the set so that it maximizes the portion of *Good* in one subset and the portion of *Bad* in the other one.

Remark 1 (Optimizations). The basic ID3 algorithm for decision tree learning suffers from the curse of dimensionality. However, decision trees are primarily applied to machine learning problems where small errors are allowed to obtain succinct trees. Hence the allowance of error is crucially used in existing solvers (such as WEKA [29]) to combat dimensionality. In particular, the error rate is

Algorithm 1. ID3 learning algorithm

Inputs: $Train \subseteq \{0,1\}^d$ partitioned into subsets *Good* and *Bad*.
Outputs: A decision tree $\mathcal{T}$ such that $\mathcal{L}(\mathcal{T}) \cap Train = Good$.
/* train $\mathcal{T}$ on positive set *Good* and negative set *Bad* */
$\mathcal{T} \leftarrow (\{Train\}, \emptyset, \{Train \mapsto^{\theta} YES\})$
while a mixed leaf ℓ exists **do**
    $bit \leftarrow$ an element of $\{1, \ldots, d\}$ that maximizes the information gain
    split ℓ on *bit* into two leaves ℓ_0 and ℓ_1, $\rho(\ell) = bit$
    $\theta(\ell_0) \leftarrow maxclass(\ell_0)$ and $\theta(\ell_1) \leftarrow maxclass(\ell_1)$
return $\mathcal{T}$

exploited in the unfolding, where the unfolding proceeds only when the information gain exceeds the error threshold. Further error is also introduced in the pruning of the trees, which ensures that the overfitting of training data is avoided.

4 Learning Winning Strategies Efficiently

In this section we present our contributions. We first start with the representation of strategies as training sets, and then present our strategy decision-tree learning algorithm.

4.1 Strategies as Training Sets and Decision Trees

Strategies as Training Sets. Let us consider a game $G = \langle S, S_1, S_2, A_1, A_2, \delta \rangle$. We represent strategies of both players using the same method. So in what follows we consider either of the players and denote by S_* and A_* the sets of states and actions of the player, respectively. We fix $\tilde{\sigma}: S_* \to A_*$, a memoryless strategy of the player.

We assume that G is an I/O game with binary variables, which means $S_* \subseteq \{0,1\}^n$ and $A_* \subseteq \{0,1\}^a$. A memoryless strategy is then a partial function $\tilde{\sigma}: \{0,1\}^n \to \{0,1\}^a$. Furthermore, we fix an initial state s_0, and let $S_*^R \subseteq \{0,1\}^n$ be the set of all states reachable from s_0 using σ against some strategy of the other player. We consider all objectives only on plays starting in the initial state s_0. Therefore, the strategy can be seen as a function $\sigma: S_*^R \to A_*$ such that $\sigma = \tilde{\sigma}|_{S_*^R}$.

Now we define

- $Good = \{\langle s, \sigma(s) \rangle \in S_*^R \times A_*\}$
- $Bad = \{\langle s, a \rangle \in S_*^R \times A_* \mid a \neq \sigma(s)\}$

The set of all training examples is a disjunctive union $Train = Good \uplus Bad \subseteq \{0,1\}^{n+a}$.

As we do not use any pruning or stopping rules, the ID3 algorithm returns a decision tree $\mathcal{T}$ that fits the training set *Train* exactly. This means that for all

$s \in S_*^R$ we have that $\langle s, a \rangle \in \mathcal{L}(\mathcal{T})$ iff $\sigma(s) = a$. Thus $\mathcal{T}$ represents the strategy σ. Note that for any sample of $\{0,1\}^{n+a} \setminus \mathit{Train}$, the fact whether it belongs to $\mathcal{L}(\mathcal{T})$ or not is immaterial to us. Thus strategies are naturally represented as decision trees, and we present an illustration below.

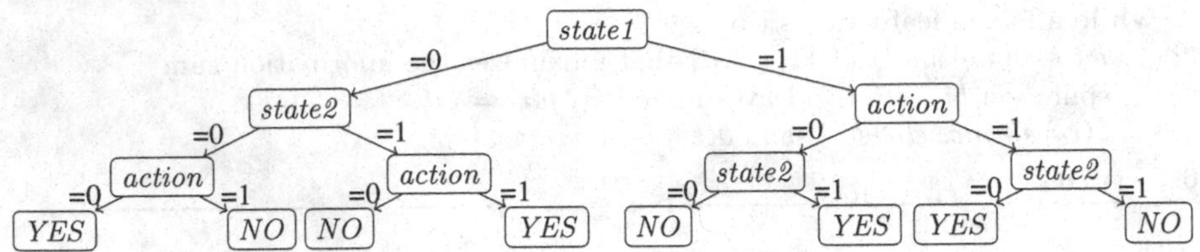

Fig. 2. Tree representation of strategy σ

Example 2. Let the state binary variables be labeled as *state1*, *state2*, and *state3*, respectively, and let the action binary variable be labeled as *action*. Consider a strategy σ such that $\sigma(0,0,0) = 0$, $\sigma(0,1,0) = 1$, $\sigma(1,0,0) = 1$, $\sigma(1,1,1) = 0$. Then

- $\mathit{Good} = \{(0,0,0,0),(0,1,0,1),(1,0,0,1),(1,1,1,0)\}$
- $\mathit{Bad} = \{(0,0,0,1),(0,1,0,0),(1,0,0,0),(1,1,1,1)\}$

Figure 2 depicts a decision tree $\mathcal{T}$ representing the strategy σ.

Remark 2. The above example demonstrates the conceptual advantages of decision trees over BDDs. First, in decision trees, different predicates can appear at the same level of the tree (e.g. predicates *state2* and *action* appear at the second level). At the same time, a predicate can appear at different levels of the tree (e.g. predicate *action* appears once at the second level and twice at the third level).

Second advantage is a bit technical, but very crucial. In the example there is no pair of samples $g \in \mathit{Good}$ and $b \in \mathit{Bad}$ that differs only in the value of *state3*. This suggests that the feature *state3* is unimportant w.r.t. differentiating between *Good* and *Bad*, and indeed the decision tree $\mathcal{T}$ in Fig. 2 contains no predicate *state3* while still representing σ. However, to construct a BDD that ignores *state3* is very difficult, since a Boolean formula is provided as the input to the BDD construction, and this formula inevitably sets the value for every sample. Therefore, it is impossible to declare "the samples of $\{0,1\}^{n+a} \setminus \mathit{Train}$ can be resolved either way". One way to construct a BDD $\mathcal{B}$ would be $\mathcal{B} \equiv \bigvee_{g \in \mathit{Good}} g$. But then $\mathcal{B}(0,0,0,0) = 1$ and $\mathcal{B}(0,0,1,0) = 0$, so *state3* has to be used in the representation of $\mathcal{B}$. Another option could be $\mathcal{B} \equiv \bigwedge_{b \in \mathit{Bad}} \neg b$, but then $\mathcal{B}(0,0,0,1) = 0$ and $\mathcal{B}(0,0,1,1) = 1$, so *state3* still has to be used in the representation.

Example 3. Consider $\mathit{Good} = \{(0,0,0,0,1)\}$ and $\mathit{Bad} = \{(0,0,0,0,0)\}$. Algorithm 1 outputs a simple decision tree differentiating between *Good* and *Bad* only according to the value of the last variable. On the other hand, a BDD constructed as $\mathcal{B} \equiv \bigvee_{g \in \mathit{Good}} g$ contains nodes for all five variables.

4.2 Strategy-DT Learning

Challenges. In contrast to other machine learning domains, where errors are allowed, since strategies in graph games must be represented precisely, several challenges arise. Most importantly, the machine-learning philosophy of classifiers is to generalize the experience, trying to achieve good predictions on any (not just training) data. In order to do so, overfitting the training data must be avoided. Indeed, specializing the classifier to cover the training data precisely leads to classifiers reflecting the concrete instances of random noise instead of generally useful predictors. Overfitting is prevented using a tolerance on learning all details of the training data. Consequently, the training data are not learnt exactly. Since in our case, the training set is exactly what we want to represent, our approach must be entirely different. In particular, the optimizations in the setting where errors are allowed (see Remark 1) are not applicable to handle the curse of dimensionality. In particular, it may be necessary to unfold the decision tree even in situations where none of the one-step unfolds induces any information gain.

Solution: Look-Ahead. In the ID3 algorithm Algorithm 1, when none of the splits has a positive information gain (see Formula (1)), the corresponding node is split arbitrarily. This can result in very large decision trees. We propose a better solution. Namely, we extend ID3 with a *"look-ahead"*: If no split results in a positive information gain, one can pick a split so that next, when splitting the children, the information gain is positive. If still no such split exists, one can try and pick a split and splits of children so that afterwards there is a split of grandchildren with positive information gain. And so on, possibly until a constant depth k, yielding a *k-look-ahead.*

Before we define the look-ahead formally, we have a look at a simple example:

Example 4. Consider $Good = \{(0,0,0,0,0,1,1),(0,0,0,0,0,0,0)\}$ and $Bad = \{(0,0,0,0,0,1,0),(0,0,0,0,0,0,1)\}$, characterising $x_6 = x_7$. Splitting on any x_i, $i \in \{1,...,7\}$ does not give a positive information gain. Standard DT learning procedures would either stop here and not expand this leaf any more, or split arbitrarily. With the look-ahead, one can see that using x_6 and then x_7, the information gain is positive and we obtain a decision tree classifying the set perfectly.

Here we could as well introduce more complex predicates such as x_6 `xor` x_7 instead of look-ahead. However, in general the look-ahead has the advantage that each of the 0 and 1 branches may afterwards split on different bits (currently best ones), whereas with x_6 `xor` x_7 we commit to using x_7 in both branches.

The example illustrates the 2-look-ahead with the following formal definition. (For explanatory reasons, the general case follows afterwards.) Consider a node $\ell \subseteq \{0,1\}^d$. For every $bit, bit_0, bit_1 \in \{1,\ldots,d\}$, consider splitting on bit and subsequently the 0-child on bit_0 and the 1-child on bit_1. This results in a partition

$P(bit, bit_0, bit_1) = \{\ell_{00}, \ell_{01}, \ell_{10}, \ell_{11}\}$ of ℓ. We assign to $P(bit, bit_0, bit_1)$ its *2-look-ahead information gain* defined by

$$IG(bit, bit_0, bit_1) = \\ H(\ell) - \frac{|\ell_{00}|}{|\ell|} H(\ell_{00}) - \frac{|\ell_{01}|}{|\ell|} H(\ell_{01}) - \frac{|\ell_{10}|}{|\ell|} H(\ell_{10}) - \frac{|\ell_{11}|}{|\ell|} H(\ell_{11})$$

The *2-look-ahead information gain of* $bit \in \{1, \ldots, d\}$ is defined as

$$IG(bit) = \max_{bit_0, bit_1} IG(bit, bit_0, bit_1)$$

We say that $bit \in \{1, \ldots, d\}$ *maximizes the 2-look-ahead information gain* if

$$bit \in \arg\max IG$$

In general, we define the *k-step weighted entropy* of a node $\ell \subseteq \{0,1\}^d$ with respect to a predicate $bit \in \{1, \ldots, d\}$ by

$$WE^k(\ell, bit) = \min_{bit_0, bit_1} WE^{k-1}(\{\boldsymbol{x} \in \ell \mid x_{bit} = 0\}, bit_0) \\ + WE^{k-1}(\{\boldsymbol{x} \in \ell \mid x_{bit} = 1\}, bit_1)$$

and

$$WE^0(\ell, bit) = |\ell| \cdot H(\ell)$$

Then we say that $\hat{bit} \in \{1, \ldots, d\}$ *maximizes the k-look-ahead information gain in* ℓ if

$$\hat{bit} \in \arg\max_{bit \in \{1,\ldots,d\}} \left(H(\ell) - WE^k(\ell, bit)/|\ell|\right) = \arg\min WE^k(\ell, \cdot)$$

Note that 1-look-ahead coincides with the choice of split by ID3. For a fixed k, if the information gain for each i-look-ahead, $i \leq k$ is zero, we split based on a heuristic on Line 8 of Algorithm 2. This heuristic is detailed on in the following subsection. Note that Algorithm 2 is correct-by-construction since we enforce representation of the entire input training set. We present a formal correctness proof in [12, Appendix B].

Remark 3 (Properties of look-ahead algorithm). We now highlight some desirable properties of the look-ahead algorithm.

- *Incrementality.* First, the algorithm presents an incremental approach: computation of the k-look-ahead can be done by further refining the results of the $(k-1)$-look-ahead analysis due to the recursive nature of our definition. Thus the algorithm can start with $k = 2$ and increase k only when required.
- *Entropy-based minimization.* Second, the look-ahead approach naturally extends the predicate choice of ID3, and thus the entropy-based minimization for decision trees is still applicable.
- *Reduction of dimensionality.* Finally, Algorithm 2 uses the look-ahead method in an incremental fashion, thus only considering more complex "combinations" when necessary. Consequently, we do not produce all these combinations of predicates in advance, and avoid the problem of too high dimensionality and only experience local blowups.

Algorithm 2. k-look-ahead ID3

Inputs: $\mathit{Train} \subseteq \{0,1\}^d$ partitioned into subsets *Good* and *Bad*.
Outputs: A decision tree $\mathcal{T}$ such that $\mathcal{L}(\mathcal{T}) \cap \mathit{Train} = \mathit{Good}$.
/* train $\mathcal{T}$ on positive set *Good* and negative set *Bad* */
$\mathcal{T} \leftarrow (\{\mathit{Train}\}, \emptyset, \{\mathit{Train} \mapsto^{\theta} \mathit{YES}\})$
while a mixed leaf ℓ exists **do**
  if $\exists \mathit{bit} \in \{1,\ldots,d\}$ with a positive 1-look-ahead information gain **then**
    $\mathit{bit} \leftarrow$ an element of $\{1,\ldots,d\}$ that maximizes the 1-look-ahead information gain
        ▷ maximum information gain is positive
  ⋮
  else if $\exists \mathit{bit} \in \{1,\ldots,d\}$ with a positive k-look-ahead information gain **then**
    $\mathit{bit} \leftarrow$ an element of $\{1,\ldots,d\}$ that maximizes the k-look-ahead information gain
        ▷ maximum k-look-ahead information gain is positive
  else
    $\mathit{bit} \leftarrow \arg\max_{i\in\{1,..,d\}} \max\left\{\frac{|\ell[i=0]\cap Bad|}{|\ell[i=0]|}+\frac{|\ell[i=1]\cap Good|}{|\ell[i=1]|}, \frac{|\ell[i=0]\cap Good|}{|\ell[i=0]|}+\frac{|\ell[i=1]\cap Bad|}{\ell[i=1]|}\right\}$
  split ℓ on *bit* into two leaves ℓ_0 and ℓ_1, $\rho(\ell) = \mathit{bit}$
  $\theta(\ell_0) \leftarrow \mathit{maxclass}(\ell_0)$ and $\theta(\ell_1) \leftarrow \mathit{maxclass}(\ell_1)$
return $\mathcal{T}$

In general, k-look-ahead clearly requires resources exponential in k. However, in our benchmarks, it was typically sufficient to apply the look-ahead for k equal to two, which is computationally feasible.

A different look-ahead-based technique was considered in order to dampen the greedy nature of decision tree construction [24], examining the predicates yielding the highest information gains. In contrast, our technique retains the greedy approach but focuses on the case where none of the predicates provides any information gain itself at all and thus ID3-based techniques fail to advance. The main goal of our technique is to capture strong dependence between the features of the training set, in order to solve a different problem than the one treated by [24]. Moreover, the look-ahead description in [24] is very informal, which prevents us from implementing their solution and comparing the two approaches experimentally.

4.3 Heuristics

Statistical Split-Decision. The look-ahead mentioned above provides a very systematic principle on how to resolve splitting decisions. However, the computation can be demanding in terms of computational resources. Therefore we present a very simple statistical heuristic that gives us one more option to decide a split. The precise formula is $\mathit{bit} =$

$$\arg\max_{i\in\{1,..,d\}} \max\left\{\frac{|\ell[i=0]\cap Bad|}{|\ell[i=0]|}+\frac{|\ell[i=1]\cap Good|}{|\ell[i=1]|}, \frac{|\ell[i=0]\cap Good|}{|\ell[i=0]|}+\frac{|\ell[i=1]\cap Bad|}{\ell[i=1]|}\right\}$$

Intuitively, we choose a *bit* that maximizes the portion of good samples in one subset and the portion of bad samples in the other subset, which mimics the entropy-based method, and at the same time is very fast to compute. One can consider using this heuristic exclusively every time the basic ID3-based splitting technique fails. However, in our experiments, using 2-look-ahead and then (once needed) proceeding with the heuristic yields better results, and is still computationally undemanding.

Chain Disjunction. The entropy-based approach favors the splits where one of the branches contains a completely resolved data set ($\ell_* \subseteq \mathit{Good}$ or $\ell_* \subseteq \mathit{Bad}$), as this provides notable information gain. Therefore, as the algorithm proceeds, it often happens that at some point multiple splits provide a resolved data set in one of the branches. We consider a heuristic that *chains* all such splits together and computes the information gain of the resulting disjunction. More specifically, when considering each *bit* as a split candidate (line 3 of Algorithm 2), we also consider (a) the disjunction of all bits that contain a subset of *Good* in either of the branches, and (b) the disjunction of bits containing a subset of *Bad* in a branch. Then we choose the candidate that maximizes the information gain. These two extra checks are very fast to compute, and can improve succinctness and readability of the decision trees substantially, while maintaining the fact that a decision tree fits its training set exactly. [12, Appendix D] provides two examples where the decision tree obtained without this heuristic is presented, and then the decision tree obtained when using the heuristic is presented.

5 Experimental Results

In our experiments we use two sources of problems reducible to the representation of memoryless strategies in I/O games with binary variables: AIGER specifications [31] and LTL specifications [42]. Given a game, we use an explicit solver to obtain a strategy in the form of a list of played and non-played actions for each state, which can be directly used as a training set. Throughout our experiments, we compare succinctness of representation (expressed as the number of inner nodes) using decision trees and BDDs.

We implemented our method in the programming language Java. We used the external library CuDD [49] for the manipulation of BDDs. We used the Algorithm 2 with $k = 2$ to compute the decision trees. We obtained all the results on a single machine with Intel(R) Core(TM) i5-6200U CPU (2.40 GHz) with the heap size limited to 8 GB.

5.1 AIGER Specifications

SYNTCOMP [32] is the most important competition of synthesis tools, running yearly since 2014. Most of the benchmarks have the form of AIGER specifications [31], describing safety specifications using circuits with input, output, and latch variables. This reduces directly to the I/O games with variables since the latches describe the current configuration of the circuit, corresponding to the state variables of the game. Since the objectives here are safety/reachability, the winning strategies can be computed and guaranteed to be memoryless.

We consider two benchmarks: scheduling of washing cycles in a washing system and a simple bit shifter model (the latter presented only in [12, Appendix D] due to space constraints), introduced in SYNTCOMP 2015 [32] and SYNTCOMP 2014, respectively.

Scheduling of Washing Cycles. The goal is to design a centralized controller for a washing system, composed of several tanks running in parallel [32]. The model of the system is parametrized by the number of tanks, the maximum allowed reaction delay before filling a tank with water, the delay after which the tank has to be emptied again, and the number of tanks that share a water pipe. The controller should satisfy a safety objective, that is, avoid reaching an error state, which means that the objective of the other player is reachability. In total, we obtain 406 graph games with safety/reachability objectives. In 394 cases we represent a winning strategy of the safety player, in the remaining 12 cases a winning strategy of the reachability player. The number of states of the graph games ranges from 30 to 43203, the size of training example sets ranges from 40 to 3359232.

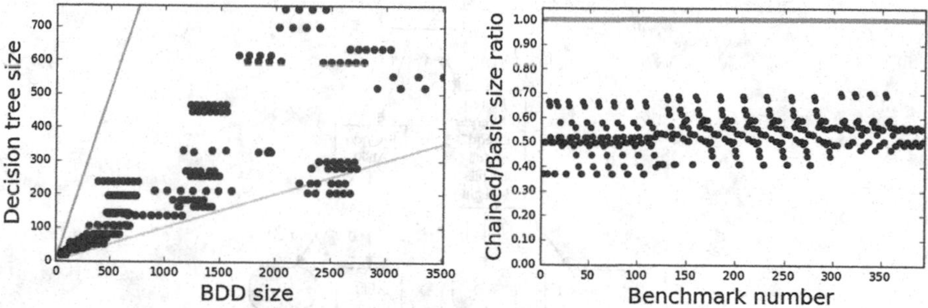

Fig. 3. Washing cycles – safety

The left plot in Fig. 3 displays the size of our decision tree representation of the controller winning safety strategies versus the size of their BDD representations. The decision tree is smaller than the corresponding BDD in all 394 cases. The arithmetic average ratio of decision tree size and BDD size is ~24%, the geometric average is ~22%, and the harmonic average is ~21%.

In these experiments, we obtain the BDD representation as follows: we consider 1000 randomly chosen variable orderings and for each construct a corresponding BDD, in the end we consider the BDD with the minimal size. As a different set of experiments, we compare against BDDs obtained using several algorithms for variable reordering, namely, Sift [47], Window4 [26], simulated-annealing-based algorithm [6], and a genetic algorithm [22]. The results with these algorithms are very similar and provided in [12, Appendix C]. Furthermore, the information about execution time is also provided in [12, Appendix C].

Moreover, in the experiments described above, we do not use the chain heuristic described in Sect. 4.3, in order to provide a fair comparison of decision trees and BDDs. The right plot in Fig. 3 displays the difference in decision tree size once the chain heuristic is enabled. Each dot represents the ratio of decision tree size with and without it.

The decision trees also allow us to get some insight into the winning strategies. Namely, for a fixed number of water tanks and a fixed empty delay, we obtain a solution that is affected by different values of the fill delay in a minimal way, and is easily generalizable for all the values of the parameter. This fact becomes more apparent once the chain heuristic described in Sect. 4.3 is enabled. This phenomenon is not present in the case of BDDs as they differ significantly, even in size, for different values of the parameter (see [12, Appendix C]). For two tanks and empty delay of one, the solution is small enough to be humanly readable and understandable, see Fig. 4 (where the fill delay is set to 7). Additional examples of the parametric solutions can be found in [12, Appendix C]. This example suggests that decision tree representation might be useful in solving parametrized synthesis (and verification) problems.

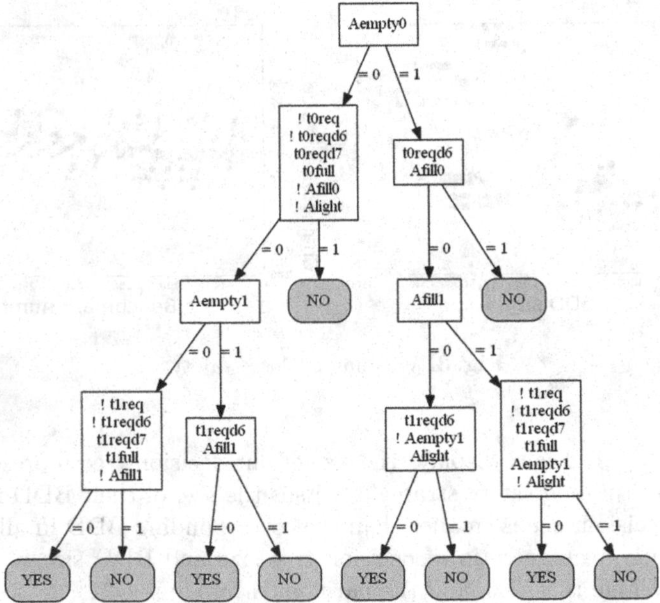

Fig. 4. A solution for two tanks and empty delay of one, illustration for fill delay of 7. Solution for other values p are the same except for replacing values p and $p - 1$ for 7 and 6, respectively. Thus a parametric solution could be obtained by a simple syntactic analysis of the difference of any two instance solutions.

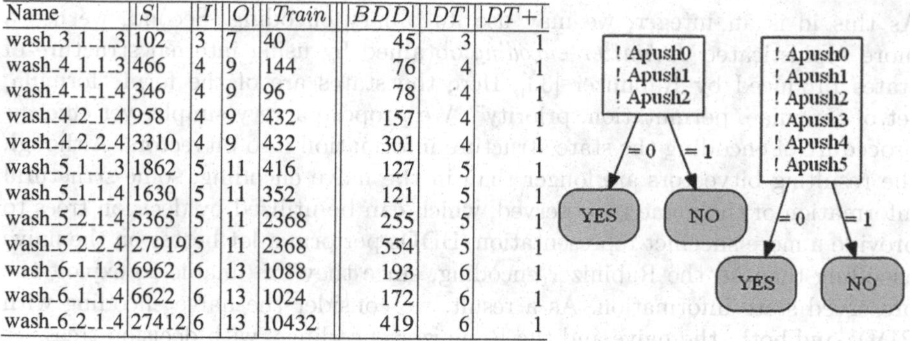

Name	$\|S\|$	$\|I\|$	$\|O\|$	$\|Train\|$	$\|BDD\|$	$\|DT\|$	$\|DT+\|$
wash_3_1_1_3	102	3	7	40	45	3	1
wash_4_1_1_3	466	4	9	144	76	4	1
wash_4_1_1_4	346	4	9	96	78	4	1
wash_4_2_1_4	958	4	9	432	157	4	1
wash_4_2_2_4	3310	4	9	432	301	4	1
wash_5_1_1_3	1862	5	11	416	127	5	1
wash_5_1_1_4	1630	5	11	352	121	5	1
wash_5_2_1_4	5365	5	11	2368	255	5	1
wash_5_2_2_4	27919	5	11	2368	554	5	1
wash_6_1_1_3	6962	6	13	1088	193	6	1
wash_6_1_1_4	6622	6	13	1024	172	6	1
wash_6_2_1_4	27412	6	13	10432	419	6	1

Fig. 5. Washing cycles – reachability

The table in Fig. 5 summarizes the results for the cases where the controller cannot be synthesized and we synthesize a counterexample winning reachability strategy of the environment. The benchmark parameters specify the total number of tanks, the fill delay, the empty delay, and the number of tanks sharing a pipe, respectively. In all of these cases, the size of the decision tree is substantially smaller compared to its BDD counterpart. The decision trees also provide some structural insight that may easily be used in debugging. Namely, the trees have a simple repeating structure where the number of repetitions depends just on the number of tanks. This is even easier to see once the chain heuristic of Sect. 4.3 is used. Figure 5 shows the tree solution for the case of three and six tanks, respectively. The structural phenomenon is not apparent from the BDDs at all.

5.2 Random LTL

In reactive synthesis, the objectives are often specified as LTL (linear-time temporal logic) formulae over input/output letters. In our experiments, we use formulae randomly generated using SPOT [23][1]. LTL formulae can be translated into deterministic parity automata; for this translation we use the tool Rabinizer [33]. Finally, given a parity automaton, we consider various partitions of the atomic propositions into input/output letters, which gives rise to graph games with parity objectives. See [12, Appendix F] for more details on the translation. We retain all formulae that result in games with at most three priorities.

Consequently, we use two ways of encoding states of the graph games as binary vectors. First, *naive encoding*, allowed by the fact that the output of tools such as [23,33] in HOA format [4] always assigns an id to each state.

[1] First, we run randltl from the Spot tool-set `randltl -n10000 5--tree-size=20..25 seed=0 --simplify=3 -p --ltl-priorities ap=3,false=1,true=1,not=1, F=1,G=1,X=1,equiv=1,implies=1,xor=0,R=0,U=1, W=0,M=0,and=1,or=1 | ltlfilt -- unabbreviate="eiMRW"` to obtain the formulae. Then we run Rabinizer to obtain the respective automata and we retain those with at least 100 states.

As this id is an integer, we may use its binary encoding. Second, we use a more sophisticated *Rabinizer encoding* obtained by using internal structure of states produced by Rabinizer [33]. Here the states are of the form "formula, set of formulae, permutation, priority". We propose a very simple, yet efficient procedure of encoding the state structure information into bitvectors. Although the resulting bitvectors are longer than in the naive encoding, some structural information of the game is preserved, which can be utilized by decision trees to provide a more succinct representation. BDDs perform a lot better on the naive encoding than on the Rabinizer encoding, since they are unable to exploit the preserved state information. As a result, we consider the naive encoding with BDDs and both, the naive and the Rabinizer encodings, with decision trees.

We consider 976 examples where the goal of the player, whose strategy is being represented, is that the least priority occurring an infinite number of times is odd.

Figure 6 plots the size ratios when we compare BDDs and decision trees (note that the y-axis scales logarithmically). For each case, we consider 1000 random variable orderings and choose the BDD that is minimal in size, and after that we construct a decision tree (without the chain heuristic of Sect. 4.3). For BDDs, we also consider all the ordering algorithms mentioned in the previous set of experiments, however, they provide no improvement compared to the random orderings.

In 925 out of 976 cases, the resulting decision tree is smaller than the corresponding BDD (in 3 cases they are of a same size and in 48 cases the BDD is smaller). The arithmetic average ratio of decision tree size and BDD size is ~46%, the geometric average is ~38%, and the harmonic average is ~28%.

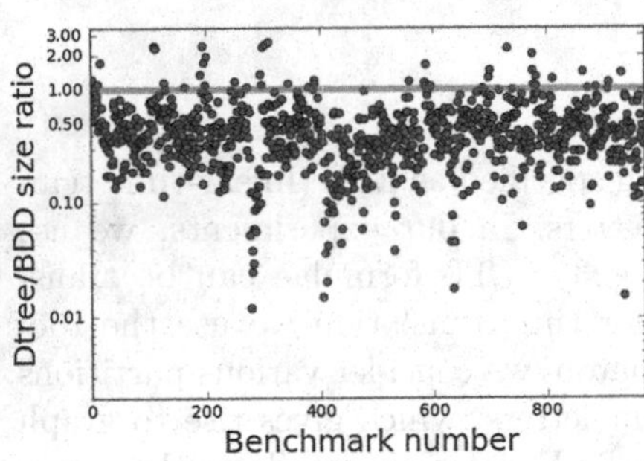

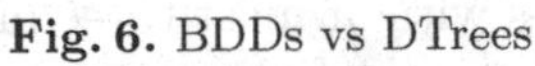

Fig. 6. BDDs vs DTrees

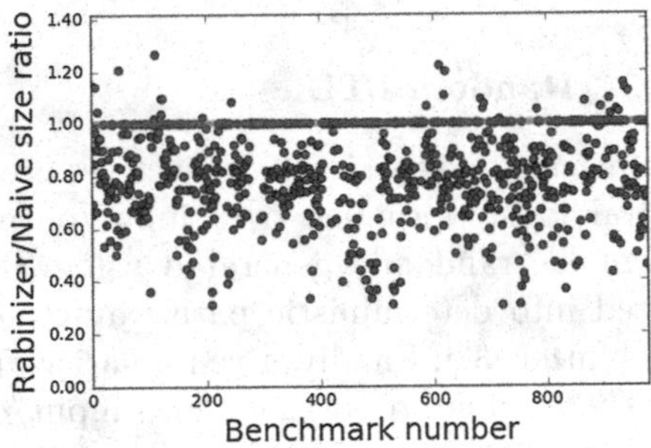

Fig. 7. DTrees improvement with Rabinizer enc.

Figure 7 demonstrates how decision tree representation improves once the features of the game-structural information can be utilized. Each dot corresponds to a ratio of the decision tree size once the Rabinizer encoding is used, and once the naive encoding is used. In 638 cases the Rabinizer encoding is superior, in 309 cases there is no difference, and in 29 cases the naive encoding is superior.

All three types of the average ratio are around 80%. In [12, Appendix E] we present the further improvement of decision trees once we use the chain heuristic of Sect. 4.3.

6 Conclusion

In this work we propose decision trees for strategy representation in graph games. While decision trees have been used in probabilistic settings where errors are allowed and overfitting of data is avoided, for graph games, strategies must be entirely represented without errors. Hence optimization techniques for existing decision-tree solvers do not apply, and we develop new techniques and present experimental results to demonstrate the effectiveness of our approach. Moreover, decision trees have several other advantages: First, in decision trees the nodes represent predicates, and in richer domains, e.g., where variables represent integers, the internal nodes of the tree can represent predicates in the corresponding domain, e.g., comparison between the integer variables and a constant. Hence richer domains can be directly represented as decision trees without conversion to bitvectors as required by BDDs. However, we restricted ourselves to the boolean domain to show that even in such domains that BDDs are designed for the decision trees improve over BDDs. Second, as illustrated in our examples, decision trees can often provide similar and scalable solution when some parameters vary. This is quite attractive in reactive synthesis where certain parameters vary, however they affect the strategy in a minimal way. Our examples show decision trees exploit this much better than BDDs, and can be useful in parametrized synthesis. Our work opens up many interesting directions of future work. For instance, richer versions of decision trees that are still well-readable could be used instead, such as decision trees with more complex expressions in leaves [40]. The applications of decision trees in other applications related to reactive synthesis is an interesting direction of future work. Another interesting direction is the application of the look-ahead technique in the probabilistic settings.

Data Availability Statement and Acknowledgments. This work has been partially supported by the Czech Science Foundation, Grant No. P202/12/G061, Vienna Science and Technology Fund (WWTF) Project ICT15-003, Austrian Science Fund (FWF) NFN Grant No. S11407-N23 (RiSE/SHiNE), ERC Starting grant (279307: Graph Games), DFG Grant No KR 4890/2-1 (SUV: Statistical Unbounded Verification), TUM IGSSE Grant 10.06 (PARSEC) and EU Horizon 2020 research and innovation programme under the Marie Skłodowska-Curie Grant No. 665385. We thank Fabio Somenzi for detailed information about variable reordering in BDDs. The source code and binary files used to obtain the results presented in this paper are available in the figshare repository: https://doi.org/10.6084/m9.figshare.5923915.v1 [11].

Appendix

A Artifact Description

We provide instructions to replicate the experimental results presented in this paper, using our artifact that is openly available at [11]. All the results can be obtained with the heap size limited to 8 GB.

Results for Scheduling of Washing Cycles (Sect. 5.1**).** Running this batch takes roughly 30 h and generates 7.1 GB of training data. Note that we did not include around 30 most resource-demanding benchmarks of this batch in the artifact. (i) in folder art, execute ./run.sh wTOTAL, (ii) observe the results at art/results/reports/reprWash{2,3,4,reach}.txt, (iii) in folder art/results, execute python plotsWash.py and observe the plots that correspond to Fig. 3. Alternatively, to run a subset of this batch that takes only 30 min to run and generates only 265MB of training data, in (i) execute ./run.sh wPART. To additionaly generate dot representation of DTs/BDDs, in (i) execute either ./run.sh wTOTALdot or ./run.sh wPARTdot.

Results for Scheduling of Washing Cycles BDD Reordering ([12, Appendix C]**).** Running this batch takes roughly 30 min. (i) make sure you have the training data obtained by running the batch above, (ii) in folder art/results, execute ./runBDDreorder.sh, (iii) observe the results at art/results/reports/BDDreorder.txt.

Results for Random LTL (Sect. 5.2**).** Running this batch takes roughly 2 h and generates 84 MB of training data. (i) in folder art, execute ./run.sh rTOTAL, (ii) observe the results at art/results/reports/reprRandomLTL{naive,encoded}.txt, (iii) in folder art/results, execute python plotsRandomLTL.py and observe the plots that correspond to Figs. 6 and 7.

Results for Bit Shifter ([12, Appendix D]**).** Running this experiment batch takes roughly 5 min. Note that we did not include two benchmarks in the artifact since they take considerable execution time. (i) in folder art, execute ./run.sh aTOTAL, (ii) observe the results at art/results/reports/reprAiger.txt.

References

1. Abadi, M., Lamport, L., Wolper, P.: Realizable and unrealizable specifications of reactive systems. In: Ausiello, G., Dezani-Ciancaglini, M., Della Rocca, S.R. (eds.) ICALP 1989. LNCS, vol. 372, pp. 1–17. Springer, Heidelberg (1989). https://doi.org/10.1007/BFb0035748
2. Akers, S.B.: Binary decision diagrams. IEEE Trans. Comput. **C-27**(6), 509–516 (1978)
3. Alur, R., Henzinger, T., Kupferman, O.: Alternating-time temporal logic. J. ACM **49**, 672–713 (2002)

4. Babiak, T., Blahoudek, F., Duret-Lutz, A., Klein, J., Křetínský, J., Müller, D., Parker, D., Strejček, J.: The Hanoi omega-automata format. In: Kroening, D., Păsăreanu, C.S. (eds.) CAV 2015, Part I. LNCS, vol. 9206, pp. 479–486. Springer, Cham (2015). https://doi.org/10.1007/978-3-319-21690-4_31
5. Blass, A., Gurevich, Y., Nachmanson, L., Veanes, M.: Play to test. In: FATES 2005 (2005)
6. Bollig, B., Lbbing, M., Wegener, I.: Simulated annealing to improve variable orderings for OBDDs. Presented at the International Workshop on Logic Synthesis, Granlibakken, CA (1995)
7. Boutilier, C., Dearden, R.: Approximate value trees in structured dynamic programming. In: Saitta, L. (ed.) ICML, pp. 54–62. Morgan Kaufmann (1996)
8. Boutilier, C., Dearden, R., Goldszmidt, M.: Exploiting structure in policy construction. In: IJCAI, pp. 1104–1113. Morgan Kaufmann (1995)
9. Brázdil, T., Chatterjee, K., Chmelík, M., Fellner, A., Křetínský, J.: Counterexample explanation by learning small strategies in Markov decision processes. In: Kroening, D., Păsăreanu, C.S. (eds.) CAV 2015, Part I. LNCS, vol. 9206, pp. 158–177. Springer, Cham (2015). https://doi.org/10.1007/978-3-319-21690-4_10
10. Brázdil, T., Chatterjee, K., Chmelík, M., Gupta, A., Novotný, P.: Stochastic shortest path with energy constraints in POMDPs: (extended abstract). In: AAMAS, pp. 1465–1466 (2016)
11. Brázdil, T., Chatterjee, K., Křetínský, J., Toman, V.: Artifact and instructions to generate experimental results for TACAS 2018 paper Strategy Representation by Decision Trees in Reactive Synthesis. Figshare (2018). https://doi.org/10.6084/m9.figshare.5923915.v1
12. Brázdil, T., Chatterjee, K., Křetínský, J., Toman, V.: Strategy representation by decision trees in reactive synthesis. arXiv.org:1802.00758 (2018)
13. Bryant, R.: Graph-based algorithms for Boolean function manipulation. IEEE Trans. Comput. **C-35**(8), 677–691 (1986)
14. Büchi, J.: On a decision method in restricted second-order arithmetic. In: Nagel, E., Suppes, P., Tarski, A. (eds.) Proceedings of the First International Congress on Logic, Methodology, and Philosophy of Science 1960, pp. 1–11. Stanford University Press (1962)
15. Büchi, J., Landweber, L.: Solving sequential conditions by finite-state strategies. Trans. AMS **138**, 295–311 (1969)
16. Calude, C.S., Jain, S., Khoussainov, B., Li, W., Stephan, F.: Deciding parity games in quasipolynomial time. In: Hatami, H., McKenzie, P., King, V. (eds.) Proceedings of the 49th Annual ACM SIGACT Symposium on Theory of Computing, STOC 2017, Montreal, QC, Canada, 19–23 June 2017, pp. 252–263. ACM (2017). https://dblp.org/rec/bib/conf/stoc/2017
17. Church, A.: Logic, arithmetic, and automata. In: Proceedings of the International Congress of Mathematicians, pp. 23–35. Institut Mittag-Leffler (1962)
18. Clarke, E., Henzinger, T., Veith, H. (eds.): Handbook of Model Checking. Springer, Heidelberg (2017). https://doi.org/10.1007/978-3-319-10575-8. Chapter: Games and Synthesis
19. de Alfaro, L., Henzinger, T.: Interface automata. In: FSE 2001, pp. 109–120. ACM (2001)
20. de Alfaro, L., Henzinger, T., Mang, F.: Detecting errors before reaching them. In: CAV 2000, pp. 186–201 (2000)
21. Dill, D.: Trace Theory for Automatic Hierarchical Verification of Speed-independent Circuits. The MIT Press, Cambridge (1989)

22. Drechsler, R., Becker, B., Gockel, N.: Genetic algorithm for variable ordering of OBDDs. Presented at the International Workshop on Logic Synthesis, Granlibakken, CA (1995)
23. Duret-Lutz, A., Lewkowicz, A., Fauchille, A., Michaud, T., Renault, E., Xu, L.: Spot 2.0 - a framework for LTL and ω-automata manipulation. In: ATVA, pp. 122–129 (2016)
24. Elomaa, T., Malinen, T.: On lookahead heuristics in decision tree learning. In: Zhong, N., Raś, Z.W., Tsumoto, S., Suzuki, E. (eds.) ISMIS 2003. LNCS (LNAI), vol. 2871, pp. 445–453. Springer, Heidelberg (2003). https://doi.org/10.1007/978-3-540-39592-8_63
25. Emerson, E., Jutla, C.: Tree automata, mu-calculus and determinacy. In: FOCS 1991, pp. 368–377. IEEE (1991)
26. Fujita, M., Matsunaga, Y., Kakuda, T.: On variable ordering of binary decision diagrams for the application of multi-level logic synthesis. In: EURO-DAC, pp. 50–54 (1991)
27. Garg, P., Neider, D., Madhusudan, P., Roth, D.: Learning invariants using decision trees and implication counterexamples. In: POPL (2016)
28. Gurevich, Y., Harrington, L.: Trees, automata, and games. In: STOC 1982, pp. 60–65. ACM Press (1982)
29. Hall, M.A., Frank, E., Holmes, G., Pfahringer, B., Reutemann, P., Witten, I.H.: The WEKA data mining software: an update. SIGKDD Explor. **11**(1), 10–18 (2009)
30. Henzinger, T., Kupferman, O., Rajamani, S.: Fair simulation. I&C **173**, 64–81 (2002)
31. Jacobs, S.: Extended AIGER format for synthesis. CoRR, abs/1405.5793 (2014)
32. Jacobs, S., Bloem, R., Brenguier, R., Könighofer, R., Pérez, G.A., Raskin, J., Ryzhyk, L., Sankur, O., Seidl, M., Tentrup, L., Walker, A.: The second reactive synthesis competition (SYNTCOMP 2015). In: SYNT, pp. 27–57 (2015)
33. Komárková, Z., Křetínský, J.: Rabinizer 3: safraless translation of LTL to small deterministic automata. In: ATVA, pp. 235–241 (2014)
34. Krishna, S., Puhrsch, C., Wies, T.: Learning invariants using decision trees. CoRR, abs/1501.04725 (2015)
35. Liu, S., Panangadan, A., Raghavendra, C.S., Talukder, A.: Compact representation of coordinated sampling policies for body sensor networks. In: Proceedings of Workshop on Advances in Communication and Networks (Smart Homes for Tele-Health), pp. 6–10. IEEE (2010)
36. Manna, Z., Pnueli, A.: The Temporal Logic of Reactive and Concurrent Systems: Specification. Springer, New York (1992). https://doi.org/10.1007/978-1-4612-0931-7
37. McNaughton, R.: Infinite games played on finite graphs. Ann. Pure Appl. Log. **65**, 149–184 (1993)
38. Mitchell, T.M.: Machine Learning, 1st edn. McGraw-Hill Inc., New York (1997)
39. Neider, D.: Small strategies for safety games. In: ATVA, pp. 306–320 (2011)
40. Neider, D., Saha, S., Madhusudan, P.: Synthesizing piece-wise functions by learning classifiers. In: Chechik, M., Raskin, J.-F. (eds.) TACAS 2016. LNCS, vol. 9636, pp. 186–203. Springer, Heidelberg (2016). https://doi.org/10.1007/978-3-662-49674-9_11
41. Neider, D., Topcu, U.: An automaton learning approach to solving safety games over infinite graphs. In: Chechik, M., Raskin, J.-F. (eds.) TACAS 2016. LNCS, vol. 9636, pp. 204–221. Springer, Heidelberg (2016). https://doi.org/10.1007/978-3-662-49674-9_12

42. Pnueli, A.: The temporal logic of programs. In: Proceedings of the 18th Annual Symposium on Foundations of Computer Science, pp. 46–57. IEEE Computer Society Press (1977)
43. Pnueli, A., Rosner, R.: On the synthesis of a reactive module. In: POPL 1989, pp. 179–190. ACM Press (1989)
44. Quinlan, J.R.: Induction of decision trees. Mach. Learn. **1**(1), 81–106 (1986)
45. Rabin, M.: Automata on Infinite Objects and Church's Problem. Number 13 in Conference Series in Mathematics. American Mathematical Society, Providence (1969)
46. Ramadge, P., Wonham, W.: Supervisory control of a class of discrete-event processes. SIAM J. Contr. Opt. **25**(1), 206–230 (1987)
47. Rudell, R.: Dynamic variable ordering for ordered binary decision diagrams. In: ICCAD, pp. 42–47. IEEE Computer Society Press (1993)
48. Schewe, S.: Solving parity games in big steps. JCSS **84**, 243–262 (2017)
49. Somenzi, F.: CUDD: CU decision diagram package release 3.0.0 (2015)
50. Thomas, W.: Languages, automata, and logic. In: Rozenberg, G., Salomaa, A. (eds.) Handbook of Formal Languages, pp. 389–455. Springer, Heidelberg (1997). https://doi.org/10.1007/978-3-642-59126-6_7
51. Wimmer, R., Braitling, B., Becker, B., Hahn, E.M., Crouzen, P., Hermanns, H., Dhama, A., Theel, O.: Symblicit calculation of long-run averages for concurrent probabilistic systems. In: QEST, pp. 27–36. IEEE Computer Society, Washington, DC (2010)
52. Zielonka, W.: Infinite games on finitely coloured graphs with applications to automata on infinite trees. Theor. Comput. Sci. **200**(1–2), 135–183 (1998)

Feature-Guided Black-Box Safety Testing of Deep Neural Networks

Matthew Wicker[1], Xiaowei Huang[2(✉)], and Marta Kwiatkowska[3]

[1] University of Georgia, Athens, USA
matthew.wicker25@uga.edu
[2] University of Liverpool, Liverpool, UK
xiaowei.huang@liverpool.ac.uk
[3] University of Oxford, Oxford, UK
marta.kwiatkowska@cs.ox.ac.uk

Abstract. Despite the improved accuracy of deep neural networks, the discovery of adversarial examples has raised serious safety concerns. Most existing approaches for crafting adversarial examples necessitate some knowledge (architecture, parameters, etc) of the network at hand. In this paper, we focus on image classifiers and propose a *feature-guided* black-box approach to test the safety of deep neural networks that requires no such knowledge. Our algorithm employs object detection techniques such as SIFT (Scale Invariant Feature Transform) to extract features from an image. These features are converted into a mutable saliency distribution, where high probability is assigned to pixels that affect the composition of the image with respect to the human visual system. We formulate the crafting of adversarial examples as a two-player turn-based stochastic game, where the first player's objective is to minimise the distance to an adversarial example by manipulating the features, and the second player can be cooperative, adversarial, or random. We show that, theoretically, the two-player game can converge to the optimal strategy, and that the optimal strategy represents a globally minimal adversarial image. For Lipschitz networks, we also identify conditions that provide safety guarantees that no adversarial examples exist. Using Monte Carlo tree search we gradually explore the game state space to search for adversarial examples. Our experiments show that, despite the black-box setting, manipulations guided by a perception-based saliency distribution are competitive with state-of-the-art methods that rely on white-box saliency matrices or sophisticated optimization procedures. Finally, we show how our method can be used to evaluate robustness of neural networks in safety-critical applications such as traffic sign recognition in self-driving cars.

1 Introduction

Deep neural networks (DNNs or networks, for simplicity) have been developed for a variety of tasks, including malware detection [11], abnormal network activity detection [31], and self-driving cars [5,6,32]. A classification network N can

D. Beyer and M. Huisman (Eds.): TACAS 2018, LNCS 10805, pp. 408–426, 2018.
https://doi.org/10.1007/978-3-319-89960-2_22

be used as a decision-making algorithm: given an input α, it suggests a decision $N(\alpha)$ among a set of possible decisions. While the accuracy of neural networks has greatly improved, matching the cognitive ability of humans [17], they are susceptible to adversarial examples [4,33]. An adversarial example is an input which, though initially classified correctly, is misclassified after a minor, perhaps imperceptible, perturbation. Adversarial examples pose challenges for self-driving cars, where neural network solutions have been proposed for tasks such as end-to-end steering [6], road segmentation [5], and traffic sign classification [32]. In the context of steering and road segmentation, an adversarial example may cause a car to steer off the road or drive into barriers, and misclassifying traffic signs may cause a vehicle to drive into oncoming traffic. Figure 1 shows an image of a traffic light correctly classified by a state-of-the-art network which is then misclassified after only a few pixels have been changed. Though somewhat artificial, since in practice the controller would rely on additional sensor input when making a decision, such cases strongly suggest that, before deployment in safety-critical tasks, DNNs resilience (or robustness) to adversarial examples must be strengthened.

A number of approaches have been proposed to search for adversarial examples (see Related Work). They are based on computing the gradients [12], along which a heuristic search moves; computing a Jacobian-based saliency map [27], based on which pixels are selected to be changed; transforming the existence of adversarial examples into an optimisation problem [8], on which an optimisation algorithm can be applied; transforming the existence of adversarial examples into a constraint solving problem [15], on which a constraint solver can be applied; or discretising the neighbourhood of a point and searching it exhaustively in a layer-by-layer manner [14]. All these approaches assume some knowledge about the network, e.g., the architecture or the parameters, which can vary as the network continuously learns and adapts to new data, and, with a few exceptions [26] that access the penultimate layer, do not explore the feature maps of the networks.

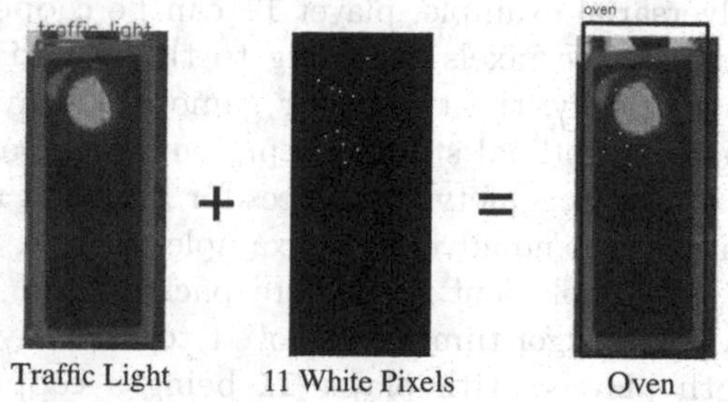

Fig. 1. An adversarial example for the YOLO object recognition network.

In this paper, we propose a *feature-guided* approach to test the resilience of image classifier networks against adversarial examples. While convolutional neural networks (CNN) have been successful in classification tasks, their feature extraction capability is not well understood [37]. The discovery of adversarial examples has called into question CNN's ability to robustly handle input with diverse structural and compositional elements. On the other hand, state-of-the-art feature extraction methods are able to deterministically and efficiently extract structural elements of an image regardless of scale, rotation or transformation. A key observation of this paper is that feature extraction methods enable us to identify elements of an image which are most vulnerable to a visual system such as a CNN.

Leveraging knowledge of the human perception system, existing object detection techniques detect instances of semantic objects of a certain class (such as animals, buildings, or cars) in digital images and videos by identifying their features. We use the scale-invariant feature transform approach, or SIFT [20], to detect features, which is achieved with no knowledge of the network in a *black-box* manner. Using the SIFT features, whose number is much smaller than the number of pixels, we represent the image as a two-dimensional Gaussian mixture model. This reduction in dimensionality allows us to efficiently target the exploration at salient features, similarly to human perception. We formulate the process of crafting adversarial examples as a two-player turn-based stochastic game, where player `I` selects features and player `II` then selects pixels within the selected features and a manipulation instruction. After both players have made their choices, the image is modified according to the manipulation instruction, and the game continues. While player `I` aims to minimise the distance to an adversarial example, player `II` can be cooperative, adversarial, or nature who samples the pixels according to the Gaussian mixture model. We show that, theoretically, the two-player game can converge to the optimal strategy, and that the optimal strategy represents a globally minimal adversarial image. We also consider safety guarantees for Lipschitz networks and identify conditions to ensure that no adversarial examples exist.

We implement a software package[1], in which a Monte Carlo tree search (MCTS) algorithm is employed to find asymptotically optimal strategies for both players, with player `II` being a cooperator. The algorithm is *anytime*, meaning that it can be terminated with time-out bounds provided by the user and, when terminated, it returns the best strategies it has for both players. The experiments on networks trained on benchmark datasets such as MNIST [18] and CIFAR10 [1] show that, even without the knowledge of the network and using relatively little time (1 min for every image), the algorithm can already achieve competitive performance against existing adversarial example crafting algorithms. We also experiment on several state-of-the-art networks, including the winner of the Nexar traffic light challenge [25], a real-time object detection system YOLO, and VGG16 [3] for ImageNet competition, where, surprisingly, we show that the algorithm can return adversarial examples even with very limited resources (e.g., running time of *less than a second*), including that in Fig. 1 from YOLO. Further, since the SIFT method is scale and rotation invariant, we can counter claims in the recent paper [21] that adversarial examples are not invariant to changes in scale or angle in the physical domain.

Our software package is well suited to safety testing and decision support for DNNs in safety-critical applications. First, the MCTS algorithm can be used *offline* to evaluate the network's robustness against adversarial examples on

[1] The software package and all high-resolution figures used in the paper are available from https://github.com/matthewwicker/SafeCV.

a given set of images. The asymptotic optimal strategy achievable by MCTS algorithm enables a theoretical guarantee of safety, i.e., the network is safe when the algorithm cannot find adversarial examples. The algorithm is guaranteed to terminate, but this may be impractical, so we provide an alternative termination criterion. Second, the MCTS algorithm, in view of its time efficiency, has the potential to be deployed on-board for *real-time* decision support.

An extended version of the paper, which includes more additional explanations and experimental results, is available from [36].

2 Preliminaries

Let N be a network with a set C of classes. Given an input α and a class $c \in C$, we use $N(\alpha, c)$ to denote the confidence (expressed as a probability value obtained from normalising the score) of N believing that α is in class c. Moreover, we write $N(\alpha) = \arg\max_{c \in C} N(\alpha, c)$ for the class into which N classifies α. For our discussion of image classification networks, the input domain D is a vector space, which in most cases can be represented as $\mathbb{R}^{\mathrm{w} \times \mathrm{h} \times \mathrm{ch}}_{[0,255]}$, where w, h, ch are the width, height, and number of channels of an image, respectively, and we let $P_0 = w \times h \times ch$ be the set of input dimensions. In the following, we may refer to an element in $w \times h$ as a pixel and an element in P_0 as a dimension. We remark that dimensions are normalised as real values in $[0, 1]$. Image classifiers employ a distance function to compare images. Ideally, such a distance should reflect perceptual similarity between images, comparable to human perception. However, in practice L_k distances are used instead, typically L_0, L_1 (Manhattan distance), L_2 (Euclidean distance), and L_∞ (Chebyshev distance). We also work with L_k distances but emphasise that our method can be adapted to other distances. In the following, we write $||\alpha_1 - \alpha_2||_k$ with $k \geq 0$ for the distance between two images α_1 and α_2 with respect to the L_k measurement.

Given an image α, a distance measure L_k, and a distance d, we define $\eta(\alpha, k, d) = \{\alpha' \mid ||\alpha' - \alpha||_k \leq d\}$ as the set of points whose distance to α is no greater than d with respect to L_k. Next we define adversarial examples, as well as what we mean by targeted and non-targeted safety.

Definition 1. *Given an input* $\alpha \in$ D, *a distance measure* L_k *for some* $k \geq 0$, *and a distance* d, *an* adversarial example α' *of class* $c \neq N(\alpha)$ *is such that* $\alpha' \in \eta(\alpha, k, d)$, $N(\alpha) \neq N(\alpha')$, *and* $N(\alpha') = c$. *Moreover, we write* $adv_{N,k,d}(\alpha, c)$ *for the set of adversarial examples of class* c *and let* $adv_{N,k,d}(\alpha) = \bigcup_{c \in C, c \neq N(\alpha)} adv_{N,k,d}(\alpha, c)$. *A* targeted safety *of class* c *is defined as* $adv_{N,k,d}(\alpha, c) = \emptyset$, *and a* non-targeted safety *is defined as* $adv_{N,k,d}(\alpha) = \emptyset$.

Feature Extraction. The Scale Invariant Feature Transform (SIFT) algorithm [20], a reliable technique for exhuming features from an image, makes object localization and tracking possible without the use of neural networks. Generally, the SIFT algorithm proceeds through the following steps: scale-space extrema detection (detecting relatively darker or lighter areas in the image), keypoint localization (determining the exact position of these areas), and keypoint descriptor assignment (understanding the context of the image w.r.t its local area). Human perception of an image or an object can be reasonably represented as a set of features (referred to as keypoints in SIFT) of different sizes and response strengths, see [35] and Appendix of [36] for more detail. Let $\Lambda(\alpha)$ be a set of features of the image α such that each feature $\lambda \in \Lambda(\alpha)$ is a tuple $(\lambda_x, \lambda_y, \lambda_s, \lambda_r)$, where (λ_x, λ_y) is the coordinate of the feature in the image, λ_s is the size of the feature, and λ_r is the response strength of the feature. The SIFT procedures implemented in standard libraries such as OpenCV may return more information which we do not use.

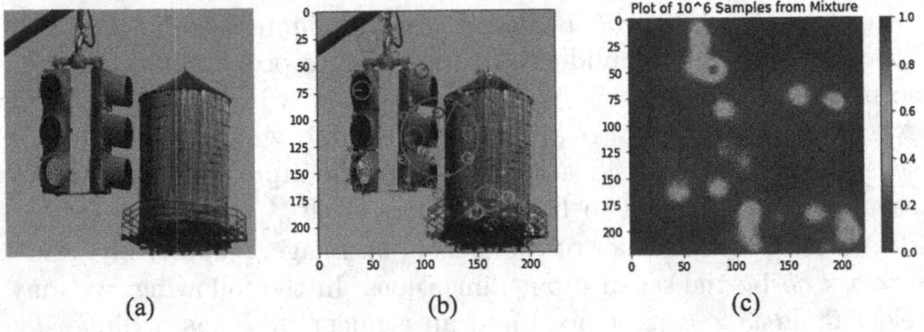

Fig. 2. Illustration of the transformation of an image into a saliency distribution. (a) The original image α, provided by ImageNet. (b) The image marked with relevant keypoints $\Lambda(\alpha)$. (c) The heatmap of the Gaussian mixture model $\mathcal{G}(\Lambda(\alpha))$.

On their own, keypoints are not guaranteed to involve every pixel in the image, and in order to ensure a comprehensive and flexible safety analysis, we utilize these keypoints as a basis for a Gaussian mixture model. Figure 2 shows the original image (a) and this image annotated with keypoints (b).

Gaussian Mixture Model. Given an image α and its set $\Lambda(\alpha)$ of keypoints, we define for $\lambda_i \in \Lambda(\alpha)$ a two-dimensional Gaussian distribution $\mathcal{G}_i$ such that, for pixel (p_x, p_y), we have

$$\mathcal{G}_{i,x} = \frac{1}{\sqrt{2\pi\lambda_{i,s}^2}} exp(\frac{-(p_x - \lambda_{i,x})^2}{2\lambda_{i,s}^2}) \quad \mathcal{G}_{i,y} = \frac{1}{\sqrt{2\pi\lambda_{i,s}^2}} exp(\frac{-(p_y - \lambda_{i,y})^2}{2\lambda_{i,s}^2}) \quad (1)$$

where the variance is the size $\lambda_{i,s}$ of the keypoint and the mean is its location $(\lambda_{i,x}, \lambda_{i,y})$. To complete the model, we define a set of weights $\Phi = \{\phi_i\}_{i \in \{1,2,...,k\}}$ such that $k = |\Lambda(\alpha)|$ and $\phi_i = \lambda_{i,r} / \sum_{j=0}^{k} \lambda_{j,r}$. Then, we can construct a Gaussian mixture model $\mathcal{G}$ by combining the distribution components with the weights as coefficients, i.e., $\mathcal{G}_x = \prod_{i=1}^{k} \phi_i \times \mathcal{G}_{i,x}$ and $\mathcal{G}_y = \prod_{i=1}^{k} \phi_i \times \mathcal{G}_{i,y}$. The two-dimensional distributions are discrete and separable and therefore their realization is tractable and independent, which improves efficiency of computation. Let $\mathcal{G}(\Lambda(\alpha))$ be the obtained Gaussian mixture model from $\Lambda(\alpha)$, and G be the set of

Gaussian mixture models. In Fig. 2 we illustrate the transformation of an image into a saliency distribution.

Pixel Manipulation. We now define the operations that we consider for manipulating images. We write $\alpha(x,y,z)$ for the value of the z-channel (typically RGB or grey-scale values) of the pixel positioned at (x,y) on the image α. Let $I = \{+,-\}$ be a set of manipulation instructions and τ be a positive real number representing the manipulation magnitude, then we can define pixel manipulations $\delta_{X,i} : \mathrm{D} \rightarrow \mathrm{D}$ for X a subset of input pixels and $i \in I$:

$$\delta_{X,i}(\alpha)(x,y,z) = \begin{cases} \alpha(x,y,z) + \tau, \text{if } (x,y) \in X \text{ and } i = + \\ \alpha(x,y,z) - \tau, \text{if } (x,y) \in X \text{ and } i = - \\ \alpha(x,y,z) \qquad \text{otherwise} \end{cases}$$

for all pixels (x,y) and channels $z \in \{1,2,3\}$. Note that if the values are bounded, e.g., $[0,1]$, $\delta_{X,i}(\alpha)(x,y,z)$ needs to be restricted to be within the bounds. For simplicity, in our experiments and comparisons we allow a manipulation to choose either the upper bound or the lower bound with respect to the instruction i. For example, in Fig. 1, the actual manipulation considered is to make the manipulated dimensions choose value 1.

3 Safety Against Manipulations

Recall that every image represents a point in the input vector space D. Most existing investigations of the safety (or robustness) of DNNs focus on optimising the movement of a point along the gradient direction of some function obtained from the network (see Related Work for more detail). Therefore, these approaches rely on the knowledge about the DNN. Arguably, this reliance holds also for the black-box approach proposed in [26], which uses a new surrogate network trained on the data sampled from the original network. Furthermore, the current understanding about the transferability of adversarial examples (i.e., an adversarial example found for a network can also serve as an adversarial example for another network, trained on different data) are all based on empirical experiments [26]. The conflict between the understanding of transferability and existing approaches to crafting adversarial examples can be gleaned from an observation made in [19] that gradient directions of different models are orthogonal to each other. A reasonable interpretation is that transferable adversarial examples, if they exist, do not rely on the gradient direction suggested by a network but instead may be specific to the input.

In this paper, we propose a *feature-guided* approach which, instead of using the gradient direction as the guide for optimisation, relies on searching fro adversarial examples by targeting and manipulating image features as recognised by human perception capability. We extract features using SIFT, which is a reasonable proxy for human perception and enables dimensionality reduction through the Gaussian mixture representation (see [29]). Our method needs neither the knowledge about the network nor the necessity to massively sample the network for data to train a new network, and is therefore a *black-box* approach.

Game-Based Approach. We formulate the search for adversarial examples as a two-player turn-based stochastic game, where player I selects features and player II then selects pixels within the selected features and a manipulation instruction. While player I aims to minimise the distance to an adversarial example, player II can be cooperative, adversarial, or nature who samples the pixels according to the Gaussian mixture model. To give more intuition for feature-guided search, in Appendix of [36] we demonstrate how the distribution of the Gaussian mixture model representation evolves for different adversarial examples.

We define the objective function in terms of the L_k distance and view the distance to an adversarial example as a measure of its severity. Note that the sets $adv_{N,k,d}(\alpha, c)$ and $adv_{N,k,d}(\alpha)$ of adversarial examples can be infinite.

Definition 2. *Among all adversarial examples in the set $adv_{N,k,d}(\alpha, c)$ (or $adv_{N,k,d}(\alpha)$), find α' with the minimum distance to the original image α:*

$$\arg\min_{\alpha'}\{sev_{\alpha}(\alpha') \mid \alpha' \in adv_{N,k,d}(\alpha, c)(or\ adv_{N,k,d}(\alpha))\} \tag{2}$$

where $sev_{\alpha}(\alpha') = ||\alpha - \alpha'||_k$ is the severity *of the adversarial example α' against the original image α.*

We remark that the choice of L_k will affect perceptual similarity, see Appendix of [36].

Crafting Adversarial Examples as a Two-Player Turn-Based Game. Assume two players I and II. Let $M(\alpha, k, d) = (S \cup (S \times \Lambda(\alpha)), s_0, \{T_a\}_{a \in \{I,II\}}, L)$ be a game model, where S is a set of game states belonging to player I such that each state represents an image in $\eta(\alpha, k, d)$, and $S \times \Lambda(\alpha)$ is a set of game states belonging to player II where $\Lambda(\alpha)$ is a set of features (keypoints) of image α. We write $\alpha(s)$ for the image associated to the state $s \in S$. $s_0 \in S$ is the initial game state such that $\alpha(s_0)$ is the original image α. The transition relation $T_I : S \times \Lambda(\alpha) \to S \times \Lambda(\alpha)$ is defined as $T_I(s, \lambda) = (s, \lambda)$, and transition relation $T_{II} : (S \times \Lambda(\alpha)) \times \mathcal{P}(P_0) \times I \to S$ is defined as $T_{II}((s, \lambda), X, i) = \delta_{X,i}(\alpha(s))$, where $\delta_{X,i}$ is a pixel manipulation defined in Sect. 2. Intuitively, on every game state $s \in S$, player I will choose a keypoint λ, and, in response to this, player II will choose a pair (X, i), where X is a set of input dimensions and i is a manipulation instruction. The labelling function $L : S \cup (S \times \Lambda(\alpha)) \to C \times G$ assigns to each state s or (s, λ) a class $N(\alpha(s))$ and a two-dimensional Gaussian mixture model $\mathcal{G}(\Lambda(\alpha(s)))$.

A path (or game play) of the game model is a sequence $s_1 u_1 s_2 u_2 ...$ of game states such that, for all $k \geq 1$, we have $u_k = T_I(s_k, \lambda_k)$ for some feature λ_k and $s_{k+1} = T_{II}((s_k, \lambda_k), X_k, i_k)$ for some (X_k, i_k). Let $last(\rho)$ be the last state of a finite path ρ and $Path_a^F$ be the set of finite paths such that $last(\rho)$ belongs to player $a \in \{I, II\}$. A stochastic strategy $\sigma_I : Path_I^F \to \mathcal{D}(\Lambda(\alpha))$ of player I maps each finite paths to a distribution over the next actions, and similarly for $\sigma_{II} : Path_{II}^F \to \mathcal{D}(\mathcal{P}(P_0) \times I)$ for player II. We call $\sigma = (\sigma_I, \sigma_{II})$ a strategy profile. In this section, we only discuss targeted safety for a given target class c (see Definition 1). All the notations and results can be easily adapted to work with non-targeted safety.

In the following, we define a reward $R(\sigma, \rho)$ for a given strategy profile $\sigma = (\sigma_{\mathtt{I}}, \sigma_{\mathtt{II}})$ and a finite path $\rho \in \bigcup_{a \in \{\mathtt{I},\mathtt{II}\}} Path_a^F$. The idea of the reward is to accumulate a measure of severity of the adversarial example found over a path. Note that, given σ, the game becomes a fully probabilistic system. Let $\alpha'_\rho = \alpha(last(\rho))$ be the image associated with the last state of the path ρ. We write $t(\rho)$ for the expression $N(\alpha'_\rho) = c \vee ||\alpha'_\rho - \alpha||_k > d$, representing that the path has reached a state whose associated image either is in the target class c or lies outside the region $\eta(\alpha, k, d)$. The path ρ can be terminated whenever $t(\rho)$ is satisfiable. It is not hard to see that, due to the constraints in Definition 1, every infinite path has a finite prefix which can be terminated. Then we define the reward function $R(\sigma, \rho) =$

$$\begin{cases} 1/sev_\alpha(\alpha'_\rho) & \text{if } t(\rho) \text{ and } \rho \in Path_{\mathtt{I}}^F \\ \sum_{\lambda \in \Lambda(\alpha)} \sigma_{\mathtt{I}}(\rho)(\lambda) \cdot R(\sigma, \rho T_{\mathtt{I}}(last(\rho), \lambda)) & \text{if } \neg t(\rho) \text{ and } \rho \in Path_{\mathtt{I}}^F \\ \sum_{(X,i) \in \mathcal{P}(P_0) \times I} \sigma_{\mathtt{II}}(\rho)(X, i) \cdot R(\sigma, \rho T_{\mathtt{II}}(last(\rho), X, i)) & \text{if } \rho \in Path_{\mathtt{II}}^F \end{cases}$$

where $\sigma_{\mathtt{I}}(\rho)(\lambda)$ is the probability of selecting λ on ρ by player I, and $\sigma_{\mathtt{II}}(\rho)(X, i)$ is the probability of selecting (X, i) based on ρ by player II. We note that a path only terminates on player I states.

Intuitively, if an adversarial example is found then the reward assigned is the inverse of severity (minimal distance), and otherwise it is the weighted summation of the rewards if its children. Thus, a strategy $\sigma_{\mathtt{I}}$ to maximise the reward will need to minimise the severity $sev_\alpha(\alpha'_\rho)$, the objective of the problem defined in Definition 2.

Definition 3. *The goal of the game is for player* I *to choose a strategy* $\sigma_{\mathtt{I}}$ *to maximise the reward* $R((\sigma_{\mathtt{I}}, \sigma_{\mathtt{II}}), s_0)$ *of the initial state* s_0*, based on the strategy* $\sigma_{\mathtt{II}}$ *of the player* II*, i.e.,*

$$\arg\max_{\sigma_{\mathtt{I}}} \mathbf{opt}_{\sigma_{\mathtt{II}}} R((\sigma_{\mathtt{I}}, \sigma_{\mathtt{II}}), s_0). \tag{3}$$

where option $\mathbf{opt}_{\sigma_{\mathtt{II}}}$ *can be* $\max_{\sigma_{\mathtt{II}}}$, $\min_{\sigma_{\mathtt{II}}}$, *or* $\mathbf{nat}_{\sigma_{\mathtt{II}}}$, *according to which player* II *acts as a cooperator, an adversary, or nature who samples the distribution* $\mathcal{G}(\Lambda(\alpha))$ *for pixels and randomly chooses the manipulation instruction.*

A strategy σ is called deterministic if $\sigma(\rho)$ is a Dirac distribution, and is called memoryless if $\sigma(\rho) = \sigma(last(\rho))$ for all finite paths ρ. We have the following result.

Theorem 1. *Deterministic and memoryless strategies suffice for player* I*, when* $\mathbf{opt}_{\sigma_{\mathtt{II}}} \in \{\max_{\sigma_{\mathtt{II}}}, \min_{\sigma_{\mathtt{II}}}, \mathbf{nat}_{\sigma_{\mathtt{II}}}\}$.

Complexity of the Problem. As a by-product of Theorem 1, the theoretical complexity of the problem (i.e., determining whether $adv_{N,k,d}(\alpha, c) = \emptyset$) is in PTIME, with respect to the size of the game model $M(\alpha, k, d)$. However, even if we only consider finite paths (and therefore a finite system), the number of states (and therefore the size of the system) is $O(|P_0|^h)$ for h the length of the longest finite path of the system without a terminating state. While the precise size of $O(|P_0|^h)$ is dependent on the problem (including the image α and the difficulty of crafting an adversarial example), it is roughly $O(50000^{100})$ for the images used in the ImageNet competition and $O(1000^{20})$ for smaller images such as CIFAR10 and MNIST. This is beyond the capability of existing approaches for exact or ϵ-approximate computation of probability (e.g., reduction to linear programming, value iteration, and policy iteration, etc) that are used in probabilistic verification.

4 Monte Carlo Tree Search for Asymptotically Optimal Strategy

In this section, we present an approach based on Monte Carlo tree search (MCTS) [9] to find an optimal strategy asymptotically. We also we show that the optimal strategy, if achieved, represents the best adversarial example with respect to the objective in Definition 2, under some conditions.

We first consider the case of $\texttt{opt}_{\sigma_{II}} = \max_{\sigma_{II}}$. An MCTS algorithm, whose pseudo-code is presented in Algorithm 1, gradually expands a *partial game tree* by sampling the strategy space of the model $M(\alpha, k, d)$. With the upper confidence bound (UCB) [16] as the exploration-exploitation tradeoff, MCTS has a theoretical guarantee that it converges to optimal solution when the game tree is fully explored. The algorithm mainly follows the standard MCTS procedure, with a few adaptations. We use two termination conditions tc_1 and tc_2 to control the pace of the algorithm. More specifically, tc_1 controls whether the entire procedure should be terminated, and tc_2 controls when a move should be made. The terminating conditions can be, e.g., bounds on the number of iterations, etc. On the partial tree, every node maintains a pair (r, n), which represents the accumulated reward r and the number of visits n, respectively. The *selection* procedure travels from the root to a leaf according to an exploration-exploitation balance, i.e., UCB [16]. After *expanding* the leaf node to have its children added to the partial tree, we call *Simulation* to run simulation on every child node. A simulation on a new *node* is a play of the game from *node* until it terminates. Players act randomly during the simulation. Every simulation terminates when reaching a terminated node α', on which a reward $1/sev_\alpha(\alpha')$ can be computed. This reward is then *backpropagated* from the new child node through its ancestors until reaching the root. Every time a new reward v is backpropogated through a node, we update its associated pair to $(r+v, n+1)$. The $bestChild(root)$ returns the child of $root$ which has the highest value of r/n. The other two cases are similar except for the choice of the next move (i.e., Line 12). Instead of choosing the best child, a child is chosen by sampling $\mathcal{G}(\Lambda(\alpha))$ for the case of $\texttt{opt}_{\sigma_{II}} = \texttt{nat}_{\sigma_{II}}$, and the worst child is chosen for the case of $\texttt{opt}_{\sigma_{II}} = \min_{\sigma_{II}}$. We remark the game is not zero-sum when $\texttt{opt}_{\sigma_{II}} \in \{\texttt{nat}_{\sigma_{II}}, \max_{\sigma_{II}}\}$.

Severity Interval from the Game. Assume that we have fixed termination conditions tc_1 and tc_2 and target class c. Given an option $\texttt{opt}_{\sigma_{II}}$ for player $\texttt{II}$, we have an MCTS algorithm to compute an adversarial example α'. Let

Algorithm 1. Monte Carlo Tree Search for $\mathtt{opt}_{\sigma_{\mathtt{II}}} = \max_{\sigma_{\mathtt{II}}}$

Input: A game model $M(\alpha, k, d)$, two termination conditions tc_1 and tc_2, a target class c
Output: An adversarial example α'
procedure MCTS($M(\alpha, k, d), tc_1, tc_2, c$)
  $root \leftarrow s_0$
  While$(\neg tc_1)$:
    While$(\neg tc_2)$:
      $leaf \leftarrow selection(root)$
      $newnodes \leftarrow expansion(M(\alpha, k, d), leaf)$
      for *node* in *newnodes*:
        $v \leftarrow Simulation(M(\alpha, k, d), node, c)$
        $backPropogation(node, v)$
    $root \leftarrow bestChild(root)$
  return *root*

$sev(M(\alpha, k, d), \mathtt{opt}_{\sigma_{\mathtt{II}}})$ be $sev_\alpha(\alpha')$, where α' is the returned adversarial example by running Algorithm 1 over the inputs $M(\alpha, k, d)$, tc_1, tc_2, c for a certain $\mathtt{opt}_{\sigma_{\mathtt{II}}}$. Then there exists a severity interval $SI(\alpha, k, d)$ with respect to the role of player $\mathtt{II}$:

$$[sev(M(\alpha, k, d), \max_{\sigma_{\mathtt{II}}}), \quad sev(M(\alpha, k, d), \min_{\sigma_{\mathtt{II}}})]. \tag{4}$$

Moreover, we have that $sev(M(\alpha, k, d), \mathtt{nat}_{\sigma_{\mathtt{II}}}) \in SI(\alpha, k, d)$.

Safety Guarantee via Optimal Strategy. Recall that τ, a positive real number, is the manipulation magnitude used in pixel manipulations. An image $\alpha' \in \eta(\alpha, k, d)$ is a τ-grid image if for all dimensions $p \in P_0$ we have $|\alpha'(p) - \alpha(p)| = n * \tau$ for some $n \geq 0$. Let $G(\alpha, k, d)$ be the set of τ-grid images in $\eta(\alpha, k, d)$. First of all, we have the following conclusion for the case when player $\mathtt{II}$ is cooperative.

Theorem 2. *Let $\alpha' \in \eta(\alpha, k, d)$ be any τ-grid image such that $\alpha' \in adv_{N,k,d}(\alpha, c)$, where c is the targeted class. Then we have that $sev_\alpha(\alpha') \geq sev(M(\alpha, k, d), \max_{\sigma_{\mathtt{II}}})$.*

Intuitively, the theorem says that the algorithm can find the optimal adversarial example from the set of τ-grid images. The idea of the proof is to show that every τ-grid image can be reached by some game play. In the following, we show that, if the network is Lipschitz continuous, we need only consider τ-grid images when τ is small enough. Then, together with the above theorem, we can conclude that our algorithm is both sound and complete.

Further, we say that an image $\alpha_1 \in \eta(\alpha, k, d)$ is a misclassification aggregator with respect to a number $\beta > 0$ if, for any $\alpha_2 \in \eta(\alpha_1, 1, \beta)$, we have that $N(\alpha_2) \neq N(\alpha)$ implies $N(\alpha_1) \neq N(\alpha)$. Intuitively, if a misclassification aggregator α_1 with respect to β is classified correctly then all input images in $\eta(\alpha_1, 1, \beta)$ are classified correctly. We remark that the region $\eta(\alpha_1, 1, \beta)$ is defined with respect to the L_1

metric, but can also be defined using $L_{k'}$, some k', without affecting the results if $\eta(\alpha, k, d) \subseteq \bigcup_{\alpha_1 \in G(\alpha,k,d)} \eta(\alpha_1, k', \tau/2)$. Then we have the following theorem.

Theorem 3. *If all τ-grid images are misclassification aggregators with respect to $\tau/2$, and $sev(M(\alpha, k, d), \max_{\sigma_{II}}) > d$, then $adv_{N,k,d}(\alpha, c) = \emptyset$.*

Note that $sev(M(\alpha, k, d), \max_{\sigma_{II}}) > d$ means that none of the τ-images in $\eta(\alpha, k, d)$ is an adversarial example. The theorem suggests that, to achieve a complete safety verification, one may gradually decrease τ until either $sev(M(\alpha, k, d), \max_{\sigma_{II}}) \leq d$, in which case we claim the network is unsafe, or the condition that all τ-grid images are misclassification aggregators with respect to $\tau/2$ is satisfiable, in which case we claim the network is safe. In the following, we discuss how to decide the largest τ for a Lipschitz network, in order to satisfy that condition and therefore achieve a complete verification using our approach.

Definition 4. *Network N is a Lipschitz network with respect to the distance L_k and a constant $\hbar > 0$ if, for all $\alpha, \alpha' \in \mathrm{D}$, we have $|N(\alpha', N(\alpha)) - N(\alpha, N(\alpha))| < \hbar \cdot ||\alpha' - \alpha||_k$.*

Note that all networks whose inputs are bounded, including all image classification networks we studied, are Lipschitz networks. Specifically, it is shown in [30] that most known types of layers, including fully-connected, convolutional, ReLU, maxpooling, sigmoid, softmax, etc., are Lipschitz continuous. Moreover, we let ℓ be the minimum confidence gap for a class change, i.e.,

$$\ell = \min\{|N(\alpha', N(\alpha)) - N(\alpha, N(\alpha))| \mid \alpha, \alpha' \in \mathrm{D}, N(\alpha') \neq N(\alpha)\}.$$

The value of ℓ is in $[0, 1]$, dependent on the network, and can be estimated by examining all input examples α' in the training and test data sets, or computed with provable guarantees by reachability analysis [30]. The following theorem can be seen as an instantiation of Theorem 3 by using Lipschitz continuity with $\tau \leq \frac{2\ell}{\hbar}$ to implement the misclassification aggregator.

Theorem 4. *Let N be a Lipschitz network with respect to L_1 and a constant $\hbar$. Then, when $\tau \leq \frac{2\ell}{\hbar}$ and $sev(M(\alpha, k, d), \max_{\sigma_{II}}) > d$, we have that $adv_{N,k,d}(\alpha, c) = \emptyset$.*

$1/\epsilon$-convergence Because we are working with a finite game, MCTS is guaranteed to converge when the game tree is fully expanded. In the worst case, it may take a very long time to converge. In practice, we can work with $1/\epsilon$-convergence by letting the program terminate when the current best adversarial example has not been improved by finding a less severe one for $\lceil 1/\epsilon \rceil$ iterations, where $\epsilon > 0$ is a small real number.

5 Experimental Results

For our experiments, we let player II be a cooperator, and its move (X, i) is such that for all $(x_1, y_1, z_1), (x_2, y_2, z_2) \in X$ we have $x_1 = x_2$ and $y_1 = y_2$, i.e., one pixel (including 3 dimensions for color images or 1 dimension for grey-scale images) is changed for every move. When running simulations (Line 10 of Algorithm 1), we let $\sigma_{\text{I}}(\lambda) = \lambda_r / \sum_{\lambda \in \Lambda(\alpha)} \lambda_r$ for all keypoints $\lambda \in \Lambda(\alpha)$ and $\texttt{opt}_{\sigma_{\text{II}}} = \texttt{nat}_{\sigma_{\text{II}}}$. That is, player I follows a stochastic strategy to choose a keypoint according to its response strength and player II is nature. In this section, we compare our method with existing approaches, show convergence of the MCTS algorithm on limited runs, evaluate safety-critical networks trained on traffic light images, and counter-claim a recent statement regarding adversarial examples in physical domains.

Comparison with Existing Approaches. We compare our approach to two state-of-the-art methods on two image classification networks, trained on the well known benchmark datasets MNIST and CIFAR10. The MNIST image dataset contains images of size 28 × 28 and one channel and the network is trained with the source code given in [2]. The trained network is of medium size with 600,810 real-valued parameters, and achieves state-of-the-art accuracy, exceeding 99%. It has 12 layers, within which there are 2 convolutional layers, as well as layers such as ReLU, dropout, fully-connected layers and a softmax layer. The CIFAR10 dataset contains small images, 32 × 32, with three channels, and the network is trained with the source code from [1] for more than 12 hours. The trained network has 1,250,858 real-valued parameters and includes convolutional layers, ReLU layers, max-pooling layers, dropout layers, fully-connected layers, and a softmax layer. For both networks, the images are preprocessed to make the value of each dimension lie within the bound $[0, 1]$. We randomly select 1000 images $\{\alpha_i\}_{i \in \{1..1000\}}$ from both datasets for non-targeted safety testing. The numbers in Table 1 are average distances defined as $\frac{1}{1000} \cdot \sum_{i=1}^{1000} ||\alpha_i - \alpha_i'||_0$, where α_i' is the adversarial image of α_i returned by the algorithm. Table 1 gives a comparison with the other two approaches (CW [8] and JSMA [27]). The numbers for CW and JSMA are taken from [8][2], where additional optimisations have been conducted over the original JSMA. According to [27], the original JSMA has an average distance of 40 for MNIST.

Table 1. CW vs. Game (this paper) vs. JSMA

L_0	CW (L_0 algorithm)	Game (timeout = 1 m)	JSMA-F	JSMA-Z
MNIST	8.5	14.1	17	20
CIFAR10	5.8	9	25	20

Our experiments are conducted by setting the termination conditions $tc_1 = 20\,\text{s}$ and $tc_2 = 60\,\text{s}$ for every image. Note that JSMA needs several minutes to

[2] For CW, the L_0 distance in [8] counts the number of changed pixels, while for the others the L_0 distance counts the number of changed dimensions. Therefore, the number 5.8 in Table 1 is not precise, and should be between 5.8 and 17.4, because colour images have three channels.

handle an image, and CW is 10 times slower than JSMA [8]. From the table, we can see that, already in a limited computation time, our game-based approach can achieve a significant margin over optimised JSMA, which is based on saliency distributions, although it is not able to beat the optimisation-based approach CW. We also mention that, in [14], the un-optimised JSMA produces adversarial examples with smaller average L_2 distance than FGSM [12] and DLV on its single-path algorithm [14]. Appendix of [36] provide illustrative examples exhibiting the manipulations that the three algorithms performed on the images.

Convergence in Limited Runs. To demonstrate convergence of our algorithm, we plot the evolution of three variables related to the adversarial severity $sev_{\alpha}(\alpha')$ against the number of iterations. The variable *best* (in blue color) is the smallest severity found so far. The variable *current* (in orange) is the severity returned in the current iteration. The variable *window* (in green) is the average severity returned in the past 10 iterations. The blue and orange plots may overlap because we let the algorithm return the best example when it fails to find an adversarial example in some iteration. The experiments are terminated with $1/\epsilon$-convergence of different ϵ value such as 0.1 or 0.05. The green plot getting closer to the other two provides empirical evidence of convergence. In Fig. 3 we show that two MNIST images converge over fewer than 50 iterations on manipulations of 2 pixels, and we have confirmed that they represent optimal strategies of the players. We also work with other state-of-the-art networks such as the VGG16 network [3] from the ImageNet competition. Examples of convergence are provided in Appendix of [36].

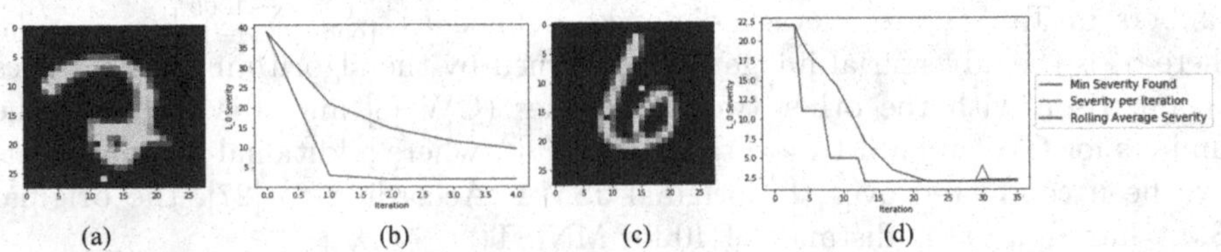

Fig. 3. (a) Image of a two classified as a seven with 70% confidence and (b) the demonstration of convergence. (c) Image of a six classified as a five with 50% confidence and (d) the demonstration of convergence. (Color figure online)

Evaluating Safety-Critical Networks. We explore the possibility of applying our game-based approach to support real-time decision making and testing, for which the algorithm needs to be highly efficient, requiring only seconds to execute a task.

We apply our method to a network used for classifying traffic light images collected from dashboard cameras. The Nexar traffic light challenge [25] made over eighteen thousand dashboard camera images publicly available. Each image is labeled either green, if the traffic light appearing in the image is green, or red, if the traffic light appearing in the image is red, or null if there is no traffic light appearing in the image. We test the winner of the challenge which scored an accuracy above 90% [7]. Despite each input being 37632-dimensional ($112 \times 112 \times 3$), our algorithm reports that the manipulation of an average of 4.85 dimensions changes the network classification. Each image was processed by the algorithm in 0.303 s (which includes time to read and write images), i.e., 304 s are taken to test all 1000 images. We illustrate the results of our analysis of the network in Fig. 4. Though the images are easy for humans to classify, only one pixel change causes the network to make potentially disastrous decisions, particularly for the case of red light misclassified as green. To explore this particular situation in greater depth, we use a targeted safety MCTS procedure on the same 1000 images, aiming to manipulate images into green. We do not consider images which are already classified as green. Of the remaining 500 images, our algorithm is able to change all image classifications to green with worryingly low severities, namely an average L_0 of 3.23. On average, this targeted procedure returns an adversarial example in 0.21 s per image. Appendix of [36] provides some other examples.

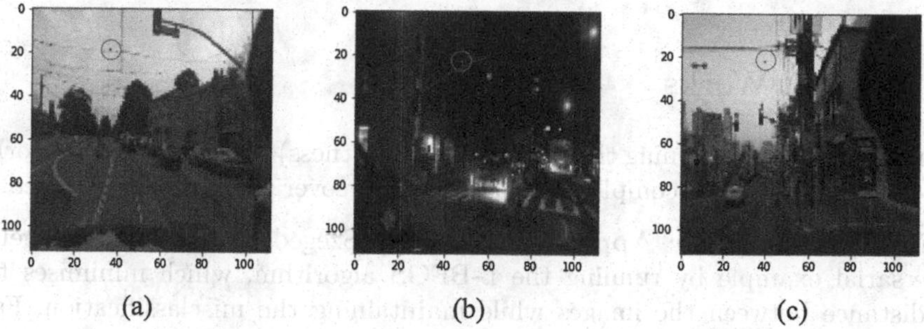

Fig. 4. Adversarial examples generated on Nexar data demonstrate a lack of robustness. (a) Green light classified as red with confidence 56% after one pixel change. (b) Green light classified as red with confidence 76% after one pixel change. (c) Red light classified as green with 90% confidence after one pixel change. (Color figure online)

Counter-Claim to Statements in [21]**.** A recent paper [21] argued that, under specific circumstances, there is no need to worry about adversarial examples because they are not invariant to changes in scale or angle in the physical domain. Our SIFT-based approach, which is inherently scale and rotationally invariant, can easily counter-claim such statements. To demonstrate this, we conducted similar tests to [21]. We set up the YOLO network, took pictures of a few traffic lights in Oxford, United Kingdom, and generated adversarial examples on these images. For the adversarial example shown in Fig. 1, we print and photograph it at several different angles and scales to test whether it remains misclassified. The results are shown in Fig. 5. In [21] it is suggested that realistic camera movements – those which change the angle and distance of the viewer – reduce the phenomenon of adversarial examples to a curiosity rather than a safety concern. Here, we show that our adversarial examples, which are predicated on scale and rotationally invariant methods, defeat these claims.

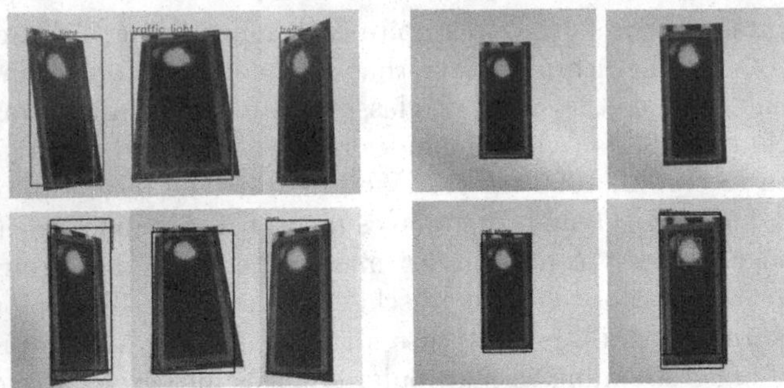

Fig. 5. (Left) Adversarial examples in physical domain remain adversarial at multiple angles. Top images classified correctly as traffic lights, bottom images classified incorrectly as either ovens, TV screens, or microwaves. (Right) Adversarial examples in the physical domain remain adversarial at multiple scales. Top images correctly classified as traffic lights, bottom images classified incorrectly as ovens or microwaves (with the center light being misclassified as a pizza in the bottom right instance).

6 Related Works

We review works concerning the safety (and robustness) of deep neural networks. Instead of trying to be complete, we aim to only cover those directly related.

White-Box Heuristic Approaches. In [34], Szegedy et. al. find a targeted adversarial example by running the L-BFGS algorithm, which minimises the L_2 distance between the images while maintaining the misclassification. Fast Gradient Sign Method (FGSM) [12], a refinement of L-BFGS, takes as inputs the parameters θ of the model, the input α to the model, and the target label y, and computes a linearized version of the cost function with respect to θ to obtain a manipulation direction. After the manipulation direction is fixed, a small constant value τ is taken as the magnitude of the manipulation. Carlini and Wagner [8] adapt the optimisation problem proposed in [34] to obtain a set of optimisation problems for L_0, L_2, and L_∞ attacks. They claim better performance than FGSM and Jacobian-based Saliency Map Attack (JSMA) with their L_2 attack, in which for every pixel x_i a new real-valued variable w_i is introduced and then the optimisation is conducted by letting x_i move along the gradient direction of $\tanh(w_i)$. Different from the optimisation approaches, the JSMA [27] uses a loss function to create a "saliency map" of the image which indicates the importance of each pixel on the network's decision. A greedy algorithm is used to gradually modify the most important pixels. In [23], an iterative application of an optimisation approach (such as [34]) is conducted on a set of images one by one to get an accumulated manipulation, which is expected to make a number of inputs misclassified. [22] replaces the softmax layer in a deep network with a multiclass SVM and then finds adversarial examples by performing a gradient computation.

White-Box Verification Approaches. Compared with heuristic search approaches, the verification approaches aim to provide guarantees on the safety of DNNs. An early verification approach [28] encodes the entire network as a set of constraints. The constraints can then be solved with a SAT solver. [15] improves on [28] by handling the ReLU activation functions. The Simplex method for linear programming is extended to work with the piecewise linear ReLU functions that cannot be expressed using linear programming. The approach can scale up to networks with 300 ReLU nodes. In recent work [13] the input vector space is partitioned using clustering and then the method of [15] is used to check the individual partitions. DLV [14] uses multi-path search and layer-by-layer refinement to exhaustively explore a finite region of the vector spaces associated with the input layer or the hidden layers, and scales to work with state-of-the-art networks such as VGG16.

Black-Box Algorithms. The methods in [26] evaluate a network by generating a synthetic data set, training a surrogate model, and then applying white box detection techniques on the model. [24] randomly searches the vector space around the input image for changes which will cause a misclassification. It shows that in some instances this method is efficient and able to indicate where salient areas of the image exist.

7 Conclusion

In this paper we present a novel feature-guided black-box algorithm for evaluating the resilience of deep neural networks against adversarial examples. Our algorithm employs the SIFT method for feature extraction, provides a theoretical safety guarantee under certain restrictions, and is very efficient, opening up the possibility of deployment in real-time decision support. We develop a software package and demonstrate its applicability on a variety of state-of-the-art networks and benchmarks. While we have detected many instabilities in state-of-the-art networks, we have not yet found a network that is safe. Future works include comparison with the Bayesian inference method for identifying adversarial examples [10].

Acknowledgements. Kwiatkowska is supported by EPSRC Mobile Autonomy Programme Grant (EP/M019918/1). Xiaowei gratefully acknowledges NVIDIA Corporation for its support with the donation of the Titan Xp GPU, and is partially supported by NSFC (no. 61772232).

References

1. CIFAR10 model for Keras. https://github.com/fchollet/keras/blob/master/examples/cifar10_cnn.py
2. MNIST, CNN network. https://github.com/fchollet/keras/blob/master/examples/mnist_cnn.py

3. VGG16 model for Keras. https://gist.github.com/baraldilorenzo/07d7802847aaad0a35d3
4. Biggio, B., Corona, I., Maiorca, D., Nelson, B., Šrndić, N., Laskov, P., Giacinto, G., Roli, F.: Evasion attacks against machine learning at test time. In: Blockeel, H., Kersting, K., Nijssen, S., Železný, F. (eds.) ECML PKDD 2013. LNCS (LNAI), vol. 8190, pp. 387–402. Springer, Heidelberg (2013). https://doi.org/10.1007/978-3-642-40994-3_25
5. Bittel, S., Kaiser, V., Teichmann, M., Thoma, M.: Pixel-wise segmentation of street with neural networks. CoRR, abs/1511.00513 (2015)
6. Bojarski, M., Del Testa, D., Dworakowski, D., Firner, B., Flepp, B., Goyal, P., Jackel, L.D., Monfort, M., Muller, U., Zhang, J., Zhang, X., Zhao, J., Zieba, K.: End to end learning for self-driving cars. CoRR, abs/1604.07316 (2016)
7. Burg, A.: Deep Learning Traffic Lights model for Nexar Competition. https://github.com/burgalon/deep-learning-traffic-lights
8. Carlini, N., Wagner, D.A.: Towards evaluating the robustness of neural networks. CoRR, abs/1608.04644 (2016)
9. Chaslot, G.M.J.B., Winands, M.H.M., Uiterwijk, J.W.H.M., van den Herik, H.J., Bouzy, B.: Progressive strategies for Monte-Carlo tree search. New Math. Nat. Comput. **4**(3), 343–359 (2008)
10. Dabkowski, P., Gal, Y.: Real time image saliency for black box classifiers. CoRR, abs/1705.07857 (2017)
11. Dahl, G., Stokes, J.W., Deng, L., Yu, D.: Large-scale malware classification using random projections and neural networks. In: Proceedings IEEE Conference on Acoustics, Speech, and Signal Processing. IEEE SPS, May 2013
12. Goodfellow, I.J., Shlens, J., Szegedy, C.: Explaining and harnessing adversarial examples. CoRR, abs/1412.6572 (2014)
13. Gopinath, D., Katz, G., Pasareanu, C.S., Barrett, C.: Deepsafe: a data-driven approach for checking adversarial robustness in neural networks. CoRR, abs/1710.00486 (2017)
14. Huang, X., Kwiatkowska, M., Wang, S., Wu, M.: Safety verification of deep neural networks. In: Majumdar, R., Kunčak, V. (eds.) CAV 2017. LNCS, vol. 10426, pp. 3–29. Springer, Cham (2017). https://doi.org/10.1007/978-3-319-63387-9_1
15. Katz, G., Barrett, C., Dill, D.L., Julian, K., Kochenderfer, M.J.: Reluplex: an efficient SMT solver for verifying deep neural networks. In: Majumdar, R., Kunčak, V. (eds.) CAV 2017. LNCS, vol. 10426, pp. 97–117. Springer, Cham (2017). https://doi.org/10.1007/978-3-319-63387-9_5
16. Kocsis, L., Szepesvári, C.: Bandit based Monte-Carlo planning. In: Fürnkranz, J., Scheffer, T., Spiliopoulou, M. (eds.) ECML 2006. LNCS (LNAI), vol. 4212, pp. 282–293. Springer, Heidelberg (2006). https://doi.org/10.1007/11871842_29
17. LeCun, Y., Bengio, Y., Hinton, G.: Deep learning. Nature **521**, 436–444 (2015)
18. LeCun, Y., Cortes, C.: MNIST handwritten digit database (2010)
19. Liu, Y., Chen, X., Liu, C., Song, D.: Delving into transferable adversarial examples and black-box attacks. In: ICLR 2017 (2017)
20. Lowe, D.G.: Distinctive image features from scale-invariant keypoints. Int. J. Comput. Vision **60**(2), 91–110 (2004)
21. Lu, J., Sibai, H., Fabry, E., Forsyth, D.: NO need to worry about adversarial examples in object detection in autonomous vehicles. ArXiv e-prints, July 2017
22. Melis, M., Demontis, A., Biggio, B., Brown, G., Fumera, G., Roli, F.: Is deep learning safe for robot vision? Adversarial examples against the iCub humanoid. CoRR, abs/1708.06939 (2017)

23. Moosavi-Dezfooli, S.-M., Fawzi, A., Fawzi, O., Frossard, P.: Universal adversarial perturbations. CoRR, abs/1610.08401 (2016)
24. Narodytska, N., Kasiviswanathan, S.P.: Simple black-box adversarial perturbations for deep networks. CoRR, abs/1612.06299 (2016)
25. Nexar. Challenge: Using deep learning for traffic light recognition. https://www.getnexar.com/challenge-1
26. Papernot, N., McDaniel, P.D., Goodfellow, I., Jha, S., Celik, Z.B., Swami, A.: Practical black-box attacks against deep learning systems using adversarial examples. CoRR, abs/1602.02697 (2016)
27. Papernot, N., McDaniel, P., Jha, S., Fredrikson, M., Celik, Z.B., Swami, A.: The limitations of deep learning in adversarial settings. CoRR, abs/1511.07528 (2015)
28. Pulina, L., Tacchella, A.: An abstraction-refinement approach to verification of artificial neural networks. In: Touili, T., Cook, B., Jackson, P. (eds.) CAV 2010. LNCS, vol. 6174, pp. 243–257. Springer, Heidelberg (2010). https://doi.org/10.1007/978-3-642-14295-6_24
29. Reynolds, D.A.: Gaussian mixture models. In: Encyclopedia of Biometrics (2009)
30. Ruan, W., Huang, X., Kwiatkowska, M.: Reachability analysis of deep neural networks with provable guarantees (2018, submitted)
31. Ryan, J., Lin, M.J., Miikkulainen, R.: Intrusion detection with neural networks. In: Jordan, M.I., Kearns, M.J., Solla, S.A. (eds.) Advances in Neural Information Processing Systems, vol. 10, pp. 943–949. MIT Press, Cambridge (1998)
32. Sermanet, P., LeCun, Y.: Traffic sign recognition with multi-scale convolutional networks. In: The 2011 International Joint Conference on Neural Networks (2011)
33. Szegedy, C., Zaremba, W., Sutskever, I., Bruna, J., Erhan, D., Goodfellow, I.J., Fergus, R.: Intriguing properties of neural networks. In: International Conference on Learning Representations (ICLR-2014) (2014)
34. Szegedy, C., Zaremba, W., Sutskever, I., Bruna, J., Erhan, D., Goodfellow, I.J., Fergus, R.:. Intriguing properties of neural networks. CoRR, abs/1312.6199 (2013)
35. Szeliski, R.: Computer Vision: Algorithms and Applications. Springer, London (2010). https://doi.org/10.1007/978-1-84882-935-0
36. Wicker, M., Huang, X., Kwiatkowska, M.: Feature-guided black-box safety testing of deep neural networks. CoRR, abs/1710.07859 (2017)
37. Yosinski, J., Clune, J., Nguyen, A., Fuchs, T., Lipson, H.: Understanding neural networks through deep visualization. In: 2015 ICML Workshop on Deep Learning (2015)

Author Index

Printed in the United States
By Bookmasters